The New International Lesson Annual

2012-2013

September–August

Abingdon Press
Nashville

THE NEW INTERNATIONAL LESSON ANNUAL 2012–2013

Copyright © 2012 by Abingdon Press

All rights reserved.

This book is printed on acid-free paper.

ISBN 978-1-4267-0957-9

ISSN 1084-872X

12 13 14 15 16 17 18 19 20 21—10 9 8 7 6 5 4 3 2 1

MANUFACTURED IN THE UNITED STATES OF AMERICA

PREFACE

Welcome! You hold in your hands a resource used by the global community of Bible students and teachers who study resources based on the work of the Committee on the Uniform Series, known by many as the International Lesson Series. *The New International Lesson Annual* is designed for teachers who seek a solid biblical basis for each session and a step-by-step teaching plan that will help them lead their classes. *The New International Lesson Annual* can be used with any student curriculum based on the International Lesson Series. In many classes, both the students and the teacher rely on *The New International Lesson Annual* as their companion to the Bible.

During the Sunday school year that extends from September 2012 through August 2013, we focus on four themes: *faith, God: Jesus Christ, hope,* and *worship.* During the fall quarter, we will explore the theme of faith by delving into Hebrews and Acts in a course titled "A Living Faith." We recognize that "Jesus Is Lord" during the winter quarter as we study three letters traditionally attributed to Paul: Ephesians, Philippians, and Colossians. "Beyond the Present Time," the course for the spring quarter, enables us to see how the theme of hope plays out in both the Old Testament (Daniel) and the New (Luke, Acts, 1 and 2 Thessalonians, 1 and 2 Peter). The summer quarter, "God's People Worship," examines Isaiah, Ezra, and Nehemiah to see how God's people are called to worship.

As you examine this book, notice the following features that are especially valuable for busy teachers who want to provide in-depth Bible study experiences for their students. Each lesson includes the following sections:

Previewing the Lesson highlights the background and lesson Scriptures, focus of the lesson, three goals for the learners, a pronunciation guide in lessons where you may find unfamiliar words or names, and supplies you will need to teach.

Reading the Scripture includes the Scripture lesson printed in both the New Revised Standard Version and the Common English Bible. By printing these two translations in parallel columns, you can easily compare them for in-depth study. If your own Bible is another version, you will then have three translations to explore as you prepare each lesson.

Understanding the Scripture closely analyzes the background Scripture by looking at each verse. Here you will find help in understanding concepts, ideas, places, and people pertinent to each week's lesson. You may also find explanations of Greek or Hebrew words that are essential for understanding the text.

Interpreting the Scripture looks at the lesson Scripture, delves into its meaning, and relates it to contemporary life.

Sharing the Scripture provides you with a detailed teaching plan. Written by your editor, who is a very experienced educator, this section is divided into two major subsections.

First, you will find a devotional reading related to the lesson for your own spiritual enrichment and ideas to help you prepare for the session.

Second, the *Leading the Class* portion begins with "Gather to Learn" activities designed to welcome the students and draw them into the lesson. Here, the students' stories and experiences or other contemporary stories are highlighted as preparation for the Bible story. The next three headings of *Leading the Class* are the three "Goals for the Learners." The first goal always focuses on the Bible story itself. The second goal relates the Bible story to the lives of the learners. The third goal encourages the students to take action on what they have learned. You will find diverse activities that may include among other strategies: listening, reading, writing, speaking, singing, drawing, conducting research, interacting with others, and meditating. The lesson ends with "Continue the Journey," where you will find closing activities, preparation for the following week, and ideas for students to commit themselves to action during the week.

In addition to these weekly features, each quarter begins with the following helps:

- **Introduction to the Quarter** provides you with a quick survey of each lesson to be studied during the quarter. You will find the title, background Scripture, date, and a brief summary of each week's basic thrust. This feature is on the first page of each quarter.
- **Meet Our Writer**, which follows the quarterly introduction, provides biographical information about each writer, including education, pastoral and/or academic teaching experience, previous publications, and family information.
- **The Big Picture**, written by the same writer who authored the quarter's lessons, is designed to give you a broader scope of the materials to be covered than is possible in each weekly lesson. You will find this background article immediately following the writer's biography.
- **Close-up** gives you some focused information, such as a timeline, chart, overview, short article, map, word study, or list that you may choose to use for a specific week or anytime during the quarter, perhaps even repeatedly.
- **Faith in Action** provides ideas related to the broad sweep of the quarter that the students can use individually or as a class to act on what they have been studying. These ideas are usually intended for use beyond the classroom.

Finally, two annual features are included:

- **List of Background Scriptures** is offered especially for those of you who keep back copies of *The New International Lesson Annual*. This feature, found immediately after the contents, will enable you to locate Bible background passages used during the current year at some future date.
- **Teacher Enrichment Article** is intended to be useful throughout the year, so we hope you will read it immediately and refer to it often. This year's article, "Teaching for Spiritual Transformation," follows the List of Background Scriptures.

We welcome your suggestions to help us make *The New International Lesson Annual* the first resource you consult when planning your lesson. Please send your questions, comments, and suggestions to me. I invite you to include your e-mail address and/or phone number. I will respond as soon as your message reaches my home office in Maryland.

> Dr. Nan Duerling
> Abingdon Press
> P.O. Box 801
> Nashville, TN 37202

All who use *The New International Lesson Annual* are blessed by the collective community of readers. As you lead this study, we pray that you and the students will be guided by the word of God and the power of the Holy Spirit so as to be transformed and conformed to the image of our Lord and Savior Christ.

> Nan Duerling, Ph.D.
> Editor, *The New International Lesson Annual*

CONTENTS

List of Background Scriptures, 2012–2013 10
Teacher Enrichment: Teaching for Spiritual Transformation 11

FIRST QUARTER

A Living Faith
September 2, 2012–November 25, 2012

Introduction: A Living Faith 15
Meet Our Writer: The Reverend Dr. Michael Fink 16
The Big Picture: The Vital Statitics of Faith 17
Close-up: Paul's Voyage to Rome 21
Faith in Action: Living Our Faith 22

UNIT 1: WHAT IS FAITH?
(September 2-30)

LESSON   PAGE
1.   Faith Calls for Perseverance 23
          September 2—Hebrews 10:19-31
2.   Faith Is Assurance 31
          September 9—Hebrews 11:1-3, 6; Psalm 46:1-3, 8-11
3.   Faith Is Endurance 39
          September 16—Hebrews 12:1-11
4.   Faith Inspires Gratitude 47
          September 23—Hebrews 12:18-29
5.   Faith Requires Mutual Love 55
          September 30—Hebrews 13:1-3; 1 Corinthians 13

UNIT 2: WHO UNDERTANDS FAITH?
(October 7-28)

6.   Stephen's Arrest and Speech 63
          October 7—Acts 6:8–7:2a
7.   Stephen's Martyrdom 71
          October 14—Acts 7:51–8:1a
8.   Simon Wants to Buy Power 79
          October 21—Acts 8:9-24
9.   Philip and the Ethiopian Eunuch 87
          October 28—Acts 8:26-39

UNIT 3: WHERE DOES FAITH TAKE US?
(November 4-25)

10.   Paul Before King Agrippa 95
        November 4—Acts 26:19-32
11.   Paul Sails for Rome 103
        November 11—Acts 27:1-2, 33-44
12.   Paul Ministers in Malta 111
        November 18—Acts 28:1-10
13.   Paul Evangelizes in Rome 119
        November 25—Acts 28:23-31

SECOND QUARTER

Jesus Is Lord
December 2, 2012–February 24, 2013

Introduction: Jesus Is Lord 127
Meet Our Writer: Dr. Jerry L. Sumney 128
The Big Picture: Paul's Prison Epistles 129
Close-up: Cities of Paul's Letters—Facts at a Glance 133
Faith in Action: Proclaiming Jesus as Lord 134

UNIT 1: VICTORY IN JESUS
(December 2-30)

LESSON   PAGE
1.   Spiritual Blessings in Jesus Christ 135
        December 2—Ephesians 1:3-14
2.   One in Jesus Christ 143
        December 9—Ephesians 2:11-22
3.   Unity in the Body of Christ 151
        December 16—Ephesians 4:1-16
4.   Live in the Light 159
        December 23—John 1:1-5; Ephesians 5:1-2, 6-14
5.   Christ's Love for the Church 167
        December 30—Ephesians 5:21–6:4

UNIT 2: EXALTING CHRIST
(January 6-27)

6.   Proclaiming Christ 175
        January 6—Philippians 1:15-26
7.   Jesus' Humility and Exaltation 183
        January 13—Philippians 2:5-11
8.   Gaining in Jesus Christ 191
        January 20—Philippians 3:7-11
9   Stand Firm 199
        January 27—Philippians 3:12-16

UNIT 3: IMITATING JESUS
(February 3-24)

10. The Supremacy of Jesus Christ 207
      February 3—Colossians 1:15-20
11. Full Life in Christ 215
      February 10—Colossians 2:6-15
12. Clothed With Christ 223
      February 17—Colossians 3:5-17
13. Spiritual Disciplines for New Life 231
      February 24—Colossians 4:2-6, 17

THIRD QUARTER

Beyond the Present Time
March 3, 2013–May 26, 2013

Introduction: Beyond the Present Time 239
Meet Our Writer: The Reverend John Indermark 240
The Big Picture: Literatures of Hope 241
Close-up: Finding Hope in Resurrection 245
Faith in Action: Offering Them Hope 246

UNIT 1: THE KINGDOM OF GOD
(March 3-17)

LESSON   PAGE
1. Daniel's Vision of Change 247
      March 3—Daniel 7:9-14
2. Daniel's Prayer 255
      March 10—Daniel 9:4b-14
3. Gabriel's Intepretation 263
      March 17—Daniel 8:19-26

UNIT 2: RESURRECTION HOPE
(March 24–April 28)

4. The Lord's Supper 271
      March 24—Luke 22:14-30
5. The Lord Has Risen Indeed! 279
      March 31—Luke 24:13-21, 28-35
6. The Lord Appears 287
      April 7—Luke 24:36-53
7. The Holy Spirit Comes 295
      April 14—Acts 2:1-13
8. Living With Hope 303
      April 21—1 Thessalonians 4:13–5:11
9. Hope Comes From God's Grace 311
      April 28—2 Thessalonians 2:1-3, 9-17

UNIT 3: A CALL TO HOLY LIVING
(May 5-26)

10.   A Living Hope 319
          May 5—1 Peter 1:3-12
11.   Equipped With Hope 327
          May 12—2 Peter 1:3-14
12.   Hope Through Stewardship 335
          May 19—1 Peter 4:1-11
13.   Hope in the Day of the Lord 343
          May 26—2 Peter 3:1-15a

FOURTH QUARTER

God's People Worship
June 2, 2013–August 25, 2013

Introduction: God's People Worship 351
Meet Our Writer: Dr. Melody Knowles 352
The Big Picture: The Proper Worship of God 353
Close-up: The Prayers of Ezra and Nehemiah 357
Faith in Action: Building Our Church 358

UNIT 1: THE PROPHET AND PRAISE
(June 2-23)

LESSON   PAGE
  1.   Holy, Holy, Holy 359
          June 2—Isaiah 6:1-8
  2.   Give Thanks 367
          June 9—Isaiah 12
  3.   Meaningless Worship 375
          June 16—Isaiah 29:9-16a
  4.   The Glorious New Creation 383
          June 23—Isaiah 65:17-21, 23-25

UNIT 2: WORSHIPING IN JERUSALEM AGAIN (EZRA)
(June 30–July 28)

  5.   Joyful Worship Restored 391
          June 30—Ezra 3:1-7
  6.   Temple Restored 399
          July 7—Ezra 3:8-13
  7.   Dedication of the Temple 407
          July 14—Ezra 6:13-22
  8.   Fasting and Praying 415
          July 21—Ezra 8:21-23
  9.   Gifts for the Temple 423
          July 28—Ezra 8:24-30

UNIT 3: WORSHIPING IN JERUSALEM AGAIN (NEHEMIAH)
(August 4-25)

10.   Festival of Booths 431
       August 4—Nehemiah 8:13-18
11.   Community of Confession 439
       August 11—Nehemiah 9:2, 6-7, 9-10, 30-36
12.   Dedication of the Wall 447
       August 18—Nehemiah 12:27-36, 38, 43
13.   Sabbath Reforms 455
       August 25—Nehemiah 13:15-22

List of Background Scriptures, 2012–2013

Old Testament

Ezra 1:1–3:1-7	June 30	Psalm 46:1-11	September 9
Ezra 3:8-13	July 7	Isaiah 6:1-12	June 2
Ezra 6	July 14	Isaiah 12	June 9
Ezra 8:21-23	July 21	Isaiah 29	June 16
Ezra 8:24-30	July 28	Isaiah 65	June 23
Nehemiah 7:73b–8:18	August 4	Daniel 7	March 3
Nehemiah 9:1-37	August 11	Daniel 9:3-19	March 10
Nehemiah 12:27-43	August 18	Daniel 8	March 17
Nehemiah 13:4-31	August 25		

New Testament

Luke 22:14-30	March 24	Philippians 2:1-13	January 13
Luke 24:1-35	March 31	Philippians 3:1-11	January 20
Luke 24:36-53	April 7	Philippians 3:12–4:1	January 27
John 1:1-14	December 23	Colossians 1:15-20	February 3
Acts 2:1-36	April 14	Colossians 2:6-15	February 10
Acts 6:8–7:53	October 7	Colossians 3:1-17	February 17
Acts 7:1–8:1a	October 14	Colossians 4:2-17	February 24
Acts 8:4-24	October 21	1 Thessalonians 4:13–5:11	April 21
Acts 8:26-39	October 28	2 Thessalonians 2	April 28
Acts 25:23–26:32	November 4	Hebrews 10:19-31	September 2
Acts 27	November 11	Hebrews 11:1-7	September 9
Acts 28:1-10	November 18	Hebrews 12:1-11	September 16
Acts 28:16-31	November 25	Hebrews 12:14-29	September 23
1 Corinthians 13	September 30	Hebrews 13:1-6	September 30
Ephesians 1	December 2	1 Peter 1:1-12	May 5
Ephesians 2–3	December 9	1 Peter 4	May 19
Ephesians 4:1-16	December 16	2 Peter 1	May 12
Ephesians 4:17–5:20	December 23	2 Peter 3	May 26
Ephesians 5:21–6:4	December 30		
Philippians 1:12-30	January 6		

TEACHER ENRICHMENT: TEACHING FOR SPIRITUAL TRANSFORMATION

In the two thousand–plus membership Methodist Episcopal church I grew up in during the 1950s, adult Sunday school was divided into two very large groups—the Women's Bible Class and the Men's Bible Class—and a much smaller class for married couples. I don't know what the couples' group studied, but my parents each took their Bible study "quarterlies" and their Bibles to these larger sessions. My maternal grandmother and grandfather joined my parents in their respective classes. These classes were often discussed over dinner, so I was aware that they were each conducted by a teacher who stood before the group and lectured. To say that the choice of curriculum and teaching styles in these groups was limited is a definite understatement. While these lectures were apparently well received, at least by my family, the classes were definitely one size fits all.

Fast-forward about fifty-five years. Adult Sunday school is still valued by many as an important means through which adults can learn how to become better conformed to the image of Christ. But we also see real changes when compared to my childhood years. Yes, those Bible study "quarterlies" are still very popular, and men's and women's classes still exist in some churches. Now, though, we have all kinds of curriculum from which to choose. Some resources, such as those based on the International Lesson Series, begin with the Bible and apply those lessons to life. Other resources begin with life issues to discern what the Bible has to say about them. Now, in addition to the "quarterly" book, curriculum is available on DVD, as downloadable lessons from the Internet, as short-term studies on specific topics, and also as longer-term studies. Current options for curriculum are almost endless. So too are options for the way in which classes are formed among groups of varying ages and interests. Some classes have been meeting for years; others agree to meet for six weeks. Certain classes are based on common interests, whereas others may be more appealing to specific age groups, such as young adults. Some classes are led by gifted lay teachers, whereas others are led by seminary-educated pastors.

While class configurations and curriculum designs have expanded over the years, have our teaching methods kept up with the changing face of our classes and the materials we have available to us? Or are we still standing before a group lecturing, perhaps inviting a few questions at the end of the session, just as the teachers of my parents' classes did decades ago? If you grew up listening to class lectures and have not had the opportunity to experience or learn about other teaching styles, you may be reluctant to try a different approach, or you may not know how to use a different approach. Lectures certainly have their place, especially if they are short and convey factual information that the students are unlikely to know. In *The New International Lesson Annual*, for example, brief lectures may be suggested for information from Understanding the Scripture. In that section, we consider names, dates, places, concepts, and occasionally Greek or Hebrew words that are useful in explaining the setting of the Scripture and learning why things happened the way they did. While it is easy to ask factual questions, such as "When did the Babylonians destroy the Temple in Jerusalem?" most adults will not be able to respond "587 B.C." If they do not know for certain, they may be afraid to guess; and if they guess and are wrong, they will feel embarrassed. So, when dealing with this kind of information, by all means consider presenting a concise lecture. Once you move beyond questions that have factual, right-or-wrong answers, though, switch to another method. This change may challenge the students who are accustomed to the teacher providing all the answers. The change may also challenge your own comfort level. But think about the purpose of an adult Sunday school class. Are you there for the kinds of information that a lecture can provide? Well, yes, but there is far more. Information is the beginning, but you need to create a learning environment that will help the adults move to a point of spiritual transformation so that they might ultimately be conformed to the image of Christ. That kind of learning requires a student who is fully engaged with the material at hand and with other adults who can help one another in their faith journeys.

Let's take one well-known Bible passage, the story of Jesus feeding the five thousand, which appears in all four Gospels, as an example and see some of the many ways that we might approach it. There are a few factual questions you could ask, such as the time of day, the number of men who were fed, the number of loaves and fish Jesus had to begin, the number of baskets of leftovers. These questions obviously do not take us very far into the heart of the story. To learn more, you may want to use the story from Matthew 14 as the main text and check the details there. Then have a volunteer read the same story from John 6 and discuss how the two different accounts are similar and how they differ. Then wonder with the group why, for example, the detail of the boy with fish and bread being present seemed important to John, whereas Matthew only reported on the "five loaves and two fish" (Matthew 14:17). Ask an open-ended question, that is, one that has multiple correct answers. In this story, you might ask how the boy in John's account felt when he first gave up his lunch and then how he felt later when he saw twelve baskets of leftovers being collected. What impact did this amazing change have on him? How did it draw him closer to Jesus? What did this miracle teach him about turning over what was his so that Jesus could use it for greater purposes? Go deeper into the story by considering the eucharistic imagery: Jesus took, blessed, broke, and gave the bread to those who were present, just as he would later take, bless, break, and give bread to the disciples in the upper room on Holy Thursday. What does this gift of bread to his followers say about his generosity and compassion for these hungry people? Another open-ended approach is to invite the participants to envision themselves as the disciples. Notice that in the story they suggested to Jesus that he order the people to leave, but he put responsibility on the disciples by saying, "You give them something to eat" (Matthew 14:16). Take this a step further: Who is Jesus calling the church to feed, both physically and spiritually, today? How are we responding? Ask a theological question, such as, "What does this story say to us about God?" Such a question will lead to a discussion about God's grace, compassion, and abundance. That discussion may include examples from the group, thus demonstrating how their personal stories intersect with the biblical story.

A discussion based on the kinds of questions we have raised will spark all kinds of ideas and potential new insights. It will enable the learners to explore how the early church heard and understood this story, not just in one community, but in two (or more). It will allow them to walk in the sandals of several important characters; it will encourage them to consider what the story says to the church today; and it will challenge them to live out the story by discerning how they can be a partner in ministry with Christ. That's quite a bit of mileage to get from one story that in John 6 is fifteen verses long and in Matthew 14 is only nine verses long! The difference between presenting a fact-based lecture and inviting the adults to enter into the story is similar to Job's response to God after God challenges him with questions about creation that he cannot possibly answer. Job replies to God, "I had heard of you by the hearing of the ear, / but now my eye sees you" (Job 42:5). We want—God wants—our classes to be places where believers and seekers alike not only have the opportunity to *hear about* God but also have a chance to *see and experience* God as they delve into the Scriptures with others.

Even with well-planned discussion questions that address the Scripture on several levels, some learners may still not see and experience God. They are not necessarily slow of wit or disinterested or skeptical. More than likely they have a different learning style that you need to tap into. Suppose you know that certain class members are very visual learners. Distribute unlined paper and pencils, and ask the class members to draw pictures of the scene of the five thousand as they envision it while you read the story. Or check the Internet or art books prior to the session for pictures depicting this story. Ask several people to retell the story based on the picture they see. Locate information about the number of hungry people in your community and make a chart or create a collage of faces.

Still other learners may not really "get it" until they have had a chance to use their senses to apprehend this story. Prior to reading the story aloud, suggest that the students be aware of what they can see, hear, taste, touch, or smell in this story. Then discuss those sensory impressions after the reading. Depending on factors such as the time of the year this story is taught, the access you have to a church lawn, and the physical mobility of the class members, you may be able to take the class outside for this session. Invite them to sit on the lawn. (You may want to have some blankets available.) Pass out some bread. Simulate the fish by using goldfish crackers. These simple actions will make the story of the feeding of the five thousand come alive.

Another group of adults may learn best through movement or music. Your hymnal may contain hymns based on this story. Or consider using a Communion hymn, such as "One Bread, One Body." Choose several class members to pantomime the story as you read it aloud. Or have a loaf of bread handy and ask two students to divide it and "move through the crowd" to give each person a piece.

Provide opportunities for learners who prefer to look inward to encounter this story in their own space by suggesting that they each write a journal entry as if they were (a) one of the disciples or (b) a person among the crowd who was fed by Jesus. If you are using the version from John's Gospel, suggest that one of the disciples write a note to the boy's mother explaining what happened to his lunch and how his willingness to share led to a miracle through Jesus' compassionate generosity.

Like most narratives, the story of Jesus feeding the five thousand lends itself to a myriad of approaches. Of course, not all of our Bible lessons are based on stories. You may encounter the poetry of prophecy or the Psalms, a historical account, a letter to a church, or another literary form. Not all teaching strategies will work with all types of lessons, but you have many options to draw readers into the passage. Maps can be very useful. For example, during the fall quarter, we will study Paul's journey to Rome and his shipwreck en route in Malta. Tracing his route on a map will allow the adults to see the relationships among the places mentioned in the Bible. You could enrich the experience further by showing pictures of Malta or drawings of ancient ships that might have plied the Mediterranean during the first century.

Sometimes, different ways of reading a passage can help learners encounter the text in a novel way. Reading a psalm silently will be helpful to some, but others will find the passage to be richer if they can participate in a responsive reading. Still others may find it useful to chant a psalm. Many hymnals have a collection of the Psalms printed responsively and with dots over certain words to indicate where the notes of a chant are to be changed.

While it is possible for you to present a lecture on the background and meaning of a passage, a more engaging way is to provide commentaries and Bible dictionaries and invite the adults to work together to find the information. You may provide a list of questions, but another plan is to ask the adults to find out as much as possible and then rewrite the passage in their own words. Most of us do not truly understand something until we can rephrase it in our own words. In a few cases, such as Philippians 2:5-11, participants could be asked to draw a diagram (in this case a V) to illustrate the movement of the passage as Jesus empties himself and is later glorified and exalted by God.

As you choose activities for each lesson, think about your students and ask yourself questions such as:

(1) How might this activity help participants encounter the Scripture passage, particularly one that is very familiar, in a new way?

(2) How will this activity help the students grow in their relationship with Jesus Christ?

(3) How will this activity engage the learners so that they have an opportunity to encounter God, rather than simply hear about God?

Teaching for spiritual transformation is challenging. Providing a wide range of activities for different types of biblical texts, for people at different places along their spiritual journeys, and for different learning styles takes a lot of work. You will not hit a home run every week. An activity that three people find enriching may leave two others scratching their heads. And let's face it: No matter how successful the lesson appears to be, you really cannot take the credit for spiritual growth in the learners. All you can do is set the table—provide the learning environment—where, through the power of the Holy Spirit, each participant may find something in the session that grabs the attention, captures the imagination, stirs the soul, and requires a response. The Spirit, not you, will be responsible for changes in attitudes and behavior that enable the learners to become more closely conformed to Christ. That's a rather humbling thought, especially when you have spent precious time preparing the lesson. But, without your careful planning designed to engage the learners, many of them may come to class, speak politely with classmates, and enjoy the coffee and donuts, only to return home without having seen the Lord. You cannot *make* anyone take a look, but as a teacher you do have the task of polishing the glass so that students who choose to can peer through and encounter the living God. What a great privilege and responsibility!

FIRST QUARTER
A Living Faith

SEPTEMBER 2, 2012–NOVEMBER 25, 2012

During September, October, and November, we will focus attention on the theme of faith. The three units in "A Living Faith" help us describe faith, and explore how the early church thought about and practiced faith. The primary books we will study are Hebrews and Acts.

The five sessions of Unit 1, "What Is Faith?" explore Hebrews 10–13. We respond obediently to God's love as revealed in Jesus Christ, and our response is an act of faith. Through these lessons, we will consider perseverance in faith, the assurance that comes with faith, those saints who serve as models of faith for us, faith as a gift, and how faith and love relate to each other. We begin on September 2 with a session from Hebrews 10:19-31, which teaches us that "Faith Calls for Perseverance." Hebrews 11:1-7 and Psalm 46:1-11 create the background for "Faith Is Assurance" on September 9. "Faith Is Endurance" as well, according to the session on September 16 from Hebrews 12:1-11. Hebrews 12:14-29, which we will study on September 23, teaches that "Faith Inspires Gratitude" when we realize it is a gracious gift from God. The unit ends on September 30 with a lesson from Hebrews 13:1-6 and 1 Corinthians 13 titled "Faith Requires Mutual Love."

The first two lessons in Unit 2, "Who Understands Faith?" focus on Stephen's faithful message and his martyrdom. In the third session we encounter Simon, who saw faith as a commodity that he could buy. The final lesson of this unit investigates the faith that both Philip and the Ethiopian seeker showed as they explored the Scriptures together. The session for October 7, rooted in Acts 6:8–7:53, reviews "Stephen's Arrest and Speech." His bold witness and strong faith resulted in "Stephen's Martyrdom," according to the lesson on October 14 from Acts 7:1–8:1a. A greedy power-monger appears on October 21 in Acts 8:4-24, where we learn that "Simon Wants to Buy Power," a purchase that he believes will allow him to use the Spirit's power to his own advantage. Acts 8:26-39 tells the story we will study on October 28, of "Philip and the Ethiopian Eunuch."

The quarter concludes with four additional sessions from Acts in Unit 3, "Where Does Faith Take Us?" As we study Paul's faith and ministry—before King Agrippa, aboard a ship to Rome, and his continuing evangelism despite his status as a prisoner—we recognize that being faithful costs us much. On November 4, we see "Paul Before King Agrippa," preaching the gospel in Acts 25:23–26:32. The apostle is again the focus of the lesson on November 11, where we read in Acts 27 how he responded to a storm as "Paul Sails for Rome." Continuing the story of his mission by preaching and healing, as told in Acts 28:1-10, we see on November 18 how "Paul Ministers in Malta." This quarter ends on November 25 as we continue to follow Paul, this time as "Paul Evangelizes in Rome," as recorded in Acts 28:16-31.

MEET OUR WRITER

THE REVEREND DR. MICHAEL FINK

This quarter's study represents the fourth contribution that Michael Fink has made to *The New International Lesson Annual*. In his blog (www.mikesthinkingaloud.blogspot.com) you would find him introduced as follows: "In my life I have been a movie projector operator, a lifeguard, a student trainee engineer, a dormitory counselor, a summer missionary, a boys camp counselor, a minister of education and music, an assistant pastor, an interim pastor, a pastor, a college professor of religion, a curriculum designer and editor of Bible study materials, a publishing manager, a staff specialist in religious publishing, a product manager for online sales, a new product development specialist, an adjunct professor, a hardware store salesman, and a retiree, in that order. Through it all I also have been a husband, father, grandfather, writer, poet, preacher, and teacher while trying to be a deeply committed follower of Jesus Christ. I invite you to join me in the journey of life—heart, soul, mind, and strength." That invitation to "the journey of life" continues as you study this quarter's lessons on "A Living Faith."

Mike's journey of life has led him to interesting places in recent years. He and his pastor spent two weeks in the Sichuan Province of China training pastors and other church leaders in Christian ministry and Christian education. Upon returning from that mission trip, one of his former students (from his years as a professor at Campbell University in North Carolina) invited him to join a group on a mission trip to South India. On that trip Mike participated in a missions conference for 180 pastors and their wives from all over India. He also provided support in three medical clinics that were conducted in the tea plantations area of South India and participated in ministry to a children's home that cares for more than 130 children from all over India.

On the home front, Mike teaches a Sunday school class primarily composed of Korean students who are attending Carson-Newman College. He and his wife have adopted five Carson-Newman students, two from the United States and three from Taiwan, Turkmenistan, and Argentina. He chairs his church's benevolence committee, which provides assistance each year to about two hundred families in the community who need help paying utility bills, buying food or prescription drugs, or meeting other needs. He also sings in the church's choir and serves on the Mission Visioning Committee. For many years Mike has worked on contract in developing the Home Daily Bible Readings and the Devotional Readings associated with the International Sunday School Lessons developed by the Committee on the Uniform Series. The lessons you are studying in *The New International Lesson Annual* are based on the Uniform Series.

Mike's wife, Evelyn, is a preschool specialist who loves gardening, music, and shepherding their family of three daughters, two sons-in-law, and four grandchildren. Their oldest daughter does part-time accounting work for the Minnie Pearl Cancer Foundation; their middle child is an administrative specialist with Dell Computer; and their youngest daughter is a pilot with Southwest Airlines. Mike and Evelyn, who reside in Dandridge, Tennessee, are active members of First Baptist Church in nearby Jefferson City.

THE BIG PICTURE:
THE VITAL STATISTICS
OF FAITH

Early in my work on the lessons for this quarter, I experienced a health crisis. I awoke in the middle of the night with an unusual sense of tightness in my chest. Since I was getting ready to leave the next morning on a vacation and was fretting about the strange cycling off and on of our home's air-conditioning system, I thought this probably was a brief attack of tension and anxiety. After the sensation in my chest failed to lessen over the next couple of hours, I awoke my wife and had her drive me to the emergency room at the nearest hospital. That proved to be a wise decision.

The emergency room personnel quickly determined that I was experiencing an episode of atrial fibrillation, and they immediately began to work to get my heart back in rhythm. Over the next three days I was examined, monitored, poked, probed, tested, assessed, and medicated by a wonderful corps of medical personnel. Things that I had once taken for granted (like the steady rhythm of my heart) suddenly became very important to me. "Vital statistics" took on new meaning. Each beat of my heart, every breath I took, every blip on the monitor suddenly was more significant for me than ever before.

When I was released from the hospital, not much had changed from the day before my "a-fib" episode. No causes had been found; no signs of permanent damage were detected; no explanation had been discovered for what caused the attack. Physically I was back to where I had been before the episode—but I really wasn't the same. I was more attuned to my body, to the tensions I experience, and to the importance of the people around me who showed they really cared. My vital statistics meant more to me, and not just the physical ones. Love, home, friends, health, and church took on new significance as I took the vital statistics of my life—which went far beyond the vital statistics of my body.

A Living Faith

This experience gave me a new perspective on my work on these lessons. We are studying "A Living Faith" this quarter, and I began to think of this study through the eyes of my recent hospitalization. If our physical lives have vital statistics, do our spiritual lives exhibit signs of vitality? When we speak of "A Living Faith" in this quarter's study theme, are we looking at faith's vitality and the evidences of its aliveness? "Vital," after all, is derived from the Latin word for "life." In fact, titling our study "A Vital Faith" would not change its focus much at all. If anything, a focus on vitality would move us beyond "a beating heart" to a focus on the power that energizes our faith and sustains it in times of crisis. That realization led me to another insight. Our study this quarter really is designed to examine, monitor, poke, probe, test, and assess the vital statistics of our faith. Maybe this study will keep us from waiting until some major crisis comes along before we begin to probe our faith, to assess its vitality, to monitor its breadth and depth, to test its vulnerabilities, and to poke at its blind spots. I hope that after we have moved through these studies together, you will look back and say, "I have gained a new perspective on my faith. My faith is coming alive. I understand faith more clearly, and I have a new willingness to pay the costs that come with faithfulness."

The Experience of a Living Faith

If you were asked to define the word "life," you would quickly recognize that this simple four-letter word really is quite complex in what it describes. From a single-celled microbe to a human being, "life" has some continuity and a whole lot of diversity. Inanimate things such as flowers and trees have life in them—in fact, the primary definition of "life" notes that "cellular biochemical activity characterized by the ingestion of nutrients, the storage and use of energy, the excretion of wastes, growth, and reproduction" are common threads in all forms of life.

Every day new things begin life, and every day some things cease to live. Every year new species of living forms are discovered, and every year some species become extinct. Of course, we humans, when we speak of life, tend to think in terms of our experience with human life. Dealing with our own experiences is not easy, for we face many crucial issues that complicate our interaction with life. When does life begin? When does it end? How much control and influence should we exercise over its beginning, continuing, and ending? What enables it to thrive? What causes it to deteriorate?

During this quarter, as we consider faith as a living experience, we will face some of the same simple/complex issues in defining the meaning, scope, and experience of faith. We want our lives to exhibit evidence of more than a list of biological functions. Since human life embodies both biological and spiritual dimensions, a living faith reflects the health of that spiritual dimension. Interestingly, a robust spiritual life requires many of the same ingredients as biological life. The spirit needs to be nourished. It needs to store spiritual energy and employ that energy appropriately. It needs to get rid of those wasteful things that rob it of vitality. It needs to grow and to reproduce its faith in the lives of others.

Too often we deal with faith as a dichotomy: It is either alive or dead. While it might be possible for faith to die and a person to continue to live without it (some would dispute that possibility on theological grounds), in most ways our spiritual lives of faith have the same kinds of characteristics, needs, experiences, and threats that physical life faces. Trying to develop criteria to monitor those spiritual dimensions, however, is difficult. A more realistic approach might be to assess the degree to which faith is alive. We may not be able to measure its vitality as easily as we measure physical life, but we will find some measuring standards this quarter that will help us.

The Metrics of a Vital Faith

"Metrics" are "standards of measurement by which efficiency, performance, progress, or quality of a plan . . . can be assessed." This term may be applied to the art of writing in meter, but in recent years the term has been applied in many new ways. Metrics, for example, frequently applies to the standards by which we determine if a person is physically healthy. When you get a physical checkup, you expect your doctor to run a series of tests to assess how well your body is functioning. Each of these tests will have a range of normal readings; and if some metric is out of range, the doctor will investigate further to see whether or not some significant health issue needs to be addressed. The "normal" range of the metrics has been developed from experience with these tests being run on many people. Some people "normally" have abnormal readings on certain tests, but being outside the normal range signals the need for further attention and evaluation.

Of course, our human metrics are never perfect. I have known people who died just days after getting a clean bill of health from their doctors. I also have seen people live for years after being told that their diseases would claim their lives in a matter of days or weeks. We don't stop testing just because our metrics are not 100 percent correct.

Imperfect metrics also arise around attempts to measure faith. Pharisaic Judaism was noted for its exacting prescriptions for what a person should and should not do in living out faith. Certain laws, traditions, and practices formed the basis for its metrics. On the other extreme, libertines dismissed all metrics as oppressive and meaningless. Faith for them involved freedom, license, and self-gratification. Every group, sect, and generation seems to develop its own peculiar set of criteria for measuring faithfulness and insisting on conformity to those metrics. Some focus on beliefs and doctrines. Others honor and preserve traditions. Most have some kind of focus on practicing the faith in daily experience. Many strive for feelings of security and confidence. Each has some central "truths" that undergird and sustain faith.

Our September studies in the Book of Hebrews will show us how traditional faith can be affected by culture, change, challenge, and crisis. We will see how Jesus can become the model for our faith. Our faith metrics will be anchored in his example—the race he ran and the victory he won. Hebrews, however, does not advocate rugged individualism. It addresses an entire community that was forced to adjust its historical understandings in light of the more complete revelation in Jesus Christ. All of the central institutions and images at the core of the Hebrew faith were raised to a higher level of spiritual accountability. The ultimate metric advocated by Hebrews is found in "the pioneer and perfecter of our faith," Jesus Christ, "who . . . endured the cross, disregarding its shame, and has taken his seat at the right hand of the throne of God" (Hebrews 12:2). A living faith, in this context, entails running with perseverance a race on the same track that Jesus pioneered.

Defining the Nature of Faith

In English the word "faith" is a noun. Generally, when we shift to a verb, we push "faith" in the direction of "believe." That is an unfortunate shift in many ways because "believe" weighs heavily on the side of "the mental acceptance of something." If we were shifting back from the verb "believe" to a noun, we generally would use "belief" rather than "faith" as the noun equivalent. This problem does not exist in the New Testament, where the same Greek root serves both the verb and the noun. While the verb in Greek can mean "believe," it carries a special sense when applied to religious beliefs. It emphasizes the idea of "trust in the power of God and God's nearness to help." This meaning presses "faith" much more deeply into the relational ideas of trust, confidence, and conviction.

Many people think that faith is mostly about doctrine. If a person holds orthodox views on the major doctrines of the faith, then his or her faith is correct and valid. Jesus and the early church certainly faced many doctrinal tensions in relation to Judaism, and we especially see these tensions reflected in Acts. The doctrinal issues, however, serve only as flashpoints in a much longer struggle to understand the nature of faith.

Judaism's roots began in an extended family headed by a series of patriarchs. Its faith was defined by a covenant with God and a familial relationship with its adherents. As the families grew, tribes or clans developed, and these tribes lived in proximity to one another but were loosely confederated. The covenant with God narrowed to an exclusive one. They jointly became the people of God, and through the covenantal law God bound them together. The people longed for a greater unity under a king, but even kingship could not hold them together. The nation split into two, and eventually the two fell under foreign domination. Through these centuries of transition, one factor after another became the binding force for the people—family, covenant, land, tribe, law, nation, king, and Temple played varying roles in defining who they were as God's people. In some ways, the same struggle for Israel's core identity continues into our own day.

Christianity emerged in the midst of this identity struggle, and in many ways it added to the struggle. Acts shows how the earliest followers of Jesus struggled with the nature of their relationship with Judaism. Were they a Jewish sect? Were they bound to the covenant, to circumcision, to the law, to kosher regulations, to the land, to the Temple? Acts 1:8 became the central call for the early church, and our studies in October and November will show how that call led to dramatic breaks beyond the boundaries of Judaism "to the ends of the earth."

Recognizing the Cost of Faith

One final element emerges in our studies during October and November. The struggle for authentic faith is not a painless one. Acts reminds us that battles will continue to be fought over the parameters that define authentic faith. Narrow vision will resist the expansion of inclusiveness. The finely defined parameters offered by legalism will resist the Spirit's attempt to draw all people into God's embrace. At one time or another almost all committed believers will resist new ideas, change, and freedom. Progress is made only through deep commitment, hard work, fearless perseverance, and staunch boldness.

Jesus, who launched the good news and blazed the trail as pioneer and perfecter of faith, set a path that led to Calvary. As painful as the brutal cross must have been, the greater pain had been that the invitation of a loving Abba was rejected right and left by the very ones chosen to bless the nations on God's behalf. All the exclusive commitment, all the pride and passion for being God's people, all the hope for establishing a kingdom ruled by God failed when exclusiveness became a barrier, when pride elevated egos, when passion was channeled into defensiveness, and when hope focused on winning a selfish victory rather than winning the lost. If that sounds somewhat anti-Semitic, let me emphasize that the very same inclinations continue in our day, in our country, in our churches, and—let's be honest—in our hearts.

Stephen, Philip, and Paul are highlighted in our studies in October and November. Two of these three disciples followed Jesus in a martyr's death. Stephen's bravery may have been an inspiring example for the other two. The apostles faced resistance, suppression, and imprisonment from the ruling authorities, but Stephen, a Hellenist who is mentioned first when a dispute arose in the early Christian community, became the first martyr. Luke described him in the most glowing terms and reserved the longest address in Acts to this bold leader.

Philip prepared the way for taking the gospel to people outside the Jewish community. True, he left Jerusalem under the threat of persecution, but he seems to have heard clearly Jesus' call to take the gospel beyond the Jewish enclave into neighboring Samaria. Philip followed Jesus, who had been the true pioneer making the first advances into Samaria (John 4:1-42).

Luke mentioned others who opened the doors of the gospel in keeping with Acts 1:8, but most of his attention focused on the work of Paul—perhaps because Luke traveled a good bit with Paul, receiving firsthand knowledge of Paul's evangelistic efforts. Though Paul's martyrdom is not referenced in Acts, he too followed in the path of suffering pioneered by Jesus. In faith, all of these strived to unfetter the gospel so that it could spread boldly and without hindrance (Acts 28:31).

May our study this quarter guide us on that same path, proclaiming the gospel and teaching about our Lord with all boldness and without hindrance.

CLOSE-UP:
PAUL'S VOYAGE TO ROME

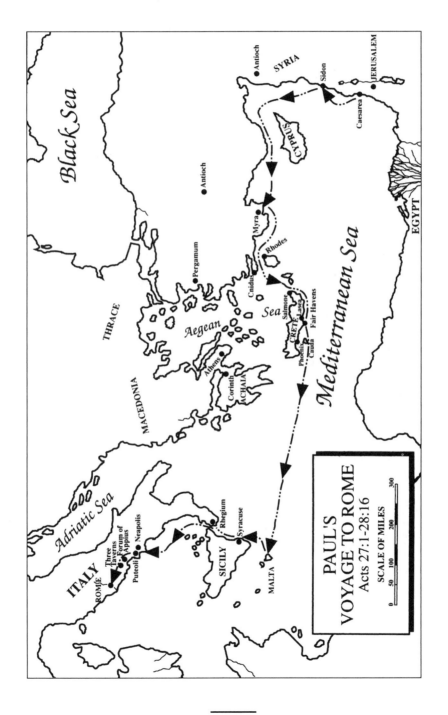

PAUL'S
VOYAGE TO ROME
Acts 27:1–28:16
SCALE OF MILES

FAITH IN ACTION: LIVING OUR FAITH

Our sessions during this fall quarter focus on describing faith, trying to understand it, and counting its cost as it takes us to places we may prefer not to go. Wrapped together, this course encourages us to live our faith in Christ. But what does that entail?

Distribute paper and pencils. Read the following sentences aloud or post them on newsprint. Encourage participants to complete the sentences in ways that reflect a lived faith. These sentences are open-ended, so there is no single correct answer but instead many alternatives. Set a time limit.

(1) To better know what God expects of faithful believers, I regularly practice the following spiritual disciplines: _____.

(2) When I encounter a person who is clearly hungry or homeless, I attempt to live faithfully by _____.

(3) When I encounter a stranger, I show God's hospitality by _____.

(4) I share my faith with others by _____.

(5) Two biblical characters who are models for my faith are _____ and _____ because _____.

(6) Two people I know personally who are models for my faith are _____ and _____ because _____.

(7) When I read about unjust structures in my society, I try to address these problems by _____.

(8) I find assurance in my faith through _____.

(9) I realize that faith is costly. One experience that taught me this is _____.

(10) I demonstrate my love of God in the following ways: _____.

(11) When crises befall me, my first response is often _____.

(12) As an expression of my faith, I worship God by _____.

(13) When I think of God's love for me, words come to mind such as _____.

(14) I live my faith by giving about _____ percent of my income to God.

(15) When I meet a newcomer to the church, I try to welcome that person by

_____.

Call the group back together when time is up. Go through the questions, encouraging volunteers to voice their responses. Talk especially about those questions where there seems to be a wide variety of answers. Suggest that the adults listen carefully and perhaps make some notes on their papers when they hear new ideas. They may wish to try something that has worked for other class members.

UNIT 1: WHAT IS FAITH?

FAITH CALLS FOR PERSEVERANCE

PREVIEWING THE LESSON

Lesson Scripture: Hebrews 10:19-31
Background Scripture: Hebrews 10:19-31
Key Verse: Hebrews 10:23

Focus of the Lesson:

People wonder about, may even envy, others who feel secure about their spiritual lives. What security is available? The writer of Hebrews tells us that our sins can be forgiven because of the blood of Jesus and that we can experience the presence of God in a new and life-giving way through faith.

Goals for the Learners:

(1) to gain knowledge about the power of faith in Jesus.
(2) to reflect on their security in Jesus Christ.
(3) to increase their confidence in sharing Jesus Christ with others.

Supplies:

Bibles, newsprint and marker, paper and pencils, hymnals

READING THE SCRIPTURE

NRSV
Lesson Scripture: Hebrews 10:19-31

[19]Therefore, my friends, since we have confidence to enter the sanctuary by the blood of Jesus, [20]by the new and living way that he opened for us through the curtain (that is, through his flesh), [21]and since we have a great priest over the house of God, [22]let us approach with a true heart in full assurance of faith, with our hearts sprinkled

CEB
Lesson Scripture: Hebrews 10:19-31

[19]Brothers and sisters, we have confidence that we can enter the holy of holies by means of Jesus' blood, [20]through a new and living way that he opened up for us through the curtain, which is his body, [21]and we have a great high priest over God's house.

[22]Therefore, let's draw near with a genuine heart with the certainty that our faith

clean from an evil conscience and our bodies washed with pure water. **²³Let us hold fast to the confession of our hope without wavering, for he who has promised is faithful.** ²⁴And let us consider how to provoke one another to love and good deeds, ²⁵not neglecting to meet together, as is the habit of some, but encouraging one another, and all the more as you see the Day approaching.

²⁶For if we willfully persist in sin after having received the knowledge of the truth, there no longer remains a sacrifice for sins, ²⁷but a fearful prospect of judgment, and a fury of fire that will consume the adversaries. ²⁸Anyone who has violated the law of Moses dies without mercy "on the testimony of two or three witnesses." ²⁹How much worse punishment do you think will be deserved by those who have spurned the Son of God, profaned the blood of the covenant by which they were sanctified, and outraged the Spirit of grace? ³⁰For we know the one who said, "Vengeance is mine, I will repay." And again, "The Lord will judge his people." ³¹It is a fearful thing to fall into the hands of the living God.

gives us, since our hearts are sprinkled clean from an evil conscience and our bodies are washed with pure water.

²³Let's hold on to the confession of our hope without wavering, because the one who made the promises is reliable.

²⁴Let's also think about how to motivate each other to show love and to do good works. ²⁵Don't stop meeting together with other believers, which some people have gotten into the habit of doing. Instead, encourage each other, especially as you see the day drawing near.

²⁶If we make the decision to sin after we receive the knowledge of the truth, there isn't a sacrifice for sins left any longer. ²⁷There's only a scary expectation of judgment and of a burning fire that's going to devour God's opponents. ²⁸When someone rejected the Law from Moses, they were put to death without mercy on the basis of the testimony of two or three witnesses. ²⁹How much worse punishment do you think is deserved by the person who walks all over God's Son, who acts as if the blood of the covenant that made us holy is just ordinary blood, and who insults the Spirit of grace? ³⁰We know the one who said,

Judgment is mine; I will pay people back.
And he also said,
The Lord will judge his people.
³¹It's scary to fall into the hands of the living God!

UNDERSTANDING THE SCRIPTURE

Introduction. The Book of Hebrews begins with a reference to "long ago" when God spoke to "*our* ancestors" through the prophets (1:1; emphasis added to highlight the author's identification with his readers). Immediately, however, the author turned to "these last days" when God "has spoken to us by a Son" (1:2). These introductory verses set the context for the entire Book of Hebrews. They establish the tensions between the past and the present for its readers. The continuity with the past was strained by an influx of new believers who had no background or history in Judaism. In fact, these new Gentile believers soon outnumbered the Jewish adherents. The old ways of living one's faith through covenant, priest, prophet, Temple, and ritual were not fully understood, appreciated, or practiced by these newcomers. An aggressive evangelistic spirit had gripped the church, and many unfamiliar with the past were flooding in. Both traditional Jews and Roman officials were trying to contain the infectious spirit of this movement. Jewish believers were caught in the middle. They were sympathetic toward the past and their roots in Judaism, but they did not welcome the repressions coming upon them (see 10:32-34).

The Book of Hebrews addressed these Jewish believers caught in the middle. Many of them were being drawn back into the comfortable expressions of their established Jewish faith, abandoning the new spirit and freedom that had been won for them through Christ. The writer encouraged his readers by reinterpreting the central tenets of the Jewish faith, viewing them through the lens of Jesus' own experience and example. Thereby he encouraged them to hold on to their new faith in Christ and not to draw away from a fellowship enfolding all believers.

Hebrews 10:19-22. Affirming a common bond with his readers by calling them "friends" (literally "brothers," 10:19), the writer focused on the significant changes that had been wrought through Jesus Christ. The writer used Old Testament images (sanctuary, blood, curtain, priest, house of God) to highlight what had been accomplished through the life, death, and resurrection of Jesus. These images held special significance for Jewish believers, but the power of the writer's arguments would have been affected by when he wrote. If he wrote before the destruction of the Jerusalem Temple by the Romans in A.D. 70, the images reflected live practices in the Temple. If he wrote following the Temple's destruction, the images embodied past memories, the hope for future restoration, and perhaps even a significant need for reinterpretation—a task that may be represented in his book.

In a fashion resembling Plato, the writer contrasted the actual practices of Jewish rituals in the earthly Temple with the redemption accomplished by Jesus' death on the cross. The former were like shadows that only dimly represented the once-for-all sacrifice that offered confident access to reconciliation with God.

Earlier in chapter 10 the writer pointed out the inadequacy of daily sacrifices of bulls and goats in the Temple (10:4). Here he points to a new and living way to God through Christ that surpasses what the high priest could do when he entered the sanctuary (the Holy of Holies behind the curtain in the Temple). References to sanctuary, curtain, great priest, house of God, hearts sprinkled clean, and bodies washed with pure water all related to the rituals associated with the once-a-year sacrifice on the Day of Atonement. This was such a sacred experience that an apocryphal tradition says that a cord was tied around the ankle of the high priest so that if he were to die from his encounter with the holy God, his body could be pulled out of the sanctuary. In sharp contrast, the new and living way opened by Jesus allowed all believers to approach God with confidence. We have in Jesus a high priest who brings us into the presence of God, and we can come in full assurance with true hearts and cleansed consciences.

Hebrews 10:23-25. Though believers could approach God with confidence because of the once-for-all sacrifice of Jesus, they still were approaching a holy God. Coming into God's presence necessitated some careful self-examination. The writer noted the consequences brought on by their current situation.

First, some believers were wavering in their faith. The hope in Christ that they once had confessed was declining. God's faithfulness could sustain them if they only would recognize it and embrace it.

Second, the love that had characterized the believers' fellowship was weakening, and the good deeds expressed through that love were declining. If they would show greater consideration for one another, they would stir up love and good deeds.

Third, some were habitually absent from the gathering of believers. Whether by intention or neglect, their participation in the body of believers was declining. They needed to be exhorted and entreated to renew their commitment to the body of Christ. The writer saw this as an urgent matter in light of the approaching day of the Lord.

Hebrews 10:26-31. The focus of the writer's concerns becomes clear in 10:26. The problems were not brought on by mere neglect; they were evidence of willful or intentional sin. To emphasize the seriousness of the problem, the writer pointed to the theological consequences of such behavior. The sacrifice for sin through the death of Christ is the once-for-all remedy for sin to those who have received the knowledge of truth. But after receiving that remedy, further willful sin has no further sacrifice to provide a remedy. The only remaining prospect is terrifying judgment and a fiery anger that consumes God's adversaries.

The law of Moses provided for a death penalty upon the testimony of two or three witnesses (Deuteronomy 17:6-7). The prospects for one who spurns the Son of God, profanes the sanctifying blood of the covenant, and insults the Spirit of grace are worse.

The writer concluded this section with a foreboding warning of how dreadful the prospects will be for those blatant sinners who fall into the hands of the Living God.

INTERPRETING THE SCRIPTURE

The Confidence to Draw Near

The writer of Hebrews strongly emphasized that believers have confidence to draw near to God because of what God had accomplished through Jesus Christ. The imagery he used to explain that confidence drew heavily upon Old Testament institutions that were familiar to "the Hebrews" to whom he wrote. They were not so familiar to the Gentile members of the early church, and they may not be familiar to contemporary Christians.

From the time of Moses, the presence of God was represented among God's people by a holy place into which only the high priest could enter. At first this holy place was in a movable tabernacle. After Solomon's Temple was built in Jerusalem, this holy place was located in the Temple. The "Holy of Holies" ("sanctuary" in NRSV; "the Most Holy Place," Hebrews 10:19 NIV) was the most sacred room in the Temple. It was entered only once a year on the Day of Atonement, when the high priest entered the sanctuary to sprinkle sacrificial blood and make atonement for the people. The sanctuary was separated by a curtain from another room where priests daily ministered before God. In the courtyards surrounding the Temple, specific areas were restricted to priests, Israelite men, or Israelite women. An altar for offering sacrifices and a basin for ritual washing were restricted to priests, though the activities there could be viewed by Israelite men and women. Outside all of these areas (and separated from them by a wall with warnings for others not to enter) was a large courtyard for Gentiles. The whole structure was designed to limit access to God and protect the people from the holiness of God.

With this structure in view, note the revolutionary changes in the traditional access to God that the writer expounds (10:19-22). Hebrews says that all believers can enter into the sanctuary—in essence we all are high priests. The blood of Jesus, which symbolizes his death on the cross, has opened a new and living way into the Holy of Holies for all believers. Our hearts have been cleansed both by the blood of Jesus and the washing of our bodies (symbolized in baptism). With true hearts in full assurance of faith, we can confidently enter into the very presence of God.

The Danger of Drifting Away

The writer of Hebrews warned readers that, in spite of the access available to God through Jesus, believers must approach God "with a true heart in full assurance of faith" (10:22). Following that admonition, the writer gave clues that all is not right in his audience. He sprinkles his letter with words and phrases such as "hold fast," "wavering," "not neglecting," "willfully persist in sin," "violated the Law," "spurned the Son of God," "profaned the blood of the covenant," and "outraged the Spirit of grace." Together these give clues of real trouble.

The writer also gives clues to how the church arrived in this trouble. In the beginning, the congregation had a full assurance of faith bolstered by hope. Cleansed and purified from an evil conscience, they lived with the law of God in their hearts and minds. As time passed, the hope that God would quickly fulfill divine promises began to waver and wane. Expectations that a faithful God would act quickly to establish a sovereign kingdom began to fade. Dissension began to rise within the congregation, and so the love and good deeds that once characterized their fellowship began to decline. To avoid the growing conflict, some members began to stay home. Eventually, their avoidance turned to neglect in meeting together.

The result of this was a drifting away from God and from the fellowship of believers when all that Christ had done for his people was designed to draw them closer to God and closer to one another. The writer of Hebrews called his readers to a steadfast faith that perseveres not only in times of difficulty but also in ordinary times when routine sets in and neglect of our faith is easier than maintaining vigilance.

Some people find a focus on the number of members on a church's roll to be unspiritual. To be concerned about how many people attend church services would be viewed by these same folks as a secular concern. While all of us know that spiritual commitment and religious devotion cannot easily be quantified, we also recognize that we "vote" by our presence. The time we give in terms of presence and attention tells much about what we value. The first sign of drifting away is absence, "neglecting to meet together" (10:25). When that absence becomes a habit, we must encourage one another and "consider how to provoke one another to love and good deeds" (10:24).

Defining the Drift

The Book of Hebrews reflects a pivotal point in time for the early Christians. Birthed from the womb of Judaism, early Christianity drew its heritage, its Scriptures, and its practices from the faith of its Jewish ancestors. As evidenced in Acts 6, however, tensions quickly developed within the Christian community between those with a Hebrew background and those with a Greek background. At first these tensions arose over practical matters of administration, but by the time of Acts 15 tensions were surfacing over foundational doctrinal issues.

The church was forced to decide how the emerging Christian community related to its Jewish foundations. How did Gentiles fit into the Christian community? Must they accept all of Judaism in order to be followers of Jesus? Was the church only a movement or sect within Judaism? If it was more, how did its Jewish heritage affect its mission "to the ends of the earth" (Acts 1:8)?

The writer of Hebrews saw that some were drifting away from the fellowship of the church, but the people to whom he wrote certainly would have disagreed over what constituted a drift. Those whose background was in Judaism (the target audience for this book) probably viewed any neglect of the basic tenets of Judaism as drifting away from the faith revealed to their ancestors. They fought hard to preserve Jewish values centered in the covenant law and in Jewish practices like circumcision, food laws, and Sabbath observance. These people could be called "Judaizers" because they wanted all believers to come under the tent of the covenant. Departure from even the minutest detail of the law would be viewed by them as drifting.

The apostle Paul championed another view. The law was merely a "tutor to lead us to Christ, so that we may be justified by faith. But now that faith has come, we are no longer under a tutor" (Galatians 3:24-25 NASB). Distinctive Jewish practices were outward symbols of an inner experience: "a person is a Jew who is one inwardly, and real circumcision is a matter of the heart—it is spiritual and not literal" (Romans 2:29). From this perspective, drifting is sliding back into literal Jewish practices rather than claiming the freedom that comes from religion of the heart.

The Book of Hebrews adopts Paul's views, but not without giving extensive evidence of how the fundamental concepts of the Jewish faith had been fulfilled in Christ. Moses and the law, the priesthood, the earthly sanctuary, and the atoning sacrifices all found their completion in Jesus Christ. The covenant had not been set aside; it had been fulfilled and indeed surpassed in Christ. In the writer's view, drifting was neither moving back toward Judaism nor moving away from Judaism. Instead, it was neglecting the fellowship of those who had been cleansed by the blood of Jesus and granted access to the holy God, those whose hearts had become true by faith and whose lives had been directed toward a new and living way.

SHARING THE SCRIPTURE

Preparing Our Hearts

Explore this week's devotional reading, found in Romans 5:1-5. Paul opens this chapter by assuring readers that they can be confident that through Christ they are now "justified," put right, with God. Verses 3-5 identify the links of a chain reaction—endurance, character, hope—that originated in suffering and result in an outpouring of God's love. Recall times of suffering in your own life. Can you see, in retrospect, how such situations produced the traits that Paul listed? Are there other traits that you would add? Have you claimed the "peace with God" that Christ offers? If not, what barriers prevent you from doing so?

Pray that you and the adult students will persevere and grow in your faith.

Preparing Our Minds

Study the background Scripture and the lesson Scripture, both of which are from Hebrews 10:19-31.

Consider this question as you prepare the lesson: *What security is available in our spiritual lives?*

Write on newsprint:
❑ information for next week's lesson, found under "Continue the Journey."
❑ activities for further spiritual growth in "Continue the Journey."

Review the "Introduction," "The Big

Picture," "Close-up," and "Faith in Action." Consider how you will use this additional information, which immediately precedes the first lesson, for this session and throughout the quarter.

Familiarize yourself with the information in Understanding the Scripture and Interpreting the Scripture so that you can add to the discussion as appropriate.

LEADING THE CLASS

(1) Gather to Learn

❖ Greet the class members. Introduce any guests and help them feel at home.

❖ Pray that the adults will experience God's presence in a new and life-giving way.

❖ Read this information: **Martin Luther, one of the great founders and theologians of the Protestant Reformation, was fearful of hell and lacking in assurance that he was saved. Even after he had been ordained in the Roman Catholic Church, he still felt very insecure about his eternal life. This anxiety continued until he recognized that he was saved by grace through faith alone (see Ephesians 2:4-8). Once Luther recognized this truth in Paul's writings, he felt assured that he was indeed forgiven and saved, not because of anything he did, but because God offered this free gift through Jesus Christ.**

John Wesley, the founder of the Methodist movement, who died 245 years after Luther, experienced the same kinds of doubts and insecurities. While attending a small religious gathering on Aldersgate Street, London, on May 24, 1738, Wesley, who was by then an ordained Anglican priest, reported a spiritual experience in which his "heart was strangely warmed." Like Luther, he realized that salvation came by faith in Christ alone.

❖ Ask: **Are you surprised that these two spiritual giants had such doubts about their salvation? Why or why not?**

❖ Read aloud today's focus statement: **People wonder about, may even envy, others who feel secure about their spiritual lives. What security is available? The writer of Hebrews tells us that our sins can be forgiven because of the blood of Jesus and that we can experience the presence of God in a new and life-giving way through faith.**

(2) Goal 1: Gain Knowledge About the Power of Faith in Jesus

❖ Read or retell "Introduction" in Understanding the Scripture to provide a context for today's reading.

❖ Choose two volunteers, one to read Hebrews 10:19-25 and the other to read verses 26-31. Discuss the following questions. Refer to Understanding the Scripture and Interpreting the Scripture for help with answers.

  (1) **What kinds of changes does the writer of Hebrews point out to his readers with respect to access to God?**

  (2) **Describe situations among the believers that are discussed in Hebrews 10:23-25. Which of these might still be seen in the church today?** (See especially "The Danger of Drifting Away" in Interpreting the Scripture.)

  (3) **What are the consequences of intentional sin, according to Hebrews 10:26-31?**

  (4) **What kind of picture does this description of the consequences of sin paint of God? How does this picture square with your own understanding of God?**

❖ Wrap up by asking: **What new knowledge have you gained about the power of faith in Jesus?**

(3) Goal 2: Reflect on the Learners' Security in Jesus Christ

❖ Read or retell "The Confidence to Draw Near" from Interpreting the Scripture.

❖ Invite individuals to tell brief stories of times when they felt that Christ would care for them and so persevered when others may have given up. Encourage them to be forthright about their fears and concerns, as well as why they remained steadfast in their faith.

❖ Post newsprint and invite the students to answer this question: **Why do you believe in Jesus Christ?**

❖ Provide a few moments of quiet time for the participants to review the list, identify those points that highlight their own reasons for belief, and mentally add any other points that are important to them.

(4) Goal 3: Increase Confidence in Sharing Jesus Christ With Others

❖ Form groups of three to do role-plays. One person will observe a conversation between an unbeliever and a friend who wants to share Christ. Provide time for each person to play at least two of the roles. Suggest that as group members play the part of the believer who wants to share his or her faith, they decide which of the points from the previous activity they will want to highlight.

❖ Call the groups together. Invite those who observed conversations to comment on strategies for sharing faith that seemed to work well and note other strategies that did not seem as effective. Suggest that they try to pinpoint why some ways of sharing faith worked, while others did not. Try to keep personalities out of the discussion; simply focus on strategies.

(5) Continue the Journey

❖ Pray that those who have come today will go forth to share their faith in Jesus Christ with others.

❖ Read aloud this preparation for next week's lesson. You may also want to post it on newsprint for the students to copy.

■ **Title: Faith Is Assurance**

■ **Background Scripture: Hebrews 11:1-7; Psalm 46:1-11**

■ **Lesson Scripture: Hebrews 11:1-3, 6; Psalm 46:1-3, 8-11**

■ **Focus of the Lesson: Because of all the conflicts in the world, people may lose hope for positive change. What prompts people to hope for positive change? By believing in God's strength, say the writers of Hebrews and the Psalms, we can be rescued and change can take place because God is with us.**

❖ Post these three activities related to this week's session on newsprint for the students to copy. Challenge the adults to grow spiritually by completing one or more of them.

(1) Talk with at least one other person about your faith in God through Jesus Christ. Follow up with this person to see if he or she seems ready to visit your church or wants to learn more about what it means to be a Christian. Be winsome in your approach.

(2) Be aware of people who are living out their faith, particularly under challenging circumstances. Talk with several of these people, if possible, to learn why their faith is so strong.

(3) Write in a spiritual journal about a time when you experienced spiritual growth because of a situation that caused your faith to deepen.

❖ Sing or read aloud "I Am Thine, O Lord."

❖ Conclude today's session by leading the class in this benediction, adapted from the key verses for September 16 from Hebrews 12:1-2: **Let us go forth to run with perseverance the race that is set before us, looking to Jesus the pioneer and perfecter of our faith.**

UNIT 1: WHAT IS FAITH?
FAITH IS ASSURANCE

PREVIEWING THE LESSON

Lesson Scripture: Hebrews 11:1-3, 6; Psalm 46:1-3, 8-11
Background Scripture: Hebrews 11:1-7; Psalm 46:1-11
Key Verse: Hebrews 11:1

Focus of the Lesson:
Because of all the conflicts in the world, people may lose hope for positive change. What prompts people to hope for positive change? By believing in God's strength, say the writers of Hebrews and the Psalms, we can be rescued and change can take place because God is with us.

Goals for the Learners:
(1) to explore the meaning of faith and its implications for our lives.
(2) to appreciate and grow from the faith of others.
(3) to develop a practice of relying on God for positive change.

Pronunciation Guide:
hypostasis (hoop os' tas is)
Paraclete (pair' uh kleet)
Selah (see' luh)

Supplies:
Bibles, newsprint and marker, paper and pencils, hymnals

READING THE SCRIPTURE

NRSV
Lesson Scripture: Hebrews 11:1-3, 6

¹Now faith is the assurance of things hoped for, the conviction of things not seen. ²Indeed, by faith our ancestors received approval. ³By faith we understand that the worlds were prepared by the word

CEB
Lesson Scripture: Hebrews 11:1-3, 6

¹Faith is the reality of what we hope for, the proof of what we don't see. ²The elders in the past were approved because they showed faith.

³By faith we understand that the universe

of God, so that what is seen was made from things that are not visible.

⁶And without faith it is impossible to please God, for whoever would approach him must believe that he exists and that he rewards those who seek him.

has been created by a word from God so that the visible came into existence from the invisible.

⁶It's impossible to please God without faith because the one who draws near to God must believe that he exists and that he rewards people who try to find him.

Lesson Scripture: Psalm 46:1-3, 8-11

¹ God is our refuge and strength,
  a very present help in trouble.
² Therefore we will not fear, though
    the earth should change,
  though the mountains shake in
    the heart of the sea;
³ though its waters roar and foam,
  though the mountains tremble with
    its tumult.   *Selah*
⁸ Come, behold the works of the LORD;
  see what desolations he has brought
    on the earth.
⁹ He makes wars cease to the end of
    the earth;
  he breaks the bow, and shatters
    the spear;
  he burns the shields with fire.
¹⁰ "Be still, and know that I am God!
  I am exalted among the nations,
  I am exalted in the earth."
¹¹ The LORD of hosts is with us;
  the God of Jacob is our refuge.   *Selah*

Lesson Scripture: Psalm 46:1-3, 8-11

¹ God is our refuge and strength,
  a help always near
    in times of great trouble.
² That's why we won't be afraid
  when the world falls apart,
  when the mountains crumble into the
    center of the sea,
³ when its waters roar and rage,
  when the mountains shake
    because of its surging waves.   *Selah*
⁸ Come, see the LORD's deeds,
  what devastation he has imposed
    on the earth—
⁹ bringing wars to an end
    in every corner of the world,
  breaking the bow
    and shattering the spear,
  burning chariots with fire.
¹⁰ "That's enough!
  Now know that I am God!
  I am exalted among all nations;
    I am exalted throughout the world!"
¹¹ The LORD of heavenly forces is with us!
  The God of Jacob is our place of safety.
                                   Selah

UNDERSTANDING THE SCRIPTURE

Introduction. The writer of Hebrews concluded his call for believers to persevere in their faith with a final word of encouragement: "We are not among those who shrink back and so are lost, but among those who have faith and so are saved" (Hebrews 10:39). "Those who shrink back" was his characterization both of those who were sliding back into comfortable Old Testament practices and those whose confident faith was being weakened by persecution and public abuse. The course he proposed was a persevering faith that leads to salvation. Psalm 46 reminds us that we can have that kind of faith because we have a great God on whom we can rely.

Hebrews 11:1-3. The kind of faith the writer propounded required further definition and illustration. In both his definition and his illustration he drew from the readers' Jewish heritage while encouraging them toward new dimensions and understandings of faith.

Two words, "assurance" and "conviction," were used to define faith. "Assurance" translates a Greek word, *hypostasis*, which has been brought over into English and literally means "to stand under." It implies a support or foundation. That foundation supports the things for which believers are presently hoping. "Things" come from the Greek root that supplies our English word "pragmatic," and it basically deals with doing practical things. A paraphrase might be "Faith is the foundation for this business we call hope."

"Conviction" ("evidence" in KJV) is a rare noun in the New Testament, but the underlying verb means to bring something to light or to convince someone of something and thus convict them or create a conviction. A more literal translation would be "Faith is being convinced of things that currently are unseen." Verse 3 expands these "things" to "the worlds" (literally, "the eons" or "the ages," which implies "eternity") where the word of God brought creation into existence out of invisible nothingness. "Prepared by the word of God" calls to mind John 1:1-5, and "prepared" also could be translated "created" here. The reference to "ancestors," "ancients" (NIV), "men of old" (NASB), or "elders" (KJV) in verse 2 points toward the "faith hall of fame" depicted in verses 4-40.

Hebrews 11:4-7. Having defined faith, the writer went on to illustrate it. Before we look at the illustrations, verse 6 should claim our attention. It emphasizes the important role that faith plays in our relationship with God. While Hebrews states it negatively ("*without* faith it is *impossible* to please God," emphasis added), Paul represented this idea positively in Galatians 5:6: "The only thing that counts is faith working through love." Faith involves both believing

and seeking—believing that the invisible God exists and seeking the Holy One diligently. On those criteria alone will God reward believers and take pleasure in them. The placement of these criteria is significant, for pleasing God was possible before Abraham (Hebrews 11:8-19); before Isaac, Jacob, and Joseph (11:20-22); before Moses (11:23-28); and before all the subsequent models of faith (11:29-38).

In Hebrews 11:4-5 the writer focused on Abel (Genesis 4:1-10), Enoch (5:18-24), and Noah (5:28–9:29) as his first examples of the kind of faith that pleases God. Abel was a copycat in following his brother's example in making an offering to God, but something about the manner in which he gave set apart his sacrifice of faith as "more acceptable" (Hebrews 11:4). Perhaps it was that he gave "the firstlings of his flock, the fat portions" (Genesis 4:4), rather than leftovers he had in hand. His spirit in giving certainly contrasted to Cain's. Abel's example of faith "still speaks" (Hebrews 11:4).

Enoch's only commendation was that he "walked with God" (Genesis 5:22, 24), but walking with God speaks of a lifetime of faith. The writer of Hebrews reminds us that faith is not merely a moment of high commitment, a one-time experience, or a point of decision; it is a lifelong walk with God.

Noah's story in Genesis 6–9 is more extensive and is not always flattering, but his example is commended because of his foundational acts of obeying God and building the ark in faith. Noah too walked with God as a just man, perfect in his generation (6:9). While the mocking and scoffing we often associate with Noah's story are not mentioned in the Genesis account, Noah held on to a firm conviction of what God expected in spite of the almost universal wickedness, violence, and debauchery of his time. God established the first covenant with Noah and through him with all humanity who followed.

Psalm 46:1-3. If faith is a matter of inner

qualities like assurance and conviction, then the examples of Abel, Enoch, and Noah add outward expression to the mix. Such a faith will be sustained in daily life, in good times and in bad. Psalm 46 is a classic example of faith being put into practice during challenging times of "trouble."

Psalm 46 focuses on the God who is the object of faith. The psalm employs two Hebrew names for God: *Elohim* (used seven times) is more closely associated with Hebrew worship, and *Yahweh* (used three times) is associated with the covenant with Abraham and the giving of the law to Moses. The same God who is yesterday, today, and forever (compare Hebrew 13:8) in creation, call, and covenant is a constant Presence with the people who acknowledge God. The Creator of the earth, mountains, and seas is still Lord over creation; and though people may feel danger, threat, and anxiety in natural disasters, God remains a strong refuge and strength for those who need help in trouble.

Psalm 46:4-7. The psalmist next assured worshipers of God's presence in the very midst of them. The "city of God" (Psalm 46:4-5) certainly refers to Jerusalem, where God was worshiped in the Temple. While Jerusalem had no "river," it was blessed with springs, fountains, pools, and a system of canals and aqueducts that supplied its need for water; and the land around it was "a good land, a land with flowing streams, with springs and underground waters welling up in valleys and hills" (Deuteronomy 8:7). The streams that gave life and gladness to the faithful were daily reminders of God in their midst. The God whose refuge of grace was enjoyed by God's faithful also brings judgment and terror to the pagan nations.

Psalm 46:8-11. God is supreme in power, and all the earth is under God's command. God can bring desolation or consolation. Evil's greatest destructive powers are under God's control. Wars can be halted, and weapons of war can be destroyed. Peace is offered to those who see God's works, reverence God's presence, and exalt God among the nations of the world. Until God's peace is established, God's faithful ones will find refuge with the Lord of hosts, who is with us.

INTERPRETING THE SCRIPTURE

Defining Faith

The word "faith" is used so widely in religious circles that we often feel we understand it perfectly. Obviously, its connection with belief in a transcendent reality or a Supreme Being is common. But the word also is used with more specific meanings. Faith can mean unquestioning belief, complete confidence, trust, reliance, or loyalty. It is used to refer to a religion (the Christian "faith") or a system of religious beliefs (the "faith" of our fathers). Its meaning can span a spectrum from a state of being, to an act, to an abstract idea. In Islam, faith includes complete submission to the will of Allah, which involves belief, profession, and the actual performance of deeds consistent with Allah's will.

The importance of faith, however, is widely disputed. Some view faith as unscientific and superstitious, contending that any beliefs held solely on the basis of faith are invalid (this view is called "logical positivism"). Devoted believers often question the ability of reason to arrive at ultimate truth. Others go so far as to contend that true belief arises only by faith and that accepting things that can be demonstrated, proved, or validated does not require faith. This faith versus reason debate has brought varied attempts at resolution from St. Augustine, who called for "faith seeking understanding," to C. S. Lewis, who called faith the virtue by which we hold on to our reasoned ideas despite moods to the contrary.

Hebrews 11:1 contains perhaps the most widely quoted definition of faith in the Bible. Since faith is at the heart of the Bible's message, such a summary naturally demands our attention. The writer holds in tension what we experience in faith ("assurance" and "conviction") with humanity's highest aspiration for reality ("things hoped for" and "things not seen"). Hope in things that we cannot see, touch, or manipulate seems a rather vague idea at first. But think of the power in this idea. When faced with ultimate reality we can be either optimistic or pessimistic. The power of hope is in its optimism. What is the best that we can conceive? Would it not be things like a benevolent Creator, a loving Father, a forgiving Savior, and a ready Paraclete beside us in all we face in life? If this hope were merely spun out of our imaginations, we would be among all people those most to be pitied as delusional. But the message of the Bible is that this hope has been revealed to us by the Creator-Father through the Savior-Son and implanted with assurance and conviction in our hearts by the Spirit-Paraclete. A faith hall of fame is filled with the names of men and women who have experienced this hope in things not seen and through assurance and conviction have pleased God. By faith, so can we!

Faith That Pleases God

The kind of faith that pleases God is something to which we all aspire. Hebrews clearly states the preeminent role that faith plays: "Without faith it is impossible to please God" (Hebrews 11:6). The writer goes on to say that whoever would approach God must demonstrate two dimensions of faith: first that God exists, and second that God rewards those who seek God. The Book of Hebrews gives some surprising insights into that kind of acknowledging and seeking faith.

Since the first recorded covenant between God and humanity is reported in the account of Noah, we cannot overlook the record that God found a faith that pleased God in the lives of Abel and Enoch, two who lived before that first covenant. While Abel gave "a more acceptable sacrifice than Cain's" (Hebrews 11:4), we cannot overlook that Cain gave the first offering (certainly an acknowledgment that God exists); he did it without any instruction, command, or evident expectation on the part of God. Could it be that Cain failed to seek God, to seek God's guidance, to discover God's expectations, or to follow God's will as he prepared his offering?

In responding to Cain's offering, God said, "If you do well, will you not be accepted? And if you do not do well, sin is lurking at the door; its desire is for you, but you must master it" (Genesis 4:7). If "doing well" and "gaining acceptance by God" are the central criteria for an acceptable offering, did Cain miss something that Abel had discovered in giving "the firstlings of his flock, their fat portions" (4:4)? Doing well and gaining acceptance by God are possibilities for all of us, though sin is always lurking at the door. If Cain had first sought God, would he have avoided the anger, the sinful impulses, and the enmity against his brother? Would he not also have pleased God?

The Assurance of Faith

Theologically, a covenant is a promise made by God to humanity and the relationship that is established by that promise. Abel and Enoch demonstrate that humanity can acknowledge and seek God and gain God's pleasure without a formal covenant. The creation of humanity, the garden of Eden, and the intimacy that God initially shared with Adam and Eve were a kind of unspoken covenant. With the exceptions of Abel and Enoch, the Bible shows that the initiative to foster relationship with humanity subsequently rested with God. God took the initiative with Noah, with Abraham, with Moses, and with David to establish a relationship that would turn all humanity from the sin that lurks at the door back toward an intimate relationship with God. The faith hall of fame in Hebrews 11 records how a faithful God bound the Creator God with creatures made in God's own image in a covenant of promise that was sustained by people who lived "by faith" (a recurring theme throughout Hebrews 11).

The relationship with God founded on the covenant offered assurance to God's people. That assurance was not a promise of perpetual peace, prosperity, good times, and happiness. Indeed, the path into the hall of fame is filled with indecision, missteps, hardships, and even death. Most important of all, however, is that their paths never reached their intended goals: "All these, though they were commended for their faith, did not receive what was promised" (11:39). While the promise ultimately was fulfilled in Jesus, we too live in between Jesus' coming and his future appearing when all the promises will be fulfilled.

Psalm 46 takes on its significance for a people living between the promise and its fulfillment. We continue to live in times of trouble. The earth is changing, mountains are trembling, nations are in an uproar, kingdoms totter, desolation plagues our world, and wars reach to the ends of the earth. In the midst of all this turmoil and trouble, we have an assurance that flows from our faith: " 'Be still, and know that I am God! I am exalted among the nations, I am exalted in the earth.' The LORD of hosts is with us; the God of Jacob is our refuge" (Psalm 46:10-11). Such is our assurance!

SHARING THE SCRIPTURE

Preparing Our Hearts

Explore this week's devotional reading, found in Psalm 27:1-6. This song of David exudes a confidence and trust in God, even in the face of extreme danger. The psalmist reminds us that we need not fear because God is our "light" and "salvation" (27:1). How does David's song give you confidence? Where do you need to experience God's light and salvation at this moment? Ponder your own degree of confidence in God.

Pray that you and the adult students will find confidence in God, especially when the storms of life are beating down upon you.

Preparing Our Minds

Study the background Scripture from Hebrews 11:1-7 and Psalm 46:1-11. The lesson Scripture is from Hebrews 11:1-3, 6 and Psalm 46:1-3, 8-11.

Consider this question as you prepare the lesson: *What prompts people to hope for positive change?*

Write on newsprint:
❑ information for next week's lesson, found under "Continue the Journey."
❑ activities for further spiritual growth in "Continue the Journey."

Review the "Introduction," "The Big Picture," "Close-up," and "Faith in Action." Consider how you will use this additional information, which immediately precedes the first lesson.

Prepare the lecture suggested for "Explore the Meaning of Faith and Its Implications for Our Lives."

LEADING THE CLASS

(1) Gather to Learn

❖ Greet the class members. Introduce any guests and help them feel at home.

❖ Pray that all who gather around the circle today will be inspired to put confident faith in God.

❖ Invite the students to identify conflicts currently raging in the world. List their ideas on newsprint. Note that some of these (probably) have been occurring for some time, perhaps over centuries, as one group holds another in contempt.

❖ Ask these questions:

(1) **What are some of the root causes of these conflicts?** (Control of land and natural resources, historic claims to certain pieces of land, and religious or ethnic differences are often to blame.)

(2) **Where do you see signs of hope that positive change may occur?**

❖ Read aloud today's focus statement: **Because of all the conflicts in the world, people may lose hope for positive change. What prompts people to hope for positive change? By believing in God's strength, say the writers of Hebrews and the Psalms, we can be rescued and change can take place because God is with us.**

(2) Goal 1: Explore the Meaning of Faith and Its Implications for Our Lives

❖ Choose a volunteer to read Hebrews 11:1-3, 6.

❖ Present a brief lecture using information from Hebrews 11:1-3 in Understanding the Scripture and "Defining Faith" from Interpreting the Scripture. The purpose of this lecture is to explain the meaning of "faith," particularly as it is described in Hebrews.

❖ Invite participants to form small groups. Read this sentence and ask them to fill in the blank: **Although I think I understand the biblical meaning of faith, when it comes to living out that faith in my own life I _____.** Encourage the groups to talk about how easy or challenging they find it to live out faith.

❖ Bring everyone together and invite anyone who chooses to lift up an idea that his or her group discussed.

(3) Goal 2: Appreciate and Grow From the Faith of Others

❖ Select several volunteers who use the same Bible translation to read Psalm 46:1-3, 8-11 in unison.

❖ Talk about how the community of faith in this psalm confesses its faith and confidence in God.

❖ Look at these expressions of faith. Read them aloud in turn and invite the adults to comment on them in terms of their own understandings of faith.

■ **Eternal life does not begin with death; it begins with faith.** (Samuel M. Shoemaker, 1893–1963)

■ **Faith does not mean believing without evidence. It means believing in realities that go beyond sense and sight—for which a totally different sort of evidence is required.** (John Baillie, 1741–1806)

■ **Faith is a reasoning trust, a trust which reckons thoughtfully and confidently upon the trustworthiness of God.** (John R. W. Stott, 1921–)

■ **Faith never knows where it is being led, but it loves and knows the one who is leading.** (Oswald Chambers, 1874–1917)

❖ Wrap up by asking: **Now that you have considered a variety of descriptions of faith written by others, how might you describe faith?** (Some participants may want to jot down their ideas, so have paper and pencils handy.)

(4) Goal 3: Develop a Practice of Relying on God for Positive Change

❖ Read together today's key verse, Hebrews 11:1.

❖ Read "The Assurance of Faith" in Interpreting the Scripture. Discuss briefly evidence of faith that participants saw in this passage from Hebrews as biblical people relied on God.

❖ Distribute paper and pencils. Encourage the students to write briefly about a situation that may feel like a brick wall to them. Suggest that they write as many positive outcomes as they can brainstorm for this situation. Recommend that they put these papers in their Bibles and refer to them throughout the week as a sign that they are relying on God to bring about some kind of positive change.

(5) Continue the Journey

❖ Pray that the students will go forth with steadfast confidence that God is able to care for them and sustain them.

❖ Read aloud this preparation for next week's lesson. You may also want to post it on newsprint for the students to copy.
- **Title: Faith Is Endurance**
- **Background Scripture: Hebrews 12:1-11**
- **Lesson Scripture: Hebrews 12:1-11**
- **Focus of the Lesson: People know that to win a race we sometimes have to suffer some pain, but we must keep our eyes on the goal. What help is available? The writer of Hebrews tells us there is a huge crowd of witnesses of the faith that have trained well, kept their eyes on God and Jesus, and have grown in grace and character.**

❖ Post these three activities related to this week's session on newsprint for the students to copy. Challenge the adults to grow spiritually by completing one or more of them.

(1) **Find definitions of "faith" in dictionaries, books of quotations, and other sources. Choose several that express your understanding of faith. Copy them into your spiritual journal and add your own definition of "faith."**

(2) **Identify historical or living people who are models of faith for you. What obstacles have they encountered? How does their faith shine forth? How might you follow their example of faithfulness?**

(3) **Name a current situation that is testing your own confidence in God. Why is this situation so difficult for you? What do you hope that God will do under these circumstances? Pray that your faith may be strengthened even as this situation is in the process of being resolved.**

❖ Sing or read aloud "Faith, While Trees Are Still in Blossom."

❖ Conclude today's session by leading the class in this benediction, adapted from the key verses for September 16 from Hebrews 12:1-2: **Let us go forth to run with perseverance the race that is set before us, looking to Jesus the pioneer and perfecter of our faith.**

UNIT 1: WHAT IS FAITH?
FAITH IS ENDURANCE

PREVIEWING THE LESSON

Lesson Scripture: Hebrews 12:1-11
Background Scripture: Hebrews 12:1-11
Key Verses: Hebrews 12:1-2

Focus of the Lesson:
People know that to win a race we sometimes have to suffer some pain, but we must keep our eyes on the goal. What help is available? The writer of Hebrews tells us there is a huge crowd of witnesses of the faith who have trained well, kept their eyes on God and Jesus, and have grown in grace and character.

Goals for the Learners:
(1) to understand that following Jesus in faith leads to persevering through any suffering we encounter and disciplining ourselves in Christian living.
(2) to declare what it means to them to follow Jesus' example in their lives.
(3) to use their faith in Jesus Christ to determine and reach spiritual goals.

Supplies:
Bibles, newsprint and marker, paper and pencils, hymnals

READING THE SCRIPTURE

NRSV
Lesson Scripture: Hebrews 12:1-11

¹Therefore, since we are surrounded by so great a cloud of witnesses, let us also lay aside every weight and the sin that clings so closely, and **let us run with perseverance the race that is set before us, ²looking to Jesus the pioneer and perfecter of our faith,** who for the sake of the joy that was set before him endured the cross, disregarding its shame, and has taken his seat at the right hand of the throne of God.

³Consider him who endured such hostil-

CEB
Lesson Scripture: Hebrews 12:1-11

¹So then **let's also run the race that is laid out in front of us,** since we have such a great cloud of witnesses surrounding us. Let's throw off any extra baggage, get rid of the sin that trips us up, ²**and fix our eyes on Jesus, faith's pioneer and perfecter.** He endured the cross, ignoring the shame, for the sake of the joy that was laid out in front of him, and sat down at the right side of God's throne.

³Think about the one who endured such

ity against himself from sinners, so that you may not grow weary or lose heart. [4]In your struggle against sin you have not yet resisted to the point of shedding your blood. [5]And you have forgotten the exhortation that addresses you as children—

> "My child, do not regard lightly
> the discipline of the Lord,
> or lose heart when you are
> punished by him;
> [6] for the Lord disciplines those
> whom he loves,
> and chastises every child
> whom he accepts."

[7]Endure trials for the sake of discipline. God is treating you as children; for what child is there whom a parent does not discipline? [8]If you do not have that discipline in which all children share, then you are illegitimate and not his children. [9]Moreover, we had human parents to discipline us, and we respected them. Should we not be even more willing to be subject to the Father of spirits and live? [10]For they disciplined us for a short time as seemed best to them, but he disciplines us for our good, in order that we may share his holiness. [11]Now, discipline always seems painful rather than pleasant at the time, but later it yields the peaceful fruit of righteousness to those who have been trained by it.

opposition from sinners so that you won't be discouraged and you won't give up. [4]In your struggle against sin, you haven't resisted yet to the point of shedding blood, [5]and you have forgotten the encouragement that addresses you as sons and daughters:

> *My child, don't make light*
> *of the Lord's discipline*
> *or give up when you are corrected by him,*
> [6]*because the Lord disciplines*
> *whomever he loves,*
> *and he punishes every son or daughter*
> *whom he accepts.*

[7]Bear hardship for the sake of discipline. God is treating you like sons and daughters! What child isn't disciplined by his or her father? [8]But if you don't experience discipline, which happens to all children, then you are illegitimate and not real sons and daughters. [9]What's more, we had human parents who disciplined us, and we respected them for it. How much more should we submit to the Father of spirits and live? [10]Our human parents disciplined us for a little while, as it seemed best to them, but God does it for our benefit so that we can share his holiness. [11]No discipline is fun while it lasts, but it seems painful at the time. Later, however, it yields the peaceful fruit of righteousness for those who have been trained by it.

UNDERSTANDING THE SCRIPTURE

Introduction. Membership in the faith hall of fame is still open. The list in Hebrews 11 of those commended for their faith was incomplete. God had promised something the forerunners had not received. The "perfect" faith eluded them because something better was on the horizon. The writer set the current race of his readers in two contexts. First, he pointed to Jesus as an example of endurance and sacrifice that believers ought to follow. Then he interpreted the readers'

circumstances in the context of discipline that prepared them for receiving the race's prize.

Hebrews 12:1-2. Previous inductees into the hall of fame now compose a "great cloud of witnesses." The Greek word translated "witnesses" is the root for our word "martyrs." While all martyrs do not die for their faith, all suffer for it. These martyr-witnesses now watch and await the completion of the final race. They have passed on the baton, and Hebrews uses "we" and "us" to describe the current runners in the race.

The faith that characterized the forerunners and toward which the readers are entreated has a new and supreme model— one who gives final definition to living in faith. That model is Jesus. As the "pioneer and perfecter" (12:2) Jesus was the "something better" (11:40) that God provided. "Pioneer" denotes a leader who blazes the trails for his followers. A "perfecter" is someone who brings something to its consummation and conclusion. The King James Version italicizes the "our" before "faith," correctly indicating that the "our" is not in the Greek text. Literally, the text says that Jesus was the trailblazer and perfecter of faith. His disciples follow in his footsteps and face similar consequences to those he faced. The perfect faith modeled by Jesus involved enduring crucifixion and "disregarding" (NRSV) or "despising" (NASB, KJV) its shame. "Disregarding" literally means "to think against or counter to" something. Jesus reinterpreted shame as "joy," and the honored "seat at the right hand of the throne of God" (12:2) replaced the despised cross. The race now belongs to his disciples, who must lay aside every back-bending burden and every ensnaring sin. Fixing their eyes on Jesus, they must run the race with perseverance.

Hebrews 12:3-4. All that Jesus did was for the sake of sinners. By enduring opposition and facing hostility, Jesus became the supreme example of what faith looks like and how it is lived. His example provides the model for how his followers can avoid the weariness and despair that trouble, hard times, and persecution inevitably bring. "Lose heart" (12:3) carries the image of fainting from extreme toil.

Hebrews 10:33-34 recounted the insults, persecutions, and confiscations of property the readers already had faced. Their persecution had not led to the loss of life, but the mention of that prospect may indicate that martyrdom was a possibility. The verb translated "resisted" in verse 4 literally means to set down or deploy troops against an enemy. The believers were waging war against sin while struggling with their own adverse circumstances. Jesus struggled with sin to the point of giving his life in order to conquer sin's power through the resurrection. His struggle unto death provided a pioneering example for his followers.

Hebrews 12:5-8. To further establish the context by which believers might interpret their race and its hardships, the writer cited Proverbs 3:11-12. He exhorted readers with words of wisdom from their Jewish heritage. He gently chided them for forgetting and failing to apply Wisdom's truths to their particular situations.

At first impression, we might think that the writer is making a dramatic shift here. He appeared earlier to blame sinners for Jesus' death. By using the possibility of the readers' facing death in their struggle with sin, he could be understood as blaming sinners outside the church for their struggles. Suddenly in verses 5-6, however, the writer appears to interpret all that the readers are experiencing as God's intentional discipline. The hardships are evidence of God's love for God's children and are part of the divine shaping of a devoted people.

God's discipline and reproof take place in the context of a familial relationship. We all are children of God, and the Lord's discipline and punishment take place in that relational context. All God's children share in that discipline. Indeed, the absence of discipline would be evidence of a lack of love and concern for the well-being of the children—in essence it would make them "illegitimate" (12:8). God does not abandon children but rather disciplines them. "Endure" (12:7) can be either an imperative ("Endure!") or indicative ("You are enduring"). "Endure for the purpose or goal of discipline" seems the likeliest meaning. As God's children, we are called to persist through trials in order to develop discipline. Persius, the first-century Roman poet, rightly said, "He conquers who endures."

Hebrews 12:9-11. To draw a deeper understanding of God's discipline, the writer compared it with the discipline of human parents. "We had parents" (12:9) actually has a durative element in Greek, meaning "we had and continue to have." "Parents" translates two nouns in Greek, "fathers" and "teachers." Their discipline is based on what seems best to them and lasts for the "short time" (12:10) until we reach maturity. In the midst of it, discipline creates a heavy sense of sorrow or pain. But when we have been trained by it, it pays back with a fruitful harvest of righteousness and peace.

The result of discipline by human parents is respect. The verb "respected" provides an interesting twist. In the active or passive voices it means "to make someone ashamed" or "to be put to shame." In the Greek middle voice, which occurs in verse 9, it means "to shame oneself" and thus to humble oneself out of respect for another. The durative element also is present here: "We respected and continue to respect" our human parents for their discipline.

All of these elements draw together in the writer's advocacy on responding to hardship. The hard race that is being run in the present is painful. The present moment, however, must be put in a larger context. It will be a short time of divine discipline through which God will bring the runners to a peaceful and just conclusion when they cross the finish line. Underlying all is a distinct understanding of faith. Faith is a respect for God that trusts God to work through the present difficult trials to bring a joyous victory.

INTERPRETING THE SCRIPTURE

Disciplining and Discipling

For most of us, the word "discipline" has both a negative and a positive meaning. Especially when used as a verb, it connotes the actions of some authority figure to correct or punish others. Discipline by parents, by school officials, and even by God easily fit that definition. Hebrews 12:5-11 reflects this kind of discipline.

Discipline involves a social system in which right and wrong are defined and behaviors outside the parameters are punished. People who are concerned about behavior that negatively affects them and the rest of society often wish for more discipline in homes, schools, businesses, courts, and even in churches. Many "law-and-order" advocates feel that clear, firm, and certain punishment is the best way to deter misdeeds. The focus of this kind of discipline is on forbidding and restraining with the assumption that positive results will follow. Few of us like to be the object of this kind of discipline, though we may like it very much when it is applied to others who have different standards and values from our own.

Conversely, discipline is greatly esteemed when it is identified with the personal characteristics associated with self-control, character, orderliness, and efficiency. Disciplined students, workers, and athletes generally are admired. They possess an inner drive that sets them apart as intensely focused, highly dedicated, and extremely competent people. They are the achievers, the movers and shakers, who possess the skills, work ethic, and courage to get things done. Jesus epitomizes this kind of discipline in Hebrews 12:2-3, and the perseverance of those who run the race all the way to the finish demands a similar discipline. This discipline involves laying aside or sacrificing some conveniences and ease in order to reach the ultimate goal. Often it also leads to envy, resentment, hatred, and hostility from those who think the disciplined person has raised the bar of expectations too high.

The words "discipline" and "disciple" come from the same Latin root. Dictionaries do not reflect the popular use of "disciple" as a verb, but the noun and the emerging verb both carry a focus on learning from and following a teacher. Jesus both discipled and disciplined through his teaching—and even more through his example. His own discipline was seen in his maintaining focus on God and God's will. His discipline of his followers was more focused on pioneering faith than on laying down and administering rules of behavior. As disciples of Jesus, we are called to run the race set before us. It is *our* race now, but we are not alone in it. We have a cheering crowd of previous racers who surround us, and we have before us the footprints of the Pioneer. If we keep our eyes fixed on Jesus, his example will lead us in becoming children of God and joint heirs with him of the race's gold medal.

Sin Outside and In

Paul noted that the first truth he received and passed on to others was this: "Christ died for our sins in accordance with the scriptures" (1 Corinthians 15:3). Hebrews extended that idea: Jesus "endured such hostility against himself from sinners" that he "endured the cross, disregarding its shame" (Hebrews 12:2-3). Additionally, 1 John 1:9 affirms that "if we confess our sins, he who is faithful and just will forgive us our sins and cleanse us from all unrighteousness." Having confessed our sins and accepted the forgiveness offered to us through Christ, we now turn our attention toward calling others to repentance, faith, and forgiveness.

Our world certainly needs that message

of hope, for, however we define it, sin is rampant in our world. Attention given to God and civility among people seem to be in steep decline. Dishonesty, greed, exploitation, violence, crime, and general moral decay surround us. From financial crises, to international disputes, to wars and conflicts, our problems can be traced back to human sin. Sin is so deeply entrenched that many believers have fallen into hopeless despair. Those who seek to share the good news often must endure hostility and rejection. The faithful face trials and tribulations on every side. Many assume that this "suffering for Jesus" is suffering like Jesus. We have been made righteous and holy; sinners are to blame for our troubles, trials, and tribulations.

Hebrews stops such thinking right in its tracks. The writer correctly points out that no we-are-holy-and-you-are-sinners distinction exists. We all are sinners and will remain so. Christ died for all. Sin is a weight that clings to us and impedes us in living out our faith as surely as it weighs on unrepentant sinners.

Hebrews 6:1-9 applies the ultimate warning to those who fail to strive for "perfection," which is maturity (compare Jesus as the "perfecter" in 12:2). We who have been enlightened must go beyond the foundation of faith (6:1), becoming fruitful (6:7). Confident of our salvation (6:9), we are to love and serve the saints (6:10), show diligence (6:11), and "through faith and patience inherit the promises" of our salvation (6:12).

As disciples of Jesus, we constantly struggle against sin. That sin, continually in us, calls for reproof, punishment, and discipline. This discipline of the Lord is how God deals with beloved children.

Shame, Respect, and Faith

The faith "perfected" by Jesus, our supreme model of faith, is the faith for which we strive as Jesus' followers and disciples. Shifting for a moment from the expression of discipleship found in Hebrews to Jesus' own model, we are called under the discipline of the Lord to take up our crosses and follow Jesus. Believers often have marveled how the cross (a cruel symbol of Roman punishment, oppression, and death) has been transformed into an altar of sacrifice (Hebrews 10:12-14), an avenue to eternal life (John 3:14-15), and a magnet that draws all people to Jesus (John 12:32). This ability to radically transform one reality into another is at the heart of the Christian faith, where desperately lost sinners become children of God and joint heirs with Christ (Romans 8:15-17).

We have noted that "disregarding" (Hebrews 12:2 NRSV) or "despising" (NASB, KJV) the shame of the cross literally means "to think against or counter to" the normal way of looking at the cross. The Romans used crucifixion to deter rebellion and intimidate opponents into submission. The person crucified generally was stripped of his clothing, bound to a cross, and left to die from dehydration, exposure, and asphyxia—a slow, painful, cruel way to die.

Transforming shame into joy is a powerful transformation. Transforming the effects of an instrument of death into an eternal place at the right hand of God is almost beyond belief. But this kind of transformation has been and continues to be at the heart of the gospel. Echoing "The Prayer of St. Francis of Assisi," we too long for a powerful transformation in our lives.

SHARING THE SCRIPTURE

Preparing Our Hearts

Explore this week's devotional reading, found in James 5:7-11. Here James, who many believe to have been Jesus' brother, writes about patience in suffering. James calls Christians to endure patiently "until the coming of the Lord" (5:7). To make his point he refers to a farmer who must wait patiently for rain. He points to prophets and Job as examples of people who patiently endured suffering. Think about your own level of endurance. Are there situations you are patiently enduring now? What help do you need to continue to endure?

Pray that you and the adult students will steadfastly endure, believing that God will faithfully uphold you.

Preparing Our Minds

Study the background Scripture and the lesson Scripture, both of which are from Hebrews 12:1-11.

Consider this question as you prepare the lesson: *What help is available to reach a goal you have set?*

Write on newsprint:
❑ steps for "Use the Learners' Faith in Jesus Christ to Determine and Reach Spiritual Goals."
❑ information for next week's lesson, found under "Continue the Journey."
❑ activities for further spiritual growth in "Continue the Journey."

Review the "Introduction," "The Big Picture," "Close-up," and "Faith in Action." Consider how you will use this additional information, which immediately precedes the first lesson.

LEADING THE CLASS

(1) Gather to Learn

❖ Greet the class members. Introduce any guests and help them feel at home.
❖ Pray that all who have come today

will focus on Jesus and the example he has set for us as "the pioneer and perfecter of our faith" (Hebrews 12:2).

❖ Read this story summarized from www.marathonguide.com: **In 2009, fifty-two-year-old Pete Van Hamersveld left the starting line to run his first marathon with a goal of finishing within the six-hour time limit, which he did, finishing in 5 hours and 55 minutes. His very presence at this event was amazing. Just six months prior to the race Pete had undergone surgery for stage 3C colon cancer. He had endured months of radiation and chemotherapy. Advised by friends to run a shorter race, Pete was determined to go the full marathon distance. Not only did he finish this race but he also raised $2,600 for the American Cancer Society.**

❖ Read aloud today's focus statement: **People know that to win a race we sometimes have to suffer some pain, but we must keep our eyes on the goal. What help is available? The writer of Hebrews tells us there is a huge crowd of witnesses of the faith who have trained well, kept their eyes on God and Jesus, and have grown in grace and character.**

(2) Goal 1: Understand That Following Jesus in Faith Leads to Persevering Through Any Suffering We Encounter and Disciplining Ourselves in Christian Living

❖ Choose someone to read Hebrews 12:1-11.

❖ Read information from Understanding the Scripture as found in Hebrews 12:1-2 and 12:3-4. Encourage the adults to add any comments or raise any questions. Use "Sin Outside and In" and "Shame, Respect, and Faith" from Interpreting the Scripture to help answer questions or make other points.

❖ Focus on verses 5-11 by discussing these questions. Use information from "Disciplining and Discipling" in Interpreting the Scripture as appropriate.

(1) **How do you define "discipline"?**
(2) **What images come to your mind when someone talks about discipline?**
(3) **How do you define "discipling"?**
(4) **What images come to mind when you think about being someone's disciple?**
(5) **What argument does the writer of Hebrews make in 12:5-11 concerning God's discipline?**
(6) **How might this type of discipline enable you to be a better follower of Jesus?**

❖ Conclude by reading today's key verses, Hebrews 12:1-2, preferably in unison.

(3) Goal 2: Declare What It Means to the Learners to Follow Jesus' Example in Their Lives

❖ Read these words from three verses of a hymn written in India during the late 1800s. Since "I Have Decided to Follow Jesus" was often sung in Sunday school, class members may know the tune.

I have decided to follow Jesus
　(sung three times)
No turning back, no turning back.
Though no one join me, I still will follow
　(sung three times)
No turning back, no turning back.
The world behind me, the cross before
　me (sung three times)
No turning back, no turning back.

❖ Invite the adults to comment on how these words may express their commitment to following Jesus.

❖ Form several small groups. Distribute paper and pencils. Ask each group to write at least one more verse, which would be sung three times and then end with "no turning back."

❖ Call everyone together and invite the groups to read or sing their verses.

(4) Goal 3: Use the Learners' Faith in Jesus Christ to Determine and Reach Spiritual Goals

❖ Prompt the class to create actions they would need to take to prepare for a race. List ideas on newsprint, though these need not be in any particular order. Responses might include *eating nutritious meals daily, purchasing comfortable running shoes and attire, establishing and maintaining a training schedule,* or *finding a coach who could help runners meet their full potential.*

❖ Distribute paper and pencils if you have not already done so. Encourage the learners to follow these steps, which you will have written on newsprint:

Step 1: Write at least three spiritual goals that you would like to meet.

Step 2: Focus on one of those goals. Write any actions you might need to take to meet this goal. For example, if your goal is to be better acquainted with the Bible, you may want to commit yourself to reading the Bible daily, attending a weekly Bible study, purchasing a Bible commentary to aid in your study, and so on.

Step 3: Talk with a partner or small group about the goals you have set and what you need to do to meet at least one of them. See if your partner would be willing to support you in prayer over the next several weeks as you work to achieve your goal.

(5) Continue the Journey

❖ Bring everyone together and pray that the adults will persevere in meeting their goals so that everyone will be able to follow in Christ's footsteps and reach the finish line of their journey in faith.

❖ Read aloud this preparation for next week's lesson. You may also want to post it on newsprint for the students to copy.

■ **Title: Faith Inspires Gratitude**
■ **Background Scripture: Hebrews 12:14-29**
■ **Lesson Scripture: Hebrews 12:18-29**
■ **Focus of the Lesson: People fear many things, especially judgment and death. What can we believe in that will relieve our fears? The writer of Hebrews says that God in Christ Jesus brought us forgiveness and the promise of eternal life.**

❖ Post these three activities related to this week's session on newsprint for the students to copy. Challenge the adults to grow spiritually by completing one or more of them.

(1) **Offer whatever support and help you can to someone who is enduring a difficult situation or suffering.**

(2) **Identify people among the "cloud of witnesses" (Hebrews 12:1) who have been important in your life. How have they enabled you to grow as Christ's disciple?**

(3) **Write in your spiritual journal about a time when you believe God was disciplining you. What happened? How did this situation enable you to grow stronger in your faith?**

❖ Sing or read aloud "Through It All."

❖ Conclude today's session by leading the class in this benediction, adapted from the key verses for September 16 from Hebrews 12:1-2: **Let us go forth to run with perseverance the race that is set before us, looking to Jesus the pioneer and perfecter of our faith.**

UNIT 1: WHAT IS FAITH?

FAITH INSPIRES GRATITUDE

PREVIEWING THE LESSON

Lesson Scripture: Hebrews 12:18-29
Background Scripture: Hebrews 12:14-29
Key Verse: Hebrews 12:28

Focus of the Lesson:
People fear many things, especially judgment and death. What can we believe in that will relieve our fears? The writer of Hebrews says that God in Christ Jesus brought us forgiveness and the promise of eternal life.

Goals for the Learners:
(1) to explore the meaning of God's forgiveness and promise of eternal life.
(2) to examine their fears about death and assurances of God's grace to relieve their fears.
(3) to repent for the ways in which they reject God's grace and to worship God with reverence and awe.

Pronunciation Guide:
Jebusite (jeb yoo site)
shalom (shah lohm′)

Supplies:
Bibles, newsprint and marker, paper and pencils, hymnals

READING THE SCRIPTURE

NRSV
Lesson Scripture: Hebrews 12:18-29

¹⁸You have not come to something that can be touched, a blazing fire, and darkness, and gloom, and a tempest, ¹⁹and the sound of a trumpet, and a voice whose words made

CEB
Lesson Scripture: Hebrews 12:18-29

¹⁸You haven't drawn near to something that can be touched: a burning fire, darkness, shadow, a whirlwind, ¹⁹a blast of a trumpet, and a sound of words that made

the hearers beg that not another word be spoken to them. [20](For they could not endure the order that was given, "If even an animal touches the mountain, it shall be stoned to death." [21]Indeed, so terrifying was the sight that Moses said, "I tremble with fear.") [22]But you have come to Mount Zion and to the city of the living God, the heavenly Jerusalem, and to innumerable angels in festal gathering, [23]and to the assembly of the firstborn who are enrolled in heaven, and to God the judge of all, and to the spirits of the righteous made perfect, [24]and to Jesus, the mediator of a new covenant, and to the sprinkled blood that speaks a better word than the blood of Abel.

[25]See that you do not refuse the one who is speaking; for if they did not escape when they refused the one who warned them on earth, how much less will we escape if we reject the one who warns from heaven! [26]At that time his voice shook the earth; but now he has promised, "Yet once more I will shake not only the earth but also the heaven." [27]This phrase, "Yet once more," indicates the removal of what is shaken—that is, created things—so that what cannot be shaken may remain. **[28]Therefore, since we are receiving a kingdom that cannot be shaken, let us give thanks, by which we offer to God an acceptable worship with reverence and awe;** [29]for indeed our God is a consuming fire.

the ones who heard it beg that there wouldn't be one more word. [20]They couldn't stand the command, *If even a wild animal touches the mountain, it must be stoned.* [21]The sight was so frightening that Moses said, "I'm terrified and shaking!"

[22]But you have drawn near to Mount Zion, the city of the living God, heavenly Jerusalem, to countless angels in a festival gathering, [23]to the assembly of God's first-born children who are registered in heaven, to God the judge of all, to the spirits of the righteous who have been made perfect, [24]to Jesus the mediator of the new covenant, and to the sprinkled blood that speaks better than Abel's blood.

[25]See to it that you don't resist the one who is speaking. If the people didn't escape when they refused to listen to the one who warned them on earth, how will we escape if we reject the one who is warning from heaven? [26]His voice shook the earth then, but now he has made a promise: *Still once more I will shake not only the earth but heaven also.* [27]The words "still once more" reveal the removal of what is shaken—the things that are part of this creation—so that what isn't shaken will remain. **[28]Therefore, since we are receiving a kingdom that can't be shaken, let's continue to express our gratitude. With this gratitude, let's serve in a way that is pleasing to God with respect and awe,** [29]because our God really is a consuming fire.

UNDERSTANDING THE SCRIPTURE

Hebrews 12:14-17. In spite of all the hardship, suffering, and persecution they had experienced, those persevering in faith were encouraged to pursue peace with everyone. The writer chose an interesting Greek word for "pursue," for the word is frequently used in the New Testament to mean "persecute." For example, the word

was employed when Jesus both blessed those who were "persecuted" (Matthew 5:11-12) and urged his followers to pray for those who "persecuted" them (5:44). In Hebrews, the zeal with which believers had been pursued by their enemies was to be returned by a zeal for peace with everyone, including their enemies.

Such a pursuit for peace could come only with a corresponding pursuit of holiness or consecration to God. The bitterness that results from being persecuted and oppressed can be removed only by a deep experience with God's grace that yields sanctification or holiness. The presence of bitterness will cause trouble in the community of believers and will defile its fellowship, even when the bitterness is directed at those outside the community. Holiness, on the other hand, will help people "see the Lord" (Hebrews 12:14) through the peacemakers. Esau (12:16) served as a warning for those who, through godless immorality, lose their blessing. He could not recapture the blessing because tears of regret cannot equate with the transformation of life and spirit that true repentance embodies (see Hebrews 6:4-7).

Hebrews 12:18-21. The writer next established a contrast between a place to which the readers "have not come" (12:18) and a place to which they "have come" (12:22). The former represents the covenant given to Moses at Mount Sinai. The latter represents the fulfillment of the new Davidic covenant through the Messiah who rules in the "heavenly Jerusalem" (12:22). Throughout Hebrews the writer attempted to draw the readers away from the former and toward the latter. At this point the readers had not lapsed back into their old ways, but the enticements were present.

Verses 18-19 draw allusions from Exodus 19:16-22; 20:18-21; and Deuteronomy 4:11-12; 5:22-27. These images focus on the terrifying events and the overwhelming fear that surrounded the giving of the covenant to Moses on Mount Sinai. The voice of God was so awesome that the people begged not to hear another word, and Moses himself trembled with fear. Access to God was highly restricted because even touching the mountain meant death. Thus, the people "have not come" there (Hebrews 12:18). The whole event was an experience of painful discipline for the nation, but it foreshadowed a kingdom where the peaceful fruit of righteousness would prevail (see 12:11).

Hebrews 12:22-24. Mount Zion stands in contrast to the forbidding mountain where the covenant was revealed to Moses. Zion is first mentioned in the Scriptures when David captured a Jebusite fortress by that name. For centuries the city surrounding the fortress had been known as Jerusalem, meaning "foundation of Shalem" (named after a Canaanite god of twilight and not originally meaning "city of peace," as is often supposed). As a result of David's conquest, Jerusalem became known as "the city of David" (2 Samuel 5:6-10), and Zion became associated with the particular area in the city where the Temple subsequently was built.

By accepting the good news of Jesus Christ, the writer contends, the readers already had come to a mountain on which stood the heavenly Jerusalem. The writer employed the perfect tense in "you have come," which in Greek connotes an action in the past whose effect continues into the present. He then identifies a series of places to which they had come, followed by a series of assemblages of which they have become a part. The places are virtual synonyms for one location and include Mount Zion, the city of the living God, and the heavenly Jerusalem. The assemblages to which they have come are a myriad of angels (or messengers) in a festive gathering, an assembly (sometimes translated "church") of the firstborn whose names have been registered or recorded in heaven, the Judge-God of all, the spirits of the righteous made perfect (see 11:40), and the mediator of Jesus' new covenant, and sprinkled (or cleansing) blood that speaks better than the blood of Abel (see Genesis 4:10). The writer used a Greek word for "new" in verse 24, emphasizing something fresh, different, and newly established rather than contrasting it with the old.

These images have a wide possible range of meanings, from heavenly to earthly, but the central message is clear: A way has been opened for the readers to "come" (Hebrews 12:22) before God through a new covenant sealed in the effective sacrifice of Jesus. One day those who have remained faithful and steadfast in running the race will cross the finish line and will join in a great celebration with the celestial hosts in the presence of God. The power of the verb form "have come" is that their present experience is part of a race whose destination already is established. The cloud of witnesses surrounding them is the first assemblage that greets them on Mount Zion.

Hebrews 12:25-29. "The one who is speaking" refers to Jesus, whose "better word" (11:24) was spoken through the sacrificial blood he shed. Hebrews 9:12-14 provides the context for the sprinkling of blood in the Holy Place by Christ, who acts both as high priest and atoning offering. Those who had been warned by Jesus during his earthly ministry and had rebuffed that warning had not escaped judgment. The chance for escape is even less for those who now are turning away from the warning coming from heaven.

The presence of God at Mount Sinai had caused the earth to tremble (Exodus 19:18). The writer quotes the prophecy of Haggai 2:6 that the heavens and the earth will be shaken one more time. This shaking will remove the material substance of all created things, and only a spiritual kingdom that cannot be shaken will remain. The awesome awareness that we will receive such a kingdom calls for thanksgiving. We ought to bow in reverent worship before such a God who consumes (see Hebrews 10:26-31) in judgment and sustains in salvation.

INTERPRETING THE SCRIPTURE

The Mediator of a New Covenant of Grace

The roles associated with Jesus in the Letter to the Hebrews are varied and are filled with deep theological significance. Jesus is the Son through whom God has spoken. He is the heir of all things who sits at the right hand of God and sustains all things by his word. He is creator of the universe, the reflection of God's glory, and an exact imprint of God's very being. He is the high priest who makes atonement for sin and at the same time is the perfect sacrifice who makes purification from sin possible. In the midst of all these roles with cosmic significance, Jesus also is our brother and our supreme example in living out our faith.

All that Jesus is and will be and all that he has done and is doing might easily be summed up in one word: "grace." No wonder then, in the midst of his encouragement for those who struggle to run the difficult race of life, the writer of Hebrews says, "See to it that not one fails to obtain the grace of God" (Hebrews 12:15). All that Jesus is has been offered to humanity as a free gift. When the Word became flesh and dwelled among us, and when Christ humbled himself and became obedient to the point of death on the cross, it was all about grace.

That grace speaks to us, and we must not refuse it. Why? Because all of us will one day face the God-Judge of all (12:23); and Jesus, the mediator of a new covenant, will be our only advocate. The sacrifice that Jesus made (his "sprinkled blood," 12:24) will speak "a better word" (surely "grace") for us than the blood (like Abel's) that cries out for justice. When the earth is shaken by the final judgment, we will have a covenant with God that promises us a place in an unshakable kingdom. With that kind of grace, we will stand shoulder to shoulder forever with the myriad of angels, the assembly of the firstborn, and the spirits of the righteous made perfect in the heavenly Jerusalem.

Holiness and Intimacy

The symbolism contrasting Mount Sinai and Mount Zion is a prominent feature in Hebrews 12. The writer of Hebrews highlighted the differences between these two symbols as a way to draw the Christians who were tempted to go back into their old ways toward a new understanding of humanity's relationship with God. In making this appeal, the writer highlighted the importance of holiness for believers who hope to see the Lord one day (12:14). This holiness is a moral quality that seeks to leave behind the old ways of sin to walk in the purity of God's love and grace. This moral orientation recognizes that sin defiles and that "immoral and godless" people like Esau lose the blessings promised by God (12:16).

Holiness represents the dedication of God's people to a "no other gods" relationship with God (Exodus 20:3). This holiness is the main focus in the Mount Sinai symbolism. Holiness emphasizes the distance between the Creator God who made heaven and earth and the creatures made in God's image. Holiness engenders reverence and an awe that closely resembles fear. Holiness focuses on the hidden aspects of God and surrounds the unknowable and incomprehensible God with distance and darkness. Holiness requires a spokesperson or representative to speak on God's behalf. Moses was "the one who warned them on earth" (12:25), and the prophets who followed him shook the earth with the prospects of God's judgment.

God "provided something better" (11:40) in the Mount Zion symbolism. God had not always been a distant and exalted Sovereign. In the beginning, God had walked in the garden with Adam and Eve. In the Mount Zion experience, God once again walked among the people, this time in the form of Jesus, the mediator of a new covenant and a new way of relating to God. With their mediator, Jesus, at their side, believers gain access to the city of the living God, the heavenly Jerusalem. Together, believers stand in the very presence of God.

Our faith is a balance between holiness and intimacy, between an exalted Sovereign and a loving and forgiving "Abba." In our daily walk with God, we need both holiness and accessibility, both reverence and relationship, both reconciliation and gracious love. We need both Mount Sinai and Mount Zion, but mostly we need the mediator, Jesus.

Zealously Pursuing Peace

Bible commentators often have noted that the biblical view of "peace" is an active concept that does not focus merely on the absence of war or conflict. The concept was so central to the Hebrew understanding of faith that it became and continues to serve today as a common greeting, "shalom," that is exchanged among people of goodwill. "Shalom" conveys nuances of safety, health, happiness, friendliness, rest, prosperity, and welfare. The greeting is a kind of blessing as well as an entreaty. It both offers a wish for God's favor to be bestowed on the friend and beckons for the return of such goodwill from the friend.

In the Greek-speaking world, "grace" was the common word of greeting, and the apostle Paul frequently used "grace and peace" as the greeting in his letters. That was a significant and insightful combination. Too often the greeting of "peace" is offered solely to friends and a fist is offered to one's enemies. Cautiousness and suspicion often are directed toward others until their goodwill can be established. Strangers might be shown hospitality, but shalom can be cautious, guarded, and tentative. When we meet new people, we commonly seek to discover whether we have common friends or some other connections before we relax with one another.

Paul's combination of "grace and peace" insightfully reflects Jesus' teaching in

Matthew 5:43-47. Warm greetings are offered only to family, friends, and neighbors in most cultures. Jesus said that if we want to be "perfect" (5:48) or complete in our growth toward becoming children of God, we must offer the same kind of peace, grace, and love even to our enemies. Zealously pursuing peace with our enemies personally and corporately is a critical challenge that will reveal how seriously we have taken our own experience with grace and love through Jesus Christ, who has healed our enmity with God and has led us to Mount Zion.

In reality, we can never fully pursue peace with our enemies until we have zealously pursued peace with God. Our lives are filled with anxiety and distress. Fears often rise up and overwhelm us. Daily life is filled with uncertainties, and death casts an ominous shadow over the present and the future. Our hearts will be troubled and afraid until we find rest from the worries of life in the loving care of God (Matthew 6:25-34). Mount Sinai still harbors fears of a distant and hidden God. Mount Zion offers the hope of forgiveness and reconciliation. Mount Calvary and the nearby empty tomb provide the assurance of a peace that triumphs over humanity's sinful brutality and our own mortality. Let us pursue that peace so zealously that our lives will show gratitude, reverence, and awe. Then we will have offered acceptable service and worship to God (Hebrews 12:28) as we present our bodies as living sacrifices, which is our spiritual worship (Romans 12:1).

SHARING THE SCRIPTURE

Preparing Our Hearts

Explore this week's devotional reading, found in 2 Thessalonians 1:1-7. Notice that Paul begins by giving thanks for the growing faith and love of the Christians at Thessalonica, the capital of Macedonia. The people here are being persecuted for their faith, yet they remain steadfast. Identify reasons that you have to be thankful for your faith. Are you enduring afflictions that are currently testing your relationship with Christ? If so, take a moment each day to write three blessings that are yours because of your faith. Give thanks for these blessings.

Pray that you and the adult students will rely on faith to inspire gratitude.

Preparing Our Minds

Study the background Scripture from Hebrews 12:14-29 and the lesson Scripture from Hebrews 12:18-29.

Consider this question as you prepare the lesson: *What can we believe in that will relieve our fears, particularly about judgment and death?*

Write on newsprint:
❑ information for next week's lesson, found under "Continue the Journey."
❑ activities for further spiritual growth in "Continue the Journey."

Review the "Introduction," "The Big Picture," "Close-up," and "Faith in Action." Consider how you will use this additional information, which immediately precedes the first lesson.

LEADING THE CLASS

(1) Gather to Learn

❖ Greet the class members. Introduce any guests and help them feel at home.
❖ Pray that all who have come today will experience God's faithfulness.

❖ Invite participants to silently identify a situation that causes them to fear.

❖ Read these words from Harry Emerson Fosdick (1878–1969): **"Fear imprisons, faith liberates; fear paralyzes, faith empowers; fear disheartens, faith encourages; fear sickens, faith heals; fear makes useless, faith makes serviceable—and, most of all, fear puts hopelessness at the heart of life, while faith rejoices in its God."**

❖ Distribute paper and pencils. Suggest that the adults create one column labeled "fear" and another labeled "faith." Read the Fosdick quotation again slowly so that they might list the characteristics of "fear" and "faith." Invite them to write the fear-producing situation they have identified under the list. Then provide a few moments for them to think silently about how their lives and attitudes could be different if they allowed their faith in Jesus to relieve that fear.

❖ Read aloud today's focus statement: **People fear many things, especially judgment and death. What can we believe in that will relieve our fears? The writer of Hebrews says that God in Christ Jesus brought us forgiveness and the promise of eternal life.**

(2) Goal 1: Explore the Meaning of God's Forgiveness and Promise of Eternal Life

❖ Set the stage by reading Hebrews 12:14-17 from Understanding the Scripture.

❖ Select a volunteer to read Hebrews 12:18-29 from the Bible.

❖ Help the students recognize the contrast in this chapter between Mount Sinai (where Moses received the Ten Commandments) and Mount Zion, "the city of the living God" (12:22) by reading or retelling "Holiness and Intimacy" in Interpreting the Scripture.

❖ Discuss these questions:

(1) **What point do you think the author is trying to make in verse 24?** (Help the group think about Jesus' blood, which was shed to bring about forgiveness and reconciliation to God, in contrast to Abel's blood, which cried out for vengeance in Genesis 4:10 after Cain had killed him.)

(2) **Based on verses 18-24, how do you see Jesus as "the mediator of a new covenant"?** (Read or retell "The Mediator of a New Covenant of Grace" in Interpreting the Scripture.)

(3) **How does today's passage help you appreciate God's forgiveness?**

(4) **As you read about the unshakable faith that is ours, what inspires you to give thanks to God for that faith?**

(3) Goal 2: Examine the Learners' Fears About Death and Offer Assurances of God's Grace to Relieve Their Fears

❖ Distribute hymnals and invite the adults to look at the second verse of "Amazing Grace," where John Newton writes of grace relieving his fears. Form groups of three and encourage the learners to tell one another how God's grace has already relieved a fear with which they have struggled.

❖ Call everyone together and ask:

(1) **What similarities did you note about the kinds of things that the people in your group fear?**

(2) **What lessons did you learn about how God's grace can and does relieve fears?**

(3) **How might other people's experiences assure you that God will remain steadfastly with you?**

❖ Point out that some fears, such as a fear of flying or public speaking or heights, can be overcome by placing oneself in the very situation that one fears. One can learn to feel comfortable speaking in front of a group, for example, by doing it. Yet a nearly universal fear—the fear of death—cannot be dispelled in this way. Ask: **How does the promise of eternal life help you cope with the fear of death?**

(4) Goal 3: Repent for the Ways in Which the Learners Reject God's Grace and Worship God With Reverence and Awe

❖ Distribute paper and pencils. Invite the students to list at least one way that they have recently rejected God, possibly by failing to trust God or trying to "engineer" their own answer to a problem without seeking God's guidance. Suggest that they write two or three sentences in which they recall this failure and ask God's forgiveness. Make clear at the outset that whatever they write is confidential.

❖ Conclude by assuring the group of God's gracious forgiveness by reading from Jude 24-25: **Now to him who is able to keep you from falling, and to make you stand without blemish in the presence of his glory with rejoicing, to the only God our Savior, through Jesus Christ our Lord, be glory, majesty, power, and authority, before all time and now and forever. Amen.**

(5) Continue the Journey

❖ Pray that all who have participated will continue to give thanks for God's amazing grace and forgiveness.

❖ Read aloud this preparation for next week's lesson. You may also want to post it on newsprint for the students to copy.

■ **Title: Faith Requires Mutual Love**

■ **Background Scripture: Hebrews 13:1-6; 1 Corinthians 13**
■ **Lesson Scripture: Hebrews 13:1-3; 1 Corinthians 13**
■ **Focus of the Lesson: People search for a workable and reliable definition of love. Is there one? The writers of both Hebrews and 1 Corinthians define love and tell us that love is greater than faith and hope.**

❖ Post these three activities related to this week's session on newsprint for the students to copy. Challenge the adults to grow spiritually by completing one or more of them.

(1) **Identify an experience you anticipate this week that creates fear or anxiety for you. Pray each day that your faith in God will remain unshakable so that you will be able to overcome this fear.**

(2) **Focus on Hebrews 12:28. Think about your experiences of God as you worship. Are you truly approaching God with "reverence and awe"? If not, what changes do you need to make to enable worship to be more authentic for you?**

(3) **Offer sincere forgiveness to someone who has harmed you.**

❖ Sing or read aloud "Give Thanks," found in *The Faith We Sing.*

❖ Conclude today's session by leading the class in this benediction, adapted from the key verses for September 16 from Hebrews 12:1-2: **Let us go forth to run with perseverance the race that is set before us, looking to Jesus the pioneer and perfecter of our faith.**

UNIT 1: WHAT IS FAITH?
FAITH REQUIRES MUTUAL LOVE

PREVIEWING THE LESSON

Lesson Scripture: Hebrews 13:1-3; 1 Corinthians 13
Background Scripture: Hebrews 13:1-6; 1 Corinthians 13
Key Verse: 1 Corinthians 13:13

Focus of the Lesson:
People search for a workable and reliable definition of love. Is there one? The writers of Hebrews and 1 Corinthians define love and tell us that love is greater than faith and hope.

Goals for the Learners:
(1) to explore the implications of love as expressed in Hebrews 13 and 1 Corinthians 13.
(2) to reflect on the ways they experience Christian love in their lives.
(3) to share Christian love with others.

Pronunciation Guide:
agape (uh gah′ pay)   *philos* (fee′ los)
paraenesis (pair eh nee′ sis)   *philoxenia* (fil on ex ee′ ah)

Supplies:
Bibles, newsprint and marker, paper and pencils, hymnals

READING THE SCRIPTURE

NRSV
Lesson Scripture: Hebrews 13:1-3
   ¹Let mutual love continue. ²Do not neglect to show hospitality to strangers, for by doing that some have entertained angels without knowing it. ³Remember those who are in prison, as though you were in prison with them; those who are being tortured, as though you yourselves were being tortured.

CEB
Lesson Scripture: Hebrews 13:1-3
   ¹Keep loving each other like family. ²Don't neglect to open up your homes to guests, because by doing this some have been hosts to angels without knowing it. ³Remember prisoners as if you were in prison with them, and people who are mistreated as if you were in their place.

Lesson Scripture: 1 Corinthians 13

[1]If I speak in the tongues of mortals and of angels, but do not have love, I am a noisy gong or a clanging cymbal. [2]And if I have prophetic powers, and understand all mysteries and all knowledge, and if I have all faith, so as to remove mountains, but do not have love, I am nothing. [3]If I give away all my possessions, and if I hand over my body so that I may boast, but do not have love, I gain nothing.

[4]Love is patient; love is kind; love is not envious or boastful or arrogant [5]or rude. It does not insist on its own way; it is not irritable or resentful; [6]it does not rejoice in wrongdoing, but rejoices in the truth. [7]It bears all things, believes all things, hopes all things, endures all things.

[8]Love never ends. But as for prophecies, they will come to an end; as for tongues, they will cease; as for knowledge, it will come to an end. [9]For we know only in part, and we prophesy only in part; [10]but when the complete comes, the partial will come to an end. [11]When I was a child, I spoke like a child, I thought like a child, I reasoned like a child; when I became an adult, I put an end to childish ways. [12]For now we see in a mirror, dimly, but then we will see face to face. Now I know only in part; then I will know fully, even as I have been fully known. **[13]And now faith, hope, and love abide, these three; and the greatest of these is love.**

Lesson Scripture: 1 Corinthians 13

[1]If I speak in tongues of human beings and of angels but I don't have love, I'm a clanging gong or a clashing cymbal. [2]If I have the gift of prophecy and I know all the mysteries and everything else, and if I have such complete faith that I can move mountains but I don't have love, I'm nothing. [3]If I give away everything that I have and hand over my own body to feel good about what I've done but I don't have love, I receive no benefit whatsoever.

[4]Love is patient, love is kind, it isn't jealous, it doesn't brag, it isn't arrogant, [5]it isn't rude, it doesn't seek its own advantage, it isn't irritable, it doesn't keep a record of complaints, [6]it isn't happy with injustice, but it is happy with the truth. [7]Love puts up with all things, trusts in all things, hopes for all things, endures all things.

[8]Love never fails. As for prophecies, they will be brought to an end. As for tongues, they will stop. As for knowledge, it will be brought to an end. [9]We know in part and we prophesy in part; [10]but when the perfect comes, what is partial will be brought to an end. [11]When I was a child, I used to speak like a child, reason like a child, think like a child. But now that I have become a man, I've put an end to childish things. [12]Now we see a reflection in a mirror; then we will see face-to-face. Now I know partially, but then I will know completely in the same way that I have been completely known. **[13]Now faith, hope, and love remain—these three things—and the greatest of these is love.**

UNDERSTANDING THE SCRIPTURE

Hebrews 13:1-6. The writer of Hebrews moved toward his conclusion with a series of moral instructions. Though only three imperatives are found in 13:1-3, the force of those commands carries throughout the verses. Greek has two forms of imperatives.

The one occurring in verse 1 has a different force than the commands used in verses 2-3, which are more like imperatives in English. The verb in verse 1 means "let continue." In English, we would understand "you" as the implied subject of this command. In Greek, however, "mutual love" is the subject, and the force is something like saying, "Mutual love, continue!" While somewhat oblique from an English perspective, the imperative force is strong in Greek. The word translated "mutual love" is literally translated into English as "philadelphia," which is the kind of love or affection shown between family members. Letting this kind of love "continue" implies that it already existed within the fellowship of the church, but as often is the case when disagreements or disputes arise within a family, even the close bonds of familial love can be challenged and threatened.

"Hospitality" (13:2) translates a word that combines the same root "phil-" (denoting family love) with the Greek word for stranger or alien. "Neglect" (literally, "letting something slip from your mind in forgetfulness") implies an awareness of Old Testament injunctions about the treatment of foreigners in the midst of the Hebrew nation (Exodus 23:9; Leviticus 19:34; 24:22; Deuteronomy 1:16; 10:17-19). That Old Testament connection is strengthened by the allusion to experiences with angels, like those of Abraham (Genesis 18:1-15) and Lot (19:1-11). "Remember" (Hebrews 13:3) is the opposite of "neglect" and introduces a kind of elaboration of the Golden Rule—visualizing yourself in the place of the prisoner in order to understand the need for empathy and ministry with those in prison. The harshness of prison life is emphasized by the reference to torture and by imagining yourself as an object of torture.

Acknowledging that the Lord is our helper and will never forsake us, the writer also counseled guarding the sanctity of marriage and avoiding greed in verses 4-6.

1 Corinthians 13:1-3. Although some traditions have connected Paul with the writing of Hebrews, that view generally is rejected today. Nevertheless, the themes that Paul developed in 1 Corinthians 13 elaborate and extend the particular focus found in Hebrews 13:1. The church in Corinth was troubled by quarrels, disputes, power struggles, rivalries, and divisions. In chapter 12, Paul used the human body as an image of how the many gifts, roles, and functions of the church should operate together in unity. One way surpassed all others in its potential for achieving that unity, and Paul made his case for that "more excellent way" (1 Corinthians 12:31) in chapter 13.

In verses 1-3, Paul highlighted some of the gifts, virtues, and characteristics that were favored among the Corinthians. These continue to be esteemed among believers today: eloquence, vision, insight, knowledge, confidence, wealth, generosity, and unselfishness. Paul emphasized the deficiencies in these expressions of faith when love is absent. The phrase "but do not have love" occurs in each verse. "Have" means to have at hand, hold, possess, preserve, or keep something. Though Paul's use of the subjunctive mood and the Greek word he uses for "not" show that he was posing possibilities rather than making strong accusations, the end results of loveless virtues are striking. Being nothing, gaining nothing, and contributing nothing more than annoying and abrasive noise are the payoffs for loveless devotion, even when the causes are worthy.

1 Corinthians 13:4-7. Having noted what the absence of love means, Paul moved on to focus on the nature of *agape* love. He bracketed a list of specific negative behaviors (introduced by a series of "not's," in verses 4c-6a) with a brief list of significant positive characteristics. The King James Version's "suffereth long" (13:4) preserves a more literal translation than the "is patient" used in other translations. The central idea is of anger, wrath, or rage patiently being held far away. "Is kind" represents the only occurrence of this verb in the New Testament, but its associated noun and adjective carry the meanings of goodness, kindness, generosity, and benevolence. "Rejoices in the truth" (13:6) provides the final bracket. It depicts love and truth rejoicing together.

Between these brackets are eight negative characteristics that poison love: being envious or jealous, boastful or vain, arrogant or prideful (13:4), rude or ill-mannered, selfish or self-centered, irritable or peevish, resentful or unforgiving (13:5), and reveling or flamboyant in doing wrong (13:6). With these kinds of attitudes and behaviors, love has no soil in which to take root.

1 Corinthians 13:8-13. Paul concluded his ode to love by focusing on love's endurance. While we might identify a number of possible beginnings for love (creation, the call of Abram, the Exodus, the birth of Jesus, the crucifixion, or the resurrection), love once begun has no end. By contrast, anything that is "partial will come to an end" (13:10). The divisive things that were disturbing the Corinthian fellowship were among these "partial" things.

Prophecies, tongues, and knowledge (13:8) were recognized as legitimate parts of the life and the giftedness of the Corinthian church (12:8-11), but they were not general gifts bestowed on all (13:28-30). They also were associated with some of the conflict and divisiveness in the church (8:1; 14:2-25), especially when they were practiced without an *agape* type of love (13:1-2). Those who possessed those gifts and who elevated their particular gifts in importance had failed to recognize the partial, incomplete, and temporal limitations of these gifts. Their current perspectives are more like dim images reflected in glass than face-to-face reality.

At some point in time, all of these partial perspectives will end. When "the complete comes" (13:10), they all will cease. Failure to recognize the limited significance of these gifts is childish thinking. Paul's readers currently were speaking, thinking, and reasoning like children. Only the maturity of adulthood will end such childish ways. Then we will know as fully as God currently knows us. In that full knowledge our petty differences will be swallowed up by three great and abiding truths: faith, hope, and love. The greatest of these—love—is the one enduring thing that can transform our present moment into something of eternal value.

INTERPRETING THE SCRIPTURE

The Quest for Unity

When I was a child attending vacation Bible school, I learned the pledges of allegiance to the American flag, to the Christian flag, and to the Bible. While the pledge to the Christian flag has undergone some revisions and changes recently to make it more theologically and politically correct, the pledge I learned expressed a goal that still touches me deeply. Under an encompassing vision of a kingdom inaugurated by the Savior, the pledge called for "one brotherhood, uniting all mankind in service and in love." A similar impetus toward unity is seen in "one nation, under God, indivisible" in the pledge to the American flag. Something in the vision of unity captures our highest aspirations, and something about the power of love to transform brokenness into oneness gives us hope.

Unity in the body of Christ was a deep concern for the apostle Paul, and his letters to the church at Corinth clearly show the depth of his concern. First-century churches like the one in Corinth were dynamic and fluid. They did not have the benefit of centuries of theological reflection, experience, and tradition that we enjoy. They were in some sense making up the rules as they went along. Paul was the rule maker, the enforcer, and the referee all rolled into one; and the church in Corinth, with all of its divisions, factions, and disputes, needed that and more.

The model Paul adopted for addressing the fractured fellowship in Corinth was one body with many members (1 Corinthians 12:12). He argued for an organic unity under Christ as the head of the body. But he celebrated the diversity of gifts, experiences, and worship styles by which God had chosen to arrange the body (12:18). He insisted that all the parts must work together for the body to function optimally while celebrating the variety of spiritual gifts that were represented in the parts. If Christ is the head and the one Spirit is the nervous system that keeps all the parts of the body working together, then love is the circulatory system that nourishes the entire body and keeps it vibrant and alive. Faith, hope, and love are integral parts of the church's life, but love is the key factor in the unified body of Christ.

Love Is the Theme

Reflections about love in the New Testament frequently point to the four Greek words that refer to different kinds of love. In reality, only two of those are found in the New Testament itself: *agape* and *philos* (*eros* and *storgo* are absent). Even that statement, however, is somewhat misleading. *Agape* is represented in three forms: as a noun, as a verb, and as a derived adjective (meaning "beloved"). *Philos* is used much more widely because it often is joined with other words to form compound words that describe various kinds of love. In a quick count, I found thirty-six different words in the Greek lexicon that start with the root of *philos*. We already have encountered in this lesson *philadelphia* (brotherly love or love for family) and *philoxenia* (hospitality, literally,

"love of strangers"). While Paul used *agape* throughout 1 Corinthians, the writer of Hebrews employed the two compounds of *philos* in chapter 13. Depending on the object loved, however, *philos* can be viewed as either good or bad. Loving money (Luke 16:14; 2 Timothy 3:2), oneself (2 Timothy 3:2), or pleasure (2 Timothy 3:4) might be viewed negatively. Loving God (2 Timothy 3:4), one's husband or children (Titus 2:4), or humanity in general (translated "loving kindness" in Titus 3:4) likely would be viewed positively. Some people might have different responses about showing hospitality (loving strangers, depending on how the strangers are perceived ["illegal aliens," for example]), but the Bible shows no such distinction in encouraging hospitality.

More truth is found in the old gospel song "Love Is the Theme" than we sometimes acknowledge, but the crucial decisions that believers face in applying love are much more critical than the song acknowledges. Jesus placed loving God and loving neighbor at the center of his gospel message (see Mark 12:29-31). In explaining the commandment to "love your neighbor as yourself," Jesus held up the example of a despised Samaritan both as a model and as a challenge to transform one's understanding of "neighbor" (Luke 10:25-37). At the same time, Jesus acknowledged a struggle at the center of our souls over which master we will love and serve (Matthew 6:24).

Paul was right in focusing on the *agape* love exemplified in Jesus' life and death rather than on *philos* love, which swings back and forth based on our perceptions of the worthiness of the objects of our affection. The *agape* love poured out on us "while we still were sinners" (Romans 5:8) is the theme of the love we have received in grace and the love we are called to show toward our neighbors.

Living by the Rules

Biblical scholars sometimes use the word *paraenesis* to describe the moral exhortations and advice found in Scripture. The Greek verb from which that word is derived occurs twice in the New Testament: in Acts 27:9 when Paul "advised" (or "admonished" in KJV) and in Acts 27:22 when Paul said "I urge" (or "I exhort" in KJV). The term often is applied to portions of Scripture like Hebrews 13:1-18, where a series of moral imperatives are recorded.

Putting love at the center of the Christian faith is a worthy reflection of Jesus' teaching, but *agape* love is more than an emotion or a warm, fuzzy feeling. *Agape* finds expression in actions. While the central core of rule making and rule keeping can lead to legalism and a repressive faith, love that does not express itself in unselfish devotion is as worthless as no love at all. "Love God and love your neighbor" well summarizes all of the Law and the Prophets, but that summary does not replace or nullify the Law and the Prophets. Love still requires concrete expression in our lives.

Fearing they might be viewed as Pharisaic or legalistic, many believers flee from any law, rule, or regulation that others might view as unfairly attacking their rights to be and do whatever they please. What these believers fail to recognize is that love of God, love of others, and even love of self are at the core of all the laws, rules, and regulations. The issue, however, is what you mean by "love." If "love" is the indecisive *philos* that draws its strength from the object being loved, then laws based on that kind of love will be reflections of whim. If "love" is the self-serving *eros*, then the laws are subject to acceptance or rejection based on the self-centered criteria of each individual. If the rules are based on *agape*, however, the self is subordinated to a larger and higher good. Each law, rule, or regulation becomes an expression of loving God, others, or yourself with a love that Jesus showed on the cross. Whether we are dealing with the Ten Commandments, the Sermon on the Mount, or the *paraenesis* recorded in Hebrews, we must find and affirm the underlying foundation provided by *agape*. Our faith in Christ requires such love.

SHARING THE SCRIPTURE

Preparing Our Hearts

Explore this week's devotional reading, found in John 13:31-35. Near the end of his life Jesus explains to his disciples that they must "love one another" in the same way that he has loved them (13:34). But Jesus is not just talking about love; rather, he is making God's love known by the way he lives. He models this love for us. If we follow his commandment, others will come to know that we are his followers because of the love we not only talk about but also enact. Try to be aware of your actions this week. In what ways are you showing Jesus' love to others?

Pray that you and the adult students will ask Jesus to guide you in demonstrating his love to other people.

Preparing Our Minds

Study the background Scripture from Hebrews 3:1-6 and 1 Corinthians 13. The lesson Scripture is from Hebrews 13:1-3 and 1 Corinthians 13.

Consider this question as you prepare the lesson: *Is there a workable and reliable definition of love?*

Write on newsprint:
❑ information for next week's lesson, found under "Continue the Journey."

❑ activities for further spiritual growth in "Continue the Journey."

Review the "Introduction," "The Big Picture," "Close-up," and "Faith in Action." Consider how you will use this additional information, which immediately precedes the first lesson.

LEADING THE CLASS

(1) Gather to Learn

❖ Greet the class members. Introduce any guests and help them feel at home.

❖ Pray that all who have come today will reflect on what it means to experience and show God's love to others.

❖ Point out that in today's lesson we are going to investigate what love means. Read the following descriptions and invite the adults to comment on how each one helps shape their own definition of love.

■ "He who is filled with love is filled with God himself." (Saint Augustine of Hippo, *On the Trinity*)

■ "Paul's description of love in 1 Corinthians 13 . . . is a portrait for which Christ Himself has sat." (C. H. Dodd, quoted in Elizabeth Urch, *Friendship*)

■ "To love as Jesus loves; that is not only the Lord's precept, it is our vocation. When all is said and done it is the one thing we have to learn, for it is perfection." (René Voillaume, *Seeds of the Desert*)

❖ Read aloud today's focus statement: **People search for a workable and reliable definition of love. Is there one? The writers of Hebrews and 1 Corinthians define love and tell us that love is greater than faith and hope.**

(2) Goal 1: Explore the Implications of Love as Expressed in Hebrews 13 and 1 Corinthians 13

❖ Choose a volunteer to read Hebrews 13:1-3.

❖ Ask these questions. Add to the discussion by reading or retelling information on Hebrews 13:1-6 from Understanding the Scripture.

    (1) What examples of mutual love continuing do you see within your congregation?

    (2) Notice that in verses 2-3 the focus is on populations that we tend to ignore: the stranger, the prisoner, and the one being tortured. How is your congregation showing love for these persons, as well as those who are otherwise living on the fringes of society?

❖ Select several students who use the same Bible translation to read 1 Corinthians 13 in unison.

❖ Ask these questions. Add to the discussion by reading or retelling information on the sections from 1 Corinthians 13 from Understanding the Scripture.

    (1) Look at verses 1-3. What do you learn about how God views the things and abilities that many people, including some Christians, hold dear?

    (2) How does Paul describe love according to verses 4-7?

    (3) According to verses 4-7, what behaviors are unloving?

    (4) What is Paul's point in verses 8-12?

    (5) According to the final verse, which is also today's key verse, love is greater than faith and hope. Do you agree? Give reasons to support your answers.

❖ **Option:** If you have access to *The United Methodist Hymnal*, invite the participants to read responsively "Canticle of Love," found on page 646. This reading includes portions of Scripture that speak directly to the notion of love. After the reading, encourage participants to talk about the implications of love that they find in these verses.

(3) Goal 2: Reflect on the Ways the Learners Experience Christian Love in Their Lives

❖ Distribute paper and pencils. Suggest that the adults reflect on this question in writing, though some may prefer just to meditate on it: **How do you experience Christian love in your life?** Think about the ways that God cares for you. Especially consider the ways that, through other people, you experience the blessings of Jesus' love.

❖ Invite volunteers to comment on ways that they have experienced Christian love.

(4) Goal 3: Share Christian Love With Others

❖ Read aloud the second paragraph of "Living by the Rules" in Interpreting the Scripture.

❖ Post a sheet of newsprint and invite the adults to answer this question: **How can we concretely share Jesus' love with our community?** Collecting food for a pantry, sending money to support a homeless shelter, or sponsoring an ecumenical Bible study are all worthy ideas. However, challenge the group to go further, to think outside the box. Could your church help children who have no place to go after school by starting a homework center staffed with volunteers? Could you match each homebound member with a "friendly caller" who will telephone at a certain time each day to be sure that all is well?

❖ Determine which option(s) the group can address. One way to do that is to ask participants to raise their hands to signify which project or idea they would personally support. Form a task force to consider the specifics of what you will do and how you will do it. The task force will ensure that the focus of the project is on sharing God's love with other people.

(5) Continue the Journey

❖ Pray that the group will continue to show God's steadfast love to others in as many ways as they can.

❖ Read aloud this preparation for next week's lesson. You may also want to post it on newsprint for the students to copy.
- **Title: Stephen's Arrest and Speech**
- **Background Scripture: Acts 6:8–7:53**
- **Lesson Scripture: Acts 6:8–7:2a**
- **Focus of the Lesson: People need a bold and perceptive leader to articulate truth in times of uncertainty. How can we find courage to speak the truth? Stephen, in the face of opposition, demonstrated the power and wisdom of the Spirit to speak the truth of Christ.**

❖ Post these three activities related to this week's session on newsprint for the students to copy. Challenge the adults to grow spiritually by completing one or more of them.
1. **Memorize 1 Corinthians 13:13 as it appears in your favorite Bible translation. If possible, try to learn the entire chapter.**
2. **Use a Bible concordance to look up the word "love" in the New Testament. Note the Greek words that are used for this one English word. Read several entries. Write your thoughts as to what "love" means to Jesus and how it is interpreted within the early church.**
3. **Take action this week to live out the love to which Jesus calls you.**

❖ Sing or read aloud "The Gift of Love."

❖ Conclude today's session by leading the class in this benediction, adapted from the key verses for September 16 from Hebrews 12:1-2: **Let us go forth to run with perseverance the race that is set before us, looking to Jesus the pioneer and perfecter of our faith.**

UNIT 2: WHO UNDERSTANDS FAITH?
STEPHEN'S ARREST AND SPEECH

PREVIEWING THE LESSON

Lesson Scripture: Acts 6:8–7:2a
Background Scripture: Acts 6:8–7:53
Key Verse: Acts 6:8

Focus of the Lesson:
People need a bold and perceptive leader to articulate truth in times of uncertainty. How can we find courage to speak the truth? Stephen, in the face of opposition, demonstrated the power and wisdom of the Spirit to speak the truth of Christ.

Goals for the Learners:
(1) to identify the risks of leadership that become known in Stephen's witness.
(2) to confront the principalities and powers of our day.
(3) to seek the power and the wisdom of the Spirit in their efforts to speak truth.

Pronunciation Guide:
Alexandrian (al ig zan' dree uhn)   *koinonia* (koy nohn ee' ah)
Cilicia (suh lish' ee uh)   Sanhedrin (san hee' druhn)
Cyrenian (si ree' nee uhn)

Supplies:
Bibles, newsprint and marker, paper and pencils, hymnals

READING THE SCRIPTURE

NRSV
Lesson Scripture: Acts 6:8–7:2a

⁸**Stephen, full of grace and power, did great wonders and signs among the people.** ⁹Then some of those who belonged to the synagogue of the Freedmen (as it was called), Cyrenians, Alexandrians, and others of those from Cilicia and Asia, stood up and

CEB
Lesson Scripture: Acts 6:8–7:2a

⁸**Stephen, who stood out among the believers for the way God's grace was at work in his life and for his exceptional endowment with divine power, was doing great wonders and signs among the people.** ⁹Opposition arose from some who belonged

argued with Stephen. [10]But they could not withstand the wisdom and the Spirit with which he spoke. [11]Then they secretly instigated some men to say, "We have heard him speak blasphemous words against Moses and God." [12]They stirred up the people as well as the elders and the scribes; then they suddenly confronted him, seized him, and brought him before the council. [13]They set up false witnesses who said, "This man never stops saying things against this holy place and the law; [14]for we have heard him say that this Jesus of Nazareth will destroy this place and will change the customs that Moses handed on to us." [15]And all who sat in the council looked intently at him, and they saw that his face was like the face of an angel.

[7:1]Then the high priest asked him, "Are these things so?" [2]And Stephen replied:

"Brothers and fathers, listen to me."

to the so-called Synagogue of Former Slaves. Members from Cyrene, Alexandria, Cilicia, and Asia entered into debate with Stephen. [10]However, they couldn't resist the wisdom the Spirit gave him as he spoke. [11]Then they secretly enticed some people to claim, "We heard him insult Moses and God." [12]They stirred up the people, the elders, and the legal experts. They caught Stephen, dragged him away, and brought him before the Jerusalem Council. [13]Before the council, they presented false witnesses who testified, "This man never stops speaking against this holy place and the Law. [14]In fact, we heard him say that this man Jesus of Nazareth will destroy this place and alter the customary practices Moses gave us." [15]Everyone seated in the council stared at Stephen, and they saw that his face was radiant, just like an angel's.

[7:1]The high priest asked, "Are these accusations true?"

[2]Stephen responded, "Brothers and fathers, listen to me."

UNDERSTANDING THE SCRIPTURE

Acts 6:8. Stephen is mentioned first among the seven (6:5) chosen by the church in Jerusalem to deal with the complaints of the Hellenists (Greek-speaking Jews) against the Hebrews (Aramaic-speaking Jews). The issue was the inequitable distribution of food to needy Hellenist widows (6:1-5). For a community that "had all things in common" and sold possessions so they could "distribute the proceeds to all, as any had need" (2:44-45), this was a significant breach of koinonia, or fellowship. The seven were chosen because of their good reputations and evidence of their being full of the Spirit and of wisdom (6:3). Stephen is singled out in the account as being both "a man full of faith and the Holy Spirit" (6:5) and "full of grace and power" who "did great

wonders and signs among the people" (6:8). Of the seven, only Stephen and Philip are mentioned subsequently in Acts. Philip is remembered as "the evangelist" (21:8), and Stephen is literally heralded as a "martyr" (though translated "witness" in 22:20). Stephen's martyrdom surely had a significant influence on Philip (as it likely had on Paul), for Stephen is the focus of Acts 6:8–8:1. The accounts of Philip's evangelistic efforts (8:5-40) begin immediately after Stephen's martyrdom.

Acts 6:9-12. Part of the mix of people living in Jerusalem at this time was a group of freed Roman slaves and their descendants. Their designation as "libertines" (translated "freedmen") is actually a Latin loanword brought over into Greek (and ultimately into English, though with an added nuance of immorality). Rome made slaves of many people they conquered, and slaves were kept by Romans wherever they lived. The Freedmen mentioned came from such disparate places as North Africa (Cyrene), Egypt (Alexandria), and Asia Minor (the Roman provinces of Cilicia and Asia). Roman slaves were not necessarily field workers. Many were educated and actually taught the children of their masters. Many were artisans, craftsmen, and highly skilled in their trades. Questions remain about the Freedmen. Had they been freed in Jerusalem and remained there? Or had they immigrated after being freed elsewhere? Why had they come or stayed in Jerusalem? Were they converts to Judaism? Was their synagogue a Jewish synagogue, or was Luke using the generic meaning of synagogue as a gathering place? Answering such questions might give us a better idea about the nature of their dispute with Stephen and why they conspired against him.

Luke does not record what Stephen was saying, unless Stephen's later defense before the council represents a parallel message. Given the fact that his words were interpreted as blasphemous against Moses and God, we can assume that Stephen was addressing issues about the law of Moses and the nature of Jesus' relationship with God. If Stephen's defense before the council in chapter 7 parallels his earlier message, the Freedmen likely were converts to Judaism who had undergone the circumcision and baptism required of proselytes. Their zeal for their new faith seems to have paralleled the zeal of Saul, who dedicated himself to stamping out the heretical sect that was pledging allegiance to Jesus as the Son of God and the promised Son of Man. Outdone by Stephen's wisdom and spiritual power, the Freedmen secretly induced others to accuse Stephen of blasphemy. Soon the incitement enveloped the Jewish elders and scribes as well, and Stephen was brought before the Sanhedrin, the supreme judicial council that interpreted and enforced the law.

Acts 6:13-15. The Sanhedrin had a checkered history, and because of its role in the accusations against Jesus, it generally is viewed critically in the New Testament. Under Roman domination, the council's influence and importance waxed and waned depending on the inclinations of the current Roman overseer. At times the council was severely restricted; at other times it was given considerable authority to oversee Jewish affairs. Much of the time it was manipulated by the Romans to ensure that Caesar's interests were established and protected. Comprising seventy-one religious leaders, the council had its own internal power struggles between various religious temperaments that also waxed and waned. Generally it was controlled by Sadducees with sympathies toward the priestly aristocrats, but the Pharisaic influence increased over time and gained control after the destruction of the Jerusalem Temple in A.D. 70.

Luke identified the people called to testify against Stephen as "false witnesses," but their testimony appears to be true in light of Luke's report, Stephen's subsequent testimony, and other New Testament records. Their testimony was "false," not because they were attesting to false facts, but because they were arguing against a greater truth that Jesus had proclaimed and Stephen had endorsed. Jesus regularly criticized abuses in the Temple, argued against the Pharisees' nitpicking application of the law, and challenged the "customs" (the Greek word is *ethos*, which speaks of the distinguishing attitudes, habits, and beliefs of a group) that had grown up around the Mosaic law. How Luke knew the impression that the council saw on Stephen's face, we cannot determine, but I think most translators have chosen the wrong meaning of "angel" to imply a heavenly messenger. I think instead they saw the face of a "messenger" absolutely convinced of the truth of his message and unwavering in his commitment to it.

Acts 7:1-53. Chapter 7 contains the longest address in the Book of Acts. It begins with a synopsis of the story of Abraham (7:2-8), followed by a brief account of Jacob and Joseph (7:9-19). The heart of Stephen's address focuses on Moses (7:20-40). After brief references to the Hebrew people's idol in the wilderness (7:41-43), the tent in the wilderness (7:44), and the period from Joshua to David (7:45-46), Stephen concludes with Solomon's construction of the Temple (7:47). Throughout his address Stephen laid the groundwork for his case. He immediately brought his listeners into the story by referring to "this country in which you are now living" (7:4). "Enslave" and "mistreat" in verse 6 hint at their current plight under the Romans. "The fulfillment of the promise that God had made to Abraham" (7:17) introduces a messianic theme that anticipates Stephen's introduction of "the coming of the Righteous One" (7:52).

Israel's rejection of Moses (7:25, 27, 35) ushers in more references to "our ancestors" (an expression used twelve times in chapter 7) with an intensifying emphasis on disobedience (7:39). Verse 51 provides the final confrontation: "You stiff-necked people, uncircumcised in heart and ears, you are forever opposing the Holy Spirit, just as your ancestors used to do." Just as their ancestors persecuted the prophets and killed those who foretold the coming of Christ, they themselves had become the betrayers and murderers of the Righteous One, for whom their ancestors had been longing for centuries. Stephen's accusations were so direct and hard that the members of the Sanhedrin "covered their ears" (7:57) to the truth and followed the example of their ancestors by putting to death the prophetic voice that indicted them.

INTERPRETING THE SCRIPTURE

Character That Counts

The word "character" speaks of the traits, qualities, attributes, and moral constitutions of people. Of course, we also apply the term to odd, eccentric persons. On closer examination, we might decide that these two definitions are not so far apart. People of true character seem rare in our day. While we may not view them as eccentric, many people find anyone of integrity to be a little out of touch with the practical realities of today's world. Compromise, where each party gets some wins and makes some concessions, is more the spirit of our times. While compromise is not always bad, too often it results in a combination of the good, the bad, and the ugly.

When difficult problems arise, we often wish for people of integrity to help us deal with the problems. Integrity in such circumstances generally will mean fair, informed, balanced, and objective guidance in dealing with the problem and arriving at a fitting solution. When the Twelve were looking for ways to deal with a disgruntled group within the Jerusalem church, they showed wisdom in addressing the problem. First, they made the concern a community-wide issue—they called together the whole community of disciples. Second, they established the criteria for the kind of leaders who could address the problem—people of good standing, full of the Spirit and of wisdom. Third, they allowed the whole community to select the leaders while reserving the right to appoint them to the task. Rather than selecting a bipartisan committee to deal with the issue, the community selected the Twelve, leaders who represented the interest of those who were disgruntled. The success of the entire venture resided not in the process followed, but rather in the criteria established for the leaders who were being chosen.

Stephen, the first listed among the leaders, demonstrated how significant the criteria were. Not only did he meet the criteria but Luke also adds that he was "full of faith and the Holy Spirit" (6:5) and was "full of grace and power" (6:8). Without a doubt, the problem was resolved because the character of the leaders ensured that a wise, compassionate, fair, and equitable solution was found.

Truth and Consequences

The phrase "truth or consequences" entered the American vernacular in 1940 when Ralph Edwards launched a radio program by that name. The program won instant popularity and in 1950 also entered the national television market. On the show, contestants had to answer off-the-wall trivia questions, and when they failed, they usually had to perform some madcap or embarrassing stunt. Bob Barker, who hosted the TV show from 1956–75, used to sign off with the phrase, "Hoping all your consequences are happy ones."

Of course, not all consequences are happy ones. Generally, bad consequences arise as a result of bad behavior, and good consequences result from good behavior. The "truth or consequences" approach actually is a way of encouraging truthfulness. Unless you tell the truth, you will suffer the consequences. It doesn't promise that you will be rewarded for telling the truth, but candor and truthfulness generally are viewed favorably. In our day, the consequences for telling the truth generally are positive, even when the truth is an admission of doing something very bad. Popular culture looks at candor and the honest admission of guilt as being almost as good as not having committed the immoral deed in the first place.

Conversely, in this day of heightened sensitivity about possible bias, many people do not want to hear the truth if it contradicts their preconceived notions. On this score, things haven't changed much since the days of Stephen. The fact that "witness" and "martyr" are both used to translate the same Greek word is a reminder of how speaking the truth often precipitates consequences— and sometimes significant consequences. Unfortunately, too many people want to witness with their words without risking anything, much less their lives. When the stakes are high and taking a stand for truth might bring repercussions, many "witnesses" shut down. Most are unwilling to face even minor slights when their views appear unpopular with the crowd. When the slightest amount of intimidation closes down our witness, the minor consequences we shun erect a wall that encloses the truth and keeps it contained. A bold witness given in the face of negative consequences not only testifies to the character of the witness but also adds power to the message. We need more bold witnesses today "speaking the truth in love (Ephesians 4:15), showing through their words and their lives the transformation that Christ has made in them.

The Open and the Closed Mind

Sometimes truth hurts. Sometimes truth heals. Sometimes truth repels. The truth, of course, never changes. What results from an encounter with truth is fully associated with the individuals confronted by the truth.

Some people, and even some churches, like to hide the truth. That could have been the case with the Jerusalem church in confronting its ethnic diversity. Publicizing your great fellowship, where each person's needs are met, is a whole lot more appealing than pulling out the dirty laundry, with its ethnic and class inequities. It is better to put on smiles and act like we all love Jesus, and let slip that part about loving your neighbor as yourself. But when the Spirit, wisdom, faith, grace, and power are present, truth can work a remarkable transformation.

Truth does not always win out, however. Sometimes the bonds of common background, experience, place, tradition, and even theology can close minds and hearts to the spirit of truth that blows like the wind through our communities. "Freedmen," indeed! Yes, they had been freed from their bonds of slavery, but they were still indentured to closed minds. When the power of wisdom and the Spirit overwhelms some folks, they do not fall on their knees and repent. Rather, they strike back with anger, uttering half-truths and labeling their opponents as infidels, and secretly plot to destroy and conquer. Some extremists cannot allow heresies to exist, so they close their ears and their minds to the truth—and try to bury the truth with its messenger under stones.

The church lost Stephen to such closed minds, but truth didn't die. Standing by, watching the stoning of Stephen, was an archenemy of the faith, Saul of Tarsus. A martyr-witness touched his life and planted a seed of truth and hope in his heart that later took root and bore great fruit. Philip also was transformed from troubleshooter to evangelist. Rather than be intimidated, Philip became one of the witnesses scattered by Stephen's martyrdom—an unexpected outcome that advanced the spread of the truth "to the ends of the earth" (Acts 1:8).

SHARING THE SCRIPTURE

Preparing Our Hearts

Explore this week's devotional reading, found in Proverbs 8:1-11. Here we see wisdom personified as a woman, just as in 1:20-33. The way of wisdom is the way of life. Chapter 8 emphasizes the righteous words that come from the lips of the wise one. Similarly, in today's reading from Acts we will witness "the wisdom and the Spirit with which [Stephen] spoke" (Acts 6:10). God's wisdom is indeed powerful. As you listen to people speak, what criteria do you use to determine whether or not they are speaking words of wisdom?

Pray that you and the adult students will both speak wisely and listen with a discerning spirit to people who claim to witness for God.

Preparing Our Minds

Study the background Scripture from Acts 6:8–7:53 and the lesson Scripture from Acts 6:8–7:2a.

Consider this question as you prepare the lesson: *How can we find courage to speak the truth, especially in times of uncertainty?*

Write on newsprint:
- ❏ questions for "Identify the Risks of Leadership That Become Known in Stephen's Witness."
- ❏ information for next week's lesson, found under "Continue the Journey."
- ❏ activities for further spiritual growth in "Continue the Journey."

Review the "Introduction," "The Big Picture," "Close-up," and "Faith in Action." Consider how you will use this additional information, which immediately precedes the first lesson.

LEADING THE CLASS

(1) Gather to Learn

❖ Greet the class members. Introduce any guests and help them feel at home.

❖ Pray that today's participants will open their hearts to discern the wisdom and truth of God's Word.

❖ Read this information: **Martin Luther, a leading figure in the Protestant Reformation, had posted his 95 Theses on the door of the Wittenberg Church in October 1517. In these statements he accused the Roman Catholic Church, of which he was a monk, of numerous heresies. Pope Leo X condemned Luther's views as heresy and demanded that he appear before the Diet of Worms in April 1521. Shown a table with books of his writings, Luther was asked to state whether he stood by what he had professed. The next day he came again before the assembly and made this historic speech: "Unless I am convinced by proofs from Scriptures or by plain and clear reasons and arguments, I can and will not retract, for it is neither safe nor wise to do anything against conscience. Here I stand. I can do no other. God help me. Amen." As a result, Luther was declared an outlaw.**

❖ Ask: **What characteristics does one need in order to courageously speak truth to power as Martin Luther did?**

❖ Read aloud today's focus statement: **People need a bold and perceptive leader to articulate truth in times of uncertainty. How can we find courage to speak the truth? Stephen, in the face of opposition, demonstrated the power and wisdom of the Spirit to speak the truth of Christ.**

(2) Goal 1: Identify the Risks of Leadership That Become Known in Stephen's Witness

❖ Choose a volunteer to read Acts 6:8–7:2a (ending with the words "listen to me").

❖ Form two groups (or multiples of two if the group is large). Assign one group to study Stephen and the other to study members of the synagogue of the Freedmen. Post a sheet of newsprint on which you have written the following questions for each group to discuss.

(1) **What can you surmise about the traits of your assigned character(s)?**

(2) **How do the characters' actions demonstrate their relationship to God and to other people?**

(3) **What motives do you think each of the characters has for acting as he does?**

❖ Bring the groups together and encourage speakers from each group to answer the questions. After each has had a turn to report, add whatever information you feel may round out or clarify the discussion from Interpreting the Scripture.

❖ Wrap up this portion of the lesson by asking: **What risks does Stephen appear to take in order to share the gospel?**

(3) Goal 2: Confront the Principalities and Powers of Our Day

❖ Read: **In a May 1963 issue of *Time* magazine, Karl Barth, a giant among Protestant theologians who was then retired, reported that years earlier he had advised young theologians to "take your Bible and take your newspaper, and read both. But interpret newspapers from your Bible." If we take Barth's mandate seriously, what issues do we as Christians need to be speaking out about today to ensure that the good news of the Bible reaches a world where sin and corruption abound?**

❖ Distribute paper and pencils. Challenge each adult to write a letter to a newspaper editor or an elected official to lay out the facts of an issue he or she feels is important and try to persuade the recipient to act in a way that ensures God's will is done in a just and loving way.

❖ Invite several volunteers to read their letters.

❖ Encourage participants to revise and send their letters from home and then to report to the class about any replies they receive.

(4) Goal 3: Seek the Power and the Wisdom
of the Spirit in the Learners'
Efforts to Speak Truth

❖ Read again Acts 6:10. Note that Stephen is not speaking on his own accord, but with God's wisdom though the Spirit.

❖ Provide quiet time for the adults to meditate on this brief prayer: **Lord, when opportunities present themselves to stand up for you, please empower me through the Holy Spirit with the wisdom and courage to speak truth even in the face of opposition.**

(5) Continue the Journey

❖ Break the silence by praying that all who have come today will have the courage to speak as the Spirit leads them, even under difficult circumstances.

❖ Read aloud this preparation for next week's lesson. You may also want to post it on newsprint for the students to copy.

■ **Title: Stephen's Martyrdom**
■ **Background Scripture: Acts 7:1–8:1a**
■ **Lesson Scripture: Acts 7:51–8:1a**
■ **Focus of the Lesson: When strong leaders confront traditional ideas, their words may incite anger and violence. What causes such violent reactions? Stephen's criticism of the religious establishment and his exaltation of Christ enraged the religious leaders, who responded by stoning him to death.**

❖ Post these three activities related to this week's session on newsprint for the students to copy. Challenge the adults to grow spiritually by completing one or more of them.

(1) Identify a major social or political issue that you feel led to speak about as a Christian. Take action by writing a letter to an elected official or newspaper, or by giving testimony to a legislative body to encourage others to agree with your position.

(2) Be aware of examples in the media of people trying to use slander or innuendo to discredit or falsely accuse someone they do not like. How does the person or group being wronged respond? What does the response suggest about this person?

(3) Select a topic in the Bible, such as covenant or love or grace, that you would like to know more about. Plan to study that theme this week in order to be able to speak from a position of knowledge and strength should you be challenged about this topic.

❖ Sing or read aloud "Stand By Me."

❖ Conclude today's session by leading the class in this benediction, adapted from the key verses for September 16 from Hebrews 12:1-2: **Let us go forth to run with perseverance the race that is set before us, looking to Jesus the pioneer and perfecter of our faith.**

UNIT 2: WHO UNDERSTANDS FAITH?
STEPHEN'S MARTYRDOM

PREVIEWING THE LESSON

Lesson Scripture: Acts 7:51–8:1a
Background Scripture: Acts 7:1–8:1a
Key Verse: Acts 7:59

Focus of the Lesson:
When strong leaders confront traditional ideas, their words may incite anger and violence. What causes such violent reactions? Stephen's criticism of the religious establishment and his exaltation of Christ enraged the religious leaders, who responded by stoning him to death.

Goals for the Learners:
(1) to explore the reasons for Stephen's martyrdom.
(2) to disclose how they feel when their beliefs are attacked.
(3) to witness peacefully and candidly for Christ, no matter the cost.

Pronunciation Guide:
martus (mar' toos)
Shekinah (shuh ki' nuh)

Supplies:
Bibles, newsprint and marker, paper and pencils, hymnals

READING THE SCRIPTURE

NRSV
Lesson Scripture: Acts 7:51–8:1a
[51]"You stiff-necked people, uncircumcised in heart and ears, you are forever opposing the Holy Spirit, just as your ancestors used to do. [52]Which of the prophets did your ancestors not persecute? They killed those who foretold the coming of the Righteous One, and now you have become his betrayers and murderers. [53]You are the ones that received the law as

CEB
Lesson Scripture: Acts 7:51–8:1a
[51]"You stubborn people! In your thoughts and hearing, you are like those who have had no part in God's covenant! You continuously set yourself against the Holy Spirit, just like your ancestors did. [52]Was there a single prophet your ancestors didn't harass? They even killed those who predicted the coming of the righteous one, and you've betrayed and murdered him! [53]You received

ordained by angels, and yet you have not kept it."

[54]When they heard these things, they became enraged and ground their teeth at Stephen. [55]But filled with the Holy Spirit, he gazed into heaven and saw the glory of God and Jesus standing at the right hand of God. [56]"Look," he said, "I see the heavens opened and the Son of Man standing at the right hand of God!" [57]But they covered their ears, and with a loud shout all rushed together against him. [58]Then they dragged him out of the city and began to stone him; and the witnesses laid their coats at the feet of a young man named Saul. [59]**While they were stoning Stephen, he prayed, "Lord Jesus, receive my spirit."** [60]Then he knelt down and cried out in a loud voice, "Lord, do not hold this sin against them." When he had said this, he died. [8:1a]And Saul approved of their killing him.

the Law given by angels, but you haven't kept it."

[54]Once the council members heard these words, they were enraged and began to grind their teeth at Stephen. [55]But Stephen, enabled by the Holy Spirit, stared into heaven and saw God's majesty and Jesus standing at God's right side. [56]He exclaimed, "Look! I can see heaven on display and the Human One standing at God's right side!" [57]At this, they shrieked and covered their ears. Together, they charged at him, [58]threw him out of the city, and began to stone him. The witnesses placed their coats in the care of a young man named Saul. [59]**As they battered him with stones, Stephen prayed, "Lord Jesus, accept my life!"** [60]Falling to his knees, he shouted, "Lord, don't hold this sin against them!" Then he died. [8:1a]Saul was in full agreement with Stephen's murder.

UNDERSTANDING THE SCRIPTURE

Acts 7:1-50. This lesson shares a common background with the previous lesson about Stephen's appearance before the Sanhedrin. Because Israel was under Roman control, the Sanhedrin functioned with some limitations. It could deal with religious matters in a kind of legislative-judicial capacity. Though some commentators claim that it lacked the power under the Romans to execute offenders, restrictions seem to have been placed on political judgments but apparently not on religious ones. Jesus was accused of blasphemy (Matthew 26:65), but political charges were made against him in the accusations before Pilate (27:11). Stephen was accused solely of blasphemy— a religious offense that called for stoning (see Leviticus 24:13-16).

The high priest's question to Stephen, "Are these things so?" (Acts 7:1), refers to the accusations in 6:11-14. Stephen did not give a yes-or-no answer. Instead he gave his accusers an abbreviated history of God's work among the people of Israel, focusing on Moses and the people's reception of him. They had questioned Moses' authority (7:35), refused to obey him, pushed him aside, and longed to return to Egypt (7:39). They made idols and worshiped the work of their hands (7:41). Even in building Solomon's Temple, the people tried to limit and confine God to one physical location (7:44-50). Stephen's negative reflection on the Temple would have been a particular concern to the priest-dominated Sanhedrin.

Acts 7:51-54. Stephen made a personal indictment against the members of the Sanhedrin and their ancestors, an especially pointed charge given that the priestly office was a hereditary one that focused on tribal purity. He used the adjectives "stiff-necked" and "uncircumcised" to describe them. The former is a compound word that combines the Greek words "hard" (from which we derive "sclerosis" and "skeleton") and "neck" or "throat" (from which we derive "trachea"). "Uncircumcised" was a term applied to Gentiles and the heathen, but a strong Old Testament tradition made a distinction between physical and the more important spiritual circumcision (Leviticus 26:41; Jeremiah 6:10, translated as "their ears are closed"; 9:25; Ezekiel 44:7-9). "Always resisting the Holy Spirit" (Acts 7:51 NASB) placed members of the Sanhedrin in line with those who persecuted and killed the prophets who foretold the coming of the Messiah, "the Righteous One." The final indictment was the most severe. The Righteous One had come, and they had betrayed and murdered him—thereby breaking the very law that they themselves contended had been transmitted from God via "angels" (or prophetic "messengers"). Such accusations prompted a deeply emotional response from the Sanhedrin.

Acts 7:55-56. From the beginning, Stephen had been described as a man "full of . . . the Holy Spirit" (Acts 6:5). Somewhat like Jesus, who at his baptism saw the heavens open, saw the Spirit of God descending like a dove, and heard a confirming voice from heaven (Matthew 3:16-17), Stephen experienced a heavenly vision. Filled with the Holy Spirit, Stephen saw "the glory of God" and "Jesus standing at the right hand of God" (Acts 7:55). The holiness of God is so sacred that only God's "glory" can be seen. Later Jewish tradition joined the word *Shekinah* with "glory" to speak particularly of the shining majesty and the weighty presence of the unseen God. Some scholars suggest that the reference in verse 56 to Jesus "standing" is an image of him giving testimony on Stephen's behalf before a heavenly jury. Luke equates "the Righteous One" (7:52), "Jesus" (7:55), and "the Son of Man" (7:56), reinforcing his testimony of who Jesus was and underscoring who had been put to death by the Jewish leaders through the actions of Pilate.

Acts 7:57-58. In one sentence (7:56), Stephen uttered a stinging condemnation of the actions of the Sanhedrin contributing to Jesus' crucifixion and an absolute confession of who Jesus was. The former was blatant boldness by a Hellenist nobody associated with a subversive sect that the Sanhedrin was seeking to extinguish. The latter was the ultimate blasphemy in associating an executed criminal with the Holy God of heaven. At its most basic, blasphemy is offensive use of God's name. Associating Jesus with the right hand of God placed him in the position of being the strength of God, the blessing of God, and the protector of God. In the Old Testament the "right hand of God" was a metaphor of the mighty power by which God created (Isaiah 48:13), waged war (Exodus 15:6, 12), and delivered God's people (Psalms 17:7; 60:5). Crying out with loud voices, covering their ears to shut out the "blasphemy," and rushing Stephen to quiet and subdue him, the Sanhedrin (apparently by common consent) sentenced him to stoning. In essence, they all became the required "witnesses" needed to convict him, and as witnesses they also were the ones designated to lay their hands on the perpetrator's head (Leviticus 24:14), symbolically placing the community's guilt upon him. Without fanfare or further introduction, Luke noted that the executioners laid their robes at the feet of the young man Saul.

Acts 7:59–8:1a. After his confrontational address before the Sanhedrin, Stephen's final words and actions were startling. As he was being stoned, Stephen prayed to "Lord Jesus"—from the perspective of the Sanhedrin, a continuation of his blasphemy and certainly justification in itself for his stoning. His prayer, however, was not vindictive. He first asked Jesus to receive his spirit, affirming that he was anticipating joining Jesus in heaven. In the final cry, as he knelt under the blows of the stones, he asked the Lord not to hold this sin against his executioners. Then, in an unexpected literary device, Luke characterized Saul's feelings about Stephen's execution. The word translated "approved" also can mean "consented to, was gratified by, or took pleasure in" the action taken against Stephen by the Sanhedrin. This seemingly offhanded observation actually prepares readers for a later question addressed to Saul, "Why do you persecute me?" (Acts 9:4).

INTERPRETING THE SCRIPTURE

Bold Witness

"Bold witness" is something we associate with dedicated martyrs or fanatical fundamentalists. Generally it is not something with which most of us feel comfortable. We prefer positive and supportive relationships with friends, cordial and genial relationships with acquaintances, and amiable and affable interactions with strangers. Our desire for peace and harmony sometimes overshadows convictions. Boldness introduces an uncomfortable, impetuous, and brusque dimension to human relationships that we prefer to avoid. The pressured sales pitch, the insistent solicitation, and the emotional altar call make us anxious, uncomfortable, and apprehensive.

Of course, boldness requires some things that we might lack—assurance, confidence, conviction, passion, and bravery. Years ago I participated in training at a summer conference center. Thousands were in attendance, and an outstanding preacher delivered some of the most moving sermons I have ever heard. His messages insistently called for change in our churches and in our lives. Recommitment and revival stirred in my heart. July 4 fell during that week, and a patriotic service was held that evening with flags, uniformed representatives of our armed forces, and stirring patriotic songs. Emotions were stirred and tears flowed freely in patriotic fervor, and that was OK. But the entire week's passion for recommitment and revival did not come close to matching that one night of patriotic enthusiasm. In reflection, I thought of the hymn "O Zion, Haste," which calls for giving our children the glorious gospel message to bear around our world, for giving our wealth to facilitate that mission enterprise, and for fervent prayer for such bold witness. I discovered that many believers have a greater sense of commitment to the cause of freedom through military might than to our divine commission to proclaim the freedom that comes through Jesus Christ.

Some still go into all the world. Some still sacrifice and suffer for the cause of Christ. Some, like Stephen, even give their lives in bold and faithful witness. Too many of us, though, lack the assurance, confidence, conviction, passion, and bravery to speak the good news to a neighbor, much less to go to distant lands. We fear not stoning, but slights, shunning, ridicule, or even rejection. Where is our boldness? What is the testimony others see in us? Maybe we should pray Paul's prayer in Ephesians 6:19, where he asks the church to pray for him "so that when I speak, a message may be given to me to make known with boldness the mystery of the gospel."

Silencing the Opposition

We find some examples of boldness "acceptable" even if we don't share the convictions ourselves. Individuals express deep commitment, active support, and strong advocacy for multitudes of causes, and as long as their convictions don't interfere with our rights, we tend to take a live-and-let-live attitude toward such bold expressions. We hardly ever try to quiet, squelch, or annihilate such bold advocates.

At some point our tolerance for other views may be stretched. Many have noted the loss of civil discourse in our society. Television commentators talk over each other while trying to drown out the opposition. Politicians avoid open forums because passionate advocates are interrupting the discourse and are shouting down opposing points of view. Attempts to reconcile differences or to compromise are ridiculed contemptuously. Dirty tricks, half-truths, scandalous accusations, and outright scorn are directed at opponents in attempts to silence their voices. If we cannot silence them, we demonize them and their views. Challenges to traditional values, conventional views, vested interests, cherished relationships, and sacred cows can generate high tensions, explosive confrontations, and violent reactions. Such was the case with Stephen before the Sanhedrin.

Stephen reinterpreted Israel's history, beginning with Abraham and God's covenant and continuing through Moses and God's law, Solomon and God's Temple, and on to the prophet whom God promised to raise up, "the Righteous One" (Acts 7:52) that Stephen's generation had betrayed and murdered. Earlier, "many of the priests became obedient to the faith" (6:7), but Stephen's theological dismantling of Israel's history, institutions, and practices was too much for the Sanhedrin. When Stephen addressed "you stiff-necked people, uncircumcised in heart and ears, . . . forever opposing the Holy Spirit, just as your ancestors used to do" (7:51), he touched sensitive nerves that struck back in reaction. In defense of the "sacred" idea, the Sanhedrin silenced the heresy, removed its advocate, and set a precedent that continues today for forcefully silencing the opposition.

Our church's choir recently has sung Craig Courtney's anthem "Silence the Stones," which is based on Luke 19:40. When the Pharisees sought to stop the crowd's acclamation of Jesus at the triumphal entry, Jesus told them that if we do not voice the truth with our words the stones will shout out. The truth cannot be silenced.

Good Things From Bad Experiences

One Greek word, *martus*, can be translated either "witness" or "martyr." We should never forget that these two things go together. When people lose their lives in total dedication to their cause, we must never forget that every martyr for truth leaves behind a witness. Good things often come from bad experiences, and Stephen's martyrdom provides an illustration of how unexpected those good outcomes can be.

Jesus' last words to his disciples before his ascension were, "You will be my witnesses in Jerusalem, in all Judea and Samaria, and to the ends of the earth" (Acts 1:8). Although we don't know the exact time interval between chapters 1 and 7, some time obviously passed as the small group of believers huddled in the upstairs room (1:13-14) grew first to three thousand (2:41) and then daily added more (2:47) until about five thousand had become believers (4:4). Soon great numbers of people came to Jerusalem from surrounding towns, attracted by the miraculous works of the apostles (5:12-16). Then, in spite of the strong opposition from the Sanhedrin (5:17-40), even some priests came to the faith (6:7). This success is clouded by one central concern: Jesus had commanded his disciples to "go into all the world and proclaim the good news to the whole creation" (Mark 16:15; compare Matthew 28:19-20). Yet none of the disciples had left Jerusalem.

Whether ironic or providential, the first result of Stephen's martyrdom was the scattering of the church in Jerusalem "throughout the countryside of Judea and Samaria" (Acts 8:1)—the first step in fulfilling Jesus' commission in Acts 1:8. The real irony is that the apostles themselves stayed in Jerusalem, certainly an act of bravery, but not yet one of obedience.

A second significant result from Stephen's martyrdom is speculative, but Luke's mention of it certainly bears drawing the implication. Saul, who had first been mentioned in Acts as concurring in Stephen's stoning (8:1), immediately afterward launched a diligent attempt to stamp out the church (8:3). Later Saul, renamed Paul, became the central character in fulfilling Acts 1:8. Saul obviously saw something in Stephen that made a lasting impression on him. Perhaps it was Stephen's new way of understanding biblical history presented to the Sanhedrin. Perhaps it was the boldness and courage Stephen exhibited in the face of certain judgment and punishment. Perhaps it was the parting words of forgiveness and grace on Stephen's lips as he died. Certainly all this was part of the preparation for Paul's hearing the words "I am Jesus, whom you are persecuting" (Acts 9:5). Perhaps Saul too saw "the face of an angel" (6:15) when Stephen died, though he never saw the face of Jesus. The martyr was a witness!

SHARING THE SCRIPTURE

Preparing Our Hearts

Explore this week's devotional reading, found in Ephesians 6:13-20. Notice the pieces of the whole armor of God that Paul calls Christians to put on to withstand evil. Paul closes this section with an admonition to "pray in the Spirit" (6:18) and a request to pray for him so that he may boldly speak the gospel message. Pray for those who labor to spread the good news, particularly in places where their lives may be threatened. Stand courageously for Christ wherever you are, especially when people ridicule your faith.

Pray that you and the adult students will be ready to put your own faith on the line and support in prayer those whose witness puts them in jeopardy.

Preparing Our Minds

Study the background Scripture from Acts 7:1–8:1a and the lesson Scripture from Acts 7:51–8:1a.

Consider this question as you prepare the lesson: *What causes such violent reactions when strong leaders confront traditional ideas?*

Write on newsprint:

❑ information for next week's lesson, found under "Continue the Journey."
❑ activities for further spiritual growth in "Continue the Journey."

Review the "Introduction," "The Big Picture," "Close-up," and "Faith in Action." Consider how you will use this additional information, which immediately precedes the first lesson.

LEADING THE CLASS

(1) Gather to Learn

❖ Greet the class members. Introduce any guests and help them feel at home.

❖ Pray that those who are present will come to understand what it means to pay the price for faith in Jesus Christ.

❖ Read this story from Persecution.com: **Seven churches in the Béjaia province of Algeria were ordered to be closed on orders of the provincial governor. Even after police delivered written notices, which church leaders refused to sign, the churches continued to hold their regular services. The notices had clearly stated that if the churches did not comply with the order, they would be subject to "severe consequences and punishments." Church** leaders suspect that these notices may be the beginning of an effort to close all except Islamic houses of worship. One bold Christian leader responded: "We must begin to make noise and to not allow this to pass over in silence, or else the authorities will crush us."

❖ Ask: **How do you think our church would respond to such threats?**

❖ Read aloud today's focus statement: **When strong leaders confront traditional ideas, their words may incite anger and violence. What causes such violent reactions? Stephen's criticism of the religious establishment and his exaltation of Christ enraged the religious leaders, who responded by stoning him to death.**

(2) Goal 1: Explore the Reasons for Stephen's Martyrdom

❖ Read or retell information from Acts 7:1-50 in Understanding the Scripture to set the scene for today's lesson.

❖ Select a volunteer to read Acts 7:51-53 as if Stephen were speaking.

❖ Add information from Acts 7:51-54 from Understanding the Scripture to help participants better understand Stephen's accusations against the religious leaders. Ask: **How would you describe Stephen's witness? Was it bold, foolish, or perhaps both?**

❖ Choose another person to read the account of his stoning in 7:54–8:1a. Ask the following questions. Use information from Understanding the Scripture as it seems helpful.

    (1) What differences do you see in the behaviors of Stephen and his accusers?

    (2) Why might Stephen's comment in verse 56 have prompted such outrage?

    (3) Why might the detail of Paul's presence and approval be important? (Notice in Acts 8:1a-3 that Paul becomes vehement in his persecution of Christians. Also notice

that in the Acts 9 account of Paul's conversion Jesus responds to Paul's question by saying in 9:5 that he is the One whom Paul is persecuting.)

(3) Goal 2: Disclose How the Learners Feel When Their Beliefs Are Attacked

❖ Read this information: **Having been harshly persecuted in Europe, members of the Amish and Mennonite churches began arriving in the New World in search of freedom to live and worship peacefully. Even here, they were outsiders because of their beliefs about education, government regulations, military service, and taxes. It was not until 1972 that the Amish were able to run their own private schools and end their children's education at the eighth grade. Due to their beliefs in pacifism, during World War I some of their conscientious objectors were abused even in camps established for those who objected to war. In 1981, a baby riding in his parents' buggy was hit and killed by a rock thrown by boys riding in a car. A series of arsons destroyed seven barns in 1992, but the Amish were stunned when $600,000 was raised by those beyond their Pennsylvania community to rebuild the barns and replace the livestock that had died.**

❖ Discuss these questions, either with the entire class or in small groups:

    (1) How might you feel if your beliefs were rejected and even vilified by others?

    (2) What personal experiences have you had of people attacking your beliefs—even attacking you because of what you believe? How did you respond?

(4) Goal 3: Witness Peacefully and Candidly for Christ, No Matter What the Cost

❖ Read or retell "Good Things from Bad Experiences" in Interpreting the Scripture.

Point out that although Stephen lost his life for his candid witness, the church of Christ moved forward as disciples were scattered and thus able to take the good news to many places.

❖ Invite several pairs to role-play this scenario, which you will read aloud: **You are attending a community meeting where folks are trying to keep a Muslim entrepreneur from getting a zoning variance to open a restaurant. Many nasty comments have been made, but none have any basis in fact in relation to this particular businessman. Recalling Jesus' teachings about loving and caring for one's neighbor, you stand to speak in favor of this variance, and one person tries to argue with you. How do you witness for Christ in this situation?**

(5) Continue the Journey

❖ Pray that all who have come today will be strengthened to make a bold witness for Christ.

❖ Read aloud this preparation for next week's lesson. You may also want to post it on newsprint for the students to copy.

■ **Title: Simon Wants to Buy Power**
■ **Background Scripture: Acts 8:4-24**
■ **Lesson Scripture: Acts 8:9-24**
■ **Focus of the Lesson: Some people try to buy power. What are the consequences of inappropriately seeking power? When Simon the magician tried to buy the power of the Holy Spirit, Peter plainly laid**

out the fatal consequences for those who think the Spirit can be bought or sold.

❖ Post these three activities related to this week's session on newsprint for the students to copy. Challenge the adults to grow spiritually by completing one or more of them.

(1) **Read stories of people currently facing persecution. If you have Internet access, Persecution.com is one source for this information. Share this information with other Christians and encourage them to join you in prayer for those who are suffering.**

(2) **Be alert for opportunities to witness for Christ, such as when people are making hurtful comments about a group of people or when someone is ridiculing Christ or his followers.**

(3) **Look at the Gospel accounts of the death of Jesus. What similarities do you see between these stories and the account of the stoning of Stephen in Acts 7:54–8:1a?**

❖ Sing or read aloud "Are Ye Able."

❖ Conclude today's session by leading the class in this benediction, adapted from the key verses for September 16 from Hebrews 12:1-2: **Let us go forth to run with perseverance the race that is set before us, looking to Jesus the pioneer and perfecter of our faith.**

UNIT 2: WHO UNDERSTANDS FAITH?
SIMON WANTS TO BUY POWER

PREVIEWING THE LESSON

Lesson Scripture: Acts 8:9-24
Background Scripture: Acts 8:4-24
Key Verse: Acts 8:18

Focus of the Lesson:
Some people try to buy power. What are the consequences of inappropriately seeking power? When Simon the magician tried to buy the power of the Holy Spirit, Peter plainly laid out the fatal consequences for those who think the Spirit can be bought or sold.

Goals for the Learners:
(1) to gain an understanding of Simon's motivation to receive the Holy Spirit.
(2) to recognize selfish desires for God's power.
(3) to nurture an authentic desire for the Holy Spirit's power in their lives and in the lives of others.

Pronunciation Guide:
Elymas (el' uh muhs)
Judaizer (joo' day iz' uhr)
Magus (may' guhs)
simony (sahy' muh nee)

Supplies:
Bibles, newsprint and marker, paper and pencils, hymnals

READING THE SCRIPTURE

NRSV
Lesson Scripture: Acts 8:9-24
⁹Now a certain man named Simon had previously practiced magic in the city and amazed the people of Samaria, saying that he was someone great. ¹⁰All of them, from

CEB
Lesson Scripture: Acts 8:9-24
⁹Before Philip's arrival, a certain man named Simon had practiced sorcery in that city and baffled the people of Samaria. He claimed to be a great person. ¹⁰Everyone,

the least to the greatest, listened to him eagerly, saying, "This man is the power of God that is called Great." [11]And they listened eagerly to him because for a long time he had amazed them with his magic. [12]But when they believed Philip, who was proclaiming the good news about the kingdom of God and the name of Jesus Christ, they were baptized, both men and women. [13]Even Simon himself believed. After being baptized, he stayed constantly with Philip and was amazed when he saw the signs and great miracles that took place.

[14]Now when the apostles at Jerusalem heard that Samaria had accepted the word of God, they sent Peter and John to them. [15]The two went down and prayed for them that they might receive the Holy Spirit [16](for as yet the Spirit had not come upon any of them; they had only been baptized in the name of the Lord Jesus). [17]Then Peter and John laid their hands on them, and they received the Holy Spirit. **[18]Now when Simon saw that the Spirit was given through the laying on of the apostles' hands, he offered them money,** [19]saying, "Give me also this power so that anyone on whom I lay my hands may receive the Holy Spirit." [20]But Peter said to him, "May your silver perish with you, because you thought you could obtain God's gift with money! [21]You have no part or share in this, for your heart is not right before God. [22]Repent therefore of this wickedness of yours, and pray to the Lord that, if possible, the intent of your heart may be forgiven you. [23]For I see that you are in the gall of bitterness and the chains of wickedness." [24]Simon answered, "Pray for me to the Lord, that nothing of what you have said may happen to me."

from the least to the greatest, gave him their undivided attention and referred to him as "the power of God called Great." [11]He had their attention because he had baffled them with sorcery for a long time. [12]After they came to believe Philip, who preached the good news about God's kingdom and the name of Jesus Christ, both men and women were baptized. [13]Even Simon himself came to believe and was baptized. Afterward, he became one of Philip's supporters. As he saw firsthand the signs and great miracles that were happening, he was astonished.

[14]When word reached the apostles in Jerusalem that Samaria had accepted God's word, they commissioned Peter and John to go to Samaria. [15]Peter and John went down to Samaria where they prayed that the new believers would receive the Holy Spirit. ([16]This was because the Holy Spirit had not yet fallen on any of them; they had only been baptized in the name of the Lord Jesus.) [17]So Peter and John laid their hands on them, and they received the Holy Spirit.

[18]When Simon perceived that the Spirit was given through the laying on of the apostles' hands, he offered them money. [19]He said, "Give me this authority too so that anyone on whom I lay my hands will receive the Holy Spirit."

[20]Peter responded, "May your money be condemned to hell along with you because you believed you could buy God's gift with money! [21]You can have no part or share in God's word because your heart isn't right with God. [22]Therefore, change your heart and life! Turn from your wickedness! Plead with the Lord in the hope that your wicked intent can be forgiven, [23]for I see that your bitterness has poisoned you and evil has you in chains."

[24]Simon replied, "All of you, please, plead to the Lord for me so that nothing of what you have said will happen to me!"

UNDERSTANDING THE SCRIPTURE

Acts 8:4-8. The scattering of Jesus' followers that resulted from Stephen's stoning began the movement Jesus had envisioned (Acts 1:8). Jerusalem had been the center of the church's initial activity, and people from around Judea had been drawn to Jerusalem by news of the apostles' activities (5:16). Just as the apostles had taught and proclaimed Jesus as the Messiah in Jerusalem even after actions were taken against them by the Sanhedrin (5:17-18, 41), the scattered disciples proclaimed "the word" as they went from place to place. Philip, one of the seven Hellenist leaders previously chosen to deal with complaints about the distribution of food (Acts 6:1-6), led in the church's next step beyond Jerusalem and Judea. He carried the message of the Messiah to Samaria.

While Samaritans in general were despised by the Jews because of their mixed heritage and competing religious institutions (see John 4:20), they shared many common religious traditions with the Jews. Jesus had deliberately visited Samaria and had demonstrated complete openness toward Samaritans. Therefore, Philip's proclaiming "the Messiah to them" (8:5) was not unexpected. And when many of the miraculous healings that had been performed in Jerusalem were repeated there, the reaction to the gospel message was enthusiastic. The whole city was filled with great joy.

Acts 8:9-13. Simon, a magician referenced in the Bible only in connection with Philip's ministry in Samaria, has an interesting place in postbiblical records. He is viewed in subsequent generations as either a Christian, a heretic, or even as the Antichrist. Even the account in Acts has confusing elements in it. The Greek text uses a verb that speaks of his previously being in the city and then shifts to the present tense, saying that he practices magic and amazes the people. He obviously was in Samaria when Philip arrived, so most translators imply that he was at that time inactive as a magician. Luke used a verb for "practiced magic" (8:9) and a noun for "magic" (8:11), but not "magician" to describe Simon—although today he is regularly called "Simon Magus." "Magus" (plural "magi") is used elsewhere in the New Testament and is translated "magician" or "wise man"—the latter with reference to the wise men who were experts in astrology and interpreted dreams (Matthew 2:7). In the Greek Old Testament the word is associated with those who cast spells, foretell the future, or communicate with the spirits of the dead. Some (like Elymas in Acts 13:6-12) interpreted omens and provided counsel to government officials. The fact that "the greatest" (8:10) listened to Simon indicates that his claim to be "someone great" (8:9) and the acclamation of the people that he was "the power of God that is called Great" (8:10) were common perceptions in Samaria.

Philip's arrival in Samaria brought significant change. He proclaimed the good news about the kingdom of God and about the name of Jesus Christ. He performed signs and great miracles. The people of Samaria embraced the gospel, believing Philip's words and accepting baptism. Even Simon believed, was baptized, and attached himself to Philip. The word translated "amazed" (8:13) conveys a level of astonishment and even confusion where amazement is mingled with awe and fear.

Acts 8:14-17. When the news of the dramatic reception to the gospel message in Samaria reached the apostles in Jerusalem, they sent Peter and John to Samaria. The selection of two of Jesus' earliest disciples (Matthew 4:18-22) made this a high-level delegation to a region that was highly suspect in Jewish circles. John 8:48 reveals the popular estimation of the Samaritans, and Jesus' reception in Samaria had been mixed (compare Luke 9:51-56; 17:11-19; and John 4:4-42). A more significant issue seems to be at work, however: the receiving of the Holy Spirit. This is a major theme in Acts beginning with references to the Holy Spirit in Acts 1:5, 8; 2:4, 17. Acts 2:38 appears to lay out a clear association that may be the guiding principle: "Repent and be baptized every one of you in the name of Jesus Christ so that your sins may be forgiven; and you will receive the gift of the Holy Spirit." Luke provides no explanation for why the gift of the Holy Spirit had been dissociated from repentance and baptism in Samaria, but the "hands of the apostles" had been referenced earlier as the instrument of "many signs and wonders" (5:12 NASB and KJV) and in the blessing of the Seven (6:6). The new believers received the Holy Spirit after prayer and the laying on of hands by the apostles. Most significantly, this was God's endorsement of the universality of the gospel embodied in Acts 1:8, rather than a vesting of power that could be transmitted solely through the apostles.

Acts 8:18-24. Luke tells us what Simon saw but not what Simon experienced. Evidently, Simon had witnessed the apostles' laying on of hands but had not experienced it himself. As one who had practiced the magical powers of the spiritual world, he lusted after this power, which was greater than any he had previously known. His old pride as someone who was "great" (8:9) and as the embodiment of "the power of God that is called Great" (8:10) overwhelmed his new faith and recent baptism. With a "heart . . . not right before God" (8:21), he lapsed into a secular mind-set and fell prey to the ways of the world. He was caught in "the gall of bitterness and the chains of wickedness" (8:23). He offered money, not to obtain the Spirit, but to gain the power to bestow the Spirit on others. In spite of Peter's curse, "May your silver perish with you" (8:20), Peter held out the hope of repentance and urged Simon to pray that the intent of his heart might be forgiven. Simon's response, "Pray for me" (8:24), is somewhat ambiguous and explains why subsequent generations could view him as a Christian, a heretic, or the Antichrist.

As Peter and John returned to Jerusalem, they proclaimed the good news in many Samaritan villages (8:25). Acts 1:8 continued to unfold.

INTERPRETING THE SCRIPTURE

The Allure of Power

Power has been an enticing attraction in every era of humankind. The ability to do, to act, and to produce is a fundamental element in assessing ourselves and others. Even the most primitive societies seem to have an innate desire to surpass the abilities, capacities, and influences of the past and of their present competitors. We too want to demonstrate vigorous, forceful, and controlling strength that sets us apart and elevates us above others. We want authority, influence, and control. Competition is not an aspect only of the business world. We see it in government, sports, education, organizations, and even in and between churches. The desire for greatness, notoriety, wealth, influence, and deference can become insatiable.

Simon Magus had already achieved notoriety. He was admired and acclaimed as someone with great powers that must have come from God. Somehow Simon was drawn to the message of the gospel. Perhaps he was attracted to the story of a humble carpenter who became a great teacher, who challenged the power brokers in Israel, was convicted of treason, crucified, and buried—but by the power of God was raised from the dead. When Peter and John demonstrated powers that Simon had never known, the allure for greater and greater power seized him. If you will look in the dictionary, you will find the outcome of his quest. He lives on in the word "simony." His grasp for power became a poor example of sacrilege.

Humility generally is seen as a Christian virtue. In Philippians 2:5-8, Paul highlighted humility in the example of Jesus. In verses 3-4, however, Paul laid out the guiding principle for us: "Do nothing from selfish ambition or conceit, but in humility regard others as better than yourselves. Let each of you look not to your own interests, but to the interests of others." Oh, if humility only had the allure of power, how different our world would be.

The Scope of the Gospel

One confusing element in the account of Philip in Acts 8 relates to the incomplete element in Philip's proclamation of the gospel in Samaria. Philip certainly was not a second-class disciple of Jesus. He originally had been chosen along with Stephen as a man "of good standing, full of the Spirit and of wisdom" (Acts 6:4). He had been prayed over by the apostles, who also had laid their hands on him (6:6).

When the church scattered after Stephen's martyrdom, Philip is the first disciple named who spread the word from place to place (8:4-5). Philip's dedication led him to Samaria—the next place Jesus had mentioned as an objective in the spread of the gospel (see Acts 1:8). His proclamation had correctly focused on "the Messiah" (8:5) and "the good news about the kingdom of God and the name of Jesus Christ" (8:12). His message was received eagerly, and he performed miraculous signs and wonders (8:6-7, 13)—a sure sign that the power of God was with him. He baptized the new believers in the name of Jesus, including baptizing such an influential man as Simon Magus (8:12-13).

When the apostles heard about Philip's success in Samaria, they sent Peter and John to Samaria. The narrative does not indicate when or how the apostles discovered that the believers in Samaria had not received the Holy Spirit, but that seems to have been a missing element either in the response to Philip's preaching or in the administration of baptism. From the Acts account, however, blame is not the issue. Though Philip is not mentioned again until his call to go south for an encounter with the Ethiopian eunuch (8:26), no evident fault is placed on him. The Samaritans received the Holy Spirit immediately after the apostles laid their hands on them (8:17) without any personal advancement beyond their first response to the gospel.

Students of Acts generally agree that Luke's account was written to defend the expansion of the gospel to all people against those who tried to keep the gospel contained within Judaism. We see evidence in the New Testament that Judaizers tried to maintain Judaism as the sole foundation for Christianity. They insisted that followers of Christ should first become Jews before they became part of the redeemed people of God. For Gentiles, this meant that they must be baptized and circumcised as proselytes. Luke's account guides readers through the expansion of the gospel to Hellenistic Jews, to heretical Samaritans, to a God-fearing eunuch, to a rabid Pharisee, to a Roman centurion and his family—until the gospel was proclaimed "without hindrance" in Rome itself (28:31). To emphasize that this was God's plan and not human ingenuity, Luke underscored the role of the Holy Spirit as the confirming evidence that the breached barriers were the work of God and no one else. The Holy Spirit received through the laying on of Peter and John's hands was a confirmation by God that the conversion of Samaritans outside of a proselytizing Judaism was the work of God.

The Hope of Repentance

The hope of the gospel lies in these words: "Repent . . . of this wickedness of yours, and pray to the Lord that, if possible, the intent of your heart may be forgiven you" (8:22). Directed by Peter to Simon Magus, the call to repentance highlights several important aspects of the way God deals with sinners.

First, note Peter's emphasis on the intent of the heart. One danger in our judging one another is that we cannot know another person's intent. First Samuel 16:7 reveals how God judges. When Samuel was examining the sons of Jesse for the one whom God had chosen as a successor to Saul, Samuel was unduly impressed by the commanding presence of Jesse's eldest son. God warned Samuel that a person's physical appearance or stature is not a good basis for evaluation: "The LORD does not see as mortals see; they look on the outward appearance, but the LORD looks on the heart." This reminds us that actions may not clearly reveal motives, and expressions of remorse may not always represent true repentance. God deals with the "intent" that underlies the "wickedness."

Second, "repent" is the driving force of Peter's invitation to Simon. While the Greek word for "repent" used here literally means to reconsider or think afterward, it is used to translate an Old Testament word that means to turn back, to return, or to change direction. Repentance is more than feeling sorry or regretting that you were caught in some misdeed. It is turning away from your wickedness back toward God.

Third, the remedy for sin is found simply in praying to the Lord. As Christians, we believe that Christ already has made the sacrifice for our sins. All we have to do to claim forgiveness is to pray sincerely for it. While that seems a simple solution, we cannot forget that the intent of our hearts and the genuineness of our repentance establish the only barriers to gracious forgiveness. While the outcome of this invitation to Simon is not clearly stated, the fact that he asks Peter to pray on his behalf (8:24) is not encouraging. He seemed more concerned that "nothing of what you said may happen to me" than that God will forgive him of his efforts to buy power that can only be received as a gracious gift from God.

SHARING THE SCRIPTURE

Preparing Our Hearts

Explore this week's devotional reading, found in 1 Corinthians 1:18-25. In today's lesson, we will discover that Simon Magus believes he can buy God's power. This passage from 1 Corinthians, though, clearly demonstrates that Christ is both the power and wisdom of God. Where do you seek power? Often we are looking for attributes of power that include wealth, status, and influence. Paul's letter to the church at Corinth teaches us that this power is to be found in the cross of Christ. Ponder that idea, especially as you encounter examples of people seeking power.

Pray that you and the adult students will recognize and respect the source of true power.

Preparing Our Minds

Study the background Scripture from Acts 8:4-24 and the lesson Scripture from Acts 8:9-24.

Consider this question as you prepare the lesson: *What are the consequences of inappropriately seeking power?*

Write on newsprint:
- ❑ questions for "Recognize Selfish Desires for God's Power."
- ❑ information for next week's lesson, found under "Continue the Journey."

❑ activities for further spiritual growth in "Continue the Journey."

Review the "Introduction," "The Big Picture," "Close-up," and "Faith in Action." Consider how you will use this additional information, which immediately precedes the first lesson.

LEADING THE CLASS

(1) Gather to Learn

❖ Greet the class members. Introduce any guests and help them feel at home.

❖ Pray that all who have come today will be sincerely motivated to seek the power of the Holy Spirit.

❖ Read the first paragraph of "The Allure of Power" in Interpreting the Scripture to consider why people seek power.

❖ Encourage the participants to call out names of famous people who have sought power at any cost. List these names on newsprint. Focus on one or two of these people and consider (1) how they tried to gain power, (2) the effect power had on them, and (3) the effect their power had on other people.

❖ Read aloud today's focus statement: **Some people try to buy power. What are the consequences of inappropriately seeking power? When Simon the magician tried to buy the power of the Holy Spirit, Peter plainly laid out the fatal consequences for those who think the Spirit can be bought or sold.**

(2) Goal 1: Gain an Understanding of Simon's Motivation to Receive the Holy Spirit

❖ Choose a volunteer to read Acts 8:9-24.

❖ Discuss these questions. Add information from Understanding the Scripture to broaden the discussion.

(1) **What do we know about Simon's life before he accepted Christ?**

(2) **Why were people attracted to him?**

(3) **What role do Peter and John play in this story?**

(4) **How did Simon respond when he saw people receiving the Holy Spirit as a result of Peter and John laying hands on them?**

(5) **How did Peter react to Simon's request?**

(6) **What seems to be Simon's motive in asking Peter to pray for him?**

(7) **What does this story suggest about how we are to view the power of the Holy Spirit?**

(3) Goal 2: Recognize Selfish Desires for God's Power

❖ Form four groups and assign each to research one of the following Bible stories about people who want God's power:

Group 1: Genesis 3:1-7—Adam and Eve are tempted to become like God by knowing the difference between good and evil.

Group 2: Ezekiel 34:1-10—Israel's shepherds abuse their power as leaders.

Group 3: Micah 3:1-12—Corrupt rulers, prophets, and priests are condemned for their abuses of power.

Group 4: Mark 10:35-40—James and John request seats of honor and power next to Jesus in his glory.

❖ Post these questions on newsprint for the groups to consider:

(1) **What are some characteristic actions and attitudes of people who grasp for divine power?**

(2) **What happens when people who are entrusted with God's power use that power for their own selfish ends?**

(3) **What is the divine response to those who attempt to usurp God's power?**

❖ Point out that selfish desires for God's power have caused people to greatly overreach their limits. There is hope, however, if one will repent and head in a new direction. Read "The Hope of Repentance" from Interpreting the Scripture.

(4) Goal 3: Nurture an Authentic Desire for the Holy Spirit's Power in the Learners' Lives and in the Lives of Others

❖ Recall that Simon wanted the power of the Holy Spirit, but his motivation was not in keeping with God's will for how we are to handle the power of the Holy Spirit. According to Acts 8:18-24, Peter corrected Simon. Discuss Peter's explanation of authentic desire for and use of the Holy Spirit.

❖ Distribute paper and pencils. Read the following statements and invite the adults to fill in the blanks.

(1) **When a person in authority abuses power, I respond by ____.**

(2) **Traits of Christian leaders who use God's power for their own ends include _____.**

(3) **Traits of Christian leaders who use God's power wisely include _____.**

(4) **I know the Holy Spirit is at work in my life when _____.**

(5) **When asked by others about how the Holy Spirit acts in the lives of believers, I say _____.**

❖ Bring everyone together. Review the five statements by asking volunteers to read their responses. After several responses have been read for each sentence, invite others in the group to raise their hands if they had similar responses.

❖ Conclude by suggesting that one important way to help others live according to the power of the Holy Spirit is to model what such a life could look like.

(5) Continue the Journey

❖ Pray that Christians will be aware of how they use power, especially when they claim to use it in God's name, and will act responsibly.

Read aloud this preparation for next week's lesson. You may also want to post it on newsprint for the students to copy.

■ **Title: Philip and the Ethiopian Eunuch**

■ **Background Scripture: Acts 8:26-39**

■ **Lesson Scripture: Acts 8:26-39**

■ **Focus of the Lesson: Some people want to prescribe who is in and who is out when it comes to membership in certain groups. Why are the boundaries of membership sometimes limited to specific people? Philip's sharing of the good news about Jesus and the baptism of the Ethiopian demonstrate the universal availability of the gospel message.**

❖ Post these three activities related to this week's session on newsprint for the students to copy. Challenge the adults to grow spiritually by completing one or more of them.

(1) **Keep an eye out for stories in the media about how people have abused power. As you learn about these abuses, ask yourself: "What would Jesus have done in this situation?"**

(2) **Identify the power brokers in the political, economic, social, or religious arenas that you know. How would you rate the way that each one is using power? Do you see God at work in these persons, or have selfish desires crowded out any opportunity to serve others and promote the greater good?**

(3) **Attune yourself to the leading of the Holy Spirit. What are you being called to do right now? How is the Spirit empowering you to act? What response will you make?**

❖ Sing or read aloud "See How Great a Flame Aspires."

❖ Conclude today's session by leading the class in this benediction, adapted from the key verses for September 16 from Hebrews 12:1-2: **Let us go forth to run with perseverance the race that is set before us, looking to Jesus the pioneer and perfecter of our faith.**

UNIT 2: WHO UNDERSTANDS FAITH?

PHILIP AND THE ETHIOPIAN EUNUCH

PREVIEWING THE LESSON

Lesson Scripture: Acts 8:26-39
Background Scripture: Acts 8:26-39
Key Verse: Acts 8:36

Focus of the Lesson:
Some people want to prescribe who is in and who is out when it comes to membership in certain groups. Why are the boundaries of membership sometimes limited to specific people? Philip's sharing of the good news about Jesus and the baptism of the Ethiopian demonstrate the universal availability of the gospel message.

Goals for the Learners:
(1) to make a connection between Philip's baptism of the Ethiopian eunuch and the universal availability of the gospel message.
(2) to examine their feelings of being excluded and their motivations for excluding others.
(3) to develop a strategy to make their church more open and inclusive.

Pronunciation Guide:
Ashdod (ash'dod)	eunuch (yoo' nuck)	Iconium (i koh' nee uhm)
Azotus (uh zoh' tuhs)	Festus (fes' tuhs)	Lystra (lis' truh)
Caesarea (ses uh ree' uh)	Frumentius	Pisidia (pi sid' ee uh)
Candace (kan' duh see)	(froo men' shee uhs)	Theophilus (thee of' uh luhs)

Supplies:
Bibles, newsprint and marker, paper and pencils, hymnals, optional basin of water

---

READING THE SCRIPTURE

NRSV
Lesson Scripture: Acts 8:26-39
   [26]Then an angel of the Lord said to Philip, "Get up and go toward the south to the road

CEB
Lesson Scripture: Acts 8:26-39
   [26]An angel from the Lord spoke to Philip, "At noon, take the road that leads from

that goes down from Jerusalem to Gaza." (This is a wilderness road.) [27]So he got up and went. Now there was an Ethiopian eunuch, a court official of the Candace, queen of the Ethiopians, in charge of her entire treasury. He had come to Jerusalem to worship [28]and was returning home; seated in his chariot, he was reading the prophet Isaiah. [29]Then the Spirit said to Philip, "Go over to this chariot and join it." [30]So Philip ran up to it and heard him reading the prophet Isaiah. He asked, "Do you understand what you are reading?" [31]He replied, "How can I, unless someone guides me?" And he invited Philip to get in and sit beside him. [32]Now the passage of the scripture that he was reading was this:

"Like a sheep he was led to the slaughter,
　and like a lamb silent before
　　its shearer,
　so he does not open his mouth.
[33] In his humiliation justice was denied him.
　Who can describe his generation?
　　For his life is taken away from the
　　earth."

[34]The eunuch asked Philip, "About whom, may I ask you, does the prophet say this, about himself or about someone else?" [35]Then Philip began to speak, and starting with this scripture, he proclaimed to him the good news about Jesus. [36]As they were going along the road, they came to some water; and **the eunuch said, "Look, here is water! What is to prevent me from being baptized?"** [38]He commanded the chariot to stop, and both of them, Philip and the eunuch, went down into the water, and Philip baptized him. [39]When they came up out of the water, the Spirit of the Lord snatched Philip away; the eunuch saw him no more, and went on his way rejoicing.

Jerusalem to Gaza." (This is a desert road.) [27]So he did. Meanwhile, an Ethiopian man was on his way home from Jerusalem, where he had come to worship. He was a eunuch and an official responsible for the entire treasury of Candace. (Candace is the title given to the Ethiopian queen.) [28]He was reading the prophet Isaiah while sitting in his carriage. [29]The Spirit told Philip, "Approach this carriage and stay with it."

[30]Running up to the carriage, Philip heard the man reading the prophet Isaiah. He asked, "Do you really understand what you are reading?"

[31]The man replied, "Without someone to guide me, how could I?" Then he invited Philip to climb up and sit with him. [32]This was the passage of scripture he was reading:

Like a sheep he was led to the slaughter
　and like a lamb before its shearer is
　　silent
　so he didn't open his mouth.
[33] *In his humiliation*
　justice was taken away from him.
　Who can tell the story of his descendants
　　because his life was taken
　　from the earth?

[34]The eunuch asked Philip, "Tell me, about whom does the prophet say this? Is he talking about himself or someone else?" [35]Starting with that passage, Philip proclaimed the good news about Jesus to him. [36]As they went down the road, they came to some water.

The eunuch said, "Look! Water! What would keep me from being baptized?" [38]He ordered that the carriage halt. Both Philip and the eunuch went down to the water, where Philip baptized him. [39]When they came up out of the water, the Lord's Spirit suddenly took Philip away. The eunuch never saw him again but went on his way rejoicing.

UNDERSTANDING THE SCRIPTURE

Acts 8:26-27a. Philip's very successful mission work in Samaria was interrupted by a new commission. The commission came through a representative of the Lord. The Greek word translated "angel" means someone who is sent, and can be applied to either a human messenger or a supernatural messenger from God. "Of the Lord" inclines this instance toward an angelic messenger who delivered divine instructions to Philip. The tense of the Greek verb translated "said" implies that the instruction was given only one time. "Got up and went" implies quick obedience. Philip's instructions sent him from Samaria north of Jerusalem to a deserted region south of Jerusalem on the travel route to Gaza, Egypt, and beyond. Without knowing exactly where he was going or why, Philip obeyed the angel's instructions.

Acts 8:27b-28. Traveling on that same route was a man described by four consecutive nouns in the Greek text: "man," "Ethiopian," "eunuch," and "court official." The two references to Ethiopia in verse 27 are the only occurrences of that noun in the New Testament. The name "Ethiopia" apparently was a combination of two Greek words that mean "scorch the face," probably a reference to the inhabitants' dark skin. The country corresponds with the Old Testament region called "Cush," which is first mentioned early in Genesis (Genesis 2:13). Some traditions posit early Israelite connections with Ethiopia. (Some contend that the lost tribe of Dan settled there or that a child of Solomon and the queen of Sheba founded an Israelite community there).

The exact implications of "eunuch" have been disputed. Some scholars think that it merely implies a court official (for example, the Hebrew equivalent is used of Potiphar in Genesis 39:1), but that would have rendered redundant the following noun in Acts translated "court official." More likely the term implies a court official who had access to the women attached to the royal court and had been castrated to ensure his trustworthiness. This was a fairly common practice in ancient palaces. Luke explained "court official" as being in charge of the queen's entire treasury. "Candace" is often mistaken for a name but likely was a title that is equivalent to queen. This explains "the Candace" in the NRSV.

The eunuch had been to Jerusalem to worship and was on his way home. His status within Judaism is difficult to define. Castration was a form of mutilation that likely would have prevented the eunuch from having full access to the Temple (Deuteronomy 23:1; but compare Isaiah 56:3-7). Acts 8:36 may imply that he had been denied baptism and thus could not become a Jewish proselyte. Most scholars describe him as a "God-fearer," rather than as a Jew or a Jewish "proselyte" (translated "devout converts to Judaism" in Acts 13:43). In Acts, Luke used a number of descriptions for Gentiles who worshiped God (16:14; 18:7) or feared God (10:2, 22) without keeping all of the Jewish laws and especially without adopting circumcision. The long distance traveled to Jerusalem and the eunuch's reading of Isaiah on the return trip seem to fit one who had accepted ethical monotheism and had some association with practicing Jews.

Acts 8:29-31. The Holy Spirit guided Philip to the Ethiopian and instructed him to join the Ethiopian's chariot on its journey toward Gaza. An opportunity for engaging in conversation was opened by the Scripture the Ethiopian was reading aloud. Philip's question, "Do you understand what you are reading?" (8:30), combined with the openness of the Ethiopian official to accept guidance from a stranger resulted in an invitation for Philip to join the official in his chariot and to ride along with him.

Acts 8:32-35. Not only was the prophetic book being read by the official a remarkable serendipity but even the Suffering Servant passage that he was reading (Isaiah 53:7-8) held messianic import that had gained full clarity through the life, death, and resurrection of Jesus Christ. The message of a prophet from centuries earlier was expounded by a disciple of the one who only recently had fulfilled that very prophecy. Just as Jesus had shown his disciples "that everything written about me in the law of Moses, the prophets, and the psalms must be fulfilled" (Luke 24:44), Philip was prepared to show how the prophecy of Isaiah had been fulfilled in Christ. Just as Jesus had "opened their minds to understand the scriptures" (24:45), in the same manner the Spirit opened the mind of the Ethiopian eunuch to the message of "good news about Jesus" (Acts 8:35). As a starting point, Philip began with the passage from Isaiah that the Ethiopian had been reading but had not understood. From that base, Philip told him the good news about Jesus. Luke's word translated "proclaimed . . . the good news" (8:35) is the Greek word from which we get "evangelize."

Acts 8:36-39. Philip's instruction in the gospel brought together all the missing pieces for the Ethiopian. When the eunuch found that the story that spanned centuries had reached its climax in the life, death, and resurrection of Jesus Christ, he responded enthusiastically. The opportune presence of water abundant enough for both the eunuch and Philip to go down into it afforded an immediate opportunity for the eunuch to embrace faith in Jesus Christ. Note that the NRSV, CEB, and NIV omit Luke 8:37. The best and oldest manuscripts of Luke do not contain this verse, and scholars have concluded that it was added many years after Luke was written. The addition probably expanded the response of the Ethiopian eunuch. Later generations wanted to clarify that a declaration of faith in Jesus Christ as the Son of God was involved. Whether the obstacle to faith had been the eunuch's unresolved questions in his study of the Old Testament or the exclusionary restriction that forbade eunuchs from being welcomed into the faith community, Philip's teaching had torn down the barrier. Philip baptized the Ethiopian eunuch, and another hindrance to the gospel for all people fell. Luke's story took another step toward an unhindered gospel (Acts 28:31). His commission fulfilled, Philip was snatched up by the Spirit of the Lord and continued his mission work in the coastal cities of Azotus (the Old Testament's Ashdod) and Caesarea. The eunuch continued his journey home rejoicing.

INTERPRETING THE SCRIPTURE

The One and the Many

Numbers are important in our society, but sometimes the numbers have become so large that we hardly can fathom them. Billions and trillions are tossed around when speaking of national debts and deficits. The farthest galaxy is so far away that we measure its distance in billions of light years because the number of miles has too many zeroes to comprehend. Even the population of our planet exceeds seven billion people.

Large numbers often are viewed as a measure of importance: higher profits, higher salaries, higher viewership, and higher attendance are symbols of success. More is better than less in almost all circumstances. And our society seems driven to own more, spend more, consume more, and accumulate more. "Less" is just that—little, insignificant, and unworthy of time and attention.

The same mind-set often infiltrates the church. In the popular view, the bigger the attendance, the budget, the building complex, and the staff, the more successful, effective, and significant is the church. How strange it seems to us that Philip would leave a successful and popular ministry in Samaria to go to some deserted area and spend time with one unnamed foreigner whom he probably would never see again.

Tradition has tried to justify Philip's efforts in abandoning the many for a ministry with one individual. Some have contended that the Ethiopian eunuch went back to his homeland and became the impetus for starting the Christian church in Ethiopia. The best historical evidence, however, says that the church in Ethiopia was started by Frumentius around A.D. 330, almost three centuries after Philip's time.

The fact that Philip virtually disappears from Luke's account after Acts 8:40 indicates that Luke's literary purpose had been fulfilled. The very brief mention of "Philip the evangelist" in Caesarea with his four unmarried daughters who prophesied (Acts 21:8-9) is a side note of Paul's story. Luke, however, had a purpose in telling Philip's story. But what was it?

Obeying the Spirit

One of Luke's purposes certainly was to emphasize obedience to the guidance of the Holy Spirit. Luke was addressing a Gentile audience that surely had some awareness of the chosen people specially called by God. With their covenant, laws, and traditions, these chosen ones had been brought into a special relationship with God for the purpose of blessing all nations. Yet in many ways, they had become self-centered and nearsighted. Jesus' vision of a witness beyond Jerusalem and Judea "to the ends of the earth" was empowered by the Holy Spirit (Acts 1:8), but cultural barriers had been raised between Jews and Samaritans, the blessed and the outcast, men and women, and the chosen and the Gentiles. Luke's story is building toward an unhindered gospel (Acts 28:31), but the intermediate stage is the Jerusalem Council in Acts 15, where the church made crucial decisions about the scope and inclusiveness of the gospel. Luke's central thesis is that God (15:4, 8, 12, 14), the Spirit (15:8-9), and Scripture (15:15-18) had chosen grace (15:11) over the "yoke" of the law (15:10) and had opened access to the gospel for all people and nations.

Luke recorded the breaking down of what Ephesians 2:14 refers to as "the dividing wall" as others were drawn to the faith: Hellenistic Jews (Acts 6:1-6); Samaritans (8:5-25); God-fearing Gentiles (8:26-39); a fervent Pharisee named Saul (9:1-22); a Gentile Roman centurion named Cornelius (10:1-48); Greeks in Antioch (11:20-24); a proconsul in Cyprus (13:4-12); and still others in Antioch in Pisidia (13:13), Iconium (14:1), and Lystra (14:8). All of this was the work of the Holy Spirit, who is mentioned twenty-eight times in Acts 6–13.

We know that Philip left his ministry in Samaria in obedience to a divine call—that's what the Bible says. If the same thing happened today, however, we would wonder if Philip were a little off in some way. How did he know this was God's call? Was not God's blessing his ministry in Samaria a sign that he was in the right place, doing the right thing? We still have dividing walls that hinder the gospel. Some are geographic, social, economic, or racial. Some are gender related, have foundations in bad theology, or are sheer examples of disobedience. Christ, however, is still in the business of breaking down the dividing wall of hostilities between people (Ephesians 2:14). But wall-busting encounters are only possible when an obedient servant of the Lord (like Philip) and an interested inquirer about the faith (like the Ethiopian eunuch) come together around God's Word under the guidance of the Holy Spirit. Where is the Spirit calling us today? What walls need to be smashed? Will we obey?

Seeking the Truth

Another of Luke's purposes certainly was to highlight the importance of seeking the truth. From the opening paragraph of the Gospel of Luke, where the stated objective was that Theophilus "may know the truth concerning the things about which you have been instructed" (Luke 1:4), to the "many convincing proofs" referenced in Acts 1:3, to the "sober truth" Paul spoke in making his defense before Festus (Acts 26:25), Luke sought to present "an orderly account . . . handed on to us by . . . eyewitnesses and servants of the word" (Luke 1:1-2).

Concern for the truth intersects Luke's account in many ways. The Ethiopian eunuch is a prime example of a search for truth. We cannot fathom today the extent of the Ethiopian eunuch's journey of more than a thousand miles each way, made in a chariot across sparse regions. Our closest comparison might be the famed Pony Express of the Old West: Horses traveled ten miles an hour, a fresh horse was provided every ten to fifteen miles, a new rider took over every seventy-five to one hundred miles, and a journey of one thousand miles took more than four days. That would have been a remarkable achievement in the Ethiopian's day. Then imagine that after traveling that far in search of new insight into the God of the Jews, you find yourself unwelcomed in the Temple, denied full status in the community of faith, and left with some confusing book of ancient prophecy as the only token of your journey. Even though he was surely discouraged, the Ethiopian did not give up his quest. As he traveled home, he pored over that book, written in a foreign language, trying to decipher the truths it offered to a people who had the kind of faith he deeply hoped to find. Only as we perceive this deep desire for truth can we appreciate what Philip's witness meant to the Ethiopian. The eunuch's response wasn't rash. It was a full embrace of the truth for which he had searched—the truth he found in Jesus Christ. Luke's account of the life of Jesus, his story of the early church's spreading the gospel, and his call from the Spirit to break down barriers to the hope for salvation are searching even today for readers who are seeking the truth and are willing to obey.

SHARING THE SCRIPTURE

Preparing Our Hearts

Explore this week's devotional reading, found in Isaiah 56:1-8. Centuries before the Messiah's birth, Isaiah prophesied that one day salvation would be available to all. The prophet specifies foreigners, eunuchs, and outcasts as those who will be valued members of the redeemed community. Our story from Acts concerns an Ethiopian official who very much wanted to become part of the community, though his status as a eunuch prevented him from offering a sacrifice in the Temple. Philip offered him hope and an opportunity to be included. How is your congregation opening wide the doors to others who may feel excluded?

Pray that you and the adult students will be aware of those who are on the margins and do whatever you can to include them.

Preparing Our Minds

Study the background Scripture and the lesson Scripture, both of which are from Acts 8:26-39.

Consider this question as you prepare the lesson: *Why are the boundaries of membership in certain groups sometimes limited to specific people?*

Write on newsprint:
- ❑ information for next week's lesson, found under "Continue the Journey."
- ❑ activities for further spiritual growth in "Continue the Journey."

Review the "Introduction," "The Big Picture," "Close-up," and "Faith in Action." Consider how you will use this additional information, which immediately precedes the first lesson.

LEADING THE CLASS

(1) Gather to Learn

❖ Greet the class members. Introduce any guests and help them feel at home.

❖ Pray that those who have gathered today, including guests, will feel that they belong here.

❖ Invite the adults to call out names of organizations to which they belong, and list these on newsprint. Choose several organizations and ask: **What are the criteria for membership in this group?**

❖ Listen carefully and then try to summarize the types of boundaries that these organizations draw. For example, one may need to (1) be either male or female to join, (2) be a businessperson, (3) have a lot of money, (4) be willing to keep certain rules and practices confidential, (5) live in a specific community, and so on. While groups have the option of limiting their membership in certain ways, the church is open to all.

❖ Read aloud today's focus statement: **Some people want to prescribe who is in and who is out when it comes to membership in certain groups. Why are the boundaries of membership sometimes limited to specific people? Philip's sharing of the good news about Jesus and the baptism of the Ethiopian demonstrate the universal availability of the gospel message.**

(2) Goal 1: Make a Connection Between Philip's Baptism of the Ethiopian Eunuch and the Universal Availability of the Gospel Message

❖ Read Acts 8:26-39 as a drama by soliciting volunteers to play the following roles:

angel, narrator, Philip, eunuch, Scripture reader (verses 32-33). If possible, have the readers stand in a semicircle around a table at the front of the group on which you have placed a basin or clear pitcher of water.

❖ Invite other participants to comment on how they might have felt had they been the Ethiopian man before he met Philip and then after he met him.

❖ Make clear that the Ethiopian was yearning to know more about God by reading or retelling "Seeking the Truth" from Interpreting the Scripture.

❖ Discuss these questions:
1. **How was the Holy Spirit active in this story?**
2. **What does this story suggest about the importance of witnessing?**
3. **What does this story suggest about the importance of knowing the gospel story?**
4. **What does this story say about the availability of the gospel to all people?**

(3) Goal 2: Examine the Learners' Feelings of Being Excluded and Their Motivations for Excluding Others

❖ Encourage adults to work in pairs to tell brief stories about times, perhaps from childhood or adolescence, when they were excluded from a team, club, social group, or some other group that was important to them. Ask them to state how being excluded made them feel.

❖ Remain in pairs but switch gears to discuss times when the class members excluded others from their group. Ask them to try to explain their motivation for excluding these people.

❖ Wrap up by inviting each team to come up with several reasons why people exclude others. The ideas may include: *the need to lord one's status over others, an unwillingness to accept members of another socioeconomic group, desire for members of "my" group to appear special.*

(4) Goal 3: Develop a Strategy to Make the Learners' Church More Open and Inclusive

❖ Point out that just as some groups exclude people, churches may also be guilty of excluding others. Ask this question and record answers on newsprint: **What could our congregation do to make people feel more welcome and included?** Here are several suggestions:

■ Encourage the entire congregation to regularly greet every person—visitor and regular attendee—who is within ten feet of their pew.

■ Ensure that the church is accessible to those with mobility, hearing, and vision challenges. Ramps, grab bars in restrooms, wireless hearing systems, and large-print hymnals and bulletins are particularly useful.

■ Invite visitors and newcomers to someone's home or to a restaurant for a get-to-know-you meal.

■ Get to know newcomers and encourage them to participate in groups that would be of interest to them.

❖ Review the list and see what needs to be done to make each one of the suggestions a reality. Consider which groups within the church need to be made aware of these ideas, but recognize that individual class members also have important roles to play.

❖ Distribute paper and pencils. Encourage the learners to write two steps they will take to help their congregation become more open and inclusive. Suggest that they put these papers in their Bibles and refer to them as they seek to be more inclusive.

(5) Continue the Journey

❖ Pray that all of today's participants will recognize their own biases in order to be open to and inclusive of all people.

❖ Read aloud this preparation for next week's lesson. You may also want to post it on newsprint for the students to copy.

■ **Title: Paul Before King Agrippa**
■ **Background Scripture: Acts 25:23–26:32**
■ **Lesson Scripture: Acts 26:19-32**
■ **Focus of the Lesson: It is difficult to stand by our convictions when other people think we are insane. Where do we find the strength to stand our ground? Confident that he spoke the truth, Paul did not back down from sharing the story of his faith in Christ.**

❖ Post these three activities related to this week's session on newsprint for the students to copy. Challenge the adults to grow spiritually by completing one or more of them.

(1) Make it a point to greet each person who worships with you next Sunday. Be especially on the lookout for those who may be new or visiting. Do all in your power to make them feel welcomed and included.

(2) Visit another church one Sunday. Notice how you are treated. Did you feel included or excluded? What behaviors or attitudes among the parishioners there contributed to your comfort or discomfort in this setting? How can you use this information to assist your own church?

(3) Help someone who is seeking to understand the Scriptures. Try, as Philip did, to answer questions and to respond to this person's desire to accept Christ.

❖ Sing or read aloud "We've a Story to Tell to the Nations."

❖ Conclude today's session by leading the class in this benediction, adapted from the key verses for September 16 from Hebrews 12:1-2: **Let us go forth to run with perseverance the race that is set before us, looking to Jesus the pioneer and perfecter of our faith.**

UNIT 3: WHERE DOES FAITH TAKE US?
PAUL BEFORE KING AGRIPPA

PREVIEWING THE LESSON

Lesson Scripture: Acts 26:19-32
Background Scripture: Acts 25:23–26:32
Key Verse: Acts 26:25

Focus of the Lesson:
It is difficult to stand by our convictions when other people think we are insane. Where do we find the strength to stand our ground? Confident that he spoke the truth, Paul did not back down from sharing the story of his faith in Christ.

Goals for the Learners:
(1) to comprehend Paul's conviction as he stood before King Agrippa.
(2) to weigh the value of keeping their convictions against the cost of losing their credibility.
(3) to examine the creeds and beliefs of the church in order to strengthen the defense of their Christian witness.

Pronunciation Guide:
Agrippa (uh grip' uh)   Caesarea (ses uh ree' uh)
Ananias (an uh ni' uhs)   Festus (fes' tuhs)

Supplies:
Bibles, newsprint and marker, paper and pencils, hymnals

READING THE SCRIPTURE

NRSV
Lesson Scripture: Acts 26:19-32

¹⁹"After that, King Agrippa, I was not disobedient to the heavenly vision, ²⁰but declared first to those in Damascus, then in Jerusalem and throughout the countryside of Judea, and also to the Gentiles, that they should repent and turn to God and do deeds

CEB
Lesson Scripture: Acts 26:19-32

¹⁹"So, King Agrippa, I wasn't disobedient to that heavenly vision. ²⁰Instead, I proclaimed first to those in Damascus and Jerusalem, then to the whole region of Judea and to the Gentiles. My message was that they should change their hearts and lives

consistent with repentance. [21]For this reason the Jews seized me in the temple and tried to kill me. [22]To this day I have had help from God, and so I stand here, testifying to both small and great, saying nothing but what the prophets and Moses said would take place: [23]that the Messiah must suffer, and that, by being the first to rise from the dead, he would proclaim light both to our people and to the Gentiles."

[24]While he was making this defense, Festus exclaimed, "You are out of your mind, Paul! Too much learning is driving you insane!" **[25]But Paul said, "I am not out of my mind, most excellent Festus, but I am speaking the sober truth.** [26]Indeed the king knows about these things, and to him I speak freely; for I am certain that none of these things has escaped his notice, for this was not done in a corner. [27]King Agrippa, do you believe the prophets? I know that you believe." [28]Agrippa said to Paul, "Are you so quickly persuading me to become a Christian?" [29]Paul replied, "Whether quickly or not, I pray to God that not only you but also all who are listening to me today might become such as I am—except for these chains."

[30]Then the king got up, and with him the governor and Bernice and those who had been seated with them; [31]and as they were leaving, they said to one another, "This man is doing nothing to deserve death or imprisonment." [32]Agrippa said to Festus, "This man could have been set free if he had not appealed to the emperor."

and turn to God, and that they should demonstrate this change in their behavior. [21]Because of this, some Jews seized me in the temple and tried to murder me. [22]God has helped me up to this very day. Therefore, I stand here and bear witness to the lowly and the great. I'm saying nothing more than what the Prophets and Moses declared would happen: [23]that the Christ would suffer and that, as the first to rise from the dead, he would proclaim light both to my people and to the Gentiles."

[24]At this point in Paul's defense, Festus declared with a loud voice, "You've lost your mind, Paul! Too much learning is driving you mad!"

[25]But Paul replied, "I'm not mad, most honorable Festus! I'm speaking what is sound and true. [26]King Agrippa knows about these things, and I have been speaking openly to him. I'm certain that none of these things have escaped his attention. This didn't happen secretly or in some out-of-the-way place. [27]King Agrippa, do you believe the prophets? I know you do."

[28]Agrippa said to Paul, "Are you trying to convince me that, in such a short time, you've made me a Christian?"

[29]Paul responded, "Whether it is a short or a long time, I pray to God that not only you but also all who are listening to me today will become like me, except for these chains."

[30]The king stood up, as did the governor, Bernice, and those sitting with them. [31]As they left, they were saying to each other, "This man is doing nothing that deserves death or imprisonment."

[32]Agrippa said to Festus, "This man could have been released if he hadn't appealed to Caesar."

UNDERSTANDING THE SCRIPTURE

Introduction. Saul, the active oppressor of early Christianity, became Paul, the staunch supporter of bearing witness to the good news of Christ "to the ends of the earth" (Acts 1:8). Based on this radical shift of allegiance, Paul's enemies among the Jews began to plot against him. The plot unfolded when Paul returned to Jerusalem after successful missionary work among the Gentiles in Asia Minor and Greece. While Acts does not give a specific reason for Paul's decision to return to Jerusalem (Acts 19:21; 20:22-24), Paul's letters indicate that he had been gathering an offering from the Gentile churches to assist the poor in Jerusalem (Romans 15:25-28; 1 Corinthians 16:1-4; 2 Corinthians 8–9). In spite of warnings of danger ahead (Acts 21:4, 10-12), Paul persisted in his plans. Shortly after Paul's arrival in Jerusalem, a riot broke out over his presence in the Temple, and he was arrested (21:27-36). When a plot to kill Paul was discovered, he was transferred to Caesarea for his safety (23:12-24). There Felix, the Roman governor of Judea, heard his case. Hoping to placate the Jews and perhaps to gain a bribe from Paul, Felix kept Paul under protective custody for two years (Acts 24). When Felix was recalled to Rome, he was succeeded by Festus (24:27). Festus quickly heard Paul's case and was preparing to return Paul to Jerusalem for trial. Recognizing the unlikely possibility of a fair trial there, Paul as a Roman citizen exercised his right and appealed his case to Caesar (25:1-12). A few days later, King Agrippa (Agrippa II, great-grandson of Herod the Great, and ruler of the region north of Judea) and his sister-consort, Bernice, paid a courtesy visit to Festus. When Festus told Agrippa about Paul's case, Agrippa expressed interest in hearing Paul (25:13-22).

Acts 25:23–26:18. Festus used the presence of King Agrippa (who was much more familiar with Jewish customs and practices than was the newly appointed Festus) as a means of gathering information about Paul to be passed on to Rome along with Paul's appeal to Caesar. Agrippa invited Paul to speak on his own behalf. Luke then provided for the third time the account of the heavenly vision of Christ that Paul had experienced on the road to Damascus (see Acts 9:1-22; 22:3-11; 26:4-23). In keeping with his Pharisaic background, Paul tied his witness to the raising of the dead (26:8): "The Messiah must suffer" but would be "the first to rise from the dead" (26:23). Paul summarized the commission he had received from Christ through Ananias (buttressed by calls from the Old Testament Scriptures): "I am sending you to open their [the Gentiles'] eyes so that they may turn from darkness to light and from the power of Satan to God, so that they may receive forgiveness of sins and a place among those who are sanctified by faith" (26:17-18). This testimony elevated the status of the Gentiles both as objects of God's concern and recipients of God's grace.

Acts 26:19-21. Addressing King Agrippa, Paul made his defense. He had been obedient to that heavenly vision and to Christ's explicit commission. By stating that negatively ("I was not disobedient," 26:19), Paul implied that to have acted otherwise would have been an offense against God worthy of punishment. You break a law by disobedience, and punishment is just. But keeping a command should be rewarded, not punished. Paul then recounted his work in carrying out Christ's commission in Damascus, in Jerusalem, in Judea, and ultimately to the Gentiles. His message was the same in all circumstances, to Jew and to Gentile: "Repent. Turn to God. Consistently practice works worthy of repentance." Paul skirted the issue of the gospel's being offered to the Gentiles. The reason he gave for his arrest in the Temple court was that the Jews themselves were unwilling to repent, turn to God, and do deeds consistent with repentance. Their attempt to kill him was evidence of extreme overreaction.

Acts 26:22-23. Although Paul had been under protective custody for two years, he still perceived the presence of God helping him. The fact that he could stand before two important political leaders like Festus and Agrippa demonstrated that God was opening doors for the "great" to hear his testimony. In his imprisonment, Paul certainly had opportunities to testify to the "small"—both his fellow prisoners and the guards and other personnel who daily worked in the prison. The verb tense of "stand" implies "I have stood and continue to stand," tying both past and present into a consistent pattern of testimony. Just as he had proclaimed the same message to Jew and Gentile, so he had testified to both the great and the small. More important, however, Paul had said nothing more than what the prophets and Moses had said would take place when the Messiah came. Verse 23 is stated as if it were the common understanding about the Messiah. But following Christ's example in Luke 24:45-49, early Christians had combed the Scriptures for support for their messianic views. Many Jews had a much more political and martial view of the Messiah, anticipating the overthrow of all foreign domination over their country. Paul's view would have been welcomed among the Roman authorities charged with maintaining peace in Judea and the surrounding areas.

Acts 26:24-32. Festus found Paul's argument so outlandish that he interrupted Paul and accused him of letting his great learning drive him insane. Paul appealed to King Agrippa, knowing that the king would be more familiar with Jewish customs and ways of thinking. Paul contended that in

order to understand what was "true and reasonable" (26:25 NIV), one needed to be aware of recent events. While Agrippa II ruled over a region neighboring Judea (including parts of Galilee) and is not mentioned in the New Testament outside of Acts 25–26, Paul was certain that he was familiar with both the Old Testament prophecies as well as the events surrounding the life and death of Jesus. Since his defense was based on Old Testament prophecy, Paul asked Agrippa directly, "Do you believe the prophets?" and then immediately affirmed, "I know that you believe" (26:27). Agrippa recognized that Paul was maneuvering him to take sides in a theological dispute over messianic prophecies. To side with Paul would be to acknowledge the truth about Jesus' messiahship. Agrippa turned Paul aside, "Do you think that in such a short time you can persuade me to be a Christian?" (26:28 NIV). Paul acknowledged that his appeal was more than a defense. He was declaring the gospel in hope that all who heard would believe as he did. Agrippa chose this uncomfortable moment (when he was being maneuvered to take sides) as an appropriate time to end the interview. He and all of his company got up and left the room. Acknowledging among themselves that Paul had committed no serious offense, they even advised Festus that Paul could have been set free if he had not already appealed to Caesar.

INTERPRETING THE SCRIPTURE

Where Does Faith Take You?

The title of this unit of Bible study poses the question "Where Does Faith Take Us?" This lesson easily affords an opportunity to personalize that question: Where does faith take me? Where does faith take you? In reality, every believer has a faith story that trav-

erses times, locations, relationships, and experiences. When we are engaged in the pilgrimage of faith, faith accompanies us wherever we go. Consciously or unconsciously, it plays a role in everything we do. It influences every relationship. It shapes every experience. Faith's role in all these aspects of life becomes the stuff from which our witness, our testimony, and our example flow.

A few months before I began work on these lessons, I joined the online Facebook community. One of the most exciting aspects of this community has been the ability to reconnect with distant family members, friends, and colleagues from the past. For me, one of the most rewarding experiences has been reconnecting with students I taught at Campbell University more than thirty years ago. In sharing our stories with one another, we have discovered that life has had its ups and downs. Life has not always been easy or kind. We have experienced some successes and some failures. Though we had sinned, we have accomplished some good. I have been touched by how many of my students are actively engaged in ministries that are making a difference in the lives of those who hurt, suffer, fail, and want to give up.

These students have a faith story that involves a faith journey. Some rub shoulders with the "great." Many touch the "small." Faith has led some to positions of significance and importance. Faith has led others to unheralded and sacrificial service. But most important, their faith is leading them—in places near and far, in places high and low, in places of prominence and anonymity, in good times and bad, in hardship and suffering, in success and achievement. I am extremely proud of them.

Paul had a faith journey that we still study almost two thousand years after the fact. His was a remarkable journey, yet it was filled with hardship, suffering, rejection, failure, and sacrifice. At the end of the journey, Paul could say, "I have fought the good fight, I have finished the race, I have kept the faith" (2 Timothy 4:7). And I expect his Master said to him, "Well done, good and trustworthy slave!" (Matthew 25:21).

What Convictions Shape Your Faith?

Earlier, in our study for September 9, Hebrews 11:1 was paraphrased this way:

"Faith is the foundation for this business we call hope; it is being convinced of things that currently are unseen." Hope and conviction are at the center of the life of faith. Both hope and conviction were clearly articulated in Paul's appearance before Festus and Agrippa.

Two sources for Paul's convictions are readily apparent in his defense before the Roman officials. The first is stated in Acts 26:22 (NIV) when Paul said, "I am saying nothing beyond what the prophets and Moses said." This reminds us of the central role that the Scriptures play in defining and shaping our faith. What we called the faith hall of fame (Hebrews 11) provides a historical and experiential connection between all who have placed their faith in God and have followed Jesus, the "pioneer and perfecter of our faith" (Hebrews 12:2). Some view Scripture as the primary source for doctrine, and neglect the stories of faith and the divine story that anchor our faith in the One whose example strengthens us so that we do "not grow weary or lose heart" (12:3). Some, like Festus, find the idea of grounding our faith in Scripture "insane" (Acts 26:24) and think that those who try to walk in the footsteps of Jesus are "out of [their] mind" (26:24). Paul's convictions were clearly based on the foundation of Scripture, and that foundation shaped his faith.

The second source is stated in his personal experience with Jesus Christ that took place on the road to Damascus. The fact that Luke recounts this experience three times in the Book of Acts certainly indicates the power of a personal encounter with Jesus Christ. Such an experience provides a strong basis for our convictions and our faith. The vast majority of us have not had and will not have an experience as dramatic as Paul's. Our faith is more a matter of conviction in things that currently are unseen. We cannot follow in the footsteps of Jesus; we cannot be his disciples; we cannot claim his promises—unless we have had some kind of personal encounter with Jesus

Christ. Our "vision from heaven" (26:19 NIV) provides the assurance that gives us hope (Hebrews 11:1).

What Is Your Witness?

The Baptist college I attended had a program where ministerial students regularly went into a region of the state and preached on Sunday at churches in that area. Having had little experience in preaching, my first attempts were somewhat of a sham. I found a book of popular sermons directed toward high school and college students. I found one sermon that spoke to me, and I basically took the outline and ideas of that sermon and made it my own. The first few times I preached that sermon, I was pleased with the response. After I had used the sermon in several places, however, I had someone come up to me one Sunday and ask if I had not taken that sermon from a book written by a famous preacher. I was nailed! I was embarrassed! Needless to say, I discovered that you shouldn't borrow someone else's sermon.

This lesson looks at Paul's experience and focuses on Paul's testimony. Some of us will be content to accept Paul's witness and think that by sharing it with others we are doing our Christian duty—and in some sense we are. Paul did use the stories from Scripture as part of his testimony; but I wonder: If Scripture is the only foundation for our convictions, where is the personal experience that gave such power to Paul's witness? Without the convictions that flow out of personal experience, our teaching is a little like my borrowed sermon. Hebrews reminds us that we are surrounded by a great "cloud of witnesses" (Hebrews 12:1), but those who are enrolled in the faith hall of fame don't share a single story. Each had a unique witness based on his or her own situation and personal encounter with God. In the light of Paul's example and the testimonies of a great cloud of witnesses, I don't want to be a copycat. So what is my witness? And what is yours? And are we both willing to stand firm on that witness, even if we, like Paul, encounter opposition to our belief?

SHARING THE SCRIPTURE

Preparing Our Hearts

Explore this week's devotional reading, found in Acts 23:1-11. Read the account of Paul's defense of his faith before the Jewish council. What strategies does Paul use to make his case? Think about your own willingness to witness. It's likely you are not in a situation where your life is at stake (see Acts 23:12-22), but you may still be challenged by people in authority. If you had just five minutes to make your case, what would be the points that you believe are critical to your faith? Write these ideas in your spiritual journal and continue to mull them over to see if you want to make any changes.

Pray that you and the adult students will witness boldly even when you have a lot to lose because of your testimony.

Preparing Our Minds

Study the background Scripture from Acts 25:23–26:32 and the lesson Scripture from Acts 26:19-32.

Consider this question as you prepare the lesson: *Where do we find the strength to stand our ground, especially when other people question our sanity?*

Write on newsprint:

❑ information for next week's lesson, found under "Continue the Journey."

❑ activities for further spiritual growth in "Continue the Journey."

Review the "Introduction," "The Big Picture," "Close-up," and "Faith in Action." Consider how you will use this additional information, which immediately precedes the first lesson.

LEADING THE CLASS

(1) Gather to Learn

❖ Greet the class members. Introduce any guests and help them feel at home.

❖ Pray that those who have gathered today will be ready to stand the ground of their convictions.

❖ Read the following words of former United Nations Secretary-General Dag Hammarskjöld (1905–1961): **"Never, for the sake of peace and quiet, deny your own experience or convictions."**

❖ Ask: **Under what kinds of circumstances do people seem willing to deny their own convictions?**

❖ Read aloud today's focus statement: **It is difficult to stand by our convictions when other people think we are insane. Where do we find the strength to stand our ground? Confident that he spoke the truth, Paul did not back down from sharing the story of his faith in Christ.**

(2) Goal 1: Comprehend Paul's Conviction as He Stood Before King Agrippa

❖ Set the scene by reading or retelling the "Introduction" in Understanding the Scripture.

❖ Note that Paul tells of his conversion experience (referred to in Acts 26:19 as "the heavenly vision") just prior to speaking to King Agrippa about the content of his preaching (26:20-23) and his invitation to Agrippa to believe in Jesus Christ (26:24-29).

❖ Select a volunteer to read Acts 26:19-23 and another to read verses 24-32.

❖ Invite the class to identify Paul's convictions as they are stated or implied in these two passages. List these ideas on newsprint. Add ideas from "What Convictions Shape Your Faith?" from Interpreting the Scripture to help the adults understand the basis of Paul's beliefs.

❖ Ask this question: **If it appears to you that Paul's convictions were firmly rooted and clearly spoken, why then do you think Festus referred to Paul as "out of [his] mind" (26:24)?**

(3) Goal 2: Weigh the Value of Keeping the Learners' Convictions Against the Cost of Losing Their Credibility

❖ Sketch on newsprint a balance scale with two pans. (Think of Lady Justice holding a scale.) Invite the adults to suggest reasons for standing firm on their convictions and list those above the pan on the left. Then ask them to think about the price they would pay in losing their credibility if they abandoned their convictions, and list those ideas on the right pan.

❖ Invite the learners to tell brief stories of times when they have chosen to stand firm on their convictions, even if that meant creating a problem or hardship for themselves. Also encourage them to give brief accounts of times when they abandoned their convictions and felt that they lost credibility because of their stance.

❖ Remind the group that there are times when compromise is necessary for people to live together in community. Faithful Christians have some major disagreements concerning how to read and interpret the Bible, and in such cases both sides can usually point to Scripture that supports their opposing perspectives. Ask: **In such cases, what criteria do you use to remain true to your convictions while recognizing that another Christian is taking a stand to remain true to his or her convictions?**

*(4) Goal 3: Examine the Creeds and Beliefs
of the Church in Order to Strengthen
the Defense of the Learner's Christian Witness*

❖ Distribute hymnals. Locate pages containing creeds of the church, particularly "The Apostles' Creed" and the "Nicene Creed." Form two groups (or multiples of two) and assign half the class to one of these creeds and half to the other. Encourage the groups to read these creeds not so much with an eye to what they as individuals may specifically agree with, but rather to understand how the church throughout history has examined and agreed upon certain convictions as important for Christians.

❖ Distribute paper and pencils. Encourage the learners to write their own creeds. They may want to use ideas (even wording) from the historic creeds.

❖ Enlist volunteers to read some ideas that best express their deepest convictions.

(5) Continue the Journey

❖ Pray that all who participated in today's session will take the time to examine and state their beliefs so that when they are challenged they might be able to respond with confidence.

❖ Read aloud this preparation for next week's lesson. You may also want to post it on newsprint for the students to copy.

- **Title: Paul Sails for Rome**
- **Background Scripture: Acts 27**
- **Lesson Scripture: Acts 27:1-2, 33-44**
- **Focus of the Lesson: In times of crises, our panic can lead us to** behave irrationally. What helps us avoid panic and act with a level head? Paul's confidence in God's faithfulness enabled him to act calmly and assure all the ship's passengers that they would survive the storm.

❖ Post these three activities related to this week's session on newsprint for the students to copy. Challenge the adults to grow spiritually by completing one or more of them.

(1) **Read about at least one missionary who faces constant challenges and yet stands firm on his or her convictions. Your denominational board of missions is a good source for locating such stories.**

(2) **Think about Scripture verses that you find compelling. Memorize several of these so that you will be prepared to take a stand should the opportunity present itself.**

(3) **Review the statement of faith you wrote in class. Pray on what you have declared and refine this document as it seems appropriate.**

❖ Sing or read aloud "Stand By Me."

❖ Conclude today's session by leading the class in this benediction, adapted from the key verses for September 16 from Hebrews 12:1-2: **Let us go forth to run with perseverance the race that is set before us, looking to Jesus the pioneer and perfecter of our faith.**

UNIT 3: WHERE DOES FAITH TAKE US?

PAUL SAILS FOR ROME

PREVIEWING THE LESSON

Lesson Scripture: Acts 27:1-2, 33-44
Background Scripture: Acts 27
Key Verse: Acts 27:44

Focus of the Lesson:

In times of crises, our panic can lead us to behave irrationally. What helps us avoid panic and act with a level head? Paul's confidence in God's faithfulness enabled him to act calmly and assure all the ship's passengers that they would survive the storm.

Goals for the Learners:

(1) to connect Paul's faith in God with his ability to remain calm in the midst of a storm.
(2) to recognize and appreciate how their relationship with God helps them cope with crises.
(3) to witness to others about how their relationship with God makes a difference in their ability to deal with crises.

Pronunciation Guide:

Adramyttium (ad ruh mit' ee uhm)   Macedonian (mas uh doh' nee uhn)
Aristarchus (air is tahr' kuhs)   Sidon (si' duhn)
Augustan (aw guhs' tuhn)   Thesmophorian (thes mah for' ree un)
eisegesis (ice' uh gee' sis)   Thessalonica (thes uh luh ni' kuh)
exegesis (ex' uh gee' sis)   Tishri (tish' ree)

Supplies:

Bibles, newsprint and marker, paper and pencils, hymnals, optional map of Paul's journey to Rome

---

READING THE SCRIPTURE

NRSV
Lesson Scripture: Acts 27:1-2, 33-44
¹When it was decided that we were to sail for Italy, they transferred Paul and some

CEB
Lesson Scripture: Acts 27:1-2, 33-44
¹When it was determined that we were to sail to Italy, Paul and some other prisoners

other prisoners to a centurion of the Augustan Cohort, named Julius. [2]Embarking on a ship of Adramyttium that was about to set sail to the ports along the coast of Asia, we put to sea, accompanied by Aristarchus, a Macedonian from Thessalonica.

[33]Just before daybreak, Paul urged all of them to take some food, saying, "Today is the fourteenth day that you have been in suspense and remaining without food, having eaten nothing. [34]Therefore I urge you to take some food, for it will help you survive; for none of you will lose a hair from your heads." [35]After he had said this, he took bread; and giving thanks to God in the presence of all, he broke it and began to eat. [36]Then all of them were encouraged and took food for themselves. [37](We were in all two hundred seventy-six persons in the ship.) [38]After they had satisfied their hunger, they lightened the ship by throwing the wheat into the sea.

[39]In the morning they did not recognize the land, but they noticed a bay with a beach, on which they planned to run the ship ashore, if they could. [40]So they cast off the anchors and left them in the sea. At the same time they loosened the ropes that tied the steering-oars; then hoisting the foresail to the wind, they made for the beach. [41]But striking a reef, they ran the ship aground; the bow stuck and remained immovable, but the stern was being broken up by the force of the waves. [42]The soldiers' plan was to kill the prisoners, so that none might swim away and escape; [43]but the centurion, wishing to save Paul, kept them from carrying out their plan. He ordered those who could swim to jump overboard first and make for the land, [44]and the rest to follow, some on planks and others on pieces of the ship. **And so it was that all were brought safely to land.**

were placed in the custody of a centurion named Julius of the Imperial Company. [2]We boarded a ship from Adramyttium that was about to sail for ports along the coast of the province of Asia. So we put out to sea. Aristarchus, a Macedonian from Thessalonica, came with us.

[33]Just before daybreak, Paul urged everyone to eat. He said, "This is the fourteenth day you've lived in suspense, and you've not had even a bite to eat. [34]I urge you to take some food. Your health depends on it. None of you will lose a single hair from his head." [35]After he said these things, he took bread, gave thanks to God in front of them all, then broke it and began to eat. [36]Everyone was encouraged and took some food. ([37]In all, there were two hundred seventy-six of us on the ship.) [38]When they had eaten as much as they wanted, they lightened the ship by throwing the grain into the sea.

[39]In the morning light they saw a bay with a sandy beach. They didn't know what land it was, but they thought they might possibly be able to run the ship aground. [40]They cut the anchors loose and left them in the sea. At the same time, they untied the ropes that ran back to the rudders. They raised the foresail to catch the wind and made for the beach. [41]But they struck a sandbar and the ship ran aground. The bow was stuck and wouldn't move, and the stern was broken into pieces by the force of the waves. [42]The soldiers decided to kill the prisoners to keep them from swimming to shore and escaping. [43]However, the centurion wanted to save Paul, so he stopped them from carrying out their plan. He ordered those who could swim to jump overboard first and head for land. [44]He ordered the rest to grab hold of planks or debris from the ship. **In this way, everyone reached land safely.**

UNDERSTANDING THE SCRIPTURE

Acts 27:1-8. The summer of A.D. 59 seems to have been the time frame for Paul's appearance before Festus and Agrippa. The word "decided" (27:1) is also the Greek word for "judged" and implies a judicial decision was made by Festus to send Paul to Rome for his appeal to Caesar. Paul and some other prisoners were placed in the custody of a Roman centurion named Julius. Julius became a popular name following the reign of Julius Caesar, who had been assassinated in 44 B.C. Our month "July" also derives from his name. The centurion was a member of the decorated Augustan Cohort ("Imperial Regiment," NIV), which probably was made up of about six hundred soldiers. Normally, a centurion commanded one hundred soldiers, who usually were drawn from the surrounding region. Luke traced the route of Paul's transfer to Rome, but more significantly, he noted that Julius treated Paul kindly and even allowed him to stay with friends in Sidon.

Acts 27:9-20. The reference to "the Fast" (27:9) provides a specific time frame that marked the end of the safe season for shipping by sea. Many assume that this was the annual fast associated with the Day of Atonement (held on the tenth day of Tishri, corresponding with our late September and early October). The Thesmophorian Fast, the most widely recognized fast in the Greco-Roman world, seems a more likely reference. It occurred closer to the cessation of all shipping (generally between November 11 and March 10 each year) and better explains the other circumstances recounted in Acts. The pressing need to find a safe harbor for the winter made the ship's pilot and its owner push on in spite of Paul's warning (27:10), and the centurion and the majority of the passengers seem to have agreed with the pilot's decision. After a few days of smooth sailing, however, a northeaster caught the ship in its violent grip. Unable to proceed on course, the ship was driven almost out of control, dragging a sea anchor to maintain stability. As the storm increased in ferocity, first the ship's cargo and a few days later even the ship's tackle were thrown overboard to lighten the ship. Soon they all abandoned hope of being saved.

Acts 27:21-32. Paul had been right in his warning, and he did not hesitate to say "I told you so." He chastised his hungry and battered shipmates for ignoring his advice and pointed out the losses they had sustained. In the midst of their desperation, however, Paul held out a message of hope given to him by an angelic messenger, who represented "the God to whom I belong and whom I worship" (27:23). The angel confirmed that Paul would make it to Rome and have his appeal to Caesar heard; he also assured Paul that all of those sailing with Paul would survive the storm, even though the ship would run aground. After fourteen days adrift, the sailors suspected that they were nearing land. They took "soundings"—an anachronism in the English translations based on the modern use of radar soundings. Actually they "heaved the lead" or dropped a lead weight attached to the end of a rope to discover the depth. The Greek word translated "fathom" means "to stretch out" and corresponds with a nautical measurement of about six feet (the distance between a man's fingertips when he stretched his arms out horizontally). When the measured depth decreased from 120 to 90 feet in just a short time, four anchors were let out. But when some of the sailors lowered a tender under the guise of attending to the anchors, Paul recognized that they were abandoning ship and had the soldiers stop them.

Acts 27:33-38. Having gone fourteen days without food and being under constant stress from the storm, all the passengers on the ship certainly were stretched to the limit. Paul urged them to take some food to renew their strength and to help them survive. He assured them again, affirming that none would lose even "a hair from your heads" (27:34). Then in eucharistic fashion, Paul took bread, gave thanks to God, broke the bread, and began to eat. Paul's example encouraged the passengers, and they all took food as well. In one of the conventions that many view as eyewitness testimony from Luke, the writer referred to "we" and gave a surprising total count of 276 people on the ship—a number comparable to two Boeing 737 aircraft. If this number is correct (alternate translations read "seventy-six" or "about seventy-six"), this was a large ocean-going vessel, not a fishing boat like those on the Sea of Galilee, where 153 large fish would strain the nets and almost sink the boat (Luke 5:6; John 21:11). After all had "satisfied their hunger," they lightened the ship again—this time throwing overboard the most precious cargo besides the passengers: the wheat. Rome was heavily dependent upon Egyptian wheat and extracted tribute from the eastern provinces to counteract its own trade imbalance. The loss of the wheat was the highest "damage and loss" (27:21) the ship could encounter, and its loss fulfilled Paul's initial premonition (27:10).

Acts 27:39-44. When dawn broke, the ship's crew did not recognize where they were. They spotted a bay with a beach and decided to try to run aground there. Casting off their anchors, they raised the foresail and, together with the oars, tried to make their way to the beach. Instead, they struck a reef where the bow became stuck. The fierce waves began to break up the ship. Fearing that their prisoners would escape, the soldiers planned to kill all of the prisoners. Julius, the centurion, however, intervened—and Luke thought that the intervention was primarily related to his desire to spare Paul. Taking charge, Julius instructed those who could swim to jump overboard first and make their way to land. Those who couldn't swim followed behind, holding on to pieces of floating debris to make their way ashore. Providentially, and in keeping with Paul's prediction, all made it ashore safely. The ship, however, was a total loss. From his departure from Caesarea until his landing in Malta, Paul had traveled at least fifteen hundred miles under generally unfavorable conditions. God had protected and preserved him, and Paul was progressing toward his goal of proclaiming the gospel in Rome.

INTERPRETING THE SCRIPTURE

Following Paul's Example

My mother used to say jokingly, "Do what I say, not what I do!" Direct instruction is often easier to follow than a personal example. The historical narrative in this lesson does not lend itself easily to application. When you have a Bible passage that intentionally teaches, you can easily apply that teaching. When you are dealing with a unique life experience, like the one Paul faced on his journey to Rome, finding intersections with our life experiences are harder. Scholars sometimes contrast legitimate exegesis (drawing meaning out of a biblical text) with twisted eisegesis (reading your own meaning into a biblical text). The theological interpretations in this lesson's narrative are not intentionally evident. We can, however, learn from the example of other believers, and that is the case with Paul. When we see how others faithfully deal with life situations, we can learn from their examples.

Paul provided an open witness both through his words and through his actions. From the time of his arrest, we hear and see his witness in the context of a host of uncomfortable circumstances. Paul certainly can provide an example for our attempts to speak and live the gospel.

Life's Spiritual GPS

Some of us go through long, wrenching crises that drag out for months or even years. At one time or another all of us have periods when nothing seems to go our way. Hard times come to us, and sometimes we get more of the hard times than we imagined possible. Paul went through one of those long, hard experiences. After being arrested in Jerusalem, he discovered a plot to assassinate him. He appealed his case and was transferred to Caesarea, where he languished in prison for two years waiting for his case to be considered. Once his case was heard, he was shipped off under guard to Rome. All of his premonitions told him that trouble was ahead, but his armed escort would not listen to premonitions. When the storm of his life struck, Paul had weeks of unceasing chaos. Every moment brought a threat of death. The strain and danger was so great that no one on the ship even thought of food for two weeks! The storm was so intense that all means of navigation were lost. Paul and his companions were blown they knew not where; no navigational instruments worked in that dark, intense, continuous storm. Even when they shipwrecked, they had no idea where they were.

Most navigation prior to the modern era was accomplished by reference to the stars. In the Northern Hemisphere, the North Star (Polaris) provided a dependable point of reference that guided ships around the world. But fourteen days in the clouds, winds, waves, and darkness cut Paul and

his travel companions off from their sure point of geographical reference. For many on that ship, that was the only reference that mattered. Not for Paul! Hear Paul's words: "I am convinced that neither death, nor life, nor angels, nor rulers, nor things present, nor things to come, nor powers, nor height, nor depth, nor anything else in all creation, will be able to separate us from the love of God in Christ Jesus our Lord" (Romans 8:38-39). Paul had a spiritual GPS (global positioning system) that assured him that he was always on God's radar screen, even in the darkest times. Like Jeremiah before him (Jeremiah 1:5), Paul was fully known by God—and so are we! God knew exactly where he was and what he was experiencing. We too have Christ's assurance: "Remember, I am with you always, to the end of the age" (Matthew 28:20).

Staying Together in Times of Trouble

What is it about humanity that causes people to "jump ship" when troubles come? After days of being battered by a horrendous storm and with a shoreline finally in sight, some of the crew on the ship transporting Paul to Italy decided they would rather take their chances on a small tender ("lifeboat," 27:30 NIV) than on the large ship. They wanted to abandon a sinking ship in the interest of personal safety. Without regard for their duties and obligations for the safety of others, they cast aside the spirit of "one for all and all for one."

We too tend to emphasize independence. We have a fascination with the quirky characters around us who thumb their noses at convention and gain notoriety by outrageous behavior. These are mere symptoms of the decline of community in our society. The solution, however, is not conformity that sacrifices our individuality. We must find a space somewhere between stifling conformity that bullies those who are different and the anarchy of self-centered individualism evident in the "it's all about me" approach to life. Earlier in his writings, Paul addressed the destructiveness of selfish insistence on having things your own way. He wrote 1 Corinthians to address the quarrelsome factions and deep divisions that plagued the church at Corinth. The center of Paul's prescription is found in 1 Corinthians 12—the unity of the body that appreciates and celebrates its individual parts. With Christ as the Head and love as the binding power, the body works together as one.

When times are good, we are surrounded by fellow travelers on the journey of life. When difficulties arise, our travel companions often seem to disappear. Too often we celebrate with a crowd and suffer alone. We know there is strength in numbers, but we are forced to fight so many of life's crucial battles single-handedly. Elisha A. Hoffman's gospel song speaks of our situations: "I must tell Jesus all of my trials. I cannot bear these burdens alone." But Jesus and the Spirit seem so ephemeral. We need real, tangible, present people who can hold us in their arms and comfort us in times of trouble; and we too must be comforters for those around us. Let's be that to one another.

"I Have Faith in God"

When everyone on the ship had given up "all hope of our being saved" (Acts 27:20), Paul had an opportunity to present a powerful testimony of his faith in God. In the face of the hopelessness of his companions, Paul made two affirmations that spoke of faith and offered hope to those who were despairing. First, he affirmed that he belonged to God ("the God to whom I belong," 27:23) and had dedicated himself to serve God ("whom I worship," 27:23). Faith goes beyond our "owning" God. It acknowledges that God owns us and we are committed to serving God in all the circumstances in our lives—good times and bad.

Second, after conveying the message God had given him through an angelic messenger, Paul stated, "I have faith in God that it will be exactly as I have been told" (27:25). Living in faith and walking by faith reveal a confidence in God—that God ultimately is in control; that God's will ultimately will be done; and that the goodness, love, and hope God represents will ultimately prevail in our lives, our churches, and our world. "I have faith in God" may be our greatest witness, especially when that faith is affirmed in times of trouble when all hope seems lost.

SHARING THE SCRIPTURE

Preparing Our Hearts

Explore this week's devotional reading, found in Romans 1:13-17. Notice that in verses 16-17 the word "faith" is used four times. Paul wants to be sure that the church in Rome, which he longs to visit but has not yet been able to see, understands that faith is an essential attribute for salvation—which as Paul defines it is deliverance from sin, from death, and from Satan. This salvation is offered to all people. According to Paul, "the one who is righteous will live by faith" (1:17).

Keep his words about faith in mind as you read the account of Paul and 275 other passengers shipwrecked off Malta in Acts 27.

Pray that you and the adult students will be prepared to live out the faith you profess, particularly when you are battered by the storms of life.

Preparing Our Minds

Study the background Scripture from Acts 27 and the lesson Scripture from Acts 27:1-2, 33-44.

Consider this question as you prepare the lesson: *In times of crises, what helps us avoid panic and act with a level head?*

Write on newsprint:

❏ information for next week's lesson, found under "Continue the Journey."

❏ activities for further spiritual growth in "Continue the Journey."

Take note of the map in "Close-up: Paul's Voyage to Rome," which you will find at the beginning of this quarter. You may also be able to locate a larger map.

Review the "Introduction," "The Big Picture," and "Faith in Action." Consider how you will use this additional information, which immediately precedes the first lesson.

LEADING THE CLASS

(1) Gather to Learn

❖ Greet the class members. Introduce any guests and help them feel at home.

❖ Pray that the students who have come today will consider how their faith can help them stay calm in a crisis.

❖ Read this quotation from American author and speaker Denis Waitley: **"The Chinese symbols for *crisis* are identical to those for the word *opportunity*. Literally translated it reads, 'Crisis is an opportunity riding the dangerous wind.' View crises as opportunities and stumbling blocks as stepping-stones to the stars."**

❖ Ask: **What do you suppose enables some people to keep calm and level-headed in the midst of a crisis while others respond to the same situation with panic?**

❖ Read aloud today's focus statement: **In times of crises, our panic can lead us to behave irrationally. What helps us avoid panic and act with a level head? Paul's confidence in God's faithfulness enabled him to act calmly and assure all the ship's passengers that they would survive the storm.**

(2) Goal 1: Connect Paul's Faith in God with His Ability to Remain Calm in the Midst of a Storm

❖ **Option:** Show the route of Paul's journey to Rome. Be sure to point out Malta, the site of the shipwreck that drives the action of today's story.

❖ Choose three volunteers, one to read Acts 27:1-2, a second for verses 33-38, and a third for verses 39-44.

❖ Look at Paul's role in this story, pointing out that he is a prisoner. Ask these questions. Use information from Interpreting the Scripture to add ideas to the discussion.

(1) What role does Paul play during the tumultuous storm?

(2) Why do you think that even those who were supposed to be in charge followed Paul's directions?

(3) Why do you think that the centurion devised a plan to save Paul, particularly when it would have been much easier to let all the prisoners drown?

(4) How do you see God at work in this story?

(3) Goal 2: Recognize and Appreciate How the Learners' Relationship With God Helps Them Cope With Crises

❖ Invite the adults to listen to the following statements that you will read aloud:

(1) Research has revealed that 25 percent of hospital patients report that they rely primarily on their religion to deal with this health crisis.

(2) Research has also shown that religion is a major resource for coping with the death of a child, spouse, or close friend.

(3) Religious people who are able to cope successfully with crises believe that God will support them and that they will be able to find greater meaning in life as a

result of these challenges. Such perceptions tend to lower psychological distress.

(4) **Religious people who view God as a judge who is testing them may feel that they have been abandoned by God. Such perceptions lead to emotional distress and depression.**

❖ Distribute paper and pencils. Encourage the learners to mull over these ideas and write a few sentences about how their relationship with God helps them cope with crises.

❖ Move directly into the next activity, where the adults will be asked to continue processing these thoughts.

(4) Goal 3: Witness to Others About How the Learners' Relationship With God Makes a Difference in Their Ability to Deal With Crises

❖ Form groups of three or four students. Suggest that each person tell the group about how their relationship with God enabled them to cope effectively with a crisis. They need not go into detail about the crisis itself, particularly if it was of a confidential nature. The focus of the discussion should be how faith in God enabled the learners to cope. Some class members may be able to talk about how they handled two crises—one before they accepted Christ and one after—to demonstrate the changes that their faith made in how they approached a serious situation.

❖ Call the groups back together and ask: **As you listened to the stories, are there any generalizations you can make about how faith in God helps people handle the unexpected challenges that life hurls at us?** (Possible answers may include *seeking God's guidance through prayer and meditation,* or *researching biblical characters and following their example.*)

❖ Wrap up this activity by reading or retelling "I Have Faith in God" from Interpreting the Scripture.

(5) Continue the Journey

❖ Pray that today's participants will be strengthened in their faith in order to better cope with crises.

Read aloud this preparation for next week's lesson. You may also want to post it on newsprint for the students to copy.

■ **Title: Paul Ministers in Malta**
■ **Background Scripture: Acts 28:1-10**
■ **Lesson Scripture: Acts 28:1-10**
■ **Focus of the Lesson: Often we can tell something about the character of people by observing how they respond in difficult situations. What conclusions might others draw from observing our actions? The people of Malta recognized something extraordinary about Paul because through his faith in Christ a man was healed.**

❖ Post these three activities related to this week's session on newsprint for the students to copy. Challenge the adults to grow spiritually by completing one or more of them.

(1) **Read the story of Jesus calming a storm from Luke 8:22-25. How might this story bolster your faith during a time of crisis or trial?**

(2) **Do whatever you can to help an individual or community in crisis. The crisis might be due to a death, serious illness, a problem with a family member, loss of job or home foreclosure. A community crisis might be due to a natural disaster or multiple deaths, particularly those caused by violence.**

(3) **Be willing to share how you handled a crisis in order to help your listener deal with his or her own crisis.**

❖ Sing or read aloud "Jesus, Savior, Pilot Me."

❖ Conclude today's session by leading the class in this benediction, adapted from the key verses for September 16 from Hebrews 12:1-2: **Let us go forth to run with perseverance the race that is set before us, looking to Jesus the pioneer and perfecter of our faith.**

UNIT 3: WHERE DOES FAITH TAKE US?
PAUL MINISTERS IN MALTA

PREVIEWING THE LESSON

Lesson Scripture: Acts 28:1-10
Background Scripture: Acts 28:1-10
Key Verse: Acts 28:8

Focus of the Lesson:
Often we can tell something about the character of people by observing how they respond in difficult situations. What conclusions might others draw from observing our actions? The people of Malta recognized something extraordinary about Paul because through his faith in Christ a man was healed.

Goals for the Learners:
(1) to connect Paul's ministry and the hospitality he received in Malta.
(2) to express awe over God's extraordinary action in their lives.
(3) to demonstrate their faith by ministering to the needs of others.

Pronunciation Guide:
Malta (mawl' tuh)   Melitene (mel i tee' nee)
Melita (mel' i tuh)   Publius (puhb' lee uhs)

Supplies:
Bibles, newsprint and marker, paper and pencils, hymnals

READING THE SCRIPTURE

NRSV
Lesson Scripture: Acts 28:1-10

¹After we had reached safety, we then learned that the island was called Malta. ²The natives showed us unusual kindness. Since it had begun to rain and was cold, they kindled a fire and welcomed all of us around it. ³Paul had gathered a bundle of brushwood and was putting it on the fire, when a

CEB
Lesson Scripture: Acts 28:1-10

¹After reaching land safely, we learned that the island was called Malta. ²The islanders showed us extraordinary kindness. Because it was rainy and cold, they built a fire and welcomed all of us. ³Paul gathered a bunch of dry sticks and put them on the fire. As he did, a poisonous snake,

viper, driven out by the heat, fastened itself on his hand. [4]When the natives saw the creature hanging from his hand, they said to one another, "This man must be a murderer; though he has escaped from the sea, justice has not allowed him to live." [5]He, however, shook off the creature into the fire and suffered no harm. [6]They were expecting him to swell up or drop dead, but after they had waited a long time and saw that nothing unusual had happened to him, they changed their minds and began to say that he was a god.

[7]Now in the neighborhood of that place were lands belonging to the leading man of the island, named Publius, who received us and entertained us hospitably for three days. [8]It so happened that the father of Publius lay sick in bed with fever and dysentery. **Paul visited him and cured him by praying and putting his hands on him.** [9]After this happened, the rest of the people on the island who had diseases also came and were cured. [10]They bestowed many honors on us, and when we were about to sail, they put on board all the provisions we needed.

driven out by the heat, latched on to his hand. [4]When the islanders saw the snake hanging from his hand, they said to each other, "This man must be a murderer! He was rescued from the sea, but the goddess Justice hasn't let him live!" [5]Paul shook the snake into the fire and suffered no harm. [6]They expected him to swell up with fever or suddenly drop dead. After waiting a long time and seeing nothing unusual happen to him, they changed their minds and began to claim that he was a god.

[7]Publius, the island's most prominent person, owned a large estate in that area. He welcomed us warmly into his home as his guests for three days. [8]Publius' father was bedridden, sick with a fever and dysentery. **Paul went to see him and prayed. He placed his hand on him and healed him.** [9]Once this happened, the rest of the sick on the island came to him and were healed. [10]They honored us in many ways. When we were getting ready to sail again, they supplied us with what we needed.

UNDERSTANDING THE SCRIPTURE

Acts 28:1. The Greek manuscripts of Acts disagree over the name of the island on which Paul and his company arrived. The earliest and best manuscripts record that they landed on "Melita," a small group of islands south of Sicily known today as Malta. The name "Malta" also is applied to the largest of those islands. Some copyists of Greek manuscripts, perhaps unfamiliar with Malta, substituted "Melitene," an island off the coast of modern-day Croatia in the northern Adriatic Sea. It sometimes was confused with Malta in ancient sources. Most scholars agree that Malta was the site of the shipwreck.

Acts 28:2-6. Not only did Paul and his

company find safety on Malta after the shipwreck, they also found a gracious people who welcomed them. Luke mentions "we" and "us" several times in his narrative, indicating his personal experience with the islanders' welcome, but interestingly, the word he applies to the "natives" is correctly reflected in the King James Version's "barbarous people" (28:2) or "barbarians" (28:4), designations often applied by the Greeks to less-civilized foreigners. The "unusual kindness" (28:2) implies extraordinary hospitality on the part of the Maltese. With 276 survivors from the ship (27:37), the care for this number of people was not a small gesture of hospitality. The provision of a fire large enough to warm this crowd of people from the rain and the cold required a good bit of firewood. Paul chose to assist in gathering wood for the fire and gathered a bundle of sticks (the Greek word implies sticks that could be used for roasting food over a fire and thus would be about the size of snakes). As the bundle was being placed on the fire, a viper (adder or similar kind of poisonous snake) hidden in the bundle attached itself to Paul's hand. The natives, perhaps noting the prisoners' chains or otherwise knowing that the ship had been transporting prisoners, assumed that the snakebite was an evil omen and that Paul must have been justly stricken because he was guilty of some notorious crime like murder. The New International Version and Common English Bible capitalize the word "Justice" (28:4), associating it with the personification of justice as a pagan goddess. The islanders expected the injury to become inflamed and for Paul to swell up or drop dead. Paul and every one of his shipmates already had miraculously survived the shipwreck. Now, when nothing happened as a result of the snakebite, the Maltese superstitiously assumed that Paul held greater powers than Justice and must be some kind of god himself. The verb translated "changed their minds" is not the expression used in the New Testament for repentance. The word Luke employed here literally means to "cast behind" or "throw over" an opinion.

Acts 28:7. Publius—whom Acts identifies as the first, foremost, chief, or leading man on the island of Malta—owned land near the site of the shipwreck. His name is Latin and means "public." The name is one of a small group of common forenames found in the culture of ancient Rome, but information is lacking for determining whether his office was a local or a Roman one. The "us" in verse 7 certainly included Paul and Luke, but it seems unlikely that all the passengers, soldiers, and prisoners from the boat were included in the hospitable reception pro-

vided by Publius. Julius, the centurion overseeing Paul's transport to Rome, likely gave Paul similar freedoms in Malta that he had in Sidon (Acts 27:3). Paul's role in saving all the passengers on the ship and the reverence shown him by the Maltese would seem to justify Julius's confidence in Paul. The word translated "entertained" more properly applies to supplying lodging, and "hospitably" implies a mind disposed toward *philos*, brotherly love and affection. "Three days" is a frequently recurring length of time in the Bible used to denote a reasonable span for a stay—neither short nor long. It conveys Paul's status as an honored guest.

Acts 28:8-9. Paul discovered during his visit that Publius's father was with his son and was bedridden with an illness involving fever and dysentery. The English word "dysentery" derives directly from the Greek word used here, and the technical designation may have been noted by Luke, a physician. It involved abdominal pain with frequent and intense diarrhea. When Paul visited with Publius's father, he prayed and placed his hands on the ill man. Publius's father was healed. The Scriptures have a long tradition that combine hands, prayer, Holy Spirit, and healing (see "Prayer, the Laying on of Hands, and Healing" in the Interpreting the Scripture section that follows). As a result of this healing, word quickly spread about what had happened. Luke doesn't provide a count but simply says that "the rest of the sick on the island came and were cured" (28:9 NIV). This implies that the sick were coming *to Paul* rather than to Publius's home. Acts 28:11 records that Paul stayed at least three months on Malta, awaiting the passing of winter and the opening of the spring shipping season. The healings likely continued during those months after Paul's visit with Publius.

Acts 28:10. Luke simply noted that the Maltese "bestowed many honors on us" (literally, "honored us with many honors"), but the associated Greek words "honor" and "honored" can have a range of meanings. The words can imply the showing of honor or respect (see John 4:44; Romans 12:10; 13:7; 1 Timothy 6:1; Hebrews 3:3), can reflect the value or price of something ("blood money," literally "price of blood" in Matthew 27:6; "sum" in Acts 7:16; "price" in 1 Corinthians 6:20; "precious" in 1 Peter 2:7), can designate the proceeds of a sale (Acts 4:34; 5:2), or can even indicate payment for services (1 Timothy 5:17-18). The furnishing of supplies when Paul, Luke, and their party set sail may have been a new aspect of "honoring" or may be continued support that the Maltese had provided during Paul's three months on Malta.

INTERPRETING THE SCRIPTURE

Hospitality and the Welcoming of Strangers

The word "stranger" obviously comes from the word "strange." In its broadest application, "strange" refers to things that are unfamiliar because they either are previously unknown to us or are uncommon in our experience. While "strange" can be used to describe something that is peculiar or odd, generally it refers to something that lies outside our knowledge or experience. A foundational issue in approaching how we relate to strangers is to recognize that fundamentally our lack of knowledge and experience is the issue. We are the ones who establish the criteria by which we characterize something as strange. "Strangeness" is not something inherent in the stranger; it is a perception within us.

When we go to a foreign country and encounter a new culture, we don't suddenly become strange. We are the same people we were in our homeland. We may be strangers to the natives, and their culture may be strange to us, but cultures and people are not strange in their own settings. The only way to bridge cultural gaps is to remove the strangeness that comes from our lack of knowledge and experience.

The Scriptures and many cultures prescribe hospitality as the avenue for addressing the strangeness that characterizes relationships with foreigners and other strangers. Hospitality opens the door for experiencing others, learning about them and their culture, and finding the common elements within humanity that make us a larger family together. Frequently, people whose culture, practices, and language seem "barbarous" to us upon our first encounter with them prove to be kind, hospitable, and generous people whose welcoming embrace quickly removes all barriers of strangeness. Often strangers in our midst are suspiciously perceived as unwanted intruders or even dangerous threats to our safety and security. If we would provide the warm, welcoming, generous hospitality shown by the Maltese toward Paul and his companions, perhaps we would discover that these strangers can bring healing to many of our ills.

Job affirmed that "the stranger has not lodged in the street; I have opened my doors to the traveler" (Job 31:32). Jesus spoke of those "blessed by my Father" who welcome the stranger and invite him in (Matthew 25:34-35 NIV). The Letter to the Hebrews, reflecting the example of Abraham in Genesis 18:1-8, admonished readers: "Do not neglect to show hospitality to strangers, for by doing that some have entertained angels without knowing it" (Hebrews 13:2). The Maltese demonstrated this kind of genuine hospitality naturally and without prompting. If only we could match their example—even with the prompting we have from our Lord. May our motto become the words of William Butler Yeats, "There are no strangers here; Only friends you haven't met yet."

Prayer, the Laying on of Hands, and Healing

Many of us are uncomfortable dealing with the spiritual powers associated with prayer or the healing power involved in the laying on of hands. In a day of advanced medical science and hand sanitizer, the presence and power of the Holy Spirit and significance of touch might seem quaint concepts. I once heard Tony Campolo tell of anointing a man with oil and praying for his healing. A few weeks later the man's wife called to tell Tony that the man had died. Feeling like a failure in the healing department, Tony began to apologize, but the woman interrupted him, "Oh, don't apologize. The last few weeks were the best of our lives. All of the anger and resentment he had harbored for years were gone. He *was* healed."

The Bible reveals an array of connections between prayer and the hands, blessing and healing, and the presence and power of the Holy Spirit. Prayer has been a central practice throughout Judeo-Christian history. Hands often were symbols of power. Uplifted or outstretched hands are associated with prayer. The laying on of hands is connected with harming, seizing, or arresting someone, but one of the earliest references in the Bible to laying on hands reflects the transfer of the guilt of sin to a sacrificial animal (Exodus 29:10). Hands also conferred blessings (Genesis 48:14; Matthew 19:13) and were involved in healing (Luke 4:40; 13:13), ordaining (Acts 6:6), commissioning (Acts 13:3), and conveying the Holy Spirit (Acts 8:17; 19:6).

The remarkable thing about these and other examples of the power of prayer and touch is the lack of an established formula by which the remarkable results were achieved. Too often today we see a kind of holy formula that involves dramatic pleading with God through prayer, dramatic strikes with the hands, and solemn beseeching for the Holy Spirit to give evidences of power by healing, by charismatic tongues, or by some remarkable miracle. Too often the evangelist, faith healer, or charismatic preacher receives more credit for the results than does God. Today we do not see many examples like Matthew 9:23-25 or Acts 9:39-40, where healing was accomplished outside the limelight.

The Holy Spirit works in mysterious ways, and we must remember that prayers are answered in different ways; people are healed in different ways; people are anointed with new visions, new commissions, and new purposes. When the Holy Spirit is present in the prayer or in the touch, we cannot anticipate what transformations will be wrought through God's power.

Providing What Is Needed

The generosity of the Maltese is seen both in the hospitality shown toward Paul and his fellow travelers after the shipwreck and in their furnishing supplies for their continued journey to Rome. Luke does not specify what supplies they provided—the original Greek is even less specific than the English translations. It states only two things: (1) the Maltese put on board (2) what was needed.

We often face the problem of finding appropriate gifts. Because so many of us have everything we need, giving gifts deals with novelty rather than necessity. Most of our giving is occasional, based on events like birthdays, anniversaries, and holidays. With necessities fully met, gifts tend to focus on wants, desires, and wishes rather than on needs. What needs we have tend to be intangible, involving time and attention rather than physical objects, but our gift-giving culture insists that we find some physical object that symbolizes our goodwill for our friends.

The Maltese were doubly effective in their giving. After the shipwreck, when all had been lost, they provided the victims with the basic necessities of lodging and food. When the shipwrecked group was ready to resume its journey, the Maltese anticipated their needs and provided exactly what they needed for the next stage in their journey.

I currently serve in our church's benevolence program in addressing the needs in our community. The aid we provide is significant, but we often ask ourselves if we are providing what really is needed by these families. We can help pay an electric bill or provide a voucher to purchase food, and those are good things to do, but the question still haunts me: Are we providing what they really need for the next stage in their journey through life? When bills have been paid, when food and clothing have been provided, when prescriptions have been filled, when transportation needs have been addressed, are there still not intangible needs and spiritual needs that will require more of our time and attention—if we are to provide what they *truly* need?

SHARING THE SCRIPTURE

Preparing Our Hearts

Explore this week's devotional reading, found in Ezekiel 34:11-16. Here we see God as the good shepherd of the flock. Notice the verbs used in verses 12-16 to show how God cares for the flock. One of those verbs is "rescue." We will see in today's Bible lesson how God rescues and cares for Paul and the company of people shipwrecked on the island of Malta. Just as God tends the flock, so the residents of Malta helped those rescued from the damaged ship. Paul, in turn, helped the people by healing the sick through the power of God. Consider: Who have you helped within the past few days? How did your assistance reflect God's care?

Pray that you and the adult students will offer hospitality to strangers, particularly those in need.

Preparing Our Minds

Study the background Scripture and the lesson Scripture, both of which are from Acts 28:1-10.

Consider this question as you prepare the lesson: *What conclusions might others draw about our character from observing our actions in difficult circumstances?*

Write on newsprint:
❑ information for next week's lesson, found under "Continue the Journey."
❑ activities for further spiritual growth in "Continue the Journey."

Review the "Introduction," "The Big Picture," "Close-up," and "Faith in Action." Consider how you will use this additional information, which immediately precedes the first lesson.

LEADING THE CLASS

(1) Gather to Learn

❖ Greet the class members. Introduce any guests and help them feel at home.

❖ Pray that those who have come today will be open to finding ways to help others.

❖ Read this information as reported by ABC News: **Kristoffer Nyborg, a twenty-four-year-old working at a Norwegian Labour party camp on Utoya island, responded heroically when a gunman, posing as a police officer, opened fire on the teen campers. The "officer" was**

Anders Breivik, who allegedly attacked the youth because he considered the Labour Party's views treasonous. Seeing the massacre unfolding, Nyborg made a "snap decision" to order about thirty campers to swim from the island to the shore. The "officer" turned his weapon on the fleeing swimmers. Although all had feared for their lives, Nyborg and three campers made it to the shore. At least one perished in the water, and others became too tired and returned to the island. A total of sixty-eight people died in this rampage.

❖ Ask: What conclusions might you draw about Kristoffer Nyborg's character, based on his response to this life-threatening situation?

❖ Read aloud today's focus statement: **Often we can tell something about the character of people by observing how they respond in difficult situations. What conclusions might others draw from observing our actions? The people of Malta recognized something extraordinary about Paul because through his faith in Christ a man was healed.**

(2) Goal 1: Connect Paul's Ministry and the Hospitality He Received in Malta

❖ Select a volunteer to read Acts 28:1-10.
❖ Ask these questions:
  (1) **What did you learn about the people of Malta?** (Use information from "Hospitality and the Welcoming of Strangers" in Interpreting the Scripture to discuss the importance of showing hospitality to those who are unfamiliar to us.)
  (2) **What did you learn about Paul?** (Add to the discussion that this story makes no mention of Paul preaching. Instead, he shares the gospel by means of praying for the sick and laying hands on them. As a result, people were cured. See "Prayer, the Laying on of Hands,

and Healing" in Interpreting the Scripture.)
  (3) **How did the people of Malta respond to Paul?** (Look especially at verses 4-6 and 8-10 to see how their response changed. Also refer to "Providing What Is Needed" in Interpreting the Scripture to see how the people tried to help Paul.)

(3) Goal 2: Express Awe Over God's Extraordinary Action in the Learners' Lives

❖ Distribute paper and pencils. Invite the adults to hold the paper horizontally and draw a straight line across the middle. On the left side of the line, ask them to put the year of their birth, and on the right, 2012. Encourage them to recall events in their lives that they believe were truly the work of God. Make a brief note about each of these events at the place along the timeline that approximates the date.

❖ Form groups of three or four. Invite the learners to talk in their groups about these important times in their lives and express their response to God's gracious action.

❖ Bring everyone together and talk for a few moments about any responses the groups seemed to have in common.

(4) Goal 3: Demonstrate the Learners' Faith by Ministering to the Needs of Others

❖ Point out that people of Malta ministered to Paul and the other shipwreck survivors, and he later ministered to them by curing their diseases.

❖ Challenge the adults to think about a way that they could minister to others in need. Post a sheet of newsprint on which you will list their ideas. Suggest that they think about specific needs in their community. Here are several ideas:
  ■ For a community with many senior citizens: Could the church offer daytime activities and a meal? Or

pair a senior with a member of the class who would make a daily call to check in? Or offer health services, such as blood pressure screening, drivers to transport seniors to medical appointments, or people who could assist seniors in filling out medical forms?

■ For a community with many college students: Could the church offer a coffeehouse or other informal gathering place? Would some members be willing to host a holiday meal for a student who was unable to return home? Or offer a clean, affordable place to live in a member's home?

■ For a community with many young children: Could the church offer a babysitting service for an occasional Parents' Night Out? Does the church offer Sunday school, vacation Bible school, and other opportunities for children to experience the love of Christ?

❖ Encourage the group to decide on one or two projects to help others in need.

(5) Continue the Journey

❖ Pray that today's participants will see in Paul and the people of Malta examples of people who are willing to reach out and share whatever they have available.

❖ Read aloud this preparation for next week's lesson. You may also want to post it on newsprint for the students to copy.

■ **Title: Paul Evangelizes in Rome**
■ **Background Scripture: Acts 28:16-31**
■ **Lesson Scripture: Acts 28:23-31**

■ **Focus of the Lesson: One paradox of human nature is that even when we have good news to share, some will ignore or reject it. What will we do when people refuse to listen? Paul persevered in faith, preaching the gospel and bringing salvation to those who would listen, even though there were many who refused to believe in the Lord Jesus Christ.**

❖ Post these three activities related to this week's session on newsprint for the students to copy. Challenge the adults to grow spiritually by completing one or more of them.

(1) **Offer to help a new neighbor or church member. Even simple things, such as recommending a restaurant or doctor, can go a long way toward helping a newcomer feel at home. Invite this person to enjoy a meal with you.**

(2) **Pray for someone who needs healing. Recognize that a cure may or may not come, but healing enables reconciliation and an opportunity to tend to unfinished business.**

(3) **Help provide provisions for those in need by contributing to your church's food pantry.**

❖ Sing or read aloud "By Gracious Powers."

❖ Conclude today's session by leading the class in this benediction, adapted from the key verses for September 16 from Hebrews 12:1-2: **Let us go forth to run with perseverance the race that is set before us, looking to Jesus the pioneer and perfecter of our faith.**

UNIT 3: WHERE DOES FAITH TAKE US?

PAUL EVANGELIZES IN ROME

PREVIEWING THE LESSON

Lesson Scripture: Acts 28:23-31
Background Scripture: Acts 28:16-31
Key Verse: Acts 28:28

Focus of the Lesson:
One paradox of human nature is that even when we have good news to share, some will ignore or reject it. What will we do when people refuse to listen? Paul persevered in faith, preaching the gospel and bringing salvation to those who would listen, even though there were many who refused to believe in the Lord Jesus Christ.

Goals for the Learners:
(1) to understand Paul's persistence in making an evangelistic witness.
(2) to reflect on times when they could affirm their belief in Christ and times when they had doubts.
(3) to continue to express their faith in Christ even when some refuse to listen.

Pronunciation Guide:
Puteoli (pyoo tee' oh lee)

Supplies:
Bibles, newsprint and marker, paper and pencils, hymnals

READING THE SCRIPTURE

NRSV
Lesson Scripture: Acts 28:23-31

23After they [local Jewish leaders in Rome] had set a day to meet with him [Paul], they came to him at his lodgings in great numbers. From morning until evening he explained the matter to them, testifying to the kingdom of God and trying to convince

CEB
Lesson Scripture: Acts 28:23-31

23On the day scheduled for this purpose, many people came to the place where he was staying. From morning until evening, he explained and testified concerning God's kingdom and tried to convince them about Jesus through appealing to the Law of them about Jesus both from the law of Moses and from the prophets. 24Some were convinced by what he had said, while others refused to believe. 25So they disagreed with each other; and as they were leaving, Paul made one further statement: "The Holy Spirit was right in saying to your ancestors through the prophet Isaiah,

26 'Go to this people and say,
You will indeed listen, but never
    understand,
and you will indeed look, but
    never perceive.
27 For this people's heart has grown dull,
    and their ears are hard of hearing,
    and they have shut their eyes;
    so that they might not look with
      their eyes,
    and listen with their ears,
and understand with their heart and
    turn—
and I would heal them.'
28Let it be known to you then that this salvation of God has been sent to the Gentiles; they will listen."

30He lived there two whole years at his own expense and welcomed all who came to him, 31proclaiming the kingdom of God and teaching about the Lord Jesus Christ with all boldness and without hindrance.

Moses and the Prophets. 24Some were persuaded by what he said, but others refused to believe. 25They disagreed with each other and were starting to leave when Paul made one more statement. "The Holy Spirit spoke correctly when he said to your ancestors through Isaiah the prophet,

26Go to this people and say:
 You will hear, to be sure,
  but never understand;
  and you will certainly see but never
    recognize what you are seeing.
27This people's senses have become calloused,
  and they've become hard of hearing,
  and they've shut their eyes
    so that they won't see with their eyes
    or hear with their ears
    or understand with their minds,
      and change their hearts and lives
        that I may heal them.
28"Therefore, be certain of this: God's salvation has been sent to the Gentiles. They will listen!"

30Paul lived in his own rented quarters for two full years and welcomed everyone who came to see him. 31Unhindered and with complete confidence, he continued to preach God's kingdom and to teach about the Lord Jesus Christ.

UNDERSTANDING THE SCRIPTURE

Acts 28:16. Departing from Malta, Paul and his fellow travelers continued their journey to Rome. At Puteoli, the major seaport for shipping to and from Rome, Paul was welcomed by fellow believers (28:13-14). The seven-day visit with these Christians demonstrates again the benevolent treatment Paul received from his guards. Word of Paul's arrival spread to believers in Rome (about 150 miles away). Some Roman believers traveled more than forty miles to greet Paul at the Forum of

Appius, and others connected with him at a layover on the road to Rome called "Three Taverns." Paul thanked God for these believers and was encouraged by their support. Upon arriving in Rome, Paul was not imprisoned. Instead, he was able to reside in private housing under the guard of one soldier (compare 28:30).

Acts 28:17-22. Paul immediately set out to establish contact with the Jewish community in Rome. Three days after arriving he called together the foremost leaders of the Jews.

"Leaders of the Jews" (28:17) is the same designation used in Acts 25:2 of the group in Jerusalem that (along with the chief priests) first made charges against Paul. Paul may have hoped that support from this group in Rome would offset the charges made by their Palestinian equals and that the charges against him would be dropped. By first addressing them as "brothers" and the Jews as "our people," Paul sought to establish an empathetic relationship with them. In defending himself, Paul did not make direct reference to the charges against him. Instead he claimed innocence for any action "against our people" or breach of Jewish "customs"—the latter being a broad term that applied both to legal prescriptions and traditional practices. In Acts 25:8, Paul had denied before the Roman tribunal any offense against the law, the Temple, or the emperor. The subtlety of Paul's argument is that fundamental differences existed within Judaism about what was prescribed by divine law and what comprised traditional practices. By focusing on these divisive matters, Paul divided his opposition and made them appear to be more interested in squabbling over minor points of religious differences than on legal issues that could appropriately be decided by Roman authorities. Such differences of religious opinion certainly would not be grounds for "the death penalty" (28:18). Paul pointed out that the Romans wanted to release him, but the Jewish leaders objected. Therefore, Paul was "forced" (28:19 NASB) to appeal to Caesar. Paul explained that his detention ultimately was for "the sake of the hope of Israel" (28:20). The Jewish leaders obviously saw in Paul's statement some connection with "this sect . . . that everywhere . . . is spoken against" (Acts 28:22). No communication about Paul had been received from Judea, however; and no one coming to Rome from Judea had reported anything against Paul. The Jewish leaders wanted to hear more of what Paul had to say, and they set a date to meet with him again.

Acts 28:23-29. When the Jewish leaders returned to meet with Paul at his lodging, a larger number came. Paul gave a lengthy explanation to this assemblage that lasted from morning until night. Luke summarized the focus of Paul's testimony in two areas: the kingdom of God and the crucial role of Jesus. The kingdom of God is widely recognized as a central theme in the teachings of Jesus, and the Gospels give much attention to the kingdom and to the role Jesus played in the kingdom. References to the kingdom in Paul's writings, however, tend to focus more intently on two aspects of the kingdom: (1) the nature of the kingdom itself (Romans 14:17; 1 Corinthians 4:20; 15:24, 50); and (2) the moral qualities of the kingdom and their implications for living as Christians in the world (1 Corinthians 6:9-10; Galatians 5:19-21; Ephesians 5:5; 1 Thessalonians 2:12; 2 Timothy 4:1). The focus of Paul's testimony on this occasion closely parallels much of what we see in the Gospels; and since Luke wrote both the Gospel and Acts, we can assume that his focus had some similarity in both. In the Gospel of Luke, 89 percent of the references to "kingdom" are recorded as spoken by Jesus. Most of the Jewish leaders would have had little difficulty in accepting the concept of the kingdom of God. They too were looking for a Messiah who would come and establish that kingdom. They would have had trouble, however, associating Jesus with that kingdom-founding Messiah. Jesus was the one whom the previous generation of Jewish leaders by political pressure had sent to a Roman cross. To counteract that historical influence, Paul followed the example of the Gospel writers (and Matthew in particular) who used references "both from the law of Moses and from the prophets" (28:23) to try to convince them that Jesus was the promised Messiah, the one who was establishing God's kingdom on earth as it was in heaven. Some Jewish leaders were convinced by Paul's argument, but others were not. In the face of that stalemate, Paul cited a prophecy from Isaiah 6:9-10 (which also is cited at least in part by all four Gospel writers—Matthew 13:14-15; Mark 4:12; Luke 8:10; John 12:40). Paul's concluding statement in Acts 28:28 extends sentiments similar to those found in Psalms 67:2; 98:3; Luke 3:6; and Acts 13:46; 18:6. Note that verse 29 is not found in many of the oldest and best manuscripts.

Acts 28:30-31. Luke concluded the Book of Acts rather quickly and abruptly, perhaps because the story of the reception of the gospel among the nations is a story that is still unfolding. Paul's story is left unfinished after the reference to "two whole years" in Rome. Traditions disagree over whether Paul was released, went to Spain, and returned to Rome and martyrdom, or whether he was martyred after the two years in Rome. In another sense, however, the story was concluded. Paul's final actions in Acts had been the goal of his life from that day on the Damascus road when he encountered the Lord—"proclaiming the kingdom of God" and "teaching about the Lord Jesus Christ" (28:31). The last words in the Greek text are thought by many to have been the theme of Luke's account in Acts. Paul's preaching and teaching were accomplished "with all boldness without hindrance."

INTERPRETING THE SCRIPTURE

The Unhindered Gospel

New Testament scholar Dr. Frank Stagg frequently focused on the significant role that the last word in the Greek text of Acts (translated literally as "unhinderedly") plays in understanding the primary purpose of Luke's work. He wrote *The Book of Acts: The Early Struggle for an Unhindered Gospel* to point out how this adverb (used only once in the New Testament and awkwardly placed at the end of Luke's two-volume history) summarizes the story.

As we read Acts, we see how barrier after barrier fell as the gospel spread from Jerusalem to Rome. The barrier of languages fell in chapters 2 and 6. The barrier between Samaritan and Jew crumbled in chapter 8, as did the barrier between Jews and God-fearing Gentiles. Next a Roman centurion and his family were converted (Acts 10), and the barriers separating Jews and Gentiles began to fall. By the conclusion of the Jerusalem Conference in Acts 15, the door for Gentiles into the kingdom was wide open. Progress was not always without difficulty, and setbacks arose time after time, but the goal of an unhindered gospel being proclaimed boldly "to the ends of the earth" (Acts 1:8) was achieved symbolically in Rome.

Of course, barriers still exist. In many places today, those who spread the good news must do so in quiet ways. Boldness and unhindered proclamation are not possible without violent consequences. But the barriers we face are not always barriers outside us. In our secularized society, many of us are intimidated by unflattering labels that are attached to faithful witnesses. We allow fear, the desire for acceptance, and the inclination to be one of the gang to conform us to the world's mold. We don't want to be too abrasive or to offend others, so we keep quiet and hide the penetrating light of the gospel under a bushel basket (Matthew 5:15).

Paul's example challenges us to ask, "How far am I willing to go to share the gospel with others?" In a day without planes, trains, and automobiles, Paul traveled more widely than many people today. He wanted to carry the good news about Christ to places where the gospel had never been proclaimed. Read 2 Corinthians 11:16–12:10 to grasp the constant challenges that Paul had faced in his service for Christ—the "weaknesses, insults, hardships, persecutions, and calamities" (12:10) he endured for the sake of Christ. Then imagine what he must have felt when suddenly the confinement of a jail cell or a house arrest prevented his mobility, limited his freedom, and restricted his interactions with the lost Gentiles to whom Christ had called him to witness. One who had been commissioned to "go into all the world and proclaim the good news to the whole creation" (compare Mark 16:15) found that he could do no more than welcome "all who came to him" (Acts 28:30). Yet Paul discovered in those adverse circumstances he still could speak boldly and without hindrance.

What artificial barriers have you allowed to restrict and restrain the gospel? What fears and apprehensions have you allowed to rob your witness of boldness? The very things that hindered the gospel in Paul's day still confront us. May Paul's example inspire us to proclaim the kingdom of God and teach about the Lord Jesus Christ with all boldness and without hindrance!

Receiving Good News

People respond to good news in different ways. Some shout for joy; others cry. Some faint; others jump up and down. Some laugh; some cry. Some respond with disbelief, insisting on proof that the good news is true. Sometimes others try to take some of the excitement out of the good news and create a sense of resentment, but the news is still good.

Because of our assumption that good news is good, we sometimes have unreasonable expectations about the reception of the gospel. If the gospel is good news, shouldn't everyone accept it, welcome it, and embrace it? The answer is no, and Jesus frequently warned his disciples about the wide ranges of response they could expect when they shared the good news. "If anyone will not welcome you or listen to your words," Jesus said, "shake off the dust from your feet as you leave that house or town" (Matthew 10:14). Perhaps the best description of the different responses we can expect in "sowing the seed of the gospel" is found in Jesus' parable of the sower (Matthew 13:1-9; Mark 4:1-9; Luke 8:4-8). Some prefer to call this the parable of the soils, for receptivity to the seed ultimately is a characteristic of the soil.

Everyone will not respond to the good news in the same way. We might think that a powerful witness like Paul would bat a thousand in sharing the good news, but the reception of the Jewish leaders shows that is not the case. The fault was not in Paul, nor was it in the good news he shared. The fault—whether hardness of heart, preconceived notions, pride, or stubbornness— finally rests with the ones who hear the good news. Matthew 13:13 summarizes the matter this way: "Seeing they do not perceive, and hearing they do not listen, nor do they understand." Our job is to share the good news, and we, like Paul, must leave the way it is received in the hands of God.

The Old, Old Story

Most scholars see the kingdom of God as the central element in Jesus' teaching. Some more skeptical scholars have proposed that Paul, who never met Jesus in the flesh, took Christianity in a different direction. The problem with that conclusion is that we do not possess much evidence of Paul's regular teaching. Most of what we know comes from letters he sent to churches that were facing particular problems in unique circumstances. We do not have a theological textbook written by Paul or a book of his sermons. Luke, however, a companion of Paul and a participant in much of his ministry, does give us a summary that shows a close alignment between the messages of Paul and Jesus.

The references to "we" in the Book of Acts are evidence of Luke's eyewitness presence in the situations he was describing. In that light, the summary that Luke provided of Paul's witness to the Jewish leaders in Rome is quite revealing. Earlier, Luke had connected Paul with "the law" and "the temple" (25:8), with support for the "customs" of his Jewish ancestors (28:17), with "the prophets and Moses" (26:22), and with the entire messianic tradition of the Old Testament ("the hope of Israel" [28:20]). Most significantly, however, when Luke described Paul's all-day exchange with the Jewish leaders, Paul's testimony focused on "the kingdom of God" as he tried "to convince them about Jesus both from the law of Moses and from the prophets" (28:23). That is a strong continuity with Jesus and his message.

We stand in that same biblical tradition by proclaiming Jesus and the reign of God in our midst. Our message, testimony, and witness today continue to focus on what the gospel songwriter Katherine Hankey called "the old, old story, of Jesus and His love."

SHARING THE SCRIPTURE

Preparing Our Hearts

Explore this week's devotional reading, found in Deuteronomy 4:32-40. This book, traditionally attributed to Moses, recounts the journey and uniqueness of Israel up until just prior to their entry into the Promised Land. They are reminded that although God created all people, Israel has a special purpose: to lead people to God. As you read this passage, think about your own relationship with God. What message do you have to share with others about how God has worked in your life? Who needs to hear your story today?

Pray that you and the adult students will recognize your own unique relationship with God and share that good news with others.

Preparing Our Minds

Study the background Scripture from Acts 28:16-31 and the lesson Scripture from Acts 28:23-31.

Consider this question as you prepare the lesson: *What will we do when people refuse to listen?*

Write on newsprint:
❏ information for next week's lesson, found under "Continue the Journey."
❏ activities for further spiritual growth in "Continue the Journey."

Review the "Introduction," "The Big Picture," "Close-up," and "Faith in Action." Consider how you will use this additional information, which immediately precedes the first lesson.

Prepare a brief lecture from Understanding the Scripture, Acts 28:16, 17-22 to present for "Understand Paul's Persistence in Making an Evangelistic Witness."

LEADING THE CLASS

(1) Gather to Learn

❖ Greet the class members. Introduce any guests and help them to feel at home.

❖ Pray that the adults who have come today will be ready to listen to good news with open hearts and minds.

❖ Read this information taken from a 2004 *Business Week* interview with Fred Smith, founder of FedEx: **The genesis of this multibillion-dollar business came from a college term paper in which Smith** pointed out the need for a new system of logistics. Although he didn't act on the idea immediately, when he did try to get venture capital from Wall Street, it was an uphill battle. Potential investors were leery of a business that had to develop both a product and a market. But from its beginnings with eight planes and thirty-five to forty cities, FedEx has become a leader in "just in time" delivery, first focused on inventory parts and later adding documents.

❖ Ask: Fred Smith certainly had good, innovative ideas to share with Wall Street, but investors at first had no interest in what proved to be a lucrative investment. Why do you think even knowledgeable people reject potentially good news?

❖ Read aloud today's focus statement: **One paradox of human nature is that even when we have good news to share, some will ignore or reject it. What will we do when people refuse to listen? Paul persevered in faith, preaching the gospel and bringing salvation to those who would listen, even though there were many who refused to believe in the Lord Jesus Christ.**

(2) Goal 1: Understand Paul's Persistence in Making an Evangelistic Witness

❖ Present the lecture you have prepared from the background Scripture (Acts 28:16-22) to set the stage for today's lesson.

❖ Choose three volunteers to read Acts 28:23-31: a narrator, Paul, and one of the Jewish leaders in Rome.

❖ Discuss these questions. Add information from Understanding the Scripture as appropriate.

　(1) **What explanation does Paul give for his imprisonment?**

　(2) **How do the local Jewish leaders in Rome respond to Paul?**

　(3) **Look at verse 23. What kinds of arguments might you imagine Paul making in order to convince the leaders about Jesus?**

　(4) **Suppose you had been one who had "refused to believe" (28:24). How might you have responded to Paul's quotation from Isaiah 6:9-10 in verses 26-27?**

　(5) **Once the leaders had departed from Paul, what might they have said to one another?**

　(6) **What does Paul's willingness to boldly proclaim the gospel, even as he is under house arrest, suggest to the church today?**

(3) Goal 2: Reflect on Times When the Learners Could Affirm Their Belief in Christ and Times When They Had Doubts

❖ Form groups of three or four. Challenge the adults to talk with one another about times when they had doubts about their faith. What triggered these doubts? Was there some crisis that precipitated them? How were they able to resolve these doubts in order to continue to affirm their faith in Christ?

❖ Word of caution: Doubts and questions are normal and necessary components of spiritual growth. Make sure that the groups do not make people feel as if they are somehow "second-class" Christians because they dared to question their faith. Their doubts and questions should be affirmed.

(4) Goal 3: Continue to Express the Learners' Faith in Christ Even When Some Refuse to Listen

❖ Choose three volunteers to role-play a scenario in which one person tries to talk with the other two about Christ. Person A will be the Christian, Person B will listen with great interest and acceptance, and Person C will listen but refuse to accept Person A's witness. Before you begin, encourage Person A to continue to express his or her faith in Christ, regardless of responses from the two who are listening.

❖ Debrief the role-play by discussing the following questions:

(1) **How did the Christian in the group handle the responses of the two listeners?**

(2) **Based on your own experience, is there anything else Person A could have said or done that might have made a difference in Person C's response?**

(3) **What ideas are useful for us to keep in mind when people do not choose to respond favorably to our witness?** (Remember that not everyone who heard Jesus chose to follow him. Not everyone who heard the good news from Paul and other disciples chose to follow Jesus. Our witness can plant the seeds, but God provides the water and the increase. We are called to be faithful, but that does not necessarily mean that we will be successful.)

(5) Continue the Journey

❖ Pray that the learners will go forth today to spread the good news.

❖ Read aloud this preparation for next week's lesson. You may also want to post it on newsprint for the students to copy.

■ **Title: Spiritual Blessings in Jesus Christ**

■ **Background Scripture: Ephesians 1**

■ **Lesson Scripture: Ephesians 1:3-14**

■ **Focus of the Lesson: All people want to feel valued and worthy. Where can we turn to receive affir-** mation? The writer of Ephesians declares that through Jesus Christ we gain an inheritance as God's own people to become recipients of forgiveness and salvation's redemption power.

❖ Post these three activities related to this week's session on newsprint for the students to copy. Challenge the adults to grow spiritually by completing one or more of them.

(1) **Identify someone who seems to be searching for something else in life. Invite this person to join you for worship, Sunday school, or an outreach project.**

(2) **Look for opportunities this week to share something that God has done in your life. Consider these opportunities to plant seeds as ways to act as a faithful disciple of Jesus.**

(3) **Look at one or more letters written by Paul. Read portions at random. Try to get a feel for how he presents the gospel. Each person will share the gospel differently, but are there any "tips" you can get from Paul that will enable you to be a better witness?**

❖ Sing or read aloud "Go, Make of All Disciples."

❖ Conclude today's session by leading the class in this benediction, adapted from the key verses for September 16 from Hebrews 12:1-2: **Let us go forth to run with perseverance the race that is set before us, looking to Jesus the pioneer and perfecter of our faith.**

SECOND QUARTER
Jesus Is Lord

DECEMBER 2, 2012–FEBRUARY 24, 2013

"Jesus Is Lord," the title for the winter's course, proclaims an essential teaching of the early church. During this quarter we will investigate the first-century church's teachings about Christ. Based on three letters often called Paul's Prison Epistles (along with Philemon)—Ephesians, Philippians, Colossians—our study will draw us into a deeper understanding of who Christ is and what it might mean for us to imitate our Lord.

Unit 1, "Victory in Jesus," explores Ephesians across five sessions. All of these sessions emphasize the exaltation of Christ over all principalities and powers from the beginning of time to the end of time. On December 2 we turn to Ephesians 1 to consider the "Spiritual Blessings in Jesus Christ," which include our adoption as God's children. Ephesians 2–3 is the background Scripture for the session on December 9, "One in Jesus Christ," which stresses our unity, though not uniformity, within the church. We learn to live together by studying Ephesians 4:1-16 on December 16 in the session titled "Unity in the Body of Christ." The background Scriptures for December 23, John 1:1-14 and Ephesians 4:17–5:20, relate to Christmas as they help us "Live in the Light." "Christ's Love for the Church" is demonstrated in our session on December 30 from Ephesians 5:21–6:4, where we are taught to be subject to one another.

We turn to a four-session study of Philippians in Unit 2, "Exalting Christ." Here we find encouragement for believers to follow the pattern Christ laid out for us and to oppose those who are enemies of his cross so that we might live in a manner worthy of the gospel. The session for January 6 about the importance of "Proclaiming Christ," is rooted in Philippians 1:12-30. The familiar hymn within Philippians 2:1-13, which we will study on January 13, presents Jesus' two paradoxical natures in "Jesus' Humility and Exaltation." On January 20, we hear Paul's teaching in Philippians 3:1-11 about "Gaining in Jesus Christ." Unit 2 concludes on January 27 with "Stand Firm," Paul's teaching about holding on to what we have attained in Christ as described in Philippians 3:12–4:1.

A study of Colossians rounds out the quarter in Unit 3, "Imitating Jesus." In these four sessions we discover the significance of the person and work of Christ as Lord of all creation and author of our peace with God. We begin on February 3 with a confessional hymn from Colossians 1:15-20 concerning the reconciling work of Christ the Redeemer in a session called "The Supremacy of Jesus Christ." Colossians 2:6-15, which we will study on February 10, teaches that we have "Full Life in Christ." In the lesson for February 17 from Colossians 3:1-17, we are called to "put to death" (3:5) our sinful lifestyle and be "Clothed with Christ." The quarter ends on February 24 with a challenge from Colossians 4:2-17 to exercise "Spiritual Disciplines for New Life" and support one another through mentoring.

MEET OUR WRITER

DR. JERRY L. SUMNEY

Dr. Jerry L. Sumney is a member of the Society of Biblical Literature and is past president for the Southeastern Region of the Society. At the national level, he also served as the chair of the steering committee for the Theology of the Disputed Paulines Group from 1996–2001 and currently serves as the chair of the steering committee for the Disputed Paulines Section. He is also currently chair for the Pauline Epistles and Literature Section of the International Meeting of the Society of Biblical Literature. He was elected to membership in the Studiorum Novi Testamenti Societas (SNTS) in 2005.

Dr. Sumney has written six books: *The Bible: An Introduction* (2010); *Colossians: A Commentary*, New Testament Library Series (2008); *Philippians: A Greek Student's Intermediate Reader* (2007); *"Servants of Satan," "False Brothers" and Other Opponents of Paul* (1999); *Preaching Apocalyptic Texts* (co-authored with Larry Paul Jones, 1999), and *Identifying Paul's Opponents* (1990). He is editor of *The Order of the Ministry: Equipping the Saints* (2002) and coeditor of *Theology and Ethics in Paul and His Interpreters* (1996) and *Paul and Pathos* (2001). Dr. Sumney also has written more than thirty articles in journals and books. He also contributed entries to the *New Interpreter's Dictionary of the Bible* and the *Dictionary of the Later New Testament and Its Developments*, and the forthcoming *Dictionary of Scripture and Ethics*. In addition, he was a contributor to *The College Study Bible*. He is currently working on a book on Romans.

Prior to joining the faculty of Lexington Theological Seminary (LTS), where he is professor of biblical studies, he taught in the religion department at Ferrum College from 1986–97. He received his B.A. from David Lipscomb University in 1978, his M.A. from Harding University in 1982, and his Ph.D. from Southern Methodist University in 1987.

Dr. Sumney has presented papers at regional, national, and international academic conferences. He has also led numerous workshops for elders and deacons, and Bible study workshops and series, at the Lay School of Theology at LTS and at the school for licensed ministers sponsored by the Kentucky region of the Christian Church. He is the regular teacher of an adult Sunday school class in his home church, Central Christian Church (Disciples of Christ) in Lexington.

Jerry and his wife, Diane, have three daughters: Elizabeth, Victoria, and Margaret.

THE BIG PICTURE: PAUL'S PRISON EPISTLES

Philippians, Colossians, and Ephesians (along with Philemon) are known as the Prison Epistles because they all say Paul is in prison as he writes them. Although all these letters identify Paul as a prisoner, they take up quite different issues and questions.

Philippians

The Philippian church have had a history of good relations with Paul. They have been faithful to him, as well as to the gospel. Paul thanks them for their financial support and tells them about his current circumstances. Since he has the freedom to write and to profit from their gifts, some think Paul must be in Rome where Acts says he was under house arrest for two years. Others, however, think he must be in Ephesus, which is much closer to Philippi. This proximity makes the regular contacts between Paul and this church more feasible. Wherever he is, he takes this opportunity to address some problems in the Philippian church.

Paul talks more about rejoicing in Philippians than in any other letter. There is much to celebrate and be thankful for within this church, but its members also have some problems. Paul warns them not to listen to teachers who want Gentile Christians (that is, most of the people in this church) to adopt practices from the Mosaic law that Paul sees as appropriate only for Jews. Particularly, he tells Gentiles they must not be circumcised, keep the sabbath, or adhere to the Jewish food regulations. Adopting these things amounts to converting fully to Judaism. Paul believes that Gentiles must remain Gentiles as a demonstration that God is the God of the whole world, not just of Jews. While the problematic teaching has not gained adherents at Philippi, Paul still issues a stern warning not to give it a hearing.

A more pressing issue involves arguments among church leaders. In chapter 4, we discover that two leaders in this church, Euodia and Syntyche, are arguing and not getting along with each other. Paul even asks other church members to help them reach some reconciliation. (We should note in passing that these two church leaders are women, which shows that Paul is not opposed to having women as leaders in his churches.) Throughout the letter, Paul emphasizes the importance of agreeing with one another and of unity, urging the Philippians not to grumble or complain. He bases this advice on the gospel itself. He recites the liturgical material of 2:6-11 (often called the Philippian hymn) to exhort the Philippians to adopt the attitude they see in Christ. This liturgy describes how Christ accepted disadvantage, even humiliation, for the good of others. Following that example, Christians, especially leaders, should put the good of others ahead of their own good.

Paul's treatment of this problem is a good example of the way he often addresses issues in his churches. He evaluates behavior and beliefs according to whether they are consistent with the gospel message. When he tells churches to stop doing or believing something, he often shows them how that belief or behavior violates an implication of the gospel. In Philippians, he sees the argument between these church leaders as inconsistent with the way Christ acted for us. Their behavior, he argues, should conform to what we see in the coming, death, and resurrection of Christ.

The other important issue Paul addresses is persecution. Gentile converts had stopped worshiping all the gods they had previously known to begin serving the one most powerful

God. It seems that such a change should make their lives better. But their experience was just the opposite; things had gotten worse. Their neighbors were hostile, people quit doing business with them, and sometimes the civil authorities punished them—as Paul's own imprisonment demonstrates. Given this turn of events, they wonder whether it was a mistake to commit themselves to this one God. Paul's response to this common experience of early Christians is rooted in the church's eschatology, its understanding of the end time.

As was true for all of the early church, Paul believed that the coming of Christ initiated a new and final era in the way God relates to the world. This is what the New Testament means when it speaks of the "last days." It does not mean that the world will end soon (a hope that was present in the very earliest times but quickly shifted so that believers acknowledged that no one knew when God would act in that dramatic way). Rather, the death and resurrection of Christ signal that God is present in new and powerful ways. Thus, the kingdom of God has entered the world through the church that is empowered by the Spirit to bear witness to God's love and justice.

It was painfully clear to the Philippians, to Paul, and to all early Christians that the kingdom of God had not taken over the world, even if it had begun to make an appearance in the church. In fact, as Paul sees things, the powers of evil have begun a drive to squash God's efforts to reestablish relationship with humanity. This is why Christians experience persecution and disadvantage. Their persecutions are manifestations of the work of powers that oppose the purposes of God. These powers still control the political, social, and economic structures of the world. Since they control these societal and cultural structures, these self-declared enemies of God do all they can to inflict harm on the church. In this way, they hope to get Christians to renounce their faith and turn back to their old way of thinking and living.

These enemies will not, however, have the last word. The resurrection of Christ demonstrates that God is more powerful than these foes and provides assurance that God will use that power to overcome such enemies and to vindicate God's people. In the time between Christ's resurrection and the end, the church exists in a world that remains under the control of evil. Thus, it experiences opposition and persecution. The church can endure these troubles and work for God's will in the world because its life is founded on the assurance of God's final vindication.

This view of the world underlies the entire New Testament and remains important for the church. When Christians suffer inexplicably and when the effects of their good works seem too impermanent, they can remember that this world is not what God wants it to be, nor does it work the way God wants it to work. But Christ's resurrection promises that the suffering and injustice of this world cannot overcome God's will to bless God's people and to bring them into the peace and goodness God intends. So the church needs a clear eschatology (teaching about the end time) to respond to questions about suffering and the continuing injustice of the world.

Colossians

Colossians addresses a different set of issues and probably comes from a later time than Philippians. Most New Testament scholars think that Colossians was written a few years after Paul's death by someone who knew his thoughts well. There are a number of differences between Colossians and the letters that are certainly penned by the apostle. The writing style and vocabulary of Colossians are different from the undisputed letters (that is, the letters everyone agrees that Paul wrote). Among the differences in theology that many see are Colossians' description of the end-time blessings. Paul usually talks about these blessings as coming at the end of time, but Colossians envisions them as already existing in heaven. Colossians also uses the image of the "body" of Christ differently. In 1 Corinthians this body is the local congregation, but in Colossians the universal church is the body that has Christ as its head. The emphasis on the cosmic nature of Christ is also more prominent in Colossians than in the undisputed letters. Finally, Colossians has Paul say, "I fill up what is lacking in the afflictions of Christ" (1:24, my translation), or as the NRSV puts it, "I am completing what is lacking in Christ's afflictions." While Paul often sees his suffering as something that benefits the church, he never speaks of filling up something lacking in Christ's sufferings. No one of these differences is so dramatic that Paul could not have said what we find in Colossians. But most scholars are convinced that the scope of these dissimilarities makes it unlikely that he would have changed in all of these ways.

When we first hear that a book of the Bible was not written by the person it claims to be from, it is disconcerting. But ideas about writing in someone else's name were different in the first century. Throughout the ancient world, many books were written in the name of a revered figure of an earlier time. Some were written several hundred years after the person's death. The authors of these books believed they were both honoring the earlier person and extending his influence in a new time by having the honored teacher address issues that are now troubling the group.

What matters for the church is not really who wrote a book, but that God speaks through it. Since it was not the equivalent of forgery, there is no reason that a later author, using Paul's name, could not write a letter to the church giving instructions about how to understand the faith. Since this writer is convinced that he understands Paul correctly, he believes he is truly having Paul address their new questions and issues. God can work in this process as easily as God could direct Paul's own reflections on the meaning of the gospel.

Colossians was written to turn its readers from a teaching that gave excessive attention to angels. Some teachers are saying either that Christians should worship angels to gain some spiritual advantage or that worshiping with angels in visions is necessary for salvation. Either way, this teaching violates the gospel proclamation of the sufficiency of faith in Christ for salvation. Colossians emphasizes that forgiveness comes through faith in Christ. The writer emphasizes that baptism is the point at which Christians receive forgiveness to argue that they already possess what the other teaching says it will give them. In baptism they have also been identified with Christ, and since Christ is more powerful than any other beings, they do not need to worry about association with angels.

Colossians devotes significant attention to the exalted position of Christ to assure the readers that Christ is all they need for salvation. Christ is seen as the creator of these beings and the one who has defeated those who are rebellious. Christ is the medium of God's presence and power in the world, in both creation and salvation.

The eschatology of Colossians also assures the readers that they do not need anything from those angelic beings. The writer says that the blessings of salvation are already awaiting them in heaven. He also emphasizes their present possession of end-time gifts. They have already been raised with Christ and have been made full. They already have the presence of God in their lives through the Spirit. Still, the writer also points to a future full consummation of those blessings at the end.

Finally, questions about spirituality underlie much of what we find in Colossians. The teachers this letter refutes argue that all Christians must have the same dramatic spiritual experience. Colossians is not opposed to mountaintop experiences, but does argue that such experiences are not required signs of salvation or spiritual depth. God's Spirit manifests itself in various ways in different people. Thus, there is no one correct kind of spiritual experience that everyone must have.

Ephesians

Ephesians comes from a bit later time than Colossians. By the time it is penned, the author is looking back to the time of the apostles and seeing them as the foundation of the church. He moves beyond Colossians in talking about the universal church as the body of Christ by identifying the church more fully as Christ's body rather than seeing Christ as just the head of the body. These ways of thinking about the church are not necessarily contradictory, but they are different. This writer knows Colossians because he borrows several distinctive phrases from it.

When Ephesians is written, the arguments about whether Gentiles must keep those parts of the law that make Jews distinctive have diminished significantly. Rather than worrying about Gentiles accepting circumcision, sabbath keeping, and food law observance, Ephesians emphasizes the connection between the church and Judaism. By this time, a significant majority of Christians are Gentiles. This is a significant change from Paul's early days as a missionary. Then, most Christians were Jewish and the church was trying to discern how to include Gentiles. In Ephesians, the church is struggling with maintaining its connection to Judaism. Some Gentile Christians wonder why they should retain contact with the roots of the faith in Judaism, and if they should, they wonder how they might do so. Just as it had been difficult for early Christians who were Jews to let Gentiles in, now Gentiles struggle with how to keep observant Jews in. The different practices of their faith make living together as a single church difficult (for example, Jews continued to keep the sabbath, but Gentiles were forbidden to keep it). Ephesians does not address a particular false teaching as most of Paul's letters do; instead, it addresses this broad question with a careful hand.

In response to questions about how Christianity is related to Judaism and the law, Ephesians asserts the essential unity of the church. The writer argues that the ties with which Christ has bound together Jews and Gentiles are stronger than the things that separate them. They now stand before God as equally in need of salvation and equally saved through Christ. The work of Christ also establishes peace between Jews and Gentiles as they recognize their equal status before God. Thus, Paul's gospel has brought them reconciliation both with God and with one another. Jews and Gentiles are now one new person in Christ. They share one Lord, one faith, one baptism, and one God. These shared beliefs, practices, and relationships inseparably relate Jews and Gentiles in Christ.

Such oneness also brings responsibilities. Since Christians are given this unity, they must live it out in their relations with one another. They must demonstrate in their life together what God has accomplished among them. This requires active relationships across ethnic lines. Thus, the church shows what God wants for the world in the ways it expresses the given unity of the whole church across racial boundaries and other boundaries that usually divide peoples.

Even the ethical instructions of Ephesians stress the unity of the church in contrast to the outside world. The struggle to live ethically is a battle between God's people and the forces of evil. This stand against the powers that oppose God reinforces the oneness of those in the church. However different Christians are, they are all engaged in the same struggle to live for God in the face of the things that oppose God's will for the world.

CLOSE-UP: CITIES OF PAUL'S LETTERS

Category	Ephesus	Philippi	Colossae
Location	Southwestern Ionia on the coast of Asia Minor	City in Macedonia in northeastern Greece	Central highlands of Asia Minor
Political association during first century	Hellenistic and Roman city	Roman colony	Roman city
Population	Estimated 400,000–500,000	Cosmopolitan area of Romans, Greeks, and Jews	Small town overshadowed by neighboring Laodicea and Hieropolis
Gods connected to the city	Artemis (temple), Roma and Divus Julius (joint temple for both)	People devoted to the Roman Empire, Jupiter, Mars, Bendis, Cybele	Artemis, Helios, Demeter, Men, Isi, Serapis
Jewish presence during first century	Little evidence exists of Jewish presence, though synagogue is mentioned in Acts 18:26 and 19:8	Jewish synagogue located outside city walls (Acts 16:13)	Cicero estimated that more than 10,000 Jewish males lived in Colossae, Laodicea, Hierapolis region
Early Christians associated with the church in this city	Church likely founded by Paul; Priscilla (Prisca), Aquila, and Apollos; Gaius; Aristarchus; Tychicus	Church founded by Paul	Probably Epaphras, a companion of Paul (see Colossians 1:7-8)
Record in Acts of Paul's visit	Acts 18:19-21 (brief) Acts 19:1–20:1 (lasted more than two years)	Acts 16:11-40 (Paul and Silas imprisoned.) Acts 20:1-6 Paul probably visited once or twice again (1 Cor. 16:5-6; 2 Cor. 2:13; 7:5)	No record of Paul ever visiting Colossae
Other biblical references to the city	One of the seven cities to receive a letter in Revelation 2:1-7 Timothy may have been first bishop (1 Tim. 1:3) Paul wrote 1 Corinthians here (see 1 Corinthians 16:8)	1 Thessalonians 2:2	None

FAITH IN ACTION: PROCLAIMING JESUS AS LORD

During this winter quarter we are exploring the letters of Ephesians, Philippians, and Colossians with an eye toward discovering who Jesus is and what it means for us to follow his example in our own lives. These three letters represent important teachings of the early church, teaching traditionally ascribed to Paul. Intended for congregations in specific locations, these letters became part of our sacred Scripture. Even as we study these letters to proclaim who Jesus is, we seek other ways to share Christ with others in both word and deed.

Distribute paper and pencils and ask the adults to write brief answers to these questions, which you will post on newsprint:

(1) **If you only had two minutes to tell someone about Jesus, what essential points would you want to make?**

(2) **What would you want to tell people about your own relationship with Jesus and the impact he has made on your life?**

(3) **Imagine that you are someone else looking at you as a model for how a Christian lives. Which of your behaviors would draw others to Christ? Which behaviors might push them away?**

(4) **Think about the witness that your congregation makes to the community.**

    (a) **What are you teaching people by the way you open your building for use by those in need (for example, a food pantry, space for Alcoholics Anonymous meetings, a child care center)?**

    (b) **What does the accessibility of your building say about who may come in and participate?**

    (c) **What do your nursery and children's Sunday school rooms say about how you value children?**

    (d) **How does the congregation show hospitality to those who come to the church for any reason?**

(5) **What ministries does your church engage in to show the love of Jesus?**

(6) **What ministries do you personally engage in to show the love of Jesus?**

Invite the learners to join with a partner or trio to discuss their ideas. Suggest that they look for and note common features that seem to define their lives together as a congregation and as individuals.

Bring the entire class together and consider this scenario:

A church consultant has visited your congregation to help you discern how you as a body and as individuals within that body proclaim that Jesus is Lord. The consultant has considered what seems to be the most important teachings here about Jesus, how individuals live out their relationship with Jesus, the witness that the church makes within the community, and the way in which parishioners support the ministries of the church. What would you expect the consultant's "bottom line" to be about how Jesus is proclaimed where you are? What recommendations might the consultant make? If change is recommended, what could this class do to help strengthen the witness of your church and its individual members?

Challenge the class members to do whatever they can to live into a more effective witness for Christ and encourage other members of the congregation to join them in this effort.

UNIT 1: VICTORY IN JESUS
SPIRITUAL BLESSINGS IN JESUS CHRIST

PREVIEWING THE LESSON

Lesson Scripture: Ephesians 1:3-14
Background Scripture: Ephesians 1
Key Verses: Ephesians 1:5-6

Focus of the Lesson:
All people want to feel valued and worthy. Where can we turn to receive affirmation? The writer of Ephesians declares that through Jesus Christ we gain an inheritance as God's own people to become recipients of forgiveness and salvation's redemption power.

Goals for the Learners:
(1) to understand Paul's explanation of being adopted by God through Jesus Christ.
(2) to express humility at God's affirmation of their worthiness.
(3) to offer praise for the remarkable gift of God's adoption of them through Jesus Christ.

Pronunciation Guide:
doxa (dox' ah)
eschatological (es kat uh loj' i kuhl)

Supplies:
Bibles (preferably several translations), newsprint and marker, paper and pencils, hymnals, optional commentaries on Ephesians

---

READING THE SCRIPTURE

NRSV
Lesson Scripture: Ephesians 1:3-14
   ³Blessed be the God and Father of our Lord Jesus Christ, who has blessed us in

CEB
Lesson Scripture: Ephesians 1:3-14
   ³Bless the God and Father of our Lord Jesus Christ! He has blessed us in Christ

Christ with every spiritual blessing in the heavenly places, ⁴just as he chose us in Christ before the foundation of the world to be holy and blameless before him in love. **⁵He destined us for adoption as his children through Jesus Christ, according to the good pleasure of his will, ⁶to the praise of his glorious grace that he freely bestowed on us in the Beloved.** ⁷In him we have redemption through his blood, the forgiveness of our trespasses, according to the riches of his grace ⁸that he lavished on us. With all wisdom and insight ⁹he has made known to us the mystery of his will, according to his good pleasure that he set forth in Christ, ¹⁰as a plan for the fullness of time, to gather up all things in him, things in heaven and things on earth. ¹¹In Christ we have also obtained an inheritance, having been destined according to the purpose of him who accomplishes all things according to his counsel and will, ¹²so that we, who were the first to set our hope on Christ, might live for the praise of his glory. ¹³In him you also, when you had heard the word of truth, the gospel of your salvation, and had believed in him, were marked with the seal of the promised Holy Spirit; ¹⁴this is the pledge of our inheritance toward redemption as God's own people, to the praise of his glory.

with every spiritual blessing that comes from heaven. ⁴God chose us in Christ to be holy and blameless in God's presence before the creation of the world. **⁵God destined us to be his adopted children through Jesus Christ because of his love. This was according to his goodwill and plan ⁶and to honor his glorious grace that he has given to us freely through the Son whom he loves.** ⁷We have been ransomed through his Son's blood, and we have forgiveness for our failures based on his overflowing grace, ⁸which he poured over us with wisdom and understanding. ⁹God revealed his hidden design to us, which is according to his goodwill and the plan that he intended to accomplish through his Son. ¹⁰This is what God planned for the climax of all times: to bring all things together in Christ, the things in heaven along with the things on earth. ¹¹We have also received an inheritance in Christ. We were destined by the plan of God, who accomplishes everything according to his design. ¹²We are called to be an honor to God's glory because we were the first to hope in Christ. ¹³You too heard the word of truth in Christ, which is the good news of your salvation. You were sealed with the promised Holy Spirit because you believed in Christ. ¹⁴The Holy Spirit is the down payment on our inheritance, which is applied toward our redemption as God's own people, resulting in the honor of God's glory.

UNDERSTANDING THE SCRIPTURE

Ephesians 1:1-2. The greeting of Ephesians establishes the authority of Paul by identifying him as an apostle who holds that position because it is God's will. At the same time, the letter identifies the recipients as saints (holy people) and as faithful. How this greeting identifies both Paul and the readers prepares for the instructions that follow.

Ephesians 1:3-6. While most Pauline letters begin with a prayer, that element of Ephesians is delayed by the insertion of a blessing. Similar periods of praise in the Hebrew Bible recognize specific acts of God or are more general acclamations of God's greatness. All of 1:3-14 is a single sentence in Greek, so it all fits together in the writer's thought as praise for the all-encompassing graciousness of God.

This blessing praises God for all of God's planning (which the writer says began before creation) and work in Christ. The writer praises God for the blessings Christians have "in the heavenly realms" (1:3 NIV) and in Christ. Thus, Christ is the sphere in which the blessings that extend throughout the entire cosmos are received.

When the writer says God chose us, he does not have in mind the selection of individuals. Instead, as a period of praise to God, the writer focuses on the sovereignty of God expressed through the preparations God has made for God's people. Rather than talking about *whom* God chose, he tells us *what* God chose us to be: holy. This is less the imposition of a requirement than it is a gift of God's love because the life of holiness brings us a fuller and more meaningful life.

More than this, God adopted us, making us heirs, indeed co-heirs with Christ. This adoption indicates that God lavishes on us the gifts of family membership and a coming inheritance. We receive this status and these gifts through and in Christ. These blessings come to us because of Christ, not through any merit of our own. God did this "to the praise of his glorious grace" (1:6). This means that these acts are expressions of God's character. They evoke praise when we recognize who God is and what God has done for us. The constant emphasis in this section of praise is that we receive all these blessings *in Christ.* And after noting that we receive holiness "in love" (1:4), the writer calls Christ "the Beloved" (1:6), intimating that God's love comes to us in and through the love God has for Christ.

Ephesians 1:7-10. The grace of God that gives us holiness also brings us redemption and forgiveness. Redemption is an unfamiliar image to us. It means that God has freed us from a hopeless situation. The church drew this image from the Exodus story. In Exodus 15:13, Moses sings that God has redeemed the people. Then Moses reminds the people that God redeemed them from Pharaoh in Deuteronomy 6:21. This image points to both God's love and our helplessness. We could no more escape the powers of evil than Israel could free itself from slavery. Redemption comes through Christ's death in the form of forgiveness of sins. We are thus freed from genuine guiltiness and from the feeling of guilt that would keep us from the full experience of God's grace. This comes to us through God's grace, a grace that overflows to us. So the redemption and forgiveness we receive are manifestations of the enormous grace that God seeks to pour out on us.

"With all wisdom and understanding" (1:8) may describe the way God's grace abounded (as the NIV translates it) or how God makes known the mystery (as the NRSV translates it). Since other descriptions of God's work in this section begin with the same preposition that begins this phrase (*en*), these words probably go with what follows (that is, with the NRSV). But the phrase may fit with both, serving as a transition to the next statement about what God has done while also describing the way God redeemed and forgave us.

God's grace brings us knowledge of the eschatological (that is, end-time) mystery. The purposes of God that were unclear before are now made known in the church. God's intention is to "gather up" (1:10) or "bring . . . together" (NIV) all things in Christ. While it is hard to know exactly what this means, even what "all" (the saved or the material world or evil powers) refers to, it locates all God's saving work in Christ. Perhaps it looks ahead to the theme of bringing together Jews and Gentiles in Christ.

Ephesians 1:11-14. God's initiative remains the main focus in these verses. The powerful will of God calls believers into Christ. Their salvation is a demonstration of God's grace and so leads to praise for God's gracious nature.

At verse 13 the pronouns change from

"we/us" to "you," along with the contrast between we who first hoped in Christ and you who believed later. This seems to point to the distinction between Jewish and Gentile Christians. Both, however, believe the "word of truth" (1:13). This designates the gospel as the genuine revelation of God and of God's activity on behalf of the world. It also marks the gospel proclaimed in Ephesians as the true gospel, possibly contrasting it with any other teaching the readers might hear.

Believing this true gospel leads to receiving the Spirit. For Ephesians, the Spirit lives in every Christian and serves as the down payment on the blessings to be received at the end. The Spirit brings a foretaste of the intimate life with God that awaits believers at the consummation of all things. The Spirit is the promissory deposit that gives believers confidence that God will bring them all the blessings of salvation. This blessing ends with a reminder that all of these gifts flow from the gracious character of God. These demonstrations of who God is, then, lead believers to offer praise to God.

Ephesians 1:15-23. Verse 15 begins the letter's prayer for its readers. The writer prays that they will recognize the gifts God has given them and realize that those blessings are secured for them by the power that raised Christ from the dead and exalted him to the highest place in the cosmos. They can, then, rest assured that nothing can wrest these blessings from them.

INTERPRETING THE SCRIPTURE

We Are Beloved

One of the clearest things this praise to God asserts is that God loves us. Throughout, it praises God for what God has done for us. God has given us all spiritual blessings, adopted us, redeemed us, forgiven us, revealed hidden mysteries to us, and come to live in us. While it is true that we need God to do many of these things because we have turned from God, they are also a powerful witness to how much God values us. We are so valuable to God that God has reached out to us to reestablish a relationship with us. God does this because we are so important to God. If we were not so precious, God would not work so extensively to make us God's own. The gift of Christ and his death for us demonstrate how much we are worth to God. And we should note that God does not just save us from condemnation; God desires relationship with us. So while we may feel unworthy when we remember that we need salvation, we should feel enormous worth when we recognize all God has done for us and the ways God wants us close.

Holiness Is a Gift

We nearly always think of living a holy life as a burden or at least as an expectation. It is certainly an expectation, but it is also a gift. This is the case not only because God grants us holiness in judgment but also because it gives us the best life now. This runs counter to the way we usually think of things. We often think that sinners get to have all the fun. But in truth the life of holiness is best suited to being human. As beings made in the image of God, our true nature is to live according to the holiness of God. While that seems difficult in a world governed by other values, the holy life is the one that brings fuller meaning to our existence (even as we forgo some immediate gratification). So even the demand to be holy is a gift of the love and grace of God.

In addition, the life of holiness is the life

appropriate to our identity as children of God. Ephesians says we have been adopted by God. Christians are children of God in a special sense. While all people are children of God in one sense, Christians have been made heirs with Christ to all of God's blessings. This way of talking about salvation envisions us being brought fully into the family of God. Being part of a family brings blessings and expectations. Since we are in the family of God, we are to live up to being in that family. Many of us have heard or said something to the effect that people in our family don't act certain ways. Adoption into God's family brings that same kind of relatedness and expectation.

Redeemed

We seldom use the language of redemption and so often do not understand fully why New Testament writers use it to speak of salvation. When something is redeemed, it is bought back. This language was used for buying a captured person out of slavery. This image troubles us for at least two reasons. First, it implies that we were unable to do something ourselves. The language of redemption says we need an outsider to rescue us. We like being self-sufficient people, but the image of redemption says we were trapped and had to be rescued. This makes us more vulnerable than we like to imagine. It means that our salvation is an act of God, who did something for us we could not do on our own. At the same time, it is another sign of how valuable we are to God.

The image of salvation as redemption also makes us ask who was paid. If we remember that redemption is a metaphor, this problem dissipates. We simply cannot push the metaphor that far. All analogies have similarities and differences. This analogy breaks down when we ask about the recipient of the ransom. It can help us if we remember that Moses uses this image to describe the acts of God in freeing the Israelites from Egypt. If we ask whom God

paid to free the people, the logical answer would be Pharaoh. But that is clearly not the case. God did not actually pay anyone, but the image of redemption expresses the depth of God's love and the extent to which God was willing to go to free us from the things that would keep us from relationship with God.

Ephesians balances this image of our helplessness by also saying that we have forgiveness. This implies that we have purposefully done things that have separated us from God. But even in the face of that rejection, God forgives because of the wealth of God's grace. This grace is not in short supply. It is like a flood that can hardly be held back. It is such a part of the nature of God that it overflows to grant us forgiveness.

One of the gifts of salvation for which Ephesians praise God is the presence of the Spirit in our lives. The indwelling of the Spirit is an initial act of God that will be completed only when we live fully in God's presence. Ephesians sees the Spirit as the down payment on what God promises to do in the time to come. This presence of God is a fundamental promise; it does not keep bad things from happening, but it does mean God is always with us in our troubles. We do not always feel the Spirit's presence in life, but the Spirit is never absent. That ever-abiding presence is a promise we receive from God at baptism.

Three times in this short passage, Ephesians says that God gave us the many gifts of salvation "for the praise of his glory" (1:6 [adapted], 12, 14). In most contexts, the term "glory" (doxa) refers to a person's reputation. When applied to God in Jewish literature it points to the radiance surrounding the presence of God and so to the nature of God. Ephesians follows this understanding so that these acts of salvation flow from the nature and character of God. They are demonstrations of who God is. The proper response to catching a glimpse of the nature of God through these saving acts is praise and worship. When we truly comprehend the gracious acts God has performed for us, praise is not so much a requirement as it is a recognition of what we have been given. If someone had saved our lives, we would respond with overflowing thanks. God has done more than simply keep us from an untimely death; God has given us life with God now and in the time to come. Worship is our thanks for the great things God has done for us. At the same time, it proclaims to all what a wonderful God we serve and so invites them to come to know God and the blessings found in Christ.

SHARING THE SCRIPTURE

Preparing Our Hearts

Explore this week's devotional reading, found in Psalm 33:8-12. This psalm praises the greatness and goodness of God the Creator and the Lord of history. Note the reference in verse 12 to "the people whom [God] has chosen as his heritage." Compare this to today's key verse, which speaks of our "adoption as [God's] children through Jesus Christ" (Ephesians 1:5). How do you respond to the notion of being God's "heritage" and an adopted child of God? How might you live differently if you were constantly aware of this relationship with God?

Pray that you and the adult students will praise God the Father for the blessings of adoption that you have through the Son, Jesus Christ.

Preparing Our Minds

Study the background Scripture from Ephesians 1 and the lesson Scripture from Ephesians 1:3-14.

Consider this question as you prepare the lesson: *Since all of us want to feel valued and worthy, where can we turn to receive affirmation?*

Write on newsprint:
❑ information for next week's lesson, found under "Continue the Journey."
❑ activities for further spiritual growth in "Continue the Journey."

Review the "Introduction," "The Big Picture," "Close-up," and "Faith in Action." Consider how you will use this additional information, which immediately precedes the first lesson, for this session and throughout the quarter.

Prepare a lecture if you choose Option 1 for "Understand Paul's Explanation of Being Adopted Through Jesus Christ."

LEADING THE CLASS

(1) Gather to Learn

❖ Greet the class members. Introduce any guests and help them feel at home.

❖ Pray that those who have come today will be ready to recognize and give thanks that God has chosen and adopted them through Christ Jesus.

❖ Invite the adults to raise their hands when you read a statement that makes them feel valued and worthy. All of these statements may prompt a positive response.

(1) **People speak to me in ways that show respect even if we don't see eye to eye.**

(2) **At least one person is willing to give me undivided attention on a regular basis.**

(3) **People listen empathetically to what I have to say.**

(4) **I have a sense of belonging within a family, church, or group.**

(5) **Other people praise me for something that I do.**

(6) I believe that I can improve, even after I've made a mistake.

❖ Ask: **How would you describe a person who feels valued and worthy as opposed to one who does not?**

❖ Read aloud today's focus statement: **All people want to feel valued and worthy. Where can we turn to receive affirmation? The writer of Ephesians declares that through Jesus Christ we gain an inheritance as God's own people to become recipients of forgiveness and salvation's redemption power.**

(2) Goal 1: Understand Paul's Explanation of Being Adopted by God Through Jesus Christ

❖ Explain that verses 3-14, although divided into six sentences in the NRSV, are actually part of just one Greek sentence. Comment that, as our author points out, "it all fits together in the writer's thought as praise for the all-encompassing graciousness of God."

❖ Invite a volunteer to read Ephesians 3:1-14 aloud.

❖ Choose one of these three options to help the learners understand this passage.

■ **Option 1:** Use information from Understanding the Scripture for verses 3-6, 7-10, 11-14 to create a lecture explaining Paul's meaning. You may wish to add other information from Interpreting the Scripture.

■ **Option 2:** Have several translations of the Bible handy. Form groups and give each one a different Bible translation. Assign each group one sentence to read and interpret. Bring the groups together and let each report, in turn, on its sentence.

■ **Option 3:** Form several small groups and give each a Bible commentary. The commentary will be useful, but encourage the learners to wrestle with the text to decide what they think it means.

(3) Goal 2: Express Humility at God's Affirmation of the Learners' Worthiness

❖ Read or retell "Redeemed" from Interpreting the Scripture.

❖ Lead the class in this guided imagery. Suggest that each person find a comfortable position and relax as you read the following script:

(1) You have been invited to attend a banquet. You arrive believing that Jesus will be the honored guest and center of everyone's attention. You enter the ballroom and look around at the lavish decorations and the feast that awaits the guests. What are you thinking? (*Pause.*)

(2) As you take your seat at the side of the room, Jesus steps up to a microphone, calls your name, and asks you to come forward. When you reach the podium, he shakes your hand and presents you with a plaque that reads "You are one of God's chosen children." Thunderous applause erupts. What are you feeling? (*Pause.*)

(3) Give humble thanks for God's affirmation of your worthiness. (*Pause.*)

❖ Invite volunteers to report on how the recognition that they are God's chosen children makes them feel. What response will they make to this awesome news?

(4) Goal 3: Offer Praise for the Remarkable Gift of God's Adoption of the Learners Through Jesus Christ

❖ Form several groups and distribute a marker and sheet of newsprint to each. Challenge the learners to write a hymn of praise for what God has done for us through Jesus and offer thanks that God has adopted us. Recommend that each group of people choose an easy hymn tune or praise song and write words to go with their selected tune.

❖ Allow time for each group to offer its praise either by singing together or by posting the words and inviting the entire class to join them.

(5) Continue the Journey

❖ Pray that those who have participated today will count their spiritual blessings in Christ Jesus.

❖ Read aloud this preparation for next week's lesson. You may also want to post it on newsprint for the students to copy.

■ Title: One in Jesus Christ
■ Background Scripture: Ephesians 2–3
■ Lesson Scripture: Ephesians 2:11-22
■ Focus of the Lesson: Adversaries sometimes search and long for ways to come together. What or who can bring the two sides together? The writer of Ephesians proclaims that it is in Christ that we, who are dead through our trespasses, are made alive in Christ and that Jesus Christ is the one who breaks down all dividing walls and brings us together as one.

❖ Post these three activities related to this week's session on newsprint for the students to copy. Challenge the adults to grow spiritually by completing one or more of them.

(1) Identify at least three spiritual blessings that you experience each day this week. Give thanks to God.

(2) Ponder your relationship with God. Do you perceive God to be far-off and inaccessible, or is God a loving father figure who wants the best for you? What difference does your perception of God make in terms of your relationship with God?

(3) Share with others this week the good news that in Christ they are chosen and blessed children of God. Be prepared to talk about what that relationship means in your own life.

❖ Sing or read aloud "They'll Know We Are Christians by Our Love," found in *The Faith We Sing.*

❖ Conclude today's session by leading the class in this benediction, adapted from the key verses for December 23 from Ephesians 5:1 and January 13 from Philippians 2:5: **Go now as the Father's beloved children, who are of the same mind as the Son, Jesus Christ, to be imitators of God.**

UNIT 1: VICTORY IN JESUS
ONE IN JESUS CHRIST

PREVIEWING THE LESSON

Lesson Scripture: Ephesians 2:11-22
Background Scripture: Ephesians 2–3
Key Verse: Ephesians 2:21

Focus of the Lesson:
Adversaries sometimes search and long for ways to come together. What or who can bring the two sides together? The writer of Ephesians proclaims that it is in Christ that we, who are dead through our trespasses, are made alive in Christ and that Jesus Christ is the one who breaks down all dividing walls and brings us together as one.

Goals for the Learners:
(1) to understand Paul's explanation of Jews and Gentiles becoming one in Christ.
(2) to express sorrow at the divisions within Christ's church and joy when divisions are overcome.
(3) to become acquainted with issues dividing the church and name strategies for addressing these issues.

Pronunciation Guide:
eschatological (es kat uh loj' i kuhl)

Supplies:
Bibles, newsprint and marker, paper and pencils, hymnals

READING THE SCRIPTURE

NRSV
Lesson Scripture: Ephesians 2:11-22

[11]So then, remember that at one time you Gentiles by birth, called "the uncircumcision" by those who are called "the circumcision"—a physical circumcision made in the flesh by human hands—[12]remember that you were at that time without Christ, being aliens from the commonwealth of Israel, and

CEB
Lesson Scripture: Ephesians 2:11-22

[11]So remember that once you were Gentiles by physical descent, who were called "uncircumcised" by Jews who are physically circumcised. [12]At that time you were without Christ. You were aliens rather than citizens of Israel, and strangers to the covenants of God's promise. In this world

strangers to the covenants of promise, having no hope and without God in the world. [13]But now in Christ Jesus you who once were far off have been brought near by the blood of Christ. [14]For he is our peace; in his flesh he has made both groups into one and has broken down the dividing wall, that is, the hostility between us. [15]He has abolished the law with its commandments and ordinances, that he might create in himself one new humanity in place of the two, thus making peace, [16]and might reconcile both groups to God in one body through the cross, thus putting to death that hostility through it. [17]So he came and proclaimed peace to you who were far off and peace to those who were near; [18]for through him both of us have access in one Spirit to the Father. [19]So then you are no longer strangers and aliens, but you are citizens with the saints and also members of the household of God, [20]built upon the foundation of the apostles and prophets, with Christ Jesus himself as the cornerstone. **[21]In him the whole structure is joined together and grows into a holy temple in the Lord;** [22]in whom you also are built together spiritually into a dwelling place for God.

you had no hope and no God. [13]But now, thanks to Christ Jesus, you who once were so far away have been brought near by the blood of Christ.

[14]Christ is our peace. He made both Jews and Gentiles into one group. With his body, he broke down the barrier of hatred that divided us. [15]He canceled the detailed rules of the Law so that he could create one new person out of the two groups, making peace. [16]He reconciled them both as one body to God by the cross, which ended the hostility to God.

[17]When he came, he announced the good news of peace to you who were far away from God and to those who were near. [18]We both have access to the Father through Christ by the one Spirit. [19]So now you are no longer strangers and aliens. Rather, you are fellow citizens with God's people, and you belong to God's household. [20]As God's household, you are built on the foundation of the apostles and prophets with Christ Jesus himself as the cornerstone. **[21]The whole building is joined together in him, and it grows up into a temple that is dedicated to the Lord.** [22]Christ is building you into a place where God lives through the Spirit.

UNDERSTANDING THE SCRIPTURE

Ephesians 2:1-10. Chapter 2 begins by reminding readers that before they were Christians they had alienated themselves from God through their sinful lives. Despite their hostility, God saved them and gave them new life in Christ.

Ephesians 2:11-13. The focus of 2:11-22 is on the way Gentiles have been brought into the blessings of God and on the way differences between Jews and Gentiles have been made irrelevant in the church. The passage is written to Gentile Christians from the perspective of a Jewish Christian. The ideas

expressed would not make good sense to people of either group who are not in the church.

Verse 11 reminds the readers of the time when they were Gentiles. This is arresting for two reasons. First, it tells us that the writer is a Jewish Christian because Jews are the only ones who made the distinction between Jews and everyone else. The term "Gentile" simply designates all non-Jews. As the Greeks defined peoples as either Greek or barbarian, so Jews saw two groups: Jews and non-Jews. Second, the verse says that one group was "formerly" Gentiles (NIV). We might ask what they are now because they did not become Jews. Verse 15 may provide the answer because it speaks of "one new" person in Christ.

Verse 12 lists Jewish blessings to which Gentiles previously had no access. Most generally, they were outside the blessings that come with citizenship in Israel. Then they were not part of the covenant that includes promises from God. They were without hope and godless. Non-Christian Gentiles would have rejected the accusation that they were without god because they worshiped many gods. Some would also have claimed hope for the afterlife. But these descriptions were standard Jewish accusations about Gentiles.

All of that separation from God's blessings and from association with God's people has ended. Gentiles have been brought into those blessings through the death of Christ and through incorporation into Christ. The following verses offer further definition of this change.

Ephesians 2:14-18. Some type of hymnic or liturgical piece may lie behind verses 14-18. The writer does not simply quote it (something like what we see in Colossians 1:15-20), but rather draws on pieces of it to make his points. The paragraph's most basic point is that all things that separate Jews and Gentiles have been rendered irrelevant. In Christ, the wall that separated them has been torn down. This is probably not a reference to the wall at the Jerusalem Temple that set the limit for how close Gentiles could come. It may refer to the law or simply be a metaphor for all things that divided them. Whatever it was, Christ has removed it. Verse 15 identifies the law as something that divided Jews and Gentiles, but which Christ has removed. Saying that Christ "abolished" the law goes beyond anything that we find in the letters scholars are certain Paul wrote. Ephesians seems to say that the law no longer has a place as a guide for God's people. But the writer is

using dramatic language that masks the nuance he might apply on other occasions. After all, in Ephesians 6:2 he cites a commandment of the law as an authority. So perhaps he has in mind those parts of the law that created differences between Jews and Gentiles.

This nullification of (parts of) the law creates a new eschatological (that is, end-time) reality that includes both Jews and Gentiles as the people of God. This discussion assumes that Jews enjoyed a relationship with God that Gentiles did not have before Christ. But now, in the time after Christ, both have been brought together to form a new people of God. Ephesians sees this as a blessing of the new era of God's activity in the world that was initiated with the life and death of Christ. In this new time, all have access to God through Christ and through the Spirit.

Ephesians 2:19-22. Parts of verses 19-22 may also quote earlier confessions of the church so that the writer is citing what the readers already believe, but putting it in a new context to draw out a new meaning. He says that Gentiles are now fellow citizens with the saints and members of God's household. The household image shifts so that together Jews and Gentiles are being made into a house. This house rests on the teaching of the apostles and prophets. These prophets are early Christian prophets who were understood to deliver genuine messages from God. Ephesians looks back to the time when the apostles were still alive and sees them and the prophets as authoritative for the church. All the authority of these teachers is based on Christ himself, here called "the cornerstone." Or perhaps the term means the capstone of an arch. In either case, Christ is the crucial element in the construction of this building of God.

This is no common building they are becoming; they are being made into the temple of God. As a temple, the church is the place of the very presence of God. Calling the church God's temple says that it is the place of the concentrated presence of God, the place where others can come to know and experience the presence of God. In Christ and through the Spirit the church is the focused dwelling place of God in the world.

Ephesians 3:1-13. Chapter 3 describes Paul's ministry to Gentiles as a work that is enabled by God's power and that reveals a mystery: the inclusion of Gentiles. His ministry proclaims that through Christ Gentiles may now enter the community that enjoys God's blessings. Before Christ they were excluded, but now God invites them to share all God's blessings.

Ephesians 3:14-21. These verses constitute a period of thanksgiving for the love of God known in Christ. This love now lavishes God's riches on both Jews and Gentiles. Indeed, they now possess "all the fullness of God" (3:19). Recognition of such blessings leads to a benediction that closes this section of the letter.

INTERPRETING THE SCRIPTURE

Reconciled to One Another

In verses 2:1-10 Ephesians focuses on the way Christians are reconciled to God. At verse 11 attention shifts to the implications this reconciliation to God has for relationships within the church. It is hard for us to imagine the division that existed between Jews and non-Jews in the ancient world. They had different and incompatible religions, different standards of morality, different ways that they lived as citizens in their cities, even different social institutions. (The synagogue served as a school and a social center, as well as a place of worship for Jews.) The distinguishing marks of Jews (sabbath keeping, food laws, and circumcision) were looked down on by their neighbors. As a result, there was significant anti-Semitism in the ancient world. At the same time, Jews saw non-Jews as deceived in their religious beliefs and at times as a threat.

Quite early, the church brought Gentiles into its membership. From the perspective of Jews within the church, this meant that Gentiles were being offered the blessings Jews had enjoyed as the people of God. Indeed, the church enjoyed the new blessings that Christ had given and invited Gentiles to partake of those. This was a dramatic step. By the time of Ephesians, there was no longer an argument about whether the church should do this. The church was probably predominantly Gentile at this point. But the distinctions between Jews and Gentiles were still evident. Belief in Christ did not eradicate the differences between Jews and Gentiles, but it did make them irrelevant when assigning status or relationship with God.

As we look to those who are different in our world, few will be more different than Jews and Gentiles in the first century. Today's Scripture asserts that those differences are unimportant to our central identity as the people who are in Christ. Life in Christ provides reconciliation and demands that we be reconciled to those who are different from us. We do not demand that others in the church become like us; rather, we share a relationship with them while they remain different. Something larger than our differences binds us together. In Christ we have been given peace with God and with one another. We begin to embody the peace with one another that God has given us by recognizing that we all stand before God on the same basis; we all depend on the work of Christ and our participation in him.

A Ministry of Reconciliation

As we think about this passage, we need to avoid seeing it as a denigration of Judaism. The whole discussion assumes that members of the Mosaic covenant enjoy genuine relationship with God. The good news for Gentiles is that what was available to Jews is now available to them. Although membership in the Mosaic covenant offers no status in Christ, that does not mean that covenant was bad. Ephesians does think that there are more blessings in Christ, but the writer knows that there were authentic blessings and relationship with God within that earlier covenant. One of the additional blessings for the church is that Gentiles are now offered peace with God.

Ephesians gives attention only to relationships within the church. Inner-church relations remain this author's interest throughout the letter. He calls the church to live out the reconciliation we have been given in how we treat one another within the church. But the reconciliation Christians experience in Christ has implications for the way we live in relation to non-Christians as well. In 2 Corinthians 5:18-20, Paul describes his ministry as a ministry of reconciliation. Just as God seeks to be reconciled to all people, so Christians work to bring reconciliation not only between God and others but also between different groups within their communities. Taking on this work is a part of accepting the gift of reconciliation that we experience in the church. Working for reconciliation is one way we show the world how God has touched our lives and what God wants for the people of the world.

New Identities

Verses 19-22 offer multiple ways to think about our identity as Christians. First, Ephesians 2:19 calls Christians fellow "citizens with the saints." This way of expressing the oneness of Jews and Gentiles in

Christ indicates that the most important allegiance of Christians is to the kingdom of God rather than any other citizenship. At the same time, it sets Christians apart as those who are to live holy lives. Ephesians adds that Christians are members of God's household. Not only are they children of God but they are also family members with one another. This identity expects a relatedness and love among members of the church that reflects the reconciliation among different groups that the previous verses proclaim.

Ephesians moves from the idea of belonging in God's household to seeing the church as a house constructed by God. The foundation of this building is the apostolic teaching. This signifies that what the church believes and does is based on the teaching that came from the apostles, the authoritative representatives of Christ. That teaching takes Christ himself as its basis. The word translated "cornerstone" can mean either a cornerstone or the keystone in an arch. While "cornerstone" seems to fit better here, either understanding designates Christ, including his teaching and his saving work, as the most important determinant of the church's identity and status. All the church's teaching is based on and held together by who we understand Christ to be and what he has accomplished for our salvation.

The Church as God's Temple

The church built on Christ and the apostolic teaching is no ordinary building; it is growing into a temple. Religions of the first century had a temple where one could go and expect that the god would be present in a special way. By the time Ephesians was written (A.D. 80–100), the Jerusalem Temple had been destroyed. This means that the God of the church had no temple. To some that could suggest that this God was too weak to maintain a place in the world or that God was not present in the world in that focused way. Ephesians sees things differently. The church's God does not need a temple in the traditional sense because the church itself is where God dwells in that intimate and powerful way. The church is the residence of the presence of God in the world. This is both a great gift and an important responsibility. It is a gift to have God dwelling directly in the midst of the gathered people of God. That presence brings comfort, joy, and the ability to live for God. At the same time, being the dwelling place of God means that others should be able to see God's presence in our midst. The church should be a demonstration of who God is, and it is to mediate the presence of God to the rest of the world. Both the ways church members treat one another and how they extend God's love into the community should be demonstrations of the character of God. When we act in love and justice to bring reconciliation among the estranged, we are living as God's temple.

SHARING THE SCRIPTURE

Preparing Our Hearts

Explore this week's devotional reading, found in Ephesians 3:14-21. Paul's prayer is actually one sentence in Greek (3:14-19). The prayer concludes with a two-verse doxology (3:20-21). Just prior to this prayer, in verses 10-12, Paul summarizes the theme of this letter: He wants to make known mysteries in the "heavenly places" and God's plan for the church to include Gentiles as the plan is made known and "carried out" through Jesus. Notice Paul's four petitions in verses 16-19. How might they relate to your own life?

Pray that you and the adult students will recognize that all people are invited to become one in Jesus Christ.

Preparing Our Minds

Study the background Scripture from Ephesians 2–3 and the lesson Scripture from Ephesians 2:11-22.

Consider this question as you prepare the lesson: *What or who can bring two opposing sides together?*

Write on newsprint:
❑ information for next week's lesson, found under "Continue the Journey."

❑ activities for further spiritual growth in "Continue the Journey."

Review the "Introduction," "The Big Picture," "Close-up," and "Faith in Action." Consider how you will use this additional information, which immediately precedes the first lesson, for this session.

LEADING THE CLASS

(1) Gather to Learn

❖ Greet the class members. Introduce any guests and help them feel at home.

❖ Pray that all who have gathered today will give thanks that through Jesus all may become one.

❖ Read this information from Ohio University: **Professor of environmental studies at Ohio University Ted Bernard coauthored *The Ecology of Hope* (1997) and authored *Hope and Hard Times* (2010). Bernard explored ways that groups worked together to create strategies for successfully handling environmental problems. This method of operating, known as "collaborative community-based conservation," often brought together groups that had been adversaries. For example, environmentalists, loggers,** fishers, millworkers, and ranchers, who at one time pulled in different directions, were able to unite to stabilize salmon runs in California's Mattole Valley watershed. As a result of people working to find solutions, problems have been solved, some so successfully that the solutions have become models for other projects.

❖ Ask: **What examples can you cite of people who have opposing points of view coming together for the common good to solve a problem?**

❖ Read aloud today's focus statement: **Adversaries sometimes search and long for ways to come together. What or who can bring the two sides together? The writer of Ephesians proclaims that it is in Christ that we, who are dead through our trespasses, are made alive in Christ and that Jesus Christ is the one who breaks down all dividing walls and brings us together as one.**

(2) Goal 1: Understand Paul's Explanation of Jews and Gentiles Becoming One in Christ

❖ Introduce today's Scripture passage by reading "A Ministry of Reconciliation" from Interpreting the Scripture.

❖ Call on a volunteer to read Ephesians 2:11-22.

❖ Discuss these questions. Use information from Understanding the Scripture to augment the discussion.

    (1) **How have Gentiles, who had no part in the covenant blessings of the Jews, been brought to God?**

    (2) **How does the image of "the household of God" (2:19) help readers understand God's intention for both Jews and Gentiles?**

    (3) **According to 2:21 (key verse) and 2:22, the church is "a holy temple" and God's "dwelling place." How well do you think the church is living up to God's expectations for a holy home today? What changes do we need to make?**

(3) Goal 2: Express Sorrow at the Divisions Within Christ's Church and Joy When Divisions Are Overcome

❖ Read this information: **As tensions rose prior to the American Civil War, the Methodist, Baptist, and Presbyterian churches all tragically split over the issue of slavery. Both sides of each denomination used biblical texts to support their positions. In the case of The Methodist Episcopal Church, the General Conference in 1844 voted that the bishop of Georgia, who was a slaveholder, must desist from fulfilling his duties as bishop. At that point Southern delegates walked out and The Methodist Episcopal Church, South was formed. Nearly one hundred years later, in 1939, The Methodist Episcopal Church, The Methodist Episcopal Church, South, and The Methodist Protestant Church (which had broken away earlier over issues related to lay participation in the governance of the church) reunited. The reunification did not solve all problems, especially those pertaining to race, but it was a step in the direction of healing divisions.**

❖ Ask: **How do internal divisions harm the church?**

❖ Recall Paul's teachings in Ephesians about unity by reading or retelling "The Church as God's Temple" in Interpreting the Scripture.

❖ Discuss these questions:

    (1) **When divisions, such as the ones that occurred during the Civil War, tear asunder the body of Christ, what kind of witness is the church then making to the world?**

    (2) **When divisions are overcome, as was the case in 1939 when splinter denominations within The Methodist Church reunited, how might the church celebrate and move forward together?**

(4) Goal 3: Become Acquainted With Issues Dividing the Church and Name Strategies for Addressing These Issues

❖ **Ask: Do you perceive any issues within your own denomination that have the potential to cause a major rift? If so, what are they?** (List answers on newsprint.)

❖ Form groups of three or four students. Tell the groups that they are to determine strategies that they might use to learn more about any of these issues and address them in a way that can help church members come together. Be sure the groups understand that they are not to debate or try to solve any issues but rather are to determine strategies for addressing them. Examples of strategies include *studying the Bible on the topic, gathering groups with different perspectives to dialogue and listen carefully to other viewpoints,* and *accepting differences by recognizing that uniformity is not essential for unity.*

❖ Call on each group to report its ideas.

(5) Continue the Journey

❖ Pray that all who have participated will recognize the importance of unity within the body of Christ.

❖ Read aloud this preparation for next week's lesson. You may also want to post it on newsprint for the students to copy.

■ **Title: Unity in the Body of Christ**
■ **Background Scripture: Ephesians 4:1-16**
■ **Lesson Scripture: Ephesians 4:1-16**
■ **Focus of the Lesson: We all feel positive about life when everything goes well after we have worked together on a project. What brings about this feeling of unity? The writer of Ephesians** says that, although each of us brings different gifts, we find true unity as we grow into Christ, who is the head of the whole body.

❖ Post these three activities related to this week's session on newsprint for the students to copy. Challenge the adults to grow spiritually by completing one or more of them.

(1) **Attend a church council meeting and listen carefully to opposing arguments as issues are being debated. Try to see all sides of each issue. If possible, articulate different points of view and help the group recognize possibilities for compromise and unity.**

(2) **Reach out to a church member with whom you have had a disagreement. Do whatever you can to bring about reconciliation.**

(3) **Become familiar with an issue that is causing division within your own denomination. Research as many angles as possible. Look for biblical support for both sides of the argument. Try to reach an informed conclusion about the points that separate the two sides and ways that might help the discussion move forward.**

❖ Sing or read aloud "Christ Is Made the Sure Foundation."

❖ Conclude today's session by leading the class in this benediction, adapted from the key verses for December 23 from Ephesians 5:1 and January 13 from Philippians 2:5: **Go now as the Father's beloved children, who are of the same mind as the Son Jesus Christ, to be imitators of God.**

UNIT 1: VICTORY IN JESUS
UNITY IN THE BODY OF CHRIST

PREVIEWING THE LESSON

Lesson Scripture: Ephesians 4:1-16
Background Scripture: Ephesians 4:1-16
Key Verses: Ephesians 4:4-5

Focus of the Lesson:
We all feel positive about life when everything goes well after we have worked together on a project. What brings about this feeling of unity? The writer of Ephesians says that although each of us brings different gifts, we find true unity as we grow into Christ, who is the head of the whole body.

Goals for the Learners:
(1) to explore characteristics of a life worthy of Christ's calling in building up the body of Christ.
(2) to identify and celebrate their gifts that help build up the body of Christ.
(3) to state an interpretation of having "one faith, one baptism, one God of all" as it relates to the building up of the body of Christ.

Supplies:
Bibles, newsprint and marker, paper and pencils, hymnals

READING THE SCRIPTURE

NRSV
Lesson Scripture: Ephesians 4:1-16

¹I therefore, the prisoner in the Lord, beg you to lead a life worthy of the calling to which you have been called, ²with all humility and gentleness, with patience, bearing with one another in love, ³making every effort to maintain the unity of the Spirit in the bond of peace. **⁴There is one body and one Spirit, just as you were called to the one hope of your calling, ⁵one Lord, one faith, one baptism,** ⁶one God and Father of

CEB
Lesson Scripture: Ephesians 4:1-16

¹Therefore, as a prisoner for the Lord, I encourage you to live as people worthy of the call you received from God. ²Conduct yourselves with all humility, gentleness, and patience. Accept each other with love, ³and make an effort to preserve the unity of the Spirit with the peace that ties you together. **⁴You are one body and one spirit just as God also called you in one hope. ⁵There is one Lord, one faith, one baptism,** ⁶and one

151

all, who is above all and through all and in all.

[7]But each of us was given grace according to the measure of Christ's gift. [8]Therefore it is said,

"When he ascended on high he made captivity itself a captive;
he gave gifts to his people."

[9](When it says, "He ascended," what does it mean but that he had also descended into the lower parts of the earth? [10]He who descended is the same one who ascended far above all the heavens, so that he might fill all things.) [11]The gifts he gave were that some would be apostles, some prophets, some evangelists, some pastors and teachers, [12]to equip the saints for the work of ministry, for building up the body of Christ, [13]until all of us come to the unity of the faith and of the knowledge of the Son of God, to maturity, to the measure of the full stature of Christ. [14]We must no longer be children, tossed to and fro and blown about by every wind of doctrine, by people's trickery, by their craftiness in deceitful scheming. [15]But speaking the truth in love, we must grow up in every way into him who is the head, into Christ, [16]from whom the whole body, joined and knit together by every ligament with which it is equipped, as each part is working properly, promotes the body's growth in building itself up in love.

God and Father of all who is over all, through all, and in all.

[7]God has given his grace to each one of us measured out by the gift that is given by Christ. [8]That's why scripture says, *When he climbed up to the heights, he captured prisoners, and he gave gifts to people.*

[9]What does the phrase "he climbed up" mean if it doesn't mean that he had first gone down into the lower regions, the earth? [10]The one who went down is the same one who climbed up above all the heavens so that he might fill everything.

[11]He gave some apostles, some prophets, some evangelists, and some pastors and teachers. [12]His purpose was to equip God's people for the work of serving and building up the body of Christ [13]until we all reach the unity of faith and knowledge of God's Son. God's goal is for us to become mature adults—to be fully grown, measured by the standard of the fullness of Christ. [14]As a result, we aren't supposed to be infants any longer who can be tossed and blown around by every wind that comes from teaching with deceitful scheming and the tricks people play to deliberately mislead others. [15]Instead, by speaking the truth with love, let's grow in every way into Christ, [16]who is the head. The whole body grows from him, as it is joined and held together by all the supporting ligaments. The body makes itself grow in that it builds itself up with love as each one does their part.

UNDERSTANDING THE SCRIPTURE

Introduction. This discussion of the importance and advantages of unity becomes even more powerful when we remember that the author is holding together Jewish and Gentile Christians. With all that could separate them, Ephesians affirms the oneness of the church and reminds readers of some of the most important things that bind the whole church into the one body of Christ.

Ephesians 4:1-6. In the previous chapter, Ephesians reminded the readers of the great blessings they have in Christ; they have been "filled with all the fullness of God" (3:19). With this basis, the writer turns to exhortation. The opening of chapter 4

hinges on the word "therefore." Because readers have these gifts, they are therefore to live worthily, to live up to what God has given them. The writer highlights maintaining unity and peace as the central elements of living worthily. He knows this will not be easy, so he encourages readers to have patience with one another and to be humble in their dealings with those who are different and yet are in the same church. The usual translation of the end of verse 2 masks how difficult this may be; both the NRSV and NIV translate it "bearing with one another." In our vernacular, these words mean "putting up with one another." The writer does not assume that maintaining unity and peace in the church means all will agree with one another or even appreciate the other. Still, through patience and humility, they can maintain unity and peace.

Peace and unity are maintained through more than force of will; the church lives in them because of all its members share. Even though they have substantive differences, whatever separates them and makes them different is overshadowed by all they have in common. The same Spirit indwells all; all hold the same hope for the future; all have the same God, the same central understanding of Christ, and the same initiation into the church. They are bound together by the God who is over all things and the way that God has acted in Christ. The series of "ones" in verses 4-6 is a powerful reminder of what unites the church. The cosmic scope of the things they share puts their differences in a new perspective, making their substantial differences seem minor.

Ephesians 4:7-12. In addition to his or her common beliefs and experiences, each person has been given a gift by Christ. Ephesians gives new meaning to Psalm 68, a psalm about God's victory over God's enemies. Ephesians 4:8 applies the words of this psalm to the ascension of Christ and the benefits the church derives from it. The writer's brief narrative of the Incarnation sees the preexistent Christ descending into the world and then ascending to heaven's highest position. From this position, Christ distributes gifts to every church member. Importantly, Ephesians says that the gift each receives is "according to the measure of Christ's gift" (4:7), that is, the gift each person has is determined by what Christ determines the church needs. This meaning becomes clear in what follows. The presence of each member, therefore, is needed because Christ has gifted each to serve the whole. This statement adds yet another commonality: They are all recipients of gifts from the same exalted and gracious giver, Christ.

All Christians receive gifts, but not the same gifts. In verse 11 Ephesians lists gifts of leadership that Christ grants to the church. Christ has made some apostles and others prophets. Both of these are authoritative teachers. Apostles were the primary authority for the church. Their interpretation of the gospel and its meaning for how to conduct one's life was accepted as the authentic understanding of the message and mission of Christ. Prophets were people in local churches who received a word from God for a particular congregation. They were seen as recipients of revelation, even though their words were to be tested by the community (see 1 Corinthians 14:29). Evangelists preached to draw in new members. Pastors and teachers are joined more closely in the grammar of the sentence. Perhaps Ephesians sees the combination as the kinds of leaders expected to be present in the church of the writer's day. The gifts of these people are in gentle leading, as the image of a shepherd (pastor) suggests, and in helping the church understand the faith clearly.

Verse 12 spells out the function of these gifts of leadership: They are to prepare the saints for the work of ministry. These leaders are not the only ones with a ministry. Here their real task is to help the rest of the church be engaged in ministry. Thus, all members are commissioned to exercise a ministry in the church. The leader's job is to prepare others to participate in the church's ministry so that the whole is built up. It is the ministry of each member to the others— not just that of leaders to non-leaders—that builds up the body of Christ, according to this verse.

Ephesians 4:13-16. Verses 13-16 describe the results of this ministry of the whole church. First, it leads the church to maturity, to what Christ wants it to be. This happens as the church attains unity in their faith and knowledge of Christ. Ephesians places a high value on holding to correct teaching. The writer knows that believing the right things is important because what we believe influences how we live. Proper maturity, he says, keeps us from believing wrong things. He sees the entrance of false teachings as a result of human sneakiness and deceitfulness. The antidote for false teaching is speaking true doctrine lovingly. This leads the church to become what it should be because it secures its connection to Christ. When the church lovingly maintains correct teaching, Christ empowers his body to retain unity. Using explicit biological language, Ephesians speaks of the way Christ holds all the members of his body together. In this unity, each member is strengthened personally and is enabled to love others and experience the love of Christ in the church.

INTERPRETING THE SCRIPTURE

Live Worthily

Our passage today begins with a powerful demand: Live in a manner that is worthy of the call you have accepted to be one of God's people. How could anyone live up to the grace and salvation we have been given in Christ? We live with this challenge always, in every aspect of our lives. The more we realize how much God has done for us, the more we recognize what we should do to reflect that gift in our lives. Ephesians focuses attention on how we live out this demand in relation to other Christians. We live worthily by exercising patience and humility, even by putting up with one another, in ways that maintain unity and peace in the church. Thus, our treatment of fellow Christians is an important aspect of how we strive to live worthily of our calling to be God's people.

Unity With Diversity and Difference

Ephesians supports this demand by listing things that already make us one. This list shows that our unity is a given. It is a part of what God grants to the church. All Christians are part of the same body of Christ, all have the same Holy Spirit living in them, all look forward to the same blessings in the presence of God, and all have been brought into these gifts through the same ritual. We are further made one by our common faith about and commitment to the same God and the same Lord, Christ. Whether we recognize it or act like it, we are all part of the one church created by these things. This impressive list of things Christians share dwarfs all the things that might seem to separate us. Nothing can be larger or more important than these things we have in common. It is our task to behave in ways that reflect that unity.

Such unity does not mean uniformity— and that is why the concept of unity is difficult. Ephesians reminds Gentile Christians that they must maintain unity with Christians who are quite different. They must recognize and enact unity with Jewish Christians. Thus, they must maintain peace and unity with people of a different cultural heritage who perhaps have different worship practices. Ephesians calls first-century Jewish and Gentile Christians to be one with people who eat different foods, keep different religious holidays, and belong to different social institutions. The gift of unity demands the same things of us. We have to recognize our unity with those who worship differently or have customs that make us uncomfortable. Unity with those who are like us is easy, at least when compared to unity with those who are different in their practices and perhaps even in their doctrinal emphases. Unity with Christians who take different positions on hot-button issues is especially difficult. But Ephesians sees it as necessary.

Such matters make it hard to live up to the unity we have been granted. We all like to think that our way of being Christian is superior to the ways others live their faith or conduct their worship. Ephesians says that some ways of being faithful are more suited to some kinds of people, while other ways are more suited to a different cultural community. Acknowledging the validity of that which is different calls for the kind of humility Ephesians asks for. The recipients of the Letter to the Ephesians needed to recognize that Jews and Gentiles have different, even contradictory, practices (as for example, some will eat pork, others will not), but that both are being faithful to God. The difference comes because of the identity of each community. We find it difficult to acknowledge that those with different ways of living their faith are as faithful as we are. But this is what Ephesians calls us to do. We must look for ways to acknowledge that our practice may be better suited to who we are, but realize that it is not the only right way to be Christian. Indeed, other ways of practicing the faith are better for other communities.

This way of understanding and practicing unity requires humility and patience, even putting up with one another. Still, Ephesians calls us to maintain the gift of unity. Accepting difference as a part of our unity in Christ is a concrete demonstration of our love for one another in Christ.

Difference and Proper Teaching

This emphasis on unity does not mean the church should accept any teaching that someone might advocate. Proper teaching is still a requirement. So the church must learn to set parameters as it also lets diversity live within those limits. Ephesians sees living in unity as one way to shield the church from false teaching. Remember that one of the things in Ephesians' list of what binds the church together is "one faith" (4:5). There is a body of teaching to which all Christians must adhere. Our difficulty comes when we try to identify the necessary components of the faith we must all share. The church constantly struggles to make this judgment correctly. If the lines are drawn too narrowly, we become sectarian and judgmental. But if we fail to draw the lines or draw them too broadly, we lose anything that is distinctly Christian and so we fail to proclaim and embody the way God was present in Christ.

Our limitations should counsel humility here. We do not fully understand God and God's will, yet we may truly understand God. Ephesians advocates maintaining proper faith, but knows that proper teaching must be done in a loving way. Only by "speaking the truth in love" (4:15) will the church become what Christ wants it to be. This manner of engaging in discussion about correct teaching enables the church to maintain unity and even strengthens its connection to Christ.

Everyone Has a Ministry

Ephesians expects the whole church to be engaged in ministry. Various New Testament books provide different lists of the gifts that Christ gives the church. Ephesians chooses to enumerate a select group of gifts of leadership. After mentioning those through whom the voice of God is heard most authoritatively and directly, the writer turns to gifts known well in the church, those of evangelist, pastor, and teacher (4:11). The task he assigns these leaders may be surprising: They are "to equip the saints for the work of ministry" (4:12). Those with these gifts are not *the* ministers; rather, they are the people who enable others in the church to do ministry. Ephesians asserts that ministry is the work of every member of the church. The writer stresses that each member has been given a gift by Christ. So the work of ministry cannot simply be assigned to people on staff or to clergy. Ministry is the work of all the church. Church members cannot simply hire clergy to do the church's work. Ephesians says all are to be involved in the church's ministry because Christ has gifted each in a way that contributes to the growth of the church. A central part of the work of leaders is to help the rest of the church be engaged in ministry, helping all recognize and use their gifts. This ministry of the whole church, in turn, builds up the body of Christ so that it begins to reflect more fully Christ's own fullness.

SHARING THE SCRIPTURE

Preparing Our Hearts

Explore this week's devotional reading, found in Romans 12:3-8. Here Paul emphasizes the diversity of gifts within the one body of Christ. Compare the list of gifts found in verses 6-8 with the list found in today's reading from Ephesians 4:11. Notice that God has given us these gifts. Moreover, our gifts do not make us better than someone else. Rather, as Ephesians 4:12 reminds us, these gifts are to build up the body of Christ. What are your spiritual gifts? How are you using them to build up Christ's body? Are there new avenues of ministry that you could undertake to bring greater strength and unity to the body?

Pray that you and the adult students will identify and use your gifts for the good of all.

Preparing Our Minds

Study the background Scripture and the lesson Scripture, both of which are from Ephesians 4:1-16.

Consider this question as you prepare the lesson: *What brings about a feeling of unity after we have worked together on a project that goes well?*

Write on newsprint:
❑ information for next week's lesson, found under "Continue the Journey."
❑ activities for further spiritual growth in "Continue the Journey."

Review the "Introduction," "The Big Picture," "Close-up," and "Faith in Action." Consider how you will use this additional information, which immediately precedes the first lesson, for this session.

LEADING THE CLASS

(1) Gather to Learn

❖ Greet the class members. Introduce any guests and help them feel at home.

❖ Pray that all who have come today will feel at one with the rest of the group.

❖ Read: **Building a Habitat for Humanity home is a project that a Sunday school class can spearhead for the entire church to create an exciting mission opportunity. Everything—from working with the local Habitat office, to raising funds, to working on the house with the selected** owner, to enjoying the celebration when the keys are handed over to the family, to raising more money to support home building in a foreign country—provides an opportunity for folks to work together, solve problems, overcome obstacles, use their gifts, and feel really good about the way everything has come together. In short, working on such a project not only builds a home but also builds up unity within the body of Christ.

❖ Ask: **What projects has our class engaged in that afforded us similar opportunities to use our gifts and feel a sense of unity as a group?**

❖ Read aloud today's focus statement: **We all feel positive about life when everything goes well after we have worked together on a project. What brings about this feeling of unity? The writer of Ephesians says that although each of us brings different gifts, we find true unity as we grow into Christ, who is the head of the whole body.**

(2) Goal 1: Explore Characteristics of a Life Worthy of Christ's Calling in Building Up the Body of Christ

❖ Introduce today's Bible passage by reading "Live Worthily" from Interpreting the Scripture.

❖ Choose a volunteer to read Ephesians 4:1-16.

❖ Look again at verses 1-3 and talk with the class about the characteristics Paul cites as being worthy of a life devoted to Christ.

❖ Read or retell Ephesians 4:7-12 and 13-16 in Understanding the Scripture to clarify the purpose of these gifts and their intended results.

❖ Provide a few moments for silent reflection and ask: **How am I working with other members of my class and church to build up the body of Christ in love? Is there anything I am doing to harm the body? If so, what steps do I need to take to change?**

(3) Goal 2: Identify and Celebrate the Learner's Gifts That Help Build Up the Body of Christ

❖ Distribute paper and pencils. Call on volunteers to read aloud slowly these lists of gifts that God gives to build up the body. As each gift is read, those adults who believe that they have this gift are to write it on their paper.
    (1) Romans 12:4-8
    (2) 1 Corinthians 12:4-11
    (3) Ephesians 4:11-13
❖ Form several small groups. Invite each adult to name the gifts on his or her list. Others in the group may add to the list, perhaps stating an example of a situation in which they observed that gift being used.

❖ Conclude by encouraging the learners to continue to identify and use their gifts to the glory of God.

(4) Goal 3: State an Interpretation of Having "One Faith, One Baptism, One God of All" as It Relates to the Building Up of the Body of Christ

❖ Begin by reading in unison Ephesians 4:4-6. Then choose one or both of the options to explore these verses.

❖ **Option 1:** Read "Unity with Diversity and Difference" from Interpreting the Scripture and discuss these questions:
    (1) **Why do you suppose that people "find it difficult to acknowledge that those with different ways of living their faith are as faithful as we are"?**
    (2) **What can we do to push out the boundaries of the church so that those who are "not like us" might feel welcomed and included without diminishing the identity of the church as the one body of Christ?** (See "Difference and Proper Teaching" in Interpreting the Scripture.)
    (3) **How can we encourage people to use God's diverse gifts to create unity within Christ's body?**

❖ **Option 2:** Distribute hymnals and invite the adults to read "One Bread, One Body" and discuss these questions:

(1) **What does this hymn suggest to you about the meaning of "one faith, one baptism, one God and Father of all" (Ephesians 4:5-6)?**

(2) **How do you see this idea of oneness being lived out in your own congregation?**

(3) **The hymn speaks of many gifts. What are some of the gifts that you see at work in members of your congregation?**

(4) **How are these gifts used in specific ministries to glorify the "one God . . . of all"?**

(5) Continue the Journey

❖ Pray that today's participants will seek the Holy Spirit's guidance in maintaining the unity of Christ's body.

❖ Read aloud this preparation for next week's lesson. You may also want to post it on newsprint for the students to copy.

■ **Title: Live in the Light**

■ **Background Scripture: John 1:1-14; Ephesians 4:17–5:20**

■ **Lesson Scripture: John 1:1-5; Ephesians 5:1-2, 6-14**

■ **Focus of the Lesson: People sometimes think their thoughts, fears, and actions are hidden or are secrets from others. What happens when these secrets are exposed to the light? The writer of Ephesians tells us that as Christians we always live in Christ's light that,** as John reminds us, overcomes all kinds of darkness.

❖ Post these three activities related to this week's session on newsprint for the students to copy. Challenge the adults to grow spiritually by completing one or more of them.

(1) **Talk with some friends at church to help one another identify and affirm spiritual gifts. Challenge yourselves to use these gifts in ways that build up the body of Christ.**

(2) **Investigate the ecumenical movement, which according to the World Council of Churches has as its main goal "the visible unity of the church." How do you see churches of different denominations coming together? What separates us?**

(3) **Make a special effort to "maintain the unity of the Spirit in the bond of peace" (Ephesians 4:3). If there is dissension within your congregation, do all that you can to promote peace.**

❖ Sing or read aloud "All Praise to Our Redeeming Lord."

❖ Conclude today's session by leading the class in this benediction, adapted from the key verses for December 23 from Ephesians 5:1 and January 13 from Philippians 2:5: **Go now as the Father's beloved children, who are of the same mind as the Son Jesus Christ, to be imitators of God.**

UNIT 1: VICTORY IN JESUS
LIVE IN THE LIGHT

PREVIEWING THE LESSON

Lesson Scripture: John 1:1-5; Ephesians 5:1-2, 6-14
Background Scripture: John 1:1-14; Ephesians 4:17–5:20
Key Verse: Ephesians 5:1

Focus of the Lesson:
People sometimes think their thoughts, fears, and actions are hidden or secrets from others. What happens when these secrets are exposed to the light? The writer of Ephesians tells us that as Christians we always live in Christ's light that, as John reminds us, overcomes all kinds of darkness.

Goals for the Learners:
(1) to explore images of Jesus as light overcoming darkness as used in John and Ephesians.
(2) to imagine living in constant light, where there are no secrets.
(3) to commit to discovering how to live a fruitful life in the light.

Supplies:
Bibles, newsprint and marker, paper and pencils, hymnals

READING THE SCRIPTURE

NRSV
Lesson Scripture: John 1:1-5

¹In the beginning was the Word, and the Word was with God, and the Word was God. ²He was in the beginning with God. ³All things came into being through him, and without him not one thing came into being. What has come into being ⁴in him was life, and the life was the light of all people. ⁵The light shines in the darkness, and the darkness did not overcome it.

CEB
Lesson Scripture: John 1:1-5

¹In the beginning was the Word
  and the Word was with God
  and the Word was God.
²The Word was with God in the beginning.
³Everything came into being
  through the Word,
  and without the Word
  nothing came into being.
  What came into being

Lesson Scripture: Ephesians 5:1-2, 6-14

¹**Therefore be imitators of God, as beloved children,** ²and live in love, as Christ loved us and gave himself up for us, a fragrant offering and sacrifice to God.

⁶Let no one deceive you with empty words, for because of these things the wrath of God comes on those who are disobedient. ⁷Therefore do not be associated with them. ⁸For once you were darkness, but now in the Lord you are light. Live as children of light—⁹for the fruit of the light is found in all that is good and right and true. ¹⁰Try to find out what is pleasing to the Lord. ¹¹Take no part in the unfruitful works of darkness, but instead expose them. ¹²For it is shameful even to mention what such people do secretly; ¹³but everything exposed by the light becomes visible, ¹⁴for everything that becomes visible is light. Therefore it says,

"Sleeper, awake!
    Rise from the dead,
and Christ will shine on you."

⁴through the Word was life,
    and the life was the light for all people.
⁵The light shines in the darkness,
    and the darkness doesn't
        extinguish the light.

Lesson Scripture: Ephesians 5:1-2, 6-14

¹**Therefore, imitate God like dearly loved children.** ²Live your life with love, following the example of Christ, who loved us and gave himself for us. He was a sacrificial offering that smelled sweet to God.

⁶Nobody should deceive you with stupid ideas. God's anger comes down on those who are disobedient because of this kind of thing. ⁷So you shouldn't have anything to do with them. ⁸You were once darkness, but now you are light in the Lord, so live your life as children of light. ⁹Light produces fruit that consists of every sort of goodness, justice, and truth. ¹⁰Therefore test everything to see what's pleasing to the Lord, ¹¹and don't participate in the unfruitful actions of darkness. Instead you should reveal the truth about them. ¹²It's embarrassing to even talk about what certain persons do in secret. ¹³But everything exposed to the light is revealed by the light. ¹⁴Everything that is revealed by the light is light. Therefore it says, *Wake up, sleeper! Get up from the dead, and Christ will shine on you.*

UNDERSTANDING THE SCRIPTURE

John 1:1-5. The Gospel of John begins with the most exalted language about Christ found in any of the Gospels. John draws on traditions within Jewish Wisdom Literature to describe the preexistent Christ. Wisdom Literature had seen Wisdom as a personification of an important characteristic of God. She was identified with God and worked as an agent of God in creation. Similarly, John identifies Christ as the Word of God who was God's agent in creation and brings knowledge of God to the world. This liturgy posits the closest possible relationship between God and Christ, so that Christ can be the clearest revelation of God's nature and will. This best revelation comes through the Incarnation. Saying that "the Word became flesh" (1:14) goes beyond anything that had been said about Wisdom and the ways God was seen in her. Through Christ the presence of God partakes of our world and reveals itself in a new and clearer way.

Calling Christ the "Word" emphasizes that one of the main saving acts of Christ is that he brings us true knowledge of God. For John the books of the Hebrew Bible bring knowledge of God. Yet he finds more and clearer revelation in the person of Jesus. God does more than speak through him: Jesus is the genuine and direct presence of God in the world. Advent calls us to remember, celebrate, and look more closely at this revelatory and direct presence of God among us. John notes that this knowledge of God is difficult to receive. The NRSV translates the verb at the end of verse 5 with "overcome," while the NIV has "understood." These translations are equally viable and both point to the difficulty the world has in understanding who God is—even in the face of the immediate presence of God found in Christ.

John 1:6-14. The Gospel introduces John the Baptist as a witness to the identity of Jesus as the light of the world and the agent of its creation. Furthermore, it is through Christ that people come to have a relationship with God; those who see God in Christ are made the children of God in a new and profound sense. This possibility comes to us through the Incarnation, God's genuine participation in our world in the person of Jesus.

Ephesians 4:17-24. This passage contrasts non-Christian life with what is expected of believers. The section lists vices that the writer sees as characteristic of non-Christian Gentiles and reminds them that they are no longer a part of that world. They have been given a new life that requires different behavior.

Ephesians 4:25-32. A list of instructions about specific behaviors begins in 4:25. The writer contrasts the unacceptable behaviors with proper conduct and sometimes grounds the exhortation in some aspect of the gospel. Some of these instructions seem to be primarily about behavior within the church because he speaks of the readers being members of the same body (4:25) and of the forgiveness that they have received in Christ (4:32). While the commands here apply to all of life, the writer is particularly concerned about relations within the church as Jews and Gentiles learn to live together as God's people.

Ephesians 5:1-5. Chapter 5 begins with a daunting exhortation: Imitate God because you are God's children. Such exhortations were not, however, uncommon among moralists of the first century. They sometimes called on readers to imitate a god in their moral lives. This did not mean becoming all-powerful or attaining aspects of a god's nature that are beyond humans. It did mean that humans should conduct their lives in ways that were patterned after the moral aspects of a god's character. This is what Ephesians intends. Specifically, Ephesians wants readers to respond to God's forgiveness by forgiving and loving others.

The appropriateness of this exhortation is reinforced by reminding readers that they are loved children of God. In the ancient world, children were to represent and imitate their parents. So Ephesians recalls that believers have been given the status of beloved children, a status that expects them to reflect the character of their parent, God.

Verse 2 expands the exhortation to include the conduct of their whole lives. Christians should live in love because God has shown them love in Christ. Christ's willingness to die for them sets the standard for how loving they should be to others. Ephesians compares Christ's death to a sacrifice offered on an altar. The writer draws on descriptions of sacrifices found in Leviticus 4:7 and elsewhere in the Hebrew Bible when he speaks of Christ's sacrifice as a "fragrant offering." This way of referring to a sacrifice has nothing to do with paying a penalty. Instead, it defines the sacrifice as a gift that gives God something pleasing. Thus, Christ's demonstration of love for us was pleasing to God and therefore calls us to please God by showing love to those around us.

Ephesians 5:6-14. These verses renew the dramatic contrast between the readers' former lives and their present state by identifying their past lives as lived in darkness and their present lives as living in light. This contrast characterizes their behavior, not their inner nature. The difference is more about the realm in which they live (which determines their behavior) than about whether they have a defect in the nature of their being. Now they live in the light of God's love and holiness, where they are able to discern what God's will is.

Verse 14 combines Isaiah 26:19 and 60:1 to emphasize that this transfer into the light and the accompanying transformation of their lives and behavior depends on Christ.

The transformation moves them from a life lived in darkness and death to a life in the light, where their lives are given new meaning and their behavior is conformed to God's holiness and love.

Ephesians 5:15-20. Believers must live out that transformation they have experienced in daily life. They must carefully discern God's will for their lives in a world that is evil and foolish. Therefore, their lives will be distinctive. At the end of this section, the writer returns his attention to life within the church, calling on readers to encourage one another through the praise in song and the thanks that they offer to God through Christ.

INTERPRETING THE SCRIPTURE

Imitate God

Ephesians 5 begins with an overwhelming exhortation: Imitate God. This command calls Christians to live by the highest imaginable standard. The command to imitate God takes us to the heart of Christian ethics. How we decide what is right is ultimately determined by whether it conforms to what God is like. At least as far back as Leviticus (for example, 11:44), moral instructions have been grounded in the character of God, particularly God's holiness. This basis for evaluating behavior is repeated in the New Testament directly (for example, 1 Peter 1:16) and even more often stands in the background, as it does here in Ephesians. All our moral judgments should be based on who God is and how we can live that out in our lives. This means we will act with love and justice in all we do, just as it means we will strive for holiness, because that reflects who God is.

Since the criteria of the character of God may seem rather vague, the writer of Ephesians gives some specifics about how his readers should live out this imitation of God. These specifics include being loving and forgiving, as well rejecting sinful behaviors. He does not, of course, list all things that might be sins or all things that Christians ought to do. Even if he had been able to do that for those first-century readers, we would need more guidance for our time. Fortunately, the life of Jesus shows us what it looks like to conform our lives to the will and character of God.

Imitate Jesus

John opens his Gospel by identifying Jesus as the Word of God. A significant part of what it means to call Jesus the Word is that he is the one who reveals who God is and what God wants for us. As Jesus tells Philip later in John, if you have seen Jesus you have seen the Father (14:8-9). Similarly, as Ephesians enumerates things Christians must put out of their lives, the writer says they "learned Christ" in a way that requires ethical living (4:20-24). For both John and Ephesians, the life of Jesus sets the standard for the kinds of attitudes and behaviors Christians must adopt. While we will not directly adopt all Jesus did in his life (for example, keeping the sabbath or the Mosaic food laws), his way of relating to God and those around him should condition the ways we make all ethical decisions. We should discern what God calls us to do by observing the life of Jesus and letting it direct how we make moral decisions.

Jesus' life shows us that living by what God wants often sets us at odds with the values of the people around us. This is clear from Jesus' exchanges with both religious and civil authorities, conflicts that eventually led to his death. Ephesians also stresses that Christians must reject much of the behavior of non-Christians as they adopt ways of living that are appropriate to being followers of Christ. It is often difficult to discern which widely accepted attitudes and behaviors Christians should reject. We sometimes do not see those faults until the world changes (for example, racism was once acceptable in the church). So the church must constantly examine how it participates in the attitudes, ideas, and practices that are conventional in the wider society.

The Gift of a New Inner Self

Calling readers to imitate God and to follow the example of Jesus sets a standard that may seem discouraging, but Ephesians offers hope and support as we strive to live for God. First, the writer notes that God strengthens us to live as we should. He says that each Christian is made a "new self" that God has created in "righteousness and holiness" (4:23-24). So part of the gift of our salvation is that God empowers us by recreating us, remaking our inner selves so we can live for God and live in the ways that make the most meaningful lives for ourselves.

These expectations may seem even more discouraging as we recognize that we do not immediately begin to live for God consistently. But we should recognize that the gift of this newness does not automatically and immediately change all our behavior. This change is a process—after all, the section we are reading gives extensive instructions about behavior to people to whom God has already given the new inner self. The need for instruction and discernment continues throughout our lives. God recognizes that we are limited in our ability to understand what God wants and in our ability to live fully according to God's will in a world that honors attitudes and actions that violate God's will. So we seek to understand God's will more fully through Christ, knowing that God continues to support and enable our discernment and our faithfulness.

Light and Darkness

Ephesians uses the metaphor of light and darkness to contrast the church with the rest of the world. Those of us who grew up in the church may find it hard to think about a time when we lived in darkness. Ephesians seems to assume that most of its readers are first-generation Christians who had a sinful pre-Christian life. But the contrast is not simply about individual lives; it points to the distinction between a life directed by the primary values of the world and one that seeks to follow the example of Jesus.

Various religious communities of the first century used the language of light and darkness to distinguish themselves from the rest of the world. Darkness was the realm of immorality and ignorance of God, while living in the light meant having the correct knowledge of God and living morally. Which sphere a person lived in determined the direction of his or her life. Ephesians reminds its readers that their lives were once dominated by the powers of evil. Now God has brought them into the realm of light, so they must not participate in the things that characterized their former lives.

The direction of their lives has changed. They possess a new relationship with God and thus experience God's goodness. And since they are in the light, they are able to discern God's will and their lives manifest righteousness (5:8-10).

By bringing us into the light, God grants us new understandings of God's will and a new ability to live for God. Even as we are told that we already live in the light, we must be encouraged to live lives that show that is where we belong. We must work to keep those elements of darkness (immorality of all sorts—personal and social) out of our lives. As we do this, we may even see some transformation of the world. Ephesians expects real progress in personal moral behavior, as we overcome the darkness in our lives. Fortunately, the writer reminds us again that we are not left to our own efforts. As we turn to God, Christ shines this light in our lives, enlightening our minds and supporting our efforts to live for God.

SHARING THE SCRIPTURE

Preparing Our Hearts

Explore this week's devotional reading, found in Psalm 97. Here the psalmist praises God, who reigns over the entire universe. Verse 11 speaks of light dawning for those who are righteous. Light is a powerful metaphor in the Bible. Although darkness is not mentioned in this psalm, the two are often contrasted, as, for example, in John 1 and Ephesians 5. In what areas of your life are you living in the light? In what areas are you in darkness? Ask God to guide you into the light.

Pray that you and the adult students will choose to follow the example of Christ by living in his light.

Preparing Our Minds

Study the background Scripture from John 1:1-14 and Ephesians 4:17–5:20. The lesson Scripture is from John 1:1-5 and Ephesians 5:1-2, 6-14.

Consider this question as you prepare the lesson: *What happens when people's secret thoughts, fears, and actions are exposed to the light?*

Write on newsprint:

❑ questions for "Commit to Discovering How to Live a Fruitful Life in the Light."
❑ information for next week's lesson, found under "Continue the Journey."
❑ activities for further spiritual growth in "Continue the Journey."

Review the "Introduction," "The Big Picture," "Close-up," and "Faith in Action." Consider how you will use this additional information, which immediately precedes the first lesson, for this session.

Be prepared for this Sunday before Christmas as some regular attendees will likely be absent and some guests may be present. You may wish to contact several members about providing some Christmas refreshments. If so, be sure to have whatever paper products and beverages you will need.

LEADING THE CLASS

(1) Gather to Learn

❖ Greet the class members. Introduce any guests and help them feel at home.

❖ Pray that those who are present today will be illumined by the light of Christ.

❖ Ask: **What are your favorite Christmas**

decorations? Students may recall decorations from childhood, as well as current items that they use. Try to bring the discussion to the common use of lights at Christmas. People put candles in the windows and strings of lights on Christmas trees. They also use spotlights on holiday door wreaths and lights to outline or accent features of their homes. Point out that it is difficult to find a home—even a business—that celebrates the holiday without lights. Ask: **What meaning do these lights have for you?**

❖ Read aloud today's focus statement: **People sometimes think their thoughts, fears, and actions are hidden or are secrets from others. What happens when these secrets are exposed to the light? The writer of Ephesians tells us that as Christians we always live in Christ's light that, as John reminds us, overcomes all kinds of darkness.**

(2) Goal 1: Explore Images of Jesus as Light Overcoming Darkness as Used in John and Ephesians

❖ Choose a volunteer to read John 1:1-5.
❖ Help the students understand this opening portion of the Prologue of John's Gospel (1:1-18) by reading or retelling John 1:1-5 from Understanding the Scripture.
❖ Select another volunteer to read Ephesians 5:1-2.
❖ Read "Imitate God" from Interpreting the Scripture and invite the adults to discuss what it means on a practical, daily basis for them to act as God does.
❖ Call on another volunteer to read Ephesians 5:6-14.
❖ Use information from "Light and Darkness" in Interpreting the Scripture to unpack the meaning of these verses. Discuss ways in which first-century understandings of light and darkness may be similar to and different from our own understandings.

(3) Goal 2: Imagine Living in Constant Light, Where There Are No Secrets

❖ Read: **Areas south of the Antarctic Circle and north of the Arctic Circle experience periods of twenty-four-hour daylight during the summer months. These lands of the "midnight sun" include all or parts of Norway, Sweden, Finland, Russia, Iceland, Canada's Northern Territories, Greenland, and Alaska. Although the idea of having twenty-four hours of daylight might sound enticing, this constant light requires sleep adjustments and is associated with an increase in mental disorders and suicides. As you think about the pros and cons of living where there is sunlight twenty-four hours a day during part of the year, think too about what it would be like to live constantly in the light of God.**

❖ Ask these questions. Provide time for silent reflection rather than discussion.

(1) **What advantages could you see to living constantly in the light of God?** (*Pause.*)
(2) **What challenges would you find in that light, particularly knowing that you would never have any secrets?** (*Pause.*)
(3) **What might be your worst fear about living in the light?** (*Pause.*)
(4) **Are there any changes that you could make now to set aside that fear?** (*Pause.*)
(5) **How might the world be different if everyone's life were continuously exposed to the light?** (*Pause.*)

(4) Goal 3: Commit to Discovering How to Live a Fruitful Life in the Light

❖ Read "Imitate Jesus" in Interpreting the Scripture.
❖ Form several groups. Ask each group to consider these questions, which you will post on newsprint:

(1) **Review together Ephesians 5:6-14. What ideas do you find there**

for living a fruitful life in the light of Christ?

(2) Verse 10 suggests that we are to "try to find out what is pleasing to the Lord." Name ways that you can do that.

(3) What kinds of actions and attitudes do you believe are off-limits for Christians?

(4) Part of verse 14 is likely a fragment from an early Christian hymn. How do you see the church today as a "sleeper" that needs to awaken and "rise from the dead"?

(5) Continue the Journey

❖ Pray that all who have come today will experience the blessings of the coming of Jesus, the light of the world, and will share those blessings with others.

❖ Read aloud this preparation for next week's lesson. You may also want to post it on newsprint for the students to copy.

■ **Title: Christ's Love for the Church**
■ **Background Scripture: Ephesians 5:21–6:4**
■ **Lesson Scripture: Ephesians 5:21–6:4**
■ **Focus of the Lesson: People struggle to balance the demands of their daily lives with their need to show love for one another. Where can people find the secret to a**

healthy life together? The writer of Ephesians states that family members should love and care for one another just as Christ loves and cares for the church.

❖ Post these three activities related to this week's session on newsprint for the students to copy. Challenge the adults to grow spiritually by completing one or more of them.

(1) **Attend a Christmas Eve candle-light service. As you light your candle, remember that you are called to live in the light of Christ.**

(2) **Take a child to see Christmas trees or other displays of light in your community. Use this opportunity to talk about how Jesus is the light of the world.**

(3) **Confess your own works of darkness to God and ask for forgiveness. Be assured that you are indeed forgiven.**

❖ Sing or read aloud "I Want to Walk as a Child of the Light."

❖ Conclude today's session by leading the class in this benediction, adapted from the key verses for December 23 from Ephesians 5:1 and January 13 from Philippians 2:5: **Go now as the Father's beloved children, who are of the same mind as the Son Jesus Christ, to be imitators of God.**

UNIT 1: VICTORY IN JESUS
CHRIST'S LOVE FOR THE CHURCH

PREVIEWING THE LESSON

Lesson Scripture: Ephesians 5:21–6:4
Background Scripture: Ephesians 5:21–6:4
Key Verse: Ephesians 5:21

Focus of the Lesson:
People struggle to balance the demands of their daily lives with their need to show love for one another. Where can people find the secret to a healthy life together? The writer of Ephesians states that family members should love and care for one another just as Christ loves and cares for the church.

Goals for the Learners:
(1) to compare Christ's love for the church with the relationships among family members.
(2) to appreciate Christ's sacrifice to show love and care for the church.
(3) to accept responsibility for showing love in the family as Christ demonstrated love for the church.

Pronunciation Guide:
Christology (kris tol' uh jee)

Supplies:
Bibles, newsprint and marker, paper and pencils, hymnals

READING THE SCRIPTURE

NRSV
Lesson Scripture: Ephesians 5:21–6:4
²¹Be subject to one another out of reverence for Christ.
²²Wives, be subject to your husbands as

CEB
Lesson Scripture: Ephesians 5:21–6:4
²¹And submit to each other out of respect for Christ. ²²For example, wives should submit to their husbands as if to the Lord.

you are to the Lord. ²³For the husband is the head of the wife just as Christ is the head of the church, the body of which he is the Savior. ²⁴Just as the church is subject to Christ, so also wives ought to be, in everything, to their husbands.

²⁵Husbands, love your wives, just as Christ loved the church and gave himself up for her, ²⁶in order to make her holy by cleansing her with the washing of water by the word, ²⁷so as to present the church to himself in splendor, without a spot or wrinkle or anything of the kind—yes, so that she may be holy and without blemish. ²⁸In the same way, husbands should love their wives as they do their own bodies. He who loves his wife loves himself. ²⁹For no one ever hates his own body, but he nourishes and tenderly cares for it, just as Christ does for the church, ³⁰because we are members of his body. ³¹"For this reason a man will leave his father and mother and be joined to his wife, and the two will become one flesh." ³²This is a great mystery, and I am applying it to Christ and the church. ³³Each of you, however, should love his wife as himself, and a wife should respect her husband.

⁶:¹Children, obey your parents in the Lord, for this is right. ²"Honor your father and mother"—this is the first commandment with a promise: ³"so that it may be well with you and you may live long on the earth."

⁴And, fathers, do not provoke your children to anger, but bring them up in the discipline and instruction of the Lord.

²³A husband is the head of his wife like Christ is head of the church, that is, the savior of the body. ²⁴So wives submit to their husbands in everything like the church submits to Christ. ²⁵As for husbands, love your wives just like Christ loved the church and gave himself for her. ²⁶He did this to make her holy by washing her in a bath of water with the word. ²⁷He did this to present himself with a splendid church, one without any sort of stain or wrinkle on her clothes, but rather one that is holy and blameless. ²⁸That's how husbands ought to love their wives—in the same way as they do their own bodies. Anyone who loves his wife loves himself. ²⁹No one ever hates his own body, but feeds it and takes care of it just like Christ does for the church ³⁰because we are parts of his body. ³¹*This is why a man will leave his father and mother and be united with his wife, and the two of them will be one body.* ³²Marriage is a significant allegory, and I'm applying it to Christ and the church. ³³In any case, as for you individually, each one of you should love his wife as himself, and wives should respect their husbands.

⁶:¹As for children, obey your parents in the Lord, because it is right. ²The commandment *Honor your father and mother* is the first one with a promise attached: ³so that things will go well for you, and you will live for a long time in the land. ⁴As for parents, don't provoke your children to anger, but raise them with discipline and instruction about the Lord.

UNDERSTANDING THE SCRIPTURE

Ephesians 5:21. Where we begin a paragraph and what we recognize as its topic sentence often greatly influence the meaning of the whole. Such is the case here. Some translations, such as the NIV, began the paragraph that opens our reading at verse 22, which calls women to submit to their husbands. Beginning the section with verse 21 significantly shifts the meaning of this section. Verse 21 calls for mutual submission of all. Thus, what follows is the epistle writer's understanding of what such submission looks like for various members of a household. The sentence structure of verse

21 in the Greek demonstrates that it belongs with verse 22. The verb "submit" appears only in verse 21 and we must infer that it is the verb of verse 22 that tells wives what to do. This is not a strange way to construct a Greek sentence. Here it shows that mutual submission is the basic topic.

Ephesians 5:22-24. Verse 22 begins a section that extends through 6:9 that is known as a household code. This literary form appears in a few other New Testament books. The form draws on earlier non-Christian literature that discusses how various members of the household (particularly husbands and wives, parents and children, and masters and slaves) should relate to one another. The household code of Ephesians is distinctive in the way it draws in the position and example of Christ to ground its instructions. The household codes of Colossians (3:18–4:1) and 1 Peter show greater dissatisfaction with the traditional hierarchical structure of first-century households than Ephesians does. Yet the way Christ is incorporated into Ephesians' discussion also reshapes relations within Christian marriages.

Ephesians reinforces the expected hierarchical structure of the household with powerful assertions based in Christology. Wives are to submit to husbands as to the Lord and to envision the relationship between Christ and the church as a parallel to that of husbands and wives. Yet we should remember that the initial command to submit is the second half of the sentence that says Christians are to submit to one another. A mixed message, then, opens this discussion of the household. Still, wives are called on to submit to husbands.

Ephesians 5:25-27. The usual instructions to husbands in discussions of how to run households involved the ways husbands should exercise dominance over wives in ways that are different from using their authority over children and slaves. In Ephesians, husbands are instead commanded to love their wives in a self-giving way. The second half of verse 25 through verse 27 constitutes a digression on Christ's love for the church. This digression begins by describing the extent of Christ's love: He gave his life for the church. The result of that self-giving is that the church is holy. The reference to water points to baptism as the point at which people enter the church and have the stain of sin removed from their lives. This cleansing provides the church with the holiness that makes its association with Christ appropriate.

Ephesians 5:28-31. After instructing husbands to love their wives as Christ loves the church, Ephesians takes a new tack in verses 28-31. The writer tells husbands to love their wives to the same extent that they love themselves, observing that people always take good care of themselves. He brings this argument back to his analogy between Christ and the church, noting that Christ takes care of the church the way people nurture their own bodies. He further grounds this argument in Genesis 2:24 where marriage is described as a melding of two people into one flesh. This supports the assertion that husbands should love and nurture their wives as much as they do these things for their own bodies.

This discussion of the husband's responsibilities shifts the emphasis of the hierarchy so that it is no longer about asserting dominance but about showing love and nurturing the other. Ephesians leaves the hierarchy in place, then, but changes what it means to be in the higher position. The superior does not demand privilege, but offers love and service. Ephesians may well see this change as the form of mutual submission that is appropriate for husbands.

Ephesians 5:32-33. The dual focus of the discussion (on Christ and husbands) remains in verse 32, as Ephesians applies the Genesis passage about marriage to the relationship between Christ and the church. If it is mysterious to think of how close people become in marriage, it is even more mysterious to contemplate the way Christ and the church have become one. The church as the body of Christ has a mysterious union with Christ that identifies the church with Christ in the most intimate way. This gives expression to Christ's great love for the church and suggests that the church has the responsibility to live up to its identification with Christ.

Verse 33 concludes these instructions to husbands and wives, repeating the call for husbands to love their wives as they love themselves and telling wives to respect their husbands. As we noted above, this retains the hierarchy but significantly shifts the responsibilities within it.

Ephesians 6:1-4. The second relationship the household code discusses is that between parents and children. For the second time, Ephesians grounds its instructions with a quotation from the Old Testament. The writer highlights the importance of the command by pointing out that this is the first commandment that comes with a special promise attached. Thus, he makes emphatic the command to obey parents. He balances that emphasis with the demand that fathers not provoke their children. Fathers had great authority over children in this era, even to the point of putting them to death (at least writers of the time assert this about Roman fathers). This command seems to limit that authority by prohibiting its unnecessary and severe use. Indeed, fathers are to nurture and encourage their children in ways that keep them in the faith. Thus, again, the person in the higher place in the hierarchy is given responsibility rather than privilege.

INTERPRETING THE SCRIPTURE

Reading Scripture

Today's reading requires us to think carefully about how we use the Bible as a guide for our lives. This becomes particularly clear in Ephesians 6:5-9, where the household code continues with instructions about how slaves and masters should act. The way we read this pair should guide our use of the rest of the code. We do not apply directly the commands we find to slaves and masters because we are convinced that there should be no slaves. To be consistent we should recognize that all of the instructions in this code address a different cultural setting and all are attempts to help the original readers think about how to be Christian in situations they cannot change. Thus, we cannot apply them directly to our time and relationships. We must think of how these instructions addressed that time and then of how that way of applying the faith should shape our lives today. Our world is different enough that how the gospel shapes our relationships will be different from the first century, as the instructions to masters and slaves indicates.

All Are Equal in Christ

One clear emphasis of the New Testament is that social class, sex, and ethnicity do not grant status or value in the church. This principle is pronounced clearly in Galatians 3:27-28, a passage that quotes a baptismal liturgy that is also cited in a different form in Colossians 3:11. This liturgy says that in Christ those distinctions that usually determine status and value in the world do not function in that way in the church. All are one, all have the same value to God, and so all must have the same value in the eyes of Christians. Much of Paul's argument with those who wanted Gentiles to convert to Judaism in order to be Christians revolved around the radical claim that God accepts and values Gentiles as Gentiles. Paul argues that Gentiles are as valuable to God as Jews, which is why the saving work of Christ is for both. The baptismal liturgy of Galatians 3 applied that same point to women and slaves, the other important social distinctions in the first century. The early church struggled to live out this oneness of all Christians as they thought about how believers should act within the structures of society that denied the equal value of each person. Our reading today is one of the church's efforts to discern how Christians could live out their faith in a society built on non-Christian values.

Just as they did, we also must think about how to embody our beliefs in our world. Our world continues to grant status and privilege based on social class, race, and sex. Statistics about prison populations, salary discrepancies, and many other indicators show that such things still matter in our society. The church has to continually think of how to conduct its life so that it is known as a place that rejects the values that grant favorable treatment to some groups within society. We must show the oneness of all in the eyes of God by the ways we treat those who are different.

Faith Influences All of Life

This discussion of how to be Christian within the family shows that our responsibilities as Christians extend into all areas of life. We sometimes separate our religious life from our business and personal lives. This passage demonstrates that such segmentation of our lives is not permissible. Households of the first century included the family business, not just spouses and children. So a discussion of the household implies that the faith should guide one's business practices as well as one's family life. Christian responsibilities go beyond our treatment of fellow Christians and family members. This may lead us to work for policies in the workplace that are based on values other than profit. Or it may lead us to favor political candidates who advocate policies that are more in line with our Christian values, even when those views may benefit others rather than ourselves. No area of our lives is exempt from our application of the principles found in the gospel, and no area is immune from seeking to exemplify what God wants for all people.

Transforming Faith

While we may be distressed to see the inequity evident in the discussion of marriage in Ephesians, we should recognize that this discussion moves the relationship between husbands and wives closer to recognizing the equal value and status of all people. As we noted in Understanding the Scripture, most discussions of household management in the ancient world focused on how the head of the household should rule over various other members of the household. Usually these discussions addressed only the head of the household. The New Testament household codes address all members of the household, thus according them status as people with responsibilities. But more substantial changes appear in Ephesians.

First, the section begins with a call for mutual submission. What follows does not sound like mutual submission to us, but in his context the author of Ephesians seems to think that his instructions do constitute it. That claim can make sense to us only if we remember that the usual instructions to husbands tell about how they should rule over wives, children, and slaves. The call for mutual submission was a dramatic shift from what was expected in first-century culture. Humility and submission were not virtues for free people in that era. Greco-Roman culture encouraged people to accumulate honor and status, even by shaming others. Thus, a call to mutual submission rejected the usual structure of the household and wider society.

Second, rather than telling husbands how to rule, Ephesians demands that they love with a self-giving love that is exemplified in Christ's giving of himself for us.

Third, the identification of the wife as one with the husband supports the command for husbands to love their wives as they love themselves. This implies that husbands will treat wives as well as they treat themselves.

These shifts in the kinds of instructions given to husbands changes the way they should envision their relationships with their wives. Wives are no longer simply subordinates; they are one with the husband's own body. To love a wife as Christ loves the church also means that she will be treated with respect and that the husband will make sacrifices for her.

Ephesians does not envision a marriage without hierarchy. Perhaps the writer was not quite able to see how such a marriage would function in the first century. But the description he gives of the duties of husbands and wives shows that his vision is changing. Being above the other person does not allow the one in the superior position to expect obedience and deference; rather, it brings responsibility and sacrifice. This acceptance of responsibility and sacrifice by both husband and wife is what this text calls for in marriages today.

SHARING THE SCRIPTURE

Preparing Our Hearts

Explore this week's devotional reading, found in John 3:16-21, which speaks of God's love as evidenced in the sending of Jesus. Read this familiar passage slowly, looking for new insights. Read it from another Bible translation, again seeking new understandings. Think about the contrast between light and darkness that is so often found in John's Gospel. Consider how you might explain this kernel of scriptural truth to a child or to someone who does not yet know Christ. Try to share your explanation with someone this week.

Pray that you and the adult students will recognize and give thanks for the love of God as you experience it in Jesus.

Preparing Our Minds

Study the background Scripture and the lesson Scripture, both of which are from Ephesians 5:21–6:4.

Consider this question as you prepare the lesson: *As people struggle to balance the demands of their daily lives with their need to show love for one another, where can they find the secret to a healthy life together?*

Write on newsprint:
- ❑ questions for "Appreciate Christ's Sacrifice to Show Love and Care for the Church."
- ❑ information for next week's lesson, found under "Continue the Journey."
- ❑ activities for further spiritual growth in "Continue the Journey."

Review the "Introduction," "The Big Picture," "Close-up," and "Faith in Action." Consider how you will use this additional information, which immediately precedes the first lesson.

LEADING THE CLASS

(1) Gather to Learn

❖ Greet the class members. Introduce any guests and help them feel at home.

❖ Pray that those who attend today will experience love and concern for one another.

❖ Read: **"If your father and mother, your sister and brother, if the very cat and dog in the house, are not happier for your being a Christian, it is a question whether you really are"** (James Hudson Taylor, 1832–1905).

❖ Ask: **In the midst of all the demands in today's fast-paced life, what key elements are necessary for maintaining a happy Christian home?**

❖ Read aloud today's focus statement: **People struggle to balance the demands of their daily lives with their need to show love for one another. Where can people find the secret to a healthy life together? The writer of Ephesians states that family members should love and care for one another just as Christ loves and cares for the church.**

(2) Goal 1: Compare Christ's Love for the Church With the Relationships Among Family Members

❖ Choose a volunteer to read Ephesians 5:21–6:4.

❖ Discuss these questions. Use information from Understanding the Scripture and Interpreting the Scripture as appropriate to clarify or expand the conversation:

(1) **In light of verse 21, how do you understand the relationship between wives and their husbands?** (See Ephesians 5:21 in Understanding the Scripture.)

(2) **In light of verse 21, how do you understand the relationship between husbands and their wives?**

(3) **Although these instructions to spouses may not impress us as progressive, how might they have been heard in the first century?** (See "Transforming Faith" in Interpreting the Scripture.)

(4) **If a letter to the church were being written today to help couples understand how to live together as Christ calls us to, what might be some of the major points?** (See

"All Are Equal in Christ" in Interpreting the Scripture.)

(3) Goal 2: Appreciate Christ's Sacrifice to Show Love and Care for the Church

❖ Read again Ephesians 5:25-27.

❖ Read these words from Understanding the Scripture: **The second half of verse 25 through verse 27 constitutes a digression on Christ's love for the church. This digression begins by describing the extent of Christ's love: He gave his life for the church. The result of that self-giving is that the church is holy. The reference to water points to baptism as the point at which people enter the church and have the stain of sin removed from their lives. This cleansing provides the church with the holiness that makes its association with Christ appropriate.**

❖ Form two groups and assign each one of the following questions, which you will post on newsprint:

(1) **Since Christ has loved us to the point of giving himself on the cross, what might we as individuals do to show our appreciation and love for him?**

(2) **Since Christ has loved us to the point of giving himself on the cross, what might we as a congregation do to show our appreciation and love for him?** (Note that this response may include sponsoring ministries that take Christ's love far beyond the walls of the church.)

❖ Call the groups together and invite a spokesperson to report. List ideas on newsprint. Challenge the adults to implement some of these ideas, both individually and as a group.

(4) Goal 3: Accept Responsibility for Showing Love in the Family as Christ Demonstrated Love for the Church

❖ Distribute paper and pencils. Tell the students that you will be reading a list of statements to which they will add information at places where you pause. Encourage them to be honest, since this information is for their eyes only.

(1) As I think about the members of my family of origin, the best words I can use to describe them are_____.

(2) As I think about the family I've chosen to create as an adult, I would describe it as_____.

(3) My favorite family member is _____ because_____.

(4) The family member who is most difficult for me to love is _____ because _____.

(5) The three most important ways that I show love to the family with whom I live are _____.

(6) If Jesus were to rate the love I show toward my family, he would give me a _____ on a scale of one to ten with ten being the top grade.

❖ Provide a few moments for the students to ponder their answers. Ask them to consider if there are any situations or attitudes they would like to change. If so, how might they start?

(5) Continue the Journey

❖ Pray that all who are present today will renew their love for their families and live with the kind of love that Christ has shown to the church.

❖ Read aloud this preparation for next week's lesson. You may also want to post it on newsprint for the students to copy.

■ Title: Proclaiming Christ
■ Background Scripture: Philippians 1:12-30
■ Lesson Scripture: Philippians 1:15-26
■ Focus of the Lesson: In a media-driven world, we hear many messages without fully knowing what

motivates the "messenger." In what ways does the messenger's motive affect the message? Paul claimed that regardless of the person's intentions, the result was still that "Christ is proclaimed in every way."

❖ Post these three activities related to this week's session on newsprint for the students to copy. Challenge the adults to grow spiritually by completing one or more of them.

(1) Do something special this week for your family. Tackle another member's chores, cook a special meal, take the family on an outing—anything that fits within your budget and shows your love for those closest to you.

(2) Help a family that is struggling to relate appropriately to one another. Even if you do not feel that you can make suggestions, act as a role model so that these people, who may be part of your own extended family, can see a Christlike way to show mutual love and respect.

(3) Review Ephesians 5:27, which refers to the church being "without a spot or wrinkle." Ponder the blemishes that you can identify within your own congregation. Pray about whatever role you may be able to play in making the church more holy.

❖ Sing or read aloud "Where Charity and Love Prevail."

❖ Conclude today's session by leading the class in this benediction, adapted from the key verses for December 23 from Ephesians 5:1 and January 13 from Philippians 2:5: **Go now as the Father's beloved children, who are of the same mind as the Son Jesus Christ, to be imitators of God.**

UNIT 2: EXALTING CHRIST
PROCLAIMING CHRIST

PREVIEWING THE LESSON

Lesson Scripture: Philippians 1:15-26
Background Scripture: Philippians 1:12-30
Key Verse: Philippians 1:18

Focus of the Lesson:

In a media-driven world, we hear many messages without fully knowing what motivates the "messenger." In what ways does the messenger's motive affect the message? Paul claimed that regardless of the person's intentions, the result was still that "Christ is proclaimed in every way."

Goals for the Learners:

(1) to comprehend Paul's message of joy in the proclamation of the gospel of Jesus Christ.
(2) to reflect on the variety of motives for proclaiming the gospel of Jesus Christ.
(3) to fashion a personal proclamation of the gospel.

Supplies:

Bibles, newsprint and marker, paper and pencils, hymnals

READING THE SCRIPTURE

NRSV
Lesson Scripture: Philippians 1:15-26

[15]Some proclaim Christ from envy and rivalry, but others from goodwill. [16]These proclaim Christ out of love, knowing that I have been put here for the defense of the gospel; [17]the others proclaim Christ out of selfish ambition, not sincerely but intending to increase my suffering in my imprisonment. [18]What does it matter? Just this, that **Christ is proclaimed in every way, whether out of false motives or true; and in that I rejoice.**

CEB
Lesson Scripture: Philippians 1:15-26

[15]Some certainly preach Christ with jealous and competitive motives, but others preach with good motives. [16]They are motivated by love, because they know that I'm put here to give a defense of the gospel; [17]the others preach Christ because of their selfish ambition. They are insincere, hoping to cause me more pain while I'm in prison.

175

Yes, and I will continue to rejoice, [19]for I know that through your prayers and the help of the Spirit of Jesus Christ this will turn out for my deliverance. [20]It is my eager expectation and hope that I will not be put to shame in any way, but that by my speaking with all boldness, Christ will be exalted now as always in my body, whether by life or by death. [21]For to me, living is Christ and dying is gain. [22]If I am to live in the flesh, that means fruitful labor for me; and I do not know which I prefer. [23]I am hard pressed between the two: my desire is to depart and be with Christ, for that is far better; [24]but to remain in the flesh is more necessary for you. [25]Since I am convinced of this, I know that I will remain and continue with all of you for your progress and joy in faith, [26]so that I may share abundantly in your boasting in Christ Jesus when I come to you again.

[18]What do I think about this? **Just this: since Christ is proclaimed in every possible way, whether from dishonest or true motives, I'm glad and I'll continue to be glad.** [19]I'm glad because I know that this will result in my release through your prayers and the help of the Spirit of Jesus Christ. [20]It is my expectation and hope that I won't be put to shame in anything. Rather, I hope with daring courage that Christ's greatness will be seen in my body, now as always, whether I live or die. [21]Because for me, living serves Christ and dying is even better. [22]If I continue to live in this world, I get results from my work. [23]But I don't know what I prefer. I'm torn between the two because I want to leave this life and be with Christ, which is far better. [24]However, it's more important for me to stay in this world for your sake. [25]I'm sure of this: I will stay alive and remain with all of you to help your progress and the joy of your faith, [26]and to increase your pride in Christ Jesus through my presence when I visit you again.

UNDERSTANDING THE SCRIPTURE

Introduction. Philippians is one of Paul's gentler letters. The church at Philippi was among his strongest supporters. His sense of relationship with them pervades the letter and undergirds the sense of joy that is present throughout, even when he must address problems they are having.

Paul is in prison when he writes this letter. This situation demands some explanation. While we expect to hear that early Christians endured persecution, that experience seemed strange to them. These Christians had abandoned the worship of the gods of their families, city, and country to serve the most powerful god in the cosmos. They expected that worshiping this God would mean that things in their lives would get better, but that had not been the case. So early Christians struggled to understand their experience of being disadvantaged because of their faith if, in fact, this God they worshiped was the most powerful god that existed.

Philippians 1:12-14. Paul's discussion of his own imprisonment is a part of his explanation of their experience of persecution. As Paul reminds the Philippians of his circumstances, they see that they are not alone in their suffering; their leader faces even worse problems. More important, Paul asserts that his troubles had contributed to the spread of the gospel. Because Paul is in prison, the Praetorian Guard (those soldiers committed particularly to the emperor) and others involved with his imprisonment have heard the gospel and have seen his faithfulness there as testimony to its truth. Not only has Paul's imprisonment spread the gospel in new places but it has also made others bolder in their proclamation because they see God working through Paul, even in his circumstances. Thus, God has used these difficult circumstances that stem from opposition to the gospel to advance God's own purposes.

Philippians 1:15-18a. Some fellow Christians, however, have used Paul's imprisonment to try to gain influence among his churches and perhaps to question his apostleship or faithfulness. Perhaps they want to displace his influence to gain prominence for themselves. He says only that they are envious and work from self-ambition, hoping that their work hurts him. He may overstate their desire to do him harm, but their behavior betrays bad motives.

Still, Paul is glad they are at work because they are proclaiming the true gospel. Even these preachers who have bad motives are accomplishing good because they proclaim the true gospel—the message that brings hearers to Christ and into genuine relationship with God. This is more important than any attempt to harm (or success at harming) Paul. The motives of the messengers are of no importance if the purposes of God are accomplished through their preaching.

Philippians 1:18b-26. Paul's second reason for being joyful is his confidence that he will remain faithful at his trial. This is not egotism; rather, he trusts the effectiveness of the Philippians' prayers and the power of the Spirit. Their praying for him gives him a sense of connectedness with them that helps him endure, but more important, their prayers assure him that God will provide the strength he needs in this circumstance. Paul trusts the Holy Spirit to empower him to remain faithful. Faithfulness is not solely dependent on the Christian. Rather, the Spirit enables and supports believers to be able to endure and be faithful (see

Philippians 2:13, where Paul says God enables believers to want to do what is right and to do it). So his certainty about his affirmation of the gospel springs from his faith in the power of God working through him, not from self-assuredness. He remains reliant on the power of God to work in him to provide boldness in his affirmation of the gospel during his trial.

Both the NRSV and the NIV end verse 19 with the word "deliverance." The word Paul uses here is the word he commonly uses for "salvation." Since verse 20 says he is not sure whether he will be released or executed, "deliverance" does not mean Paul will be acquitted. It refers to his confidence that the power of the Spirit and their prayers will bring his ultimate salvation despite his troubles. Thus, his difficulties do not separate him from God's final blessings. Furthermore, his goal is not to be released but to honor Christ, no matter how the trial goes.

Honoring Christ dominates the rest of Paul's comments about his trial's outcome. Since he has more work to do among the Philippians, he expects God will use him to strengthen their faith through his continuing presence. At this point, his presence advances their faith more than his death would. His faith in God to grant him salvation also appears in these verses, as he asserts that it would be better for him to die so he can be with Christ. Yet his desire is to strengthen their faith when they see the effectiveness of their prayers (what he means by their "boasting"—1:26) through his return to them.

Philippians 1:27-30. The verb Paul uses when he tells the Philippians to live "in a manner worthy of the gospel" (1:27) is based on the word that means "citizenship." Thus, he is saying they should live as citizens of the realm determined by the gospel. Their citizenship is no longer a citizenship of their city or country; rather, they are citizens of the kingdom of God. This "citizenship" is in direct competition with all other citizenships. When they give their allegiance to the gospel and its claims on their lives, they should expect opposition from those around them.

Throughout today's reading, Paul emphasizes the overriding significance of the advance of the gospel. He voluntarily accepts difficulties so that the Philippians can continue to grow and have joy in the faith. Furthermore, he is willing to have people harm him so others can hear and respond to the gospel. In these ways, he imitates Christ, who suffered for them. In what follows this lesson, Paul will encourage them to pattern their interactions with one another after this way of being.

INTERPRETING THE SCRIPTURE

A Surprising Situation

Christians often find it hard to understand why they experience difficulties that they do not bring on themselves. We assume that if we are faithful, God will take care of us and make our lives easy. Of course, we know this does not always happen. When troubles do come, we want to know why the world does not work as it should. Or sometimes we blame ourselves, looking for things we must have done to deserve this treatment. Such problems often make us feel that God has abandoned us. Many early Christians had similar experiences and feelings. When Paul wrote his Letter to the Philippians, both he and the Philippian church faced this kind of hard-to-understand situation. They were serving God faithfully, and yet they had many problems in their lives. In fact, they experienced hardships for reasons that few of us know: Their difficulties and disadvantages were the direct result of their faithfulness to the gospel. This root cause makes the problem even worse. Paul intends to comfort them and help them understand these circumstances by talking about his own imprisonment.

Surprising Outcomes

The main way Paul responds to his imprisonment in our reading is to say that it has actually turned out that his suffering has advanced the gospel. You would think that seeing Christians suffer would turn people away from the faith, but Paul says that in his case the opposite has been true. When he bears the difficulties of his imprisonment faithfully, it leads people to ask him how he can endure them as he does. This becomes an occasion for sharing his faith, for telling people how his faith sustains him even in these circumstances. It is powerful testimony to the gospel's power to give us meaning and relationship with God when we see someone maintain faithfulness in trying times. Paul's commitment to the gospel has given occasion for him to proclaim the faith to others.

Beyond this, other preachers have become bolder in their proclamation because they see the way Paul endures persecution. These Christians are strengthened in their faith and in their resolve to share it when they see God continuing to be with and continuing to work through Paul, even though he is in prison. Paul says he is pleased that his suffering can lead to this surprising outcome.

Even More Surprising Outcomes

The next consequence of his suffering is yet more surprising. He says his imprisonment has led other preachers to try to take advantage of what has happened to him.

Perhaps they are suggesting that he suffers because he is not faithful or does not have enough faith, or perhaps they are simply seeking to advance their position in the vacuum left by Paul's absence. Paul's general accusations about them simply name their motives as false and self-serving, intended to hurt Paul personally. That others attacked him is not a surprise to Paul; the result of these attacks is. The preaching by these people with bad motives spreads the genuine gospel. Their evil intentions do not keep the proclamation of Christ from being heard.

Paul is so convinced that the purposes of God are being advanced by these people that he says he is happy about their work—he rejoices, that is, gives thanks to God for them. He refuses to be discouraged by them and will not let others dissuade him from his thanksgiving for them. Despite their motives, God works through them. God is able to accomplish good in the world even through the acts of people who intend their conduct to be harmful. This amazing expression of faith can give us confidence.

We know how difficult, perhaps impossible, it is to do anything with completely pure motives. Today's reading talks about people whose motives are clearly bad, and yet God accomplishes divine purposes through them. Knowing this, we can be assured that when we try to serve God, God can work through us—even if our motives are not wholly unmixed. Thus, when we recognize our own self-serving motivations, we do not need to be overly discouraged because God is able to achieve good through flawed people. If God can accomplish good through those who intend to do harm, how much more is God able to advance the gospel through those who are trying to do good.

Faithfulness Through Prayer

Paul does not suppose he can maintain his faithfulness through his own willpower. Paul can be confident that he will remain faithful *because* he depends on prayers offered for him and he relies on the power of the Holy Spirit working in him. The prayers of the Philippians give him strength in his troubles. Both knowing that they care enough to pray for him and believing that God hears those prayers give Paul strength to remain faithful and to see God at work in any good that comes from his difficulties. Christians draw strength through their participation in a community of those with like faith. Christianity is not an individualistic faith. Faith in Christ draws us into a community that provides support through acts of caring (and this church has sent Paul a gift) and through prayer. The church is a place where shared beliefs allow us to share our burdens and be strengthened by the love of others. Paul feels this support even though he is separated from them, in a different city and in prison.

More than the assurance of a loving community helps Paul remain faithful; he is empowered by the Spirit. God has not left him to his own devices. The Spirit that lives in Christians enables them to live for God. Christians can live as God wants because God's presence and strength are with them, even in dark times. In those times when we seem unable to sense the presence of God, Paul's faith tells him that the Spirit is still with him. The Spirit of God does not just bring comfort; it brings strength to endure. This ability to maintain our faith is one of the gifts of salvation. This reliance on God is what gives Paul confidence that he can remain faithful. Likewise, it is God's power that enables all Christians to do God's will.

It is crucial to see that the love of fellow Christians and the strength Paul gets from the Spirit are not guarantees that he will not have to endure hardship. Although he is fairly sure he will be released, he recognizes the possibility that he will be killed. The Spirit does not spare believers from suffering; it enables them to keep their faith in the midst of trouble. Even if things turn out for the worst, that outcome is no sign that God has abandoned us. Paul's confidence is that God will be with him even in death. In fact, this confidence extends beyond death. Paul sees God claiming him after death, perhaps especially because he entrusted himself to God even if that meant dying for his faith. Christians can trust God to be with them, enabling them to live for God through suffering and death because they trust God to work goodness and justice for them and for all beyond the grave. Paul can be faithful in difficulty and death because he knows he will be with God in Christ no matter what happens.

SHARING THE SCRIPTURE

Preparing Our Hearts

Explore this week's devotional reading, found in Psalm 119:169-176. This psalm, which stretches to 176 verses, praises God's law, or teaching. It takes the form of an alphabetical acrostic and is categorized as a wisdom psalm. The psalmist has presented his need to God and in these verses he urges God to provide what he needs. Notice in verse 176 that the writer confesses to having gone astray from God's teaching, but he trusts that God knows the depth of his love for God. What do you need to ask God about right now?

Pray that you and the adult students will offer prayers of praise and petition, believing that God will answer you and supply your needs.

Preparing Our Minds

Study the background Scripture from Philippians 1:12-30 and the lesson Scripture from Philippians 1:15-26.

Consider this question as you prepare the lesson: *In what ways does a messenger's motive affect the message, especially in our media-driven world?*

Write on newsprint:
❑ information for next week's lesson, found under "Continue the Journey."
❑ activities for further spiritual growth in "Continue the Journey."

Review the "Introduction," "The Big Picture," "Close-up," and "Faith in Action." Consider how you will use this additional information, which immediately precedes the first lesson, for this session.

LEADING THE CLASS

(1) Gather to Learn

❖ Greet the class members. Introduce any guests and help them feel at home.

❖ Pray that all who gather today will be ready to examine their motives for speaking about Christ.

❖ Read this quotation from A. W. Tozer (1897–1963): **"It is not what a man does that determines whether his work is sacred or secular; it is why he does it."**

❖ Discuss these questions:
(1) **What kinds of motivations do you think God finds pleasing?**
(2) **What sorts of motivations tarnish the apparently godly words or deeds of someone claiming to act in the name of Christ?**
(3) **Is it possible to proclaim the good news with impure motives and still help others find Christ? Explain your answer.**

❖ Read aloud today's focus statement: **In a media-driven world, we hear many messages without fully knowing what motivates the "messenger." In what ways does the messenger's motive affect the message? Paul claimed that regardless of** the person's intentions, the result was still that "Christ is proclaimed in every way."

(2) Goal 1: Comprehend Paul's Message of Joy in the Proclamation of the Gospel of Jesus Christ

❖ Set the scene by reading or retelling the "Introduction" and "Philippians 1:12-14" from Understanding the Scripture.

❖ Choose one volunteer to read Philippians 1:15-18a and another to read verses 18b-26.

❖ Discuss these questions using information from Understanding the Scripture to add to the discussion where appropriate:

    (1) What is Paul's current situation?

    (2) How would you describe his mood or emotional state?

    (3) What does he have to say about the motives of some who proclaim the gospel?

    (4) What is Paul's attitude concerning the proclamation of those whose motives may be suspect? (Be sure to note that his concern is the proclamation itself, even if the motivations of the speakers are not pure.)

    (5) Why is Paul ambivalent about living or dying? What are the benefits of each to him? What are the benefits of each to the community at Philippi?

❖ Read "Faithfulness Through Prayer" from Interpreting the Scripture.

❖ Invite the participants to be in an attitude of prayer as they name persons who need prayer support, particularly as they undertake challenging ministries. Conclude this prayer time by leading the group in the Lord's Prayer.

(3) Goal 2: Reflect on the Variety of Motives for Proclaiming the Gospel of Jesus Christ

❖ Post a sheet of newsprint and invite the class to brainstorm answers to this question: **Why do people proclaim the gospel?** Note that some students may hear this question as one asking for motives as to why people entered ordained ministry. Certainly affirm these answers, but do not limit the scope of the question. Try to elicit positive and negative motives, such as *(1) want to share with others what Christ has done in my life; (2) have a sense of gratitude for something special God did for me; (3) want to impress other people with my knowledge of the Bible; (4) want people to see me as a really good person.*

❖ Review the list by asking:

    (1) Which of these answers reflects what you think Jesus would consider a good motivation?

    (2) Which of these reasons do not reflect a real desire to speak and act for God?

    (3) While we need to be very careful about judging the motives of other people, what signs do you look for when you want to test the authenticity of someone else's witness?

    (4) Ask yourself: *Which of these motives have prompted me to speak on behalf of Jesus? Do I need to make some changes?*

(4) Goal 3: Fashion a Personal Proclamation of the Gospel

❖ Form several small groups and distribute paper and pencils. Invite the groups to talk together about what they believe are the key points of the good news. Encourage the group members to talk among themselves as to why these points are key. Help them recognize that not everyone will agree on all points.

❖ Call time and challenge each person to write several statements or list several points that he or she would use in proclaiming the gospel to someone else.

❖ Call time again and bring everyone back together. Ask volunteers from the groups to state what their key points are. Talk together about the points that most members agreed on.

(5) Continue the Journey

❖ Pray that today's participants will proclaim the gospel message with motivations that God would approve.

❖ Read aloud this preparation for next week's lesson. You may also want to post it on newsprint for the students to copy.

- **Title: Jesus' Humility and Exaltation**
- **Background Scripture: Philippians 2:1-13**
- **Lesson Scripture: Philippians 2:5-11**
- **Focus of the Lesson: Sometimes people who are driven by the need to succeed exploit others and abuse power as they fight their way to the top. What honor is there in success won at the expense of others? God exalted Jesus because of Jesus' selflessness, obedience, servanthood, and humility.**

❖ Post these three activities related to this week's session on newsprint for the students to copy. Challenge the adults to grow spiritually by completing one or more of them.

(1) **Proclaim the gospel in a medium of your choice, such as singing a** song you have written, performing a hymn on YouTube, adding a gospel proclamation to your website, drawing a picture, or talking with someone. Pray that your witness will inspire others to seek Christ.

(2) **Review your day each evening this week. As you reflect on your words and deeds, ask yourself,** *What motivated me to act that way? Why would my actions be pleasing or displeasing to God? How do I hope tomorrow will be better?*

(3) **Read about contemporary Christians who, like the Philippians, are suffering for the sake of the gospel. What might you be able to do to support these brothers and sisters? Whom might you enlist to join you in your efforts?**

❖ Sing or read aloud "How Shall They Hear the Word of God."

❖ Conclude today's session by leading the class in this benediction, adapted from the key verses for December 23 from Ephesians 5:1 and January 13 from Philippians 2:5: **Go now as the Father's beloved children, who are of the same mind as the Son Jesus Christ, to be imitators of God.**

UNIT 2: EXALTING CHRIST

Jesus' Humility and Exaltation

PREVIEWING THE LESSON

Lesson Scripture: Philippians 2:5-11
Background Scripture: Philippians 2:1-13
Key Verse: Philippians 2:5

Focus of the Lesson:
Sometimes people who are driven by the need to succeed exploit others and abuse power as they fight their way to the top. What honor is there in success won at the expense of others? God exalted Jesus because of Jesus' selflessness, obedience, servant-hood, and humility.

Goals for the Learners:
(1) to analyze Paul's description of God's exaltation of Jesus based on sacrifice and self-lessness rather than power.
(2) to value selfless behavior over power.
(3) to adopt Christ-like humility as a personal lifestyle.

Pronunciation Guide:
Christology (kris tol' uh jee)
Jochebed (jok' uh bed)

Supplies:
Bibles, newsprint and marker, paper and pencils, hymnals

READING THE SCRIPTURE

NRSV

Lesson Scripture: Philippians 2:5-11

⁵Let the same mind be in you that was in Christ Jesus,

  ⁶ who, though he was in the form of God,

CEB

Lesson Scripture: Philippians 2:5-11

⁵Adopt the attitude that was in Christ Jesus:

  ⁶ Though he was in the form of God,

did not regard equality with God
    as something to be exploited,
7 but emptied himself,
    taking the form of a slave,
    being born in human likeness.
    And being found in human form,
8   he humbled himself
    and became obedient to the
        point of death—
    even death on a cross.
9 Therefore God also highly exalted him
    and gave him the name
    that is above every name,
10 so that at the name of Jesus
    every knee should bend,
    in heaven and on earth and
    under the earth,
11 and every tongue should confess
    that Jesus Christ is Lord,
    to the glory of God the Father.

he did not consider being equal
    with God something to exploit.
7 But he emptied himself
    by taking the form of a slave
    and by becoming like human beings.
When he found himself
    in the form of a human,
    8he humbled himself by becoming
        obedient to the point of death,
    even death on a cross.
9 Therefore, God highly honored him
    and gave him a name above all names,
10 so that at the name of Jesus everyone
    in heaven, on earth,
    and under the earth might bow
11 and every tongue confess
    that Jesus Christ is Lord,
    to the glory of God the Father.

UNDERSTANDING THE SCRIPTURE

Philippians 2:1-4. In Philippians 2:1-13, Paul's attention focuses on intra-church relations. He first reminds the Philippians of blessings they have in Christ. The "if" at the beginning of verse 1 does not imply there is any doubt that there is encouragement, comfort, fellowship, or love. The sense of the word is "since," meaning "since we have these things." Verse 2 exhorts the Philippians to be united, exhibiting mutual love and adopting proper attitudes toward one another. The various expressions of "same" and "one" emphasize the need for unity. This emphasis suggests (and chapter 4 confirms) that relations within this church needed improvement.

Their oneness needs to express itself in how they treat one another. They need to reverse the usual order of priorities: Each person should put the good of others ahead of his or her own good. This radical demand is the most basic command of the section,

indeed of the whole letter, and is the primary way of thinking Paul wants them to adopt.

Philippians 2:5. This verse contains the command that the material in verses 6-11 supports. Paul tells them to adopt the attitude we see in Christ. The preceding verses indicate that this attitude involves putting the good of others ahead of one's own good.

Philippians 2:6-11. These verses contain what is often called "the Philippians hymn," a liturgical piece that existed before Paul quoted it in this letter. Paul inserts it because he knows that the Philippians already know it. He assumes they will recognize it and agree with its content. He uses it to support his exhortation for them to put the good of others above their own good. So while it is among the New Testament's richest texts in its statements about Christ, it was not inserted here to teach about Christology (that is, the study of the nature and work of Christ) but to support an exhortation.

This liturgical material has two basic movements. The first tells of Christ's descent to earth (2:6-8); the second of his exaltation by God (2:9-11). Together they take the reader from some time before the Incarnation to the end of time when all acknowledge Christ.

Verse 6 emphasizes the unparalleled place of Christ with God. Only Christ could claim not only to possess the form of God but also equality with God. Just what it means for Christ to exist in the "form" of God is unclear. Still, this assertion about Christ has played an important role in the development of the church's theology, especially its development of the doctrine of the Trinity and doctrine of the Incarnation of Christ that asserts that Jesus was both fully divine and fully human. If we try to hear this passage as the Philippians did, it remains vaguer than those later doctrinal developments. The language of liturgy is not the language of systematic theology or of philosophy, so we should expect less specificity but more praise and adoration.

The liturgy speaks of the high place of Christ to contrast it with what he was willing to do for humanity. Verses 7-8 are intentionally dramatic. Just as Christ was in the "form" of God (2:6), so verse 7 says Christ takes the "form" of a slave. Saying that Christ took the form of a slave accentuates just how diminishing the Incarnation was to Christ. He did not just become a servant, but a slave. The main verb of verse 7 emphasizes this radical contrast, declaring that Christ "emptied himself." He gave up all position and status to become human. The writer here makes the distance between the place of the preexistent Christ and his life as a human impossible to calculate.

But there is more. Beyond becoming human, he accepted a humiliating death at the hands of the ones he came to save. Christ did this out of love for us, but this is not the explicit point of the liturgy. This piece emphasizes the obedience of Christ to the command of God. Both the Incarnation and the Crucifixion are acts of obedience here. We shy away from thinking about the Crucifixion as a part of God's plan, much less thinking of it as a demand from God. But this passage identifies the death of Christ as an act of obedience, obedience that demanded accepting humiliation. This obedience was voluntary on Christ's part: He "emptied *himself*" (2:7, emphasis added) and "humbled *himself*" (2:8, emphasis added). Thus, the Incarnation and Crucifixion are at once acts of both self-giving love and obedience.

God responded to Christ's self-giving and obedience by exalting Christ to the highest place in the cosmos. This response by God elevates Christ so that all beings everywhere will be required to recognize his superiority. Christ's position and title are the public manifestation of the power of God to all, even to those who oppose God's will.

This magnificent act of God will lead some to turn to God in thankfulness and confess, even proclaim, the place of Jesus. But not all the bowing and "confessing" will be voluntary. Those powers of the cosmos that remain opposed to God's purposes will be forced to acknowledge Christ and his place over all. So while some will joyfully confess his name and devote themselves to him, others will only acknowledge his power. Importantly, this liturgy ends by declaring that Christ exercises this authority to give honor to God.

Philippians 2:12-13. Paul now applies the liturgy to the Philippians, telling them to obey as Christ obeyed. As verses 14-16 indicate, the command they need to obey involves how they treat one another. It sounds a bit odd when Paul tells them to "work out your own salvation" (1:12). He does not mean they earn their salvation; rather, they are to live out their salvation. That is, they should live in ways that reflect the salvation they have been given.

The central point Paul makes with this liturgy is that believers should put the good of others ahead of their own good, just as Christ did for us.

INTERPRETING THE SCRIPTURE

Christ Our Savior and Example

This passage contains one of the most powerful statements about Christ's nature and work in all of the New Testament. The liturgy commonly called the "Christ hymn" identifies Christ as a preexistent being and as a human. Paul uses this piece for much the same reason that pastors today sometimes recite the lines of well-known hymns or poetry. This kind of material adds weight to what the speaker says because hearers already grant some type of authority to what is being quoted. This allows Paul to cite a powerful example of what he wants the Philippians to do and avoid being heavy-handed because he is not simply demanding that they obey him. It also makes his argument more attractive because it draws on the saving work of Christ from which they had all received benefit.

The Person and Work of Christ

While the language of this liturgy is suggestive rather than precise, it proclaims that the human Jesus was the incarnation of one who had the "form of God" (2:6). The liturgy passes over this astonishing and confusing statement without comment, assuming that all acknowledge its truth. It emphasizes the willingness of Christ to humble himself by taking this form, describing the distance that Christ descends as "emptying himself" and becoming a "slave" (2:7). It is hard for us to comprehend how Christ could become human; even this liturgy tiptoes around the matter. It uses words like "form" and "likeness" to speak of the human form of Christ. Later creedal statements are bolder and more direct because many early Christians were reticent to acknowledge either the full humanity or the full divinity of Jesus Christ. In our time, it is easier for most people to see Jesus as fully human. This does less to disrupt our scientific view of the world. Saying that Jesus is the appearance of God within the natural structures of the world suggests that the way we say natural law works may be wrong, or that it can at least be suspended. Such a view is hard to defend today in the marketplace of ideas. For other reasons, it was difficult then too. But this liturgy declares that the preexistent Christ truly entered this world.

This liturgy finds the descent of Christ into human form to be even more amazing because he did not come to reign but to obey and serve. Rather than taking a high place as a human, he humbles himself by being obedient to God's will. This obedience is willing obedience; he did not submit to God's will because he was forced to but because he was willing to. His willingness to obey extended all the way to accepting a humiliating death.

Christ as Our Example

The point of the liturgy, the reason Paul quotes it, is to present Christ's work as an example. Christ's willingness to accept severe disadvantage for our good sets the pattern for the way Christians should live their lives. Christ's example calls Christians to act with humility toward one another. But Christ's example demands even more, that we accept disadvantage for the good of others. That sounds unfair, but Paul says Christians should adopt the attitude we see in Christ: He left the highest place in heaven to serve us; he was willing to accept even death to serve us. This is the example Paul points us to when we think about how to shape our lives. The things Christ gave up make any sacrifice we make for others seem rather small. Putting the good of others ahead of our own good was as countercultural then as it is now. But the example of Christ calls us not just to be humble or even just to consider the good of others; it calls us to see their good as more important than our own. Such a demand should lead us to reevaluate all of our relationships with those around us.

We see this kind of sacrifice for others as exceptional behavior. People like Mother Teresa do this, but not regular Christians with their many responsibilities. But Paul does not exhort just a few people to follow this example of Christ; he makes it an expectation for all Christians. All are to treat their fellow Christians in ways that reflect the sacrificial love of Christ. Just as Christ put our good before his own as an act of obedience, so we obey God when we put others first. We can move toward acting this way because we have received the benefits of Christ's putting us above his own good. This gift of salvation and relationship with God can motivate us to do for others, on a small scale, what Christ has done for us.

God's response to Christ's sacrificing his status and humbling himself for us is to exalt Christ to the highest place in the cosmos. This pattern is part of the reason Christians can make sacrifices for others. They know that God exalts those who act with humility to benefit others. But this exaltation was not a part of this life for Christ. His exaltation came only after his shameful death. Similarly, Christians should not expect a monetary or this-worldly reward for their sacrificial service to others. God does not shower financial blessings on or remove difficulties from the lives of those who serve others. Still, we can be certain that God's justice and love will respond to those deeds of kindness, even if that response comes in ways or times that the world does not see.

Working Out Your Salvation

We expect to hear Paul say that justification (salvation) comes to us through faith, not works. So what Paul says in verse 12 shocks and worries us. It is bad enough that he says we should "work out" our salvation, but then he adds that we should do it fearing God's judgment. Paul nowhere says simply that salvation is by faith without works, but neither does he think Christians earn their salvation. The meaning of "work out" is that Christians should put their salvation into practice; they must live out of their salvation. Their lives ought to reflect what Christ has done for them. Perhaps this is another way to say we must follow Christ's example.

Paul expects Christians to adopt a manner of life that reflects who God is and how God has acted to save them. Adopting this way of life is part of "faith" for Paul. In Paul's usage, the word "faith" does not mean just what you believe; it includes faithfulness in the way you orient your life toward God. This does not imply that our salvation is in jeopardy every time we sin, but it does mean that we remain accountable to God for how we live. Just as we are sometimes ashamed to admit some things about our behavior in front of people we respect, Paul envisions us having to account for ourselves to God. In some ways this is daunting. In other ways this is good to hear because it means that we are important enough to God that how we live our lives matters to God.

SHARING THE SCRIPTURE

Preparing Our Hearts

Explore this week's devotional reading, found in James 3:13-18. Here James, the leader of the church in Jerusalem who may have been the brother of Jesus, is writing about wisdom as a gift from God. In contrast to earthly wisdom, God's wisdom is pure, peaceable, willing to yield, merciful, fruitful, and lacking in hypocrisy (3:17). Think about your perceptions of wisdom. How do they stack up against James's description of God's wisdom? Notice that one's life and works reveal the source of one's wisdom. What is your life saying about the source of wisdom that guides you?

Pray that you and the adult students will set aside earthly wisdom that creates disorder and continue to reach for God's wisdom.

Preparing Our Minds

Study the background Scripture from Philippians 2:1-13 and the lesson Scripture from Philippians 2:5-11.

Consider this question as you prepare the lesson: *What honor is there in success won at the expense of others?*

Write on newsprint:

❑ information for next week's lesson, found under "Continue the Journey."

❑ activities for further spiritual growth in "Continue the Journey."

Review the "Introduction," "The Big Picture," "Close-up," and "Faith in Action." Consider how you will use this additional information, which immediately precedes the first lesson, for this session.

LEADING THE CLASS

(1) Gather to Learn

❖ Greet the class members. Introduce any guests and help them feel at home.

❖ Pray that all who have come today are willing to assume the humble attitude of Christ.

❖ Post a sheet of newsprint titled "The Use and Abuse of Power." Draw a line down the center. To the left write "Power Rooted in God's Love" and on the right write "Power Rooted in Selfish Motives." Invite the adults to identify characteristics for each type of power. They may name some historical or contemporary public figures who exhibit one type or the other.

❖ Read aloud today's focus statement: **Sometimes people who are driven by the need to succeed exploit others and abuse power as they fight their way to the top. What honor is there in success won at the expense of others? God exalted Jesus because of Jesus' selflessness, obedience, servanthood, and humility.**

(2) Goal 1: Analyze Paul's Description of God's Exaltation of Jesus Based on Sacrifice and Selflessness Rather Than Power

❖ Introduce today's passage by reading Philippians 2:1-4 from Understanding the Scripture.

❖ Choose one volunteer to read Philippians 2:5-8 and another to read verses 9-11.

❖ Discuss these questions using pertinent information from Understanding the Scripture to enhance the discussion:

(1) What does this passage tell you about Jesus?

(2) Are there comments here about Jesus that you find difficult to fully grasp? If so, what are they?

(3) What does this passage tell you about God?

(4) Why did God exalt Jesus?

(5) What do you learn about humanity's response to the exalted Jesus?

❖ Review today's key verse by inviting students who have several different translations to read aloud verse 5 and then ask:

(1) **What does this verse mean to you?**

(2) **Given what this passage reveals about God, how might you follow our Lord's example and set your mind on the things of Christ?**

(3) Goal 2: Value Selfless Behavior Over Power

❖ Do a Bible study that illustrates selfless behavior over power by selecting several volunteers to read aloud Exodus 1:8–2:10. Invite the adults to describe the following by working with the whole class or in small groups:

(1) **the way in which the taskmasters exercised their power.**

(2) **the way in which the midwives exercised their power.** (Note that they quietly subverted the king's power by refusing to follow his order and then concocting a story to explain why they could not act on the order to kill all newborn Hebrew males.)

(3) **the way in which Moses' mother Jochebed exercised power to care for her son.**

(4) **the way in which Moses' sister Miriam used her power to care for Moses.**

(5) **the way in which Pharaoh's daughter exercised her power to adopt Moses.**

(6) **the ways in which Pharaoh exercised power.** (Be sure to note that he had plans to destroy the Hebrews, first by ordering hard physical labor; then by trying to have the midwives kill the baby boys; then by ordering all Egyptians to kill the Hebrew boys.)

❖ Conclude by asking: **In the end, did selfless behavior of either those who seemingly had no power or those who had royal power win out in these situations? Why do you think this was the case?** (Be sure to note that each of Pharaoh's destructive plans was subverted by women who acted selflessly to protect life.)

(4) Goal 3: Adopt Christ-like Humility as a Personal Lifestyle

❖ Read "Christ as Our Example" from Interpreting the Scripture.

❖ Post a sheet of newsprint. Encourage the learners to call out characteristics of Jesus. Ask them, if possible, to give an example or cite a biblical story where this characteristic is seen. Record their ideas.

❖ Distribute paper and pencils. Challenge the adults to review the list and then select several ideas that they would like to use in order to live with Christ-like humility. They may add ideas not included on the class list. Encourage them to state in concrete terms how they would live out each characteristic.

❖ Call the group together. Solicit volunteers to state what they intend to do.

❖ Affirm the class members' ideas and encourage them to take action this week.

❖ **Option:** Suggest that the class members pair off so that they can support one another in prayer and hold one another accountable for taking steps on the action they committed to take.

(5) Continue the Journey

❖ Pray that all who have come today will not only give thanks for Christ's sacrificial love but also strive to follow his example in as many ways as they can.

❖ Read aloud this preparation for next week's lesson. You may also want to post it on newsprint for the students to copy.

■ **Title: Gaining in Jesus Christ**

■ **Background Scripture: Philippians 3:1-11**

■ Lesson Scripture: Philippians 3:7-11

■ Focus of the Lesson: The self-worth of many people resides in the things they have accomplished in life. What is the true value of our lives when stripped of our achievements? Paul believed that none of the achievements of this life are worth anything when compared to the surpassing value of knowing Christ Jesus.

❖ Post these three activities related to this week's session on newsprint for the students to copy. Challenge the adults to grow spiritually by completing one or more of them.

(1) Write a prayer of gratitude for Christ's sacrificial love. Think not only about what Christ has done for you personally but also about what he has done for all humanity.

(2) Read a biography of someone who has held great wealth or exercised major power. How did this individual get to the top? What would Jesus say about how he or she rose to this position? What lessons—positive or negative—can you learn from this person?

(3) Read Colossians 1:15-20, which is another passage exalting Christ. This may have been a fragment of an early hymn, just as today's passage was. Look at these two hymns. How are their comments about Christ similar? How are they different? What do these hymns tell you about the beliefs of the early church?

❖ Sing or read aloud "Jesus! the Name High over All."

❖ Conclude today's session by leading the class in this benediction, adapted from the key verses for December 23 from Ephesians 5:1 and January 13 from Philippians 2:5: **Go now as the Father's beloved children, who are of the same mind as the Son Jesus Christ, to be imitators of God.**

UNIT 2: EXALTING CHRIST
GAINING IN JESUS CHRIST

PREVIEWING THE LESSON

Lesson Scripture: Philippians 3:7-11
Background Scripture: Philippians 3:1-11
Key Verse: Philippians 3:7

Focus of the Lesson:
The self-worth of many people resides in the things they have accomplished in life. What is the true value of our lives when stripped of our achievements? Paul believed that none of the achievements of this life are worth anything when compared to the surpassing value of knowing Christ Jesus.

Goals for the Learners:
(1) to discover Paul's attitude about the value of knowing Christ Jesus.
(2) to compare feelings of achieving honors with feelings of living life in Christ.
(3) to establish a lifelong goal of measuring their achievements against the value of knowing Jesus Christ.

Pronunciation Guide:
Epaphroditus (i paf ruh di' tuhs)

Supplies:
Bibles, newsprint and marker, paper and pencils, hymnals

READING THE SCRIPTURE

NRSV
Lesson Scripture: Philippians 3:7-11

7Yet whatever gains I had, these I have come to regard as loss because of Christ. 8More than that, I regard everything as loss because of the surpassing value of knowing Christ Jesus my Lord. For his sake I have suffered the loss of all things, and I regard them as rubbish, in order that I may gain

CEB
Lesson Scripture: Philippians 3:7-11

7These things were my assets, but I wrote them off as a loss for the sake of Christ. 8But even beyond that, I consider everything a loss in comparison with the superior value of knowing Christ Jesus my Lord. I have lost everything for him, but what I lost I think of as sewer trash, so that I might gain Christ

Christ ⁹and be found in him, not having a righteousness of my own that comes from the law, but one that comes through faith in Christ, the righteousness from God based on faith. ¹⁰I want to know Christ and the power of his resurrection and the sharing of his sufferings by becoming like him in his death, ¹¹if somehow I may attain the resurrection from the dead.

⁹and be found in him. In Christ I have a righteousness that is not my own and that does not come from the Law but rather from the faithfulness of Christ. It is the righteousness of God that is based on faith. ¹⁰The righteousness that I have comes from knowing Christ, the power of his resurrection, and the participation in his sufferings. It includes being conformed to his death ¹¹so that I may perhaps reach the goal of the resurrection of the dead.

UNDERSTANDING THE SCRIPTURE

Philippians 3:1. In chapter 2 Paul provides a number of good examples whose attitudes the Philippians should adopt (Christ, Paul himself, Timothy, and Epaphroditus). In 3:2 he starts talking about teachers whom he introduces as bad examples. These teachers were not currently a threat to this church, but they serve as his example of who not to be like.

Philippians 3:2-6. Paul warns the Philippians in no uncertain terms, telling them to "watch out for" (3:2 NIV) the dogs, evil workers, and mutilators. This sudden outburst seems out of place in the calm of Philippians. But Paul inserts this shocking statement to emphasize the difference between the good people of chapter 2 and the dangerous people he refers to here. Paul's rhetoric is so strong because he has been arguing with these people for many years. Paul has strong feelings about them, even when just using them as bad examples.

These "evil workers" are Christians who advocate that Gentiles fully convert to Judaism in order to be members of the church. The label "mutilators" refers to their insistence that Gentile Christians receive circumcision. Paul rejects their teaching, arguing (elsewhere) that Gentiles must be saved as Gentiles as a demonstration that God is the God of all people.

Paul makes the astonishing claim in verse 3 that his Gentile converts are "the circumcision," even though they are not literally circumcised. He asserts that they are the people of God who serve God by the power of the Spirit and depend on Christ for their relationship with God. What makes them people of God is reliance on Christ, not the ancestral covenant with its sign of circumcision. To show that he does not take this position because he is unable to claim membership in Israel, Paul sets out his own pedigree—one that demonstrates that he has the right to a place of honor within the Mosaic covenant (3:4-6).

Verses 5-6 tell of Paul's participation in Judaism: He was a good Pharisee who kept the law conscientiously, and he was so dedicated to preserving the faith that he persecuted the church. He does not tell us what made the church seem dangerous. Perhaps the best options are either that the church's claims about the exalted Christ seemed perilously close to worshiping a second god or that the church was admitting Gentiles as full members of the people of God without requiring them to keep the commandments (particularly circumcision, food laws, and the sabbath). Paul was not a guilt-ridden person before joining the church. He was not seeking a way to escape a burden of sin;

he had a relationship with God and understood himself to be serving God well. He just had not recognized the new act of God in Christ and the gifts Christ offers.

Philippians 3:7-9. We must be careful with the next few verses. They have often been used to denigrate Judaism. But these verses do not suggest that Judaism is of no value or that it does not provide a relationship with God. For Paul's argument to work, what Jews have must be very valuable. If he says he gave up what he had to gain something greater, what he gave up must have a high value for knowledge of Christ to be worth much. He gave up real and valuable blessings to gain Christ. Participation in Christ led him to give them up, but they were valuable.

This evaluation of Christ was a change in his thinking. After his experience of the risen Christ, he stopped seeing Christ as a danger and recognized the blessings that belonging to Christ entails. Now he relies on a more secure foundation for his relationship with God; that foundation is the work of Christ. God grants the benefits of Christ's work to the one who has faith. Paul had once thought that claims about what Christ supplies were false. Now he knows them to be true and to be worth losing claims of status based on other ways of being in relationship with God.

Philippians 3:10-11. Receiving God's righteousness brings both blessing and responsibility. This righteousness brings into Paul's life the experience of knowing God and the experience of the power of God, the astonishing power that raised Christ. Sharing the suffering of Christ is also part of what comes to Christians. Being a first-century Christian meant accepting disadvantage and persecution because of one's faith. Most Christians of that era faced economic and social disadvantages, and some experienced government-sponsored persecution. The power of God did not take them out of those circumstances, but it enabled them to endure those sufferings with faith and hope.

To understand what Paul means in verse 10 by "becoming like [Christ] in his death" we should remember the hymnic section of Philippians 2:6-11. Christ's death was the ultimate expression of his obedience and his willingness to put the good of others before his own good. Conforming to Christ's death does not simply mean being willing to die for one's faith; it means adopting the attitudes of humility, obedience, and love for others that we see exemplified in that death. Romans 6:1-11 speaks of baptism as the place where believers identify with Christ's death in a way that ends their old way of life and that commits them to a new way of living. So this conforming to the death of Christ begins at baptism and continues throughout the Christian's life.

Philippians 3:11 does not suggest that Paul doubts his salvation. Rather, he expresses amazement that such a wonderful blessing as the resurrection is awaiting his completion of a faithful life. His life with God is secured by Christ, but his understanding of faith includes the necessity of faithful living—not a perfect life, but a life that remains oriented toward God and God's will. The power of God that works in him, according to verse 10, assures him that he will be able to live faithfully and so participate in the resurrection. Thus, even the required faithfulness is a gift from God.

INTERPRETING THE SCRIPTURE

Coming to Understand God More Clearly

Joining the church and accepting Christ required Paul to reevaluate things he had earlier held dear in his walk of faith. As a person of deep faith, he was moved to change his understanding of Christ. He did not decide that things he previously celebrated were worthless, but he did see that God had even more to offer him. He speaks in exaggerated language in this reading, saying that he considered his marks of status in the Mosaic covenant something he gave up; they were a loss. He gave them up to claim something in Christ that was even more valuable. This signaled a dramatic break in his life. He was granted new insight into how God had acted in the world, and the implications of that insight led him to accept Christ and join the church. Our walk with God demands a constant reevaluation of how we serve God and how we recognize God's activity in the world. We sometimes have to admit we were wrong about something profound, as Paul had to change his mind about whether God was working in the ministry of Jesus. More often we will be called on to be open to new ideas about how to be a presence for God in our geographic, social, and church location. Openness to such change is difficult but necessary as we bring our deepening understanding of the gospel to bear on our world.

This is a dangerous passage. It has often been used to assert that Judaism has no validity or value. Thus, it has supported a good deal of anti-Semitism. But Paul does not say that the blessings available in Judaism are invalid or even that they are few. He says only that he has received even more blessings through Christ. We should not use this passage to denigrate Judaism as a legalistic religion. Jews knew that the covenant was initiated and sustained by God's grace. Paul's change was not from being a legalist to being a person who recognized God's grace, but his understanding of God's presence in the world did undergo significant change. Recognizing the work and presence of God in Christ led Paul to see more clearly the ways in which God was now reaching out in love to the whole world.

Losing All Things

When Paul came to understand Christ as Savior and Lord, he lost more than status within Judaism. This shift in the way he saw the presence of God in the world and his commitment to proclaim that message required him to reevaluate all things in his life. The level of education that his letters seem to indicate suggests that Paul enjoyed many social and economic advantages. Such an education and skills placed Paul in a position to attain the status and honor that so many craved in the first century. Both within his religious community and in the broader society, Paul was poised to rise to a social level that many others would covet.

What Paul had to consider loss because of his acceptance of Christ included all these kinds of advantages and benefits. Becoming a member of the church changed Paul's outlook on everything, things in both his religious and secular life. This reorientation was dramatic, not minor. These things were not simply less important; he says he now considers them "rubbish" (3:8). This is a comparative statement rather than an absolute one. Paul still knows there are advantages to possessing wealth and education. Indeed, his access to those things had allowed him to become the apostle he was. But in comparison with the blessings one receives in Christ, those advantages are completely insignificant. The gospel calls us to adopt this same outlook on possessions and power. All the trappings and comforts such advantages buy are without value when compared to what God gives us in Christ.

It is hard for Christians to develop and retain the understanding of status and wealth that Paul expresses here. Then and now, the messages of our culture tell us that the value of people's lives is determined by the wealth and power they accumulate. What we learn about God and about life through Christ shows this value system to be wrong. In Christ we see that God's love gives us value and that if we live in that love our lives will have the meaning and significance that makes life good. Paul emphasizes in this passage that this blessing of fullness of life in Christ is not something we attain through our own righteousness. It is a gift from God.

Present Change and Coming Transformation

Paul speaks here of the blessings he already enjoys because of his faith in Christ. His life and outlook have already been transformed. He has been given the relationship with God that enriches life, and he has been given righteousness. This righteousness includes the forgiveness we receive from God in Christ, as well as the relationship with God that this forgiveness enables. This righteousness also entails living as God expects, which requires us to discern God's will in the various places in which we find ourselves. This discernment may lead us to discover that we need to change our views on some issues and questions. This righteousness is a life of faithfulness that is patterned on the faithfulness of Christ, a faithfulness that we are constantly trying to understand more fully. We are

granted this life through faith and we must constantly grow in it so that our righteousness conforms more and more to the example of righteousness we see in Jesus. These efforts do not allow us to make a claim on God. Even as Paul talks about all he has given up and all he has already received, he looks forward to the resurrection and life in God's presence as a gift that is almost too good to be true. The coming and final transformation of our lives is the ultimate confirmation of the value system that Paul has adopted and calls us to discern and adopt.

God Enables Us to Be Conformed to Christ

Paul defines the required response to receiving grace in Christ as being conformed to Christ's death. This highlights the contrast with the values of the rest of the world. How could patterning life after a humiliating death make life good? This statement points to and calls us to adopt the attitude of Christ described in last week's lesson: Just as Christ put the good of others ahead of his own good, so we must do the same. We can adopt this outlook because we know that the cross was not the last word. The Resurrection shows us that Jesus' manner of life is what God wants and that God vindicates that way of life, no matter what it seems to cost.

Paul ends this section noting that he must remain vigilant in his quest to live for God. He recognized the necessity of constantly reaffirming our commitments to God. We must remember that this demand comes on the heels of his affirmation that it is the power that raised Christ that enables him to fulfill the expectation of faithfulness.

SHARING THE SCRIPTURE

Preparing Our Hearts

Explore this week's devotional reading, found in Matthew 13:44-46. These two familiar parables from Jesus quite accurately reflect today's lesson from Philippians. In both cases, the people in the parable had something of great value. Yet they were willing to sacrifice what they had to get something of far greater value. Notice that in both stories the "finder" sells all of his possessions to buy the treasure or pearl. Notice too that the "finder" was apparently looking for something. What are you seeking? Is the kingdom of heaven a treasure that you are willing to give your all to attain? If not, what is holding you back? What steps can you take to remove this stumbling block?

Pray that you and the adult students will be willing to lose something of value in order to gain far greater value in God's kingdom.

Preparing Our Minds

Study the background Scripture from Philippians 3:1-11 and the lesson Scripture from Philippians 3:7-11.

Consider this question as you prepare the lesson: *What is the true value of our lives when stripped of our achievements?*

Write on newsprint:

❑ **option:** statements for "Establish a Lifelong Goal of Measuring the Learners' Achievements Against the Value of Knowing Jesus Christ."

❑ information for next week's lesson, found under "Continue the Journey."

❑ activities for further spiritual growth in "Continue the Journey."

Review the "Introduction," "The Big Picture," "Close-up," and "Faith in Action." Consider how you will use this additional information, which immediately precedes the first lesson, for this session.

LEADING THE CLASS

(1) Gather to Learn

❖ Greet the class members. Introduce any guests and help them feel at home.

❖ Pray that those in attendance today are willing to assess their lives in the light of Christ.

❖ Discuss these questions:

(1) **What does our society say makes a person valuable?**

(2) **What do Jesus' teachings and actions suggest about what makes a person valuable?**

❖ Read this quotation from Erwin W. Lutzer (1941–): **"If the value of an article is dependent upon the price paid for it, Christ's death made our value skyrocket. Let no one say we are worthless. God is not a foolish speculator; he would never invest in worthless property."** Invite volunteers to determine where this quotation fits along the spectrum of value that they just discussed.

❖ Read aloud today's focus statement: **The self-worth of many people resides in the things they have accomplished in life. What is the true value of our lives when stripped of our achievements? Paul believed that none of the achievements of this life are worth anything when compared to the surpassing value of knowing Christ Jesus.**

(2) Goal 1: Discover Paul's Attitude About the Value of Knowing Christ Jesus

❖ Read Philippians 3:1 and 3:2-6 from Understanding the Scripture to set the stage for today's lesson.

❖ Invite a volunteer to read Philippians 3:7-11.

❖ Form several small groups. Encourage participants to talk about what

Paul believes he has lost and what he has gained.

❖ Encourage the groups to talk about their findings with the entire class. Use "Losing All Things" in Interpreting the Scripture to enhance the discussion.

(3) Goal 2: Compare Feelings of Achieving Honors With Feelings of Living Life in Christ

❖ Distribute paper and pencils. Encourage the adults to make a list of the three to five most important achievements in their lives. These might relate to any area of life: family, profession, wealth, or fulfilling personal goals. Next, ask them to write a short paragraph about how the honor accompanying each of these achievements compares to how they feel about living in Christ. Urge the class members to be honest in assessing their feelings.

❖ Call on several volunteers to read their paragraphs.

❖ Ask these questions and encourage everyone to join in the discussion:

(1) **If you feel that you get great satisfaction from living as society prods you to live, what factors do you think inhibit you from experiencing an authentic relationship with Christ?**

(2) **If you feel you get great satisfaction from living life in Christ, what strategies have you used to set aside the demands of the world? Are there experiences that you can talk about to demonstrate how you live?**

(4) Goal 3: Establish a Lifelong Goal of Measuring the Learners' Achievements Against the Value of Knowing Jesus Christ

❖ Read aloud these values statements and invite the learners to rate themselves on a scale of one to five, with five being greatest agreement with the statement and one being least agreement. The students are to write the answers on the back of the papers you previously distributed. They need not share their responses with others. If you prefer, post these statements on newsprint and let the adults work at their own pace.

(1) **As a Christian, I am guided by the ethics of love.**

(2) **I find it necessary sometimes in business to go along with certain practices to get ahead, even though I disagree with some of these practices.**

(3) **In social situations, I keep my faith to myself.**

(4) **I want my family and close friends to view me as a success.**

(5) **A large measure of my self-esteem depends upon my honors and achievement.**

(6) **I want people to value me for what I can do.**

(7) **My relationship with Christ is more important to me than my possessions and accomplishments.**

(8) **I want to relate to Jesus, but I also want to be well respected among my peers who have different values.**

❖ Suggest that the learners think about how their ratings will help them measure their earthly achievements against the value of knowing Jesus Christ. Notice that for some statements, such as the first one, students will want to rank high (5), whereas others, such as the second one, they will want to rank low (1).

❖ Conclude by reading or retelling "Coming to Understand God More Clearly" from Interpreting the Scripture.

(5) Continue the Journey

❖ Pray that all who have gathered today will weigh whatever they have lost by being Christians against the gains, both temporal and eternal, that have come their way.

❖ Read aloud this preparation for next week's lesson. You may also want to post it on newsprint for the students to copy.

- ■ Title: Stand Firm
- ■ Background Scripture: Philippians 3:12–4:1
- ■ Lesson Scripture: Philippians 3:12-16
- ■ Focus of the Lesson: Sometimes it is difficult to sustain energy to achieve goals that have lasting value. What motivates us to press on toward a goal? Maintaining a strong relationship with Christ now prepares us for the relationship we will have with Christ in eternity.

❖ Post these three activities related to this week's session on newsprint for the students to copy. Challenge the adults to grow spiritually by completing one or more of them.

(1) Review your life. How has your self-evaluation changed over time? Do you think that Jesus would put the same value on you as you put on yourself? If not, are you possibly using different criteria than he would use? What changes might you need to make?

(2) Talk with someone who is struggling with his or her faith. Encourage this person to begin looking inside through the eyes of Christ. What new value might he or she discover? How might this discovery transform his or her life?

(3) Recall your baptism. If possible, read again the baptismal liturgy of your denomination, which is often found in the hymnal. How might the recollection of baptism—dying to self and rising with Christ—refocus your life and your values? Ponder these ideas.

❖ Sing or read aloud "And Can It Be That I Should Gain."

❖ Conclude today's session by leading the class in this benediction, adapted from the key verses for December 23 from Ephesians 5:1 and January 13 from Philippians 2:5: Go now as the Father's beloved children, who are of the same mind as the Son Jesus Christ, to be imitators of God.

UNIT 2: EXALTING CHRIST
STAND FIRM

PREVIEWING THE LESSON

Lesson Scripture: Philippians 3:12-16
Background Scripture: Philippians 3:12–4:1
Key Verse: Philippians 3:16

Focus of the Lesson:

Sometimes it is difficult to sustain energy to achieve goals that have lasting value. What motivates us to press on toward a goal? Maintaining a strong relationship with Christ now prepares us for the relationship we will have with Christ in eternity.

Goals for the Learners:

(1) to become familiar with what Paul says about living so that one attains eternity with Jesus Christ.
(2) to appreciate that the journey of Christian living is demanding and a quest for something eternal.
(3) to pledge to stand firm so as not to jeopardize the gift of Jesus Christ they have received.

Pronunciation Guide:

eschatological (es kat uh loj' i kuhl)

Supplies:

Bibles, newsprint and marker, paper and pencils, hymnals

READING THE SCRIPTURE

NRSV
Lesson Scripture: Philippians 3:12-16

¹²Not that I have already obtained this or have already reached the goal; but I press on to make it my own, because Christ Jesus has made me his own. ¹³Beloved, I do not consider that I have made it my own; but this one thing I do: forgetting what lies behind and straining

CEB
Lesson Scripture: Philippians 3:12-16

¹²It's not that I have already reached this goal or have already been perfected, but I pursue it, so that I may grab hold of it because Christ grabbed hold of me for just this purpose. ¹³Brothers and sisters, I myself don't think I've reached it, but I do this one

forward to what lies ahead, ¹⁴I press on toward the goal for the prize of the heavenly call of God in Christ Jesus. ¹⁵Let those of us then who are mature be of the same mind; and if you think differently about anything, this too God will reveal to you. ¹⁶Only **let us hold fast to what we have attained.**

thing: I forget about the things behind me and reach out for the things ahead of me. ¹⁴The goal I pursue is the prize of God's upward call in Christ Jesus. ¹⁵So, all of us who are spiritually mature should think this way and if anyone thinks differently, God will reveal it to him or her. ¹⁶Only **let's live in a way that is consistent with whatever level we have reached.**

UNDERSTANDING THE SCRIPTURE

Introduction. Today's reading explains what Paul means when he says he has not yet attained to the resurrection in verse 11. Verses 12-16 also prepare readers for the exhortation to imitate Paul (and others) in 3:17.

Philippians 3:12. Paul says he has not yet received all the gifts God has for believers—no one has. Paul constantly affirms that Christians now experience a measure, but only a partial measure, of the end-time blessings. The presence of the Spirit in their lives is one of the blessings Christians have now that foreshadows their place in the full presence of God at the end. All Christians live in this state of the partial fulfillment of God's promises. But this beginning of fulfillment also guarantees that God will complete the giving. In 2 Corinthians 1:22 and 5:5 Paul calls the Spirit's presence the down payment of God's gifts. Thus, he still looks forward to full possession of those gifts.

He also acknowledges that he has not "been made perfect" (NIV). The NRSV makes this phrase more parallel with the previous statement by rendering it "already reached the goal." Both translations capture the sense that Paul's Christian life has not reached its ultimate outcome. That is true when talking about both moral perfection and the full experience of the Resurrection.

Paul says that he pursues the goal of resurrection so he can attain it. But Paul does not strive for it on his own. He pursues it because Christ has already "made [Paul] his own" (3:12). Thus, while Paul can be confident of his place with God, that relationship includes the expectation that he will strive to live the way God wants, as he prepares for his reception of resurrection life.

Philippians 3:13-16. The NRSV begins verse 13 with "Beloved," while the NIV has "Brothers." The NIV is literally correct. The NRSV inadequately renders the meaning of "brothers" here (and other places) because "beloved" loses the familial meaning Paul intends to convey. The better translation is "brothers and sisters" (CEB) because Paul intends both men and women and he wants them to understand and relate to fellow Christians as family members.

Again acknowledging that he has not attained all God has for him or all that God expects of him, Paul says he has adopted a perspective that moves him toward fulfilling God's will. He refuses to remain burdened with mistakes of the past—and this from an admitted former persecutor of the church. Instead of looking back, he steadfastly reaches forward toward what God promises and expects. Thus, he pursues the goal, the prize awarded to those who heed God's call. Paul works strenuously, just as athletes strive to achieve their goal of winning a contest. And as they receive a prize, so he expects to receive a prize appropriate to the privileged calling he has received from God, the calling he received in Christ. Perhaps he views it as a high calling because it prepares him for participation in the kingdom of God (see discussion of verse 20).

Paul concludes his explanation and begins his exhortation with verses 15-16. He asserts that all who are mature in their faith adopt the way of thinking he has described in verses 12-14. Further, he expresses confidence that God will show the less mature that this is the proper way to think and live. He concludes the paragraph by encouraging them to be diligent in retaining what they have received, even if they have not achieved the level of maturity into which he expects them to grow.

Philippians 3:17-19. In verses 17-19 Paul again teaches by using examples. He tells the Philippians to imitate him and others who live as he does, and that they must not to be like those "enemies of the cross."

First-century moralists regularly called on people to imitate the behavior of their teacher. Some who wrote to others said things such as "I wish I could be there so you could see how I live." They did not say these things because they were arrogant, but because they believed that a living example was the best teacher. The substance and nuance of a manner of life are clearer in a personal example than on a page. In the ancient world, people thought that if a teacher of morality did not live by the morals he advocated, then he should stop teaching them. Paul's exhortation, then, is in line with contemporaneous expectations. Note also that he is not the sole example they are to imitate; others in their church serve as examples as well.

Since this call for imitation immediately follows Paul's recognition that he has not attained all God wants for or from him, he does not think he must be perfect to call people to imitate him. Indeed, his recognition of the need to continue to strive to live for God is part of what he calls them to imitate. The orientation of his life is what they should emulate.

Philippians 3:20-4:1. The assertion that their "citizenship is in heaven" (3:20) is powerful in this letter. Since Philippi was settled by Roman army veterans, many there had Roman citizenship. But Paul claims church members for a different kingdom, one that must take precedence over allegiance to all other nations. Christians are granted this citizenship by Christ, the Savior and ruler who has come from heaven. With citizenship comes the promise of the transformation of Christians' bodies that enables them to live in that realm. Christ effects this transformation, but does it through the power of God who made Christ the ruler of all things.

This turn to eschatological (that is, end-time) matters supports the exhortations that precede and follow these verses. Paul's assurance of future transformation provides the confidence readers need to remain faithful, even as it reminds them that God will assess their lives. Keeping the edge off any threat, Paul expresses confidence in and love for them. Perhaps because they are his joy, he ends with the exhortation to remain faithful.

INTERPRETING THE SCRIPTURE

Confident Striving

As Paul confesses that he is not yet everything God wants him to be, there is no hint that he is worried about his salvation. Rather, he strives because he knows what God has done for him. He knows the forgiveness given him, the relationship with God he has been granted, and the promise of the Resurrection. These blessings bring with them the further gift of the expectation that he live as God requires. Living according to God's commands is not a burden we have to accept because we want salvation. Instead, the demand that we live the Christian life is one of the blessings God gives us. It is a blessing because God's demands lead us to have more meaningful lives; they keep us from inflicting harm on ourselves in our short-sighted evaluations of what will be good for us. While we are accustomed to thinking of expectations as a burden, God's commands are a gift that helps us live as God made us to live. Thus, they bring us the manner of life that creates a sustainable, happy, and meaningful existence.

Part of what enables us to live for God is the realization that God constantly forgives our shortcomings. Paul speaks of forgetting the things that are past. He does not mean that he does not remember them, but that he does not allow them to determine who he is in his relationship with God. This former persecutor of the church can say with confidence that God has forgiven those things of the past. His prior evil deeds make the sins of most of us pale in comparison, yet he is certain that God has forgiven him so completely that he can have a secure relationship with God and look forward to life with God. At the same time, Christians must exert themselves in their efforts to live the Christian life. Paul compares the Christians' efforts with those of an athlete in training

and in the midst of the competition. Knowing what God has done for him motivates him to try harder to please God. We can make this effort because we know that God is not holding a grudge about our former mistakes but rather helps us to live as we should.

Paul can be confident about God's forgiveness because he lives in a genuine relationship with God, as do all Christians. Relationships entail more than keeping a tally of what someone has done for me and of how they have hurt me. Relationships involve commitment that goes beyond scorekeeping; we live in ways that please the other person in our relationships, not because we fear punishment but because we care about the other person. Paul knows that God is committed to remaining in relationship with us, not looking for a reason to leave us. Being in Christ brings Christians into the loving and committed relationship that God has with Christ. Thus, we can be certain that God will not let our past interfere with bringing us into God's full blessings. Being secure in this relationship should also motivate us to live in ways that please the God whose deep commitment to us is shown to us in the sending of Christ.

Maturing Spiritually

Paul recognizes that the outlook he has just described does not come easily. It is hard for us to let go of past mistakes. We often tend to let the past overly determine what we will become in our spiritual lives. Paul probably knows this from his own experience. Refusing to let his conduct as a persecutor define his life must have been difficult. But his experience of the risen Christ changed him in a way that helped him reorient everything in his life. Our own experience of God's grace and our relationship with God that is an element of that grace can help us begin to look forward to God's future with us rather than dwelling on mistakes of the past. Instead of dragging him down, Paul's memory of his past serves only to motivate him to greater service because he knows the overwhelming grace of God is more powerful than anything in his past. Thus, he urges Christians to adopt this forward-looking orientation. The powerful presence of God in the present urges us to live for God through troubles as we are reminded of the blessings God intends for us in the future. Paul sees adopting this way of approaching life as the view of the spiritually mature because this is the outlook that enables a peaceful and joyful life with God.

Reject Sin

Paul reminds the Philippians that some ways of living and viewing life are unacceptable for Christians. He does not supply specifics about the "enemies of the cross" (3:18) he mentions, but only speaks of their direction in life: "Their minds are set on earthly things" (3:19). Paul uses dramatic language that we should not take literally. These people do not actually go around bragging about their participation in acts they think are shameful. The description of this type of life, however, does suggest that their way of living violates God's will for humanity by bringing degradation on those who give themselves to that way of being. Such a manner of life makes one an enemy of the cross because it involves supporting values and ideas that violate what God wants for human life. The cross shows us both God's love for us and serves as an example of the way God wants us to live for others. Those who reject its message and the way of life it exemplifies are, then, enemies of the cross. Christians must adopt ways of living that are compatible with the cross, and then stand firm on those ways. That is, we must constantly be thinking of how the love of God shown there can be expressed in our lives.

Live a Life Worthy of Imitation

Paul tells the Philippians to imitate him and others who live as he does. This makes us nervous. We think that telling people to imitate us suggests that we think we are perfect and so means we are arrogant. That is not necessarily so. Paul has already told the Philippians that he is not perfect, yet he says they should imitate him. He does not mean they should be like him in every detail of his life; rather, he wants them to adopt the outlook on life and on relationship with God that he has just described. Whether we like it or not, others look at us as examples of what it means to be Christians and of how to live out the faith. People are either drawn to faith or sent away because of the ways they see Christians live. Just as ancient moralists knew that seeing a way of life is more powerful than hearing about it, we need to acknowledge that it is part of our Christian life to serve as an example of what it means to be a follower of Christ. Notice that Paul does not call them to imitate just him but also others in their church who form their lives around their relationship with God as he does. Being an example is the task of us all.

SHARING THE SCRIPTURE

Preparing Our Hearts

Explore this week's devotional reading, found in Matthew 25:14-29, which is the familiar parable of the talents. Contrast the two slaves who were good stewards of the money that had been entrusted to them with the one slave who simply hid what he had been given. Think about yourself. Are you, like the first two slaves, carefully tending to God's kingdom so that you will be rewarded as a "good and trustworthy slave" (25:23)? Or are you neglecting your kingdom work as the third slave did? How are you standing firm as a disciple of Christ?

Pray that you and the adult students will press on to attain the goal of the kingdom.

Preparing Our Minds

Study the background Scripture from Philippians 3:12–4:1 and the lesson Scripture from Philippians 3:12-16.

Consider this question as you prepare the lesson: *What motivates us to press on toward a goal?*

Write on newsprint:

❏ questions for "Appreciate that the Journey of Christian Living Is Demanding and a Quest for Something Eternal."

❏ information for next week's lesson, found under "Continue the Journey."

❏ activities for further spiritual growth in "Continue the Journey."

Review the "Introduction," "The Big Picture," "Close-up," and "Faith in Action." Consider how you will use this additional information, which immediately precedes the first lesson, for this session.

Prepare the suggested lecture for "Become Familiar With What Paul Says About Living so That One Attains Eternity With Jesus Christ."

LEADING THE CLASS

(1) Gather to Learn

❖ Greet the class members. Introduce any guests and help them feel at home.

❖ Pray that those who have gathered will continue to grow toward spiritual maturity.

❖ Read this information: **Inventor Thomas Alva Edison (1847–1931) was recognized as a genius. Despite being home-schooled after a teacher labeled him "addled" and then losing most of his hearing at age twelve, Edison pressed on. He would continue trying, never giving up until he met his goal. He is quoted as saying, "I have not failed. I've just found ten thousand ways that won't work." His best-known inventions included the phonograph, electric light system, incandescent light bulb, and motion picture camera. Some of his creations, such as the electric vote recorder that he patented in 1869, were so far ahead of their time that people were wary about using these new gadgets. Although he decided to focus on inventions that had commercial value, he never backed away from the challenge of hard work.**

❖ Ask: **What do you think gave Edison the motivation to continue trying to invent useful products?**

❖ Read aloud today's focus statement: **Sometimes it is difficult to sustain energy to achieve goals that have lasting value. What motivates us to press on toward a goal? Maintaining a strong relationship with Christ now prepares us for the relationship we will have with Christ in eternity.**

(2) Goal 1: Become Familiar With What Paul Says About Living so That One Attains Eternity With Jesus Christ

❖ Choose a volunteer to read Philippians 3:12-16.

❖ Discuss these questions:

(1) **Paul writes about the past and the future. What did he say about the past? What did he say about the future?** (Note that he apparently has forgotten about his prior status as discussed in verses 6 and 7. He now has status in Christ and therefore looks ahead to resurrection from the dead.)

(2) **What seems to motivate Paul to press on toward the goal?** (See "Confident Striving" in Interpreting the Scripture.)

(3) **Recall that in Philippians 2:5 Paul wrote about having "the same mind . . . that was in Christ Jesus." In 3:15 he tells those who are spiritually mature to be of the same mind. We recognize that we do not all think alike, so what do you think Paul means when he writes about being of the "same mind"?**

(4) **In verse 16, today's key verse, Paul encourages his readers to "hold fast" to what they have attained. How would you describe what you have attained in Christ Jesus? How are you "holding fast" to that?**

❖ End this portion of the session by presenting a lecture that you have prepared from Understanding the Scripture to help the students delve deeper into Paul's message.

(3) Goal 2: Appreciate That the Journey of Christian Living Is Demanding and a Quest for Something Eternal

❖ Read "Maturing Spiritually" from Interpreting the Scripture.

❖ Form several small groups. Invite participants to talk about challenges they faced that had the potential to throw them off course on their spiritual journeys. Suggest that they consider questions such as these, which you will read aloud and may want to post on newsprint:

(1) **How did the challenge affect your relationship with God?**

(2) **Why did you keep pressing on, or turn aside?**

(3) **What lessons did you learn about the demands of the Christian life?**

❖ Bring the groups together and call on volunteers to state briefly how demanding legs of their spiritual journeys have helped them grow closer to Christ.

(4) Goal 3: Pledge to Stand Firm so as Not to Jeopardize the Gift of Jesus Christ the Learners Have Received

❖ Distribute paper and pencils. Instruct the learners to draw an oval in the center of their papers. Then have them draw as many straight lines as they choose from each side of the oval, extending outward. Inside the oval they are to write a few words to remind them of the gift of Jesus Christ. On the lines, they are to write actions they will take to ensure that they will not jeopardize that gift. Each person will have different ideas, so assure them there is no "correct" answer.

❖ Conclude this activity by suggesting that the learners put this paper in a place at home where they will see it often, thus encouraging them to stand firm.

(5) Continue the Journey

❖ Pray that today's participants will stand firm so as to gain the heavenly prize that Christ Jesus has for them.

❖ Read aloud this preparation for next week's lesson. You may also want to post it on newsprint for the students to copy.

■ **Title: The Supremacy of Jesus Christ**

■ **Background Scripture: Colossians 1:15-20**

■ **Lesson Scripture: Colossians 1:15-20**

■ **Focus of the Lesson: Because of the immediate availability of** images of greatness, from athletics to space to technology, our grasp of the amazing becomes desensitized. What does it take to inspire true awe that commands reverence? Paul's use of metaphor strongly conveys Christ's supremacy, which helps us realize who Christ is.

❖ Post these three activities related to this week's session on newsprint for the students to copy. Challenge the adults to grow spiritually by completing one or more of them.

(1) Write in your spiritual journal about a failure you experienced. What were you trying to achieve? What happened? What did you learn from this experience? Did you grow spiritually? If so, how?

(2) Try to be of the same mind as a church member with whom you have a disagreement. Look at the situation from his or her point of view. Is there any way that the two of you can move closer together? Is this issue so important that you insist on pursuing it?

(3) Observe what motivates you to act in a variety of circumstances. On a scale of one to ten, with one being a secular motivation and ten being a motivation rooted in the kingdom of God, how would you rate your motivations? If you discover that you are often motivated by worldly goals, what changes will you make?

❖ Sing or read aloud "O Jesus, I Have Promised."

❖ Conclude today's session by leading the class in this benediction, adapted from the key verses for December 23 from Ephesians 5:1 and January 13 from Philippians 2:5: **Go now as the Father's beloved children, who are of the same mind as the Son Jesus Christ, to be imitators of God.**

UNIT 3: IMITATING JESUS

THE SUPREMACY OF JESUS CHRIST

PREVIEWING THE LESSON

Lesson Scripture: Colossians 1:15-20
Background Scripture: Colossians 1:15-20
Key Verse: Colossians 1:19

Focus of the Lesson:
Because of the immediate availability of images of greatness, from athletics to space to technology, our grasp of the amazing becomes desensitized. What does it take to inspire true awe that commands reverence? Paul's use of metaphor strongly conveys Christ's supremacy, which helps us realize who Christ is.

Goals for the Learners:
(1) to understand Paul's description of Jesus Christ's supremacy.
(2) to express feelings of awe at the supremacy of Jesus Christ.
(3) to describe to others the awe-inspiring preeminence of Christ for bringing reconciliation.

Pronunciation Guide:
christological (krist uh loj' i kuhl)

Supplies:
Bibles, newsprint and marker, paper and pencils, hymnals, pictures of great people or objects, thumbtacks or tape

---

READING THE SCRIPTURE

NRSV
Lesson Scripture: Colossians 1:15-20
  [15]He is the image of the invisible God, the firstborn of all creation; [16]for in him all things in heaven and on earth were created,

CEB
Lesson Scripture: Colossians 1:15-20
  [15]The Son is the image
    of the invisible God,
    the one who is first over all creation,

things visible and invisible, whether thrones or dominions or rulers or powers—all things have been created through him and for him. ¹⁷He himself is before all things, and in him all things hold together. ¹⁸He is the head of the body, the church; he is the beginning, the firstborn from the dead, so that he might come to have first place in everything. **¹⁹For in him all the fullness of God was pleased to dwell,** ²⁰and through him God was pleased to reconcile to himself all things, whether on earth or in heaven, by making peace through the blood of his cross.

¹⁶Because all things were created by him:
　　both in the heavens and on the earth,
　　the things that are visible
　　　and the things that are invisible.
　　Whether they are thrones or powers,
　　or rulers or authorities,
　　all things were created
　　　through him and for him.
¹⁷He existed before all things,
　　and all things are held together
　　　in him.
¹⁸He is the head of the body, the church,
　　who is the beginning,
　　　the one who is firstborn
　　　　from among the dead
　　　so that he might occupy
　　　　the first place in everything.
¹⁹Because all the fullness of God
　　was pleased to live in him,
²⁰and he reconciled all things to himself
　　through him—
　　whether things on earth
　　or in the heavens.
　　He brought peace
　　　through the blood of his cross.

UNDERSTANDING THE SCRIPTURE

Introduction. Colossians 1:15-20 is a poetic liturgy that proclaims the exalted position of Christ as a participant in creation and as Savior of the world. While many interpreters identify these verses as a hymn, its structure does not quite fit this category. The author uses this liturgy to support his assertions in verses 12-14 and 21-23 that believers have already been forgiven, been made citizens of God's kingdom, become heirs of God's blessings, been reconciled to God, and given holiness. These assertions are central to the purpose of Colossians. The letter argues that its readers should reject a teaching that presents them with new requirements that some say are needed to attain these blessings.

Colossians argues that believers have already received these things in Christ and at baptism. This liturgy reminds the readers of who Christ is and what he has already accomplished for them.

Colossians 1:15-16. The liturgy first celebrates Christ's involvement in creation. It identifies Christ closely with God, calling him the image of God. While many christological debates have used this verse, we cannot know exactly what the expression means. It does, however, clearly assert that Christ reveals God to us. This point is highlighted by calling God invisible or unseen. The liturgy proclaims that the unseen God is known to us through Christ. Further, Christ is "firstborn of all creation" (1:15).

Chronology is not the central point but rather the position of Christ. That is, calling Christ "firstborn" does not suggest that Christ is a created being. The Bible often uses the title "firstborn" to designate rank rather than priority of birth. For example, Israel is God's firstborn (Exodus 4:22; Jeremiah 31:9) and the king is the firstborn in Psalm 89:27. So calling Christ firstborn sets him above all others in creation, regardless of whether he is created or eternal.

Verse 16 asserts that Christ is firstborn because all things in all realms of creation were made through him. Christ is the agent of all of God's acts of creation. The "thrones," "dominions," "rulers," and "powers" in verse 16 are beings of the higher realms of the cosmos who exercise power and control in the world. First-century people envision the cosmos as a place populated with spiritual beings who influence things in this world. Such beings support the governmental, social, political, and economic structures of the world. So they are connected to real physical powers that dominate the world. However overwhelming these structures seem, believers in Christ do not need to fear them in any ultimate sense because Christians are associated with the One who created them all and so is more powerful than them all. Indeed, those beings were created for Christ's use in accomplishing God's purposes.

Colossians 1:17-18a. Verse 17 and the first half of verse 18 constitute an interlude between the two stanzas of the liturgy. They form a transition from praising Christ for his role in creation to proclaiming his place as Savior and head of the church. Verse 17 declares that Christ's cosmic work continues: He was not only active in creation, but it is through him that the cosmos continues to exist. Thus, the position of Christ is unrivaled. He was God's agent in creation and he continues to be the One through whom God sustains the existence of the creation.

Verse 18 then asserts that this exalted Christ is the head of the church. By identifying the church as his body, the liturgy claims that the church has an intimate association with the creator and sustainer of the cosmos. People who are part of Christ's body have nothing to gain from association with any other beings because all others are Christ's inferiors. Believers are already in the sphere of God's highest blessings and already have the closest relationship with God because they are incorporated into the body of Christ.

Colossians 1:18b-20. Paralleling the proclamation of Christ as firstborn of creation in verse 15, verse 18 declares that he is "firstborn from the dead," that he is the first to attain the permanent resurrection from the dead. This assertion includes a chronological priority that gives him the highest rank. He has authority over the church because he possesses the status of the firstborn. Calling Christ the "beginning" and "the firstborn from the dead" asserts that Christ is the source of the new creation, just as he is of the original creation. Thus, Christ is the source of the end-time blessings that the church already possesses (such as forgiveness, reconciliation, the Spirit) and of those it will receive at the Second Coming.

Christ has this position and power because the fullness of God's presence resides in him. Thus he is the one authorized to exercise God's power in all the cosmos. All that God is can be known through Christ and his work.

Verse 20 relates how that power of God is brought to bear for the church: It gives reconciliation with God and makes peace with God. Ironically, this power is exercised through Christ's death on the cross. Instead of a display of force, God's saving power is known in what looks like defeat. The love and desire of God to be in relationship with us is shown to us in the cross.

When the liturgy speaks of the cross reconciling the things in the heavens, it envisions a kind of resolution. The beings who have turned against the will of God in other realms are defeated in the cross and

Resurrection, as Christ is reaffirmed as Lord of all realms. Many in the early church understood the work of Christ to include defeating those cosmic powers that try to keep humans from God. Those forces have not completely surrendered, but their defeat is assured through the cross because the Resurrection demonstrates that the love of God has the power to defeat evil. Thus, the same act demonstrates God's love for us and effects the defeat of the forces that oppose God's will.

INTERPRETING THE SCRIPTURE

The Cosmic Christ

The liturgy of Colossians 1:15-20 makes astounding claims about Christ, claims that are cosmic in scope. From very early times the church understood Christ to be a preexistent being who was present with God before the creation of the world. Christ was not only present and the one through whom God created the world but he is also the image of God. Thus, Christ bears the character of God and shows us what the unseen God is like. So calling Christ the image of God speaks of both his nature and his function as the one who reveals God to us.

This passage makes claims that opposed the pluralism of the first century. The first century was a very pluralistic era. People who worshiped the god of a particular area saw the worship of other gods as equally valid for people of another region. People also worshiped various gods for various needs such as rain, crops, and business dealings; nearly everyone worshiped multiple gods. Even people who were priests of a particular god worshiped other gods. There was a hierarchy of gods, but the higher gods did not expect people who worshiped them to refrain from worshiping lower gods. The exceptions to this were Jews, Christians, and a few philosophers.

When members of the church made the exalted claims about Christ that we hear in today's reading, they were rejecting that kind of pluralism. The church expected its members to worship only God because they declared that others were worshiping false gods. It was not that those other gods did not exist, only that they were not really gods; the beings were real, but they should not be worshiped because God demands singular allegiance. This could be an expectation because God through Christ is the creator and sustainer of all other beings. Thus, worshiping them impugned God's sovereignty. The "thrones," "dominions," "rulers," and "powers" in verse 16 included these beings that most people worshiped as gods. This liturgy, then, makes radical claims about Christ, about his relationship to God, and about his preeminence over other supposed gods.

Such claims about Christ should also shape our thought about participation in our pluralistic world. The cosmic claims of our passage assert that Christ is over all other gods and is the clearest manifestation of God for the whole world. For Colossians, it is not just that *the church* finds the clearest manifestation of God in Christ but that Christ is that best revelation of God for all people, even for the entire cosmos. After all, the fullness of God is found in Christ. Colossians rejects the idea that all religions (or even a select few) are equal. That does not mean there is no true revelation of God anywhere else. Particularly, New Testament writers recognize true revelation of God in Judaism. At the same time, they are not reticent to claim that the revelation in Christ is yet clearer.

The Cross and Reconciliation

These claims about Christ also mean that he has all authority within the church. He is its originator and remains its head. Thus, the church must submit to Christ in all things. His resurrection attests to his preeminence within the church. Christ's resurrection inaugurates and opens the way to a new life for Christians now and in the time to come. The resurrection of Christ is an act of God that will culminate in the resurrection of God's people. It is, then, both Christ's nature and his saving work that make him the head of the church.

Colossians identifies the cross as the place where God effects the reconciliation of all people to God. The images of reconciliation and making peace assume that we have turned away from God and made ourselves enemies of God. Verse 21 expands on this notion, saying that we had estranged ourselves by the ways we have thought and acted toward God and toward one another. As it is envisioned here, the cross works to help us realize how much God loves us and what God is willing to do to reestablish a relationship with us. The very image of God dies shamefully to reveal this love to us; the cross is the height of the revelation of God's love.

The cross is also the moment of defeat for all powers that would try to separate us from God. The reconciliation of "all things" (1:20) in the heavens does not happen peacefully. Christ must defeat those things that turn us from God. The Resurrection is the sign that those powers have been defeated by Christ. They could not prohibit God's vindication of Christ's way of life and willingness to die for others. We know that there are still many things that try to turn us from God. The final defeat of all those things will not come until the end of time. But the death and resurrection of Christ are the guarantee from God that those death-inducing powers do not have the last word. God has shown in Christ's death and resurrection that God has the power and the will to conquer them. All such rebellion against God must submit to God's will in the end.

Living as a Reconciling Church Under the Lordship of Christ

As the church looks forward to that day, it must be an example of the reconciliation that God offers to all. We have experienced the beginnings of the reconciliation and peace with God that will one day be complete. Our proper response is to become agents of that reconciliation in the world. We will not eradicate evil in the world, but the church should stand as a sign of what God wants for the world. We are to be the demonstration of how those who have been reconciled to God are also reconciled to one another. We are to proclaim the gospel that God gives peace and to embody that message in our lives. In both ways we summon others to accept this relationship with God.

Accepting the offer of peace with God includes the demand that we recognize the lordship of Christ in all aspects of our lives. Since Christ has all authority in the church, he is Lord of our entire lives. Colossians' talk of the rulers and powers acknowledges that there are forces that do not act according to God's will. While we are not inclined to personify the forces that shape our world, we can recognize that our social and economic systems do not operate according to the principles of God's kingdom. Greed and desire for status are not Kingdom values. The lordship of Christ bids us to identify and reject those things around us that violate God's will for the world. The church everywhere struggles with how to embody its acceptance of Christ's lordship in the midst of the cultures that shape our living. In all cultural settings the lordship of Christ requires the church to advocate for social and economic systems that reflect God's will. Furthermore, this lordship reaches into our personal lives, demanding that we submit to God's will in all aspects of life so that we act like the people who constitute the body of Christ.

SHARING THE SCRIPTURE

Preparing Our Hearts

Explore this week's devotional reading, found in Ephesians 1:17-23. Paul offers prayers of thanksgiving and intercessions for the readers, whom he apparently does not know, since he refers to hearing of their faith in verse 15. In these verses Paul describes how God used Jesus to bring about God's will and purposes. As you read the descriptions of Christ and his work, allow yourself to be awed by his greatness. Give thanks to God for all that Jesus has done for you. Offer prayers of thanksgiving and intercession.

Pray that you and the adult students will be aware of all the promises that God has made and fulfilled in Christ Jesus.

Preparing Our Minds

Study the background Scripture and the lesson Scripture, both of which are from Colossians 1:15-20.

Consider this question as you prepare the lesson: *What does it take to inspire true awe that commands reverence?*

Write on newsprint:

❑ questions from the section "Understand Paul's Description of Jesus Christ's Supremacy."

❑ information for next week's lesson, found under "Continue the Journey."

❑ activities for further spiritual growth in "Continue the Journey."

Review the "Introduction," "The Big Picture," "Close-up," and "Faith in Action." Consider how you will use this additional information, which immediately precedes the first lesson, for this session.

Locate pictures of several people (historical or contemporary) or objects (either part of God's created world or manufactured) that you consider great. If you have limited access to such pictures, enlist the help of several class members. Prior to the session, post these pictures around the room where the adults can see them.

Become very familiar with both the Understanding the Scripture and Interpreting the Scripture portions. You will need to intersperse this information as appropriate during the discussion for "Express Feelings of Awe at the Supremacy of Jesus Christ."

LEADING THE CLASS

(1) Gather to Learn

❖ Greet the class members. Introduce any guests and help them feel at home.

❖ Pray that today's participants will experience the true greatness of Jesus Christ.

❖ Direct the students' attention to the pictures of great people or objects you have posted and ask these questions:

(1) Which of these pictures best illustrates greatness for you?

(2) Does this picture leave you with a sense of awe? Why or why not?

❖ Read aloud today's focus statement: **Because of the immediate availability of images of greatness, from athletics to space to technology, our grasp of the amazing becomes desensitized. What does it take to inspire true awe that commands reverence? Paul's use of metaphor strongly** conveys Christ's supremacy, which helps us realize who Christ is.

(2) Goal 1: Understand Paul's Description of Jesus Christ's Supremacy

❖ Set the stage for today's Scripture passage by reading "The Cosmic Christ" from Interpreting the Scripture.

❖ Select a volunteer to read Colossians 1:15-20.

❖ Discuss these questions:
   (1) What words does this passage use to tell us about Christ? (List ideas on newsprint. Encourage adults with different Bible translations to add words to the list so as to give a wider meaning to the text.)
   (2) What does each of the words or phrases we identified really mean? (For example, what does it mean to say that "in him all the fullness of God was pleased to dwell" (1:19)? Use information from Understanding the Scripture and Interpreting the Scripture as it is helpful in enhancing the discussion.)
   (3) What questions does this passage raise for you about who Christ is and what he has come to earth to do?
   (4) What does this passage affirm for you about Christ?

❖ Form three groups to do a comparative Bible study focused on this passage from Colossians. One group is to look at John 1:1-4, 10-18; a second group, Philippians 2:5-11 (which we studied on January 13); and a third group, Hebrews 1:1-4. Distribute paper and pencils so that the adults can jot down ideas. Each group is to focus on these questions, which you will post on newsprint:
   (1) What does our assigned passage teach us about Christ?
   (2) How does what we learn from our assigned passage compare with what Paul writes in Colossians 1:15-20?

❖ Bring everyone together to report on what they have learned about the supremacy of Christ.

(3) Goal 2: Express Feelings of Awe at the Supremacy of Jesus Christ

❖ Distribute hymnals. Remind the adults that often our deepest feelings are expressed in music. Encourage them to locate hymns that lift up Christ and select one for study. Here are some examples: "Jesus Shall Reign," "All Hail the Power of Jesus' Name," "At the Name of Jesus," "Majesty, Worship His Majesty." If you use *The United Methodist Hymnal*, recommend that students check the section from pages 153–94, titled "In Praise of Christ." (Check other hymnals prior to the session for a similar section.)

❖ Form small groups and invite each person to talk with the group members about how the selected hymn expresses his or her sense of awe at the supremacy of Christ. Suggest that the adults look for specific words and images that prompt or express their feelings.

❖ Call the groups together. Solicit names of hymns that the adults selected. As time permits, sing a verse or two of the songs that were often chosen.

(4) Goal 3: Describe to Others the Awe-inspiring Preeminence of Christ for Bringing Reconciliation

❖ Have a student read again Colossians 1:19-20.

❖ Ask the students what they mean by the word "reconciliation." The word can be defined in various ways, but in a Christian context the word refers to the restoration of harmony and renewal of friendship. In both cases humanity is being reconciled and restored to God the Father through the Son Jesus Christ.

❖ Read "The Cross and Reconciliation" from Interpreting the Scripture.

❖ Ask these questions:

(1) **What is the relationship between Jesus' supremacy and his resurrection?**

(2) **Why is the cross so important in terms of reconciliation?**

(3) **How does the cross reveal God's reconciling love?**

❖ **Option**: If you have access to *The United Methodist Hymnal*, conclude this portion of the session by inviting the adults to turn to page 888 and read responsively the "Affirmation from 1 Corinthians 15:1-6 and Colossians 1:15-20."

(5) Continue the Journey

❖ Pray that today's participants will recognize and give thanks for the greatness of Jesus.

❖ Read aloud this preparation for next week's lesson. You may also want to post it on newsprint for the students to copy.

■ **Title: Full Life in Christ**

■ **Background Scripture: Colossians 2:6-15**

■ **Lesson Scripture: Colossians 2:6-15**

■ **Focus of the Lesson: We regularly try but fail to live up to human expectations and traditions. How can we overcome our failures and shortcomings? Through Jesus, God forgives all our trespasses and triumphs over all earthly rulers and authorities.**

❖ Post these three activities related to this week's session on newsprint for the students to copy. Challenge the adults to grow spiritually by completing one or more of them.

(1) **Find a picture of Christ that for you illustrates his headship of the church or how he holds all things together. Study this picture, noting its colors, composition, and lines. If you were to put into words what this picture says about Christ, what words would you use?**

(2) **Recall that many commentators believe that Paul quoted a hymn of the early church in writing Colossians 1:15-20. Write your own poem or hymn of praise in which you express awe for the greatness of Christ.**

(3) **Tell someone else about the greatness of Christ as you experience it.**

❖ Sing or read aloud "Christ Is the World's Light."

❖ Conclude today's session by leading the class in this benediction, adapted from the key verses for December 23 from Ephesians 5:1 and January 13 from Philippians 2:5: **Go now as the Father's beloved children, who are of the same mind as the Son Jesus Christ, to be imitators of God.**

UNIT 3: IMITATING JESUS
FULL LIFE IN CHRIST

PREVIEWING THE LESSON

Lesson Scripture: Colossians 2:6-15
Background Scripture: Colossians 2:6-15
Key Verse: Colossians 2:10

Focus of the Lesson:
We regularly try but fail to live up to human expectations and traditions. How can we overcome our failures and shortcomings? Through Jesus, God forgives all our trespasses and triumphs over all earthly rulers and authorities.

Goals for the Learners:
(1) to discover Paul's message describing a full life in Christ.
(2) to express thanksgiving for God's forgiveness through Jesus Christ.
(3) to pursue an understanding of life in the fullness of Jesus Christ and to be thankful to him.

Supplies:
Bibles, newsprint and marker, paper and pencils, hymnals

READING THE SCRIPTURE

NRSV
Lesson Scripture: Colossians 2:6-15

⁶As you therefore have received Christ Jesus the Lord, continue to live your lives in him, ⁷rooted and built up in him and established in the faith, just as you were taught, abounding in thanksgiving.

⁸See to it that no one takes you captive through philosophy and empty deceit, according to human tradition, according to the elemental spirits of the universe, and not according to Christ. ⁹For in him the whole fullness of deity dwells bodily, ¹⁰and

CEB
Lesson Scripture: Colossians 2:6-15

⁶So live in Christ Jesus the Lord in the same way as you received him. ⁷Be rooted and built up in him, be established in faith, and overflow with thanksgiving just as you were taught. ⁸See to it that nobody enslaves you with philosophy and foolish deception, which conform to human traditions and the way the world thinks and acts rather than Christ. ⁹All the fullness of deity lives in Christ's body. ¹⁰And **you have been filled by him, who is the head of every ruler and authority.**

you have come to fullness in him, who is the head of every ruler and authority. [11]In him also you were circumcised with a spiritual circumcision, by putting off the body of the flesh in the circumcision of Christ; [12]when you were buried with him in baptism, you were also raised with him through faith in the power of God, who raised him from the dead. [13]And when you were dead in trespasses and the uncircumcision of your flesh, God made you alive together with him, when he forgave us all our trespasses, [14]erasing the record that stood against us with its legal demands. He set this aside, nailing it to the cross. [15]He disarmed the rulers and authorities and made a public example of them, triumphing over them in it.

You were also circumcised by him. This wasn't performed by human hands—the whole body was removed through this circumcision by Christ. [12]You were buried with him through baptism and raised with him through faith in the power of God, who raised him from the dead. [13]When you were dead because of the things you had done wrong and because your body wasn't circumcised, God made you alive with Christ and forgave all the things you had done wrong. [14]He destroyed the record of the debt we owed, with its requirements that worked against us. He canceled it by nailing it to the cross. [15]When he disarmed the rulers and authorities, he exposed them to public disgrace by leading them in a triumphal parade.

UNDERSTANDING THE SCRIPTURE

Colossians 2:6-7. Colossians begins its direct opposition to false teaching in 2:6-15. The writer makes an impassioned plea for the readers to reject that teaching, implying that their salvation is at stake. At the same time, he makes the other teaching as unattractive as possible.

He begins in verses 6-7 by exhorting the readers to hold to the teaching they received at the beginning of their Christian lives. This teaching is what brought them into contact with Christ and so with salvation. Consequently, all of these false teachings must be rejected.

Colossians 2:8-10. Verse 8 contains a series of disapproving evaluations of the other teaching and its promoters. The writer calls those other teachers people who want to take the Colossians captive through their regulations. So they are not the kind of people one should trust. The first evaluation of their teaching is that it is "hollow and deceptive philosophy" (2:8 NIV). Philosophy was a broad term that referred to any

kind of teaching in the first century, not just what we think of as philosophy (as opposed to religion). So this expression simply rejects that teaching as useless. He next describes this doctrine as something that comes from humans rather than from God. His third evaluation is that it is according to the "elemental spirits of the universe" (2:8). Scholars debate the meaning of this phrase, but we can be certain that it asserts that this teaching has its origin in things of the unredeemed world. That becomes clear in the next phrase that says the teaching is "not according to Christ." Thus, he describes the teaching as contrary to what Christians should believe. This teaching is also contrary to what he has said believers should hold to in verse 6. These evaluations tell us nothing about the alternative teaching except that it takes the Colossians away from Christ.

Verses 9-10 explain why they must hold to Christ. Verse 9 affirms both the presence of God in Christ and the Incarnation. All the fullness of deity is in Christ, so believers need contact with no other heavenly beings. Nothing could be better than association with Christ. He can grant them the fullness of God's blessings because the fullness of God is in him. This also means that he is over all other beings with whom the Colossians might want to be associated.

Colossians 2:11-12. The writer uses a new metaphor in verse 11 to speak of the blessings believers possess in Christ: They have received "spiritual circumcision." Circumcision was a sign of being in the covenant. Thus this metaphor asserts that receiving Christ brings Christians fully into covenant relationship with God. The other teaching can offer nothing beyond this true relationship with God. This initiation into the covenant occurs at baptism; that is where the "circumcision of Christ" (2:11) takes place. Colossians 2:12 also uses the images of dying and being raised to speak of what happens at baptism. This way of describing baptism was well known in Pauline churches. It describes baptism as the place where one's old life ends and where God grants new life. The writer assures the Colossians that they have received this new life by reminding them that the God who gave them this life is the same God who raised Christ from the dead.

Colossians 2:13-15. Colossians continues its description of the blessing Christians already possess by widening the meaning of the images of death and resurrection. The writer says the readers' old, dead existence came to an end in baptism; now they have been made alive. Their sins and separation from the covenant (their uncircumcision) meant that they were spiritually dead. Now because of Christ they have received forgiveness and so have been raised from that lifeless state.

Verses 14-15 describe how the work of Christ brings forgiveness, but these are some of the most difficult verses in the New Testament. They have often been given meanings that denigrate Judaism, but those meanings are unlikely in the historical setting of Colossians. These verses do not assert that the Mosaic covenant has been nailed to the cross.

Colossians says forgiveness is given because Christ erased "the record that stood against us" (2:14). This same language is used in other writings of the era to speak of registers of debts and so in some Jewish literature for the ledger in heaven that contains the record of each person's deeds. This is the most likely meaning here. Forgiveness in Christ means that the record of our sins has been erased. The next phrase, "with its legal demands," refers to either the rules each person violated or the decree of judgment that issued from their sins. Since Colossians was written to Gentiles who were never expected to follow the Mosaic commandments, it cannot refer to those commands specifically. What Christ nailed to the cross was the record of our sinful deeds that brought us condemnation.

To destroy the record of our sin, Christ also had to defeat the powers that keep that record. In earlier times, keeping the record of sinful behavior was seen as the duty of an angel that God assigned to the task, but by the first century many thought that beings in league with the devil or at least beings who wanted to see humans condemned had taken over the task of recording sins and prosecuting people before God. These are the beings Christ disarms and publicly shames. Thus, they are powerless to accuse God's people. There is no more record of our sin because the beings who kept that record have been overcome and shown for what they are. Ironically, this is done through the cross. The cross may have appeared to be a triumph for evil, but in it Christ removes those who seek to condemn humans. Since Christ has done all of this, the Colossians can depend on their association with Christ to bring them forgiveness and full relationship and life with God.

INTERPRETING THE SCRIPTURE

Live in Christ

The writer of Colossians is concerned to keep his readers away from any teaching that diverts their attention from the lordship of Christ. Verse 8 issues a particularly strong warning against "human tradition, according to the elemental spirits of the universe." However, any teaching that turns Christians from their singular devotion to God in Christ is destructive. The idea that certain kinds of spiritual experiences are necessary accompaniments of salvation deflects attention from the lordship of Christ. When Colossians tells its readers to "live your lives in him [Christ]" (2:6), the writer wants Christians to live out the recognition of Christ's lordship in every aspect of their lives. This begins with the proper recognition of the exalted place Christ holds in the cosmos and thus in our lives.

Christians must give regular attention to maintaining their allegiance to Christ. We do this in part by examining all areas of our lives to see where other allegiances may have begun to displace Christ. These commitments may be to good things, but if they take precedence over our allegiance to Christ, they are out of place. Since we live in a world that does not recognize his reign, it is easy to lose sight of what his lordship demands in our lives. Our regular participation in worship and study can help us maintain vigilance in living out our belief that Jesus is Lord. When worship reminds us of Christ's sovereignty and gives us opportunities to affirm it, we are encouraged to grant him lordship in the rest of our lives.

The Lordship of Christ in the World

This passage envisions the lordship of Christ to be in conflict with other powers that influence both this world and an unseen world. Colossians says these powers have been defeated by Christ; they have lost in the decisive battle. Even though Christ has defeated them, they have not stopped exercising their power to influence the world. They continue to struggle to exert their power to turn people away from the purposes of God, even though they know that they cannot ultimately withstand the power of Christ. The final end of their influence will only come at the end of time, when the will of God reigns over all things. The work of Christ and his resurrection guarantee that God will put a stop to their activity in the end. But in the meantime, in the time between the resurrection of Christ and the resurrection of all God's people, the church must contend with their influence.

We recognize these powers in the institutions and systems of our world that do not operate in accordance with the will of God. They are the values, structures, and systems that inflict injustice and violence on those who cannot resist. When social and economic systems do not conform to the values of God's kingdom, the church's task is to oppose them. Thus, our devotion to the lordship of Christ sometimes puts us in conflict with such structures. Being loyal to Christ leads Christians to stand against ways of constructing legal, economic, and cultural systems that do not conform to God's will, even when that means accepting disadvantage. Members of the early church often suffered economic and social disadvantages because of their allegiance to Christ. Since our world's values continue to be formed by values that are inconsistent with God's will, our living these alternative values will still sometimes bring us the same kinds of disadvantage.

God's Determined Love

This passage also brings us the good news that God is determined to be in relationship with us. The Incarnation is an unmistakable sign of this resolve. The fullness of deity was present in the incarnate Christ. God participated directly in our world through Christ, reaching out to offer forgiveness and relationship. God still reaches out, even when we are unwilling and unable to return to God. We were, Colossians says, spiritually dead because of our own doing, our deliberate turning from God. Sin is turning against God because it signals our collaboration with things that harm God's children and creation. Despite our involvement in these things, God acts to save us. The language of Colossians is dramatic: God raises us from the dead with the same power God used to raise Christ. In this new life, God lives in relationship with us. Thus, it is not only a fresh start but also a commitment to remain in relationship with us and to nurture us in that relationship so that we can conform more fully to God's will.

Nailing Condemnation to the Cross

Verses 14 and 15 have often been read as pronouncements about the Mosaic covenant, as declarations that it has been invalidated. Such a reading runs contrary to much that we find in Paul's letters, particularly in Romans 9–11. But this reading also limits the good news that these verses intend to proclaim.

Reading these verses as a declaration of the end of the Mosaic covenant would be of little import to Gentiles, who were the primary audience of Colossians. The law was never intended for Gentiles, and the church had, for the most part, already rejected the idea that church membership required full conversion to Judaism. Some non-Christian Jews thought Gentiles could participate in the messianic age as "righteous Gentiles" who were still not expected to follow those commands that made Jews distinct from Gentiles (for example, the food laws). Thus, Christian Gentiles would not have been worried about any judgment that related to the Mosaic law. Plus, Jews commonly saw the law as a blessing rather than a burden. It was a guide for how to live as the chosen people of God. The law was the way to have the best life and to adhere to the covenant God had made with them. Jesus argued with various religious leaders about how to keep the law, but we never see him telling Jews not to obey the law. Near the end of Acts (which was probably written after Colossians) we hear of people who accuse Paul of telling Jews they do not need to keep the law. He denies this and demonstrates that he remains observant by worshiping at the Temple (Acts 21:20-26). So it is unlikely that Colossians would say that the Mosaic law or covenant had been nailed to the cross.

The proclamation in Colossians 2:14-15 is broader and richer than the traditional reading allows: It says that all account of our sin has been erased, not just that related to Jews (or Jews and Gentiles) observing the Mosaic law. But there is good news even beyond this: These verses declare that the powers that cause us to sin and want to condemn us are disabled and defeated. The death and resurrection of Christ show violence, oppression, and sin for what they are. Christ frees us from fear of those powers so we can serve God with gratitude. By holding to and growing in our relationship with Christ, we live "in him" (2:6) and the salvation he brings, which inspires thanksgiving and joy.

SHARING THE SCRIPTURE

Preparing Our Hearts

Explore this week's devotional reading, found in Romans 8:31-39. In the midst of rhetorical questions here, Paul seeks to show us that God is for us and faithful to us. God's love is seen in its fullness in the incarnate Christ, who was crucified and raised and now intercedes for us. Nothing on earth or in heaven can separate us from God's love. Paul's words are true, even as we suffer hardship and persecution. But do we really believe what Paul writes? Are there times in our lives when challenges or losses raise the question: If God really loves me, why is this happening to me? What assurance do you have that in all circumstances the God of love is truly on your side?

Pray that you and the adult students will recognize that you can trust and count on God's love for you in all situations.

Preparing Our Minds

Study the background Scripture and the lesson Scripture, both of which are from Colossians 2:6-15.

Consider this question as you prepare the lesson: *How can we overcome our failures and shortcomings?*

Write on newsprint:

❑ information for next week's lesson, found under "Continue the Journey."
❑ activities for further spiritual growth in "Continue the Journey."

Review the "Introduction," "The Big Picture," "Close-up," and "Faith in Action." Consider how you will use this additional information, which immediately precedes the first lesson, for this session.

LEADING THE CLASS

(1) Gather to Learn

❖ Greet the class members. Introduce any guests and help them feel at home.

❖ Pray that all who have come today will celebrate the full and wonderful life we have in Jesus Christ.

❖ Read the following comments, each of which says something about the expectations that one person had of another:

■ **In 1895 Albert Einstein's teacher said to his father, "It doesn't matter what he does, he will never amount to anything."**

■ **Thomas Edison was a poor student. When a schoolmaster called Edison "addled," his furious mother took Edison out of the school and proceeded to teach him at home. Edison said many years later, "My mother was the making of me. She was so true, so sure of me, and I felt I had someone to live for, someone I must not disappoint."**

■ **Henry Ford once remarked, "If you think you can do a thing or think you can't do a thing, you're right."**

❖ Ask: **In your opinion, how do expectations affect one's ability to do what people think you should be able to do?**

❖ Read aloud today's focus statement: **We regularly try but fail to live up to human expectations and traditions. How can we overcome our failures and shortcomings? Through Jesus, God forgives all our trespasses and triumphs over all earthly rulers and authorities.**

(2) Goal 1: Discover Paul's Message Describing a Full Life in Christ

❖ Read "Live in Christ" in Interpreting the Scripture to introduce today's lesson.

❖ Choose a volunteer to read Colossians 2:6-15.

❖ Form two groups or multiples of two if the class is large. One group is to focus on what this passage says about life in Christ; the other group is to focus on the attributes of Christ that are described here. Provide paper and pencils.

❖ Bring the groups together and encourage them to report on the ideas they discussed.

❖ Discuss these questions together:

(1) **If this passage contained the sum of your knowledge about Christ and the kind of life one can live in him, would you choose to be a Christian? Why or why not?**

(2) **How might you experience the lordship of Jesus to be in conflict with the traditions and philosophies of this world?** (Look at "The Lordship of Christ in the World" in Interpreting the Scripture for additional information.)

(3) **What activities support growth in your faith? How often do you engage in these life-enhancing activities?**

(3) Goal 2: Express Thanksgiving for God's Forgiveness Through Jesus Christ

❖ Ask someone to read again Colossians 2:13-14.

❖ Retell "God's Determined Love" from Interpreting the Scripture.

❖ Lead the class in this guided imagery to help them acknowledge God's forgiveness and give thanks for it. Invite the adults to get comfortable and, if they choose, to close their eyes to imagine the scene as you read it.

(1) **You are in a deserted place where you feel alone and uncomfortable. You begin to think about sins you have committed and feel great shame and regret.** (*Pause.*)

(2) **Suddenly Jesus enters the scene. The place no longer seems isolated, but you still carry the guilt and shame of your sin. You hesitate, not knowing whether to talk** **with Jesus or to slip away quietly so that he won't have the opportunity to take you to task. But you just can't move. At that moment, Jesus, as if reading your mind about the sins you've committed, begins to speak to you. Listen to what he has to say.** (*Pause.*)

(3) **You look up and as quickly as Jesus came, he has gone. Yet you have somehow been changed. He has forgiven you. You are a new person with a brand-new chance. Imagine yourself telling someone who is dear to you how you feel now.** (*Pause.*)

❖ Invite the learners to open their eyes and come back together as they feel ready. Offer volunteers an opportunity to share a new insight about forgiveness.

(4) Goal 3: Pursue an Understanding of Life in the Fullness of Jesus Christ and Be Thankful to Him

❖ Lead the group in a unison reading of today's key verse, Colossians 2:10.

❖ Recall that earlier in the session we talked about expectations, which often become self-fulfilling prophecies. That simply means that we get what we expect. Distribute paper and pencils if you have not already done so and ask the adults to jot down answers to this question: **What do you expect living in the fullness of Christ to be like?**

❖ Provide an opportunity for the students to share their answers with a partner or the entire group. People may have focused on different ideas here, but be sure everyone understands that by living in the fullness of the incarnate Christ we are also living in the fullness of God. Our lives are radically transformed by the life, death, and resurrection of the One who has triumphed over all powers and rulers.

(5) Continue the Journey

❖ Pray that those who have attended today's session will go forth to live in the fullness of life that Christ offers to them.

❖ Read aloud this preparation for next week's lesson. You may also want to post it on newsprint for the students to copy.

- **Title: Clothed with Christ**
- **Background Scripture: Colossians 3:1-17**
- **Lesson Scripture: Colossians 3:5-17**
- **Focus of the Lesson: Our lives are guided by basic principles. How do we decide which principles to follow? Those who believe in Christ are guided by his example.**

❖ Post these three activities related to this week's session on newsprint for the students to copy. Challenge the adults to grow spiritually by completing one or more of them.

(1) **Think about traditions that you have been taught to observe, particularly in your home or church. Are there any that perhaps you should abandon because they are no longer valuable to you? Begin to make changes.**

(2) **Recall that Paul warned us against becoming a "captive through philosophy and empty deceit" (2:8). What claims are you hearing that do not square with your beliefs as a Christian? How do you handle such claims?**

(3) **Share with a new or nominal Christian your understanding of the role of Christ in the life of a believer. Be sure to come across as a fellow seeker who tries to make progress each day in the journey with Christ.**

❖ Sing or read aloud "Ask Ye What Great Things I Know."

❖ Conclude today's session by leading the class in this benediction, adapted from the key verses for December 23 from Ephesians 5:1 and January 13 from Philippians 2:5: **Go now as the Father's beloved children, who are of the same mind as the Son Jesus Christ, to be imitators of God.**

UNIT 3: IMITATING JESUS
CLOTHED WITH CHRIST

PREVIEWING THE LESSON

Lesson Scripture: Colossians 3:5-17
Background Scripture: Colossians 3:1-17
Key Verse: Colossians 3:14

Focus of the Lesson:
Our lives are guided by basic principles. How do we decide which principles to follow? Those who believe in Christ are guided by his example.

Goals for the Learners:
(1) to gain an impression of principles of living in Christ.
(2) to imagine how their life principles and behavior are different because they follow Christ.
(3) to evaluate their treatment of others and to make changes where necessary as demanded by a life lived in Christ.

Pronunciation Guide:
Scythian (sith ee' uhn)

Supplies:
Bibles, newsprint and marker, paper and pencils, hymnals, pieces of clothing as suggested

---

READING THE SCRIPTURE

NRSV
Lesson Scripture: Colossians 3:5-17
⁵Put to death, therefore, whatever in you is earthly: fornication, impurity, passion, evil desire, and greed (which is idolatry). ⁶On account of these the wrath of God is coming on those who are disobedient. ⁷These are the ways you also once followed, when you were living that life. ⁸But now you must get rid of all such things—anger, wrath, malice,

CEB
Lesson Scripture: Colossians 3:5-17
⁵So put to death the parts of your life that belong to the earth, such as sexual immorality, moral corruption, lust, evil desire, and greed (which is idolatry). ⁶The wrath of God is coming upon disobedient people because of these things. ⁷You used to live this way, when you were alive to these things. ⁸But

slander, and abusive language from your mouth. ⁹Do not lie to one another, seeing that you have stripped off the old self with its practices ¹⁰and have clothed yourselves with the new self, which is being renewed in knowledge according to the image of its creator. ¹¹In that renewal there is no longer Greek and Jew, circumcised and uncircumcised, barbarian, Scythian, slave and free; but Christ is all and in all!

¹²As God's chosen ones, holy and beloved, clothe yourselves with compassion, kindness, humility, meekness, and patience. ¹³Bear with one another and, if anyone has a complaint against another, forgive each other; just as the Lord has forgiven you, so you also must forgive. **¹⁴Above all, clothe yourselves with love, which binds everything together in perfect harmony.** ¹⁵And let the peace of Christ rule in your hearts, to which indeed you were called in the one body. And be thankful. ¹⁶Let the word of Christ dwell in you richly; teach and admonish one another in all wisdom; and with gratitude in your hearts sing psalms, hymns, and spiritual songs to God. ¹⁷And whatever you do, in word or deed, do everything in the name of the Lord Jesus, giving thanks to God the Father through him.

now set aside these things, such as anger, rage, malice, slander, and obscene language. ⁹Don't lie to each other. Take off the old human nature with its practices ¹⁰and put on the new nature, which is renewed in knowledge by conforming to the image of the one who created it. ¹¹In this image there is neither Greek nor Jew, circumcised nor uncircumcised, barbarian, Scythian, slave nor free, but Christ is all things and in all people.

¹²Therefore, as God's choice, holy and loved, put on compassion, kindness, humility, gentleness, and patience. ¹³Be tolerant with each other and, if someone has a complaint against anyone, forgive each other. As the Lord forgave you, so also forgive each other. **¹⁴And over all these things put on love, which is the perfect bond of unity.** ¹⁵The peace of Christ must control your hearts—a peace into which you were called in one body. And be thankful people. ¹⁶The word of Christ must live in you richly. Teach and warn each other with all wisdom by singing psalms, hymns, and spiritual songs. Sing to God with gratitude in your hearts. ¹⁷Whatever you do, whether in speech or action, do it all in the name of the Lord Jesus and give thanks to God the Father through him.

UNDERSTANDING THE SCRIPTURE

Colossians 3:1-4. Chapter 3 continues the argument against the false teaching by showing that a rejection of its regulations does not suggest that there are no rules for Christian conduct. The author now explains how those who have received God's blessings should live. Just as chapter 2 developed the meaning of baptism as the place where God gives new life and salvation, so chapter 3 will explain what the reception of those gifts means for the conduct of one's life. These opening verses of chapter 3 begin this discussion of proper Christian living by reminding the Colossians that they had died to their former lives and have new life in Christ. Their lives, then, should reflect their current life with Christ and their coming eternal life with God.

Colossians 3:5-7. Using dramatic imagery, the author tells his readers in verse 5 to "put to death" (or "kill," New Jerusalem Bible) those parts of themselves that are sinful. He is not suggesting amputation, but emphasizing the effort they should exert. He is also drawing on the imagery of baptism. He said in 2:20 that they already died "with Christ"; now they must enact that death in their conduct. Their old way of living must be snuffed out. Adopting the new way of living is implicit in their baptism, but it takes effort to embody it.

The primary focus of the vices mentioned in verse 5 is sexual ethics. The various terms urge readers to refrain from extramarital sex. Even covetousness (translated in the NRSV as "greed") may draw on the Decalogue's injunction against coveting your neighbor's wife. But Colossians broadens the meaning of coveting, saying it amounts to idolatry. Coveting constitutes idolatry when the thing one desires takes higher priority in life than God.

The Colossians must avoid these sins because they are a reason for God's coming judgment. Such behaviors violate what God wants for the world; they oppose God's holiness, faithfulness, and love and harm those involved. Such harm to God's people requires a response from God.

Colossians 3:8-11. The list of vices that they must put away in verse 8 focuses on behavior within community. "Anger" and "wrath" are probably synonymous here, with both included to make them emphatic. The believers must avoid slander and abusive talk because these evidence a lack of proper valuing of the other person. Finally, they must not lie "to one another." This phrase puts the emphasis on intra-church relations; the writer is particularly concerned with how his readers treat fellow Christians.

The theological basis for these demands appears in verses 9-10: Believers have put off the old self and put on the new. This again points to baptism, the point of transfer into God's kingdom. Verse 10 also assures them that God helps them reject these behaviors. The new self is renewed constantly. The passive voice here indicates that this renewal is from God, not achieved by their own efforts. And this renewal brings them more and more into conformity with God's own character. Their holiness is

a reflection of God's character. Through their cognitive and experiential knowing of God, they become more like God. This verse echoes Genesis 1:27 and so perhaps suggests that this becoming like God means that they are living out their true nature and what God has always intended for humans.

Verse 11 expands the baptismal liturgy that is also quoted in Galatians 3:27-28. This expanded version intends more explicitly to encompass the whole world; it takes in all places, ethnic groups, and social classes. These distinctions continue to exist, but they grant no status or privilege. What matters in the church is only that all are in Christ and that Christ is the defining element of the new reality in which they exist.

Colossians 3:12-15. As Colossians has enumerated unacceptable behaviors, it now lists virtues that its readers should adopt. But before the writer catalogs those virtues, he reminds the believers of their identity to reinforce that only this kind of living is appropriate to who God has made them. They are chosen by God; as such they are holy and loved. Since God is holy and has shown them love, they should be holy and loving. Again the focus is on how they treat one another within the church.

This list of virtues has a distinctively Christian outlook. Humility was not a virtue in Greco-Roman culture, where competition for honor and status was important. But the example of Christ made humility a virtue for the church. Christ's willingness to put the good of others before his own good is the church's model of humility and love. The distinctiveness of the list culminates in identifying love as the virtue that holds together and enables all the other virtues. This virtue directly mirrors God's treatment of believers; they are God's beloved so they must love others.

Verse 15 exhorts readers to let the peace of Christ rule in their hearts because this is the state of mind God intends for God's people. Even in the face of opposition, arguments about what to believe, and troubles in life, God's love for them should continually ground their lives.

Colossians 3:16-17. Verse 16 gives us a glimpse of early Christian worship. It included singing different types of songs (including the Old Testament psalms and perhaps Philippians 2:6-11 and Colossians 1:10-15) that not only offered praise but also were to teach and encourage. We are not certain what the differences were among these types of songs, but congregational singing would have been antiphonal recitation (rhythmic chanting of a line by part of the congregation followed by the other part of the congregation chanting the next line).

Verse 17 summarizes the preceding exhortations and introduces the following instructions about living within the setting of the household. This verse provides the overriding perspective for all of life. Christians are to conduct all of their lives, both within the church and in the world in a way that honors the Lord Jesus. Jesus is the master of our existence and so has authority over all of life. Living under his authority is one of the ways Christians give thanks to God for all the blessings they receive in Christ.

INTERPRETING THE SCRIPTURE

Christ as Our Model

The vice and virtue lists in Colossians have much in common with other first-century lists from moralists, but they also have some distinctive features. Others did not see humility as a virtue and did not have love as the highest virtue. The work of Christ, however, shaped Christian morality from its beginning. The love of Christ, shown by his willingness to put the good of others above his own good, serves as the primary guide for how Christians should live. His self-giving is our clearest revelation of God's character, which is the basis for all Christian morality. We live holy lives because God is holy; we forgive one another because God has forgiven us. Our lives are to be mirrors of God's love and holiness.

To live as our model, Christ, we are called to put on a new self. When Colossians says we have put off ("stripped off," 3:9) the old self and put on the new ("clothed," 3:10), it is echoing language associated with baptism. These are words used for getting undressed and dressed. They suggest that baptism gives a person a new identity because different social classes dressed differently in the first century. There were even kinds of cloths only Roman senators were allowed to wear; others could be arrested for wearing them. This vocabulary, then, suggests how different the new self is to be. Christians should live in a manner that makes them distinctive in the world. They seek to live according to God's will in ways that others do not.

Part of living as the new self is that as we begin to conform to what God is like, we begin to take on the image of the one who made us (3:10). We are not left to do this on our own. Even in the middle of exhortations, Colossians notes that this renewal is accomplished by God. Thus, God enables us to live according to the standards God sets.

At the same time, this statement implies that we are becoming what God always intended humans to be. When we live according to the image of God, we are living according to our true nature as human beings. While this is not the way most people live, it is the manner of life that brings fulfillment of our genuine selves. In our salvation our very nature is renewed. God does not simply take away guilt and shame, God renews our true humanity. With that renewal God also gives renewed expectations about how we should live. Since these moral expectations fit our true nature, they are the way to true happiness, not just obedience to imposed commands.

Our passage today shows us that Christian ethics includes both personal and communal morality. Different groups within the church tend to stress either social issues or personal morality. Colossians shows us that we must give attention to both because it contains instructions about both. The character of God seen in the life of Jesus must direct all aspects of life.

Our New Life in Christ

In verse 11, Colossians expands a baptismal liturgy by adding a list of opposites that includes geographic extremes (barbarian and Scythian) to proclaim that living in Christ transcends all ethnic and social distinctions. People do not stop being these things—Gentiles are still Gentiles and slaves remain slaves—but these distinctions do not define status in the church as they do in other contexts. All of these kinds of identity are secondary to our identification with Christ. Since Christians are one in Christ, we can transcend the things that separate people. Enacting this unity remains a task that the church must constantly engage in because such distinctions continue to grant privilege in the world. Thus we must continue to work at making the church a demonstration of the oneness of all Christians.

At the end of its virtue list, Colossians turns attention to the inner life of the Christian, encouraging us to let Christ's peace rule in our hearts. This peace flows from our knowledge of the security of our salvation. If it rules in our hearts, it determines the attitude that directs our lives. The writer does not want the accumulation of expectations to bring discouragement or fear. Life in the church does more than require things of us; it also gives to us. God intends for the Christian life to bring us peace. This is not freedom from difficulties in life. Christians continue to have problems and failures, but in the midst of them we can know that God loves us and continues to be with us. This is a part of the peace God gives us. We are called to this peace in the one body, that is, in the church. When the church lives by the virtues set out in the previous verses, it extends the peace of Christ to its members. Thus, while being in the church places demands on us, it also nurtures us.

Everything in the Name of Christ

Perhaps the most powerful exhortation in all of Colossians, perhaps in the whole of the New Testament, appears in verse 17: Everything we say or do is to be done in the name of the Lord Jesus. This is more than avoiding evil or obeying the correct instructions. All of our conduct is to be authorized by the lordship of Jesus. Because Christ is Lord of the whole cosmos, he reigns over all aspects of our lives. Think of how it would shape our lives if we asked ourselves whether each act, each interaction with others, and each thing we say would be authorized by Christ. We are not asking if it violates a command, but if this is an action or word that Christ would authorize. Colossians would have us ask ourselves if this is an act that represents Christ and his will, that is, if it could be done in Christ's name.

This all-encompassing exhortation imbues every aspect of life with deep meaning. We do not simply live for ourselves; we are embodiments of the lordship of Christ. Our moral behavior should exhibit to others that Christ is Lord. Thus, our lives become proclamations of the gospel.

Being Thankful

Colossians speaks twice near the end of our passage of being thankful (3:15, 17). The first comes between the exhortation to let Christ's peace rule in you and to let Christ's word live richly in you. Both expressions describe how Christ's presence should fill our lives. Our recognition of what that presence brings us leads to thanksgiving. The second reference to thanksgiving concludes our passage. Living in accord with the lordship of Jesus includes thanking God for the gifts we receive in Christ. Thanksgiving is more than saying thank you or offering praise; it is to be our mode of existence. Our whole life is colored by gratitude for the gifts of salvation and new life that we have in Christ. We learn to live in gratitude as we experience the fullness of life God gives us now through our new manner of life and the way we are enabled to live it. That presence of God with us is a foretaste of our future life with God. How can we help but give thanks?

SHARING THE SCRIPTURE

Preparing Our Hearts

Explore this week's devotional reading, found in Psalm 107:1-9. Here the psalmist gives thanks to God for deliverance from distress. We are called to give thanks for God's "steadfast love," which "endures forever" (107:1). This God "satisfies the thirsty," and feeds the hungry (107:9). What aspects of your life feel like deserted wastelands? What do you need to ask God to do to help you find refuge? Seek God's guidance now.

Pray that you and the adult students will thank the God who loves and delivers from trouble.

Preparing Our Minds

Study the background Scripture from Colossians 3:1-17 and the lesson Scripture from Colossians 3:5-17.

Consider this question as you prepare the lesson: *How do we decide which principles to follow?*

Write on newsprint:
❑ information for next week's lesson, found under "Continue the Journey."
❑ activities for further spiritual growth in "Continue the Journey."

Review the "Introduction," "The Big Picture," "Close-up," and "Faith in Action."

Consider how you will use this additional information, which immediately precedes the first lesson, for this session.

Locate different types of clothing for "Gather to Learn." Contact class members if you would like specific items that you do not own.

LEADING THE CLASS

(1) Gather to Learn

❖ Greet the class members. Introduce any guests and help them feel at home.

❖ Pray that participants will seek to follow the example of Christ.

❖ Display a variety of clothing, including clothes for doing gardening or working around the house, play or lounge clothes, church clothes, clothes to wear to your job. Hold up individual pieces and ask: **What would you expect to be doing if you wore this item of clothing?**

❖ Note that today's session is titled "Clothed with Christ" and read the key verse from Colossians 3:14.

❖ Read aloud today's focus statement: **Our lives are guided by basic principles. How do we decide which principles to follow? Those who believe in Christ are guided by his example.**

(2) Goal 1: Gain an Impression of Principles of Living in Christ

❖ Choose someone to read about new life in Christ from Colossians 3:5-17.

❖ Post a sheet of newsprint with a line drawn vertically down the center. On the left write "Take Off" and on the right side write "Put On." Note that the writer of Colossians is using baptismal imagery here. Invite the learners to call out qualities or principles of living that they are (a) to rid themselves of or (b) to clothe themselves with. Encourage words from as many Bible translations as possible so as to create a richly nuanced list.

❖ Form small groups, distribute paper and pencils, and challenge the participants to create a list of principles for living in Christ based on this passage from Colossians 3.

❖ Reassemble together and invite the groups to share what they have discerned. Summarize their findings by trying to rate the top three to five principles that the groups have identified.

(3) Goal 2: Imagine How the Learners' Life Principles and Behavior Are Different Because They Follow Christ

❖ Help the learners understand that their baptism was a watershed mark in terms of following Christ by reading "Christ as Our Model" from Interpreting the Scripture.

❖ Consider these questions, but monitor the discussion carefully so that names of individuals and families are not used:

(1) **If outsiders were to view the attitudes and behaviors of the members of our congregation, what differences would they see between us and those who do not claim to follow Christ?**

(2) **If we have found it difficult to identify clear-cut differences, what kinds of changes do we need to make as a congregation to follow Christ more nearly?**

(3) **If we can see noticeable differences, what steps can we take to help others choose to follow Christ?**

(4) Goal 3: Evaluate the Learners' Treatment of Others and Make Changes Where Necessary as Demanded by a Life Lived in Christ

❖ Read "Everything in the Name of Christ" from Interpreting the Scripture.

❖ Look especially at verse 17 and ask: **What does this verse suggest about how we are to treat others, no matter who they are?**

❖ Provide a few moments of silence for the students to consider personal changes they might need to make to live according to this verse.

❖ Read aloud these scenarios and invite several adults to either role-play "the rest of the story" or simply describe how they think the story should end.

Scenario 1: You have made a suggestion to a coworker that truly would help your department improve. His response is to start yelling, cursing, and telling you that he knows how to do his job and doesn't need any interference from you. How do you handle this situation in a Christ-like way?

Scenario 2: You and your spouse are in a restaurant when someone at a nearby table makes pointed comments about the behavior of children at another nearby table who are of another racial or ethnic group. The loudmouth attributes this behavior to their racial or ethnic "inferiority." You recognize that the children are misbehaving but take issue with the root cause of the problem. How do you handle this situation in a Christ-like way?

❖ Invite the adults to read in unison today's key verse, Colossians 3:14. Suggest that they memorize this verse. Challenge them to remember that by acting in Christ's love, which binds them "in perfect harmony," they will be able to live a Christ-like life.

(5) Continue the Journey

❖ Pray that today's class members will continue to assess their behavior and attitudes and do all they can to bring them in line with Christ's example.

❖ Read aloud this preparation for next week's lesson. You may also want to post it on newsprint for the students to copy.

- ■ **Title: Spiritual Disciplines for New Life**
- ■ **Background Scripture: Colossians 4:2-17**
- ■ **Lesson Scripture: Colossians 4:2-6**
- ■ **Focus of the Lesson: Once we commit ourselves to a new routine, it is helpful to have guides, partners, or mentors to strengthen our resolve. Where do we find mentors who will keep us faithful to our commitment? Paul names spiritual disciplines and faithful persons as examples of support for living a new life in Christ.**

❖ Post these three activities related to this week's session on newsprint for the students to copy. Challenge the adults to grow spiritually by completing one or more of them.

(1) **Think about Jesus and your baptism as you get dressed each day this week. How are you putting on Christ so that your life may reflect his characteristics of "compassion, kindness, humility, meekness, and patience" (3:12)?**

(2) **Review Colossians 3:5. What bad habits or attitudes do you need to "put to death"? What new habits or attitudes do you need to develop to be more Christ-like? Work on one of these habits at a time for a month until it becomes ingrained. Then select another new habit to add.**

(3) **Forgive someone who has wronged you. Be genuine, and be sure that the person understands why you are offering forgiveness. Sometimes we assume that others know they have hurt us when they are truly unaware of any offense.**

❖ Sing or read aloud "I Want a Principle Within."

❖ Conclude today's session by leading the class in this benediction, adapted from the key verses for December 23 from Ephesians 5:1 and January 13 from Philippians 2:5: **Go now as the Father's beloved children, who are of the same mind as the Son Jesus Christ, to be imitators of God.**

UNIT 3: IMITATING JESUS
SPIRITUAL DISCIPLINES FOR NEW LIFE

PREVIEWING THE LESSON

Lesson Scripture: Colossians 4:2-6, 17
Background Scripture: Colossians 4:2-17
Key Verse: Colossians 4:17

Focus of the Lesson:
Once we commit ourselves to a new routine, it is helpful to have guides, partners, or mentors to strengthen our resolve. Where do we find mentors who will keep us faithful to our commitment? Paul names spiritual disciplines and faithful persons as examples of support for living a new life in Christ.

Goals for the Learners:
(1) to recognize the importance of spiritual disciplines in maintaining a Christian life.
(2) to reflect on those people in their lives who mentor them in faith.
(3) to accept the role of mentor for a young or newly committed Christian.

Pronunciation Guide:
Archippus (ahr kip' uhs)
Epaphras (ep' uh fras)
kairos (ki' rohs)

Supplies:
Bibles, newsprint and marker, paper and pencils, hymnals

READING THE SCRIPTURE

NRSV

Lesson Scripture: Colossians 4:2-6, 17

²Devote yourselves to prayer, keeping alert in it with thanksgiving. ³At the same time pray for us as well that God will open to us a door for the word, that we may

CEB

Lesson Scripture: Colossians 4:2-6, 17

²Keep on praying and guard your prayers with thanksgiving. ³At the same time, pray for us also. Pray that God would open a door for the word so we can preach the

declare the mystery of Christ, for which I am in prison, ⁴so that I may reveal it clearly, as I should.

⁵Conduct yourselves wisely toward outsiders, making the most of the time. ⁶Let your speech always be gracious, seasoned with salt, so that you may know how you ought to answer everyone.

¹⁷And say to Archippus, "See that you complete the task that you have received in the Lord."

secret plan of Christ—which is why I'm in chains. ⁴Pray that I might be able to make it as clear as I ought to when I preach. ⁵Act wisely toward outsiders, making the most of the opportunity. ⁶Your speech should always be gracious and sprinkled with insight so that you may know how to respond to every person.

¹⁷And tell Archippus, "See to it that you complete the ministry that you received in the Lord."

UNDERSTANDING THE SCRIPTURE

Colossians 4:2. The concluding exhortations in 4:2-6 are divided into two parts. Verses 2-4 address prayer and the Colossians' participation in the Pauline mission, while verses 5-6 focus on relations with non-Christians. The beginning exhortation urges the Colossians to be devoted to prayer. This may be encouragement to pray often or to live constantly in an attitude of prayer. Either way it reminds them of the sure and constant access they have to God. God is always open to receiving their requests and their praise. Telling them to "keep alert in it" may be a reminder that they always live in the light of the second coming of Christ. The verb used here often has that connotation in the New Testament (for example, Matthew 25:13; Mark 13:34-37). The preceding two verses have mentioned the coming judgment to encourage slaves who are treated unjustly by reminding them that God will respond to the injustice inflicted on them and to remind slave owners that they have a master who will evaluate their conduct. So this more general reference to Christ's return reminds readers of both their accountability and their coming salvation. Thus, constant attention to prayer orients their lives toward God's will.

The verses just before Colossians' instructions about how various people should live within the Greco-Roman house-

hold summoned the readers to give thanks (3:15, 17). Now in 4:2 a call to give thanks appears immediately following those instructions. This suggests that they are to give thanks despite the difficulties they experience in their lives. Giving thanks reminds them of the blessings they have now as Christians and of the salvation they will receive in the future. These thanksgivings may also spring from their remembrances of God's coming justice for their oppressors.

Colossians 4:3-4. After the general exhortation to mindfulness about prayer, they are asked to pray for the Pauline mission. The first request is for receptive hearers. The writer asks them to pray that the hearts of those who hear the gospel will be open to accepting the message. Perhaps this includes a request that Paul and his companion will be able to preach without extraordinary obstacles. Mentioning that Paul is imprisoned for the sake of the gospel strengthens his argument against the false teaching that the whole letter combats by reminding them that he suffers for the truth he proclaims. It reinforces his position as a trustworthy teacher—he stands for truth even when he must suffer for it.

The reminder of Paul's circumstances also gives urgency to the second request about his mission. He wants them to pray that he will continue to have the courage he needs to preach the gospel, even as a prisoner. Opening the door for the gospel seems to entail an act of God on both the hearers and the preacher. Thus, Paul acknowledges his dependence on God, just as the previous exhortation to constant prayer implies the Colossians' dependence on God.

In verse 3 Paul calls the gospel the "mystery of Christ." The identity and work of Christ are the content of this mystery. How God was present in Christ and how he brings salvation are beyond our full comprehension. Yet these certainties are at the heart of the gospel. In response to them, we give thanks for the new life God has given us.

Colossians 4:5-6. The final instructions in our reading indicate that there was significant tension between the church and non-Christians. The different values by which Christians lived made them different enough that they experienced opposition and oppression. Colossians first urges them to live wisely among non-Christians. This probably means they were not to flaunt their differences in unnecessary ways. If Christian households were significantly different from others, they could provoke opposition and perhaps governmental persecution. So they must discern how to live in accord with their beliefs without inciting unnecessary opposition. Still, by designating non-Christians as "outsiders," the church takes on the responsibility of becoming a demonstration of God's will for all.

While acting wisely, they are to "redeem the time" (the more literal translation of what the NRSV renders "making the most of the time"). This expression may work in two related directions. First, it suggests that Christians use the remembrance of Christ's return to shape their conduct. The word used for "time" (*kairos*) often points to the end time in New Testament texts. Given what follows, redeeming the time may also

encourage them to share the gospel with others, giving those "outsiders" the opportunity to participate in the coming blessings.

The final directive instructs the Colossians to be able to respond to questions about their faith. We should envision these questions to include hostile confrontations and interested inquiries. Since this church does not seem to be experiencing an extraordinary amount of persecution, perhaps the balance between these types of questions is relatively close. Whichever type of question it is, Colossians sees it as the duty of all Christians to be prepared to discuss and share their faith. These responses are to be graceful and persuasive. "Seasoned with salt" was a well-known idiom that meant "pleasing." This gracious and pleasing speech should be Christians' response to hostile questioning, as well as to friendly inquiry. Such speech is powerful testimony to the meaning of the gospel when it is a response to fierce opposition. This manner of response also demands that Christians not adopt an air of arrogance about the blessings they enjoy. Instead, their conversation must reflect God's love and goodness. Thus, by their manner of speaking they invite others into the sphere of salvation.

Colossians 4:7-17. Ancient letters often included a series of greetings sent from the author and people with him to various people at the letter's destination. By asking for their prayers and connecting Paul with several people who are known by their church, the author makes the readers participants in the Pauline mission. Simultaneously, the status of the persons mentioned is bolstered by their association with the apostle. The final person mentioned, Archippus, is reminded of a ministerial task he has been given. By addressing this exhortation to the congregation, the writer draws them all into this ministry.

INTERPRETING THE SCRIPTURE

A Life of Prayer

In the midst of our busy lives, we find it difficult to devote ourselves to prayer. We have so many commitments and obligations that it is daunting to think of adding new tasks. Our reading today encourages Christians to take time to orient our lives so that we are conscious of living in God's presence. It asks us to take up a spiritual discipline. Christians have profited from these kinds of spiritual exercises throughout the centuries. They draw us closer to God and help us live in the light of God's presence.

We sometimes think of devoting oneself to prayer as something that religious professionals do, not Christians who are fully engaged in the business world. But this exhortation addresses the whole church. Colossians urges us all to prayer that helps us focus attention on God's blessings. Perhaps our narrow understanding of prayer makes us reticent to commit ourselves to it. Prayer can be more than time spent in contemplation or in the recitation of requests or praise. These forms of prayer are important, but not the only way to take up the spiritual discipline Colossians urges on us. Our reading's exhortation may well intend something broader than having a schedule of times to pray. Devoting ourselves to prayer involves developing an attitude and outlook that continually recognizes our dependence upon God. A few moments spent in conversation with God or in thoughts of praise, perhaps through music we listen to on the way to work, can begin to shape our day. Those moments give us touch points that remind us of the ways we are valued and loved by God. As those practices become constants in our routine, such moments begin to come back to us throughout the day, just as a song can get stuck in our heads. Such reminiscences

influence how we experience the rest of the day and how we relate to others. As such thoughts start to infuse our minds, we become devoted to prayer.

Thankfulness is an important element in developing an attitude of prayerfulness. In verse 2, Colossians exhorts us to prayer that reminds us of the blessings God has for us. Since being watchful in prayer points to remembering God's future blessings, it also leads to such thanksgiving. Cultivating a prayerful life, then, can also help us endure in difficult times by keeping us aware of the hope we have in God's promise of fullness of life beyond this world.

This reading also urges us to engage in intercessory prayer on behalf of the church and the world. Praying for others builds a relationship with those we pray for. Beyond lifting them into the presence of God, it encourages us to become participants in God's work with them. When others know we are praying for them, that alone often provides support in the circumstances they are in or in the work they are doing. Perhaps one of the important ways they can encourage Archippus to fulfill his ministry is through such intercessory prayer.

Witnesses

Unlike the early church, most of us face little opposition because of our faith. Still, we need to exercise wisdom in the way we conduct our lives in relation to non-Christians. We show this wisdom by becoming demonstrations of the benefits that derive from our relationship with God. Our lives should also show others how God wants people to live. We should reflect God's faithfulness, love, and justice in our personal and business relationships. Thus, we not only live as God intends but we also display how such living creates a richer and fuller life.

In addition to modeling our faith for others, Colossians urges us all, not just pastors and theologians, to be prepared to respond to inquiries about our faith and what it means in our lives. While this may take some preparation, it does not demand that we become scholars of religion. This exhortation does expect us to be open about what our faith means to us and to have a reasonable explanation of our basic beliefs. Without this kind of thought and reflection, our faith will not have the depth required to sustain us in difficult times. So this level of exploration of our faith is good for us, even as it prepares us to share our faith with others.

It is important to notice how Colossians describes appropriate communication with outsiders. Evangelism has a bad name in many places because of the way it has sometimes been done, particularly when the message has been used to frighten people into conversion. But the church cannot abandon the task of inviting others into relationship with God. Colossians says that our conversations about the faith need to be gracious and pleasing, as well as persuasive. We need to engage in genuine dialogue about our faith that is inviting and convincing, without resorting to threats. This gracious engagement is more consistent with the message of a loving God who has reached out to us in Christ. Conversations that tell others about the faith should exhibit the characteristics of the community into which we are inviting people. Thus, just as appropriate conduct in the church reflects who God is and how God loves us, so our interactions with those outside the church should be modeled on God's nature as we see it in Christ.

Mutual Concern

All of Colossians is written out of concern for the well-being of its recipients. The writer is convinced that they must avoid certain teachings to retain their connection to Christ. In the last verses of the letter, we see that the readers are also concerned about Paul's welfare. The writer mentions people who will soon visit the readers to tell them about Paul's circumstances and so comfort them. This section gives evidence of the kinds of relationships that early Christians had with one another. These readers cared deeply about Paul even though they had never met him. The bonds of Christian love and fellowship were strong even without direct interaction.

Epaphras exemplifies this love (4:12). As the founder of their congregation, he is devoted not just to the gospel but also to them. He suffers for them and he constantly prays earnestly for them. He is a laudable example for ministers and for all Christians. Even the little we know about him shows us what it looks like to follow Christ's example of putting others before our own good.

Being Mentors

One of the reasons all these people are mentioned at the end of Colossians is that they are being held up as examples of what Christians should be. Mature Christians can serve as such mentors and examples today. Some may mentor people new to the church; others may work with children or youth. Whether or not mature Christians are trained or actively seeking to be mentors, they serve as examples of what it means to be Christians for those younger or newly committed Christians who observe their manner of life. This inescapable function gives the mature a significant responsibility. If they explicitly embrace the role, they will provide important help to those they mentor and their own faith will be invigorated by their relationship with those who are newer to the faith.

SHARING THE SCRIPTURE

Preparing Our Hearts

Explore this week's devotional reading, found in 1 Corinthians 9:19-27. Here Paul explains his evangelistic strategy to the church in Corinth. In a nutshell, he is willing to "become all things to all people" (9:22)—even "a slave to all" (9:19)—so that he might preach the gospel and bring all people to Christ. Notice in verse 27 that Paul exercises a high degree of self-discipline and self-control. What about you? Are you willing to do whatever is necessary to serve others? If you cannot honestly answer yes, what is holding you back? Are there changes you are willing to make?

Pray that you and the adult students will be the kind of servants and mentors to others that Paul was to the people he encountered.

Preparing Our Minds

Study the background Scripture from Colossians 4:2-17 and the lesson Scripture from Colossians 4:2-6.

Consider this question as you prepare the lesson: *Where do we find mentors who will keep us faithful to our commitment?*

Write on newsprint:

❑ information for next week's lesson, found under "Continue the Journey."
❑ activities for further spiritual growth in "Continue the Journey."

Review the "Introduction," "The Big Picture," "Close-up," and "Faith in Action." Consider how you will use this additional information, which immediately precedes the first lesson, for this session.

Talk with your pastor, Sunday school superintendent, or youth counselors about how you might implement ideas found under "Accept the Role of Mentor for a Young or Newly Committed Christian."

LEADING THE CLASS

(1) Gather to Learn

❖ Greet the class members. Introduce any guests and help them feel at home.

❖ Pray that those in attendance today will give thanks for those persons who have served as examples and mentors for them in their Christian journey.

❖ Read this information gleaned from a United Methodist website: **"Spiritual direction is a formal covenant arrangement between a director and his/her directee for the purpose of enabling the directee to find the spiritual path to which God is calling him/her." The director's purpose, working under the guidance of the Holy Spirit, is to be both a soul-friend and mentor to the one who sought direction. The director acts as a sounding board to help the directee hear the voice of God and move into the future to which God calls.**

❖ Invite the class members to share any experiences (though not personal details) they have had with a spiritual director or one who has served as a spiritual friend, even without a formal agreement. Ask the group: **Would you like to work with someone who can help you discern God's will? Why or why not?**

❖ Read aloud today's focus statement: **Once we commit ourselves to a new routine, it is helpful to have guides, partners, or mentors to strengthen our resolve. Where do we find mentors who will keep us faithful to our commitment? Paul names spiritual disciplines and faithful persons as examples of support for living a new life in Christ.**

(2) Goal 1: Recognize the Importance of Spiritual Disciplines in Maintaining a Christian Life

❖ Invite a volunteer to read Colossians 4:2-6.

❖ Ask the adults to rephrase Paul's instructions. Here are possibilities:

(1) Pray constantly.
(2) Pray that Paul might be able to preach the good news.
(3) Conduct yourself in such a way so as to bring outsiders into the kingdom of God.
(4) Let your speech be clear and compelling.

❖ Note that praying is one of many spiritual disciplines, including but not limited to worshiping, tithing, fasting, journaling, studying the Bible, and living simply. In this session, we are focusing on praying.

❖ Invite participants to define prayer, and write their ideas on newsprint. Use information from "A Life of Prayer" in Interpreting the Scripture to enhance the discussion. Recognize that the students will suggest fairly specific definitions, such as "calling on God on behalf of someone else" or "praising God" or "asking God to meet a certain need of mine." Reread this sentence to help set a definition of prayer in a more life-transforming way: "Devoting ourselves to prayer involves developing an attitude and outlook that continually recognizes our dependence upon God." Ask: **How does this broader definition square with your own ideas of prayer?**

(3) Goal 2: Reflect on Those People in the Learners' Lives Who Mentor Them in Faith

❖ Note that Paul requests prayer so that he might reveal Christ to others. Distribute paper and pencils. Invite the adults to list several people who have mentored them in the faith. Suggest that they write a sentence or two next to each person's name to describe why this individual was so helpful and special to them.

❖ Form groups of three or four. Encourage everyone to talk about his or her mentors. Try to identify characteristics that made them so helpful.

❖ Call the class back together. List on newsprint any characteristics that seemed common to most mentors.

(4) Goal 3: Accept the Role of Mentor for a Young or Newly Committed Christian

❖ Recommend that the students review the list they just completed and silently identify characteristics that describe them.

❖ Encourage those who believe that they could act as mentors to consider partnering with a child, teen, or new adult Christian in your congregation. Explain whatever you have been able to work out with your pastor, Sunday school superintendent, or youth counselor about pairing a seasoned Christian from this class with someone who is just beginning a relationship with Christ. For example, the pastor may match a new member with a class member. Be sure to follow any regulations of your church or denomination regarding background checks and safety issues for adults working with children or youth.

❖ Invite class members who are willing to act as mentors to raise their hands so that you may make a list and pass it on to the pastor.

(5) Continue the Journey

❖ Pray that today's participants will practice spiritual disciplines, as well as give and receive support for their faith journey through mentoring.

❖ Read aloud this preparation for next week's lesson. You may also want to post it on newsprint for the students to copy.

■ **Title: Daniel's Vision of Change**
■ **Background Scripture: Daniel 7**
■ **Lesson Scripture: Daniel 7:9-14**
■ **Focus of the Lesson: We live in the hope that the future will be better than the past. How can we learn from the past and apply it to the future? Daniel's vision tells of the Ancient of Days seated on a**

throne, ruling forever, and giving dominion and power to a messiah.

❖ Post these three activities related to this week's session on newsprint for the students to copy. Challenge the adults to grow spiritually by completing one or more of them.

(1) **Try to connect with God in prayer on a continuing basis by constantly recognizing your dependence upon God.**

(2) **Thank someone who has been a spiritual mentor to you. Send a note, treat him or her to lunch, or give a small gift. If that special person is now deceased, make a donation in this person's name to a church project that he or she would have supported.**

(3) **Be aware of someone in your life who needs spiritual guidance. Act as a mentor to this person. Locate a book on spiritual direction if this practice is unfamiliar to you.**

❖ Sing or read aloud "Go Forth for God."

❖ Conclude today's session by leading the class in this benediction, adapted from the key verses for December 23 from Ephesians 5:1 and January 13 from Philippians 2:5: **Go now as the Father's beloved children, who are of the same mind as the Son Jesus Christ, to be imitators of God.**

THIRD QUARTER
Beyond the Present Time

MARCH 3, 2013–MAY 26, 2013

The course for the spring quarter, "Beyond the Present Time," focuses on the theological theme of hope as discussed in both the Hebrew and Christian Scriptures. We will explore this theme as it appears in the books of Daniel, Luke, Acts, 1 and 2 Thessalonians, and 1 and 2 Peter. This study not only prompts us to think about apocalyptic and resurrection hope but also calls us to holy living as we await the fulfillment of these hopes.

Unit 1, "The Kingdom of God" considers the apocalyptic hope—that is, hope for the end of time—found in three chapters of Daniel. These sessions help us connect the hope found in Daniel's prophecy with the Christian's resurrection hope. On March 3 we will examine Daniel 7 to learn about the better days ahead seen in "Daniel's Vision of Change." On March 10, we will consider "Daniel's Prayer," a prayer of confession on behalf of sinful Judah and Israel found in Daniel 9:3-19. This unit ends on March 17 with an exploration of Daniel 8 in which we read "Gabriel's Interpretation" of a vision that Daniel had related to "the time of the end."

The six sessions in Unit 2, "Resurrection Hope," move us into the Easter season. On Palm Sunday (March 24), the lesson from Luke 22:14-30 focuses on "The Lord's Supper," where Jesus talks about the privilege of serving others. The session on March 31 tells the Easter story from Luke 24:1-35 in which hope is restored as the travelers on the road to Emmaus and the disciples they visit in Jerusalem declare that "The Lord Has Risen Indeed!" According to Luke 24:36-53, which we will read on April 7, "The Lord Appears" to the disciples to teach them that his promises have been fulfilled, and then he ascended. On April 14 we read that "The Holy Spirit Comes," which is the story of the outpouring of the Spirit on Pentecost as recounted in Acts 2:1-36. The expectation that the Lord will come again encourages the early Christians to be "Living with Hope" as Paul writes in 1 Thessalonians 4:13–5:11, the background Scripture for April 21. This unit concludes on April 28 with a session from 2 Thessalonians 2 where Paul explains that "Hope Comes from God's Grace."

Unit 3, "A Call to Holy Living" is a four-lesson study of 1 and 2 Peter that begins on May 5. "A Living Hope" is, in the words of 1 Peter 1:1-12, available to us "through the resurrection of the Jesus Christ from the dead" (1:3). On May 12 we explore 2 Peter 1 to see that through Christ's divine power we are "Equipped with Hope." On Pentecost Sunday, May 19, we will reflect on "Hope Through Stewardship," as discussed in 1 Peter 4. In the final session on May 26, we return to 2 Peter, chapter 3, to see what this letter reveals to us about "Hope in the Day of the Lord."

MEET OUR WRITER

THE REVEREND JOHN INDERMARK

John Indermark lives in the town of Naselle, located in the southwest corner of Washington State. His wife, Judy, works as an E-911 dispatcher for their county. Their son, Jeff, works on a team that oversees the counseling programs in the Juvenile Rehabilitation Administration facilities of the state of Washington.

John grew up in St. Louis, graduating from Northwest High School, St. Louis University, and Eden Theological Seminary. Ordained in the United Church of Christ, John served as a parish pastor for sixteen years before shifting to a ministry of the written word. He has also served in a variety of interim and extended pulpit supply positions for Presbyterian, United Methodist, and Lutheran congregations in southwest Washington and northwest Oregon.

John's ministry of writing focuses on spiritual formation books and Christian education curricula. Among his most recent books are the volume on Luke in the Immersion Bible Studies series and *Do Not Live Afraid*. The curricula projects he presently writes for include *Feasting on the Word*, *The Present Word*, and *The New International Lesson Annual*. He wrote the New Testament materials for youth and leaders in *Crossings: God's Journey with Us*, a confirmation resource published by Logos Productions, Inc., and also did a revision of that resource for use with adults.

In their spare time, John and Judy enjoy walking their region's trails and logging roads, and traveling in Canada, the Southwest, and Hawaii.

THE BIG PICTURE: LITERATURES OF HOPE

"Hope is . . ." How would you finish that sentence? What images come to your mind when you hear the word "hope" spoken in the public arena or as you think about your own life and dreams? How do you hear your church in worship, or your church at budget time, completing that sentence? Hope is . . .

This quarter's sessions delve into the understanding and practice of hope for the community of God's people. Three passages from the Old Testament Book of Daniel will frame the first unit's exploration of views related to God's kingdom or sovereign realm that form the background for the preaching of Jesus and the early church. The second unit, "Resurrection Hope," will draw its insights from four passages in the Luke–Acts materials and two more from the Thessalonian correspondence. Finally, the way in which such hopes come to be formulated and "institutionalized" in the early church will be taken up in the third unit, "A Call to Holy Living," with passages drawn from 1 and 2 Peter.

Before turning to those units and the passages and books upon which they are based, this section will first explore a body and style of writings that form an important background for the biblical testimonies to hope: apocalyptic.

Apocalyptic Writings

"Apocalyptic" comes from a Greek word that means "to uncover" or "to reveal" (a related expression for such writings is "eschatological," from a word meaning "last or end things"). These writings share a belief system that expects a radical (and often imminent) transformation of this world into the promised realm of God. Such literature is filled with extremes in imagery, often employing stark contrasts between this age and the age to come. The element of "hiddenness" in such literature comes from an emphasis upon God's plans and purposes being hidden from general knowledge, only revealed to an individual writer or select few to prepare the community for what is about to occur (and often times, to help the community endure difficult and oppressive present times).

While there are elements of apocalyptic thought in Isaiah 24–27, it seems that Jewish apocalyptic writing emerged most forcefully following the return from exile. The influence of Persian and then Hellenistic dualism (and their often repressive political regimes that ruled over what had been Israel) are pointed to as sources that inspired the development of Jewish apocalyptic writing and thought.

The Book of Daniel is the Old Testament's primary example of apocalyptic literature. The prevalence of visions and dreams that transport the seer (and with him, the community who heeds his words) outside the "containment" of this world and age and provide knowledge of the future otherwise hidden is a clear mark of apocalyptic. As noted in the sessions on the Book of Daniel, while set in the era of the Babylonian and then Persian empires, the Book of Daniel was believed to have been composed in the mid-second century B.C. during a time of great political and religious repression under the Seleucid (Syrian) ruler named Antiochus Epiphanes IV. While there are other sections of the Old Testament identified as apocalyptic (Isaiah 24–27 and Zechariah 9–14), the bulk of Jewish apocalyptic writings did not gain acceptance into the canon of the Old Testament but still exist. Perhaps most famous among them, especially for their potential insights into the context of the New Testament era, are many of the writings of the Qumran or Dead Sea Scroll communities. The existence of all these writings, some of which precede the New Testament era and some of which may well have come from that time or at least prior to the destruction of Jerusalem by Rome in A.D. 70, make clear that apocalyptic visions of hope were clearly present and vying for attention during the time of Jesus and the earliest church.

The gospel's message of hope had to compete with these other, often quite militant visions (as with the Zealots, who are believed to have revolted against Rome on the basis that their actions would usher in the final times and God's intervention). It is also worth noting that the three Synoptic Gospels all have sections of Jesus' teachings, set in his final week in Jerusalem, that are highly apocalyptic in style and imagery (Matthew 24; Mark 13; Luke 21). Unless these teachings are attributed to the later church, the evangelists thus connect Jesus' own teachings on the theme of hope with apocalyptic views (as is also the case when, on trial, Jesus quotes Daniel 7:13-14 in response to the high priest's question if Jesus was the Messiah, found in Matthew 26:64).

The appeal of apocalyptic literature in times of turmoil is readily apparent. When the present, and those powers that dominate within it, holds out no hope, it is natural that hope comes to be seen in dramatic breaks with the world as it is. In that sense, the books of Daniel and Revelation have a great deal in common, beyond the fantastic imagery and cryptic language. The Jews under Antiochus, and the Christians weathering the persecutions of Rome, suffered under similar oppressions. The language of hope for both came to find expression in apocalyptic terms, when "Babylon" (whether a code name for the Seleucid or Roman empires) would fall and God's kingdom would be ushered in as "coming with the clouds of heaven" (Daniel 7:13) and where "the first heaven and the first earth had passed away" (Revelation 21:1).

But apocalyptic visions of the end times are not the only expressions and literature of hope available. In the Gospels, hope is most fundamentally and characteristically witnessed to in the narratives of Jesus' passion and resurrection—and in another vein, in the promise and gift of Pentecost. In the Epistles, hope becomes a calling and vocation to live as individuals and communities of faith, even when the once imminently expected return of Jesus has not taken place. So first we will turn to an overview of the Daniel passages, and then on to the narratives from the Gospels and Acts, and finally to the texts from 1 and 2 Peter.

Daniel's Vision of the Kingdom

If you were to ask the members of your congregation what one thing they associate most with the Book of Daniel, what responses would you expect? I suspect "Daniel and the lions' den" (chapter 6) might be high on the list of responses. Others might point to the story of the three young men in the fiery furnace (chapter 3), or perhaps Daniel's interpreting of dreams or the "writing on the wall" at Belshazzar's feast (chapter 5). The first six chapters of Daniel are full of these and other stories. Beginning with chapter 7, however, the Book of Daniel veers sharply into the realm of apocalyptic visions that are not nearly as likely to be part of one's upbringing in Sunday school as stories of lions and furnaces. It is this abundance of apocalyptic material that may account for why the Book of Daniel has more fragments among the Dead Sea Scrolls than any other biblical book except Isaiah. In these final six chapters of Daniel are visions of beasts (not unlike those in Revelation), and perhaps most important for New Testament studies, the already alluded to vision quoted by Jesus at his interrogation before the high priest.

The three passages for this first unit of this study come from Daniel 7, 9, and 8. The first explores the vision of the "Ancient One" that includes the reference to "one like a human being [another translation of this is "son of man"] coming with the clouds of heaven" (Daniel 7:13). The vision itself is set in context with a vision Daniel had of four beasts, representative of four empires under which Daniel's people had been governed (Babylon, Medes, Persia, and Greece, beginning with Alexander the Great). Please see Understanding the Scripture in the first session for more detail on this imagery. The second session takes up an extended prayer of Daniel in chapter 9 on behalf of his people. It in itself is not apocalyptic in nature, but a liturgical plea for forgiveness. Still, the reference in the prayer to the "calamity [that] has come upon us" (9:13) is a reminder of the dangerous situation with which the visions before and after are concerned. The hope of God's deliverance in those visions here, in the prayer, takes on the nature of hope in God's grace and forbearing. The third and final session, from Daniel 8, considers a passage where a vision Daniel has had is given interpretation by an angel named Gabriel. Assurance and hope come in Gabriel's words about the final breaking of oppressive rule that will come "not by human hands" (8:25)—that is, God will intervene decisively.

Hope in Luke–Acts

The second unit opens with four passages drawn from the Gospel of Luke and the Acts of the Apostles. While scholars may debate the fine points of whether Luke actually wrote Acts, thematically and theologically and geographically Acts is the sequel to Luke. One way of viewing their connection is by using the image of a series of concentric circles. At the outset, the birth of Jesus begins in Luke 2:1-4 with the broad circle of the Roman Empire, narrowing to the district of Syria, then from Galilee and Judah to the town of Bethlehem. The Gospel moves almost entirely within those spheres of Galilee and Judah, until the climax of Crucifixion and Resurrection in Jerusalem, closing with the disciples rejoicing in the Temple.

But then, in Acts, the circle begins to expand once more. When crowds make pilgrimage to Jerusalem and the Temple for a harvest festival named Pentecost, that festival finds new meaning as the Spirit is bestowed. At first, Acts' story of the church is restricted to Jerusalem. But then, persecution comes in 8:1, and what happens? The church arcs outward to Judea and Samaria. The movement continues when the new convert Paul sets sail for Tarsus (Acts 9:30) on the south edge of present-day Turkey, while Peter ends up at a seaport named Joppa (Acts 9:38-39) and moves on to a Roman seaport known as Caesarea (Acts 10). The widening circle of geographical expansion is accompanied by even more radical expansions. The conversion of a Gentile centurion. A missionary journey to Cyprus. Paul ventures into Asia Minor, only to be told by the Spirit to cross over to Greece (Acts 16:6-10). Eventually, the widening circle of the gospel's proclamation reaches imperial Rome itself (28:11 and following). Acts ends where Luke's Gospel had begun, only now, the seat of imperial power has been breached by the gospel of a new sovereign and realm. In other words, in Luke–Acts, geography becomes theology. The reach of hope includes the whole world, in the same way in which Jesus' ministry in Luke broke boundaries with God's expansive grace.

The distinctive nature of that theology, and hope, in Luke–Acts, as with the other Gospels, comes in the core stories of Jesus' suffering and dying and raising, of God's bringing new life to the Beloved, and bestowing the Holy Spirit upon the community called to be the ongoing body of Christ on earth long after Jesus' ascension. Such hope finds tabled expectation in this unit's first session in the narrative of the Lord's Supper. Jesus' words of institution mingle with Jesus' anticipation of the table to be spread and shared again in God's kingdom. The second and third sessions focus on hope revealed in resurrection appearances to the women and the other disciples. The fourth session takes up the Pentecost narrative in Acts to explore the Spirit's gift as empowering the church to live in resurrection's hope.

Two other sessions round out this unit on resurrection hope. Both come from the Thessalonian epistles of Paul. These two letters are of peculiar importance to understanding resurrection hope because of their antiquity. That is, it is generally believed that at least 1 Thessalonians may be the first New Testament material set to writing, predating even the Gospel of Mark. The importance of this for resurrection hope comes in two crises facing those congregations. At this early stage, it sounds very much like Christ's return had been an imminent expectation, and the death of some believers before that return caused anxiety about their fate. Also, some apparently taught that the return had already occurred. Both of these crises form the setting for Paul's reassurances and admonitions to those communities that they in turn might "encourage one another and build up each other" (1 Thessalonians 5:11).

A Call to Holy Living

The final unit considers four passages from the epistles of 1 and 2 Peter. Many more questions surround the authorship of these epistles than that of Thessalonians. Even more pertinent to their consideration in this quarter is the situation "on the ground" for the Petrine audience than that of the Thessalonians. For as 1 and 2 Thessalonians are considered among the earliest New Testament materials, 1 and 2 Peter are reckoned among the very latest, perhaps from the final two decades of the first century or even later. A church still very much from the formative stage has now become much more "institutional." As much as forty or fifty years have passed since Jesus' resurrection. Hope in terms of an imminent return is less a factor than in Thessalonians. The crisis now is one of how to sustain hope, particularly in the midst of societal and imperial powers that are increasingly uneasy about this new religion. Some even suggest that 1 and 2 Peter were written in the midst of imperial persecutions, though that is by no means clear or settled.

For the author of the Petrine Epistles, much attention is paid to hope that becomes expressed in the way life is conducted (hence the unit's title, "A Call to Holy Living"). The first session considers a passage that lays out the call to live one's faith on the basis of hope that trusts in God's presence and grace ("although you have not seen him, you love him," 1 Peter 1:8). Such trust would be needed to face the trials the author identifies in the previous verses. The second and third sessions confirm the strength needed for such living to be a gift to us from God. Of such gifts we are called to be stewards (a term whose meaning runs closer to "manager") of God's grace. That is, the gifts are not "ours" in the sense of our ability to summon or will them up on our own, but they are entrusted to us for the sake of faithful living and in particular for the sake of serving others and building up the community. The final session of the unit urges, as does the passage it considers, a faithful patience that waits upon God's promises and does not grow discouraged or cynical. God's time is in God's hands, not ours. Waiting for God's promised realm is not a state of inactivity, but an active state of continuing growth and service. Both 1 and 2 Peter offer not the extravagant visions of apocalyptic hope but the patient and trusting discipleship that lives hopefully in the interim between this age and the next, whose turning, while seeming slow, will come. For as Jews and Christians, we are a people called to live by hope.

Close-up: Finding Hope in Resurrection

Six of our sessions for this quarter concern "Resurrection Hope." To understand these lessons, we need to have a good understanding of what "resurrection" entails. Help the learners better understand "resurrection" by working through the suggestions in this activity.

The *Westminster Theological Wordbook of the Bible* describes "resurrection" this way:

Our English word "resurrection" translates the Greek noun *anastasis*—with the prefix *ana*, which may mean "up" or "again," connected to the noun *stasis*, which here means "existence," "continuance," or "standing," signifying either a rising *up* of someone who has been in reclining position or a coming to life *again* of someone who has died. In its basic sense "resurrection" denotes restoration to "existence" or "life" after . . . an interval in the realm of the dead (as with a person or people). Our English expression "raise up" translates the Hebrew word *qum* and the Greek verbs *anistemi* and *egeiro*. The noun *anastasis* (or *exanastasis*) and the verbs *anistemi* and *egeiro* appear throughout the NT for both the resurrection of Christ and the resurrection of the people in the eschatological [end time] future.

Ask: **How does this word study help you better understand what "resurrection" means?**
Spend some time looking at references to "resurrection." If you have a concordance, you may wish to check all of the places where this word is used in the New Testament. Or you may wish to check these selected citations, all of which use the word *anastasis* unless noted otherwise:

Matthew 27:53 (*egersis*)	1 Corinthians 15
John 11:17-27	Philippians 3:7-11 (verse 11—*exanastasis*)
Acts 1:22	1 Peter 1:3-5; 3:21-22
Romans 6:5	Revelation 20:5-6

Ask: **As you read and consider these passages, what hope do you find there?**
C. H. Robinson recognizes that there are Christians who do not accept the reality of Jesus' resurrection, yet he writes the following, which you may read aloud:

Whether we are prepared or not to accept the occurrence of the Resurrection as a fact of history, we cannot deny the influence that a belief in it has exercised in the world. We cannot deny that it has brought life and immortality to light as no other belief could conceivably have done, that it has substituted for the fear of death, for a large portion of the human race, that sure and certain knowledge of God which is eternal life; that it has permeated our customs, our literature, and our language with a glory and a hope that could have been derived from no other source.

Ask: **If Jesus' resurrection has as many positive facets as Robinson suggests, what do you think hinders people from accepting this event as a fact of history?**
Conclude by asking: **As you consider the meanings of "resurrection," selected Bible passages where the word "resurrection" is found, and the words of a writer who finds "a glory and a hope that could have been derived from no other source," what new insights do you have about "resurrection"? How might the prospect of resurrection give you hope for the future?**

FAITH IN ACTION: OFFERING THEM HOPE

During this spring quarter we are focusing on the theme of hope. We will see hope for the future as we study the Book of Daniel. We will also consider hope in light of Jesus' resurrection and what that means to us. Finally, we will view hope through the lens of suffering, as was the case for the early Christians to whom the first and second letters of Peter were addressed. Although hope can be viewed from these and other angles, in all cases our hope is deeply rooted in God.

As followers of Christ, we are called to share God's hope with others. Post these ideas on newsprint for the class to discuss. Encourage them to select two or three ideas that would mesh well with the talents the class members have to offer and would meet needs in your community or denomination. Not every suggested project will be appropriate for each class, but all of these suggestions have the potential to bring hope to someone.

(1) Choose a type of relief kit (cleaning, bedding, birthing, layette, health, school, or sewing) from the United Methodist Committee on Relief's website, http://new.gbgm-umc.org/umcor/getconnected/supplies. Specific directions are given on the website for creating each kit. Set a goal together and challenge the class to assemble and send as many of these kits as possible. Your contribution will be directed to the area in need of emergency relief.

(2) Assist one or more farmers who may need help with crops, livestock, or the repair of barns or outbuildings.

(3) Collect nonperishable food for your church (or community) food pantry. Encourage class members to help pack and distribute the food.

(4) Work with a church-sponsored or community shelter to give hope and dignity to those who are homeless. Many communities have ecumenically sponsored shelters housed in church buildings, at least during the coldest months of the year.

(5) Volunteer to work in a youth center to help students with homework, sports, or other recreational activities that will keep them out of harm's way.

(6) Check to see how you might help with a halfway house or other agency that deals with those who need hope as they try to overcome addictions.

(7) Contact a shelter for victims of domestic violence. Offer supplies or volunteer time to work with the women and children who are temporarily housed there.

(8) Partner with your dog or cat to do pet therapy in a place where people often feel forgotten and hopeless, such as a nursing home or residential treatment center. You and your well-behaved, neatly groomed animal will need special training, certification, and appropriate immunizations to do this work. Many communities have pet therapy groups that can help you meet requirements and place your team in a facility.

(9) Engage in a prison ministry to bring hope to inmates as they work to turn their lives in a positive, God-centered direction.

(10) Reach out to immigrants in the community by opening your church doors as a tutoring center where these newcomers can learn English and get help with learning basic skills needed to thrive in their new homeland.

UNIT 1: THE KINGDOM OF GOD

DANIEL'S VISION OF CHANGE

PREVIEWING THE LESSON

Lesson Scripture: Daniel 7:9-14
Background Scripture: Daniel 7
Key Verse: Daniel 7:14

Focus of the Lesson:
We live in the hope that the future will be better than the past. How can we learn from the past and apply it to the future? Daniel's vision tells of the Ancient of Days seated on a throne, ruling forever, and giving dominion and power to a messiah.

Goals for the Learners:
(1) to connect Daniel's dream with the historical incidents to which it is related.
(2) to share their feelings about the relationship between their dreams and reality.
(3) to articulate their vision for future change.

Pronunciation Guide:
Antiochus Epiphanes (an ti' uh kuhs i pif' uh neez)
Belshazzar (bel' shaz' uhr)
Nabonidus (nab uh ni' duhs)
Nebuchadnezzar (nub uh kihd nez' uhr)
Seleucid (si loo' sid)
theophany (thee of' uh nee)

Supplies:
Bibles, newsprint and marker, paper and pencils, hymnals

READING THE SCRIPTURE

NRSV
Lesson Scripture: Daniel 7:9-14
⁹ As I watched,
  thrones were set in place,
    and an Ancient One took his throne,
  his clothing was white as snow,

CEB
Lesson Scripture: Daniel 7:9-14
⁹ As I was watching,
  thrones were raised up.
  The ancient one took his seat.
    His clothes were white like snow;

and the hair of his head like
    pure wool;
his throne was fiery flames,
    and its wheels were burning fire.
10 A stream of fire issued
    and flowed out from his presence.
A thousand thousands served him,
    and ten thousand times ten
      thousand stood attending him.
The court sat in judgment,
    and the books were opened.

[11]I watched then because of the noise of the arrogant words that the horn was speaking. And as I watched, the beast was put to death, and its body destroyed and given over to be burned with fire. [12]As for the rest of the beasts, their dominion was taken away, but their lives were prolonged for a season and a time. [13]As I watched in the night visions,

    I saw one like a human being
      coming with the clouds of heaven.
    And he came to the Ancient One
      and was presented before him.
14 To him was given dominion
    and glory and kingship,
    that all peoples, nations, and languages
      should serve him.

**His dominion is an everlasting
    dominion
    that shall not pass away,
and his kingship is one
    that shall never be destroyed.**

his hair was like a lamb's wool.
His throne was made of flame;
    its wheels were blazing fire.
10 A river of fire flowed out
    from his presence;
    thousands upon thousands
      served him;
    ten thousand times ten thousand
      stood ready to serve him!
The court sat in session;
    the scrolls were opened.

[11]I kept watching. I watched from the moment the horn started bragging until the beast was killed and its body was destroyed, handed over to be burned with fire. [12]Then the authority of the remaining beasts was brought to an end, but they were given an extension among the living for a set time and season.

[13]As I continued to watch this night vision of mine, I suddenly saw

    one like a human being
      coming with the heavenly clouds.
    He came to the ancient one
      and was presented before him.
14 Rule, glory, and kingship
    were given to him;
    all peoples, nations, and languages
      will serve him.

**His rule is an everlasting one—
    it will never pass away!—
    his kingship is indestructible.**

UNDERSTANDING THE SCRIPTURE

Introduction. You will find it helpful to first review "Daniel in Context" under Interpreting the Scripture to familiarize yourself with the historical context that undergirds this passage and the whole Book of Daniel. The material related to the Book of Daniel in "The Big Picture: Literatures of Hope" will also shed further light on these verses.

Daniel 7:1. The connecting of this passage to the opening of King Belshazzar's reign underscores that this dream/vision arises in, and is addressed to, a time of ongoing transition in power. The notation of Daniel having a dream and visions of his head as he lay in his bed are near verbatim descriptions of two earlier experiences of Daniel regarding the Babylonian king

Nebuchadnezzar (2:28 and 4:5). While reigns and even empires change around him, Daniel remains the visionary, and God remains the One behind the dreams and their import. No powers can prevent the dreams and hope God instills.

Daniel 7:2-8. These verses relate without interpretation the vision of the four beasts. Three of the beasts are identified as lion, bear, and leopard, all predatory, while the fourth is identified as "different" from the others. Intriguingly, Hosea 13:7-8 invokes the same three beasts (and a fourth only spoken of as a "wild animal") to depict how God will come to render judgment. The "great sea" in Daniel 7:2 was the ancient designation of the Mediterranean Sea. Beyond that, the sea also symbolized the powers of chaos, not only in Judaism but also in the Babylonian creation stories. In the vision and interpretation that begins in verse 7, the word "horn(s)" recurs through verse 24. None of the aforementioned beasts has horns in the natural world. Thus the usage here is symbolic, where the horn is an image of power.

Daniel 7:9-12. Daniel's vision moves now from the beasts unleashed upon the earth to the throne(s) room of God. Notice that "thrones" is plural in verse 9, though Daniel leaves unclear who the other thrones are for. The verse identifies God as the "Ancient One" ("Ancient of Days" in KJV). Modern depictions of God as a white-haired and clothed figure come from this verse along with a verse it very likely influenced, Revelation 1:14. The association of God's presence with fire is well established in Judaism, most notably with Moses' experience of theophany (a "God appearance") in the burning bush (Exodus 3:2) and on Mount Sinai (Exodus 19:18). The passage numbers the attendants of God at "ten thousand times ten thousand" (7:10). With no word for "million," ancient Hebrew designated "ten thousand" as the highest number. Thus its squaring to represent the heavenly court would have represented the practical equivalent of infinity, and likely intends to dwarf the report of the mere "thousand" gathered for the feast of King Belshazzar in Daniel 5:1. There are two key words in this section that form the passage's theme: "dominion" (7:12, 14) and "kingdom/kingship" (7:14). Like the imagery of horns, the vision is grounded in the revelation of who holds ultimate power.

Daniel 7:13-14. In verse 13 a figure appears described as like a "human being"; other translations render this "Son of Man." Who or what the Son of Man is here remains a mystery. Ezekiel (for example, 36:16; 37:3, 11, 16) also frequently invokes a figure so named (though the NRSV there translates the words there as "mortal"). The Gospels make particular use of this shadowy term, especially in Mark, where its mystery fits well with Mark's theme of the messianic secret. Daniel, however, was not writing to the church, but to the audience of his day. While we perhaps cannot read Daniel within the church without being aware of associations made with the coming or ministry of Jesus, it is critical to begin first with the meaning of Daniel apart from those later associations. Taking Daniel's witness on its own allows us to hear how it influenced Christian Scripture, and not the other way around. A clear case in point comes with verse 14's listing of royal authority being entrusted to "one like a human being," a list that closely parallels and likely strongly influenced the later apocalyptic visions in Revelation 5:12-13; 11:15.

Daniel 7:15-27. In the narrative of the text the vision of the four beasts is now interpreted by one of the attendants to God whom Daniel approaches for explanation. The theme of dominion and power in the vision is made explicit when verse 17 indicates that the four beasts represent four kings (or empires?). Also newly introduced into the passage in this section are the "holy ones," most likely a representation of the community whom Daniel addresses. Their situation, according to both verses 21 and 25, is precarious. The fourth beast, different from the others, threatens them. Those scholars who trace the writing or at least compilation of Daniel to the crisis posed by the Seleucid ruler Antiochus IV identify him as the unnamed fourth beast or at least its "mouth speaking arrogantly" (7:8, 20). The clue they draw from the text is verse 25's charge that he "shall attempt to change the sacred seasons and the law," seen as a reference to his reign's attempt to undermine Jewish practices and change Temple observances. The end of this figure in verse 26, as in verse 10, is not in some long, drawn-out, protracted struggle. It comes decisively, without elaboration. Daniel is not interested in spectacle. Daniel simply declares who holds the power.

Daniel 7:28. The account of the vision now closes. Perhaps unexpectedly, given the resolution depicted in verses 26-27, Daniel observes that his thoughts "greatly terrified" him (7:28), using similar words as in verse 15 to interpret how the visions affected him, and because of which he sought one of the attendants at God's throne for interpretation (7:16). Verse 28 closes with the trouble continuing. In that, Daniel 7:28 may reflect the community, the "holy ones," whom he addresses. The vision of God's dominion has been revealed, the hope has been instilled, to both prophet and people. But Daniel, like his community, waits with hope, but on this side of upheaval.

INTERPRETING THE SCRIPTURE

Daniel in Context

In a session—and entire quarter—grounded in the theme of hope, one might wonder, why bother with the past? In his book titled *The Life of Reason*, George Santayana observed: "Those who cannot remember the past are condemned to repeat it." The Book of Daniel and the vision recorded here in Daniel 7:9-14 do not happen in a vacuum, apart from history. Daniel's vision of hope arises out of significant historical settings (plural) whose understanding brings even further depth and power to these words.

The first historical context comes from Daniel 7:1, which prefaces the vision: "in the first year of King Belshazzar of Babylon." Belshazzar was an ill-fated ruler. First, he never possessed power only to himself; his father, Nabonidus, merely had the son rule in his place during an extended absence. Second, Belshazzar never lived to succeed his father, but was killed (Daniel 5:30) prior to Babylon's fall to the Persian Empire

under Cyrus. This was the same Cyrus whom Isaiah 45:1 depicts as God's "anointed" for his decree that allowed the return of Jewish exiles to Jerusalem and Judea.

Placing the vision in the context of Belshazzar's time serves as a reminder that even imperial power can be fleeting, and the appearances of who actually holds power can be misleading. It also asserts that hope remains alive in times of transition. God can and does work in unexpected ways, as God shortly will in this instance through Cyrus, for the only constant is the dominion and power of God.

A second historical context informs the vision of Daniel. Many scholars agree that while portions of Daniel may well record stories that came down from the time of the Babylonian and then Persian eras, the audience to whom this book, and this vision, is addressed lived in the mid-second century B.C. during the reign of the infamous Seleucid ruler Antiochus Epiphanes IV. Antiochus sought to impose by his power a variety of changes upon the practices of Judaism and the Temple rituals. The upheaval and revolt those actions triggered are reflected in the apocryphal books of the Maccabees. It is believed Daniel was finally compiled at this time as a protest against the ruler's arrogance. But more than a protest, it served as a powerful urging of hope. Hope that the powers and dominions of this world do not have the final say or authority. Such hope belongs, as Daniel reveals in the vision, to an "Ancient One," to God.

For people and communities of faith today, this vision remains both protest and assertion of hope. From Daniel, we remember that the likes of Belshazzar and later Antiochus may have their days of power, and they may be terrible. We, too, may face times of upheaval, whether wrought by political winds or devastating earthquakes. But in the end, God strips away the arrogance of those who unwisely presume power to be theirs and theirs alone. And Daniel's vision gives to us, as to its original audience, hope to live, not simply for some distant day, but also in this day.

Dreams and Dominion

Daniel does not stand alone among the biblical books as the sole source of dreams and dreamers. And perhaps it is no coincidence that the most dream-inspired and vision-oriented stories and works in the biblical witness play off of the theme of dominion. Joseph has his dreams in Genesis, dreams that first land him in trouble with and exile from his brothers (Genesis 37). In the end, dreams and their interpretations restore Joseph not only to family but also to prominence in Egypt, the most powerful dominion in the biblical world of that day (Genesis 40–41).

As the New Testament opens, another Joseph has a dream that warns him of Herod the King's attempt to secure his throne by ridding himself of a child born in Bethlehem. Joseph and Mary flee, and the Magi become accomplices in that sheltering of the child as they disobey a king's orders because of a dream (Matthew 2:12-13). As the New Testament closes, the vision that is called Revelation plants hope in a community that has been ravaged by the excesses of Roman imperial power.

This pairing of visionary and "daring to dream" hope in God's dominion in the face of and ultimately in triumph over oppressing dominions of the day serves as the concluding "doxology" of Daniel 7:14, today's key verse. This verse, it should be noted, is echoed in Revelation 5:12-13; 11:15.

Why might dreams and visions be so closely connected, not only in these writings of old but also in present-day yearnings? Faith is about transformation. Some focus such transformation on personal conversion, and that has its place. But Daniel, and the other dreamers and visionaries of the biblical witness, and those same ones in the history of the church past and present, realize that the transformation God promises and the hope God assures are universal in scope. Daniel's vision of the Ancient One is about the direction and destination of history. Dominions that seek to parcel off power for and unto themselves, whether political or social, economic or even religious, will not succeed. That is what Daniel sees in dreams and visions, because sometimes the "static" of current powers-that-be dull everyday sight with illusions of control or dominance. They even may be capable of producing nightmares. But as Daniel reveals, the Ancient One alone assures that dreams and visions of everlasting realm and solid hope will not pass away, and will survive all the onslaughts of pretenders to the one throne.

Trusting and Living as Visionaries

We now come to the question of what we ourselves will make of Daniel. By that, I do not mean to ask what category of religious writing this was, or what each of the symbols may or may not mean, or whether Daniel intended the "one like a human being" ("Son of man" in 7:13 KJV) to be Israel or the angel Michael or Jesus, as have all been proposed. No, the more pressing question is, what will we make of Daniel in terms of whether we will choose, as he apparently did, to live and trust and work as visionaries, dreamers of the hopes of God? And if we live and choose to trust as Daniel did, what dreams and visions form our hope for the future and its changes, and thus inform how we will live and serve in their light?

Those are the real matters that concern the integration of Daniel 7:9-14 into the lives we lead and the communities we seek and the witness we would bring. The world waits to hear and see from us what gospel our vision will produce. Not only that, the world longs for dreams and visions that anchor hope. There are plenty of nightmares to go around. There are more than enough blind spots to human need or cries for justice. Daniel 7:9-14 reminds us that our calling as people of God is to bring a vision that will lift up hope out of despair, possibilities out of closed doors, and new ways of seeing and speaking that may not always fit in with conventional wisdoms and rutted routines. We are called, through Daniel, to see the throne where dominion truly resides, and then to live our lives on its basis.

SHARING THE SCRIPTURE

Preparing Our Hearts

Explore this week's devotional reading, found in Daniel 6:25-28. Here we read the words of a royal decree charging that people "tremble and fear before the God of Daniel" (6:26). What does this Persian king's decree say about Daniel's God? What does it say about God's kingdom? How do these descriptions square with what you know about God and the kingdom? How are these descriptions helpful to you at a time when worldly dominions seem to have complete control over the earth? How do the descriptions in Daniel give you hope?

Pray that you and the adult students will recognize that God's dominion will rule in the end, even if other leaders seem to be ruling right now.

Preparing Our Minds

Study the background Scripture from Daniel 7 and the lesson Scripture from Daniel 7:9-14.

Consider this question as you prepare the lesson: *How can we learn from the past and apply it to the future?*

Write on newsprint:
- ❑ information for next week's lesson, found under "Continue the Journey."
- ❑ activities for further spiritual growth in "Continue the Journey."

Review the "Introduction," "The Big Picture," "Close-up," and "Faith in Action." Consider how you will use this additional information, which immediately precedes the first lesson, for this session and throughout the quarter.

Use information from Understanding the Scripture and "Daniel in Context" from Interpreting the Scripture to prepare a lecture for "Connect Daniel's Dream with the Historical Incidents to Which It Is Related."

LEADING THE CLASS

(1) Gather to Learn

❖ Greet the class members. Introduce any guests and help them feel at home.

❖ Pray that all who have come today will find new hope as a result of encountering Daniel's vision.

❖ Invite those participants who have attended a world's fair or other place where ideas of the future are showcased to talk about what they experienced there. Discuss how the ideas for tomorrow gave the students hope that the future might be better. Encourage comments on how these prototype gadgets and ideas became part of our daily lives, or disappeared completely.

❖ Read aloud today's focus statement: **We live in the hope that the future will be better than the past. How can we learn from the past and apply it to the future? Daniel's vision tells of the Ancient of Days seated on a throne, ruling forever, and giving dominion and power to a messiah.**

(2) Goal 1: Connect Daniel's Dream With the Historical Incidents to Which It Is Related

❖ Set the scene for today's study by presenting the lecture you have prepared from Understanding the Scripture and Interpreting the Scripture. Recognize that biblical scholars have debated the date of composition of this book, which does include several sections, including parts written in Aramaic (Daniel 2:4b–7:28). Stay focused on the purpose in this session to see how Daniel's vision provides hope for the future.

❖ Choose someone to read Daniel 7:9-14.
❖ Ask these questions:
   (1) How might Daniel's vision give hope to the Israelites, who were persecuted and suffering?
   (2) What hope does this vision give you for a better future?

(3) Goal 2: Share Feelings About the Relationship Between the Learner's Dreams and Reality

❖ Read or retell "Dreams and Dominion" from Interpreting the Scripture.

❖ Distribute paper and pencils. Invite the adults to write one or two hopes they had for their future. Ask them to describe these hopes and then write about how these dreams did, or did not, become reality, or perhaps how they played out in ways the students did not anticipate.

❖ Encourage each person to talk with a partner or small group about how he or she felt when his or her dreams became reality—or when he or she realized that those dreams would never become reality. The students may reveal the hope itself or choose to keep that private. The focus here is on feelings. How did they see God at work in these dreams? If the dreams did not materialize, did they blame God, or could they see some other reason? Did something else happen on which they can now look back and say it was better for them?

❖ Bring everyone together and ask them to silently consider this question: **What would you want to say to Jesus about your feelings concerning this dream that did or did not come true?**

(4) Goal 3: Articulate Each Learner's Vision for Future Change

❖ Read "Trusting and Living as Visionaries" from Interpreting the Scripture.
❖ Form several small groups. Provide newsprint and a marker for each group. Challenge group members to identify one situation in their community that they would like to see change. For example, perhaps they want poor people to have greater access to the food and shelter they need. Or possibly they want teens to have a safe, alcohol-free, and drug-free place for recreation. Maybe they want their political leaders to be more responsive to the will of the people. Suggest that the groups list on their newsprint:
   ■ **a statement of the problem.**
   ■ **a vision of how things would be different if they could solve the problem.**

■ some steps or ideas they would need to take to bring about their vision for a future change.

❖ Call everyone together and encourage each group to report its ideas. Set a time limit so that each group will have equal time.

❖ Conclude by asking:

(1) How will our ideas bring hope to the community?

(2) How do our ideas reflect the fact that we live under the reign of God?

(3) What steps might we take to turn our vision into reality?

(5) Continue the Journey

❖ Pray that today's participants will go forth with a new vision of God's reign and how that reign will affect their lives.

❖ Read aloud this preparation for next week's lesson. You may also want to post it on newsprint for the students to copy.

■ **Title: Daniel's Prayer**
■ **Background Scripture: Daniel 9:3-19**
■ **Lesson Scripture: Daniel 9:4b-14**
■ **Focus of the Lesson: Even though our hopes for the future are grounded in God's past actions, we are human and become fearful. What should we do when fear encroaches? Daniel went to God in prayer.**

❖ Post these three activities related to this week's session on newsprint for the students to copy. Challenge the adults to grow spiritually by completing one or more of them.

(1) Consider the changes that you would like to see happen in your personal life, family, church, or workplace. Summarize each of these changes in a sentence or two. What can you do to move toward these changes? Whose help do you need? What steps can you take this week?

(2) Be aware of media coverage of governments that are acting contrary to your understanding of God's will. If the government in question is your own, contact an appropriate legislator to voice your concern as a Christian and suggest ways that the government can better care for and represent its citizens.

(3) Keep a notebook and pencil by your bed. Record any dreams you can remember as you awaken. Check books and Internet sources for interpretations of the symbols and actions. Do you feel that God is speaking to you through these dreams? If so, what action are you being led to take?

❖ Sing or read aloud "Come, Thou Almighty King."

❖ Conclude today's session by leading the class in this benediction, based on the key verses for April 28 from 2 Thessalonians 2:16-17: **Now may our Lord Jesus Christ himself and God our Father, who loved us and through grace gave us eternal comfort and good hope, comfort your hearts and strengthen them in every good work and word.**

UNIT 1: THE KINGDOM OF GOD
DANIEL'S PRAYER

PREVIEWING THE LESSON

Lesson Scripture: Daniel 9:4b-14
Background Scripture: Daniel 9:3-19
Key Verse: Daniel 9:9

Focus of the Lesson:

Even though our hopes for the future are grounded in God's past actions, we are human and become fearful. What should we do when fear encroaches? Daniel went to God in prayer.

Goals for the Learners:

(1) to hear the passionate words of Daniel's prayer to God.
(2) to express the passions that earnest prayer evokes in them.
(3) to identify elements in Daniel's prayer that they can use to frame their prayers.

Pronunciation Guide:

Antiochus Epiphanes (an ti' uh kuhs i pif' uh neez)
hesed (hee' sid)
Seleucid (si loo' sid)
Shema (shuh mah')

Supplies:

Bibles, newsprint and marker, paper and pencils, hymnals

READING THE SCRIPTURE

NRSV

Lesson Scripture: Daniel 9:4b-14

⁴"Ah, Lord, great and awesome God, keeping covenant and steadfast love with those who love you and keep your commandments, ⁵we have sinned and done wrong, acted wickedly and rebelled, turning aside from your commandments

CEB

Lesson Scripture: Daniel 9:4b-14

⁴Please, my Lord—you are the great and awesome God, the one who keeps the covenant, and truly faithful to all who love him and keep his commands: ⁵We have sinned and done wrong. We have brought guilt on ourselves and rebelled, ignoring

and ordinances. [6]We have not listened to your servants the prophets, who spoke in your name to our kings, our princes, and our ancestors, and to all the people of the land.

[7]"Righteousness is on your side, O Lord, but open shame, as at this day, falls on us, the people of Judah, the inhabitants of Jerusalem, and all Israel, those who are near and those who are far away, in all the lands to which you have driven them, because of the treachery that they have committed against you. [8]Open shame, O LORD, falls on us, our kings, our officials, and our ancestors, because we have sinned against you. **[9]To the Lord our God belong mercy and forgiveness, for we have rebelled against him,** [10]and have not obeyed the voice of the LORD our God by following his laws, which he set before us by his servants the prophets.

[11]"All Israel has transgressed your law and turned aside, refusing to obey your voice. So the curse and the oath written in the law of Moses, the servant of God, have been poured out upon us, because we have sinned against you. [12]He has confirmed his words, which he spoke against us and against our rulers, by bringing upon us a calamity so great that what has been done against Jerusalem has never before been done under the whole heaven. [13]Just as it is written in the law of Moses, all this calamity has come upon us. We did not entreat the favor of the LORD our God, turning from our iniquities and reflecting on his fidelity. [14]So the LORD kept watch over this calamity until he brought it upon us. Indeed, the LORD our God is right in all that he has done; for we have disobeyed his voice."

your commands and your laws. [6]We haven't listened to your servants, the prophets, who spoke in your name to our kings, our leaders, our parents, and to all the land's people. [7]Righteousness belongs to you, my Lord! But we are ashamed this day—we, the people of Judah, the inhabitants of Jerusalem, all Israel whether near or far, in whatever country where you've driven them because of their unfaithfulness when they broke faith with you. [8]LORD, we are ashamed—we, our kings, our leaders, and our parents who sinned against you. **[9]Compassion and deep forgiveness belong to my Lord, our God, because we rebelled against him.** [10]We didn't listen to the voice of the LORD our God by following the teachings he gave us through his servants, the prophets. [11]All Israel broke your Instruction and turned away, ignoring your voice. Then the curse that was sworn long ago—the one written in the Instruction from Moses, God's servant—swept over us because we sinned against God. [12]God confirmed the words he spoke against us and against our rulers, bringing great trouble on us. What happened in Jerusalem hasn't happened anywhere else in the entire world! [13]All this trouble came upon us, exactly as it was written in the Instruction of Moses, but we didn't try to reconcile with the LORD our God by turning from our wrongdoing or by finding wisdom in your faithfulness. [14]So the LORD oversaw the great trouble and brought it on us, because the LORD our God has been right in every move he's made, but we haven't listened to his voice.

UNDERSTANDING THE SCRIPTURE

Daniel 9:3-4a. The "answer" Daniel seeks most likely refers to verse 2, which closes on the note of Jeremiah's prophecy (Jeremiah 25:11; 29:10) regarding seventy years as the period of exile. The linkage of "fasting and sackcloth and ashes" in verse 3 with Daniel's ensuing prayer suggests the prayer's two main movements: confession of sin and a plea for deliverance. "Sackcloth and ashes" are traditional accompaniments of mourning (for example, Esther 4:1-3), and this prayer's confession of sin repeatedly mourns Israel's breakings of covenant. Fasting carries additional associations with preparing oneself for revelations from God (for example, Exodus 34:28) as well as accompanying prayers for deliverance.

Daniel 9:4b-6. The ascription of verse 4b of God as the one who keeps covenant and practices steadfast love closely parallels the opening of the prayer of Nehemiah (Nehemiah 1:5 and following), a prayer that also was prefaced with fasting. Daniel 9:5 abruptly moves from God's unquestioned nature to Israel's gross breaches of covenant. Daniel uses no less than five different expressions for those misdeeds: sin, do wrong, act wickedly, rebel, and turn aside. The language argues for a multitude of missteps. Verse 6 follows with a summary word for all of that: "not listened." That Hebrew word appears later in verse 10 ("not obeyed"), verse 11 ("refusing to obey"), and verse 14 ("disobeyed"). That word, as is the case with its Greek parallel, means both to "hear" and to "obey." The multitudinous ways of falling short are matched in verse 6 by the inclusive listing of those who have transgressed: kings, princes, ancestors, "all the people of the land." The only possible exception for Daniel are the prophets—although other passages make it clear that even prophets contributed to the disaster (Jeremiah 5:31).

Daniel 9:7-8. A stark contrast between God and people is drawn. Righteousness belongs to God, shame belongs to the people. "Open shame" in the NRSV translates what the King James Version renders as "confusion of faces" (9:7). A similar visual, though with a different Hebrew word for "shame," is conveyed when Jeremiah describes the effects of exile as "We are put to shame . . . dishonor has covered our *face*" (Jeremiah 51:51, emphasis added). This shame belongs not simply to those carried off to Babylon but to all those dispersed in consequence of their collective guilt. At the end of verse 7, Daniel reflects what other prophets affirmed. Exile came as God's action in response to the people's guilt. In Hebrew poetry, a repeated line or stanza serves as an underscoring of a point, and while verse 8 adds nothing new to verse 7, its repetition of the message makes clear its importance.

Daniel 9:9-14. These verses underscore all that has been said before, and add a few new notes. There is the hint of how deliverance may come in attributing to God the qualities of "forgiveness" and "mercy" (9:9). This latter word, appearing again in the prayer at verse 18 in the midst of Daniel's plea for deliverance, connotes "compassion." The remainder of these verses, however, quickly returns to the theme of confession and to the imagery of God and people being opposed to one another (9:11 of people, 9:12 of God). Daniel does not question God's role in what has happened. As God's "righteousness" had been affirmed in verse 7, so now do these verses close with Daniel asserting God is "right" in what has been done. The theme of negative consequences to breaks in covenant is given covenantal expression as Daniel points to the "curse and the oath" (9:11) written in the law of Moses as being poured out upon them. (Deuteronomy 28:15-68 records an extensive listing of curses brought by disobedience, with verses 47-57 especially depicting exilic experiences.) Daniel uses the term "calamity" not once but three times (Daniel 9:12 and following) to describe the experienced captivity and exile. The term is even more ominous when it is noted that the Hebrew word is frequently translated as "evil."

Daniel 9:15-16. The linkage of Daniel's prayer to older covenant traditions becomes more explicit in verse 15's opening confession of God as the One who brought the people out of the land of Egypt. The words closely parallel the prologue to the Decalogue (Ten Commandments) in Exodus 20:2 and Deuteronomy 5:6. Another covenant connection relates to one of the fundamental promises in Israel's covenant tradition: the land. In Daniel 9:16, as a result of the people's sins, it is the land (city, mountain) of those previous promises now jeopardized. Daniel contrasts the disgrace that has befallen Jerusalem and God's people with God's previous action in deliverance that "made your name renowned" (9:15). This contrast may be a subtle plea on Daniel's part to remind God that disgrace upon the land and people, in one sense, deflects from the renown or reputation of God's name in the sight of others. Daniel returns to this language of the place and people who bear God's name in verses 18-19 with his plea on behalf of that city and that people. In doing so, Daniel's prayer moves beyond confession of sin to lament that urges God to act out of integrity to God's own name.

Daniel 9:17-19. This surprising move in the prayer from confession to lament takes intriguing form in these concluding verses, beyond even the plea on behalf of those who bear God's name. Look at the imperatives that begin each of these final three verses: "God, listen . . . Incline your ear, O my God, and hear . . . O Lord, hear . . . forgive . . . listen and act and do not delay." God is summoned to hear—and in hearing, to act. The movement reflects a surprising reversal of one of Israel's foundational confessions in Deuteronomy 6:4 sometimes called the "Shema" (from the Hebrew verb "to hear"): "Hear, O Israel: The LORD is our God." In the Deuteronomy covenant, Israel is summoned to hear—and in hearing, to keep covenant. In Daniel 9:17 and following, God is summoned to hear—and in hearing, to restore covenant! So Daniel prays on behalf of Israel, and all who long for covenant's restoration when such healing exceeds our capabilities.

INTERPRETING THE SCRIPTURE

The Covenant God

The visions and dreams in the Book of Daniel in chapters 7–8 have a decidedly future orientation. Their subsequent interpretations in the church have led to all manner of speculation relating to the end of days. Much of Daniel's imagery clearly influences the extravagance of the Book of Revelation and its vivid metaphors of beasts and times and final judgment. But now in chapter 9, Daniel pivots to an entirely different genre. In place of fantastic images and symbol-laden mysteries, the prophet prays to God.

For one who is so intensely interested in the future, Daniel begins the prayer by addressing God with one of Israel's most ancient and formative of confessions of what it means to be in relationship with God: covenant. "Ah, Lord, great and awesome God, *keeping covenant and steadfast love*" (Daniel 9:4, emphasis added).

As much as the future might portend upheaval and turmoil as the kingdom of this world becomes the kingdom of our Lord, this much remains the same: God is the One who bids us into covenant—and God is the One who keeps covenant, even when we come up short. That second part will be crucial for the prayer Daniel is about to bring to God, as we will soon see. But laying this foundation of who God is represents no mere formality of address. For on covenant hangs the hope of Israel; and through Israel, our hope.

Notice, too, how Daniel links God's covenant keeping with "steadfast love." "Steadfast love" translates a Hebrew word, *hesed*, in other places translated as "mercy" or "loving kindness." I recall my Old Testament professor in seminary describing *hesed* as loyalty that exceeds purely legalistic legal requirements, that "goes the extra mile" so to speak. For a liturgical perspective on how *hesed* underlies not only covenant but also all creation, read Psalm 136. Every one of its twenty-six verses, which celebrate God's work in creation and deliverance and providence, has the identical refrain: "for his steadfast love [*hesed*] endures forever." Not only Israel but all of creation is sustained by God's loyalty to those fashioned for relationship and redeemed for that same purpose.

So Daniel begins his prayer, and latches his and his people's hope, to the One known and confessed to keep covenant. Why? That covenant is in jeopardy. Its restoration will need to rely on a God so committed to relationship, and a prophet so audacious as to summon God to covenant-keeping *hesed*.

Praying It Like It Is

There is rawness and passion to Daniel's prayer that refuses to gloss over what has led to the crises at hand. The people have sinned, which is to say, they have broken covenant with God. As noted in Understanding the Scripture, the breadth and depth of this breach of covenant comes not only in the numerous expressions Daniel employs for such infidelity but also in across-the-board denunciations of those who have been involved. It is not one sector of society that has fallen short. Daniel's recital prefigures Paul's later indictment in Romans 3:23 that "all have sinned and fall short of the glory of God."

The question in Daniel (and for us) is: Why is there such passion and repetition on the note of accountability? Three options come into play, then and now.

The first is the threat posed by denial and blame. Perhaps some in this crisis Daniel faced wanted to place the blame upon faulty leaders, or inept followers, or corrupted religious institutions, as if finding blame in another can justify one's own innocence. Such denial interrupts the possibility of renewal by falsifying the situation with flights from personal responsibility.

A second and related threat follows the first: If sin and failures in responsibility, personal or corporate, go unconfessed, it is not as if they then magically go away. The disease of unrepented sin and guilt works inside of our lives and institutions, eroding us from the inside. Psalm 32:3-4 makes explicit the internal damage done when this happens. Confession makes possible the loosing of what would otherwise eat away at us by opening us to God's forgiveness and grace—and just as important, to the Spirit's renewal and transformation. Confession is not just about facing up to old ways but also about stepping forward into God's new ways.

A third element behind the passion and starkness of Daniel's confession on behalf of the people is a warning. That is, the destruction of covenant through such actions in the past needs to be admitted, so those same wanderings do not recur. Daniel is a prophet, and in the prophetic tradition of Amos and Isaiah and others, Daniel makes clear that actions carry consequences. Covenant-keeping actions build up, and covenant-breaking actions tear down, and God is free to be part of either set of consequences.

Cautionary Whispers Between the Lines

Daniel's prayer presumes a cause and effect, made especially clear in verses 11-14. Namely, Israel sinned and God punished. As might be expected of a prophet who sees visions of things unfolding in the future that have been long planned (and now announced), Daniel sees the crisis of exile and presumably that of the Seleucid era in which the book was compiled as clearly wrought by God with forethought: "So the LORD kept watch over this calamity until he brought it upon us" (9:14). The disaster of exile and the ascendancy of Antiochus Epiphanes represent acts of God in response to human sinfulness.

But does this tell the whole tale? Does human suffering always fall in lockstep with clear cause-and-effect rationales, even those couched in religious terms? More than once, Jesus challenged attitudes in his day that too easily attributed illness or disaster to personal responsibility (John 9:1 and following; Luke 13:1-5). Perhaps the most devastating challenge in the twentieth century to such a view came in the wake of the Jewish Holocaust. Was the death of six million Jews an act of God's retributive justice? Life is more complex than simple cause-and-effect logic or theology. Jesus pointed us in this direction not only in the texts mentioned above but also in the Sermon on the Mount's assertion that God "makes his sun rise on the evil and the good, and sends rain on the righteous and the unrighteous" (Matthew 5:45).

To return to Daniel, the prophet's passion in confessing sin and pronouncing God's hand behind the disasters needs to be held in tandem with the truth that none of us knows fully the mysteries underlying God's working in the world and even our personal experience. As a result, what underlies covenant with God is not only our keeping of its commands but also our foundational trust of the One who engages us in relationship. Consider where Daniel's prayer begins and ends. Its first words in verse 4 address God as the One who keeps covenant and steadfast love. Its final words in verses 17-19 invoke a series of pleas for God to hear, and in listening, to act. That action is nothing less than the renewal of covenant. Confession may acknowledge the truth of what has gone wrong on our part, but confession alone does not restore covenant. Only grace can do that: The grace of God evidenced in covenant's enactment (Deuteronomy 7:7-8), the grace of God that in the conclusion of Daniel's prayer becomes covenant's final hope. So Daniel prays, not simply in confession of the people's covenant breaking, but in hope of God once again being the God of covenant making and remaking.

SHARING THE SCRIPTURE

Preparing Our Hearts

Explore this week's devotional reading, found in James 5:13-18. In this passage James, the leader of the Jerusalem church and possibly Jesus' brother, writes about the effectiveness of prayer. He uses the prophet Elijah's prayer for drought—and his prayer three and a half years later for rain—as examples of the power of the prayers of the righteous. These righteous pray-ers have the unwavering faith that James writes

about in 1:6. What are your current prayer requests? Offer these prayers each day.

Pray that you and the adult students will be mindful of the power of prayer and pray that God's kingdom might come as a result of our prayers.

Preparing Our Minds

Study the background Scripture from Daniel 9:3-19 and the lesson Scripture from Daniel 9:4b-14.

Consider this question as you prepare the lesson: *What should we do when we feel fearful?*

Write on newsprint:

❏ information for next week's lesson, found under "Continue the Journey."

❏ activities for further spiritual growth in "Continue the Journey."

Review the "Introduction," "The Big Picture," "Close-up," and "Faith in Action." Consider how you will use this additional information, which immediately precedes the first lesson, for this session.

LEADING THE CLASS

(1) Gather to Learn

❖ Greet the class members. Introduce any guests and help them feel at home.

❖ Pray that those who have come today will value the opportunity to pray to God, knowing they will be heard.

❖ Read aloud this Scottish prayer that the class members may have heard as children:

**From ghoulies and ghosties
And long-leggedy beasties
And things that go bump in the night,
Good Lord, deliver us!**

❖ Ask: **Although we no longer fear the beasties in the closet and monsters lurking under the bed that we imagined as children, we still have fears. What are some of the fears that many adults face? Where do we seek support as we face our fears?**

❖ Read aloud today's focus statement: **Even though our hopes for the future are grounded in God's past actions, we are human and become fearful. What should we do when fear encroaches? Daniel went to God in prayer.**

(2) Goal 1: Hear the Passionate Words of Daniel's Prayer to God

❖ Select a volunteer to read Daniel 9:4b-14.

❖ Post a sheet of newspaper and encour-

age the adults to call out attributes of God that Daniel mentions.

❖ Read "The Covenant God" from Interpreting the Scripture. Add any other attributes that this reading suggests.

❖ Post a second sheet of newsprint and this time list attributes of God's people that are evident in Daniel's prayer.

❖ Read "Praying It Like It Is" in Interpreting the Scripture. Add attributes of the people as suggested in this reading.

❖ Discuss these questions:

(1) What seems to be Daniel's motivation for praying?

(2) Many churches use a prayer of confession during worship. How would you compare such prayers to the prayer of Daniel? (Many prayers of confession are sincere, but they are more general and not as deeply heartfelt as Daniel's appears to be.)

❖ Wrap up this portion of the lesson by challenging the learners to remember and imitate Daniel's passionate attitude as he approached God's throne of grace.

(3) Goal 2: Express the Passions That Earnest Prayer Evokes in the Learners

❖ Read these quotations about prayer, pausing after each one to invite comment about what it may mean to the students.

■ **"A prayer is not holy chewing gum and you don't have to see how far you can stretch it." (Rabbi Lionel Blue, *Kitchen Blues*)**

■ **"Is prayer your steering wheel or your spare tyre?" (Corrie ten Boom)**

■ **"Prayer is the sum of our relationship with God. We are what we pray. The degree of our faith is the degree of our prayer. Our ability to love is our ability to prayer." (Carlo Carretto, *Lessons from a Desert*)**

■ "God is not a cosmic bell-boy for whom we can press a button to get things." (Harry Emerson Fosdick, *The Meaning of Prayer*)

■ "Every Christian needs an half hour of prayer each day, except when he is busy, then he needs an hour." (St. Francis de Sales)

❖ Form several small groups and encourage the adults to talk about how any of these quotations may evoke passion for prayer. Ask them to consider what drives them to offer prayer. What do they expect from God when they pray? Are they seeking answers and action from God? Or is God's presence sufficient for them?

❖ Bring the groups back together and invite the adults to contemplate this question silently: **How does prayer enable you to be closer to God and to experience divine love, mercy, and forgiveness?**

(4) Goal 3: Identify Elements in Daniel's Prayer That the Learners Can Use to Frame Their Prayers

❖ Distribute paper and pencils. Encourage the students to review Daniel 9:4b-14 in their Bibles to find ideas or phrases that may be useful to them as they create prayers of their own.

❖ Provide time for the adults to write their own prayers. Some may choose to rewrite Daniel's prayer in contemporary English using current words or images. They may want to frame the prayer in terms of a contemporary problem that concerns them.

❖ Allow time for most participants to complete their prayers. Form a circle, if possible, and invite volunteers to read their prayers.

(5) Continue the Journey

❖ Pray that today's participants will wrap their fears and concerns into a prayer that they lift up to God.

Read aloud this preparation for next week's lesson. You may also want to post it on newsprint for the students to copy.

■ **Title: Gabriel's Interpretation**
■ **Background Scripture: Daniel 8**
■ **Lesson Scripture: Daniel 8:19-26**
■ **Focus of the Lesson: Hope points us toward the future. Where can we find help as we seek to discern what the future may hold for us? When he did not understand his vision, Daniel received help from Gabriel to clarify its meaning.**

❖ Post these three activities related to this week's session on newsprint for the students to copy. Challenge the adults to grow spiritually by completing one or more of them.

(1) Make a list of your fears. Think about why each one concerns you. Take time in prayer to hand each one over to God.

(2) Select someone you find difficult to get along with or someone who seems weighed down with life's cares. Pray for this person at least once daily. Be alert for any changes you can see in this person's behavior or attitude.

(3) Recall that Daniel's prayer was focused on confession. Offer prayers of confession for yourself and for your church community.

❖ Sing or read aloud "Sweet Hour of Prayer."

❖ Conclude today's session by leading the class in this benediction, based on the key verses for April 28 from 2 Thessalonians 2:16-17: **Now may our Lord Jesus Christ himself and God our Father, who loved us and through grace gave us eternal comfort and good hope, comfort your hearts and strengthen them in every good work and word.**

UNIT 1: THE KINGDOM OF GOD
GABRIEL'S INTERPRETATION

PREVIEWING THE LESSON

Lesson Scripture: Daniel 8:19-26
Background Scripture: Daniel 8
Key Verse: Daniel 8:26

Focus of the Lesson:
Hope points us toward the future. Where can we find help as we seek to discern what the future may hold for us? When he did not understand his vision, Daniel received help from Gabriel to clarify its meaning.

Goals for the Learners:
(1) to analyze Daniel's vision and Gabriel's interpretation of the vision.
(2) to express their uncertainties when trying to make decisions that affect their future.
(3) to develop spiritual friendships with others who are seeking the kingdom of God.

Pronunciation Guide:
Antiochus Epiphanes (an ti' uh kuhs i pif' uh neez)
apocalyptic (uh pok uh lip' tik)
Belshazzar (bel shaz' uhr)
Maccabee (mak' uh bee)
Nebuchadnezzar (neb uh kuhd nez' uhr)
Seleucid (si loo' sid)

Supplies:
Bibles, newsprint and marker, paper and pencils, hymnals, Bible dictionaries, Bible commentaries

---

READING THE SCRIPTURE

NRSV
Lesson Scripture: Daniel 8:19-26
    [19]He [Gabriel] said, "Listen, and I will tell you what will take place later in the period of wrath; for it refers to the appointed time

CEB
Lesson Scripture: Daniel 8:19-26
    [19]He said, "Now, I am going to tell you what will happen during the time of doom that is coming, because at the appointed

of the end. [20]As for the ram that you saw with the two horns, these are the kings of Media and Persia. [21]The male goat is the king of Greece, and the great horn between its eyes is the first king. [22]As for the horn that was broken, in place of which four others arose, four kingdoms shall arise from his nation, but not with his power.

[23] At the end of their rule,
     when the transgressions have reached
         their full measure,
     a king of bold countenance shall arise,
         skilled in intrigue.
[24] He shall grow strong in power,
     shall cause fearful destruction,
     and shall succeed in what he does.
He shall destroy the powerful
     and the people of the holy ones.
[25] By his cunning
     he shall make deceit prosper
         under his hand,
     and in his own mind he shall be great.
Without warning he shall destroy many
     and shall even rise up against
         the Prince of princes.
But he shall be broken, and not
     by human hands.

[26]**The vision of the evenings and the mornings that has been told is true.** As for you, seal up the vision, for it refers to many days from now."

time there will be an end. [20]The two-horned ram you saw represents the kings of Media and Persia. [21]The long-haired he-goat is the king of Greece, and the big horn between its eyes is the first king. [22]The horn that snapped so that four came up in its place means that four kingdoms will come from one nation, but these four won't have the strength of the first one.

[23]When their kingship nears its end
     and their sins are almost complete,
     a king will step forward.
He will be stern
     and a master of deception.
[24]At the height of his power,
     he will wreak unbelievable destructions.
He will succeed in all he does.
     He will destroy both the mighty
         and the people of the holy ones.
[25]Along with his cunning,
     he will succeed by using deceit.
In his own mind, he will be great.
     In a time of peace,
         he will bring destruction on many,
     opposing even the supreme leader.
But he will be broken—
     and not by a human hand.

[26]**Now this vision of evening and morning, which has been announced, is true.** But you must seal it up, because it is for days far in the future."

UNDERSTANDING THE SCRIPTURE

Daniel 8:1-4. The specificity regarding time ("third year of the reign of King Belshazzar," 8:1) serves here, as it did in the vision explored in our first session (7:1 and following), to anchor these words in a time of political and social transition that created great uncertainty. Thus, Daniel's ensuing vision encompassing what will come offers a sense of stability in times otherwise unstable. The specific geographical references (the particular city, province, and river that serve as the vision's initial setting) provide a degree of tangible grounding in what is soon to be a highly symbolic and dynamic vision. The detail about Daniel "seeing himself" in those locations reminds us that Daniel was situated in Babylon. His visionary transport to this distant location parallels similar ecstatic movements by Ezekiel (Ezekiel 3:12-16; 37:1 and following). They also affirm God's ability to move freely across boundaries thought to be controlled by the empires in question. The horns of the ram, as noted in previous comments on 7:2-8 (see lesson for March 3), serve as an image of power. The three directions indicated in verse 4 are suggestive of the movement of imperial and military expansion, the identity of which will later be identified by Gabriel (8:20-22).

Daniel 8:5-8. The more fantastic elements of the vision now begin to emerge out of its initially time- and place-specific beginnings in the opening verses. The detail of the male goat moving "without touching the ground" (8:5) is a reference to the speed with which this advancing imperial force moved. It is as if there were no natural obstacles to its relentless drive eastward. Three times in these verses the NRSV uses the word "power." The brutality of the power unleashed in the vivid imagery of the battle between ram and goat captures well the rage and force used when one empire drives another into the dust. It is all about power. The breaking of horns, first of the ram and, by the end, of the goat, reveals that even the most entrenched of political and military supremacies will always come to their end. Mortality is not only a mark of human existence but of empires as well. Even the four new horns that grow out of the broken horn of the goat have their days numbered.

Daniel 8:9-13. That reckoning, and rivalry, among the four horns comes quickly, as a "little" horn emerges from one. "Little" may be a subtle insult of this soon-to-be identified power. As the vision unfolds, it is clear that this horn is the one most troubling and immediate in Daniel's vision, and in all likelihood is the most troublesome to the later community and era in which the Book of Daniel was finally composed. Images of this power's "trespassing" on holy places emerge in several ways in this portion of the vision. Growing "as high as the hosts of heaven" (8:10) implies a spiritual pride and arrogance. Likewise, the Temple/ritual language of this power inter-

rupting the "burnt offerings" and overthrowing "the place of his sanctuary" (8:11): More and more the vision is pushing its listeners to connect the symbolic imagery so described with specific acts that beset faithful Jewish worshipers in the middle of the second century B.C. A cry rises up within the vision—and likely within Daniel's eventual second-century audience—that asks God "how long?" The phrase is common in psalms of lament. Those psalms often are attributed to Israel's experience in exile. In this vision, a new "exile" is faced, one where the multiple ritual references (burnt offering, sanctuary) suggest the crisis centers around the Temple.

Daniel 8:14-18. The answer to "how long?" comes in language couched in ritual and symbolism. The ritual reference alludes to the twice-daily sacrifices at the Temple. The symbolism is that the actual days referenced here (divided by two because of the twice-daily sacrifices) would come to 1,150 days. Rendered another way that number comes to almost 3.5 years (half of "7," a number with all manner of symbolic meaning). Daniel's inability to understand the vision is met by an unnamed voice that calls upon Gabriel to help Daniel understand. This is the first time in the Hebrew Scriptures that an angel is named. Gabriel appears in later Jewish apocalyptic writings (1 Enoch, among others). In the New Testament, Gabriel appears to Zechariah and Mary in preparation for the births of John the Baptist and Jesus, respectively. Here, however, Gabriel's role is specifically to explain the meaning of the vision to Daniel.

Daniel 8:19-25. The "period of wrath" suggests times of judgment (Psalm 69:24; Isaiah 10:5). That phrase in verse 19, along with "the end," clearly sets this vision within the framework of apocalyptic literature that anticipates and awaits history's fulfillment by God's hand. In verses 20-21, Gabriel is quite specific in naming the ram as Media/Persia and the goat as the "king of Greece"; certainly Alexander the Great is in mind. At Alexander's death, his empire was divided among four of his generals. Eventually three smaller imperial regimes emerged; in Syria (which included Israel) it was the Seleucid Empire. Scholars agree that the "little horn," the one described here in verses 23-25, was a Seleucid ruler named Antiochus Epiphanes IV. The role of divine intervention in the defeat of Antiochus during the time of the Maccabees is underscored in this passage's cryptic closing statement: "He shall be broken, and not by human hands" (8:25).

Daniel 8:26-27. Gabriel's final word assures that Daniel has not been imagining this vision on his own, but rather it is "true." "Sealing up" the vision (a command repeated in 12:4) suggests keeping a secret of these things. The final verse of the chapter provides a somewhat human touch to all this. So affected by the vision, Daniel becomes ill. Beyond that, Daniel confesses not only dismay but that he "did not understand it." Apocalyptic writing can be troubling, and even when explained, if we trust this verse in Daniel, it can still escape understanding. This means, among other things, there must be more to the entrusting of this vision than simply "knowing" what's going to happen. What that might be will be considered in the final section of Interpreting the Scripture.

INTERPRETING THE SCRIPTURE

Help Offered and Received

Have you ever been in a situation where you have needed the help of another to guide you in understanding some complex or difficult situation? How have you fared when that help was forthcoming—and when it was not? Today's text recounts Gabriel's stepping forward to help Daniel understand the meaning of this vision given to him.

Keep in mind that Daniel had earlier demonstrated a prowess for interpreting dreams (2:24-49; 4:19-27) and "handwriting on the wall" (5:5-29). In two of those instances (2:48; 5:29), Daniel's gift of interpretation resulted in elevation to high rank in the Babylonian regimes of Nebuchadnezzar and Belshazzar. Given that background, it is important to recognize Daniel's openness to receiving help in interpretation. Sometimes, then as now, folks are reluctant to seek help in areas where they are supposed to be authorities or have skills, or to be the ones themselves who may be used to giving the help. Such pride can get in the way when times and situations arise where help is needed. This can be as true in family and vocational situations as it is in our spiritual journeys. Too much confidence in what we know and think we can do (sometimes because we have done it before) can throw up a roadblock when our knowledge and our abilities come up against walls not anticipated or encountered before. One reaction is to dig in, to deny, to not admit our need of others. Another, as evidenced in this passage, is to be open to the help that is available, even and especially when it comes in unexpected ways. For example, did Daniel presume that the response to his "trying to understand" would come in angelic form?

The passage also affirms God as One who would guide us in situations that perplex and defy our understanding, much less our control. The God revealed in Daniel is not an absentee landlord who stays in the wings, leaving us to muddle our way through alone. To be sure, the vehicle for God's help is not always an angel. But there are times when the guidance we find from the faith community or a fellow sojourner, expected or unexpected, might seem to be "angelic" in terms of the helpfulness we receive in timely and gracious ways. So don't be afraid to ask for help, and don't be afraid to offer it as well.

Future Times

Apocalyptic visions (and speculations) about the future did not cease with the Book of Daniel. We have similar examples in our own time: *The Late Great Planet Earth*, the Left Behind series of books (for children and "graphic novels" for adults) and now video games, a "Bible Code Digest" website and software that purports among other things that "codes" for the last names of Prime Minister Benjamin Netanyahu of Israel and President Barack Obama of the United States occur in several apocalyptic passages in Ezekiel 37-40. The imagery reflected in Daniel 8's vision and Gabriel's interpretation lend themselves, as do other such writings including the Book of Revelation, to depictions of the future times as ominous and foreboding places.

Gabriel's interpretation of the vision anchors it in events beginning with Israel's exile in Babylon and ending with the abuses (and downfall) of the Seleucid ruler Antiochus Epiphanes in the middle of the second century B.C. But because Daniel's vision and Gabriel's interpretation are expressed in highly symbolic and "transparent" imagery, they, along with any number of other such writings in the Old and New Testament, have been "reinterpreted" down through history to bring them into compliance with modern-day events (and fears, as witnessed by the Netanyahu and Obama "codes" in Ezekiel).

So what constitutes appropriate use of end-times imagery and interpretations? Does it only have meaning if we can connect it to wars in the Middle East or dislikes of particular national leaders? There can be a certain arrogance of "modernism" abroad when we presume its meaning is only fully known or applicable in our time—whether "our time" was the approach of the year 1000, or the Reformation, or the decades of the twenty-first century. Such a view diminishes the very real power this vision likely had for the community facing Antiochus Epiphanes.

But if we risk taking the Scripture out of context if we transport it to our time, does this mean it is simply an ancient document whose "end" has come and gone? I think not. Listen to the vision's and interpretation's description of what happens when power goes unchecked. Brutality and imperial inflictions of unchecked power are by no means limited to ancient kingdoms and rules. And for those who engage in such abandonment of ethic and compassion and justice for the sake of extending authority and control among us, the message of the vision is clear: All such power runs its course. If "absolute power corrupts absolutely," as Lord Acton asserted in 1887, so then Daniel's and Gabriel's words also affirm that absolute power comes to an end absolutely. The imagery of once-proud horns that now go broken are a contemporary word the church is urged to continue to bring when power and privilege presume they go on forever. They do not. In spite of hard times that may well come, as they have always come, God remains sovereign. That is our vision for the future—that it belongs to the kingdom of our Lord and of his Christ.

Living by Trust

"The vision of the evenings and the mornings that has been told is *true*" (8:26, key verse, emphasis added). Gabriel asserts to Daniel that what he has seen will come to pass. He can trust that to be the case.

In the end, the vision does come down to a matter of trust—trust that the God who has provided this glimpse of what will come to be can be depended upon. Notice something else that is critical in what Gabriel is affirming. As you reread the interpretation, and even the vision itself, there are very few specifics of what the "end game" will be. There is a great deal that will come to pass in the process, but not so much stating how things will be after the fact. In other words, the vision Gabriel affirms to be true is also inherently incomplete. There are a great many details left open. Sometimes the church and its "seers" go a bit far in filling in all those details—whether with timetables or twenty-first century "revisions" of who the beasts are, or whether rapture is premillenial or postmillenial. We occupy ourselves with all these things, as if they can somehow make us feel any more secure.

They cannot. For in the end, it will not be knowledge of apocalyptic details that saves us but trust in God. Trust that God's kingdom and realm are irresistible, despite all sorts of protestations to the contrary by powers that want to hold on tight and do as they please. Trust that God's kingdom and realm will come in all its goodness and grace, despite all of the invocations of fear to summon up faith. Faith is not fear. Faith is trust.

Gabriel's command to "seal up the vision" (8:26) might be a refreshing word in our time. For perhaps we then could set aside our speculations and anxieties and arguments about the future times, and exchange them for such trust in God as revealed in acts of service and love in this time. After all, what do you think God most values for revealing this kingdom we say we so long for?

SHARING THE SCRIPTURE

Preparing Our Hearts

Explore this week's devotional reading, found in Psalm 91:1-12. This psalm, which soldiers have often carried into battle, expresses the writer's absolute confidence that God will protect him in all circumstances. No matter how terrifying the situation, God can be depended upon to offer refuge from enemies and evil. Do you share the psalmist's trust in God as a refuge and fortress? Call upon God now to keep you safe.

Pray that you and the adult students will continually seek the God upon whom you can rely.

Preparing Our Minds

Study the background Scripture from Daniel 8 and the lesson Scripture from Daniel 8:19-26.

Consider this question as you prepare the lesson: *Where can we find help as we seek to discern what the future may hold for us?*

Write on newsprint:
❑ information for next week's lesson, found under "Continue the Journey."
❑ activities for further spiritual growth in "Continue the Journey."

Review the "Introduction," "The Big Picture," "Close-up," and "Faith in Action." Consider how you will use this additional information, which immediately precedes the first lesson, for this session.

Prepare the suggested lecture for "Analyze Daniel's Vision and Gabriel's Interpretation of the Vision."

LEADING THE CLASS

(1) Gather to Learn

❖ Greet the class members. Introduce any guests and help them feel at home.

❖ Pray that those who have come today

will be open to seeking help to discern God's will for their lives.

❖ Invite the adults to recall times in their lives when they had an urgent concern about the future, and then discuss these questions:

(1) **What prompted your concern?** (Perhaps, for example, a change in job, location, or family status caused some anxiety.)

(2) **What steps did you take to try to discern what your course of action should be?**

(3) **To whom did you turn for help in deciding what to do?**

❖ Read aloud today's focus statement: **Hope points us toward the future. Where can we find help as we seek to discern what the future may hold for us? When he did not understand his vision, Daniel received help from Gabriel to clarify its meaning.**

(2) Goal 1: Analyze Daniel's Vision and Gabriel's Interpretation of the Vision

❖ Present a lecture based on Daniel 8:1-4 and 8:14-18 of Understanding the Scripture to provide background for today's Scripture lesson. This portion of Scripture describes the vision that Gabriel will later interpret for Daniel.

❖ Choose a volunteer to read Daniel 8:19-26.

❖ Read aloud again today's key verse, Daniel 8:26. Read or retell "Living by Trust" in Interpreting the Scripture.

❖ Form four groups. Give commentaries to two groups and encourage them to learn all they can about Gabriel's interpretation of Daniel's vision. Invite students with study Bibles to consult them for help as well. If possible, give at least one copy of *The New International Lesson Annual* to a group. Give Bible dictionaries to the other two groups. Suggest that one group research Alexander the Great (represented by the male goat in verse 21) and another group research

Antiochus IV Epiphanes, the "king of bold countenance" introduced in verse 23.

❖ Call the groups together and ask each one to report its findings. Conclude by pointing out verse 26, in which Gabriel assures Daniel that the vision is "true" and that it "refers to many days from now."

(3) Goal 2: Express Uncertainties When Trying to Make Decisions That Affect the Future

❖ Distribute paper and pencils. Invite the learners to number their papers from one through five. Read aloud this list and invite the learners to write True or False in each space.

(1) **I put off making a decision as long as I can because I worry about making a mistake that I cannot undo.**

(2) **I feel very unsure of my own ability to make decisions, so I rely heavily upon other people to advise me.**

(3) **Even after I make a decision, I often review my reasoning to see if I should change my mind.**

(4) **I am fearful about the future, no matter what decisions I make.**

(5) **The world is such an uncertain place that I am filled with anxiety when I begin to think about what the future might hold for me.**

❖ Note that although there are no right or wrong answers, the more Trues one has selected, the greater that person's uncertainty about making decisions that affect the future. Challenge those who have a lot of Trues to think about why they feel so uncertain. Is there anything they can do, or anyone they can seek out, to help them feel more confident that the future is in God's hands?

(4) Goal 3: Develop Spiritual Friendships With Others Who Are Seeking the Kingdom of God

❖ Read "Help Offered and Received" from Interpreting the Scripture.

❖ Point out that although Daniel was able to receive help from an angel, we can all have spiritual friends who are able to help us as we seek God's kingdom. Invite the class members to call out characteristics of a Christian friend whom they would be likely to consult when help is needed. Record these ideas on newsprint.

❖ Provide time for the adults to consider the characteristics that are most important to them. Also ask them to identify people they know who may possess these traits and write these names on their papers. They need not share these names with other class members.

❖ Challenge the students to contact at least one of the people they have identified to see how the two might work together, perhaps helping each other as spiritual friends.

(5) Continue the Journey

❖ Pray that today's attendees will go forth assured that because God is in charge, fear and suffering will ultimately end.

❖ Read aloud this preparation for next week's lesson. You may also want to post it on newsprint for the students to copy.
- ■ **Title: Resurrection Hope**
- ■ **Background Scripture: Luke 22:14-30**
- ■ **Lesson Scripture: Luke 22:14-30**
- ■ **Focus of the Lesson: Humans seek to exaggerate their own importance. How can we overcome the burning desire to serve ourselves first and others later? Jesus says**

those who serve others will eat the bread and sip the wine at the table he has set for them in heaven.

❖ Post these three activities related to this week's session on newsprint for the students to copy. Challenge the adults to grow spiritually by completing one or more of them.

(1) **Act as a sounding board for someone who needs guidance. Although you cannot provide definitive answers, do whatever you can to help this person see what the options are and where each of these choices might lead.**

(2) **Research the lives and work of Alexander the Great and Antiochus IV Epiphanes, both of whom are highlighted in today's reading.**

(3) **Use a concordance to locate other examples of dreams in both the Old and New Testaments. Notice especially those of Joseph in Genesis and those of another Joseph in Matthew. Who interprets these dreams?**

❖ Sing or read aloud "Be Thou My Vision."

❖ Conclude today's session by leading the class in this benediction, based on the key verses for April 28 from 2 Thessalonians 2:16-17: **Now may our Lord Jesus Christ himself and God our Father, who loved us and through grace gave us eternal comfort and good hope, comfort your hearts and strengthen them in every good work and word.**

UNIT 2: RESURRECTION HOPE
THE LORD'S SUPPER

PREVIEWING THE LESSON

Lesson Scripture: Luke 22:14-30
Background Scripture: Luke 22:14-30
Key Verse: Luke 22:26

Focus of the Lesson:

Humans seek to exaggerate their own importance. How can we overcome the burning desire to serve ourselves first and others later? Jesus says those who serve others will eat the bread and sip the wine at the table he has set for them in heaven.

Goals for the Learners:

(1) to understand the connection between the Lord's Supper and Jesus' teaching on service during that meal.
(2) to value the ideal of serving others in contrast to being served.
(3) to identify ways to express humility as exemplified by Christ.

Supplies:

Bibles, newsprint and marker, paper and pencils, hymnals, bread, plate, grape juice, cup

---

READING THE SCRIPTURE

NRSV
Lesson Scripture: Luke 22:14-30

¹⁴When the hour came, he took his place at the table, and the apostles with him. ¹⁵He said to them, "I have eagerly desired to eat this Passover with you before I suffer; ¹⁶for I tell you, I will not eat it until it is fulfilled in the kingdom of God." ¹⁷Then he took a cup, and after giving thanks he said, "Take this and divide it among yourselves; ¹⁸for I tell you that from now on I will not drink of the fruit of the vine until the kingdom of God comes." ¹⁹Then he took a loaf of bread, and when he had given thanks, he broke it and

CEB
Lesson Scripture: Luke 22:14-30

¹⁴When the time came, Jesus took his place at the table, and the apostles joined him. ¹⁵He said to them, "I have earnestly desired to eat this Passover with you before I suffer. ¹⁶I tell you, I won't eat it until it is fulfilled in God's kingdom." ¹⁷After taking a cup and giving thanks, he said, "Take this and share it among yourselves. ¹⁸I tell you that from now on I won't drink from the fruit of the vine until God's kingdom has come." ¹⁹After taking the bread and giving

gave it to them, saying, "This is my body, which is given for you. Do this in remembrance of me." ²⁰And he did the same with the cup after supper, saying, "This cup that is poured out for you is the new covenant in my blood. ²¹But see, the one who betrays me is with me, and his hand is on the table. ²²For the Son of Man is going as it has been determined, but woe to that one by whom he is betrayed!" ²³Then they began to ask one another which one of them it could be who would do this.

²⁴A dispute also arose among them as to which one of them was to be regarded as the greatest. ²⁵But he said to them, "The kings of the Gentiles lord it over them; and those in authority over them are called benefactors. ²⁶But not so with you; rather the greatest among you must become like the youngest, and the leader like one who serves. ²⁷For who is greater, the one who is at the table or the one who serves? Is it not the one at the table? But I am among you as one who serves.

²⁸"You are those who have stood by me in my trials; ²⁹and I confer on you, just as my Father has conferred on me, a kingdom, ³⁰so that you may eat and drink at my table in my kingdom, and you will sit on thrones judging the twelve tribes of Israel."

thanks, he broke it and gave it to them, saying, "This is my body, which is given for you. Do this in remembrance of me." ²⁰In the same way, he took the cup after the meal and said, "This cup is the new covenant by my blood, which is poured out for you.

²¹"But, look! My betrayer is with me; his hand is on this table. ²²The Human One goes just as it has been determined. But how terrible it is for that person who betrays him." ²³They began to argue among themselves about which of them it could possibly be who would do this.

²⁴An argument broke out among the disciples over which one of them should be regarded as the greatest.

²⁵But Jesus said to them, "The kings of the Gentiles rule over their subjects, and those in authority over them are called 'friends of the people.' ²⁶But that's not the way it will be with you. Instead, the greatest among you must become like a person of lower status and the leader like a servant. ²⁷So which one is greater, the one who is seated at the table or the one who serves at the table? Isn't it the one who is seated at the table? But I am among you as one who serves.

²⁸"You are the ones who have continued with me in my trials. ²⁹And I confer royal power on you just as my Father granted royal power to me. ³⁰Thus you will eat and drink at my table in my kingdom, and you will sit on thrones overseeing the twelve tribes of Israel."

UNDERSTANDING THE SCRIPTURE

Introduction. This second unit shifts from the apocalyptic style and imagery of Daniel to New Testament passages more "mainstream" in their style. Prophetic visions give way to narratives and reflections on hope in light of Jesus' resurrection. But first, on this Sunday of Palms and Passion, this session explores Luke's

account of the Last Supper, where hope takes tabled form.

Luke 22:14-16. The "hour" of the Passover meal refers to the meal's traditional beginning at sundown. Luke's use of "apostles" here and five other times in his Gospel, rather than identifying them as "disciples," stands in stark contrast to Mark, who uses "apostles" twice, and Matthew, who use the term only once in his Gospel. Tables of this era were low, as guests typically reclined on cushions rather than sitting on chairs. The words for "Passover" and "suffer" are almost identical in Greek (both words are reflected in the English "paschal," a term used in some traditions in celebrations of communion where Jesus is the "paschal lamb"). Jesus' words, "I will not eat it until it is fulfilled in the kingdom of God," could sound as if he might not have eaten this meal with the disciples. Most scholars, however, conclude that verse 16 indicates his not eating this meal *again* until the kingdom's fulfillment, pointing to his expressed eager desire to share this meal with them.

Luke 22:17-20. Contextual and textual issues make these verses intriguing. To begin with, in contrast to the accounts of the Lord's Supper in Matthew (26:26-29), Mark (14:22-25), and 1 Corinthians (11:23-26) (John records a foot washing, not a meal), Luke has not one cup that follows the bread, but two cups, one before and one after the bread. It is also to be noted that verses 19b-20, which speak of the cup given after supper, are not included in some manuscripts in Luke. The NRSV and most other translations accept the weight of manuscript evidence that argues for their inclusion. The matter of two cups versus one might find explanation in Passover meal traditions. In present-day Judaism (and there are issues as to whether these traditions were in place at the time of Jesus), the table liturgy of the Passover meal in Jewish homes involves a series of cups. As in verse 16, verse 18 connects the meal with anticipations of the kingdom's fulfillment. Hope is as much ingrained in this table as is remembrance. This section closes by specifying this table's connection to covenant making.

Luke 22:21-23. As with the other Gospels, Luke narrates the betrayal of Judas as part of the table's setting. But Luke differs in one regard. In Matthew (26:21) and Mark (14:18), the announcement of betrayal at hand precedes the sharing of bread and cup, leaving the door open as to whether Judas might not have stayed for the meal. No such doubt is in Luke's account. Granted, this chapter opened with Judas conferring with the authorities as to how Judas might betray Jesus. But in Luke, Jesus clearly shares bread and cup with all the apostles. For when he announces the imminent betrayal, he does so by saying the hand of the betrayer is "with me . . . on the table" (22:21). The declaration of "woe to that one" hearkens back to Luke's narration of Jesus' Beatitudes in 6:20-26, where blessings are paired with woes. The apostles' ensuing questioning of one another reveals that their discussion was not so much soul searching (*am I the one?*) as it was a reflexive effort to assign blame (*are you the one?*).

Luke 22:24-27. The apostles next engage in a dispute over who was to be seen as greatest among them. Luke does not provide any background details for what might have generated this argument (Mark 10:35-45 relates a similar story, though setting it well before the Lord's Supper). Some suggest that the dispute may have been generated by their places of seating (reclining) at the table, out of traditions relating prestige of position with place at table. Jesus draws a sharp contrast between the way power (the fundamental measure of greatness) is typically exercised in the world around them with the way greatness is to be viewed and practiced among them. The term "benefactor" is highly ironic. The word's component syllables in English, as in Greek, literally mean "good doer." Yet benefactors were creations of a system where wealth and power were concentrated in a few, whose "charity" gained them this title while leaving the inequalities intact. The truly key word in this passage is "serves." It translates a Greek verb that describes the action of a table servant. In his Gospel Luke often uses themes of reversal (the songs of Zechariah and Mary, the story of the rich man and Lazarus). Here the reversal is seeing the role and identity of a lowly table servant as precisely the answer to the question of who is the greatest. Jesus' teaching is not merely theoretical, as verse 27 closes with the insight that Jesus himself stands among them as one who "serves tables."

Luke 22:28-30. These final verses of the Lord's Supper account return to a theme stressed in its opening verses: the kingdom of God. Once again there is irony in Jesus' words that "you are those who have stood by me in my trials" (22:28). In the next few hours, the apostles will be nowhere close to Jesus when literal trials descend into crucifixion. These words here frame an attitude of grace to those whose faltering has not come to an end. Such grace is also evident in the "conferral" of the kingdom and seats on thrones. What the apostles had earlier argued over, places of greatness, will now come not because of striving but from the free hand of God. The closing image of the apostles sitting in judgment finds something of a parallel in Matthew 19:28, though, as with Mark's parallel account of the arguments over greatness, Matthew's words occur before the Lord's Supper and even before Holy Week.

INTERPRETING THE SCRIPTURE

Lord's Supper as Enacting Covenant

When Jesus speaks the word "covenant" in Luke 22:20, he brings to the table the rich traditions and imagery of covenant within Judaism. Experiences of covenant making form key turning points in the Old Testament. After the Flood, God makes a covenant with Noah and all the earth that "never again" (9:11) will waters seek to destroy all life (Genesis 9:8-17). Covenant making next occurs with Abram in Genesis 15. After deliverance from Egypt, God engages in covenant making with Israel at Sinai in the giving of Torah (Exodus 19:5; 20). In the midst of exile, Jeremiah foresees God's making of a new covenant, where law comes engraved not on stone but on the heart (Jeremiah 31:31).

So before we jump too hastily from this meal directly into our understanding of it as initiation of the sacrament of communion, we need to hold it in its very Jewish context of covenant making: "the new covenant in my blood" (Luke 22:20). For to rightly understand the Lord's Supper involves a grasp of what covenant making meant to a very Jewish Jesus and disciples gathered on Passover.

The thrust of Old Testament covenant making is to fashion new community. With Noah, the newness brought to community entails no longer having to live in fear of being inundated by God. With Abraham, the newness brought to community is a promised people borne of what seemed to be a barren couple. With Moses at Sinai, the newness brought to community is a clear statement of how a covenant community is to conduct its relationships with God and with one another. With Jeremiah, the newness brought to community is the hope of God's favor and wisdom engraved on human hearts.

The Lord's Supper, as an act of covenant making in that long line of Jewish traditions, likewise aims at a new community: a community made new by remembrance of life given and service rendered for our sake, a community made new by this table's implicit commission to go and do likewise. The Lord's Supper, as an act of covenant making, lifts our sometimes divisive squabbling over the mystery of the real presence of Christ in bits of bread and wine or juice and restores us, individually and as communities, to the meal's overarching gratitude. Such gratitude bids us to live our lives in the example Christ gives us: in a loaf broken, in a cup poured out, in a life of service rendered for others.

Embodying the Servanthood of Jesus

Servanthood finds its first expression at the table in the symbols of bread and cup. But symbolism sometimes needs to be unpacked, particularly when actions are not seen beneath their surface. That clearly seems to be the case with the apostles, who shortly after sharing bread and cup suddenly get all tangled up in an argument as to who among them was the greatest. *Oh, those befuddled followers*, we may think with two thousand years of hindsight to enlighten us, not to mention protect us. How could they not get it?

To which they might reply, were they to be given the opportunity to speak across the ages, "Why didn't we get it? Look around, why don't you get it after all this time?"

Why might they say such a thing? Read the words of Jesus in Luke 22:25-27. Do they describe how power is always exercised in your congregation, whether in the leadership meetings or around the midweek coffee tables? Are local and regional church structures entirely absent of "lording it over" when it comes to authority? Do the servants among us really rise to the top, as Jesus seeks? Or do we, from time to time, engage in contemporary versions of disputes over greatness (as in "who should get the final word among us")?

The liturgy of the Evangelical and Reformed Church, in which I grew up, called for the *Agnus Dei* ("Lamb of God, who takes away the sins of the world, have mercy on us") to be used immediately before Communion, even though a prayer of confession already occurred earlier. Looking back, I see why. Even when we get to the table, like those disciples of old, we sometimes can't get over old habits.

Yet Christ bids us come, and in coming, to embody in our lives the servanthood embodied in Christ. That in itself is an act of grace. God opens the table, knowing what kind of company the Christ will be keeping. God entrusts the task and challenge to be the body of Christ on earth today to folks like us—not perfect ones, not ones who have all the answers, not ones who never let their words run ahead of their actions. We, not somebody else, are to live and serve in ways that do not lord it over others, or that do not dwell on pride of position, ecclesial or otherwise. We, not somebody else, are called to serve as the Christ who came among us as one who serves, and who comes even now in remembered bread and cup, in anticipated reign of God.

Tabled Hope

As noted earlier in the Understanding the Scripture portion, the passage and the table open and close with references to the kingdom of God, which is to say, the passage and table begin and end on the note of hope. Whenever we gather to remember and celebrate the meal Jesus shared with disciples, we are to do so with hope.

There is hope, in the table's opening, of reunion with Christ, where our gathering now anticipates that promise of Christ sharing it again with us when the kingdom's fulfillment comes. Think of those with whom you will gather the next time you celebrate this meal, and think about those with whom you once shared this meal but cannot any longer, whether because of distance or death. This table's hope brings the anticipation of other reunions as well. We have this hope not for the sake of nostalgia but for the sake of our laboring now as servants, trusting we do not do so in vain. For our trust is in the fulfillment of God's promised realm.

There is hope, in the table's closing, of our being given places at Jesus' table in that time of fulfillment. Sometimes, we lose our "place" in life, or grieve as others do. The loss of place may come from estrangement or shame. The loss of place may come from violence or Alzheimer's. If all we had were this life's horizons, we might lose confidence as so many wanderers, without place or mooring. On the other hand, sometimes we become so engaged in making a place for ourselves, carving out our own legacy on our own terms, we miss the gift and grace of knowing ourselves loved beyond our résumés or titles. The hope of this table is for place given to us by the grace of God in Jesus Christ: a gift that can be either extraordinarily uplifting or remarkably humbling. However that may be for us, and sometimes it may be a bit of both, we have this tabled hope that assures us of place— and in that assurance, emboldens our servanthood of the Christ. Share the bread, share the cup, and share the service that this table offers to us for the sake of life.

SHARING THE SCRIPTURE

Preparing Our Hearts

Explore this week's devotional reading, found in 1 Corinthians 10:14-22. Here Paul refers to the cup and bread as a "sharing" (10:16). The Greek root is the same as "partners," which are referred to in verses 18 and 20. This Greek word is also where we get our word "communion." People may choose to worship God or to worship idols, but those who choose God must have nothing to do with idols. Believers cannot be "partners" or in "communion" with idols. Paul therefore challenges his readers to turn their backs on pagan rituals. What practices do you need to turn away from to strengthen your relationship with God?

Pray that you and the adult students will serve God and God alone.

Preparing Our Minds

Study the background Scripture and the lesson Scripture, both of which are from Luke 22:14-30.

Consider this question as you prepare the lesson: *How can we overcome the burning desire to serve ourselves first and others later?*

Write on newsprint:

❑ information for next week's lesson, found under "Continue the Journey."

❑ activities for further spiritual growth in "Continue the Journey."

Review the "Introduction," "The Big Picture," "Close-up," and "Faith in Action." Consider how you will use this additional information, which immediately precedes the first lesson, for this session.

Plan to bring a loaf of bread, a plate, a cup, and some grape juice (or wine) to set on a table as a visible reminder of the elements of Jesus' Last Supper. If you would like the class to take Communion, invite your pastor to be present, since in most faith traditions only an ordained elder is authorized to consecrate the elements.

LEADING THE CLASS

(1) Gather to Learn

❖ Greet the class members. Introduce any guests and help them feel at home.

❖ Pray that all who have come on this Palm/Passion Sunday will enter into the humble service of Jesus.

❖ Tell this story: **At a summer conference held at a large church campground, participants noticed a young man who seemed very much out of place. In contrast to the neatly dressed and appropriately groomed campers, this man was raggedy** and unkempt. He didn't really bother anyone or ask for anything, but he didn't fit in either. People just ignored him. The message of the closing service was based on Matthew 25:45: "Just as you did not do it to one of the least of these, you did not do it to me." Imagine the audience's surprise when this apparent misfit stepped forward to preach. He was the pastor the organizers had selected to bring this message. He told the stunned congregation: "No one tried to include me in anything. No one asked me if I needed help. No one invited me to the dining hall. No one sat down to listen to my story. . . . My appearance offended you, and you left me out."

❖ Ask: **Why do you think most people are so reluctant to serve those in need?**

❖ Read aloud today's focus statement: **Humans seek to exaggerate their own importance. How can we overcome the burning desire to serve ourselves first and others later? Jesus says those who serve others will eat the bread and sip the wine at the table he has set for them in heaven.**

(2) Goal 1: Understand the Connection Between the Lord's Supper and Jesus' Teaching on Service During That Meal

❖ Ask: **What do you think about or meditate on when you participate in the Lord's Supper?**

❖ Select a volunteer to read Luke 22:14-30. Advise the adults to be aware of what the disciples were thinking about when they were at the table with Jesus.

❖ Discuss these questions:
(1) **What were the disciples thinking about?** (Be sure the class understands that even in the midst of these final hours with Jesus the disciples were focused on their own greatness.)
(2) **Note that in verse 20 Jesus refers to "the new covenant in my blood." How does this covenant relate to prior covenants that God**

has made with people such as those with Abraham and Moses? (Use information from "Lord's Supper as Enacting Covenant" in Interpreting the Scripture to expand the discussion. Be sure to include the idea of forming a new community.)
(3) **How do you experience a connection between the Lord's Supper and serving others?**

❖ Conclude this portion by reading "Embodying the Servanthood of Jesus" from Interpreting the Scripture.

(3) Goal 2: Value the Ideal of Serving Others in Contrast to Being Served

❖ Invite the adults to meditate on the meaning of this quotation attributed to Corrie ten Boom and the way that it might apply to their own lives: **"Life is a lot like tennis—the one who can serve best seldom loses."**

❖ Ask these questions:
(1) **How does ten Boom's statement go against the grain of what society teaches about service?**
(2) **How does this statement reflect what Jesus was teaching his disciples in Luke 22?**
(3) **In what ways do you see this statement being enacted by your congregation?**

(4) Goal 3: Identify Ways to Express Humility as Exemplified by Christ

❖ Point out the bread and cup of Communion that you have placed on a table. Note that by sacrificially giving his body and blood Jesus humbled himself in ways that are unimaginable to us.

❖ Post a sheet of newsprint and invite the participants to call out ways that they too can express humility. *Serving those in need, valuing the opinions of others, taking the time to listen and interact with others, and showing impartiality to all persons* are but a few examples.

❖ **Option:** If you have made arrangements for your pastor to serve the Lord's Supper, do so now. Remind the adults that in partaking of the Supper they are also participating in the humble service of Jesus.

(5) Continue the Journey

❖ Pray that all who have come today will go forth to serve.

❖ Read aloud this preparation for next week's lesson. You may also want to post it on newsprint for the students to copy.

- **Title: The Lord Has Risen Indeed!**
- **Background Scripture: Luke 24:1-35**
- **Lesson Scripture: Luke 24:13-21, 28-35**
- **Focus of the Lesson: Sometimes humans are caught up in their sense of gloom and despair. How can we be encouraged to see and take advantage of the good news surrounding us? Jesus opened the eyes of two followers he encountered on the road to Emmaus, and they recognized that Jesus had risen.**

❖ Post these three activities related to this week's session on newsprint for the students to copy. Challenge the adults to grow spiritually by completing one or more of them.

(1) Borrow a hymnal and review the service(s) there for the Lord's Supper. Compare the service(s) with the biblical accounts, particularly the one from Luke 22:14-23, to see how your faith tradition incorporates these accounts into its liturgy.

(2) Identify at least one individual or group whom you could serve this week. Do whatever you can, remembering that you are performing this service on behalf of Jesus.

(3) Immerse yourself in the events of Holy Week. What do Jesus' actions and teachings from Passion/Palm Sunday through Good Friday teach you about service in God's kingdom? How might you enter into such service?

❖ Sing or read aloud "For the Bread Which You Have Broken."

❖ Conclude today's session by leading the class in this benediction, based on the key verses for April 28 from 2 Thessalonians 2:16-17: **Now may our Lord Jesus Christ himself and God our Father, who loved us and through grace gave us eternal comfort and good hope, comfort your hearts and strengthen them in every good work and word.**

UNIT 2: RESURRECTION HOPE

THE LORD HAS RISEN INDEED!

PREVIEWING THE LESSON

Lesson Scripture: Luke 24:13-21, 28-35
Background Scripture: Luke 24:1-35
Key Verse: Luke 24:31

Focus of the Lesson:

Sometimes humans are caught up in their sense of gloom and despair. How can we be encouraged to see and take advantage of the good news surrounding us? Jesus opened the eyes of two followers he encountered on the road to Emmaus, and they recognized that Jesus had risen.

Goals for the Learners:

(1) to review the story of the walk to Emmaus by Cleopas and the other disciple, who have a life-changing meeting with the risen Lord.
(2) to identify with the travelers on the Emmaus road in order to raise their awareness of the places Jesus meets them in their personal journeys.
(3) to celebrate jubilantly the risen Christ.

Pronunciation Guide:

Cleopas (klee' oh puhs)
Emmaus (i may' us)

Supplies:

Bibles, newsprint and marker, paper and pencils, hymnals

READING THE SCRIPTURE

NRSV
Lesson Scripture: Luke 24:13-21, 28-35

¹³Now on that same day two of them were going to a village called Emmaus, about seven miles from Jerusalem, ¹⁴and talking with each other about all these things that had happened. ¹⁵While they were talking

CEB
Lesson Scripture: Luke 24:13-21, 28-35

¹³On that same day, two disciples were traveling to a village called Emmaus, about seven miles from Jerusalem. ¹⁴They were talking to each other about everything that had happened. ¹⁵While they were discussing

and discussing, Jesus himself came near and went with them, [16]but their eyes were kept from recognizing him. [17]And he said to them, "What are you discussing with each other while you walk along?" They stood still, looking sad. [18]Then one of them, whose name was Cleopas, answered him, "Are you the only stranger in Jerusalem who does not know the things that have taken place there in these days?" [19]He asked them, "What things?" They replied, "The things about Jesus of Nazareth, who was a prophet mighty in deed and word before God and all the people, [20]and how our chief priests and leaders handed him over to be condemned to death and crucified him. [21]But we had hoped that he was the one to redeem Israel. Yes, and besides all this, it is now the third day since these things took place."

[28]As they came near the village to which they were going, he walked ahead as if he were going on. [29]But they urged him strongly, saying, "Stay with us, because it is almost evening and the day is now nearly over." So he went in to stay with them. [30]When he was at the table with them, he took bread, blessed and broke it, and gave it to them. [31]**Then their eyes were opened, and they recognized him;** and he vanished from their sight. [32]They said to each other, "Were not our hearts burning within us while he was talking to us on the road, while he was opening the scriptures to us?" [33]That same hour they got up and returned to Jerusalem; and they found the eleven and their companions gathered together. [34]They were saying, "The Lord has risen indeed, and he has appeared to Simon!" [35]Then they told what had happened on the road, and how he had been made known to them in the breaking of the bread.

these things, Jesus himself arrived and joined them on their journey. [16]They were prevented from recognizing him.

[17]He said to them, "What are you talking about as you walk along?" They stopped, their faces downcast.

[18]The one named Cleopas replied, "Are you the only visitor to Jerusalem who is unaware of the things that have taken place there over the last few days?"

[19]He said to them, "What things?"

They said to him, "The things about Jesus of Nazareth. Because of his powerful deeds and words, he was recognized by God and all the people as a prophet. [20]But our chief priests and our leaders handed him over to be sentenced to death, and they crucified him. [21]We had hoped he was the one who would redeem Israel. All these things happened three days ago."

[28]When they came to Emmaus, he acted as if he was going on ahead. [29]But they urged him, saying, "Stay with us. It's nearly evening, and the day is almost over." So, he went in to stay with them. [30]After he took his seat at the table with them, he took the bread, blessed and broke it, and gave it to them. [31]**Their eyes were opened and they recognized him,** but he disappeared from their sight. [32]They said to each other, "Weren't our hearts on fire when he spoke to us along the road and when he explained the scriptures for us?"

[33]They got up right then and returned to Jerusalem. They found the eleven and their companions gathered together. [34]They were saying to each other, "The Lord really has risen! He appeared to Simon!" [35]Then the two disciples described what had happened along the road and how Jesus was made known to them as he broke the bread.

UNDERSTANDING THE SCRIPTURE

Luke 24:1-7. Luke alone among the Gospels does not name the women who come to the tomb at the beginning of the Easter narrative; their names do not appear until verse 10. In one sense, Luke had already placed them in the "scene" as keeping vigil, so their names are not needed until it comes time to identify who brought the news of Easter to the disciples. He already reported that they had seen the tomb, prepared the burial elements, and rested on the Sabbath (23:55-56). Luke says two men greet the women in the tomb, in contrast to Matthew (28:2-3) and Mark (16:5), who indicate there is but one. Interestingly, the kernel of their message to the women that appears in Luke and Mark and Matthew—"he is not here, but has risen"—is missing from some manuscripts of Luke. The reference to Galilee in verse 6 underscores that Jesus' teaching of not only passion and crucifixion but also raising had not been held back until the final days in Holy Week, but had been part of the journey that led to Jerusalem.

Luke 24:8-12. All four Gospels agree that Mary Magdalene was among the women who went to the tomb. Mary the mother of James also appears in Mark 16:1, and may be the "other Mary" referenced in Matthew 28:1. Joanna appears in no other Gospel's Easter narrative besides Luke (she is first mentioned in 8:3 as one of the women who provided resources for Jesus and the disciples, where she is also identified as the wife of Herod's steward named Chuza). The women's remembrance of Jesus' words refers to the angels' encouragement to "remember how he told you" in verse 6.

The reporting of their experience to the apostles is ironic, as "apostle" became a technical term in the church for one "sent out" (the literal meaning of the word) to witness to Jesus' resurrection (Acts 1:21-22). Thus, the witnesses first had to have the witness of the women. The response of the apostles to their "apostling" by the women's witness to resurrection is underwhelming, to say the least. These eventual witnesses consider the women's proclamation to be an "idle tale" (24:11). While Peter does run to the tomb afterward, Luke mentions only amazement, not faith, as his response. It should be noted that not all ancient manuscripts of Luke contain verse 12. In those writings, Easter morning ends with the disciples not believing.

Luke 24:13-16. Luke alone tells the Emmaus road story, though Mark 16:12-13 apparently alludes to it. The exact location of Emmaus is unclear. Some Lukan manuscripts say Emmaus is seven miles away ("sixty stadia," an ancient measure of distance), while others indicate the distance as 160 stadia. Two villages bearing this name exist at those approximate distances (one would reflect a round-trip of the textual "60 stadia"). The inability of the two disciples to recognize Jesus is not attributed to any fault or grief on their part, but rather "their eyes were kept from recognizing him" (24:16). The lack of recognition parallels the Easter account in John 20:14-15, where Mary Magdalene sees Jesus but mistakes him for a gardener. Sight alone, particularly in John but also here in Luke, is not a synonym for faith. One does not see God in order to trust. If anything, the reverse would be more accurate.

Luke 24:17-24. In the dialogue between the two disciples and Jesus, it is Cleopas who first carries the bulk of the conversation. Jesus is confessed as standing in the prophetic line of Israel, a possibility ironically also held (and feared) by Herod (9:7-8). Hopes are confessed of his being the one who would redeem Israel, an echo of Zechariah's prophecy at the beginning of Luke (1:68-69). "Astounded" is as far as these and the other disciples can go in response to the women's testimony (24:22).

Luke 24:25-27. Jesus' critique of the disciples in verse 25 as "foolish" and "slow of heart to believe" calls to mind an earlier upbraiding of disciples who failed to heal a possessed child ("you faithless and perverse generation," 9:41). In both cases, the issue of faith (and the lack thereof) is paramount in Jesus' words and concern. Luke depicts Jesus' interpreting "all the scriptures" by referencing "Moses and all the prophets" in verse 27. There had not yet been a final decision, at the time of Jesus, as to what parts of the materials categorized as "Writings" would be included in the Old Testament canon of Torah (attributed to Moses) and Prophets.

Luke 24:28-32. Hospitality was an honored tradition in Judaism and in the Middle Eastern region in general. Thus, the invitation by the two for Jesus to stay with them likely intended not only a meal but also a resting place for the night. Luke does not reveal whether one of the disciples was from Emmaus, and had a place to stay already, or whether some other arrangement for food and lodging had been made. The actions at the table ("took bread, blessed, broke, gave") mirror not only the Passover meal account (22:19) but also the feeding of the five thousand (9:16). Luke does not detail the *means* by which their eyes were opened but only the *time* of opening ("then," as in when bread was blessed and broken and given). As mysteriously as recognition came to the two, so Jesus "vanished from their sight" (24:31). Luke uses the verb "opened/opening" to describe both the disciples' experience at table with Jesus and (in hindsight) to their experience of this "stranger" interpreting the Scriptures earlier when they were traveling.

Luke 24:33-35. In spite of the hour (they had earlier urged their unrecognized companion to stay because it was "almost evening"), they return to Jerusalem immediately. This detail suggests the seven-mile distance of Emmaus (perhaps even roundtrip) to be the preferred one, rather than anticipating they would set out on a twenty-or-so mile jaunt at night. Upon return, they told their story to "the eleven *and their companions*" (24:33, emphasis added). Luke excels among the Gospels for reminding us the community of Jesus' followers was consistently larger than just the disciples alone. The exchanges in 24:34-35 make clear that, by now, more than the women and these two traveling disciples have heard and accepted the good news of Easter. Easter night ends as Easter morning began: with the news that "the Lord has risen."

INTERPRETING THE SCRIPTURE

Emmaus Journeys

Have you ever taken a long walk to think through some perplexing situation? Have you ever pondered again and again in your mind some experience that, no matter which way you looked at it, still escaped understanding? Have you ever held high hopes, only to find them scattered and torn through experiences you could not control?

If any of those are true, you have journeyed toward Emmaus.

The details Luke provides suggest the journey by Cleopas and the other disciple to have been an exceptionally difficult one. They are sad. Their great hopes in the One they had anticipated to redeem their people and land had been hung with him on a cross to die. They are headed out of Jerusalem, leaving behind the wider community, on this two-person retreat to somewhere else. Maybe anywhere else.

On that way, they have been discussing the things that happened. Have you ever told and retold a story you wished had come out differently, going over it again and again in hopes of seeing something you missed, something that might have turned things around differently? Such is their conversation on the way—a way joined by the One who is, at the moment, a stranger to them.

It is worth remembering that Emmaus journeys, for these two and for us, do not close us off from others. Even with the questions, even with the sadness, these two admit another traveler into their company. They speak honestly and frankly of hope that had been extinguished. They admit not being able to wrap their minds and beliefs around the message of the women.

To be on the road to Emmaus is to bare one's spirit and experiences, and not just the ones that put us in a good light. To be on the road to Emmaus does not necessarily presume to understand what is expected to be found at the end of day or days. It is, however, to journey. It is to engage with others. It is to offer hospitality to those who share that journey with us. Our own Emmaus journeys, thanks to the hindsight provided by these two, open to the possibility that no matter where the path leads, God will be upon it—and God will be with us, even when that presence is not yet perceived.

Sacraments of Word and WORD

In the baptismal liturgy of my denomination's *Book of Worship*, sacrament is defined as "an outward and visible sign of the grace of God." While the church has come to traditionally affirm only two sacraments (or seven in Roman Catholic tradition), it can be argued that any "visible sign" that conveys the reality or presence of God's grace serves a sacramental function. That is, it reveals God to us.

Two such "sacramental" occurrences take place on the road to Emmaus. First, in hindsight, the two disciples speak of their hearts moved when the stranger-turning-out-to-be-Jesus was "opening the scriptures." The two experienced the sacramental revealing of God's grace in the opening of the written word to them. Second, at the table, the two disciples have their eyes (and faith) opened when bread is taken, blessed, broken, and given. The two experienced the sacramental revealing of Christ's presence in the recognition of the living WORD in their midst. Their experience sheds light upon our own sacramental encounters of the gracious presence of God.

As the two disciples discovered, Scripture can serve as the "visible sign" that brings us into awareness and recognition of the presence of God. The written word is a means of inspiration, of opening us to God's workings. But as with those disciples of old, Scripture in and of itself is not the "sacred presence." The disciples knew the stories. Their hopes were grounded in the Old Testament language of an expected redeemer. They saw Jesus as a prophet. But knowing such things, and knowing Scripture, is not the endgame of discipleship. Discipleship comes in recognition and service of the risen Christ. Jesus' "interpreting" of the Scriptures on the Emmaus road begins the transformation that is only realized fully in hindsight ("Were not our hearts burning within us while he was talking to us on the road," 24:32). Scripture is sacramental in that it points beyond itself (the Word that is written) to sacred presence (the WORD who is Jesus Christ).

For two disciples and for us, the table can serve as the "visible sign" that brings recognition of the risen One in our midst. Bread and cup are means of opening us to Christ's gracious presence and workings. But as with those disciples of old, the table in and of itself is not the sacred presence. We sit at table with common elements, made uncommon not by what they are but by Whom they signify. We leave the table as those graced by holy presence—and called, as Christ reminded his disciples at the first table, that greatness resides not in being served but in serving.

Openings!

Openings abound in today's passage. Eyes were opened, and the risen Christ came to be recognized at table—and then just as quickly vanished. So opened to holy presence, the two Emmaus disciples begin to piece together what—and Who—had been there all along. The opening, they perceived, had already begun on the road in the experience of Scripture being interpreted in its present-day (for them) meanings.

So what do you do when you experience your life, and truly the life of all creation, opened in such a dramatic way? Earlier, on the Mount of Transfiguration, disciples who witnessed the awe-filled encounter of Jesus with Moses and Elijah wanted to freeze the moment and build a shrine (9:28-33). The two Emmaus disciples realize that being opened to holy presence, and holy possibilities, is not a cause for standing still but for moving out. Their flight from Jerusalem and the community they left in grief becomes a return to that same city and community to share the news and joy.

Is that how it is with you? Is that how it is with your congregation? Having been surprised and astounded by the Easter news of resurrection, just what has been opened for you? And where might those openings lead you, individually and as a community?

It might seem as if those disciples of old had an advantage: They got to hear and see it all for the first time. The Emmaus pair had the opportunity to recognize Jesus sitting with them. But remember: He immediately vanished. They too had to travel not on the basis of continual sightings of the risen One but in trust of Christ's journeying with them, unseen. Easter may still be hard to accept, as the reception of the disciples to the women's message made clear. There are so many non-Easter experiences in this world to bear with now and then. If you wonder about that, listen in to Cleopas as he explains what happened in Jerusalem.

In the end, Easter still relies not on irrefutable proofs but God-given openings. Openings to the possibility of life raised from death. Openings to the breaking open of holy presence in the act of breaking bread or interpreting Scripture. Openings to recognition of the risen One who may be more apt to surprise us on our journeys than to conform to all our presumptions. Christ is risen, he is risen indeed! It's not just that a tomb has been opened by God. Life has been opened.

SHARING THE SCRIPTURE

Preparing Our Hearts

Explore this week's devotional reading, found in Luke 24:22-26, which is part of our background Scripture. Here, Cleopas and an unnamed disciple are walking along the Emmaus road, unaware that the companion who has joined them is actually the risen Lord. They tell Jesus about the women's astonishing reports concerning the empty tomb that they had discovered earlier that morning. Imagine the hope that this news must have given Jesus' followers. What gives you hope? How does your relation-

ship with Jesus enable you to continue to hope even when circumstances appear bleak?

Pray that you and the adult students will experience hope anew as you rejoice in the resurrection of Jesus Christ.

Preparing Our Minds

Study the background Scripture from Luke 24:1-35 and the lesson Scripture from Luke 24:13-21, 28-35.

Consider this question as you prepare the lesson: *How can we be encouraged to see and take advantage of the good news surrounding us?*

Write on newsprint:

❑ information for next week's lesson, found under "Continue the Journey."

❑ activities for further spiritual growth in "Continue the Journey."

Review the "Introduction," "The Big Picture," "Close-up," and "Faith in Action." Consider how you will use this additional information, which immediately precedes the first lesson, for this session.

LEADING THE CLASS

(1) Gather to Learn

❖ Greet the class members. Introduce any guests and help them feel at home.

❖ Pray that all who have come today will celebrate the resurrection of Jesus.

❖ Invite the students to think about a play or film that ended on a negative note, or with an outcome that was disappointing to them. Encourage the class to talk together or in small groups about this play or film, how it captured their attention and drew them in so that they really cared what happened to the characters, and why the ending was bleak for them. Discuss how they might have rewritten the ending to create a more positive outcome.

❖ Read aloud today's focus statement: **Sometimes humans are caught up in their sense of gloom and despair. How can we be encouraged to see and take advantage of the good news surrounding us? Jesus opened the eyes of two followers he encountered on the road to Emmaus, and they recognized that Jesus had risen.**

(2) Goal 1: Review the Story of the Walk to Emmaus by Cleopas and the Other Disciple, Who Have a Life-changing Meeting With the Risen Lord

❖ Familiarize the adults with the geographical location of today's Bible passage by reading "Luke 24:13-16" from Understanding the Scripture.

❖ Choose three volunteers to play the parts of Cleopas, his companion, and Jesus. Select a fourth person to narrate. Ask this cast to read Luke 24:13-21, 28-35.

❖ Discuss these questions:

(1) What do Cleopas and his companion believe about Jesus?

(2) What hopes had they pinned on Jesus?

(3) What did Jesus say or do to restore their hopes?

(4) What happened that enabled Cleopas and his companion to open their eyes and see Jesus?

(5) What does this story teach Jesus' followers, from then and now, about the Resurrection and its significance?

(3) Goal 2: Identify With the Travelers on the Emmaus Road in Order to Raise the Learners' Awareness of the Places Jesus Meets Them in Their Personal Journeys

❖ Read "Emmaus Journeys" from Interpreting the Scripture.

❖ Do this guided imagery exercise with the adults. Begin by asking them to assume a comfortable position and close their eyes.

❖ **Imagine yourself walking a dusty road with Cleopas and his companion on that first Easter evening when an unknown person appears. Envision yourself telling this stranger about the events of the day and about Jesus.** (Pause.)

❖ **This person interprets Scripture for you and then takes, blesses, breaks, and gives you bread, just as Jesus did in the upper room. You know now that this stranger is actually Jesus, but he immediately vanishes. Speak to Cleopas about what you have experienced.** (Pause.)

❖ **See yourself walking along your own street. Jesus comes to you and meets you where you are, just as he met Cleopas and his companion. Talk with Jesus about your** own hopes and how they have been dashed, fulfilled, or still seem to be on hold. Listen to what he says and feel assured that he meets you where you are and goes with you on every step of your journey. (Pause.)

❖ Invite the adults to open their eyes and share any insights about how they recognize that Jesus is with them on their journeys and how he makes himself known to them.

*(4) Goal 3: Celebrate Jubilantly
the Risen Christ*

❖ Read or retell "Openings!" from Interpreting the Scripture.

❖ Distribute hymnals. Encourage the adults to call out favorite hymns that celebrate the resurrection of Christ. Sing a verse or two of each suggestion, depending on the time you have available.

❖ Wrap up by asking the adults to comment on the reasons these hymns empower them to celebrate. Perhaps the words, melody, tempo, or something else inspire them to worship and celebrate.

(5) Continue the Journey

❖ Pray that all of the participants will go forth to share the good news that Jesus is risen; he is risen indeed!

❖ Read aloud this preparation for next week's lesson. You may also want to post it on newsprint for the students to copy.

■ **Title: The Lord Appears**
■ **Background Scripture: Luke 24:36-53**
■ **Lesson Scripture: Luke 24:36-53**
■ **Focus of the Lesson: People find that promises are easy to make but**

hard to keep. Which promises can be relied on without reservation? Through the Resurrection, Jesus kept his word and fulfilled the words of prophecy about him.

❖ Post these three activities related to this week's session on newsprint for the students to copy. Challenge the adults to grow spiritually by completing one or more of them.

(1) **Talk with a friend who seems dejected about a loss, family crisis, or personal problem. Look for openings in the conversation to witness to the hope that you find in Jesus.**

(2) **Take a walk. Think about how your relationship with Jesus has changed your life. How do you need to grow? Give thanks for your journey with Jesus so far and pray for guidance as you continue.**

(3) **Do something special to celebrate the resurrection of Jesus. Perhaps you will serve others, or write a song, or do a dance, or experience a retreat. Whatever you do, focus on the hope and new awakenings that Jesus' resurrection creates in you.**

❖ Sing or read aloud "Christ the Lord Is Risen Today."

❖ Conclude today's session by leading the class in this benediction, based on the key verses for April 28 from 2 Thessalonians 2:16-17: **Now may our Lord Jesus Christ himself and God our Father, who loved us and through grace gave us eternal comfort and good hope, comfort your hearts and strengthen them in every good work and word.**

UNIT 2: RESURRECTION HOPE
THE LORD APPEARS

PREVIEWING THE LESSON

Lesson Scripture: Luke 24:36-53
Background Scripture: Luke 24:36-53
Key Verse: Luke 24:44

Focus of the Lesson:
People find that promises are easy to make but hard to keep. Which promises can be relied on without reservation? Through the Resurrection, Jesus kept his word and fulfilled the words of prophecy about him.

Goals for the Learners:
(1) to review the story of Jesus' postresurrection appearance and ascension.
(2) to imagine how the disciples felt when Jesus made himself known to them and how the learners feel about his presence in their lives.
(3) to rest in God's promises and share them with others.

Pronunciation Guide:
Cleopas (klee' oh puhs)
Docetist (do ce' tist)
Emmaus (i may' us)
martus (mar' toos)
pneuma (nyoo' muh)

Supplies:
Bibles, newsprint and marker, paper and pencils, hymnals

READING THE SCRIPTURE

NRSV

Lesson Scripture: Luke 24:36-53

³⁶While they [the disciples] were talking about this, Jesus himself stood among them and said to them, "Peace be with you." ³⁷They were startled and terrified, and

CEB

Lesson Scripture: Luke 24:36-53

³⁶While they were saying these things, Jesus himself stood among them and said, "Peace be with you!" ³⁷They were terrified and afraid. They thought they were seeing a ghost.

thought that they were seeing a ghost. ³⁸He said to them, "Why are you frightened, and why do doubts arise in your hearts? ³⁹Look at my hands and my feet; see that it is I myself. Touch me and see; for a ghost does not have flesh and bones as you see that I have." ⁴⁰And when he had said this, he showed them his hands and his feet. ⁴¹While in their joy they were disbelieving and still wondering, he said to them, "Have you anything here to eat?" ⁴²They gave him a piece of broiled fish, ⁴³and he took it and ate in their presence.

⁴⁴Then he said to them, **"These are my words that I spoke to you while I was still with you—that everything written about me in the law of Moses, the prophets, and the psalms must be fulfilled."** ⁴⁵Then he opened their minds to understand the scriptures, ⁴⁶and he said to them, "Thus it is written, that the Messiah is to suffer and to rise from the dead on the third day, ⁴⁷and that repentance and forgiveness of sins is to be proclaimed in his name to all nations, beginning from Jerusalem. ⁴⁸You are witnesses of these things. ⁴⁹And see, I am sending upon you what my Father promised; so stay here in the city until you have been clothed with power from on high."

⁵⁰Then he led them out as far as Bethany, and, lifting up his hands, he blessed them. ⁵¹While he was blessing them, he withdrew from them and was carried up into heaven. ⁵²And they worshiped him, and returned to Jerusalem with great joy; ⁵³and they were continually in the temple blessing God.

³⁸He said to them, "Why are you startled? Why are doubts arising in your hearts? ³⁹Look at my hands and my feet. It's really me! Touch me and see, for a ghost doesn't have flesh and bones like you see I have." ⁴⁰As he said this, he showed them his hands and feet. ⁴¹Because they were wondering and questioning in the midst of their happiness, he said to them, "Do you have anything to eat?" ⁴²They gave him a piece of baked fish. ⁴³Taking it, he ate it in front of them.

⁴⁴Jesus said to them, **"These are my words that I spoke to you while I was still with you—that everything written about me in the Law of Moses, the Prophets, and the Psalms must be fulfilled."** ⁴⁵Then he opened their minds to understand the scriptures. ⁴⁶He said to them, "This is what is written: the Christ will suffer and rise from the dead on the third day, ⁴⁷and a change of heart and life for the forgiveness of sins must be preached in his name to all nations, beginning from Jerusalem. ⁴⁸You are witnesses of these things. ⁴⁹Look, I'm sending to you what my Father promised, but you are to stay in the city until you have been furnished with heavenly power."

⁵⁰He led them out as far as Bethany, where he lifted his hands and blessed them. ⁵¹As he blessed them, he left them and was taken up to heaven. ⁵²They worshipped him and returned to Jerusalem overwhelmed with joy. ⁵³And they were continuously in the temple praising God.

UNDERSTANDING THE SCRIPTURE

Luke 24:36-37. The opening, "while they were talking about this," refers to the preceding conversation after Cleopas and the other disciple rejoined the group following the Emmaus road encounter. At this point (24:34), the disciples acknowledge Jesus'

resurrection and attest to an unrecorded appearance to Peter. But has Easter faith really taken root? Jesus suddenly appears, his greeting in verse 36 of "peace be with you" paralleling the greeting reported in John 20:19 on Easter evening (and John

20:26 on the appearance when Thomas is present a week later). This greeting is missing in some ancient manuscripts of Luke. With or without greeting, however, the manuscripts of Luke uniformly report the disciples as "terrified" at the appearance, using the same verb to describe their reaction as the reaction of the women at the appearance of the two men in the tomb (24:5). The disciples believe they are seeing a "ghost" (*pneuma*, a Greek word that can also mean "spirit" or "breath" or "wind").

Luke 24:38-43. The disciples' presumption that they were in the presence of an immaterial spirit evokes Jesus' challenging them to judge his "physicality" for themselves in the series of verbs used in verse 39: "look," "see," "touch," "see." In addition to serving as a counter to the disciples' misunderstanding, the "bodily" emphasis on Jesus' appearance distinguishes resurrection from prevailing Greek philosophical views that only the "soul" was or could be immortal. Luke's risen Jesus is no disembodied phantom. The pointed directions to view "hands and feet," the site of Jesus' wounds upon the cross, may have been a subtle witness against ideas that would later take formal shape among those called "Docetists" (from a Greek word meaning "to seem"). This group argued that Jesus only "seemed" to die, since they held that the Christ was a spiritual being who was neither incarnate nor capable of suffering, much less dying. Even with the sight of the wounds, the disciples remain somewhat befuddled. As verse 41 recounts, "their joy" intermingles with "disbelieving" and "wondering." "Wonder" is a neutral word in Luke: It signifies neither belief nor disbelief in and of itself. Jesus' eating of the fish provides yet another Lukan emphasis upon the humanity of the risen Jesus (see John 21:9-13).

Luke 24:44-46. Earlier, in the Emmaus account, Luke records that Jesus interpreted the Scriptures "beginning with Moses and all the prophets" (24:27). It was noted in last week's Understanding the Scripture comments on this verse that during this era the Old Testament canon consisted of the Law and the Prophets (a phrase that occurs often in Scripture). Tradition holds that the acceptance of what are now called the "Writings" into the canon did not fully come until near the end of the first century A.D. But notice in verse 44 that Jesus mentions "the law of Moses, the prophets, and the psalms." The Psalms had for centuries been integral to Jewish worship and teaching. Among the hallmarks for inclusion of other "writings" into the canon of Hebrew Scriptures, community usage (especially worship) over time provided the Psalms with a strong argument for inclusion, as Jesus includes it here with the Law and Prophets. The "openings" that had occurred in the Emmaus experience (24:31-32) now recur in verse 45 as Jesus opens the minds of the gathered disciples. The opening, however, is not just used to understand the past in terms of Jesus as a suffering, dying, and rising Messiah.

Luke 24:47-49. The opening goes on in verse 47 to include the disciples, now to become apostles, discerning their future vocation ("repentance and forgiveness of sins is to be proclaimed"). The familiar Lukan theme of inclusion of outsiders is joined to this commission, as such proclamation is to be made "to all nations" (see Matthew 28:19 for a similar charge). There is no doubt left as to who will bring this proclamation: "you are witnesses" (24:48). The Greek word for witness is *martus*, the root word for the English "martyr." The Greek word does not in the original language carry the connotation of one who dies. That meaning came to be added as a result of experiences of the early church, where those who bore witness sometimes did suffer death because of it. Now "martyr" is almost exclusively understood as bearing that cost, whereas in texts like these in Luke, the call is simply to be a witness. The sending of the Spirit is imbedded in the instructions to remain in the city

(Jerusalem) in verse 49. The language resembles Acts 1:4-5, where before his ascension Jesus speaks of the Father sending the Spirit. The anticipation of receiving power (as Spirit) from on high echoes a promise in Isaiah 32:15, where the prophet's listing of the woes of approaching exile is tempered by hope: "until a spirit from on high is poured out on us, and the wilderness becomes a fruitful field." Just as the Spirit promised restoration then, so now in Luke, the promise of Spirit promises power to take on the commission to be witnesses.

Luke 24:50-53. Bethany was a small village east of Jerusalem, on the lower slope of the Mount of Olives. The lifting up of hands was a traditional physical gesture (again, Luke's emphasis on "embodiment" following resurrection) of blessing. What follows is an abbreviated account of Jesus' ascension, compared to the account in Acts 1:6-11 (a work also traditionally attributed to Luke). Acts asserts that a forty-day period had separated resurrection from ascension, a period summarized as one of Jesus' teaching about the kingdom of God (Acts 1:3). No such interval is specified in Luke 24. Some Lukan manuscripts do not contain "and was carried up into heaven," perhaps as an attempt to synthesize two accounts of ascension into one (Acts alone). Following the ascension in Luke, the disciples return to Jerusalem, as instructed in 24:49. The Gospel of Luke ends with the disciples in the Temple, which is, likely not coincidentally in Luke's careful construction, the site of the first scene in the Gospel (1:5-23), where Zechariah receives the promise of the birth of a son to "make ready a people prepared for the Lord," 1:17). Luke's Gospel has come full circle.

INTERPRETING THE SCRIPTURE

Peace and Fear, Wounds and Fish

The disciples have heard the testimony of the women regarding Easter. Belief does not follow. By the night of Easter, two of their company return from a journey to Emmaus, full of excitement about their encounter with the risen Christ in bread broken and Scripture interpreted. The pair's enthusiasm is met by the larger group's own confession: "The Lord has risen" (24:34). It would seem all questions are settled, all struggles ended.

They are not. Even the most central of Christian affirmations, "Christ is risen" is rhetorical doctrine divorced from reality without experience of the risen One. For when, in our text for today, Jesus suddenly appears pronouncing "peace," what seizes the disciples is fear. They are terrified. They do not see resurrection embodied; they see a ghost.

Lest we judge those disciples too severely, let us remember times and ways in which faith has rolled too loosely off of our tongues. It is easy to say a creed in worship. It is not always so easy to live by that creed's affirmations or hopes in the world outside of sanctuary. We line up stalwartly behind "God is love" and "love your neighbor as yourself" until, of course, we encounter that neighbor we do not particularly care for. It might be because of her politics. It might be because of his sexual orientation. It's OK to talk about God creating heaven and earth, so long as we don't take too seriously the notion, therefore, that God created (and loves) those very ones that grate our nerves or contradict our careful constructions of those deserving (in our estimation) God's grace.

Faith, to be faith and not mere opinion, requires embodiment. God does not love in general. God loves particular persons and peoples. Faith requiring embodiment is one of the subtexts of Luke's resurrection appearance stories. The disciples' "The Lord has risen" quickly dissolves in a fog of disembodied confusion as they thought they were seeing a ghost. Jesus' response to them seeks to bring them back to the startling truth of resurrection: There is a body here. He encourages the disciples to engage their senses of sight and touch. When even that does not convince them ("in their joy they were disbelieving and wondering," 24:41), Jesus pushes the embodiment theme further. He asks for something to eat.

Resurrection faith is not about theories of immaterial spirits floating their way through the ethereal plane. Resurrection faith is about hope embodied. We need not stumble on abstract discussions on how the body is to be resurrected in cases of cremation or pure and simple decomposition back into the earth. The God who fashioned creation out of chaos can surely figure that out. What Luke's Easter appearances assert is that faith is not a separate "spiritual" category apart from the rest of who we are and what we do. Faith involves embodiment.

Fulfillment of the Scriptures

Twice in the appearance stories, Luke portrays Jesus as interpreting the Scriptures (24:27, 44-46) in regards to his Messianic identity and vocation. The force of these details makes the same point as Jesus' teaching in the Sermon on the Mount: "I have not come to abolish [the Law or the Prophets] but to fulfill" (Matthew 5:17). In other words, Jesus did not come to institute a rival faith to Judaism, but to fulfill Judaism's teachings and hopes for God's Messiah.

Why then the ensuing conflict anticipated in Jesus' run-ins with some religious leaders of his time, culminating in the eventual separation of the synagogue from the church? Before we leap on the bandwagon of denigrating Judaism for its lack of perceptiveness to the Messiah come in the person of Jesus, let us humbly recall that the church has created more than its share of divisive conflicts within itself. The Pauline correspondence makes clear that within the first or, at latest, the second generation of the church, "believers" found cause to choose factions (1 Corinthians 3). Later, separations came when Eastern Orthodox and Roman Catholic traditions parted ways, and when Roman Catholic and Protestant traditions branded each other as out of the fold. The divisions since have only increased. One has only to look at a list of denominations within just the United States to understand we do not easily get along with one another.

So in terms of Jesus' fulfilling the Scriptures, many Jews in that era did not come to that same conclusion. The outcome of that ought to be one of continued dialogue over the differences, not the labeling of others as "opponents" or "Christ killers." The church is called to proclaim the Messiah, not browbeat or force conversions of those who hold different viewpoints, yet who share with us the same Hebrew Scriptures and the traditions that nurtured the one we call Christ.

The Church of the Ascension

Luke's resurrection appearances do not end on the note of simply who Jesus is. Luke's Gospel closes on the note of who the church is called to be.

In a word, that call is to be Christ's witnesses: "Repentance and forgiveness of sins is to be proclaimed" (Luke 24:47). Luke used those same words to identify the ministry of John the Baptist (3:3). The point is more than coincidental. John's ministry prepared the people for the coming of God's Messiah. So, too, the ministry of the church continues to be one of preparing the people for the coming of God's Messiah and that

Messiah's kingdom. Like John, the attention is not focused on ourselves, but on the One in whom we ground our trust and our hope.

The capability of engaging in such a mission is not left to the disciples to accomplish alone and unaided. The promise of the Father will be sent, resulting in their being "clothed in power" (24:49). Clearly, Luke is setting the stage for the story of Pentecost that will be taken up in great detail near the beginning of the Book of Acts, another work attributed to Luke. The same Spirit that led Jesus into the wilderness (4:1) and empowered Jesus in ministry (4:14) will lead the church in mission whose reach goes far beyond the borders of Judah and Galilee to encompass "all nations" (24:47).

But for the church's mission and the Spirit's empowerment to take place, one more thing must happen: "While [Jesus] was blessing them, he withdrew from them and was carried up into heaven" (24:51; see also Acts 1:5-11).

So what is the point of this story? Recall the earlier emphasis on Jesus' physicality in verses 39-43, and consider that in light of a New Testament image for the church: the body of Christ. The ascension marks a type of passage to responsibility. To this point, Jesus has been the primary actor on the Gospel's stage. But now, for the disciples to become apostles, for the church to be the body of Christ, they (we) need to take responsibility for the commission entrusted. We do not do so unaided, for the Spirit is promised. By that Spirit's power, the church of the Ascension is called to be the community that serves as Christ's embodied emissary of God's love, grace, and justice. Christ is with us, only not as before. For now, others rely on coming to encounter Christ through our words, our actions, our presence. We are so blessed, and we are so commissioned.

SHARING THE SCRIPTURE

Preparing Our Hearts

Explore this week's devotional reading, found in 1 Corinthians 15:1-8. Here Paul writes about the purpose of Jesus' death, his burial, resurrection, and postresurrection appearances. Why do you think it was so important for the early church to know that Jesus had appeared to more than five hundred people? Had you been one of the first to hear the news about Jesus, would the testimony of others influence your willingness to believe in Jesus, or would that testimony have had no effect had you not seen him yourself? Ponder the role that Jesus' resurrection plays in your own faith and relationship with him.

Pray that you and the adult students will live in the confidence that Jesus is alive and that his promises are true.

Preparing Our Minds

Study the background Scripture and the lesson Scripture, both of which are from Luke 24:36-53.

Consider this question as you prepare the lesson: *Which promises can be relied on without reservation?*

Write on newsprint:
❑ information for next week's lesson, found under "Continue the Journey."
❑ activities for further spiritual growth in "Continue the Journey."

Review the "Introduction," "The Big Picture," "Close-up," and "Faith in Action." Consider how you will use this additional information, which immediately precedes the first lesson, for this session.

Use the Understanding the Scripture

portion to prepare the suggested lecture for "Review the Story of Jesus' Postresurrection Appearance and Ascension."

LEADING THE CLASS

(1) Gather to Learn

❖ Greet the class members. Introduce any guests and help them feel at home.

❖ Pray that those who have gathered for study today will recognize God as a promise keeper.

❖ Mention that in the United States elections were recently held on November 6, 2012. Invite the students to recall campaign promises that were made. List these ideas on newsprint. Ask:

    (1) Which of these promises made by winning candidates are already being addressed?

    (2) How would you rate the chances of a particular promise that you recall being kept by this newly elected official?

    (3) If your rating is high, what kind of support do you see for this promise?

    (4) If your rating is low, why do you think that the promise does not have a chance of fulfillment?

❖ Read aloud today's focus statement: **People find that promises are easy to make but hard to keep. Which promises can be relied on without reservation? Through the Resurrection, Jesus kept his word and fulfilled the words of prophecy about him.**

(2) Goal 1: Review the Story of Jesus' Postresurrection Appearance and Ascension

❖ Recall that last week we studied the encounter between Cleopas and his companion on the Emmaus road as they met the risen Christ. Select a volunteer to read Luke 24:36-53, which recounts other postresurrection appearances.

❖ Present a lecture based on Understanding the Scripture in which you make clear how Jesus made himself known to those gathered in Jerusalem, how these disciples responded, and what role they were to play now that Jesus had been bodily resurrected.

❖ Discuss these questions:

    (1) Why is it so important to recognize that Jesus is not a "ghost" but rather appears in a body that is capable even of eating?

    (2) How does this appearance of Jesus equip the disciples to go forth with good news?

    (3) How does Jesus' ascension relate to the founding of the church? (See "The Church of the Ascension" in Interpreting the Scripture.)

(3) Goal 2: Imagine How the Disciples Felt When Jesus Made Himself Known to Them and How the Learners Feel About His Presence in Their Lives

❖ Ask these questions:

    (1) Have you ever seen someone you thought you knew but didn't expect to see? If so, how did this person's unexpected appearance affect you?

    (2) How do you think the disciples must have felt when they saw Jesus, whom they did not expect to see?

❖ Distribute paper and pencils. Invite the students to draw an oval in the center of the page with spokes coming out of it. Then ask them to write the name "Jesus" inside the oval. On the spokes, they are to write words that describe how his presence in their lives makes them feel. Point out that the descriptions may be both positive and negative. For example, Jesus may bring peace and comfort to many, but some may find that his presence convicts them of sin or makes them uncomfortable because they know they are not living according to his example and teachings.

❖ Encourage the adults to talk with a partner or small group about their feelings concerning Jesus' presence in their lives.

❖ Bring the groups together and invite the students to comment on similarities they found in their responses, as well as any major differences. Accept these comments without judgment.

(4) Goal 3: Rest in God's Promises and Share Them With Others

❖ Lead the class in reading together Luke 24:44, today's key verse.

❖ Read or retell "Fulfillment of the Scriptures" from Interpreting the Scripture. Invite the students to talk about how Scriptures fulfilled are in fact promises of God that are kept. Suggest that they identify several examples of fulfilled Scriptures that are dear to them.

❖ Continue that theme by looking at Luke 24:49. Ask: **What has God promised?** (Look at Acts 1:4-5, 8; 2:33 to discern that Jesus is speaking about the coming of the Holy Spirit, which will empower the disciples to be his witnesses.)

❖ Conclude this portion of the session by asking several volunteers to bear witness to the difference that the fulfilled promises of God have made in their lives.

(5) Continue the Journey

❖ Pray that all who have participated today will rejoice in the presence of the Lord.

❖ Read aloud this preparation for next week's lesson. You may also want to post it on newsprint for the students to copy.

■ **Title: The Holy Spirit Comes**

■ **Background Scripture: Acts 2:1-36**
■ **Lesson Scripture: Acts 2:1-13**
■ **Focus of the Lesson: We often face experiences that produce dramatic changes in our lives. How can positive and lasting change be initiated? The Holy Spirit provides life-transforming power.**

❖ Post these three activities related to this week's session on newsprint for the students to copy. Challenge the adults to grow spiritually by completing one or more of them.

(1) Look at the postresurrection appearances of Jesus found in Matthew 28; Mark 16; John 20–21; and 1 Corinthians 15:1-11. What do you learn about Jesus? What do you learn about his followers? What impact do these appearances have on your own faith?

(2) Recall a promise you made but have not yet fulfilled. Take action to keep that promise.

(3) Note that Luke 24:32, 44-45 speak about Jesus opening minds to understand the Scriptures. Seek opportunities to share the Scriptures with people who want to know more about Jesus and the kingdom of God.

❖ Sing or read aloud "Hail Thee, Festival Day."

❖ Conclude today's session by leading the class in this benediction, based on the key verses for April 28 from 2 Thessalonians 2:16-17: **Now may our Lord Jesus Christ himself and God our Father, who loved us and through grace gave us eternal comfort and good hope, comfort your hearts and strengthen them in every good work and word.**

UNIT 2: RESURRECTION HOPE

THE HOLY SPIRIT COMES

PREVIEWING THE LESSON

Lesson Scripture: Acts 2:1-13
Background Scripture: Acts 2:1-36
Key Verse: Acts 2:4

Focus of the Lesson:

We often face experiences that produce dramatic changes in our lives. How can positive and lasting change be initiated? The Holy Spirit provides life-transforming power.

Goals for the Learners:

(1) to review the dramatic story of the coming of the Holy Spirit and discover its meaning for their lives.
(2) to relate the feelings of the people present at Pentecost to the learners' feelings when surprising events occur.
(3) to identify ways they sense the presence of the Holy Spirit in their lives as they experience change.

Pronunciation Guide:

Cappadocia (kap uh doh' shee uh)   Pamphylia (pam fil' ee uh)
Cretan (kree' tuhn)   Parthian (pahr' thee uhn)
Cyrene (si ree' nee)   Phrygia (frij' ee uh)
Elamite (ee' luh mite)   Pontus (pon' tuhs)
Mede (meed)   Septuagint (sep' too uh jint)
Mesopotamia (mes uh puyh tay' mee uh)

Supplies:

Bibles, newsprint and marker, paper and pencils, hymnals

READING THE SCRIPTURE

NRSV
Lesson Scripture: Acts 2:1-13

¹When the day of Pentecost had come, they were all together in one place. ²And suddenly from heaven there came a sound

CEB
Lesson Scripture: Acts 2:1-13

¹When Pentecost Day arrived, they were all together in one place. ²Suddenly a sound from heaven like the howling of a fierce

like the rush of a violent wind, and it filled the entire house where they were sitting. [3]Divided tongues, as of fire, appeared among them, and a tongue rested on each of them. **[4]All of them were filled with the Holy Spirit and began to speak in other languages, as the Spirit gave them ability.**

[5]Now there were devout Jews from every nation under heaven living in Jerusalem. [6]And at this sound the crowd gathered and was bewildered, because each one heard them speaking in the native language of each. [7]Amazed and astonished, they asked, "Are not all these who are speaking Galileans? [8]And how is it that we hear, each of us, in our own native language? [9]Parthians, Medes, Elamites, and residents of Mesopotamia, Judea and Cappadocia, Pontus and Asia, [10]Phrygia and Pamphylia, Egypt and the parts of Libya belonging to Cyrene, and visitors from Rome, both Jews and proselytes, [11]Cretans and Arabs—in our own languages we hear them speaking about God's deeds of power." [12]All were amazed and perplexed, saying to one another, "What does this mean?" [13]But others sneered and said, "They are filled with new wine."

wind filled the entire house where they were sitting. [3]They saw what seemed to be individual flames of fire alighting on each one of them. **[4]They were all filled with the Holy Spirit and began to speak in other languages as the Spirit enabled them to speak.**

[5]There were pious Jews from every nation under heaven living in Jerusalem. [6]When they heard this sound, a crowd gathered. They were mystified because everyone heard them speaking in their native languages. [7]They were surprised and amazed, saying, "Look, aren't all the people who are speaking Galileans, every one of them? [8]How then can each of us hear them speaking in our native language? [9]Parthians, Medes, and Elamites; as well as residents of Mesopotamia, Judea, and Cappadocia, Pontus and Asia, [10]Phrygia and Pamphylia, Egypt and the regions of Libya bordering Cyrene; and visitors from Rome (both Jews and converts to Judaism), [11]Cretans and Arabs—we hear them declaring the mighty works of God in our own languages!" [12]They were all surprised and bewildered. Some asked each other, "What does this mean?" [13]Others jeered at them, saying, "They're full of new wine!"

UNDERSTANDING THE SCRIPTURE

Acts 2:1-4. Pentecost was an existing Jewish harvest festival, one of three pilgrimage feasts (along with Passover and Tabernacles/Booths). Pentecost, as its prefix suggests, came fifty days following Passover. "They were all together" in verse 1 references not only the whole community (numbered at 120 in Acts 1:15) but also the status of a community "in one accord" or "like-minded" with one another (see 2:46 and 5:12 for this meaning in other uses of the word "together"). Notice that Luke carefully constructs the outbreak of Pentecost in simile: The sound was "like" a violent wind, the divided tongues were "as" of fire. The association of God's Spirit with phenomena "like" wind and fire echoes the account of the theophany ("appearing of God") on Mount Sinai prior to the giving of the commandments (Exodus 19:16). This association of Pentecost with the giving of law may be more than coincidental, as later Judaism (it is debated whether this was the case at the time of Acts) connected the giving of law with the "harvest" celebrated at Pentecost. "All of them" in verse 4 would suggest that all 120 members of the community, not just the eleven apostles, received the Spirit's gift.

Acts 2:5-13. While the outburst of diverse languages spoken attracted the crowd's attention, it is not simply speaking but "hearing" that becomes crucial to the episode that unfolds (2:6, 8, 11). The recognition that the speakers are Galileans may suggest a prior knowledge of this community. (Luke's Gospel depicted them after the ascension as "continually in the temple blessing God," Luke 24:53.) Two elements merit special attention in the listings in the crowd within verses 9-11. One is geographical: The list of nations and peoples moves east to west. Jesus in Acts 1:8 had spoken of an expanding circle of witness, beginning in Jerusalem and arcing outward "to the ends of the earth." The movement of the gospel narrated in Acts is, essentially, east to west. The second note is historical: Some of those listed no longer existed at the time of Acts. The gospel's expansion might thus be seen as crossing borders not only of place but time. "Proselytes" refers to non-ethnic Jews, that is, Gentile converts to Judaism. That theme of Gentile conversion will soon play a large and occasionally conflicted role in Acts. The astonishment of the crowd also solicits mocking explanations of the outburst: drunkenness (2:13).

Acts 2:14-21. While the whole community seems included in the Spirit's bestowal, the eleven apostles now come to the fore in the narrative. Peter in particular, as spokesman of the community, can be seen earlier in the process that led to the choosing of Matthias to replace Judas (1:15-26). Peter uses irony, if not outright sarcasm, to dismiss the charge of drunkenness (2:15). In the first of several quotations of Hebrew Scripture that will form the core of his "sermon," Peter first appeals to the prophet Joel (Joel 2:28-32) to explain what truly accounts for the Pentecost outburst. Peter adds a phrase not found in Joel at the very outset of his words: "in the last days" (Acts 2:17). Earlier, the disciples had asked Jesus about

the nearness of the coming of God's kingdom (1:6-8). While revealing that no one but God knows these times, Jesus immediately shifts the conversation from "last days" to witness days. For Peter, the coming of the Spirit forms the beachhead for the last days foreseen by Joel, days whose primary sign would be the outpouring of the Spirit. What makes Joel's prophecy so in synch with Luke's theology is its inclusive nature. Not only will recipients of Spirit be young and old, men and women, slave and free, but the fruits of the witness of those so inspired also will cut across all boundaries. "*Everyone* who calls on the name of the Lord will be saved" (2:21, emphasis added).

Acts 2:22-31. Peter aims his remarks now at the "Israelites," a designation less ethnic and more geographical. The reason is that the sermon now focuses upon the events that had come to pass when Jesus entered Jerusalem. The attribution of those events to the "definite plan and foreknowledge of God" (2:23) is not a formal argument for predestination, but rather an underscoring of the truth that what had happened was not accident or coincidence. Instead, it was part of salvation history. At the center of this section is an extended quotation from Psalm 16:8-11 and then an allusion to Psalm 132:11. If the passages so quoted seem somewhat different than the psalm wording in your Bible, it is not simply a matter of English translation. Luke employed the Greek version of the Bible called the Septuagint. The readings often are at variance with the Hebrew text of the Old Testament that is the basis of our translations. The address of "fellow Israelites" in verse 29 asserts that Peter understands himself as part of the continuing Jewish community in that region as well as kin in faith to the pilgrims who have come.

Acts 2:32-36. For the second time (see 2:24), Peter proclaims Christ's resurrection as an act of God. As the earlier quotation from Joel sought to interpret Pentecost's outpouring of Spirit from Jewish prophetic tradition, Peter now declares that Pentecost's outpouring is a direct result of Jesus' resurrection and ascension. Another psalm is quoted (110:1) to continue the contrast of Jesus with David that had implicitly begun earlier in verse 25 (where Peter subtly makes David himself a witness concerning Jesus: "For David says *concerning him*," emphasis added). The sermon comes to its pointed conclusion with Peter's witness to God making Jesus "Lord" (Greek title equivalent in the Septuagint for the name of YHWH in the Old Testament) and "Messiah." The contrast of what God has done regarding Jesus is multiplied, in a way that has sometimes been dangerously misapplied in anti-Semitism, by the closing "this Jesus whom *you* crucified" (2:36, emphasis added). "You" is best heard there in the "every one of us" sense embraced in the old gospel song "Were You There," rather than as a blanket indictment of Jews as Christ killers, as has been done in tragic and blasphemous ways in history and in church.

INTERPRETING THE SCRIPTURE

The Community Context of Pentecost

Pentecost unsettles the church year. At Christmas, we can get cozy with a stabled child in a manger, and comfortable singing carols we have been hearing in the department stores for weeks on end. At Easter, we take heart in the hope that the grave does not have the last word, and in services that fill our pews and with air scented with lilies. But Pentecost? Perhaps we wear red in honor of the fire. But by Pentecost, school is almost out and the crowds of Easter are nowhere to be found. And the details of the story itself may seem disconnected if not a bit disconcerting. Sounds like a rushing wind? Divided tongues as of fire? An outburst of languages that the speakers seem to have no choice about? No wonder some leave Pentecost to the Pentecostals. It all seems so, well, out of control. Maybe we wear red in some distant acknowledgment of fiery tongues. Maybe we allow a cake with "Happy Birthday, Church" so that the children get some "taste" of this day's meaning. But let's not go overboard.

Or is Pentecost truly about letting the Spirit flow, come what may?

The detail of the apostolic community being "all together" (2:1) reminds us that the day of Pentecost has a specific community context: preparation and expectation. It is the same context provided earlier in 1:14, where the followers are depicted as "constantly devoting themselves to prayer." It is the same context called for even earlier when Jesus invited the community to "stay here in the city until you have been clothed with power from on high" (Luke 24:49).

An argument can be made that Pentecost unfolds because of this community context of preparation and expectation. This is not to say that community, then or now, can manipulate the Spirit to be given. Rather, it is an invitation to consider that communities opening themselves to the Spirit will not be disappointed. They (we) may be surprised, for Spirit may not come according to our expectations of either time or manifestation. Nowhere in Acts is any hint given that the community knows the outpouring of Spirit will lead to charismatic speaking (and hearing; more on that later). But surprise is not a bad thing, as any child opening a package under a Christmas tree can tell you. The surprising movement of the Spirit on Pentecost, in conjunction with community that prepares and waits for God's promised activity, gave birth to the church.

And if the truth be told, in the surprising

movement of the Spirit today, in conjunction with communities that prepare and wait for God's promised activity (and do not dictate beforehand what those activities must be), the church continues to be reborn and renewed in our time.

Bewildered, Amazed, Astonished, Perplexed

Crowds often get a reputation for fickleness, and rightly so, not only in the biblical accounts but in our own lives. Demagogues can whip up the emotional frenzy of a crowd, leading them to actions that individuals within that mass might on their own question or even find repugnant. Crowds in the Gospels routinely misconstrued the moments in which they found themselves, as evidenced by the attempt to make Jesus a "king" after he fed them (John 6:15) or by being manipulated by a few to cry for a murderer's release and an innocent's crucifixion (Mark 15:6-15).

But here in Acts, the crowd got it right, at least in terms of affording us a totally understandable response to the pyrotechnics and sounds of Pentecost: bewilderment, amazement, astonishment, and perplexity. Something radically new was happening, and they reacted accordingly.

Their reaction provides insight into our own encounters with the wholly extraordinary—or the Holy. Think of times and occasions when you have been bowled over by some circumstance or event. Maybe it was the birth of a child. Maybe it was an incredible—in the literal sense of that word, as unbelievable—experience in nature or in a human relationship. Maybe it was the moment when you came face-to-face, or spirit-to-spirit, with the presence of God in an act of worship or service or fellowship. Unless we erect solid walls of reason around us and within us, such moments do come in life. When they do, our feelings can be overwhelmed with the sense of being in the presence of something new to us. It is right to be awestruck, as was this crowd.

But the other insight this crowd offers to us is their openness that allowed the experience and newness to run its course. To be sure, a few wags made wisecracks about somebody having got into the wineskins early. But notice this: When Peter began to speak, the crowd was still there. Not only were they there, they listened. Amazement and astonishment can close us down and shut us off to what is going on around us. But such feelings can also open us up, releasing us to see where, and to whom, the amazement might lead. There is no sermon by Peter without an audience—and there is no audience, no congregation, without amazement that opens to hearing. Perhaps the crisis in preaching today is less a matter of preaching skill, and more a concern of whether folks come with anything like amazement—and then be opened by it to new words and ways.

Spirit-ed Hearing

For some of its critics and its most fervent practitioners, a key feature of Pentecost is speaking in languages understood by the listeners but unknown to the speakers themselves. Both would point to the detail in verse 6 that it was the "sound" that gathered the crowd. Noise of all sorts can gather crowds, and often does.

But what keeps crowds is not just noise and sounds that are just so much babble. People want to hear something that includes them in the discourse. That forms one of the chief critiques today, not only of those whose charismatic practice of speaking in tongues is purely for their own benefit but also of preachers whose pulpit babblings leave parishioners absolutely untouched by any gospel proclamation, whether because they talk over folks' heads or because they never address where folks actually live.

In the Pentecost narrative, charismatic speaking is linked to charismatic hearing, that is, speaking and hearing empowered and enabled by God's Spirit. "In our languages, we *hear* them speaking about God's deeds of power" (2:11, emphasis added). That is the miracle of Pentecost: that in multiple tongues, the gospel was heard. Such hearing leads to the critical question that follows in the next verse: "What does this mean?"

"What does this mean?" That question gets the crowd to stick around for Peter's sermon. That is the question that truly should inform and motivate any community gathered in worship that hears the reading and interpretation of Scripture. For "what does this mean?" leads inevitably to the question (raised later in Acts 2:37) that energizes persons and communities for repentance and mission: "What should we do?"

The day and traditions of Pentecost are not intended to be archaic remnants of a spirituality that is foreign to us. Pentecost reminds us we are a community led and empowered by Spirit. Pentecost challenges us to speak the gospel in ways it can be heard and understood. Pentecost means we are a people born of Spirit, whose life-transforming power continues to renew the church in ways surprising and gracious.

SHARING THE SCRIPTURE

Preparing Our Hearts

Explore this week's devotional reading, found in John 15:1-7. Here Jesus uses the metaphor of the vine and its branches to help his disciples understand the importance of abiding in him and bearing fruit for the kingdom. What metaphor would you use to describe your own relationship with Christ? Are you as organically related as a vine and branch, or would you find it possible to easily separate yourself from Jesus? Draw the metaphor you have chosen and write a brief explanation as to why it so aptly describes your relationship.

Pray that you and the adult students will constantly stay connected to Christ.

Preparing Our Minds

Study the background Scripture from Acts 2:1-36 and the lesson Scripture from Acts 2:1-13.

Consider this question as you prepare the lesson: *How can positive and lasting change be initiated?*

Write on newsprint:
❏ information for next week's lesson, found under "Continue the Journey."
❏ activities for further spiritual growth in "Continue the Journey."

Review the "Introduction," "The Big Picture," "Close-up," and "Faith in Action." Consider how you will use this additional information, which immediately precedes the first lesson, for this session.

Prepare to read today's Bible lesson from Acts 2:1-13. Use the Pronunciation Guide as needed.

Make sure as you teach this session that the students understand that although we are studying Pentecost today we will not celebrate it until May 19 this year.

LEADING THE CLASS

(1) Gather to Learn

❖ Greet the class members. Introduce any guests and help them feel at home.

❖ Pray that those who have come today will experience the power and presence of the Holy Spirit.

❖ Post a sheet of newsprint and invite the adults to call out experiences that can create dramatic change. Some changes have a positive impact on our lives, whereas others can have a negative, even devastating, impact. Here are some examples: marriage, birth of a child, starting college, loss of a home, retirement, loss of a job, moving to a new city, death of a loved one, or serious illness.

❖ Ask: **What support did you need to make any of these changes? Who provided you with this support?**

❖ Read aloud today's focus statement: **We often face experiences that produce dramatic changes in our lives. How can positive and lasting change be initiated? The Holy Spirit provides life-transforming power.**

(2) Goal 1: Review the Dramatic Story of the Coming of the Holy Spirit and Discover Its Meaning for the Learners' Lives

❖ Read this information from Understanding the Scripture to set the scene: **Pentecost was an existing Jewish harvest festival, one of three pilgrimage feasts (along with Passover and Tabernacles/ Booths). Pentecost, as its prefix suggests, came fifty days following Passover. . . . The association of God's Spirit with phenomena "like" wind and fire echoes the account of the theophany ("appearing of God") on Mount Sinai prior to the giving of the commandments (Exodus 19:16). This association of Pentecost with the giving of law may be more than coincidental, as later Judaism (it is debated whether this was the case at the time of Acts) connected the giving of the law with the "harvest" celebrated at Pentecost.**

❖ Invite the learners to close their eyes and imagine the scene as you read expressively the account of Pentecost from Acts 2:1-13.

❖ **Option:** Distribute paper and pencils. Encourage the adults to sketch any image or scene they hear described as you read. Provide a few moments for volunteers to show their sketches and explain why these images caught their attention.

❖ Encourage the students to act as eyewitnesses by telling what they saw, heard, touched, tasted, or smelled. Suggest that they do this from memory.

❖ Discuss these questions:
  (1) **What signs suggested the presence of God in this story?**
  (2) **The disciples were speaking the languages of many people in Jerusalem to celebrate Pentecost. But the emphasis in the story is on the hearing, not the speaking. What message are the people hearing?**
  (3) **Read the third through fifth paragraphs under "Spirit-ed Hearing" in Interpreting the Scripture. How do you experience the Spirit's transforming power working in the church today?**

(3) Goal 2: Relate the Feelings of the People Present at Pentecost to the Learners' Feelings When Surprising Events Occur

❖ Invite the adults to open their Bibles to Acts 2:1-13 and call out any words that convey the emotions of the eyewitnesses. List ideas from any translations that the students use. The words as they appear in the NRSV include "bewildered," "amazed," "astonished," "perplexed."

❖ Form several small groups and invite participants to discuss feelings they have experienced when a surprising event occurs.

❖ Bring the groups together and ask:
  (1) **What connections can you draw between the way people experienced the first Pentecost and the way you feel when a surprising event occurs?**

(2) **How can the feelings of your own surprising event help you better relate to an amazing biblical event?**

❖ Wrap up this portion by reading "Bewildered, Amazed, Astonished, Perplexed" from Interpreting the Scripture.

(4) Goal 3: Identify Ways the Learners Sense the Presence of the Holy Spirit in Their Lives as They Experience Change

❖ Mention that just as we might experience fierce wind in a hurricane or the blazing heat of a forest fire, so we can sense the presence of God's Spirit in our lives.

❖ Call on volunteers to briefly tell a story of a time, perhaps in the midst of change or crisis, when they knew that God was present and working in their lives.

❖ Thank the volunteers for sharing their stories and challenge the group to go forth to tell their stories to others.

(5) Continue the Journey

❖ Pray that today's group will be filled with the Spirit's Pentecostal power so that they might witness boldly to others.

❖ Read aloud this preparation for next week's lesson. You may also want to post it on newsprint for the students to copy.

■ **Title: Living with Hope**
■ **Background Scripture: 1 Thessalonians 4:13–5:11**
■ **Lesson Scripture: 1 Thessalonians 4:13–5:11**

■ **Focus of the Lesson: People find themselves in situations that can be destabilizing, disheartening, and despairing. How do we find stability, courage, and hope? Paul assures us that the promise of Christ's return provides us with comfort and hope.**

❖ Post these three activities related to this week's session on newsprint for the students to copy. Challenge the adults to grow spiritually by completing one or more of them.

(1) **Offer to help someone who is experiencing wanted or unwanted change.**

(2) **Use a map to locate the countries of the peoples mentioned in Acts 2. Give thanks for the inclusive nature of God's pouring out of the Spirit.**

(3) **Look for signs of the Spirit's activity within your own congregation today. What are people being empowered to do?**

❖ Sing or read aloud "O Spirit of the Living God."

❖ Conclude today's session by leading the class in this benediction, based on the key verses for April 28 from 2 Thessalonians 2:16-17: **Now may our Lord Jesus Christ himself and God our Father, who loved us and through grace gave us eternal comfort and good hope, comfort your hearts and strengthen them in every good work and word.**

UNIT 2: RESURRECTION HOPE
LIVING WITH HOPE

PREVIEWING THE LESSON

Lesson Scripture: 1 Thessalonians 4:13–5:11
Background Scripture: 1 Thessalonians 4:13–5:11
Key Verse: 1 Thessalonians 5:9

Focus of the Lesson:
People find themselves in situations that can be destabilizing, disheartening, and despairing. How do we find stability, courage, and hope? Paul assures us that the promise of Christ's return provides us with comfort and hope.

Goals for the Learners:
(1) to discover signs of hope and encouragement in the promise of Christ's return.
(2) to identify and communicate the feelings they experience because of the promise of Christ's return.
(3) to encourage one another by identifying signs of hope in the midst of difficulty.

Pronunciation Guide:
chronos (kroh' nohs)
eschatological (es kat uh loj' i kuhl)
kairos (ki' rohs)
parousia (puh roo' zhee uh)

Supplies:
Bibles, newsprint and marker, paper and pencils, hymnals, candles, matches, art supplies

---

READING THE SCRIPTURE

NRSV

Lesson Scripture: 1 Thessalonians 4:13–5:11

¹³But we do not want you to be unin-formed, brothers and sisters, about those who have died, so that you may not grieve as others do who have no hope. ¹⁴For since

CEB

Lesson Scripture: 1 Thessalonians 4:13–5:11

¹³Brothers and sisters, we want you to know about people who have died so that you won't mourn like others who don't have any hope. ¹⁴Since we believe that Jesus died

we believe that Jesus died and rose again, even so, through Jesus, God will bring with him those who have died. [15]For this we declare to you by the word of the Lord, that we who are alive, who are left until the coming of the Lord, will by no means precede those who have died. [16]For the Lord himself, with a cry of command, with the archangel's call and with the sound of God's trumpet, will descend from heaven, and the dead in Christ will rise first. [17]Then we who are alive, who are left, will be caught up in the clouds together with them to meet the Lord in the air; and so we will be with the Lord forever. [18]Therefore encourage one another with these words.

[5:1]Now concerning the times and the seasons, brothers and sisters, you do not need to have anything written to you. [2]For you yourselves know very well that the day of the Lord will come like a thief in the night. [3]When they say, "There is peace and security," then sudden destruction will come upon them, as labor pains come upon a pregnant woman, and there will be no escape! [4]But you, beloved, are not in darkness, for that day to surprise you like a thief; [5]for you are all children of light and children of the day; we are not of the night or of darkness. [6]So then let us not fall asleep as others do, but let us keep awake and be sober; [7]for those who sleep sleep at night, and those who are drunk get drunk at night. [8]But since we belong to the day, let us be sober, and put on the breastplate of faith and love, and for a helmet the hope of salvation. **[9]For God has destined us not for wrath but for obtaining salvation through our Lord Jesus Christ,** [10]who died for us, so that whether we are awake or asleep we may live with him. [11]Therefore encourage one another and build up each other, as indeed you are doing.

and rose, so we also believe that God will bring with him those who have died in Jesus. [15]What we are saying is a message from the Lord: we who are alive and still around at the Lord's coming definitely won't go ahead of those who have died. [16]This is because the Lord himself will come down from heaven with the signal of a shout by the head angel and a blast on God's trumpet. First, those who are dead in Christ will rise. [17]Then, we who are living and still around will be taken up together with them in the clouds to meet with the Lord in the air. That way we will always be with the Lord. [18]So encourage each other with these words.

[5:1]We don't need to write to you about the timing and dates, brothers and sisters. [2]You know very well that the day of the Lord is going to come like a thief in the night. [3]When they are saying, "There is peace and security," at that time sudden destruction will attack them, like labor pains start with a pregnant woman, and they definitely won't escape. [4]But you aren't in darkness, brothers and sisters, so the day won't catch you by surprise like a thief. [5]All of you are children of light and children of the day. We don't belong to night or darkness. [6]So then, let's not sleep like the others, but let's stay awake and stay sober. [7]People who sleep sleep at night, and people who get drunk get drunk at night. [8]Since we belong to the day, let's stay sober, wearing faithfulness and love as a piece of armor that protects our body and the hope of salvation as a helmet. **[9]God didn't intend for us to suffer his wrath but rather to possess salvation through our Lord Jesus Christ.** [10]Jesus died for us so that, whether we are awake or asleep, we will live together with him. [11]So continue encouraging each other and building each other up, just like you are doing already.

UNDERSTANDING THE SCRIPTURE

Introduction. Biblical scholars generally assess 1 Thessalonians to be the oldest of the New Testament works. Thessalonica itself was a city in Macedonia situated on a major trade route linking Rome with its eastern colonies. The city cultivated its ties to Rome, economically and politically. Later conflict experienced by Paul and then the Thessalonian Christian community itself may owe in part to the gospel's rival claims to those promoted by imperial Rome (for example, see the comments on 5:3 below). The epistle's concern with Christ's return (*parousia*), and what happens to those who have died prior to it, reflects an immediate expectation of Christ's return apparently held in the early church (as later reflected into the Gospels, such as Matthew 16:28; John 21:20-23).

1 Thessalonians 4:13-14. Paul's address of the Thessalonian community as "brothers and sisters" occurs thirteen times in this brief epistle, underscoring the personal nature of Paul's relationship with this community as akin to family. Twice in verses 13-14, Paul makes reference to those who "have died." In Greek, this verb literally means "to sleep." In some New Testament texts it is used in its literal sense, while here and in other texts it is used as a metaphor for death. Some hold that such usage implicitly argues for death as a state of sleep while awaiting resurrection, though that is a matter of considerable debate. The absence of hope, not grief, is what Paul rejects here, thus affirming the grief of his beloved community for loved ones who have died. "Jesus died and rose again" is the foundational assurance of hope he proclaims—and, indeed, the early church's most basic confession and creed.

1 Thessalonians 4:15-17. Paul personally reflects the expectation of Christ's imminent return at this early stage of his ministry by his use of "we": "we who are alive, who are left until the coming of the Lord" (4:15; see also 4:17). The word translated as "coming" in verse 15 is *parousia*—a word that has been adopted into English in specific reference to Christ's return. In the Greco-Roman culture, *parousia* (whose literal meaning includes "presence" and "arrival") came to be associated with the visit of royalty or some other dignitary. A vivid description of this second "coming" unfolds in verses 16-17. Using imagery and symbolism (archangel, trumpet of God) common to Jewish apocalyptic writings, Paul writes to assure those grieved in the community that their deceased loved ones will "rise first." Then, the descending Lord will be met "halfway" as those yet alive will "meet the Lord in the air" (4:17). "Clouds" also bring a symbol freighted with theological weight to this scene, both in Judaism's remembrances of Sinai, where God's presence came to be associated with the clouds that enveloped Mount Sinai prior to the giving of the commandments (Exodus 19:16), and Jesus' ascension as "a cloud took him out of their sight" (Acts 1:9).

1 Thessalonians 4:18. See comments on 5:11.

1 Thessalonians 5:1-5. "Times and seasons" reflect two basic understandings of time. The first (in Greek, *chronos*—where we get the English "chronology") refers to time as measured by clocks and calendars; the moment by moment passage of specific "lengths." The second (*kairos*) refers to time as discerned by opportune or appropriate moments. Immediately before his Ascension, and in response to the disciples' wondering if this were the time when Christ would "restore the kingdom to Israel," Jesus had told them that it was "not for [them] to know the times or periods that the Father has set" (Acts 1:6-7). Here in Thessalonians, Paul echoes the same point regarding "the times and the seasons." The association of the "day of the Lord" (5:2) with apocalyptic themes traces back to the Hebrew prophets (Joel 2:1-2; Amos 5:18). Likewise, its coming "like a thief in the night" hearkens back to Jesus' teachings regarding the latter days (Matthew 24:43-44). First Thessalonians 5:3 speaks of unnamed declarers of "peace and security." This may be one of those points of contention that brought the community into conflict with its Roman authorities, for "peace and security" was precisely the rationale for the exercise of Rome's imperial power. Defying those who falsely claim peace echoes the challenge offered by Hebrew prophets to complacent audiences (Jeremiah 6:14; Ezekiel 13:10). The association of the upheaval with the pains of childbirth brought by this coming day—which is, for Paul's audience, actually the cause of hope—anticipates Paul's later image in Romans 8:18-25, where creation's "groaning in labor pains" (8:22) is a precursor to the hope of redemption.

1 Thessalonians 5:6-10. The metaphor of sleep now shifts from death to a lack of vigilance. Paul's urges the Thessalonians to adopt a stance of wakefulness and sobriety, that is, of individuals and a community acutely aware of, not dulled to, the world around them. The directions regarding employing the defensive armor of breastplate and helmet is a much briefer depiction of such imagery used in a later writing attributed to Paul (Ephesians 6:14-17). First Thessalonians 5:9 provides yet another perspective on the hope that Paul seeks to instill in the community: God's purpose, even in the coming day of the Lord, is not destruction or anger but rather salvation. Those saving purposes are grounded in the next verse in Christ's death that in turn offers the hope to those who live and to those who have already died that salvation promises life with God through Christ.

1 Thessalonians 5:11; 4:18. These two verses are taken together, because both express Paul's hope that these words be used by the community for encouragement of one another. The closing verse adds on to this purpose the related idea of "build each other up," an image employing a verb used for house construction. For Paul, this call to encouragement and community building is grounded not only in the hope of what God has promised in Christ but also in recognition of what the Thessalonians are already doing (5:11). Thus, the passage that affirms and encourages hope ends on a note of hope embodied by this community of Paul's "brothers and sisters" (5:1, 12).

INTERPRETING THE SCRIPTURE

Parousia: The Return of the King

The final installment of J. R. R. Tolkien's *Lord of the Rings* trilogy has for its title *The Return of the King*. That "return" was not simply accomplished in the final vanquishing of enemies, but in the ensuing establishment of peace and a new age in Middle Earth. The irony in the trilogy is that Middle Earth's "king" had been there all along. The recognition of his presence and the heralding of his arrival as sovereign formed a primary plotline throughout the three books.

The Christian hope of the "return of the king" as captured in the expectation of Christ's second coming, or *parousia*, has similar motifs. Or perhaps it would be better to say Tolkien's "return" may have been influenced by the motifs of the Christian concept of *parousia*. For while we long and hope for that promised coming, there is truth in the assertion that the One whose return we await has, in many ways, been among us all along.

To be sure, the theology of Christ's ascension marks a new phase in that presence. Christ is not among us now in the same way Jesus walked with the disciples and among the people of his day. Ascension theology urges a responsibility upon the church to be the "body of Christ" upon the earth while we await Christ's *parousia*. We are to be the hands and feet and voice of the risen and ascended One. We do so with the hope, especially crucial in the face of trying circumstances and delayed promises, that it is not all left up to us, even with the gift of the Spirit. This age continues to turn toward God's coming kingdom, and that turning will be completed in Christ's return. That is the hope Paul impresses upon the Thessalonians, and in so doing urges upon us, for the return of the Sovereign One.

But again, as with Tolkien's trilogy, it can rightly be said that even now, the Sovereign One is among us. At the table of Communion, in broken bread and shared cup, we encounter the risen Christ among us. As Jesus himself taught: In actions of self-giving service, we encounter the risen Christ in one another, particularly the ones who come to us hungry and thirsty and imprisoned. We hold on to the hope of Christ's return with tenacity, for we experience even now breakthroughs of that promised hope in experiences of grace and mercy, given and received.

Come, Lord Jesus, be our guest.

Discerning and Practicing Hope

"We believe that Jesus died and rose again" (4:14). With those words, Paul enunciates the most basic Christian confession. It is not that nothing else matters; it is that everything else comes to be seen in its light. The Hebrew Scriptures and their stories and teachings remain vital for understanding the roots and foundations of our hope. It is just that, in the light of resurrection, all these things come to be seen through the prism of Christ's raising. The life and ministry of Jesus, and the subsequent stories of Christian community as reflected in Gospels and Epistles, remain crucial for forming our views and practices as disciples of Jesus and members of Christ's body. Yet even all these matters take on significance through—and, it could be argued, would not have been remembered without—the radical assertion of Jesus' being raised by God. That is our hope, and that becomes the lens by which we interpret our lives and this world so that we may live with courage and endurance.

While Paul makes the case more extensively in 2 Thessalonians, even in this passage's conclusion Paul is quite clear that living with hope means practicing it. "Falling asleep" is the condition he challenges the community to avoid. Consider how that phrase lends itself to the call to discipleship. Hope is not a matter of "sleepwalking" through life until Jesus plucks us up into the air, as if nothing else matters. Life matters greatly. Service matters greatly. Witness matters greatly. Resurrection hope leads us into, not out of, daily living. Verse 3 of chapter 5 even suggests that resurrection hope has a clearly countercultural dimension to faithful discipleship. Like the prophets of old who warned against those who cried "peace, peace!" when there was no peace, so now does Paul warn against the seductive mantra of "peace and security," a justification for all manner of political and economic mischief and worse, and not just by the Romans in their time.

Where does "peace and security" seek to seduce our values today, attempting to put our ethics and values to sleep for the sake of authoritarian dreams of squelching dissent? What does it mean for individuals and communities today to live as "children of the light?" (5:5). We are called to hope, not just as an interior attitude, but as an outward practice.

Encouragement, Not Entanglement

Not once, but twice, Paul punctuates the teaching of Christ's return and the call to live by hope with the words "therefore encourage one another." And in the second of those statements (5:11), Paul supplements the call to encouragement with its related "build up each other." For Paul, eschatological ("end times") proclamation is not speculative theory arising from presumed timetables. Such proclamation is for encouragement in difficult times. Such proclamation is for building up Christ's community as we strive to live and serve with hope.

The irony, and tragedy, of this passage has come in its frequent usurping by those who obsess on timetables or dwell on what the signs of the final times are. Words meant to instill hope have instead become battlegrounds for whether one is a premillenial or postmillenial tribulationist, or are seen in fantasy-oriented visions and bumper stickers telling what will happen when drivers or pilots are "raptured"—visions and slogans that often bear no small degree of smugness in knowing who is "in" and who is "left behind." In place of hope that encourages, too often we have been sold pottages of end-times entanglements in matters that have nothing to do with building up the body of Christ.

Resurrection hope summons us to reclaim Christ's return from the swamp of speculative fantasies back to the passage's concrete concern for encouragement. Paul writes to comfort bereaved followers: Resurrection hope seeks proclamation where grief looms large today. Paul writes to encourage a community to live faithfully in the face of seductive imperial power: Resurrection hope seeks embodiment in the face of false claims that "peace and security" reside anywhere other than in the One who raised Jesus. In 5:6, Paul summons the Thessalonian community to "keep awake and be sober": Resurrection hope seeks awareness of the world around us as it is, as well as the promises that we have been given, so that our witness in these days can be grounded in authentic hope and not in mere wishful thinking or dreamy escapism.

Why does Paul urge encouraging one another and building up each other, and not say hope is a purely individualistic matter between a believer and Jesus alone? Because in the light of resurrection hope, Paul recognizes he does not address singular individuals who stand in isolation from him and from themselves. These are Paul's "brothers and sisters" in Christ. In the light and hope of Christ's resurrection, we are sisters and brothers to one another—for we are sisters and brothers of Christ.

Therefore, encourage one another. Therefore, build up each other. In hope.

SHARING THE SCRIPTURE

Preparing Our Hearts

Explore this week's devotional reading, found in Psalm 38:9-15. In this psalm a penitent individual cries to God for healing. Despite the hurt and alienation that the psalmist has experienced, he waits for God and trusts that God will answer. What situation prompts you to cry out to God right now? Even if you have felt abandoned by friends and family because of this challenge, do you have confidence that God will care for you? How does this confidence sustain you? Where do you see signs of hope in this situation?

Pray that you and the adult students will recognize that God is always on your side and acting in your best interest.

Preparing Our Minds

Study the background Scripture and the lesson Scripture, both of which are from 1 Thessalonians 4:13–5:11.

Consider this question as you prepare the lesson: *How do we find stability, courage, and hope in difficult situations?*

Write on newsprint:
❑ information for next week's lesson, found under "Continue the Journey."
❑ activities for further spiritual growth in "Continue the Journey."

Review the "Introduction," "The Big Picture," "Close-up," and "Faith in Action." Consider how you will use this additional information, which immediately precedes the first lesson, for this session.

Locate candles or tea lights and matches, preferably enough so that you can give one candle to each person. If your congregation holds candlelight services, you may be able to borrow candles, which will only be lit for a brief period. Decide the safest way to allow each person (or at least representatives) to light these candles.

Gather drawing implements (markers, colored pencils, or crayons), plain paper, and scissors. These art supplies are likely available in your Sunday school office.

Familiarize yourself with the information in the Understanding the Scripture portion.

LEADING THE CLASS

(1) Gather to Learn

❖ Greet the class members. Introduce any guests and help them feel at home.

❖ Pray that today's participants have come with great expectations about what God can and will do in their lives.

❖ Read: **Due to the difficult economy, workers of the baby boom generation who lose their jobs face greater challenges in being rehired and longer periods of unemployment as they must counter perceptions that they are overqualified, inflexible, won't fit in, will leave as soon as better opportunities come along, and other negative stereotypes. Jim Jimenez, a professional with more than thirty years of experience, had been out of work for several years and feared, in his words, "that I will never again get to do the things I was so truly good at." His fears are surely shared by many whose lives have been unexpectedly turned upside down by workforce reductions.**

❖ Ask: **What can the church do to help such people find the hope and courage to move forward?**

❖ Read aloud today's focus statement: **People find themselves in situations that can be destabilizing, disheartening, and despairing. How do we find stability, courage, and hope? Paul assures us that the promise of Christ's return provides us with comfort and hope.**

(2) Goal 1: Discover Signs of Hope and Encouragement in the Promise of Christ's Return

❖ Choose a volunteer to read 1 Thessalonians 4:13–5:11.

❖ Do an in-depth study of this passage by forming five groups to look at the following passages: Group 1: 4:13-14; Group 2: 4:15-17; Group 3: 5:1-5; Group 4: 5:6-10; Group 5: 5:11 and 4:18. Each group is to discuss these questions, which you will read aloud:

    (1) What is Paul saying about Christ's return?
    (2) How do Paul's words bring hope and comfort to his readers?

❖ Call the groups back together and, in turn, discuss the ideas they discovered in their assigned passages. Be prepared to add information from Understanding the Scripture.

(3) Goal 2: Identify and Communicate the Feelings the Learners Experience Because of the Promise of Christ's Return

❖ Read again today's key verse, 1 Thessalonians 5:9.

❖ Distribute paper, scissors, and drawing implements (markers, colored pencils, or crayons). Encourage the adults to think about how the promise of Christ's return makes them feel and express that feeling using the art supplies you have available. Artistic ability is not important. Here are some possible strategies: (1) color all or part of a sheet of paper with a single crayon that expresses feelings about this promise simply by color; (2) draw something that depicts one's feelings; (3) cut out a shape that conveys feelings; or (4) fold the paper to create a symbol.

❖ Suggest that the learners show their creations to a small group to see the variety of feelings expressed about Christ's return and how these feelings may be represented even without words.

(4) Goal 3: Encourage One Another by Identifying Signs of Hope in the Midst of Difficulty

❖ Brainstorm answers to this question: **Where do you see signs of hope in the midst of difficulties that seem common among the residents of our community?** Record ideas on newsprint. Here are some examples: *A new owner is negotiating to buy a factory that has been shuttered for several years; vegetation is growing on land that wildfires had charred; a new recreation center is creating wholesome opportunities for teens; blighted housing is being purchased and renovated.*

❖ Set out candles or tea lights on a table. Invite the learners to gather around the table and have each light one candle as a sign of hope that change is coming, just as surely as Christ himself is coming again.

❖ Conclude by reading the last two paragraphs of "Encouragement, Not Entanglement" in Interpreting the Scripture.

(5) Continue the Journey

❖ Pray that today's participants will go forth with a renewed hope and zest for living because they know the One who holds the future.

❖ Read aloud this preparation for next week's lesson. You may also want to post it on newsprint for the students to copy.

▪ **Title: Hope Comes from God's Grace**
▪ **Background Scripture: 2 Thessalonians 2**
▪ **Lesson Scripture: 2 Thessalonians 2:1-3, 9-17**
▪ **Focus of the Lesson: Information about the future comes to us from a variety of sources. How can we know which sources to trust? Paul warns us against the deception that can come from satanic sources.**

❖ Post these three activities related to this week's session on newsprint for the students to copy. Challenge the adults to grow spiritually by completing one or more of them.

(1) **Encourage someone who feels discouraged about a demoralizing situation caused by forces outside of that person's control, such as the loss of a job or a serious illness. Be careful about being glib or minimizing the severity of the situation, but do help the person see potential for new beginnings.**

(2) **Write a psalm or poem expressing the hope that you have because of the promise of Christ's second coming. Consider sharing your thoughts with someone who may need to hear these words of hope.**

(3) **Listen to music that you find upbeat. Create a dance or simply move to this music to enact in your own body the hope you feel because you believe Jesus' promise that he will come again.**

❖ Sing or read aloud "Hymn of Promise."

❖ Conclude today's session by leading the class in this benediction, based on the key verses for April 28 from 2 Thessalonians 2:16-17: **Now may our Lord Jesus Christ himself and God our Father, who loved us and through grace gave us eternal comfort and good hope, comfort your hearts and strengthen them in every good work and word.**

UNIT 2: RESURRECTION HOPE

HOPE COMES FROM GOD'S GRACE

PREVIEWING THE LESSON

Lesson Scripture: 2 Thessalonians 2:1-3, 9-17
Background Scripture: 2 Thessalonians 2
Key Verses: 2 Thessalonians 2:16-17

Focus of the Lesson:

Information about the future comes to us from a variety of sources. How can we know which sources to trust? Paul warns us against the deception that can come from satanic sources.

Goals for the Learners:

(1) to understand the stark contrasts between the message from satanic sources and the message of Paul about the coming of Christ.
(2) to evaluate how they feel when someone they trust deceives them.
(3) to hold fast to the truth they have been taught about God as they make daily choices.

Pronunciation Guide:

Antiochus Epiphanes (an ti' uh kuhs i pif' uh neez)
apostasia (ap os tas ee' ah)
Caligula (kuh lig' yuh luh)
parousia (puh roo' zhee uh)

Supplies:

Bibles, newsprint and marker, paper and pencils, hymnals

READING THE SCRIPTURE

NRSV
Lesson Scripture: 2 Thessalonians 2:1-3, 9-17
[1]As to the coming of our Lord Jesus Christ and our being gathered together to him, we

CEB
Lesson Scripture: 2 Thessalonians 2:1-3, 9-17
[1]Brothers and sisters, we have a request for you concerning our Lord Jesus Christ's

beg you, brothers and sisters, [2]not to be quickly shaken in mind or alarmed, either by spirit or by word or by letter, as though from us, to the effect that the day of the Lord is already here. [3]Let no one deceive you in any way; for that day will not come unless the rebellion comes first and the lawless one is revealed, the one destined for destruction. [9]The coming of the lawless one is apparent in the working of Satan, who uses all power, signs, lying wonders, [10]and every kind of wicked deception for those who are perishing, because they refused to love the truth and so be saved. [11]For this reason God sends them a powerful delusion, leading them to believe what is false, [12]so that all who have not believed the truth but took pleasure in unrighteousness will be condemned.

[13]But we must always give thanks to God for you, brothers and sisters beloved by the Lord, because God chose you as the first fruits for salvation through sanctification by the Spirit and through belief in the truth. [14]For this purpose he called you through our proclamation of the good news, so that you may obtain the glory of our Lord Jesus Christ. [15]So then, brothers and sisters, stand firm and hold fast to the traditions that you were taught by us, either by word of mouth or by our letter.

[16]**Now may our Lord Jesus Christ himself and God our Father, who loved us and through grace gave us eternal comfort and good hope,** [17]**comfort your hearts and strengthen them in every good work and word.**

coming and when we are gathered together to be with him. [2]We don't want you to be easily confused in your mind or upset if you hear that the day of the Lord is already here, whether you hear it through some spirit, a message, or a letter supposedly from us. [3]Don't let anyone deceive you in any way. That day won't come unless the rebellion comes first and the person who is lawless is revealed, who is headed for destruction. [9]When the person who is lawless comes, it will happen through Satan's effort, with all kinds of fake power, signs, and wonders. [10]It will happen with every sort of wicked deception of those who are heading toward destruction because they have refused to love the truth that would allow them to be saved. [11]This is why God will send them an influence that will mislead them so that they will believe the lie. [12]The result will be that everyone will be judged who is not convinced by the truth but is happy with injustice.

[13]But we always must thank God for you, brothers and sisters who are loved by God. This is because he chose you from the beginning to be the first crop of the harvest. This brought salvation, through your dedication to God by the Spirit and through your belief in the truth. [14]God called all of you through our good news so you could possess the honor of our Lord Jesus Christ. [15]So then, brothers and sisters, stand firm and hold on to the traditions we taught you, whether we taught you in person or through our letter. [16]**Our Lord Jesus Christ himself and God our Father loved us and through grace gave us eternal comfort and a good hope.** [17]**May he encourage your hearts and give you strength in every good thing you do or say.**

UNDERSTANDING THE SCRIPTURE

2 Thessalonians 2:1-3. As in his first letter to the Thessalonians, Paul once more takes up the topic of Christ's coming, or *parousia*, an event anticipated as before with reunion ("being gathered together to him," 2:1). But whereas the crisis evoking the teachings on Christ's coming in the first letter had to do with grief over the death of loved ones prior to that return, now the crisis arises out of teachings that claimed the Second Coming had already taken place, teachings that had apparently "shaken" and "alarmed" the community (2:2). The reference to "by spirit or by word or by letter" in verse 2 suggests the claim may have been made in one or more of these ways ("spirit" most likely referred to some form of ecstatic speech attributed to the Spirit). Paul makes clear at the end of verse 2 and on into verse 3 that any such claims made in his name or authority are false, and their intent is to deceive the community. "Rebellion" translates the Greek word *apostasia*, from which we get the English "apostasy." With that, Paul introduces the mysterious figure identified only as the "lawless one," whose works and threats are taken up in the next sections of the passage.

2 Thessalonians 2:4-8. Historical figures ranging from Antiochus Epiphanes IV to Caligula (who threatened to erect statues bearing his likeness in Jerusalem in A.D. 40) have been suggested for the identity or at least inspiration of the "lawless one." However, the passage at hand offers no decisive statement on the precise identity of this figure. Another mystery involves the two references in these verses as to what (2:6) and who (2:7) "restrains" the lawless one. Paul apparently had done some teaching among the Thessalonians regarding such claims or deceptions, as he appeals in verse 5 to "remember that I told you [of] these things when I was still with you." It would seem, however, the distress referred to earlier in verse 2 has clouded those remembrances, necessitating Paul now to speak again, although in this highly symbolic and obscure passage regarding the "mystery" of lawlessness already at work that somehow is related to the assertion that Christ had already come again. What is clear at the very end of the passage, however, is that the threat posed by the lawless

one need not be overwhelming. For when Christ does return, verse 8 assures that his coming will bring destruction of whatever/whoever is represented by the figure of the lawless one.

2 Thessalonians 2:9-12. Paul does introduce in these verses the connection of this figure with "the working of Satan" (2:9). In the Old Testament, Satan (from the Hebrew word meaning "accuser") was a part of the heavenly court (see Job 1:6-12). Over time, especially in some Jewish apocalyptic writings, Satan came to be more and more portrayed in the demonic terms familiar to contemporary depictions. The association of Satan in verse 9 with "lying wonders" parallels John 8:44, where Satan ("the devil") is portrayed as "the father of lies." If this passage presents readers difficulties over the identity of the lawless one or the meaning of who or what "restrains" him, perhaps an even larger challenge comes in verse 11. There, Paul's wording suggests that God also engages in deception: deluding those who are perishing by leading them to believe what is false. Various ideas have been suggested for interpreting or "softening" these words, but none prove completely satisfying. Perhaps the closest biblical parallel would be the story leading up to the Exodus from Egypt, where God tells Moses about Pharaoh: "I will harden his heart, so that he will not let the people go" (Exodus 4:21; see also 7:3; 11:10).

2 Thessalonians 2:13-15. Paul shifts now from warning to thanksgiving, lifting up the Thessalonian community in gratitude. Addressing them as "brothers and sisters" underscores, as noted in last week's Understanding the Scripture, the feeling of kinship with which Paul holds the members of this community. The cause of Paul's thanksgiving is God's choosing them for salvation. The means of that salvation, as Paul goes on to say in verse 13, comes "through sanctification by the Spirit and through belief in the truth." God's choosing them is a subtle reminder that they need not feel inferior to those who claim special knowledge about Christ's second coming having already occurred. God's choice, not human opinions, formed this community. Similarly, the affirmation of "belief in the truth" asserts that the community's faith and trust in what is true (that is, "of God," given the previous identification of Satan with lies and deception) places them on firm footing against their opponents. For that reason, then, Paul encourages the community in verse 15 to "stand firm" and "hold fast." They have the traditions (literally, "what has been given over") that comprise the "truth" to which Paul previously referred. In an ironic parallel to the warning against false sources claiming to be from Paul in verse 2, Paul declares the Thessalonians have those traditions "taught by us, either by word of mouth or by our letter" (2:15). Truth is not only in what is said but also in the person from whom it comes.

2 Thessalonians 2:16-17. The final two verses of the passage take the form of a benediction or commissioning offered to the community. The first half affirms what has come to the Thessalonians, and to all, through Christ and God: love and grace. Such love and grace become the basis for the community's comfort (recall the earlier letter's concern over those grieved) and hope. Such gifts from God, in Paul's benediction, lend themselves to internal well-being ("comfort your hearts") and external witness ("strengthen them in every good work and word," 2:17). Notice in verse 16 the verb tense Paul uses for God's action: "loved us . . . gave us." The Thessalonians need not wait for love and grace to come at some distant future moment. Although Christ has not come again, love and grace have come and remain with them. Those gifts strengthen the community and form the basis for hopeful expectation and faithful living.

INTERPRETING THE SCRIPTURE

The Future Will Bring . . .

How would you complete the sentence begun by the title of this section? Will it bring only the "same old same old," a cyclical repetition of what has been and nothing more? Will it make all of your dreams come true—or bring all of your hopes to an end?

What we think about the future makes a difference in how we conduct our lives now. If the future is seen as a place of hope, we will likely find it possible to live with hope now. If the future is seen as a bleak landscape of despair, we will likely live in ways that yield to despair, whether in sullen resignation or in a "grab all you can get now because the party won't go on forever" grasping.

Paul writes to the Thessalonians out of

concern, basically, for what they see the future holding. Interestingly, the crisis seems to arise out of some individuals or groups promoting the idea that we needn't wait for Christ to return because the return has already happened! The implications of that misjudgment could go in a number of directions. For if Christ has returned, why haven't things changed? Or if Christ has returned, then the waiting for, and the serving of, the kingdom is over. We can just sit back and let Christ take care of things.

Christ, however, did not return as some apparently believed. Unfortunately, the church has often suffered under the claims of those who thought they knew when the return would take place, only to be disappointed by false hopes. The church has also suffered under those whose vision of the future seemed, or seems, to be a mirror image of their brand of theologies and social mores and even political leanings, rather than a realm in which the grace of God is free to embrace whomever God chooses and loves.

The Thessalonian community, and every Christian community since, is called to ministries that are consistent with the qualities and hopes of the Christ's anticipated realm. Think about what you do in your personal exercise as discipleship, and what your congregation does in its ministries and programs. What do these say to you—and what do they say to those for whom you are consciously or unconsciously a witness—about what you really think the future will bring?

Discerning Truth and Deception

One of my favorite TV characters of all time was Jim Rockford, played by James Garner in *The Rockford Files*. Officially, he was a private detective. But actually, he was what is sometimes called a "con artist." The "con" is not in reference to someone who spent time in jail (though Rockford had). Rather, "con" refers to "confidence." A con artist is someone who can make you believe (have confidence) in whatever he or she is saying or presenting to you.

Rockford was a good-hearted character whose cons were done to help clients out of a jam. But not all sellers of confidence are so altruistic. Perhaps the biblical con man par excellence was Jacob, who sold his father, Isaac, on the untruth that he was really Esau, so as to usurp the blessing usually reserved for the elder son. The saga of religious purveyors of false confidence by no means ends there. Not many years ago, David Koresh sold his followers in the Branch Davidian movement on the notion that he was the second coming of Christ. The "confidence" they invested in his delusion bore horrific fruits.

It is unavoidable that the Christian church must constantly be vigilant when it comes to matters of truth or deception conveyed in the name of faith. Part of the struggle involves maintaining a spirit of openness to unexpected sources of truth, remembering God is free to move and work as God chooses. Moses was not the likeliest choice for a religious leader, not only for his reluctance in speaking but also for his once having committed a murder. Peter likewise stands as a case in point of God working through someone with a tainted past of denial and bravado. Part of the struggle when it comes to discerning truth and deception likewise turns on the way in which God brings new truths into our awareness or assumptions. Witness the opening of the gospel to Gentiles, or the far-too-long delayed rejection of slavery by the church. We need to be humble when it comes to discerning what is true and what is false.

But when the times come, we also need to be clear when truth is victimized and deception is employed, whether to sway the allegiance of would-be followers or to carry out actions, religious or political, that are not as they are portrayed.

In the end, the discernment of truth and deception relies greatly upon trust. Whom do we trust, and why? Is it those who tell us what we want to hear, or is it those who tell us what we need to hear? If it is only what we want to hear, then we set ourselves up for deception. But if it is what we need to hear, we will be more apt to exercise wise and faithful judgment, especially if we link our seeking of what we need to hear with prayerful seeking of what God would lead us to see and whom God would lead us to trust. And for those who equate trust in them with trust in God, hold on to your wallet and keep your distance!

Graced to Live With Hope

Imagine what it would be like to live without hope. Relationships would always have a "catch." Outcomes would inevitably face a downward devolution. Life itself would be, at best, an "eat, drink, and be merry while you can," or at worst, a slide into nothingness. But we do not have to live without hope. By the love and grace of God, Paul writes to the Thessalonians, we have been given "good hope" (2:16). Good hope. The future is not a place of hostility or indifference. The future holds the realm of God. Good hope.

But notice Paul does not end his benediction with verse 16's affirmation of "good hope." Such hope is entrusted for a purpose, for a calling, that we might be strengthened "in every good work and word" (2:17). Good hope is not simply an attitude adjustment; it is a call to embody the promises of God into the present conduct and witness of our daily lives, as individuals and as communities of faith.

Here is where Paul's vision of hope and Christ's coming differ radically from some escapist versions of those promises. The promise of Christ's return is not a ticket out of here while the rest of the world gets left behind. The promise of Christ's return is an ethical imperative to live lives and construct communities that reflect the qualities of God's kingdom, and that celebrate God's love and grace for all, not just the few "enlightened" ones.

Listen to Paul's words in verses 16-17 not simply as addressing an ancient community; listen to them as addressing you. You are loved, you are graced, by God.

With such assurance yours is the heart to be comforted, and yours are the works and words to be strengthened by this hope. Thanks be to God!

SHARING THE SCRIPTURE

Preparing Our Hearts

Explore this week's devotional reading, found in Titus 3:1-7. Here we are reminded that God has saved us, not because of our merit, but through Christ because of divine mercy. Having received by grace the Holy Spirit, we can have hope for eternal life. What do you hope for? Recall major examples of your hopes being fulfilled. How have you experienced God's grace acting in your own life?

Pray that you and the adult students will be aware of "God sightings" in your life that infuse you with hope.

Preparing Our Minds

Study the background Scripture from 2 Thessalonians 2 and the lesson Scripture from 2 Thessalonians 2:1-3, 9-17.

Consider this question as you prepare the lesson: *How can we know which sources to trust for reliable information?*

Write on newsprint:
❏ information for next week's lesson, found under "Continue the Journey."
❏ activities for further spiritual growth in "Continue the Journey."

Review the "Introduction," "The Big Picture," "Close-up," and "Faith in Action." Consider how you will use this additional information, which immediately precedes the first lesson, for this session.

LEADING THE CLASS

(1) Gather to Learn

❖ Greet the class members. Introduce any guests and help them feel at home.
❖ Pray that those who are present today will be able to discern the difference between true teachings of God and those teachings that come from other sources.

❖ Read the first two paragraphs of "Discerning Truth and Deception" from Interpreting the Scripture.

Discuss these questions:

(1) If you are familiar with the Jim Rockford character, would you have trusted him? Why or why not?

(2) Although we know the tragic end of the Branch Davidian story in Waco, Texas, why do you think people trusted David Koresh and thought of him as a true man of God?

(3) How can we know whom to trust?

❖ Read aloud today's focus statement: **Information about the future comes to us from a variety of sources. How can we know which sources to trust? Paul warns us against the deception that can come from satanic sources.**

(2) Goal 1: Understand the Stark Contrasts Between the Message From Satanic Sources and the Message of Paul About the Coming of Christ

❖ Select one volunteer to read 2 Thessalonians 2:1-3, a second to read verses 4-8 (background Scripture), and another to read verses 9-17.

❖ Read the information for "2 Thessalonians 2:1-3" from Understanding the Scripture to help the adults understand the situation that has caused people to become upset.

❖ Post a sheet of newsprint that you have divided in half with a vertical line. On the left write "Lawless One and His Message" and on the right, "Paul and His Message." Invite the students to look at their Bibles and call out information that belongs under each column. Talk about how these two messages stand in contrast to each other.

❖ Conclude this section by asking: **We often are drawn in by smooth talk. How** can we evaluate those messages that come from God in opposition to those that come from ungodly sources?

(3) Goal 2: Evaluate How the Learners Feel When Someone They Trust Deceives Them

❖ Read aloud this list of familiar practices:

■ A retailer advertises an item at a reduced price, but when a buyer goes into the store the clerk tries hard to convince the customer to purchase a more expensive item.

■ A car owner extols the virtues of the vehicle to a prospective buyer but fails to mention that the car was in a serious accident.

■ An ad for a weight-loss product makes amazing claims, indicating in the fine print that these losses are not obtained by all or even most users.

■ A stockbroker encourages a client to buy a stock that is not in the client's best interest but does pay a hefty commission to the broker.

■ A family member convinces you to lend money, based on a false story.

❖ Discuss these questions:

(1) How do you feel when you realize that someone has deceived you?

(2) Are your feelings different if you know this person reasonably well?

(3) How do you treat or talk to someone who has deceived you?

(4) Do you think you will ever trust this person's promises or claims again? Why or why not?

(4) Goal 3: Hold Fast to the Truth the Learners Have Been Taught About God as They Make Daily Choices

❖ Read "Graced to Live with Hope" in Interpreting the Scripture.

❖ Distribute paper and pencils. Challenge the adults to think about the hope that they have for the future and the choices they make each day that may fulfill or squelch that hope.

❖ Ask them to look again at 2 Thessalonians 2:13-15 and list on their papers "the traditions" they have been taught in the community of faith. These teachings need not be "traditions" as such but rather truths they have been taught that guide their daily choices. Here are some examples: *Jesus calls us to be servants; God is Sovereign and in charge; believers are saved by God's grace; God keeps promises.*

❖ Encourage volunteers to read one or two of their ideas. After each reading ask: **How does this teaching influence you as you make daily choices?**

❖ Talk with the group about how deceptions and untruths, as well as true teachings, may influence their daily choices.

❖ Challenge the learners to review their lists and hold fast to those items that enable them to make good choices based on God's truth.

(5) Continue the Journey

❖ Pray that today's participants will recognize and hold fast to the teachings that God by grace has given believers.

❖ Read aloud this preparation for next week's lesson. You may also want to post it on newsprint for the students to copy.

- **Title: A Living Hope**
- **Background Scripture: 1 Peter 1:1-12**
- **Lesson Scripture: 1 Peter 1:3-12**
- **Focus of the Lesson: Life's trials and tribulations cause us to experience hopelessness. Where can**

one go to find new hope and reassurance for a joyous future? Peter writes that a new birth into a living hope can be found in the resurrection of Jesus Christ.

❖ Post these three activities related to this week's session on newsprint for the students to copy. Challenge the adults to grow spiritually by completing one or more of them.

(1) Be aware of instances this week when you tell a lie or shade the truth. What prompted you to do that? What changes do you need to make to be more truthful?

(2) Discern God's truth as you read books or listen to broadcasts by persons claiming to speak for God. Does what they say reflect what you know to be the truth of Scripture? If you are unsure, do some biblical research to test the truth.

(3) Think about your hopes for the future. Has anyone made promises to you about the future? Who? (Perhaps a stockbroker, employer, spouse, grown child, or friend has made promises.) Why do you trust this person to fulfill these promises?

❖ Sing or read aloud "God of Grace and God of Glory."

❖ Conclude today's session by leading the class in this benediction, based on the key verses for today's lesson from 2 Thessalonians 2:16-17: **Now may our Lord Jesus Christ himself and God our Father, who loved us and through grace gave us eternal comfort and good hope, comfort your hearts and strengthen them in every good work and word.**

UNIT 3: A CALL TO HOLY LIVING
A LIVING HOPE

PREVIEWING THE LESSON

Lesson Scripture: 1 Peter 1:3-12
Background Scripture: 1 Peter 1:1-12
Key Verse: 1 Peter 1:3

Focus of the Lesson:
Life's trials and tribulations cause us to experience hopelessness. Where can one go to find new hope and reassurance for a joyous future? Peter writes that a new birth into a living hope can be found in the resurrection of Jesus Christ.

Goals for the Learners:
(1) to interpret Peter's message of hope rooted in the death and resurrection of Jesus.
(2) to appreciate Jesus' resurrection from the dead as a source of hope and a reason for living.
(3) to identify situations to which they could bring hope.

Pronunciation Guide:
Cephas (see' fuhs)   shalom (shah lohm')
Domitian (duh mish' uhn)   Trajan (tray' juhn)
Petrine (pee' trine)

Supplies:
Bibles, newsprint and marker, paper and pencils, hymnals

READING THE SCRIPTURE

NRSV
Lesson Scripture: 1 Peter 1:3-12

³**Blessed be the God and Father of our Lord Jesus Christ! By his great mercy he has given us a new birth into a living hope through the resurrection of Jesus Christ from the dead,** ⁴and into an inheritance that is imperishable, undefiled, and unfading, kept in heaven for you, ⁵who are being pro-

CEB
Lesson Scripture: 1 Peter 1:3-12

³**May the God and Father of our Lord Jesus Christ be blessed! On account of his vast mercy, he has given us new birth. You have been born anew into a living hope through the resurrection of Jesus Christ from the dead.** ⁴You have a pure and enduring inheritance that cannot perish—an

tected by the power of God through faith for a salvation ready to be revealed in the last time. [6]In this you rejoice, even if now for a little while you have had to suffer various trials, [7]so that the genuineness of your faith—being more precious than gold that, though perishable, is tested by fire—may be found to result in praise and glory and honor when Jesus Christ is revealed. [8]Although you have not seen him, you love him; and even though you do not see him now, you believe in him and rejoice with an indescribable and glorious joy, [9]for you are receiving the outcome of your faith, the salvation of your souls.

[10]Concerning this salvation, the prophets who prophesied of the grace that was to be yours made careful search and inquiry, [11]inquiring about the person or time that the Spirit of Christ within them indicated when it testified in advance to the sufferings destined for Christ and the subsequent glory. [12]It was revealed to them that they were serving not themselves but you, in regard to the things that have now been announced to you through those who brought you good news by the Holy Spirit sent from heaven—things into which angels long to look!

inheritance that is presently kept safe in heaven for you. [5]Through his faithfulness, you are guarded by God's power so that you can receive the salvation he is ready to reveal in the last time.

[6]You now rejoice in this hope, even if it's necessary for you to be distressed for a short time by various trials. [7]This is necessary so that your faith may be found genuine. (Your faith is more valuable than gold, which will be destroyed even though it is itself tested by fire.) Your genuine faith will result in praise, glory, and honor for you when Jesus Christ is revealed. [8]Although you've never seen him, you love him. Even though you don't see him now, you trust him and so rejoice with a glorious joy that is too much for words. [9]You are receiving the goal of your faith: your salvation.

[10]The prophets, who long ago foretold the grace that you've received, searched and explored, inquiring carefully about this salvation. [11]They wondered what the Spirit of Christ within them was saying when he bore witness beforehand about the suffering that would happen to Christ and the glory that would follow. They wondered what sort of person or what sort of time they were speaking about. [12]It was revealed to them that in their search they were not serving themselves but you. These things, which even angels long to examine, have now been proclaimed to you by those who brought you the good news. They did this in the power of the Holy Spirit, who was sent from heaven.

UNDERSTANDING THE SCRIPTURE

Introduction. The epistles of 1 and 2 Peter provide the passages for this quarter's sessions. The shift from the Thessalonian epistles is considerable. While 1 Thessalonians is believed to be the earliest of the New Testament materials, predating even the Gospels, the Petrine Epistles are believed to be among the latest. While few doubts have been raised about Paul's authorship of 1 Thessalonians, the attribution of authorship to Peter faces strong challenges. Would a Galilean fisherman be proficient in writing with the sophisticated style of Greek apparent in these letters?

Also, Peter was martyred probably between A.D. 64 and A.D. 68 in Rome, which is generally accepted as the epistles' place of origin (1 Peter 5:13, "Babylon" being a frequent symbol for Rome). However, most scholars place the writing of these epistles in the latter quarter of that century, or even in the opening decades of the second century. One prominent theme in the epistles is suffering. Whether widespread imperial persecutions or more limited local harassments of the communities addressed in Asia Minor are in mind, the audience of the Petrine Epistles clearly faces a troubled situation—one where hope would not be a given but a genuine act of faith and even defiance.

1 Peter 1:1-2. "Peter" is the Greek equivalent of the Aramaic Cephas ("rock"), the name given to Simon by Jesus (John 1:42). "Exiles of the dispersion" draws a parallel between the scattered Christian communities who live as minorities within the Roman Empire with the Jewish communities scattered during the Babylonian exile. The five place names in verse 2 are all provinces in Asia Minor (the Anatolian Peninsula, which is part of modern Turkey). The reference in verse 2 to being "sprinkled with his blood" calls to mind ritual gestures in Leviticus connected to sin offerings (Leviticus 4) and the Day of Atonement (Leviticus 16:11-19). The use of "chosen and destined" in verse 2 introduces an emphasis on the community's sure status with God that continues throughout the letter. The verse concludes with the offering of "grace" (a typical greeting in Greek letters) and "peace" (reflecting the common Semitic greeting of *shalom*).

1 Peter 1:3-5. The language of "new birth" parallels thoughts expressed not only in this epistle (1:23) but more famously in Jesus' encounter with Nicodemus (John 3:3-9). The phrase is also indicative of the situation "on the ground" in the early church, where few would have been born and nurtured within Christian community. The birth imagery also forms a natural connec-tion to the ensuing language about "inheri-tance." The author of 1 Peter here implicitly contrasts the usual "material" nature of children's inheritances with those that are, by the gift of God, "imperishable, undefiled, and unfading" (1:4). We miss the cadence of these three adjectives in English translation as, in Greek, they literally form a rhyme that underscores the author's emphasis. Christ's resurrection is affirmed as the guarantor of such hope of new life and its inheritance. "Being protected by the power of God" (1:5) hints at the need for protection in times of crisis such as these communities faced, as they trust in the salvation whose coming awaits "the last time" (1:5).

1 Peter 1:6-7. The author introduces the sometimes difficult balance here between rejoicing in the hope and salvation promised, and the present difficulties that weigh upon the communities. As noted in the introduction, "suffer various trials" in verse 6 may address all-out persecution by the empire (as in Emperor Domitian's alleged persecutions in the last decade of the first century or the more documented persecutions by Trajan in the first decade of the second century), or more local harassments of Christian communities similar to reactions narrated in Acts (for example, Acts 17:1-9; 19:21-41). Such difficulties as "character builders" are alluded to in this passage when the author speaks of how these trials provide a "test by fire" (1:7). This idea parallels other biblical musings on trials testing faith (1 Corinthians 3:13; James 1:2-4).

1 Peter 1:8-9. One clue as to the possible lateness of this epistle comes at the beginning of verse 8, when the author writes to his audience as those who "have not seen him [Christ], [yet] you love him." This and the ensuing description of these communities as not seeing Christ now but believing echoes Jesus' encounter with Thomas on the evening of Easter, where Jesus blesses those who do not see yet believe (John 20:29). In verse 6 rejoicing by the community was commended in the face of trials. Here again, the author affirms the communities' rejoicing without benefit of physical sight. Such joy is traced here to the reception of faith's end in salvation.

1 Peter 1:10-12. These final verses in this passage connect the salvation for which the community rejoices through faith with the ministry of the Hebrew prophets. The mention again here in verse 11 of "sufferings" underscores how real and pressing an issue this was for the early church. The link to the prophets accomplishes two things. First, the prophets themselves were associated with suffering, as the life of Jeremiah reveals, or that which one sees in Isaiah's familiar passage on the "suffering servant" of God (Isaiah 52:13–53:12, the Fourth Servant Song). Second, by tracing the theme of suffering back to the prophets, the author of the Petrine correspondence can confirm to these communities that what is happening to them is not new within salvation history. Suffering need not be proof of unfaithfulness; in some times, as in this one, it becomes a sign of faithfulness. The author of 1 Peter also affirms that the role of the prophets was not only for their immediate audience; rather, "they were serving not themselves but you" (1:12). These ancient words, and their purposes, have present meaning and power, which affirm, among other things, the continuing role and importance of the Hebrew Scriptures for Christian readers and communities.

INTERPRETING THE SCRIPTURE

Easter Gifts

One of the most enduring associations of Christmas is with gift giving, whether presents under the tree or the gift of the mangered child. But Easter, too, has its gifts. The author of 1 Peter singles out two such gifts that come to us through Christ's resurrection: a "new birth into a living hope" (1:3) and a heaven-kept "inheritance" (1:4).

The language of new birth has sometimes become something less than a means of extending gifts and more a battleground for views of conversion (where "have you been born again?" sounds less like an invitation and more like an inquisition). First Peter's linking of new birth with Easter provides one avenue for rescuing "new birth" from theological disputations to gracious opportunity. For if the word of resurrection is true, hopes given up may take heart. Lives resigned to quiet desperation in fear of death can be "reborn" to hope-filled embodiments of the qualities of God's sovereign realm. For with Easter, we find testimony that nothing, not even death, will stand in the way of God's purposes for compassion and justice, mercy and good. And if nothing stands in the way of such things, we find the encouragement to live with such qualities ourselves. Hope is not merely to be held in life. Hope is to be lived—even as the One in whom our hope resides himself lives, Jesus Christ, crucified and risen.

The second gift of Easter comes in the language of inheritance. Have you ever received something from a loved one, passed down to you and intended quite specifically for you? We tend to treasure such inheritances, for they keep alive in our memory the relationship and experiences shared with that one. In Christ's resurrection, the inheritance God entrusts to us is likewise to be treasured—but not for memories alone. Its treasuring directs us toward the hope of our salvation: knowing ourselves loved by God, trusting that God's resurrecting power is not a once-and-done event in Christ but rather the promise of such power to be extended toward us and all creation.

Such gifts as these are not outgrown or worn out. Such gifts as these intend to transform who we are in light of what God has done in Jesus Christ, what God continues to do within our own lives, and what God will continue doing until the final revealing of salvation in the last time, which will, in truth, become the beginning of all time beyond time.

Hope: Living by Trust

Once upon a time it may have been said that children, especially young children, were the ones who wanted things right then, whose only sense of time was of the present. In our age—rife with consumerism, an economic culture bent on taking no thought for the future when it comes to earth's resources or debt piled upon generations for the sake of immediate gratifications, and the politics of take no prisoners when it comes to using whatever means necessary to undermine someone on the other side of the aisle regardless of the effect upon the greater whole and wider good— little children have a lot of company. The willingness to live by trust rather than instant gratification—including gospels that purport God's blessing upon what more seemly times have viewed as unseemly pursuits of material wealth and power—may be becoming a lost art.

In stark contrast to such pursuits and philosophies, the author of 1 Peter testifies to a faith lived not on the basis of the success you can scramble after, or the security you can defend at any cost, and not even on the God you can claim to see and invoke to carry out your wishes. No, 1 Peter testifies to life that must be lived and hope that must be found by trust. For remember, the author does not write to a community that comprises the movers and shakers of his day, well insulated from ordinary turmoil

because of their congeniality with God and imperial authorities. First Peter is directed to a community acquainted with suffering and grief, to borrow an image from Isaiah about the nature of God's Messiah and affirmed by the early church in reference to Christ. First Peter is written to a community whose standing is not assured because they can lay eyes on Jesus but rather because they can love Jesus and one another— friend, stranger, and even enemy. For that is the gospel Christ taught. "Although you have not seen him, you love him" (1:8). How do we love Christ beyond the securities of liturgy and the safety of like-minded pewmates? How do we trust God, when all is not going as planned and "Christian" is not a synonym for majority status? If it is in God we trust, let us so live and hope and rejoice.

Salvation: Past as Prologue

Like Jews and Muslims, we are a people of the Book. We value the teachings of the past, and have chosen to deem as peculiarly authoritative for our lives and community certain writings. We do so, not in the delusion that we can live in the past, but in the trust and wisdom that we can learn from it. We look to the biblical works, in particular, to be led to critical insights into the nature and call of God upon us and in all of creation.

One might have thought that a letter such as 1 Peter, so interested in the promises of God's salvation and its accompanying hope for the future, might have little regard for the past. Instead, the author repeatedly brings allusions from the Hebrew Scriptures into the epistle's urging of hope. That connecting of what has been to what lies ahead comes to the fore in verses 10-12 of today's passage from 1 Peter. Of particular concern is the work of the prophets.

For those who conceive of prophets merely as religious fortune-tellers, that might seem obvious. But a close reading of the prophets will reveal that they are less "predictors" than they are "convictors"; that is, the prophets preach and write to bring transformation into the lives of their contemporaries. The fact that the future sometimes plays a large role in their prophesying does not owe to gazes into crystal balls but to firm trust that God is sovereign of the future as well as the present.

In that sense, for the author of the Petrine Epistles and the congregations he addressed, the prophetic past was indeed the prologue to the promised future. The emphasis in this particular passage that the prophets were "serving not themselves but you" (1:12) in their work is a very pertinent reminder for us today. Faith is not limited, either in its hopes or in its understanding, to a single generation, whether sixth-century B.C. Judaism or first-century early church or twenty-first-century contemporary Christianity. We do well to remember that God would have us live in such a way that shows concern for those who will follow us. They may well depend upon our witness for their own journey of faith. We live not to ourselves: We live in the light of those who went before us; we live for the sake of those who come after. For we live in hope.

SHARING THE SCRIPTURE

Preparing Our Hearts

Explore this week's devotional reading, found in Lamentations 3:19-24. In the midst of the lament about the fall of Jerusalem to the Babylonians in 587 B.C. the grieving poet has hope (3:21). His hope is not related to the dire circumstances of his beloved city but rather centered on God. The writer praises the never-ending love and mercy of God, who is always faithful. Are there losses in your life that cause you to grieve? Are you able to find hope in God? Write a few sentences about your own experience, expressing your confidence in God.

Pray that you and the adult students will recognize God's loving presence in all circumstances, and give thanks.

Preparing Our Minds

Study the background Scripture from 1 Peter 1:1-12 and the lesson Scripture from 1 Peter 1:3-12.

Consider this question as you prepare the lesson: *When trials and tribulations cause hope-* *lessness, where can one go to find new hope and reassurance for a joyous future?*

Write on newsprint:
- ❑ information for next week's lesson, found under "Continue the Journey."
- ❑ activities for further spiritual growth in "Continue the Journey."

Review the "Introduction," "The Big Picture," "Close-up," and "Faith in Action." Consider how you will use this additional information, which immediately precedes the first lesson, for this session.

LEADING THE CLASS

(1) Gather to Learn

❖ Greet the class members. Introduce any guests and help them feel at home.

❖ Pray that today's participants will seek signs of mercy and hope in God.

❖ Distribute paper and pencils. Tell the adults that what they will write is confidential—just between them and God. Ask them to list one to three situations in their lives, or the lives of people they know well, that may create a sense of hopelessness.

They are to write about the situation, why it feels so hopeless, and a brief prayer seeking God's reassurance that in the end all will be well.

❖ Encourage the students by reading "Hope: Living by Trust" from Interpreting the Scripture.

❖ Ask: **Where do you find the hope to trust in God, especially when the situation does not appear to change?**

❖ Read aloud today's focus statement: **Life's trials and tribulations cause us to experience hopelessness. Where can one go to find new hope and reassurance for a joyous future? Peter writes that a new birth into a living hope can be found in the resurrection of Jesus Christ.**

(2) Goal 1: Interpret Peter's Message of Hope Rooted in the Death and Resurrection of Jesus

❖ Create a transition between our study of the Thessalonian correspondence and a study of Peter's epistles by reading the "Introduction" from Understanding the Scripture.

❖ Use "1 Peter 1:1-2" from Understanding the Scripture to introduce Peter's audience, their location, and their situation to your class.

❖ Choose two volunteers, one to read 1 Peter 1:3-9, and the other to read verses 10-12.

❖ Discuss these questions:
   (1) **What do you learn about Peter's understanding of who God is and what God has done?**
   (2) **What do you learn about salvation?**
   (3) **What do you learn about suffering—both that of Jesus and of this faith community?**
   (4) **What do you learn about the prophets?**

❖ End this portion of the session by reading "Salvation: Past as Prologue" in Interpreting the Scripture. Point out that we can endure suffering because we have hope and trust that our salvation is secure.

(3) Goal 2: Appreciate Jesus' Resurrection From the Dead as a Source of Hope and a Reason for Living

❖ Read: **The Gospels all affirm that Jesus was bodily resurrected from the dead. They record postresurrection appearances of an embodied Jesus to numerous people. In 1 Corinthians 15:13-19 Paul argues that belief and preaching are useless if Christ was not raised from the dead. In other words, the bodily resurrection of Jesus is foundational for our faith. The Nicene Creed, written in the fourth century, also affirms Jesus' resurrection: "On the third day he rose again in accordance with the Scriptures." Modern writer John R. Stott bluntly writes: "Christianity is in its very essence a resurrection religion. The concept of resurrection lies at its heart. If you remove it, Christianity is destroyed." Yet some Christians will not accept the notion of a bodily resurrection.**

❖ Form several groups to discuss this question: **Why do you think that people will believe that there is no future for them rather than accept accounts that Jesus was in fact raised from the dead?**

❖ Call the groups together and invite the adults to share their ideas.

(4) Goal 3: Identify Situations to Which the Learners Could Bring Hope

❖ Brainstorm answers to this question and list them on newsprint: **Where are the direst needs in the world?** Encourage the class to think about natural disasters and political instability that have caused people to live on the margins, perhaps barely surviving. They may live in tents. Maybe they are refugees traveling to find food. Possibly they lack food or clean drinking water but cannot leave their location. Prompt the adults to think about situations that are currently in the news or have been in the news within the last year or so. Major disasters are no longer top news stories after a few days or weeks, but the need to help people rebuild their lives continues for quite some time.

❖ Continue brainstorming by asking the students to identify those situations where, as a class, they could bring hope. Try to reach consensus regarding one or two projects. Encourage the students to name ideas they could implement and add them to the paper. Challenge those who are willing to become involved to raise their hands and mention what they intend to do.

(5) Continue the Journey

❖ Pray that the class will move into the future with a sense of hope that is grounded in the resurrection of Jesus.

❖ Read aloud this preparation for next week's lesson. You may also want to post it on newsprint for the students to copy.
- ■ **Title: Equipped with Hope**
- ■ **Background Scripture: 2 Peter 1**
- ■ **Lesson Scripture: 2 Peter 1:4-14**
- ■ **Focus of the Lesson: Many people feel they are ineffective, unproductive, and unable to make the right choices in life. Where can we find the strength to surmount this sense of despair? Peter says that the inner strength needed to face life with new assurance and hope comes because of our knowledge of and faith in our Savior, Jesus Christ.**

❖ Post these three activities related to this week's session on newsprint for the stu-

dents to copy. Challenge the adults to grow spiritually by completing one or more of them.

(1) Seek out people who need hope as the result of a natural disaster. Do what you can to support them financially, in prayer, and if possible in person to help them rebuild their lives.

(2) Ponder your own future and ultimate death. How does knowledge of your salvation and Jesus' resurrection give you hope for eternal life?

(3) Be an encourager within your congregation. Perhaps your church has reasons to feel less than hopeful due to dwindling attendance, inadequate finances, declining neighborhood, or some other issue. What steps can you take to help the church members focus on the hope they have in Christ?

❖ Sing or read aloud "My Hope Is Built."

❖ Conclude today's session by leading the class in this benediction, based on the key verses for April 28 from 2 Thessalonians 2:16-17: **Now may our Lord Jesus Christ himself and God our Father, who loved us and through grace gave us eternal comfort and good hope, comfort your hearts and strengthen them in every good work and word.**

UNIT 3: A CALL TO HOLY LIVING
EQUIPPED WITH HOPE

PREVIEWING THE LESSON

Lesson Scripture: 2 Peter 1:3-14
Background Scripture: 2 Peter 1
Key Verse: 2 Peter 1:3

Focus of the Lesson:
Many people feel they are ineffective, unproductive, and unable to make the right choices in life. Where can we find the strength to surmount this sense of despair? Peter says that the inner strength needed to face life with new assurance and hope comes because of our knowledge of and faith in our Savior, Jesus Christ.

Goals for the Learners:
(1) to realize how Peter tried to help early Christians be effective and fruitful followers of Jesus Christ.
(2) to reflect on the ways faith, goodness, knowledge, self-control, endurance, godliness, mutual affection, and love are present in their lives.
(3) to identify ways they can become more effective and fruitful Christians.

Pronunciation Guide:
exodos (ex' od os)

Supplies:
Bibles, newsprint and marker, paper and pencils, hymnals

READING THE SCRIPTURE

NRSV
Lesson Scripture: 2 Peter 1:3-14

³His [Christ's] divine power has given us everything needed for life and godliness, through the knowledge of him who called us by his own glory and goodness. ⁴Thus he has given us, through these things, his precious and very great promises, so that

CEB
Lesson Scripture: 2 Peter 1:3-14

³By his divine power the Lord has given us everything we need for life and godliness through the knowledge of the one who called us by his own honor and glory. ⁴Through his honor and glory he has given us his precious and wonderful promises,

through them you may escape from the corruption that is in the world because of lust, and may become participants of the divine nature. [5]For this very reason, you must make every effort to support your faith with goodness, and goodness with knowledge, [6]and knowledge with self-control, and self-control with endurance, and endurance with godliness, [7]and godliness with mutual affection, and mutual affection with love. [8]For if these things are yours and are increasing among you, they keep you from being ineffective and unfruitful in the knowledge of our Lord Jesus Christ. [9]For anyone who lacks these things is nearsighted and blind, and is forgetful of the cleansing of past sins. [10]Therefore, brothers and sisters, be all the more eager to confirm your call and election, for if you do this, you will never stumble. [11]For in this way, entry into the eternal kingdom of our Lord and Savior Jesus Christ will be richly provided for you.

[12]Therefore I intend to keep on reminding you of these things, though you know them already and are established in the truth that has come to you. [13]I think it right, as long as I am in this body, to refresh your memory, [14]since I know that my death will come soon, as indeed our Lord Jesus Christ has made clear to me.

that you may share the divine nature and escape from the world's immorality that sinful craving produces.

[5]This is why you must make every effort to add moral excellence to your faith; and to moral excellence, knowledge; [6]and to knowledge, self-control; and to self-control, endurance; and to endurance, godliness; [7]and to godliness, affection for others; and to affection for others, love. [8]If all these are yours and they are growing in you, they'll keep you from becoming inactive and unfruitful in the knowledge of our Lord Jesus Christ. [9]Whoever lacks these things is shortsighted and blind, forgetting that they were cleansed from their past sins.

[10]Therefore, brothers and sisters, be eager to confirm your call and election. Do this and you will never ever be lost. [11]In this way you will receive a rich welcome into the everlasting kingdom of our Lord and savior Jesus Christ.

[12]So I'll keep reminding you about these things, although you already know them and stand secure in the truth you have. [13]I think it's right that I keep stirring up your memory, as long as I'm alive. [14]After all, our Lord Jesus Christ has shown me that I am about to depart from this life.

UNDERSTANDING THE SCRIPTURE

2 Peter 1:1-3. Even more questions of authorship surround this second epistle attributed to Peter than surround 1 Peter (see last week's "Introduction" to Understanding the Scripture). In contrast to the first epistle, these opening verses omit any geographical reference to a particular audience or set of communities. Rather, this epistle is simply addressed to those who have received "a faith as precious as ours" (1:1). The first verse also identifies Jesus as "Savior." That title is remarkably infrequent

in the New Testament. It is used only three times in the Gospels, while here in 2 Peter the title is used five times. The combining of traditional Greek and Hebrew greetings—grace and peace—parallels the opening of 1 Peter, and may be suggestive that the epistle is addressed to both Jewish Christian and Gentile Christian audiences. The two references to "knowledge" (1:2, 3) in terms of relationship with God may also signify a subtle shift from an earlier understanding of faith as primarily relational to one now centered in a particular set of knowledge (doctrine) about God. Such an emphasis may grow out of this epistle's wider concern with false teachers, who spread knowledge that goes beyond what the author considers the core of Christian teaching (see 1:16).

2 Peter 1:4-9. The epistle's concern with false teaching is not simply about misunderstandings, but mal-practices ("corruption") that result. The need to resist such corruption is given positive motivation in the promise that the faithful may become "participants of the divine nature" (1:4), though the nature of that participation with the divine is not spelled out here. Verse 5 introduces the first of three urgings (here and in verse 10 for the faithful; in verse 15 for the author) to "make every effort" and "be all the more eager." The Greek verb in those verses literally means "haste." What is a matter of haste and urgency in verses 5-7 that is embodying the series of intertwined virtues listed there? Such lists of virtues were frequent in Greek and Roman writings of the day, even as they are found in other New Testament epistles (for example, Galatians 5:22-23). Second Peter's invocation of these virtues is not merely for attitude adjustment but to assure fruitful and effective lives grounded in the knowledge of Christ.

2 Peter 1:10-11. These verses open with the second urging ("be all the more eager") that is now related to the confirmation of the believers' "call and election." Those two terms assert the God-derived status of the believers' standing in the church. That is, they are part of the community neither by accident nor of human accord (though their decision in faith was involved). Rather, they belong to the community because of the action of God, whose summons in Christ to faith (call) validates the divine purpose in their belonging (election). Call and election form a subtle (or, perhaps, not so subtle) rebuke to teachers who might have been seeking to sway them by saying their faith was somehow incomplete without these

teachers' "additional" insights. The author declares, in call and election, that the faith of the community is grounded in God, not in human persuasion.

2 Peter 1:12-14. The author's task in writing is twice revealed in verses 12-13 to be one of evoking remembrance ("keep on reminding you . . . refresh your memory") regarding these matters. The author also clarifies that his work of calling to remembrance is not one of passing on new truths (as the opponents likely claimed for themselves) but rather has to do with things known by the community already—truths in which they have been already "established." What highlights the urgency of the epistle author's task is the disclosure of his impending death. There is no indication here whether this means the author is imprisoned and has been sentenced to execution, or suffers from a fatal disease. All that is communicated concerning the impending passing is that "Christ has made [this] clear to me" (2:14).

2 Peter 1:15-18. The attack on "cleverly devised myths" (1:16) contrasts the speculations of the opponents with the author's claimed eyewitness testimony of Christ that follows. One of the arguments in favor of Peter's authorship of this epistle comes in this claim that the author was an eyewitness to the event known in the Gospels as Transfiguration. (The only disciples there were Peter, James, and John). Besides recounting that event, and the affirmation of the divine voice declaring Jesus as "Son, my Beloved; with whom I am well-pleased" (1:17), there is another connection to Transfiguration tucked away in the language of verse 15. Having spoken in verse 14 about his impending death, the author relates to the present urgency of his work by connecting it to his "departure." The account of Jesus' transfiguration in Luke 9:31 declares this about the conversation between Moses and Elijah and Jesus on the mountain: "They appeared in glory and were speaking of his *departure*" (emphasis added). The same Greek word occurs in Luke and 2 Peter, a word that occurs twice in all of the New Testament: *exodos*, a word that brings strong associations with narratives of redemption.

2 Peter 1:19-21. The opening chapter of the epistle concludes with an appeal to the author's prophetic credentials ("we have the prophetic message more fully confirmed," 1:19). One way for other teachers to claim new words and ways other than those held by the author would have been through prophecy: the Spirit shedding new light not earlier or otherwise known. The author's claiming the prophetic mantle in this concluding section aims at negating the possibility of such an argument. The denial of prophecy in regard to Scripture as a matter of "one's own interpretation" (1:20) likewise takes aim at individual figures who make such claims versus the weight of the apostolic (wider community) authority claimed by the epistle's writer. The writer closes by affirming the movement by God's Spirit as the basis of prophecy, not the exercise of human will: Prophecy is what God stirs, and not the work that precocious and religiously opinionated individuals generate on their own.

INTERPRETING THE SCRIPTURE

Matters of Urgency

When was the last experience you had of something that needed to be done or said with urgency? Right now! No delay! What was it in the situation—what was it in yourself—that justified taking immediate measures, whether by you or another?

The church is not always an institution we associate with urgency. Ideas for action typically need to be filtered through committees and gatekeepers before action is taken. In many instances the lack of rush is prudent and wise. But in some instances, urgency outweighs caution. A lack of urgency can at times erode momentum or decisiveness. A lack of urgency can miss an opportune moment that may not come again.

The second epistle attributed to Peter opens with a sense of urgency. The author has not as yet revealed the specific cause, but twice in the first ten verses he weighs in upon the community to respond with all due haste. In the first instance, every effort is to be made to practice in one's life a set of seven virtues: goodness, knowledge, self-control, endurance, godliness, mutual affection, love (1:5-7). There is urgency in that. Faith is not a matter of deciding to follow the way of Christ, so long as changes to one's ethical or relational conduct can be put off. Augustine is famously said to have prayed: "Grant me chastity and continence, but not yet." The integrity of faith with practice is urgent, then and now.

In the second instance, the urgency involves the community being "all the more eager to confirm your call and election" (1:10). In other words, there is urgency in taking seriously the call of Christ upon your life and the realization that you are one whom God has chosen to love. The urgency of that message impresses upon us our sense of both responsibility and being graced. Faith calls us to a new way of living, not simply a new way of talking about God. But along with that, faith as election assures us that God values us and chooses us for relationship. Sometimes we need to add humility to that, so that we do not allow election to become a badge of exclusivity, as if God is gracious only to the likes of me and mine. God is gracious to whom God chooses, and to know oneself so valued and chosen and loved is urgently needed in times when we feel we are without worth or value or love.

The third instance of urgency is one that cuts across the board of human experience: the urgency brought about by the sense of one's mortality. For the author, this is not a cause of despair, but of rekindled fervor to live faithfully. How that can be is the hope generated by faith grounded in Christ crucified and raised. Our urgency to live to the fullest before we die is not because all will then be lost. Our urgency to live life to the fullest is because we know our efforts have lasting value. That human community is in urgent need of such hope and courage as faith can provide.

Where, and what, is faith's urgency for you?

Linkage

Buffets can be intriguing places, what with all the choices of salads and entrées and desserts. While my enjoyment of them has increased (along with my waistline) in recent years, I also remember old-school cafeterias in my hometown of St. Louis, whose steam tables presenting German or Italian specialties stretched beyond the capacity of my plate to sample them all. I really had to think it over and decide which ones I would savor and which ones I would have to pass on until the next lunch there.

Second Peter 1:5-7 offers a smorgasbord of sorts: a span of Christian virtues spread across the passage's table. But there is one glaring difference between the cafeterias' overabundance and the Scripture's feast. While you can pick randomly what dishes you want for your meal, you don't get to pick and choose from discipleship's menu of virtues. They are linked: You choose one and you are committed to them all. For in discipleship, we do not get to decide that today we will be bad, and that self-control or love can wait until tomorrow. These qual-

ities are all interdependent, as is discipleship's reliance upon them.

The list does not appear to be rigidly constructed as a template of faith development, whereby faith leads to goodness, and goodness to knowledge, and so on until we finally arrive at love. An example of that is Romans 5:3-4, where Paul sets up a sequencing that goes, "suffering produces endurance, and endurance produces character, and character produces hope." Rather, the author of 2 Peter presents a set of seven virtues that are fundamental for individuals—and it could be argued for communities—of faith. But while these virtues are not sequential (we can't wait that long to get around to love), they are linked. Nor is there a specific number of virtues. (Note that Paul lists nine in Galatians 5:22-23.) Can faith be devoid of goodness without becoming cynical? Can self-control be devoid of love without becoming puritanical? Can godliness be devoid of mutual affection without becoming self-righteous?

Discipleship is not a buffet line where we get to pick and choose whatever virtues suit our particular tastes of piety of the day and either leave the rest for others so inclined or say we will eventually get around to them. The new life to which Christ calls us, and the Spirit empowers us, is called to partake of the whole feast of Christ-directed virtues.

Remembrance and Practice

As the writer of this passage from 2 Peter 1 closes, the role of memory and remembrance comes to the fore. That is an apt transition from the imagery of feast in the paragraphs above, because in the Christian liturgy, feast and remembrance are intrinsically bound in the table of Communion.

In 2 Peter 1, the remembrance is not of the table Christ shared—at least, it is not so directly or explicitly. The author's purpose in writing these things is to "keep reminding you" (1:12) and to "refresh your memory" (1:13). Why? Because remembrance impacts practice: What we do grows out of what we remember about ourselves, about others, and about God. The writer earlier tipped his hand that his aim is to keep the audience he addresses from "being ineffective, unfruitful in the knowledge of the Lord Jesus Christ" (1:8). Which is to say, the writer seeks more than head or even heart knowledge; the writer seeks the doing of what is inside.

And the place that begins is instilling remembrance. For in the logic of this epistle—and in the logic of the Eucharist—what is remembered by us will ideally be practiced by us. We remember we are loved by God, and in remembering, we love. We remember we have hope in God's grace, and in remembering, we live hopefully and graciously.

Does faithful remembrance guarantee faithful practice? No. We do tend to forget some things, especially when it is convenient or less costly to do so. But faithful remembrance lays the foundation to live with integrity to what—and Who—is recalled as the source and hope of our lives.

Jesus' remembrance of us is the source of our strength to live the new life—and our remembrance of Jesus is to be evidenced in its living.

SHARING THE SCRIPTURE

Preparing Our Hearts

Explore this week's devotional reading, found in Psalm 130. In this individual lament, we hear a cry for God's help in verse 1. The psalmist's thrust is that he will wait, not in despair, but in hope that God will act. Obviously, he seems quite confident, since in verses 7-8 he encourages all the people to hope in God, through whose love and power people are redeemed and forgiven. Where do you place your hope? Who needs to hear from you today that God is the One in whom we can securely place our hope and trust?

Pray that you and the adult students will recognize the security and affirmation that God brings to your life.

Preparing Our Minds

Study the background Scripture from 2 Peter 1, the lesson Scripture from 2 Peter 1:4-14, and key verse from 2 Peter 1:3.

Consider this question as you prepare the lesson: *If people feel they are ineffective, unproductive, and unable to make the right choices in life, where can they find the strength to surmount this sense of despair?*

Write on newsprint:
❑ information for next week's lesson, found under "Continue the Journey."
❑ activities for further spiritual growth in "Continue the Journey."

Review the "Introduction," "The Big Picture," "Close-up," and "Faith in Action." Consider how you will use this additional information, which immediately precedes the first lesson, for this session.

LEADING THE CLASS

(1) Gather to Learn

❖ Greet the class members. Introduce any guests and help them feel at home.

❖ Pray that those who have come today will be reminded that as they are equipped with hope, they can face the challenges that life brings.

❖ Read this information from a *New York Times* article dated February 8, 2009: **After eighteen years of owning their home in Lehigh Acres, a woman and her** husband were forced to vacate due to fore-closure. This exurb of Fort Meyers, Florida, which was created in the 1950s, had been rocked by recession. Numerous homes were vacant, and the residents who remained were finding it difficult to make ends meet. Churches and social service agencies worked hard to meet the basic needs of those who had lost jobs, homes, and hope. The tragedy is that this community is not alone. Many others have experienced the sting of hard economic times.

❖ Ask: **How can people who have gone from being productive citizens to losing their homes to standing in line for food find the strength to surmount the despair that many feel?**

❖ Read aloud today's focus statement: **Many people feel they are ineffective, unproductive, and unable to make the right choices in life. Where can we find the strength to surmount this sense of despair? Peter says that the inner strength needed to face life with new assurance and hope comes because of our knowledge of and faith in our Savior, Jesus Christ.**

(2) Goal 1: Realize How Peter Tried to Help Early Christians Be Effective and Fruitful Followers of Jesus Christ

❖ Read "Matters of Urgency" from Interpreting the Scripture.
❖ Invite the adults to keep these matters in mind as a volunteer reads 2 Peter 1:3-14, which includes today's key verse.
❖ Discuss these questions:
   (1) **While it is important to have knowledge of God, Peter also teaches that we must lead a virtuous life. How, according to Peter, might we do that?**
   (2) **What are signs indicating that a Christian may be ineffective or unfruitful?**
   (3) **In verses 12-14 Peter wants to refresh the memory of his readers prior to what he believes is his**

impending death. Why? (See "Remembrance and Practice" in Interpreting the Scripture.)

(3) Goal 2: Reflect on the Ways Faith, Goodness, Knowledge, Self-control, Endurance, Godliness, Mutual Affection, and Love Are Present in the Learners' Lives

❖ Read "Linkage" from Interpreting the Scripture. Emphasize that these virtues are linked, though not sequential. We do not have to wait for one to be ingrained to progress to the next.
❖ Distribute paper and pencils. Suggest that the learners list these virtues from 2 Peter 1:5-7 on their papers. Next to each one, they are to write several words explaining how they see this particular virtue within their own lives. In cases where they feel they are lacking, recommend that they write briefly about why they need to improve in a particular area and how they might be able to do that. The adults will not be asked to share what they have written.
❖ Bring the group back together. Give them the opportunity to list other virtues. Galatians 5:22-23 will be helpful, but encourage the students to suggest their own ideas.

(4) Goal 3: Identify Ways the Learners Can Become More Effective and Fruitful Christians

❖ Discuss these questions:
   (1) **What do you mean when you say that you want to be a more effective and fruitful Christian?**
   (2) **How would you describe the behaviors, attitudes, and motivations of such a person? List ideas on newsprint.** (You may want to direct attention back to today's Scripture lesson for ideas.)
   (3) **How does your specific congregation help people become these faithful, fruitful Christians? List ideas on newsprint.** (Think about

committees, such as worship and education; the role of lay and clergy leaders in equipping members for ministry; and opportunities for mission and outreach.)

(4) As you compare the two lists, what else do you think your congregation needs to do to help people become the kind of faithful, fruitful Christians that you envision?

(5) Continue the Journey

❖ Pray that the students will go forth to help others find the hope that makes faithful living possible.

❖ Read aloud this preparation for next week's lesson. You may also want to post it on newsprint for the students to copy.

■ **Title: Hope Through Stewardship**
■ **Background Scripture: 1 Peter 4**
■ **Lesson Scripture: 1 Peter 4:1-11**
■ **Focus of the Lesson: The perilous world in which we live sometimes tempts us to accept the lifestyles and values of others in order to be successful. How can we avoid losing sight of our own integrity and yet find hope for a better life? First Peter 4 tells us that God will strengthen us to serve as good stewards of God's manifold grace.**

❖ Post these three activities related to this week's session on newsprint for the students to copy. Challenge the adults to grow spiritually by completing one or more of them.

(1) Think about the Christian wisdom and values that you would like to pass on to the next generation. Write in a list or an essay about these important underpinnings of the Christian life. Begin to pass your ideas on to children, grandchildren, and other young people.

(2) Review 2 Peter 1:3, this week's key verse. Be aware that you have "everything needed for life and godliness." Count the blessings that God has given you. Make notes about these blessings and give thanks.

(3) Recall that Peter was facing death as he wrote this letter (1:13-15). Do you know someone who apparently will soon be facing death? If so, do all in your power to support this person by your prayers, presence, and service.

❖ Sing or read aloud "All Hail the Power of Jesus' Name."

❖ Conclude today's session by leading the class in this benediction, based on the key verses for April 28 from 2 Thessalonians 2:16-17: **Now may our Lord Jesus Christ himself and God our Father, who loved us and through grace gave us eternal comfort and good hope, comfort your hearts and strengthen them in every good work and word.**

UNIT 3: A CALL TO HOLY LIVING
HOPE THROUGH STEWARDSHIP

PREVIEWING THE LESSON

Lesson Scripture: 1 Peter 4:1-11
Background Scripture: 1 Peter 4
Key Verse: 1 Peter 4:10

Focus of the Lesson:
The perilous world in which we live sometimes tempts us to accept the lifestyles and values of others in order to be successful. How can we avoid losing sight of our own integrity and yet find hope for a better life? First Peter 4 tells us that God will strengthen us to serve as good stewards of God's manifold grace.

Goals for the Learners:
(1) to understand the cost and the discipline required of good stewards of the manifold grace of God.
(2) to discern how they are stewards of God's grace.
(3) to define one act of service that each learner could carry out to demonstrate stewardship of a gift received from God.

Pronunciation Guide:
theodicy (thee od' uh see)

Supplies:
Bibles, newsprint and marker, paper and pencils, hymnals

READING THE SCRIPTURE

NRSV
Lesson Scripture: 1 Peter 4:1-11

¹Since therefore Christ suffered in the flesh, arm yourselves also with the same intention (for whoever has suffered in the flesh has finished with sin), ²so as to live for the rest of your earthly life no longer by human desires but by the will of God. ³You

CEB
Lesson Scripture: 1 Peter 4:1-11

¹Therefore, since Christ suffered as a human, you should also arm yourselves with his way of thinking. This is because whoever suffers is finished with sin. ²As a result, they don't live the rest of their human lives in ways determined by human desires

have already spent enough time in doing what the Gentiles like to do, living in licentiousness, passions, drunkenness, revels, carousing, and lawless idolatry. [4]They are surprised that you no longer join them in the same excesses of dissipation, and so they blaspheme. [5]But they will have to give an accounting to him who stands ready to judge the living and the dead. [6]For this is the reason the gospel was proclaimed even to the dead, so that, though they had been judged in the flesh as everyone is judged, they might live in the spirit as God does.

[7]The end of all things is near; therefore be serious and discipline yourselves for the sake of your prayers. [8]Above all, maintain constant love for one another, for love covers a multitude of sins. [9]Be hospitable to one another without complaining. **[10]Like good stewards of the manifold grace of God, serve one another with whatever gift each of you has received.** [11]Whoever speaks must do so as one speaking the very words of God; whoever serves must do so with the strength that God supplies, so that God may be glorified in all things through Jesus Christ. To him belong the glory and the power forever and ever. Amen.

but in ways determined by God's will. [3]You have wasted enough time doing what unbelievers desire—living in their unrestrained immorality and lust, their drunkenness and excessive feasting and wild parties, and their forbidden worship of idols. [4]They think it's strange that you don't join in these activities with the same flood of unrestrained wickedness. So they slander you. [5]They will have to reckon with the one who is ready to judge the living and the dead. [6]Indeed, this is the reason the good news was also preached to the dead. This happened so that, although they were judged as humans according to human standards, they could live by the Spirit according to divine standards.

[7]The end of everything has come. Therefore, be self-controlled and clearheaded so you can pray. [8]Above all, show sincere love to each other, because love brings about the forgiveness of many sins. [9]Open your homes to each other without complaining. **[10]And serve each other according to the gift each person has received, as good managers of God's diverse gifts.** [11]Whoever speaks should do so as those who speak God's word. Whoever serves should do so from the strength that God furnishes. Do this so that in everything God may be honored through Jesus Christ. To him be honor and power forever and always. Amen.

UNDERSTANDING THE SCRIPTURE

1 Peter 4:1-4. The experience of suffering weighs heavily upon the community, whether in terms of present persecution or ominous threats, and the connection here to Christ's sufferings illustrates a bond between the community's experience and that of Christ. "Finished with sin" (4:1) is not a claim to infallibility, but rather is more of an assertion that when one is no longer being led to actions related to inappropriate desires, there is a turning away from sin's attraction and seduction. The overwhelming likelihood that the community(ies) addressed were partially or largely composed of Gentile Christians means hearing the contrast of what the "Gentiles" like to do as a more general reference to Gentile nonbelievers (the older term still used in some commentaries would be "pagans"). The listing of vices in verse 3 echoes similar listings in New Testament epistles and the wider culture. Verse 4 follows through on the contrast with the actions of the "Gentiles" who have not accepted Christ with those who have. The refusal of the letter's audience to participate in what they had "already spent enough time in doing" (4:3) has led to malicious talk against the community. The word "blaspheme," beyond its more popularly understood meaning of speaking ill of God, can more broadly mean to speak evil against others. An alternative reading in the NRSV is "they malign you."

1 Peter 4:5-6. This portion raises the implicit background of a coming day of judgment (made explicit in verse 7) that will hold folks accountable for words and for actions. Verse 6 raises major questions as to what exactly is meant by the gospel being proclaimed to the dead (a similar line of thought comes in 1 Peter 3:19-20). These two references likely came into play in the theology of the Apostles' Creed ("he descended into hell")—a phrase, interestingly, entirely omitted by the later Nicene Creed. Whatever is specifically intended in verse 6's obscure reference, it does in its own way underscore the more foundational assertion in verse 5 of God in Christ as judge of both living and dead. The realm and judgment of God do not have any corners hidden from them.

1 Peter 4:7-11. First Peter 1:20 earlier asserted Christ's revealing "at the *end* of ages" (emphasis added). That theme of end times returns to the forefront in verse 7 with a sense of imminence ("near") even more pronounced than in 1:20. As with Jesus' teachings regarding the closing of this age (Mark 13:32-37 and especially Luke 21:34-36 with its listing of vices to be avoided that resonate with 1 Peter 4:3), the coming of the end brings with it a summons to practices and ethics of faithful living. The ensuing listing of actions in verse 8 (maintain love, be hospitable, serve one another) forms a community-centered counter to the behaviors in verse 3 that by nature focus on individual gratification. This listing of actions parallels other such calls to the practical, "lived" consequences of faith (Philippians 2:1-4; Colossians 3:12-14). As Paul does in 1 Corinthians 13, the author of 1 Peter 4 likewise asserts love as the hallmark of faithful living and community connection—making love even a means of "covering" of sin. "Steward" in verse 10 uses a term that typically references a manager of a household (for example, John 2:9). The writer closes this section with words of praise. Its pairing of "the glory and the power" is also used in Jesus' teaching regarding the end of times in Matthew 24:30.

1 Peter 4:12-16. The urging to not be taken by surprise at the "fiery ordeal" makes use of the same verb in 4:12 that the writer used to describe the "surprise" of the community's opponents that the community no longer participates in the actions described in verse 4. The author gives no particular details that would shed light as to what this ordeal consisted of—only that it is interpreted as a "test" for the community. Beyond that, the community is encouraged not to see what is happening as "strange," but rather an indication that it is a sign they are sharing in Christ's sufferings (as in the bond suggested in the comments on verse 1). Verses 13-14 commend the community's rejoicing and note they are blessed because they are reviled as a result of faithfulness. These ideas closely parallel in thought and even wording Jesus' conclusion to his teachings known as the Beatitudes (Matthew 5:11-12). Suffering in general, however, is not regarded here as an automatic sign of faithfulness. The author lists (a favorite strategy of his!) several causes for suffering that carry no faithful or redemptive value. Perhaps the most intriguing one singled out for critique is "mischief maker," a word the King James Version translates as "busybody." At the end, however, the writer returns to affirming suffering for Christ not as a cause of shame but rather an occasion to glorify God.

1 Peter 4:17-19. "The time has come for judgment to begin" (4:17) carries on the theme of the immediacy of end-time expectations. What stands out, however, is that this beginning of judgment is aimed not in the direction of the opponents, but toward "the household of God," that is, the church. The difficulty of such judgment is clear: Its "hardness" for the righteous portends even greater trouble for those identified as the "ungodly and sinners" (4:18). The text's assertion of judgment beginning with the church certainly implies that the church can never rest content or consider itself above accountability to God, even in the name of grace. That is certainly the emphasis contained in the opening section's call to separate from the vices listed there, and in the middle section's call to embody and enact the qualities of love and hospitality and service. Even in the closing verse, that emphasis holds true. While calling upon the community to entrust themselves to a "faithful Creator," the author urges the community's continuing ethical responsibilities "while continuing to do good" (4:19). The end is not something for which we sit back and wait. Instead, it is something toward which we move and by which our lives are transformed.

INTERPRETING THE SCRIPTURE

Suffering and the Struggle for New Life

In 1981, Rabbi Harold Kushner's *When Bad Things Happen to Good People* was first published. According to the cover of its 2004 edition, more than 4 million copies have sold. It is easy to understand why. The problem of evil (sometimes called "theodicy") and the related issue of why the innocent suffer vex us. If only the world were such that good always triumphed, that evil always reaped its rewards—and in both cases, that such outcomes were immediate and obvious. They are not. As Jesus himself noted in the Sermon on the Mount: "[God] makes his sun shine on the evil and on the good, and sends rain on the righteous and on the unrighteous" (Matthew 5:45).

First Peter devotes considerable attention to the theme of suffering, as noted in the opening comments on verses 1-4 in Understanding the Scripture. That attention grows out of the experience of the community being addressed, and quite likely the writer who gathered these thoughts together. But rather than seeing suffering as a repudiation of faithfulness, or the faithful, the epistle challenges its hearers, then and now, to associate their current sufferings with the suffering of Christ. That is to say, the path of discipleship and covenant community follows One who was acquainted with sorrows and grief.

That is a hard lesson to accept, particularly for theologies that revel in militant triumphalism or that promise material prosperity in exchange for following Jesus. These are not the gospel messages that the author of 1 Peter proclaims. Rather, the new life to which we are called, individually and in community, is associated with sharing in the sufferings of Christ, rather than gorging on the "me-first" desires of self-gratification alluded to in verse 3. The effort to move toward such new life involves struggle. Dominant models of culture—and church—that still promote material gain and the *lack* of suffering do not take such countermovements quietly. By failing to join in with popular-at-the-moment religious (and political) movements, contemporary Christians (as their counterparts in 1 Peter 4) sometimes suffer by way of dwindling memberships in their churches or by charges of their not being "real" Christians. If they were "real," their cause would not be suffering so. But as 1 Peter 4 reminds us, suffering and faithfulness are not at all opposites. Sometimes, they are necessarily twinned. The struggle of the new life in Christ is not how to avoid suffering. The struggle of the new life in Christ is how to be faithful within suffering, as was Christ.

Stewards of God's Grace

Several options exist when folks believe the end to be near, whether the end be the cessation of a relationship or, as seems to be the case in 1 Peter, the belief in some parts of the early Christian community in Peter's time, the end of the world. One option is to sit back, kick up one's feet, and do nothing, because what a person does or does not do is not going to matter anyway. This seems to have been an issue for the community addressed in the Thessalonian correspondence, where Paul repeatedly warns against "idlers" and "idleness" (1 Thessalonians 5:14 and 2 Thessalonians 3:6-8). Another response to end times of any sort is to take advantage of the situations to do whatever one pleases, because it's going to be all over. In our times, this might be seen in a "short-timer" at work who spends his last days doing all sorts of things that would have gotten him fired—but his job is over already, so who cares? More seriously, it may be seen in the tendency of some religious cults who view the end as near to justify unconscionable actions, such as the multiple sexual partners of the Branch Davidians and the acceptance and coercion of mass suicide at Jonestown, Guyana, by Jim Jones and that group's leaders. The end is coming, so anything I choose to do will make no difference.

In stark contrast, 1 Peter 4 urges a community toward an end-time ethic of covenantal responsibility toward one another, grounded in our active stewardship, or "management," of God's grace in our serving of one another.

Consistent with Jesus' primary ethic of love, 1 Peter 4:8 urges that the community "maintain constant love." That is, love is not a passing phase through which we go as we move on to some higher spiritual knowledge. Love is the constant, consistent sign of discipleship, no matter what "time" is involved. Beyond that, "hospitality" (4:9) is urged. The word in Greek used here is a compound word that literally means "love of stranger." Hospitality is thus not simply hosting friends and family for dinner. Gospel hospitality is welcoming any and all from the community, including those whom we have not yet met. Beyond that, the author clearly delineates an ethic of faithful stewardship that engages "whatever gift each of you has received" (4:10) in service and ministry directed toward others.

Notice that every ethic of stewardship for the sake of ministry identified here is something that brings us into contact with others, and is for the sake of the community. To live in light of the kingdom's approach is not an "every man or woman for himself or herself" scattering to be ready for Jesus' return. To live in the light of the Kingdom's approach is to engage in actions and words that draw us together and fashion us as a faithful, expectant people.

To live with the end in view is, thus, to live for one another in the name of the coming Christ.

Life as Doxology

In the midst of struggle and suffering, in the labor of living out the ethics to which God has called us in these times, God is to be praised. Discipleship and service, witness and stewardship, are meant to flow into a liturgy deep with praise and hope.

We may not often think of liturgy and hope or liturgy and calling as synonyms, but in some senses they are. They certainly can be seen in the closing of 1 Peter 4:11. For the goal and direction of our sharing in Christ's sufferings and our serving as stewards of God's grace for the sake of others is "so that God may be glorified in all things through Jesus Christ." In the face of the suffering, in the midst of the struggle, in the labors to render love and welcome and service, God will hold the final word. God's glory and God's power are without end. Worship is the act that celebrates and declares God is Sovereign, and God's realm will be established. Because of that, we have hope. And out of that hope, we may joyously and confidently live lives of faithful stewardship. That is why doxology and hope are one. For in liturgy, we recite—and we rehearse—what is finally true for us and all creation: the love and grace of God, the power and authority of God. That is where creation is heading, and that is why and how we may "serve one another with whatever gift" (4:10) we have received. For whether we encounter suffering or peace upon our way, we may trust the faithful Creator whose gifts sustain us on the way and give us cause for hope.

SHARING THE SCRIPTURE

Preparing Our Hearts

Explore this week's devotional reading, found in Luke 16:10-13. In these verses Jesus explains the implications of the parable of the dishonest steward (16:1-9). He talks about the relationship between caring for a little and caring for a lot. Those who are faithful with little are also faithful when they are given much to oversee. Likewise, those who are dishonest with little are unable to handle more. Jesus concludes by stating, "You cannot serve God and wealth" (16:13). How would you rate yourself as a steward of money? Are you able to handle money wisely and honestly? If not, what changes do you need to make?

Pray that you and the adult students will live holy lives by being good stewards of the material resources that God has entrusted to you.

Preparing Our Minds

Study the background Scripture from 1 Peter 4 and the lesson Scripture from 1 Peter 4:1-11.

Consider this question as you prepare the lesson: *In a world filled with temptations, how can we avoid losing sight of our own integrity and yet find hope for a better life?*

Write on newsprint:
❑ information for next week's lesson, found under "Continue the Journey."
❑ activities for further spiritual growth in "Continue the Journey."

Review the "Introduction," "The Big Picture," "Close-up," and "Faith in Action." Consider how you will use this additional information, which immediately precedes the first lesson, for this session.

LEADING THE CLASS

(1) Gather to Learn

❖ Greet the class members. Introduce any guests and help them feel at home.

❖ Pray that those who have come today will experience Christ in their midst.

❖ Read about these religious leaders who yielded to temptation to live a lifestyle that violated their integrity as Christians:

■ Televangelist Jim Bakker not only cheated on his wife but also defrauded his PTL Club of $158 million.

■ Dr. Henry Lyons, president of the National Baptist Convention, USA, was sentenced to five and a half years in prison for racketeering and grand theft.

■ Austrian bishop Kurt Krenn was blamed for a scandal in the Roman Catholic seminary he oversaw after forty thousand lewd images, including child pornography, were found on a seminarian's computer.

❖ Ask: **What factors do you think lead to the downfall of such revered Christian leaders?**

❖ Read aloud today's focus statement: **The perilous world in which we live sometimes tempts us to accept the lifestyles and values of others in order to be successful. How can we avoid losing sight of our own integrity and yet find hope for a better life? First Peter 4 tells us that God will strengthen us to serve as good stewards of God's manifold grace.**

(2) Goal 1: Understand the Cost and the Discipline Required of Good Stewards of the Manifold Grace of God

❖ Choose a volunteer to read 1 Peter 4:1-11.

❖ Discuss these questions:

(1) **This epistle is written to a community that is faced with persecution and suffering (1:6; 2:12; 3:14-17; 4:12; 5:9). According to 4:1, believers are to be prepared to suffer as Christ suffered. Why is this reality apparently so difficult for contemporary Christians in free societies to accept?** (See the second and third paragraphs of "Suffering and the Struggle for New Life" in Interpreting the Scripture.)

(2) **What actions does Peter urge this congregation to take in order to show themselves well-disciplined followers of Jesus?** (See "1 Peter 4:7-11" in Understanding the Scripture and "Stewards of God's Grace" in Interpreting the Scripture.)

(3) **This letter was written to a congregation that believed "the end of all things is near" (4:7). What difference does it make in how one lives if Christ's return is seen as imminent—or will continue to be long delayed? Should there be a difference in behaviors? Why or why not?**

(4) **What relationship do you see between living as God has called you to live and praising God?** (See "Life as Doxology" in Interpreting the Scripture and 1 Peter 4:11.)

(3) Goal 2: Discern How the Learners Are Stewards of God's Grace

❖ Read in unison today's key verse, 1 Peter 4:10.

❖ Distribute paper and pencils. Invite each learner to write his or her name at the top of the sheet. Then ask the students to pass the paper to the person on the right, who will list a gift or two that he or she discerns in the person whose name is at the top. The one responding should write initials next to the gift. Ask again for the sheets to be passed to the right. Repeat this process for whatever time you can allow. Then have the papers returned to their owners.

❖ Encourage each person to view the list of gifts written on his or her sheet.

❖ Read these directions: **Are there gifts listed here that surprise you? If so, go to the person whose initials are beside that gift and ask for examples that can enable you to see how you are using this gift. Return to your seat when you have finished.**

❖ Conclude with a few moments for silent reflection and thanksgiving for the gifts that God has given.

(4) Goal 3: Identify One Act of Service That Each Learner Could Carry Out to Demonstrate Stewardship of a Gift Received From God

❖ Refer to "Faith in Action: Offering Them Hope," found on page 246.

❖ Discuss the ideas found there with the class. Add other acts of service that the learners may suggest.

❖ Distribute paper and pencils if you have not already done so. Invite each adult to list two or three projects that would make good use of his or her God-given gifts and talents.

❖ Go through the list as it appears on page 246, adding the name(s) of each interested person beside the project.

❖ Allow time for groups to form around common interests to decide what they might do and set a time to meet outside of class to finalize their plans.

(5) Continue the Journey

❖ Pray that today's participants will go forth with renewed hope to serve one another.

❖ Read aloud this preparation for next week's lesson. You may also want to post it on newsprint for the students to copy.

■ **Title: Hope in the Day of the Lord**
■ **Background Scripture: 2 Peter 3**
■ **Lesson Scripture: 2 Peter 3:1-15a**
■ **Focus of the Lesson: There have always been people who believe that what has been and what is will always be. What will inspire them to look more positively toward the future? The writer of 2 Peter urges his readers to pre-**pare for the day of the Lord by being patient and by living holy, godly lives.

❖ Post these three activities related to this week's session on newsprint for the students to copy. Challenge the adults to grow spiritually by completing one or more of them.

(1) **Take one or more spiritual gifts inventories available online or in books to discover (or affirm) your own spiritual gifts. Consider the work you do and decide if you are making the best use of your gifts.**

(2) **Research the history of Pentecost, which we observe today. Compare the way your congregation celebrates Pentecost to other ways you have found in your research.**

(3) **Study lists of positive and negative behaviors found in today's reading, along with Galatians 5:19-21, 22-23; 1 Timothy 3:2-7, 8-13; 2 Timothy 3:2-5; and 1 Peter 4:3. What do you learn from these lists about appropriate Christian behavior?**

❖ Sing or read aloud "Many Gifts, One Spirit."

❖ Conclude today's session by leading the class in this benediction, based on the key verses for April 28 from 2 Thessalonians 2:16-17: **Now may our Lord Jesus Christ himself and God our Father, who loved us and through grace gave us eternal comfort and good hope, comfort your hearts and strengthen them in every good work and word.**

UNIT 3: A CALL TO HOLY LIVING

HOPE IN THE DAY OF THE LORD

PREVIEWING THE LESSON

Lesson Scripture: 2 Peter 3:1-15a
Background Scripture: 2 Peter 3
Key Verse: 2 Peter 3:9

Focus of the Lesson:

There have always been people who believe that what has been and what is will always be. What will inspire them to look more positively toward the future? The writer of 2 Peter urges his readers to prepare for the day of the Lord by being patient and by living holy, godly lives.

Goals for the Learners:

(1) to examine what 2 Peter teaches about being prepared for the day of the Lord.
(2) to express their feelings about the many viewpoints on the Second Coming.
(3) to identify ways they can prepare for the day of the Lord.

Pronunciation Guide:

Petrine (pee' trine)

Supplies:

Bibles, newsprint and marker, paper and pencils, hymnals

READING THE SCRIPTURE

NRSV
Lesson Scripture: 2 Peter 3:1-15a

¹This is now, beloved, the second letter I am writing to you; in them I am trying to arouse your sincere intention by reminding you ²that you should remember the words spoken in the past by the holy prophets, and the commandment of the Lord and Savior spoken through your apostles. ³First of all you must understand this, that in the last

CEB
Lesson Scripture: 2 Peter 3:1-15a

¹My dear friends, this is now my second letter to you. I have written both letters to stir up your sincere understanding with a reminder. ²I want you to recall what the holy prophets foretold as well as what the Lord and savior commanded through your apostles. ³Most important, know this: in the last days scoffers will come, jeering, living by

days scoffers will come, scoffing and indulging their own lusts [4]and saying, "Where is the promise of his coming? For ever since our ancestors died, all things continue as they were from the beginning of creation!" [5]They deliberately ignore this fact, that by the word of God heavens existed long ago and an earth was formed out of water and by means of water, [6]through which the world of that time was deluged with water and perished. [7]But by the same word the present heavens and earth have been reserved for fire, being kept until the day of judgment and destruction of the godless.

[8]But do not ignore this one fact, beloved, that with the Lord one day is like a thousand years, and a thousand years are like one day. **[9]The Lord is not slow about his promise, as some think of slowness, but is patient with you, not wanting any to perish, but all to come to repentance.** [10]But the day of the Lord will come like a thief, and then the heavens will pass away with a loud noise, and the elements will be dissolved with fire, and the earth and everything that is done on it will be disclosed.

[11]Since all these things are to be dissolved in this way, what sort of persons ought you to be in leading lives of holiness and godliness, [12]waiting for and hastening the coming of the day of God, because of which the heavens will be set ablaze and dissolved, and the elements will melt with fire? [13]But, in accordance with his promise, we wait for new heavens and a new earth, where righteousness is at home.

[14]Therefore, beloved, while you are waiting for these things, strive to be found by him at peace, without spot or blemish; [15]and regard the patience of our Lord as salvation.

their own cravings, [4]and saying, "Where is the promise of his coming? After all, nothing has changed—not since the beginning of creation, nor even since the ancestors died."

[5]But they fail to notice that, by God's word, heaven and earth were formed long ago out of water and by means of water. [6]And it was through these that the world of that time was flooded and destroyed. [7]But by the same word, heaven and earth are now held in reserve for fire, kept for the Judgment Day and destruction of ungodly people.

[8]Don't let it escape your notice, dear friends, that with the Lord a single day is like a thousand years and a thousand years are like a single day. **[9]The Lord isn't slow to keep his promise, as some think of slowness, but he is patient toward you, not wanting anyone to perish but all to change their hearts and lives.** [10]But the day of the Lord will come like a thief. On that day the heavens will pass away with a dreadful noise, the elements will be consumed by fire, and the earth and all the works done on it will be exposed.

[11]Since everything will be destroyed in this way, what sort of people ought you to be? You must live holy and godly lives, [12]waiting for and hastening the coming day of God. Because of that day, the heavens will be destroyed by fire and the elements will melt away in the flames. [13]But according to his promise we are waiting for a new heaven and a new earth, where righteousness is at home.

[14]Therefore, dear friends, while you are waiting for these things to happen, make every effort to be found by him in peace—pure and faultless. [15]Consider the patience of our Lord to be salvation.

UNDERSTANDING THE SCRIPTURE

2 Peter 3:1-2. The writer of 2 Peter addresses his audience as "beloved" four times in the concluding chapter of this letter (the fifth "beloved" is in reference to Paul in verse 15). This term evokes a strong sense of familial bonding with these communities beyond the theological connection they share. In a type of summary, the author declares here that his purpose in writing has been to "arouse" faithful remembrance of what they had been instructed in. The breadth of that instruction encompasses the Hebrew Scriptures (particularly the Prophets) and the teachings of Christ conveyed to them through the apostles. This mediating of those teachings through the apostles (in particular Peter, in whose name at least this epistle is written, if not in fact written by him) implicitly poses a rebuke to the opponents who have brought teachings based upon their own opinions (2:1, 17-18).

2 Peter 3:3-7. The thematic emphasis in both Petrine Epistles of the imminence of the "last days" is once again asserted here. These verses connect the approach of these days with "scoffers," who ridicule or mock the approach of any day of reckoning or coming of God. The prophets Amos (9:10) and Malachi (2:17) both recognized and condemned those who engaged in such derision in their own declarations of God's coming judgment. For the opponents or scoffers addressed by 2 Peter, their theology seems to view God as an "absentee landlord" unengaged in the world or its transformation since the beginning of creation (3:4). Not only do they apparently fail to make connections between creation's origins in the speaking of God's word but they also ignore any further speaking of that word in terms of coming judgment. The author of 2 Peter goes into some detail regarding creation's being not only formed "out of water" but later "deluged" with water in judgment (in reference to the Noah story) to insist that the speaking of God's word continues to have power—and that the word of God's coming day is not one to be dismissed as if it bears no power or authority.

2 Peter 3:8-10. These verses address the community's experience of delay (compounded by their suffering, a theme not explicit in these verses but clearly in the context of 1 and 2 Peter) in terms of the promises of God's coming taking place. One line of explanation of the delay given in verse 8 solicits the wisdom of Psalm 90:4, that what we experience as a "thousand years" (far more than one lifetime of waiting) may be to God as but one day. In verse 9, another line of explanation of the delay is less chronological in nature and more redemptive. That is, the "slowness" perceived by the community, which is not slowness to God, arises out of God's desire for all to come to repentance. That is, more time is allowed to make possible more individuals and communities coming into faith and salvation, an idea shared in a slightly different expression in Romans 2:4. Verse 10 proposes the image of the day of the Lord coming "like a thief" (Revelation 3:3; 1 Thessalonians 5:2, 4). The verse goes on to speak of the consequences of its coming as a "passing away" and "dissolution" and with it, a disclosure of "everything that is done" on earth. That is, the unethical behaviors engaged in by the opponents (2:18-19) will be brought to the light of day and judgment.

2 Peter 3:11-13. The dissolution of this present age in God's coming is now presented as a challenge and opportunity to live righteously. The invitation in verse 11 takes the form of a question posed to the readers and hearers of the epistle ("What sort of persons ought you to be?") Twice in these verses (12, 13) the writer uses a Greek verb translated here as "waiting" (in the King James Version, as "look for"). The prefix "pro" implies movement or action toward or on behalf of something. Thus, in these verses, "waiting" is a natural accompaniment to "leading lives." Waiting engages us in movements or actions that look toward the expected coming of God and God's realm. Verse 13 brings a clear focus upon what results of this coming: "new heavens and a new earth." That same expression of hope in "new heavens and a new earth" is voiced by Isaiah 65:17 and Revelation 21:1. The "dissolution" witnessed to in verses 10 and 12 is not creation's annihilation but rebirth. And in contrast to the injustice that has too often taken hold in this present age, the promised time is one that the epistle's writer declares will be "where righteousness is at home" (3:13).

2 Peter 3:14-15. The author returns once again to the theme of waiting, now for this new creation. Again, in these verses, such waiting is not proposed as a passive "sitting back" but an active striving. The aim of this striving is to be found by God (on the day awaited) "at peace." "Without spot or blemish" is a phrase from sacrificial language about animals that are appropriate to be offered to God. In contrast to the opponents, whose lives and ethics are found greatly wanting, the writer thus encourages the community addressed to live lives worthy of presentation to God. The other part of the striving is to "regard the patience of our Lord as salvation" (4:15). The encouragement is to strive in those times when natural questions arise as to "will this ever be" to maintain such hope and trust in God's good purposes.

2 Peter 3:16-18. The reference to Paul is a collegial one, though its accompanying detail that "there are some things in [Paul's letters] hard to understand" is curious, and no clue is given as to what those may be. What is clear, however, is the opponents twist those or any words of Scripture to their own ends, and thus threaten the community with instability. In contrast to their unsettling ways, the writer closes the epistle by urging the community to "grow" in Christ. It ends with a final ascription of praise to God in this day and to "the day of eternity," a final reference to the day of God's coming, so central to the whole of 1 and 2 Peter.

INTERPRETING THE SCRIPTURE

Mockers, Fault-finders, and the Loss of Hope

In 1807, the American engineer and inventor Robert Fulton launched the first commercial steamboat in a time when the novelty still had more naysayers than proponents. The naysayers said that the engine's weight would cause instability and an eventual rollover. Others believed the steam contraption would blow up and take the ship down. After all, ships had always relied on sails or oars—and the doubters dubbed it "Fulton's Folly." Within a couple of generations, steamships were the norm for cargo and transportation.

It can be difficult for any of us to "think outside of the box." We can become set in our ways of thinking and doing. We become cemented into beliefs that are not explored. And in doing so, we can come to the conclusion that "as much as things change, things really stay the same." And in circumstances where "things as they are" are bleak, hope can give way to either despair or fear.

The writer of the Petrine Epistles addressed communities for whom hope in God's coming had generated stresses and strains. On the one hand were opponents who were every bit the spiritual ancestors of the detractors of Robert Fulton. Teachings of God's coming, or of "new heavens and a new earth" (3:13) were preposterous. Nothing changes. Things are as they always have been. It is not clear whether their mocking and faultfinding with the proclamation of the coming of God's realm were more out of despair from what they experienced, or more out of fear of not having their carefully balanced worlds and theologies of God's absenteeism thrown into disarray. So the epistle addressed the communities of its writer's time.

But what of our time? What of our openness to the word of God's coming and the radical promise of new heavens and a new earth? Have those obsessed with rapture and being "left behind" and timetables for God's coming so turned us off by their preoccupations that we discard any expectation of God's transformative redemption of all creation?

If so, we risk siding with the mockers and naysayers of this epistle. In one sense, we allow the "obsessors" with end-time teachings and hopes to win the day with their bizarre and often self-centered positions. To have hope in God's coming is part of what it means to live in the faith of a resurrected Christ and his promised realm.

Patience and the Relativity of Time

The relativity of time need not be as complicated as theories of physics involving the speed of light and whether one could travel back in time if you could travel fast enough. The relativity of time can be experienced in moments of great crisis and moments of great joy. In some cases, time flies for us. It seems like only yesterday the graduate on the stage at school was the infant we cradled in our arms. In some cases, time stands still. When we are waiting for help, when we are waiting for news, time can slow to a crawl.

Second Peter takes up this issue of time's relativity in regard to the need for patience. The patience at hand regards the wait involved before God's coming. The early

church is generally believed to have had some, if not many, who believed in the imminence of Christ's return, in their lifetime. But what happens when those expectations slow time down to a crawl as they remain unfulfilled? Despair can set in: It hasn't happened yet, so it never will. And in the yielding to despair comes the loss of hope, to which 2 Peter counsels patience, then and now.

It is a patience that invites us to regard, in the reasoning of this epistle, that God's experience of time and ours are not necessarily the same. What is for us a millennium may be, for God, like a single day. To be sure, that may not be in and of itself entirely reassuring to folks in the midst of crisis. Telling you, as you face some bodily pain or the grief of a loved one who has died, that, well, what seems to you an eternity is only like a day to God may not be all that comforting. But 2 Peter means here to speak—and be heard—in ways that go beyond the way we measure time on a watch or calendar.

Patience invites not just an acknowledgment of time's relativity, but more important, a trust in the One who is its giver. That is, patience engages the willingness to entrust ourselves, including our destiny, into the God who is confessed to hold all our times in God's hands (Psalm 31:15). Patience is not mindless resignation to an indifferent fate but a seasoned trust in a gracious God whose time will come in saving ways.

In the Mean-time

"Meantime." The dictionary definition of that word suggests "the time between one occurrence and another." But look again at that word, and you may see something of what lies in the background of this epistle. For the time between "one occurrence and another"—the time between now and the time of God's coming—has, for the communities here addressed, become somewhat mean. Clearly the epistle addresses a meanness of spirit brought to these times by the falsehoods of the opponents. Beyond that, the overall tone and association of the community with "suffering" in both 1 and 2 Peter suggests strongly that times have become mean if not downright lethal in some regards. So how does this epistle speak of what it means to live in both sets of "mean-times": the time between now and God's coming, and the times that have become violent and threatening?

As has been consistent with the other passages studied this quarter from the Petrine Epistles, the call is to live in faithfulness to God—faithfulness not simply in what we believe about God and the future but also in what we do about those beliefs: "leading lives of holiness and godliness" in terms of 2 Peter 3:11.

Beyond that, and in truth motivating that, faithfulness to God engages us in practices borne of hope. To have hope in God's coming is to ground one's life in higher purposes than "what's in it for me," and it is also to resist other powers in this world that would put themselves in the role of God, whether they use that language or not. To have hope in God's coming is to live also by the qualities and virtues associated not only with the Christ, whose way we follow, but also with the sovereign realm Christ's own ministry and teaching sought to embody. So, for example, when 2 Peter 3:13 commends us to "wait for new heavens and a new earth, where righteousness is at home," we are called not only to a generalized hope for a new age but also to exhibit its quality of righteousness, which is another way of speaking about justice. To live in the meantime is to be a people who embody hope and justice in our daily lives and communities, even as it is to live as those who love God and one another—even as the gospel graces us with the gift of being ourselves named "beloved," as 2 Peter 3 repeatedly says.

SHARING THE SCRIPTURE

Preparing Our Hearts

Explore this week's devotional reading, found in John 14:1-7. In this passage, where Jesus states the familiar phrase "I am the way, and the truth, and the life" (14:6), he also talks about preparing a place for us and then returning for us in order to take us there. Ponder your own beliefs about the day of the Lord. Are you really expecting Christ to return? If so, what preparations are you making? How is your life different from those who have no hope that Christ will come again?

Pray that you and the adult students will be ready and waiting for Jesus' return.

Preparing Our Minds

Study the background Scripture from 2 Peter 3 and the lesson Scripture from 2 Peter 3:1-15a.

Consider this question as you prepare the lesson: *What will inspire people who believe that what has always been will always be to look more positively toward the future?*

Write on newsprint:
❑ information for next week's lesson, found under "Continue the Journey."
❑ activities for further spiritual growth in "Continue the Journey."

Review the "Introduction," "The Big Picture," "Close-up," and "Faith in Action." Consider how you will use this additional information, which immediately precedes the first lesson, for this final session.

LEADING THE CLASS

(1) Gather to Learn

❖ Greet the class members. Introduce any guests and help them feel at home.

❖ Pray that the students who have come today will consider Christ's second coming and how it may influence the way they live.

❖ Read the first paragraph of "Mockers, Fault-finders, and the Loss of Hope" in Interpreting the Scripture and then ask: **What other successful inventions or ideas did people mock because they thought there was no way that such change was possible?**

❖ Read aloud today's focus statement: **There have always been people who believe that what has been and what is will always be. What will inspire them to look more positively toward the future? The writer of 2 Peter urges his readers to prepare for the day of the Lord by being patient and by living holy, godly lives.**

(2) Goal 1: Examine What 2 Peter Teaches About Being Prepared for the Day of the Lord

❖ Choose one volunteer to read 2 Peter 3:1-7 and another to read verses 8-15a (ending with "Lord as salvation").

❖ Discuss these questions, adding appropriate ideas from Understanding the Scripture:

(1) **Why is Peter writing to this congregation?**

(2) **How does the writer encourage his readers to respond to those who do not believe that Christ will come again?**

(3) **Why do you suppose the writer counsels his readers to remember the words of the prophets and the commandments of Jesus?** (The scoffers have their own ideas, but the epistle writer is encouraging the congregation to look at the deeply rooted traditions upon which their faith is built.)

(4) **How does the writer explain Christ's delay in returning?** (See "Patience and the Relativity of Time" in Interpreting the Scripture and today's key verse, 2 Peter 3:9.)

(5) **How does the writer describe the end?**

(6) **What does the writer urge the congregation to do in the meantime?** (See "In the Mean-time" in Interpreting the Scripture.)

(3) Goal 2: Express Feelings About the Many Viewpoints on the Second Coming

❖ Provide a few moments for the adults to gather their own beliefs about Christ's second coming.

❖ Note that people hold very different views about what the end of time will be like. Many of these views concern the one thousand years, the millennium, referred to in Revelation 20. Form small groups. Ask the adults to scan Revelation 20 and discuss how these images compare with their own ideas. Remind class members that Revelation contains very poetic images, and that no one knows exactly what the end will be like, though some claim to have knowledge about this coming time. Also remind them that Jesus himself said no one knows when this will happen (see Mark 13:32). He reiterated that point in Acts 1:6-7. Following his ascension into heaven, "two men in white robes" (1:10) told Jesus' followers that he would "come in the same way as [they] saw him go into heaven" (1:11).

❖ Call the group together and invite volunteers to state highlights of their discussion. Point out that although the Bible avows that Jesus will return, we need to express our viewpoints with humility since the details are unclear.

*(4) Goal 3: Identify Ways the Learners Can
Prepare for the Day of the Lord*

❖ Look again at 2 Peter 3:11, which asks, "What sort of persons ought you to be in leading lives of holiness and godliness" as you await the day of the Lord? Also look again at verses 14-15a.

❖ Post a sheet of newsprint. Encourage the learners to call out attitudes and behaviors that befit a person who is "at peace, without spot or blemish" (3:14). They may suggest a wide variety of options, but all should describe someone who is living a life of serious discipleship in a close personal relationship with Jesus.

❖ Conclude by challenging the adults to *continue* with attitudes and behaviors that will find them ready and waiting, *jettison* those things that create stumbling blocks to preparedness, and *add* other attitudes and behaviors that will help them be better prepared for Christ's return.

(5) Continue the Journey

❖ Pray that those who have come today will go forth to live ready for the day of the Lord, whenever that may come.

❖ Read aloud this preparation for next week's lesson. You may also want to post it on newsprint for the students to copy.

- ■ **Title: Holy, Holy, Holy**
- ■ **Background Scripture: Isaiah 6:1-12**
- ■ **Lesson Scripture: Isaiah 6:1-8**
- ■ **Focus of the Lesson: People seek a power beyond themselves worthy of praise and worship. How do people respond when they find the higher power to praise and worship? Isaiah, hearing the extravagant praises and worship directed to God, responded by**

accepting the call to become God's messenger.

❖ Post these three activities related to this week's session on newsprint for the students to copy. Challenge the adults to grow spiritually by completing one or more of them.

(1) **Find a book or article about the end times that expresses a different viewpoint from the one you espouse. How might this reading either prompt you to take a second look at a different belief or prompt you to hold fast to your own belief?**

(2) **Find the Charles Wesley hymn "Lo, He Comes with Clouds Descending" in a hymnal or online. How does Wesley's portrait of Christ's return compare or contrast with your own?**

(3) **Talk with someone who feels that God has been slow in resolving a troubling situation. Listen to this person's concerns, and assure him or her that God will act in God's time, according to God's will and purpose. Affirm that although it is difficult to wait when one is so anxious for change to come about, God is a promise keeper.**

❖ Sing or read aloud "This Is a Day of New Beginnings."

❖ Conclude today's session by leading the class in this benediction, based on the key verses for April 28 from 2 Thessalonians 2:16-17: **Now may our Lord Jesus Christ himself and God our Father, who loved us and through grace gave us eternal comfort and good hope, comfort your hearts and strengthen them in every good work and word.**

Fourth Quarter
God's People Worship

JUNE 2, 2013–AUGUST 25, 2013

"Worship" is the theme highlighted during the summer quarter. Our lessons are rooted in three books from the Hebrew Scriptures: Isaiah, Ezra, and Nehemiah. During this course, "God's People Worship," we will learn about the worship practices highlighted by Isaiah and those described by Ezra and Nehemiah after a remnant of Israelites returns home from their captivity in Babylon. Although some of their practices were good and pleasing unto God, other practices needed to be changed. As we study these ancient worship practices, we can reflect on how Christians can honor and worship God in our contemporary communities of faith.

The four sessions of Unit 1, "The Prophet and Praise," begin on June 2. "Holy, Holy, Holy" recounts the story found in Isaiah 6:1-12 of the prophet seeing a dramatic vision in the Temple as he is called to his ministry. On June 9 we turn to Isaiah 12, where the people are summoned to "Give Thanks" and praise to God for comfort, salvation, strength, and might. The background Scripture for the session on June 16 is Isaiah 29, which deals with "Meaningless Worship." The final session on June 23 spotlights Isaiah 65, where we read about "The Glorious New Creation" that assures the exiles in Babylon that they do have a future with God.

Shifting to the time after the exiles begin to return home in 539 B.C., Unit 2, "Worshiping in Jerusalem Again (Ezra)" considers how the people renew their worship. "Joyful Worship Restored," the lesson for June 30, looks at Ezra 1:1–3:7 as the people celebrate a meaningful festival. The scene in Ezra 3:8-13, which we will encounter on July 7, shows the "Temple Restored" as the foundation is laid for a new Temple that will replace the one that was destroyed. People worshiped with joy at the "Dedication of the Temple," completed just in time to celebrate Passover, as described in Ezra 6 for our study on July 14. On July 21 we will explore an account in Ezra 8:21-23 of the people "Fasting and Praying" for God's protection during a journey. The session for July 28 from Ezra 8:24-30, "Gifts for the Temple," concerns the silver and gold offerings for the Temple.

The four lessons for Unit 3, "Worshiping in Jerusalem Again (Nehemiah)" are a continuation of Unit 2, though from the perspective of Nehemiah. This unit opens on August 4 with a description from Nehemiah 7:73b–8:18 of the joyous "Festival of Booths," also known as "Sukkoth" or the "Feast of Tabernacles." Worship also includes admitting our shortcomings, as we will see on August 11 in the study "Community of Confession," based on Nehemiah 9:1-37. On August 18 we rejoice with the people and the pride they take in their accomplishment at the "Dedication of the Wall," as reported in Nehemiah 12:27-43. The final session for this quarter—and for this Sunday school year—on August 25 examines Nehemiah 13:4-31, in which Nehemiah, who is greatly concerned about inappropriate actions, makes "Sabbath Reforms" that include keeping the sabbath day holy.

MEET OUR WRITER

DR. MELODY KNOWLES

Melody Knowles is Associate Professor of Hebrew Scripture at McCormick Theological Seminary in Chicago. Her principal teaching and research interests include the religion of Israel and the reworking of historical traditions within the Bible. She has also been involved in archaeological excavations at sites from ancient Israel.

Dr. Knowles was born in Canada, and received her bachelor of arts degree from Trinity Western University. She earned her M.Div. and Ph.D. from Princeton Theological Seminary. Her various publications include *Centrality Practiced: Jerusalem in the Religious Practice of Yehud and the Diaspora in the Persian Period* (2006), *Contesting Texts: Jews and Christians in Conversations About the Bible* (2007), and several additional articles.

Melody has been active in the life of the church since her birth into a family of Salvation Army officers and soldiers. She is an ordained priest in the Episcopal Church, and works with Brent House (the Episcopal chaplaincy at the University of Chicago) and the Catechesis of the Good Shepherd program at Christ Church in Poughkeepsie, New York, where she also serves as priest-associate. With her husband, John Knight, she has two young children. Together they enjoy skiing in the winter and picking raspberries in the summer.

THE BIG PICTURE:
THE PROPER WORSHIP
OF GOD

Reading texts from the books of Isaiah, Ezra, and Nehemiah allows one to trace the development of several significant themes through a broad stretch of biblical history. The earliest texts in this unit come from the first part of the Book of Isaiah, and these passages relate to the preexilic era in the mid-to-late eighth century (around 742–701 B.C.), when the Assyrians were in political control of the region of Jerusalem and its province of Judah. By the time we get to Ezra and Nehemiah, we are in the postexilic period in the late sixth century B.C. and the Persians are now the political force in the area.

Within the several centuries that these writings represent (and within the several political upheavals as well), most of the texts that we will study will say something about the proper worship of God. "Proper worship" in this context relates to more than following liturgical rules and protocol. Throughout the study we will see that geography, ethics, theology, politics, and national identity all come into play. And so, to set the context for further study of the worship of God in specific passages, this introduction will consider two foundational issues: the historical and theological profile of Jerusalem and its Temple, and the various ways that God's people defined themselves as community.

Jerusalem and Its Temple

The very first passage that we encounter in this unit takes place in the context of the Temple. In the vision in Isaiah 6, God appears to the prophet sitting on a high and lofty throne, "and the hem of his robe filled the temple" (Isaiah 6:1). The prophecies throughout the first part of the book (Isaiah 1–39) occur in a context in which the Temple is still standing, and in which the people assume that God will always protect it from destruction.

The basis for this assumption of the Temple's inviolability is what is known as the "Zion tradition." The central idea of this tradition is that God defeated enemy forces on Mount Zion and chose the city as the place of the divine throne and Temple. This choice implies an ongoing protective relationship to the city. Thus, if the city were ever to fall into enemy hands, the assumption would be that the enemy's god was more powerful than Israel's Lord.

A significant test of these assumptions came in the context of Sennacherib's siege on Jerusalem in 701 B.C. In rebellion against Assyria, Judah joined with Egypt and Babylon. But soon King Hezekiah realized the error of his ways and tried to assuage the Assyrians with valuable gifts, including silver from the Temple and the gold that decorated the Temple's doors. But Hezekiah's gifts came too late. Sennacherib and his armies set out in retribution against Judah and its capital city. In the middle of the Assyrian siege against Jerusalem, Hezekiah consulted the prophet Isaiah, and heard this amazing oracle from God: "I will defend this city to save it, for my own sake and for the sake of my servant David" (2 Kings 19:34). According to the biblical accounts, the angel of the Lord set out that night and killed 185,000 people in the Assyrian camp (2 Kings 19:35). In his own report, Sennacherib gloats about the siege ("I shut up Hezekiah in Jerusalem . . . like a bird in a cage") but doesn't give the reason he and his company suddenly decamped from the city.

It is in this context that Isaiah emphasizes God's freedom within the traditions about Zion. Even though God has promised to protect Jerusalem, the Zion tradition cannot preserve the city and its Temple if the inhabitants constantly provoke God with their deeds of injustice and cultic impurity. Central to the prophet's message is the coming destruction of the city and the utter desolation of the land (Isaiah 6:11). Although God preserved it from the assault of Sennacherib, the danger was still real.

Just over one hundred years after Sennacherib's siege, Nebuchadnezzar and his Neo-Babylonian Empire rose in power over the Assyrians and they too came up against Jerusalem. This time, the city fell. The first defeat occurred in 597 B.C., when King Jehoiachin of Judah surrendered the city. At this point, Nebuchadnezzar deported the city's elites and artisans to Babylon, and took possession of the Temple's holy treasures (2 Kings 24). After a second rebellion in the city, Nebuchadnezzar's captain returned in 586 B.C. and totally destroyed it: "He burned the house of the LORD, the king's house, and all the houses of Jerusalem" (2 Kings 25:9). He also broke down the bronze pillars in the Temple and carried the remaining treasure and cultic vessels to Babylon. Most of the people who remained in the city were also exiled, and the only people who were left were "some of the poorest people of the land to be vinedressers and tillers of soil" (2 Kings 25:12). Tragically, Isaiah's prophecies came to pass. The city was destroyed, and according to Isaiah, its destruction came with the consent of God.

Just as the Assyrians were defeated by Nebuchadnezzar, so eventually the Neo-Babylonian Empire fell as well, and this changed political context had new implications for Jerusalem and its Temple. During the mid-sixth century B.C., the Persian Empire emerged under the leadership of Cyrus the Great from the Achaemenid dynasty. During his reign from 559–530 B.C. he successively conquered most of the land in the ancient Near Eastern world (with Egypt a notable exception), beginning with the Median Empire and going on to conquer the Neo-Babylonian Empire as well.

With the conquest of Babylon in 539 B.C., Cyrus changed the policy that his predecessors took regarding the forced migration of political captives: Instead of relocating population groups, he decided that it was more expedient to return captives to their homelands. In addition, he also returned the various god statues that had been captured in war and repaired their ruined temples. Aspects of this policy are seen in the "Cyrus Cylinder," a document inscribed on a barrel-shaped stone and written in the voice of the emperor: "I also gathered all their former inhabitants and returned to them their habitations" Cyrus' edict with which the Book of Ezra opens has a similar content: "Thus says King Cyrus of Persia: 'The LORD, the God of heaven, has given me all the kingdoms of the earth, and he has charged me to build him a house at Jerusalem in Judah. Any of those among you who are of his people . . . are now permitted to go to Jerusalem in Judah and rebuild the house of the LORD' " (Ezra 1:2-3).

It is right here at the very beginning of Ezra that we are able to trace the arc of the Zion tradition that appears in various forms in all three books in our course. The shocking destruction that Isaiah foretold has come to pass at the hands of the Neo-Babylonians. And then, during Cyrus's reign, we now also see the restoration of the city. Isaiah 40 contains the good news that the time of Jerusalem's punishment has come to an end: "Speak tenderly to Jerusalem and cry to her that she has served her term, that her penalty is paid, that she has received from the LORD's hand double for her sins" (Isaiah 40:2). With God's forgiveness and Cyrus's new policy of return, the city and its people were poised to reclaim the city as God's chosen dwelling place and to reinstitute their worship in the Temple.

Defining Community

Of course, this process of reclamation did not always run so very smoothly. Many of the disputes about Jerusalem and its Temple can be related to the various ways that groups defined their communal boundaries in relation to God's chosen city.

At the most basic level, it is clear that not all those who left Jerusalem and the province of Judah during the exile returned again to their homelands. Some settled in Egypt, and there is evidence that they remained and worshiped the Lord in colonies such as Elephantine long into the second century B.C. From biblical texts as well as tax records, we know that others remained in Babylon. And then there were the people who never left the vicinity of Jerusalem at all, referred to as "some of the poorest people of the land," who stayed to cultivate the abandoned territory (2 Kings 25:12).

Those who did return referred to themselves as the "golah" and understood themselves to be distinct from other communities who also might have worshiped the Lord. But even this "golah" maintained several internal divisions. For example, they did not all return at the same time, but came back in several waves over many decades. There was no single mass exodus back to the land during the early years of Cyrus's reign (even though this might be the initial impression from a quick reading of Ezra 1–2). Textual and archaeological evidence suggests rather that there were several waves of incremental returns—after the initial return around 538 B.C. (Ezra 1–2), we hear of additional returns such as that led by Ezra (Ezra 7–8) and then Nehemiah's own journey as well (Nehemiah 2:11).

Alongside these distinctions in return dates, there was also a great emphasis placed on determining the "true Israel" or "holy seed" (Isaiah 6:13) among the returned community. In Isaiah 65 (a text from the postexilic period) there is an image of the good grapes being separated from the bad, and wine being "found in the cluster" (Isaiah 65:8). Clearly the prophet understands that God intends to search out the true Israel that may be currently mixed together with outsiders. We also see a reliance on genealogical records to clarify communal relations. Ezra 2:62 tells of returnees from priestly lineages excluded from the priesthood because they could not prove their heritage. Related to this is the concern for the "holy seed" that might be threatened by intermarriage with foreigners (Ezra 9:1–10:44 and Nehemiah 13:23-27).

One of the clearest examples that we see of the interaction between communal boundaries and the worship of God concerns the rebuilding of the Temple in Jerusalem. In the context of the Zion tradition (and of Cyrus's edict in Ezra 1), it is likely to assume that the returnees would make quick work to rebuild God's holy Temple. And indeed, Ezra 3 tells of an initial attempt to set up the altar and lay the foundation by those who first returned to Jerusalem. But in this building campaign, the "golah" community explicitly refused any help from those who had remained in the land during the exile: "You shall have no part with us in building a house to our God. We alone will build to the LORD, the God of Israel, as King Cyrus of Persia has commanded us" (Ezra 4:3).

Perhaps it is surprising that the building campaign never really got off the ground until 520 B.C., almost twenty years after Cyrus's decree. This may be the result of the kind of disagreements seen in Ezra 4. It may also be the result of what appears to be the very slow economic recovery of Jerusalem and the province of Judah (now called "Yehud" in the Persian administration). Of course, during the exile the city shrank considerably in size, approximately back to the size it was during the time of David. But it is interesting that, after the exile, there was no great expansion for a very long time. Indeed, the city seems to have stayed at its pre-eighth-century size until the second century B.C. Although texts like Ezra and 2 Chronicles 36 imply that settlement surged after the exile, Jerusalem remained sparsely inhabited in the postexilic period.

This impoverished picture of Jerusalem is mirrored in the picture of the surrounding province of Yehud. During the postexilic period there is a sharp decrease in both the number and the size of settlements throughout the province. From the remains, it seems that most of these were either military strongholds or administrative centers.

Eventually the completion of the Temple was celebrated in 515 B.C. (Ezra 6:15), but the communal boundaries of those who claimed relation to it continued to be negotiated. Nehemiah's struggles with rebuilding Jerusalem's walls reflect similar conflicts about the identity (and leadership) of the true Israel. Clearly, God's relationship to the people and to the city of Jerusalem was in negotiation during this period. And so a study of the worship of God is of particular interest not just for liturgical purposes but also as a means of looking at the ways in which politics and theology shape worship practices.

Reading More Broadly: Isaiah, Ezra, and Nehemiah in Their Biblical Context

Other biblical books overlap and interact with these narratives and it can be interesting to consider the texts along with texts from similar periods within the canon. The historical background to several of Isaiah's oracles that we will read in this unit can be found also in the books of 1 and 2 Kings. Certain aspects of Ezra and Nehemiah can be "filled out" by reading the oracles in Haggai and Zechariah 1–8, which date within the books to 520 B.C., and relate to the renewed push to rebuild the Temple. In Haggai 1:8 God delivers a divine command that the community get to work on the Temple: "Go up to the hills and bring wood and build the house, so that I may take pleasure in it and be honored."

The postexilic community and its Temple are also a central concern throughout the historical narratives in the books of 1 and 2 Chronicles. Although 2 Chronicles *ends* with Cyrus's declaration that the people may return to Jerusalem, the author's prior retelling of the history of Israel and Judah reflects the concerns of the postexilic period (including the role of Jerusalem and its Temple, as well as communal identity and the place of foreigners). For example, it is interesting to note that although the books of Ezra and Nehemiah have a fairly narrow definition of their community, the books of 1 and 2 Chronicles present a much broader interpretation. Repeatedly the author includes the northern tribes as participants in worship at Jerusalem (2 Chronicles 30:1; 35:18). In addition, the author introduces people from outside Israel into the nation's genealogies: Judah marries the Canaanite woman Bath-Shua (1 Chronicles 2:3), and David marries Maacah from Gesher (1 Chronicles 3:2). Instead of being a threat to the "holy seed" as they are in Ezra and Nehemiah, intermarriage with foreigners is a core means of biological expansion in the books of 1 and 2 Chronicles.

Readers who are particularly interested in the historical context of the books of Isaiah, Ezra, and Nehemiah are encouraged to read the other biblical books that relate to the same time periods to hear other voices and encounter other perspectives.

CLOSE-UP: THE PRAYERS OF EZRA AND NEHEMIAH

The primary theme of this summer's lessons is worship. We see evidence of worship throughout our lessons, but in this article we will focus on several prayers of Ezra and Nehemiah. These two leaders faced many challenges from within the ranks of the returning Israelites as well as enemies of the people who did not want the Temple or the city walls rebuilt. To stay the course to which they were called, Ezra and Nehemiah frequently turned to God in prayer.

Ezra Prays

Ezra 8:21-23. Having told King Artaxerxes that God would protect the people on their homeward journey, Ezra was "ashamed" to ask for a military escort. Yet he and the returning Israelites were taking with them, as decreed by the Persian king, precious metals and treasures from the Temple that the Babylonians had sacked and burned. The people and their cargo were vulnerable and needed protection. Having declared a fast, Ezra and the people prayed to God for a safe journey, and they believed that God had heard their prayer.

Ezra 9:5-15. After hearing about and denouncing the mixed marriages that the Israelites had entered into, Ezra again fasted, this time as one in mourning (9:3-5). He again was "ashamed and embarrassed" (9:6) by the unfaithful actions of the people, who have broken covenant with God. He confesses these sins on behalf of the people.

Nehemiah 8:5-6. Here Ezra offers a blessing upon God to which the people respond worshipfully with uplifted hands and a twofold "amen."

Nehemiah 9:6-37. After praising God the Creator who made covenant with Abraham and remained faithful to the people for generations despite their disobedience, Ezra confesses their presumptuous (9:16), rebellious (9:26) behavior. He prays that God will "not treat lightly all the hardships that have come upon [them]" (9:32), for they are "in great distress" (9:37).

Nehemiah Prays

Nehemiah 1:4-11. Nehemiah fasted and wept when he learned that the walls of Jerusalem and its gates had been burned. He begins his prayer with praise for the "great and awesome God who keeps covenant" (1:5). His prayer is one of confession for the sins of the people and his own sins. He calls God to remember not only the threat that the unfaithful would be scattered but also that those who returned to God would be gathered.

Nehemiah 5:19. Contrasting himself with "the former governors" (5:15), Nehemiah prays that God will remember the good that he has done for the people.

Nehemiah 6:9, 14. Having been intimidated by Sanballat, Tobiah, and Geshem, Nehemiah prays for strength to continue the work (6:9). He also asks God to "remember" (6:14) his enemies and their attempts to stop the building of the wall.

Nehemiah 13:22, 29, 31. To prevent sabbath violation—caused by merchants selling their wares at the gates—from tainting the holiness of Jerusalem, Nehemiah closed the city gates. He prays for God to "remember" those who "have defiled the priesthood" (13:29). He also asks God to "remember" him favorably for the good he has done (13:22, 31).

FAITH IN ACTION: BUILDING OUR CHURCH

Throughout this summer quarter we are looking at how God's people worshiped during the period following the return of exiles from Babylon. Several of our lessons concern the rebuilding of the Temple and its dedication. These stories were important to the Israelites, since they had been removed from their homeland and their Temple had been destroyed. Being able to rebuild the edifice and renew worship in Jerusalem was of momentous importance.

Similarly, most congregations have stories to tell about building, expanding, and rebuilding their own physical facilities. Depending upon when these events occurred, they may be fresh in people's minds—or they may be distant memories. Younger generations and older newcomers to the congregation may have no recollection of these events at all. Thus, it is important to research this history and find ways to tell it to the children, youth, and adults so that they will know why their church came into being, who was responsible for making this happen, and how milestones were celebrated. Insofar as possible, try to make this an intergenerational project. Older adults may have memories to share, but teens and young adults may have skills in technology to bring these memories to life in a variety of creative ways.

Here are some ideas for the class to consider:

(1) Research the history: Begin by researching any written records of the building and dedication of your church's sanctuary, educational building, or other structures. You may find bulletins or programs from the dedications of these buildings. You may also discover pictures. See if there are members who were present at the dedication who can share their recollections.

(2) Create a written account: Some churches do have a written history, but many do not. If yours is in the latter category, work together to write such a history. Someone may use a graphic design program to publish this information in a booklet or add it to the church's website.

(3) Record an oral history: If possible, interview members who were present at the time of the building. Capture their comments on video. Be sure to include any personal photographs or other materials they may have that show the building as it was under construction or being dedicated.

(4) Assemble an album or collage: Borrow pictures from older members and copy them. Put them together in an album, labeling the people and dating the pictures as accurately as possible. Use additional pictures to create a collage that may be displayed in a high-traffic area, preferably one where Sunday school children can see these photographs of their church.

(5) Design a PowerPoint presentation: Use pictures, brochures, or other printed materials to put together a PowerPoint presentation. Present this at a fellowship time, during church suppers, or at other church-wide events to strengthen the bonds of community. Also show this report of the congregation's history to confirmation classes and new members' classes.

(6) Observe an anniversary: Research may bring to mind an important date, such as the anniversary of the founding of the congregation and dedication of its first building or a subsequent building. These occasions should be recognized. Allow appropriate time to plan an anniversary celebration.

UNIT 1: THE PROPHET AND PRAISE
HOLY, HOLY, HOLY

PREVIEWING THE LESSON

Lesson Scripture: Isaiah 6:1-8
Background Scripture: Isaiah 6:1-12
Key Verse: Isaiah 6:3

Focus of the Lesson:
People seek a power beyond themselves worthy of praise and worship. How do people respond when they find the higher power to praise and worship? Isaiah, hearing the extravagant praises and worship directed to God, responded by accepting the call to become God's messenger.

Goals for the Learners:
(1) to connect praise and worship of God with Isaiah's call and response of commitment.
(2) to recall a meaningful worship experience during which they made some level of commitment.
(3) to identify means of worship that include contemporary components of worship similar to those included in Isaiah's vision.

Pronunciation Guide:
Ahaz (ay haz')   seraph (ser' uf)
Amoz (ay' muhz)   Shiphrah (shif' ruh)
Hezekiah (hez uh ki' uh)   theophany (thee of' uh nee)
Jotham (joh' thuhm)   Tiglath-pileser (tig lath pi lee' zuhr)
Puah (pyoo' uh)   Uzziah (uh zi' uh)

Supplies:
Bibles, newsprint and marker, paper and pencils, hymnals, optional picture of seraphs, incense, matches, something hot to touch

---

READING THE SCRIPTURE

NRSV
Lesson Scripture: Isaiah 6:1-8
¹In the year that King Uzziah died, I saw the Lord sitting on a throne, high and lofty;

CEB
Lesson Scripture: Isaiah 6:1-8
¹In the year of King Uzziah's death, I saw the Lord sitting on a high and exalted

and the hem of his robe filled the temple. [2]Seraphs were in attendance above him; each had six wings: with two they covered their faces, and with two they covered their feet, and with two they flew. [3]And one called to another and said:

"Holy, holy, holy is the LORD of hosts; the whole earth is full of his glory."

[4]The pivots on the thresholds shook at the voices of those who called, and the house filled with smoke. [5]And I said: "Woe is me! I am lost, for I am a man of unclean lips, and I live among a people of unclean lips; yet my eyes have seen the King, the LORD of hosts!"

[6]Then one of the seraphs flew to me, holding a live coal that had been taken from the altar with a pair of tongs. [7]The seraph touched my mouth with it and said: "Now that this has touched your lips, your guilt has departed and your sin is blotted out." [8]Then I heard the voice of the Lord saying, "Whom shall I send, and who will go for us?" And I said, "Here am I; send me!"

throne, the edges of his robe filling the temple. [2]Winged creatures were stationed around him. Each had six wings: with two they veiled their faces, with two their feet, and with two they flew about. [3]They shouted to each other, saying:

"Holy, holy, holy is the LORD of heavenly forces! All the earth is filled with God's glory!"

[4]The doorframe shook at the sound of their shouting, and the house was filled with smoke.

[5]I said, "Mourn for me; I'm ruined! I'm a man with unclean lips, and I live among a people with unclean lips. Yet I've seen the king, the LORD of heavenly forces!"

[6]Then one of the winged creatures flew to me, holding a glowing coal that he had taken from the altar with tongs. [7]He touched my mouth and said, "See, this has touched your lips. Your guilt has departed, and your sin is removed."

[8]Then I heard the Lord's voice saying, "Whom should I send, and who will go for us?"

I said, "I'm here; send me."

UNDERSTANDING THE SCRIPTURE

Isaiah 6:1. The sixth chapter of Isaiah begins with politics. With the mention of King Uzziah, Isaiah situates his call in the political reality that is central to his entire work. Significantly, the whole book begins with a reference to the several kings of Judah who ruled the nation and fought to preserve it in the context of Assyrian domination during the last half of the eighth century B.C.: "The vision of Isaiah son of Amoz, which he saw concerning Judah and Jerusalem in the days of Uzziah, Jotham, Ahaz, and Hezekiah, the kings of Judah" (1:1). In 742 B.C., the Assyrian ruler Tiglath-pileser III was ruling Assyria (he reigned

from 744–727 B.C.), and quickly conquered the land from Mesopotamia up to the edge of the Egyptian border. In his prophetic ministry, Isaiah strove to tell of God's designs for Judah and Israel in the context of the Assyrian threat.

Of course, the prophet's call is also associated with the worshiping community as God speaks in the context of the Temple. The call begins with a vision of God on a throne, "high and lofty." Significantly, in a religious tradition that consistently emphasizes that God cannot be contained to any one area or in any one image, Isaiah's vision hints at God's magnitude: "the *hem* of his robe filled the temple" (emphasis added). According to the vision, even the nation's largest holy space could not fully encompass God.

Isaiah 6:2. "Seraphs" (literally, "fiery ones") were creatures associated with gods and goddesses throughout the ancient world. They often had composite bodies (a human head with eagle's wings attached to a lion's body, to take one example), and in Isaiah 6 they each have six wings, mouths that could speak words discernible to the prophet, and the ability to manipulate tongs (6:2, 3, 6). Ezekiel, in his own call vision, also sees several composite creatures that guard God's throne. These are described as having human form, each with four heads, four wings, and soles like that of a calf's foot that sparkled as burnished bronze (Ezekiel 1:5-11).

The creatures in Isaiah 6 and Ezekiel 1 are all associated with God's glory, and probably represent a kind of "ministering spirit" or divine courtier whose job it is to serve God night and day. They also effectively guarded the separation between the divine and human spheres. Traversing this boundary without following the proper protocols entailed great danger and even death, and this danger probably explains why even the seraphs needed to cover their eyes so as not to risk looking upon the holy God.

Isaiah 6:3. In the midst of this awe-invoking vision, suddenly the seraphs begin to sing, as if calling to one another. There is a sense of a fugue here, with different voices starting at different times, singing out their lines in a grand layering of sound. The music and the lyrics may have derived from an actual hymn sung at the Temple, but we can't be sure. At any rate the picture of God that is sung in this heavenly music is all powerful ("the LORD of hosts") and all-present ("the whole earth is full of his glory"). The threefold repetition "Holy, holy, holy" that begins the hymn is an acknowledgment of God's transcendence over all of creation—the holy God is wholly

other and not under the control of anyone or anything. The church has often interpreted the threefold "holy" as an allusion to the Trinity, the threefold entity that is transcendent over any attempt to confine its personhood into singleness. The church also sings the seraph's song during the Eucharist (Holy Communion) to praise the holy God who came to earth to save.

Isaiah 6:4. The hymnic revelation of God's holiness and glory is met with a response from the cosmos. The text tells us that the "pivots" of the Temple doors that were set in the foundation stones (NRSV), or "the doorposts and thresholds" (NIV), all "shook." The house also "filled with smoke." In other parts of the Bible we hear of the natural world responding to the presence of God appearing in a theophany. In Exodus 19, when God was giving Moses the Ten Commandments, the encounter was marked by thunder, lightning, and a thick cloud. In Deborah's account of a time when God went out in war to fight Israel's enemies, the divine march causes the earth to "tremble" and the clouds to "pour water" (Judges 5:4). The prophet Habakkuk also describes a march of God coming to save the people that is marked by the shattering of mountains, the splitting of the earth with rivers, and the moon standing still (Habakkuk 3). In Isaiah 6, it is as if the entire Temple and the foundation on which it stood likewise shuddered with the realization of God's near presence.

Isaiah 6:5-7. The prophet is cleansed from his sin by the application of a live coal taken from the altar applied to his lips by one of the seraphs. In the ancient world, incense was used in worship as a type of protection for the priests who ministered between God and humanity. The clouds of sweet-smelling smoke would purify and obscure the human actors from the near presence of God. In the Book of Leviticus, God tells Moses that when his brother, Aaron, enters the Holy of Holies in his role as priest, he must use enough incense to "cover the mercy seat . . . or he will die" (Leviticus 16:12-13). In Isaiah 6, the coal from the altar also functions to purify the human actor who is in God's holy presence.

Isaiah 6:8-12. The message that God gives to the prophet has less to do with a specific content and more to do with its effect: "Keep listening, but do not comprehend; keep looking, but do not understand" (6:9). A more literal translation of the first part of verse 10 would be something like "make the heart of this people fat"—a command to render the people's center of decision making incapable of understanding the consequences of their deeds. In the language of lament, the prophet asks God how long the divine punishment will endure, and God responds with the heaviest of answers: until the land is "utterly desolate" (6:11).

INTERPRETING THE SCRIPTURE

God's Call: Confrontation
With the Divine King

Throughout the Bible, we hear of God "calling" people in different ways. Often, a subtle but discernible call is found in the predictable duties of daily life. For example, the midwives Shiphrah and Puah preserved the life of Hebrew infants simply by continuing to do their job (even though Pharaoh commanded them otherwise in Exodus 1). Or one is confronted with a crisis that must be responded to personally, such as when Nehemiah heard that Jerusalem's walls had been destroyed (Nehemiah 1). In these accounts, we are not told that Shiphrah, Puah, or Nehemiah had any particular encounter with God in which any specific instructions were given. These three folk, like so many people before and after them, enacted God's plan simply by faithful living and responding to the needs that confronted them.

At points, though, we are also told of people who had a dramatic encounter with God during which they are given a specific task to do. Because these encounters often involve a call to prophetic ministry and reflect a similar pattern, scholars refer to these encounters recorded in the Bible as "prophetic call narratives." The basic outline of the encounter is fairly simple: God confronts someone and gives that person a task to do. The called one immediately protests, claiming that he or she is somehow unable to complete the assignment. God then responds with some kind of reassurance, usually in the form of a sign meant to convince the prophet that God will be with him or her. Examples of this genre include Exodus 3–4 when God confronts Moses ("Moses, Moses!" 3:4) and commissions him to go to Pharaoh so that the Israelites might be liberated from Egypt. Moses protests several times, claiming that he is unable to reveal God's true name and that he does not have the eloquence to carry out the divine request. Each time God responds to reassure Moses that he has all that that is necessary for the great task: God reveals the divine name YHWH, and provides Aaron as a spokesperson. In Jeremiah 1, we also read of that prophet's call when God appointed him "a prophet to the nations," only to be met with the response "Truly I do not know how to speak, for I am only a boy!" (Jeremiah 1:5-6). God then reassured the prophet by putting divine words in his mouth.

Although they all follow the same basic pattern, the small deviations in the written account of each individual call narrative can give us clues as to the particular emphases in each prophet's future ministry. It is significant to notice, for example, that in the account of Isaiah encountering the divine in Isaiah 6, the very first feature of this "call" is not a word or even an assigned task but rather the revelation of God as the divine king of the universe. According to the account, the prophet is first overwhelmed by the vision of the enthroned God ("I saw the LORD sitting on a throne . . . my eyes have seen the King!" 1:1, 5). Accompanying this vision is the seraph's song that emphasizes God's majesty over all creation ("the whole earth is full of his glory," 1:3). With the entire Temple shaking in response, the prophet realizes that he is in the presence of the supreme God without God having to say a single word. The Book of Isaiah will continue to emphasize God's great glory and kingship, and assert God's greatness even as the nations confront the king of Assyria's growing powers.

God's Call: Cleansing From Sin

When the prophet finally responds to the divine confrontation (in which God does not speak a single word), Isaiah's expression reflects the same inner convulsing that shook the foundations of the Temple: "Woe is me!" (6:5). On account of his vision of the enthroned God accompanied by the seraph's cry and the shaking of the Temple, he is suddenly confronted with his own humanness. In comparison to this holy God he immediately knows that he and his people are sinful and have "unclean lips" (6:5). His cry of woe is uttered in fear for his life.

As with the divine confrontation, Isaiah's response also subtly deviates from the typical pattern of the prophetic call narrative. Often, the prophets will protest that there is a physical attribute that disallows them from proclaiming God's word: Moses complains that he can't speak well enough (Exodus 4:10) and Jeremiah claims that he is too young to bear God's message (Jeremiah 1:6). Isaiah, however, cites the spiritual malady of guilt and uncleanness.

And it is right here that God again responds with the reassurance that the prophet will be up to the task ahead. In immediate reply to Isaiah's cry of woe, one of the seraphs touches his lips with a coal from the altar and declares, "Your sin is blotted out" (6:7). Although a reassuring response from God may be an expected feature of the call narrative, the particularities of this response show that this majestic and holy God is very closely involved in all of creation. Isaiah is responded to by both a deed and an act. In each recorded call narrative the "reassurance" is different, and uniquely addresses the particular fears of the prophet as she or he considers the task ahead. The cleansing with the coal and proclamation of forgiveness reassure Isaiah that he will be able to take on the task that God has set for him.

The Response to God's Call: Send Me!

After his purification, Isaiah overhears a question that God poses to the heavenly council: "Whom shall I send?" (6:8). At this point, the prophet's original call "woe is me!" is dramatically changed to "Here am I; send me!" (6:8). Although this response has been preceded by several steps (the divine confrontation, response, assurance, and so on), the reader is still struck by Isaiah's wholehearted and immediate response to God. Even though he has not heard the content of his mission, he does not hesitate to pledge his full and total participation.

Although the passage that we are considering ends in verse 8, the full significance of Isaiah's moving response is deepened when we continue to read the content of the divine proclamation. Quickly we realize that Isaiah's fullest commitment will be necessary because God's message for the prophet is grim. Isaiah is to participate in the prevention of the people's repentance: "Make the mind of this people dull . . . so that they may not . . . comprehend with their minds, and turn and be healed" (6:10).

As we will read in the following lessons, the story of God's commitment to the people will play out in some surprising ways. But throughout every chapter in the Book of Isaiah, the prophet retains his core loyalty to his God even in the most difficult of situations. Literally, the name "Isaiah" means "Salvation [is or is from] the LORD," and although there is much judgment in this book, the prophet also declares throughout that God will save those who are faithful.

SHARING THE SCRIPTURE

Preparing Our Hearts

Explore this week's devotional reading, found in Joshua 24:14-24. In this passage recounting the renewal of God's covenant with the people as they begin life in the Promised Land, we hear Joshua's familiar words: "As for me and my household, we will serve the LORD" (24:15). Perhaps less well known is Joshua's challenge to the people that they "cannot serve the LORD, for he is a holy God" (24:19). The vast difference between God's holiness and human sinfulness is an issue that is raised repeatedly in Scripture. We will see that issue again in today's reading from Isaiah 6. Where do you see yourself in relation to God's holiness?

Pray that you and the adult students will choose to serve the holy God, despite our numerous sins and imperfections.

Preparing Our Minds

Study the background Scripture from Isaiah 6:1-12 and the lesson Scripture from Isaiah 6:1-8.

Consider this question as you prepare the lesson: *How do people respond when they find the higher power to praise and worship?*

Write on newsprint:
❑ information for next week's lesson, found under "Continue the Journey."
❑ activities for further spiritual growth in "Continue the Journey."

Review the "Introduction," "The Big Picture," "Close-up," and "Faith in Action." Consider how you will use this additional information, which immediately precedes the first lesson, for this session and throughout the quarter.

LEADING THE CLASS

(1) Gather to Learn

❖ Greet the class members. Introduce any guests and help them feel at home.

❖ Pray that today's participants will experience a taste of the holiness of God.

❖ Discuss these questions:
  (1) Who or what do people worship? (Consider figures in sports, music, fashion, politics, and other powerful arenas. Also think about power and status in the workplace and society that come from certain jobs, living in the "right" neighborhood, or driving the "best" car.)
  (2) Why do you think people seek out people and things other than God to worship?

❖ Read aloud today's focus statement: **People seek a power beyond themselves worthy of praise and worship. How do people respond when they find the higher power to praise and worship? Isaiah, hearing the extravagant praises and worship directed to God, responded by accepting the call to become God's messenger.**

(2) Goal 1: Connect Praise and Worship of God With Isaiah's Call and Response of Commitment

❖ Choose a volunteer to read Isaiah 6:1-8. Suggest that the listeners close their eyes and try to experience this scene as if they were present.

❖ Ask: **What did you see, hear, taste, touch, or smell as you imagined yourself in the Temple with Isaiah?** (If the class is large, form small groups to discuss this question.)

❖ Option: Bring a picture of seraphs, incense to burn, and something hot to touch. Set up these items and invite volunteers to experience each one. Encourage them to comment on how this object might draw them to a deeper experience of worship.

❖ Consider these questions:

(1) **How does the cosmos react to this appearance of God?** (See the paragraph on "Isaiah 6:4" in Understanding the Scripture.)

(2) **Why did Isaiah, who may have been a priest, seem to be upset during this visionary worship experience?** (He recognizes his personal sinfulness and the sinfulness of his people. Isaiah has seen the Lord [6:1]. Since people believed that one who saw God would immediately die, Isaiah declares in verse 5 that he is "lost.")

(3) **What meaning do you see in the seraph touching a live coal to Isaiah's lips?** (As a prophet, Isaiah needed to be able to speak divine words that came from purified lips. See "God's Call: Cleansing from Sin" in Interpreting the Scripture and "Isaiah 6:5-7" in Understanding the Scripture.)

(3) Goal 2: Recall a Meaningful Worship Experience During Which the Learners Made Some Level of Commitment

❖ Read "The Response to God's Call: Send Me!" in Interpreting the Scripture. Point out that Isaiah's response was made in the midst of a worship experience.

❖ Distribute paper and pencils. Invite the learners to recall a worship experience during which they made some commitment to God. What was the commitment? Why do they think this call and their response came in the midst of this particular worship experience?

❖ Encourage several volunteers to tell their stories.

(4) Goal 3: Identify Means of Worship That Include Contemporary Components of Worship Similar to Those Included in Isaiah's Vision

❖ Look again at today's Scripture reading. Point out that everywhere Isaiah turned he saw evidence of God. Everything in this Temple scene calls attention to God and to divine majesty, power, and holiness. Think about your own sanctuary and services and discuss these questions:

(1) **Where do you see, hear, taste, touch, or smell evidence of God's majesty and glory in your church?**

(2) **Notice in verse 3 that the seraphs chant to one another. What role does music play in your worship experience?**

❖ Post newsprint and invite the class to brainstorm answers to this question: **If we were to create a contemporary service that included components similar to Isaiah's vision, what would we include?** (Here are some ideas: *music of praise, prayer of confession, words of assurance, call for commitment, and response. Our whole being could be included in worship by appealing to the senses. The altar may be adorned in a way to visually represent the Bible reading. Holy Communion* *may be served, which would whet our appetites. An aroma, such as burning incense or baking bread, would link the Bible passage to our sense of smell.)*

❖ Conclude by asking: **How might a change in our way of worshiping, along with a change in our expectations about what God will do during worship, help us worship God more fully and faithfully?**

(5) Continue the Journey

❖ Pray that as the adults go forth (perhaps to attend worship) that they will experience the awe of a God whose holiness is beyond description.

❖ Read aloud this preparation for next week's lesson. You may also want to post it on newsprint for the students to copy.

- ■ **Title: Give Thanks**
- ■ **Background Scripture: Isaiah 12**
- ■ **Lesson Scripture: Isaiah 12**
- ■ **Focus of the Lesson: People who experience life-saving blessings are grateful and speak words of thanksgiving. To whom do people direct their praise and thanksgiving for life's blessings? Isaiah gives thanks to God for salvation with joyous songs of praise.**

❖ Post these three activities related to this week's session on newsprint for the students to copy. Challenge the adults to grow spiritually by completing one or more of them.

(1) **Spend time in prayer before you leave home to attend worship and again when you arrive at church. Pray that you will be open to encountering God in a transforming, awe-inspiring way.**

(2) **Talk with someone who is searching for God about a meaningful encounter that you have had with God. Try to put into words what you learned about God and yourself from this encounter.**

(3) **Attend a service in your own church or a neighboring church that is structured differently from the service you normally attend. For example, if you usually participate in a traditional service, attend a contemporary or emergent service. Compare how these two types of services open the door for you to encounter God.**

❖ Sing or read aloud "Holy, Holy, Holy! Lord God Almighty."

❖ Conclude today's session by leading the class in this benediction, adapted from the key verse for June 9 from Isaiah 12:4: **Let us go forth continually giving thanks, proclaiming God's mighty deeds, and exalting God's holy name.**

UNIT 1: THE PROPHET AND PRAISE
GIVE THANKS

PREVIEWING THE LESSON

Lesson Scripture: Isaiah 12
Background Scripture: Isaiah 12
Key Verse: Isaiah 12:4

Focus of the Lesson:
People who experience life-saving blessings are grateful and speak words of thanksgiving. To whom do people direct their praise and thanksgiving for life's blessings? Isaiah gives thanks to God for salvation with joyous songs of praise.

Goals for the Learners:
(1) to discover reasons Isaiah was thankful to God and the ways he displayed his gratitude.
(2) to discern their beliefs about the connection between gratitude and natural, spontaneous praise.
(3) to proclaim thanksgiving and praise publicly.

Pronunciation Guide:
Gihon (gi' hon)
proleptic (proh lep' tik)
Shear-jashub (shee uhr ay' shuhb)

Supplies:
Bibles, newsprint and marker, paper and pencils, hymnals

READING THE SCRIPTURE

NRSV

Lesson Scripture: Isaiah 12
1　You will say in that day:
　　I will give thanks to you, O LORD,
　　　　for though you were angry with me,
　　your anger turned away,
　　　　and you comforted me.

CEB

Lesson Scripture: Isaiah 12
1You will say on that day:
　　"I thank you, LORD.
　　　　Though you were angry with me,
　　　　your anger turned away
　　　　　　and you comforted me.

2 Surely God is my salvation;
       I will trust, and will not be afraid,
   for the LORD GOD is my strength
       and my might;
       he has become my salvation.
   ³With joy you will draw water from the wells of salvation. ⁴And you will say in that day:

> **Give thanks to the LORD,**
>   **call on his name;**
> **make known his deeds among**
>   **the nations;**
>   **proclaim that his name is exalted.**

5 Sing praises to the LORD, for he has
       done gloriously;
   let this be known in all the earth.
6 Shout aloud and sing for joy,
       O royal Zion,
       for great in your midst is the Holy
       One of Israel.

²God is indeed my salvation;
    I will trust and won't be afraid.
Yah, the LORD, is my strength
    and my shield;
    he has become my salvation."
³You will draw water with joy
    from the springs of salvation.
⁴And you will say on that day:

> **"Thank the LORD; call on God's name;**
>   **proclaim God's deeds**
>   **among the peoples;**
>   **declare that God's name is exalted.**

⁵Sing to the LORD,
    who has done glorious things;
    proclaim this throughout all the earth."
⁶Shout and sing for joy, city of Zion,
    because the holy one of Israel
    is great among you.

UNDERSTANDING THE SCRIPTURE

Isaiah 12:1. The short phrase "in that day" encompasses a great swath of history, pointing both back to the prophecies given in earlier chapters, and to the future in which these prophecies will be fulfilled. Throughout chapters 10 and 11 of the Book of Isaiah, "on that day" refers to the day in the future in which God will finally break the power of Assyria and restore Israel from the countries in which it has been dispersed (10:27 and 11:11). Before "that day" of victory, however, both Israel and Judah will be punished by God for their great misdeeds. In their mistreatment of the poor, substituting political alliances for trust in God, and deviations from prescribed worship, the nation has come under the censure of God. Before Assyria will be punished "on that day," that nation too will be brought very low by the hand of God. But the prophet foretells that, in the future, God's wrath will come to an end, and the people will be restored. Strikingly, "on that day" is also when "the root of Jesse shall stand as a signal to the peoples," a kind of center around which the nations shall gather for guidance (11:10).

Both 12:1 and 12:4 begin with the phrase "You will say in that day." It is likely that this functions as a kind of liturgical rubric, that is, instructions for the proper recitation of what follows. (The term "rubric" derives from the red ink by which the instructions were distinguished from the text written in black in liturgical prayer books and missals.) Although it is undetectable in English translations, the "you" in verse 1 is singular, but plural in verse 4. That is, the literal sense of the thanksgiving in 12:1-3 gestures toward an individual speaker. However, remembering that this chapter is based upon the national prophecies given in earlier chapters, the literary context suggests that the individual in these verses could be read as representing the collective voice of the nation. Thus, the remembrance of God's anger and comfort could be expressed by individuals and still incorporate the experience of the whole people of God.

Isaiah 12:2. The close juxtaposition of the "LORD" with "my salvation" here is a subtle allusion to Isaiah's name. "LORD" is the English translation of the divine name "Yahweh," and this name is often shortened to "Yah" when it is found in proper names (rendered "iah" in our English translations). In some poetic texts of the Hebrew Bible, God's name also appears simply as "Yah." Literally, the two names for God found in the middle of 1:2 ("the LORD GOD" in the NRSV) is actually "Yahweh Yah" in the original Hebrew. As mentioned in the previous lesson, the prophet's name, "Isa-iah," means, literally, "salvation [is or is from] Yah," and both of these terms are present in the final half of this verse.

Isaiah 12:3. The water ritual described here may have a specific background in the celebration of the Feast of Tabernacles that occurs in the fall (September–October). During this celebration, water would be drawn from the Gihon spring (the water source for the city of Jerusalem, located near the city's walls). It was then transported to the Temple and poured out in front of the altar in thanksgiving for the harvest of the past year and in the hope that next year's harvest would be fruitful.

Isaiah 12:4-5. The international focus of this communal praise of God ("let this be known in all the earth," 12:5) is a thread that is repeated in this chapter and in the entire Book of Isaiah. In 12:4, the people were commanded to make known God's deeds "among the nations" (12:4). Just as the nations of Israel and Judah will be destroyed at the hands of the nations (Assyria in particular), so God's ultimate victory will also be known outside the borders of God's chosen land. Thus, the coming trouble and deliverance are both praised in an international context as both coming from the hand of God.

In a moving vision, the prophet also declares that, after Judah's destruction by Assyria, the "root of Jesse" will stand "as a signal to the people" (11:10), a witness to the international prominence of Judah in the coming age. The trouble that is to come will not have the final word, and Judah's significance will be known.

Isaiah 12:6. Careful readers will note that there are two possible translations at the beginning of this verse, and the NRSV and NIV have made different choices. The entity that is being asked to shout aloud with joy is either "people of Zion" (NIV) or "royal Zion" (NRSV). Most other English translations render the text as some kind of variation of "inhabitants of Zion."

The phrase "in your midst" probably refers to God's presence in the Temple, the context of Isaiah's call back in chapter 6. Designating God as the "Holy One" also relates to earlier sections of the book: One of the first titles given to God in the entire book is "the Holy One of Israel" (1:4). The prophet continues using this title in texts such as 5:19, 24; 10:20; 17:7; 29:19; 30:11, 12, 15; and 37:23. The designation emphasizes God's separateness from the rest of reality, and the boundary between humanity and the divine. Since the holiness of God cannot help but consume every impurity, the title highlights the inevitable destruction of any people who harbor sin. By placing "the Holy One of Israel" in the "midst" of the nation, the prayer looks forward to the day when the people have been completely purified and able to live together with their holy God.

INTERPRETING THE SCRIPTURE

Giving Thanks to God

Although we often don't distinguish between "thanksgiving" and "praise" in common parlance, scholars who study biblical prayers will often differentiate expressions of who God is (praise) from expressions of what God has done (thanksgiving). Most prayers in the Bible and in contemporary worship settings incorporate both types of expressions, but they are usually distinguishable and one aspect is often emphasized within a single prayer.

The twelfth chapter of Isaiah is a prayer consisting predominantly of thanksgiving. Throughout this prayer we are told of the specific acts of God that should cause us to erupt in praise. God was once angry, but this rage was soon appeased: "Your anger turned away, and you comforted me" (12:1). God also worked wondrous deeds for the people: "He has done gloriously" (12:5). Although the specific expressions of this "anger," "comfort," and glorious deeds are not given in any detail, Isaiah 12 functions somewhat as a testimony that witnesses to God's saving deeds in the past. Here, God is given thanks for what God has done.

Giving Thanks for the Future Ahead

The curious feature about the thanksgiving in Isaiah 12 is that its actual content lay in the future. Taken out of its literary context, the words seem to be a straightforward expression of thanksgiving for God's accomplished deeds. Yet when one reads Isaiah 1–11, it is clear that these deeds have yet to be fully realized.

Because the Book of Isaiah combines historical narratives with prophecies both of judgment and salvation, it is sometimes difficult to discern a complete "plot" of any kind. But there is an overarching "storyline" that can be detected. The book begins with chapter after chapter of accusations that Judah has committed grave crimes. God's first words in the book are a sharp and stinging accusation against the nation: "I reared children and brought them up, but they have rebelled against me" (1:2). The offenses that are eventually named largely have to do with injustice and religious unfaithfulness. Jerusalem, the city once full marked by righteousness, is now full of wrongdoing: "Everyone loves a bribe and runs after gifts. They do not defend the orphan, and the widow's cause does not come before them" (1:23). In addition, the land is full of idols and their worshipers who "bow down to the work of their hands, to what their own fingers have made" (2:8). God promises to restore the city and the nation, but only after a purifying destruction: "I will smelt away your dross as with lye and remove all your alloy" (1:25). Or, in the words of Isaiah 6 that we just studied in the previous lesson, God promises "healing" only after "the land is utterly desolate" (6:10, 11). In an utterly shocking move, God will use the power of Assyria to bring about this divine destruction: "Ah, Assyria, the rod of my anger—the club in their hands is my fury! Against a godless nation I send him, and against the people of my wrath I command him, to take spoil and seize plunder, and to tread them down like the mire of the streets" (10:5-6). After Assyria wreaks its destruction, God will bring that nation down as well: The Holy One "will burn and devour his thorns and briers in one day" (10:18).

It is only after the destruction of Israel, Judah, and Assyria that God's people will be restored, and God's "comfort" will be known to the people (12:1). The thanksgiving in Isaiah 12, thus, is proleptic—a vision of a future hope that is not currently discernible in the present except with the eyes of faith.

This may indeed be a difficult reality to accept, but the prophet himself has forged the way forward to the coming reality with two provocative names that are given to children in the book. The first is one of his own sons: Shear-jashub (7:3). The name means, literally, "a remnant shall return" and speaks of the prophet's own hope for the future even as he is fully aware of the extent of God's anger. The second is the name for another child, Immanuel, a son whose name reminds the nation of the Lord's constant presence as "God with us" (7:14). Both boys carry in their own names the reminder of the nation's ultimate restoration by the hand of God.

In Isaiah 12, prayer functions as a kind of pledge on the future. Just as surely as God's judgment will come, so too will the redemption follow in its path. The line "you will say in that day" (12:4), followed by words of thanks and memories of comfort and healing, is a difficult but ultimately hopeful prayer. This is a prayer that is not unmoored from reality in a kind of theological wish-land. Rather, it is a prayer that is able to face the difficult reality head-on, and declare that, come what may, the Lord has done glorious deeds. The threats are real, but so is the reality of God's ultimate salvation.

For the Future, Echoes of the Past:
A "Borrowed" Thanksgiving

Readers who know their Bibles well will hear echoes of several other biblical texts within Isaiah 12. The claim that YHWH is "my strength and my might; he has become my salvation" (12:2) is almost exactly the same as that made by the people in their celebration of God's deliverance at the Red Sea in Exodus 15:2. The psalmist repeats this claim as well while testifying to God's strong help in the midst of a battle with opposing forces so strong and numerous that surrounded the author "like bees, they blazed like a fire of thorns" (Psalm 118:12, 14).

Contemporary sensibilities may insist that each new experience of God's great work demands a new expression that is unique to the specific occasion. Repeating extant lines may seem inadequate and reflect a theological conservatism or even a form of liturgical laziness. But much like falling in love, perhaps one's own particular emotions can sometimes be most fully expressed in lines and verses that poets have penned centuries beforehand and other lovers have repeated countless times since.

But there is also something deeper at stake here in Isaiah 12 than simply finding the most adequate expression of a particular experience of God's deeds. "Borrowing" lines from the past praises of Israel can be read both as a statement of fidelity and as a statement of faith. For a people whom God accuses of religious misdeeds such as importing idols into worship (10:11), reciting lines from the tradition may gesture toward a renewed commitment to that tradition in religious practice. Further, for a people who still must endure the force of God's judgment, repeating the praises of those who have survived great ordeals gives hope for the future. No matter what is to come, the people know that they will, eventually, sing the same praise to the same God who brought them through the Red Sea and other fierce battles. Even as their ancestors walked through times of great trials and tribulations, so too will they. And they, like their ancestors, will survive to praise their God with a great prayer of thanksgiving.

SHARING THE SCRIPTURE

Preparing Our Hearts

Explore this week's devotional reading, found in Psalm 92:1-8. In this "Song for the Sabbath Day," an individual gives thanks to God for creation ("the works of your hands," 92:4) and for God's faithful, steadfast love (92:2). What prompts you to "give thanks" and "sing praises" (92:1) to God? Make a list of those attributes of God that you find praiseworthy. Make another list of things that God has done recently for which you want to give thanks. In verse, in song, or in prose, offer your praise and thanksgiving to God.

Pray that you and the adult students will be aware of who God is and what God does so that you may offer thanksgiving.

Preparing Our Minds

Study the background Scripture and the lesson Scripture, both of which are from Isaiah 12.

Consider this question as you prepare the lesson: *To whom do people direct their praise and thanksgiving for life's blessings?*

Write on newsprint:

❏ information for next week's lesson, found under "Continue the Journey."
❏ activities for further spiritual growth in "Continue the Journey."

Review the "Introduction," "The Big Picture," "Close-up," and "Faith in Action." Consider how you will use this additional information, which immediately precedes the first lesson, for this session.

LEADING THE CLASS

(1) Gather to Learn

❖ Greet the class members. Introduce any guests and help them feel at home.

❖ Pray that the class members will join with the prophet in praising God.

❖ Read this excerpt from Abraham Lincoln's October 1863 proclamation declaring that the citizens of the United States should set aside a day to give thanks to God: **"The year that is drawing towards its close, has been filled with the blessings of fruitful fields and healthful skies. To these bounties, which are so constantly enjoyed that we are prone to forget the source from which they come, others have been added,** **which are of so extraordinary a nature, that they cannot fail to penetrate and soften even the heart which is habitually insensible to the ever watchful providence of Almighty God. In the midst of a civil war of unequaled magnitude and severity, which has sometimes seemed to foreign States to invite and to provoke their aggression, peace has been preserved with all nations, order has been maintained, the laws have been respected and obeyed, and harmony has prevailed everywhere except in the theatre of military conflict. . . . No human counsel hath devised nor hath any mortal hand worked out these great things. They are the gracious gifts of the Most High God, who, while dealing with us in anger for our sins, hath nevertheless remembered mercy. It has seemed to me fit and proper that they should be solemnly, reverently and gratefully acknowledged as with one heart and one voice by the whole American People. I do therefore invite my fellow citizens in every part of the United States, and also those who are at sea and those who are sojourning in foreign lands, to set apart and observe the last Thursday of November next, as a day of Thanksgiving and Praise to our beneficent Father who dwelleth in the Heavens."**

❖ Ask: **What do you think motivated President Lincoln to issue a proclamation such as this?**

❖ Read aloud today's focus statement: **People who experience life-saving blessings are grateful and speak words of thanksgiving. To whom do people direct their praise and thanksgiving for life's blessings? Isaiah gives thanks to God for salvation with joyous songs of praise.**

(2) Goal 1: Discover Reasons Isaiah Was Thankful to God and the Ways He Displayed His Gratitude

❖ Read "Giving Thanks for the Future Ahead" from Interpreting the Scripture to provide a context for today's Scripture passage.

❖ Select four volunteers to read, in turn, verses 1, 2, 3-4, and 5-6.

❖ Invite the learners to review this passage and then list on newsprint reasons why Isaiah is thankful to God. (*Isaiah appreciates that God's anger turned to comfort; God is Isaiah's salvation, strength, and might; God's deeds are glorious.*)

❖ Discuss these questions:

(1) **How does Isaiah express his gratitude to God?** (*Isaiah trusts in God and is not afraid; he encourages others to call on God's exalted name and make God's deeds known to the nations; he sings praises and shouts aloud.*)

(2) **What additional ways can you think of to offer thanks for God's amazing deeds?**

(3) Goal 2: Discern the Learners' Beliefs About the Connection Between Gratitude and Natural, Spontaneous Praise

❖ Read "Giving Thanks to God" from Interpreting the Scripture.

❖ Assign volunteers one of the following passages from the Psalms to read aloud and indicate the reason the psalmist sings this song. Reasons may be found as superscriptions and explained more thoroughly in the footnotes of study Bibles:

■ Psalm 7:17 (an innocent individual asks God for help)

■ Psalm 28:7 (an individual asks God for help and offers thanks for that help)

■ Psalm 30:12 (an individual thanks God for healing from serious illness)

■ Psalm 35:9-10, 18 (an individual seeks deliverance from enemies)

■ Psalm 75:1 (the community thanks God for wondrous deeds)

■ Psalm 95:2 (a hymn that praises the Lord as the King of the universe and calls people to worship and obey)

■ Psalm 100:4 (a hymn summoning all people to praise the Lord)

■ Psalm 118:19, 21 (an entrance liturgy for worship adapted from a psalm of thanksgiving for deliverance from danger)

❖ Discuss these questions:

(1) **What kinds of reasons did you hear to offer praise and thanksgiving?**

(2) **What other reasons might individuals or communities have to praise God?**

(3) **What reasons does your congregation have to praise God right now?**

(4) Goal 3: Proclaim Thanksgiving and Praise Publicly

❖ Provide a few moments for silent reflection so that individuals may answer this question: **What reasons do I have to praise and thank God today?** Note that some participants may have a major reason, such as finding a job or welcoming a new grandchild; others may have joys of a lesser magnitude, but all of these reasons are important to God.

❖ Form a circle, if possible, in your space. Go around and ask each person to offer a sentence or two in which they state a reason to praise and thank God. After each person's prayer, the group is to respond: **We give you thanks and praise, O God.**

(5) Continue the Journey

❖ Close the circle time by praying that those who have gathered today will continue to give thanks to God and make God's wondrous deeds known to others.

❖ Read aloud this preparation for next week's lesson. You may also want to post it on newsprint for the students to copy.

■ Title: Meaningless Worship
■ Background Scripture: Isaiah 29
■ Lesson Scripture: Isaiah 29:9-16a
■ Focus of the Lesson: People sometimes ritualistically repeat words or phrases that have little or no meaning for them. What is the danger involved in insincere speaking? Isaiah announces that those who honor God with their lips but not their hearts will face divine judgment.

❖ Post these three activities related to this week's session on newsprint for the students to copy. Challenge the adults to grow spiritually by completing one or more of them.

(1) Identify a situation in your own life that evoked great thanksgiving to God. Think about how you might share this situation with others, even if you choose not to reveal details. Look for an opportunity to tell someone what God has done for you.

(2) Express thanks artistically by drawing a poster or creating a collage from magazine pictures that illustrate reasons you have to be thankful to God.

(3) Lift up a situation during a public prayer time for which you are thankful. Let people know how God has blessed you.

❖ Sing or read aloud "Give Thanks," found in *The Faith We Sing*.

❖ Conclude today's session by leading the class in this benediction, adapted from the key verse for June 9 from Isaiah 12:4: **Let us go forth continually giving thanks, proclaiming God's mighty deeds, and exalting God's holy name.**

UNIT 1: THE PROPHET AND PRAISE
MEANINGLESS WORSHIP

PREVIEWING THE LESSON

Lesson Scripture: Isaiah 29:9-16a
Background Scripture: Isaiah 29
Key Verse: Isaiah 29:13

Focus of the Lesson:
People sometimes ritualistically repeat words or phrases that have little or no meaning for them. What is the danger involved in insincere speaking? Isaiah announces that those who honor God with their lips but not their hearts will face divine judgment.

Goals for the Learners:
(1) to discover what Isaiah says about meaningless, insincere worship.
(2) to examine the meanings and emotions associated with the words they use in worship.
(3) to "freshen" a common component of worship that has come to be "mere words."

Pronunciation Guide:
Ariel (air' ee uhl)
Jebus (jee' buhs)

Supplies:
Bibles, newsprint and marker, paper and pencils, hymnals

READING THE SCRIPTURE

NRSV
Lesson Scripture: Isaiah 29:9-16a
9 Stupefy yourselves and be in a stupor,
    blind yourselves and be blind!
  Be drunk, but not from wine;
    stagger, but not from strong drink!
10 For the Lord has poured out upon you
    a spirit of deep sleep;
  he has closed your eyes, you prophets,

CEB
Lesson Scripture: Isaiah 29:9-16a
9Be shocked and stunned;
    blind yourselves; be blind!
  Be drunk, but not on wine;
    stagger, but not on account of beer!
10The Lord has poured on you
    a spirit of deep sleep,
    and has shut your eyes, you prophets,

and covered your heads, you seers.

[11]The vision of all this has become for you like the words of a sealed document. If it is given to those who can read, with the command, "Read this," they say, "We cannot, for it is sealed." [12]And if it is given to those who cannot read, saying, "Read this," they say, "We cannot read."

[13] The Lord said:
　　Because **these people draw near**
　　　　with their mouths
　　　　and honor me with their lips,
　　　　while their hearts are far from me,
　　and their worship of me is a human
　　　　commandment learned by rote;

[14]　so I will again do
　　　　amazing things with this people,
　　　　shocking and amazing.
　　The wisdom of their wise shall perish,
　　　　and the discernment of the
　　　　　　discerning shall be hidden.

[15]　Ha! You who hide a plan too deep for
　　　　the LORD,
　　　　whose deeds are in the dark,
　　　　and who say, "Who sees us?
　　　　Who knows us?"

[16]　You turn things upside down!
　　　　Shall the potter be regarded as
　　　　　　the clay?
　　　Shall the thing made say of its maker,
　　　　　"He did not make me"?

and covered your heads, you seers.

[11]This entire vision has become for you like the words of a sealed scroll. When they give it to one who can read, saying, "Read this," that one will say, "I can't, because it's sealed." [12]And when the scroll is given to one who can't read, saying, "Read this," that one will say, "I can't read."

[13]The Lord says:
　　Since **these people turn toward me**
　　　　with their mouths,
　　　　and honor me with lip service
　　　　while their heart is distant from me,
　　and their fear of me is just a human
　　　　command that has been memorized,

[14]I will go on doing amazing things
　　　　to these people,
　　　　shocking and startling things.
　　The wisdom of their wise will perish,
　　　　and the discernment of their
　　　　　　discerning will be hidden.

[15]Doom to those who hide
　　　　their plan deep, away from the LORD,
　　　　whose deeds are in the dark,
　　　　who say, "Who sees us?
　　　　Who knows us?"

[16]You have everything backward!
　　　　Should the potter
　　　　　be thought of as clay?
　　　Should what is made say of its maker,
　　　　　"He didn't make me"?
　　　Should what is shaped
　　　　　say of the one who shaped it,
　　　　　"He doesn't understand"?

UNDERSTANDING THE SCRIPTURE

Isaiah 29:1-2. God continues to proclaim judgment against Jerusalem throughout this chapter, and uses the name "Ariel" for the city (here in verse 1, as well as in verse 2 and again in verse 7). The Bible has several names for Jerusalem: "Zion" (Psalms 137:1; 147:12), "Jebus" (Judges 19:10, 11), "the city of David" (2 Samuel 5:9), and others.

Although "Ariel" is also the name of one of the leaders during the postexilic period (Ezra 8:16), Isaiah 29 is the only place where it is used to designate Jerusalem. Literally, "Ariel" might mean "lion of God [El]," but it can also designate the altar of burnt offering in the rebuilt Temple (Ezekiel 43:15). Given the destruction that God is bringing to the city in Isaiah 29, perhaps the name is used here as a synonym for a burnt offering. This would fit well with the concern throughout the book for the worship practices of Jerusalem.

The cry "Woe!" (sometimes translated "Ah!") often begins oracles of judgment in the prophets, and is usually followed by a list of indictments. Although "festivals" in the Bible are holy celebrations to the Lord, in this context they have become tainted. The exact cause of this indictment is not clear. Perhaps the people have become overconfident in the festivals' effect upon God, or perhaps they have abandoned the inner meaning of the celebration.

Isaiah 29:3. David's initial assault and capture of the city is described in 2 Samuel 5:6-10 and 1 Chronicles 11:4-8. At that time there was most probably a battle, with the inhabitants telling David, "You will not come in here" (1 Chronicles 11:5). Yet we hear nothing specifically about any "towers" or "siegeworks." This type of military architecture is most prominently associated with the Assyrians.

Isaiah 29:4. Jerusalem's destruction is portrayed here as though the city has been changed into a corpse, and whispering like a ghost speaking "deep from the earth . . . out of the dust."

Isaiah 29:5. Ironically, dust is also used in the depiction of Jerusalem's enemies, but now the image is one of strength rather than weakness. With the strategic word "but," dust now in verse 5 represents the innumerable forces that are coming to fight the city, a "multitude . . . like small dust, and the multitude of tyrants like flying chaff."

Isaiah 29:6-8. In this section, we have yet another reversal. Now the "dust" and "flying chaff" that just attacked Jerusalem will itself be dispersed by a violent attack of the Lord of hosts. Bringing thunder, whirlwind, and flame as part of the divine military retinue, the multitudes of Jerusalem's attackers will suddenly disappear "like a dream, a vision of the night" (29:7). The God who

brought Jerusalem low in 29:4 now suddenly becomes the destroyer of the city's enemies.

Isaiah 29:9-10. Here the prophet moves from speaking about Jerusalem to directly addressing other prophets. The words are harsh, but for those who have studied Isaiah's call in chapter 6, they are not entirely surprising. Central to the message that God gave to the prophet in his call was the insensibility of the people: "Keep listening, but do not comprehend; keep looking, but do not understand" (6:9). Strikingly, it is God who has brought on the blindness of the prophets and the seers in 29:10.

Isaiah 29:11-12. Although the NRSV prefers the more literal translation "sealed document," the NIV is correct in referring to the object as a scroll since larger documents were always rolled up.

Isaiah 29:13-14. The logic of these verses follows the typical prophetic pattern of stating the offense followed by the punishment. Here, empty worship will be punished with "shocking and amazing" deeds that will be insensible to the wise and discerning.

Isaiah 29:15-16. As in 29:1, the term "Woe!" in the NIV (or "Ha!" here in the NRSV) begins a statement of judgment in which the reasons for the indictment are first given. The offenses listed include the ways in which the people try to hide their plans from God and think that their deeds are hidden by the dark. The hidden "plan" and "deeds" here may refer to a political plot that the leaders have devised against Assyria.

Isaiah 29:17-20. In the rest of the chapter, God sets out the divine response to the indictment in the previous verses, and the theme is one of radical reversal. In a dramatic departure from typical prophetic oracles, God's response to the people's sin is not their destruction but rather their flourishing. Given the context, it seems that "Lebanon" (29:17) is a metaphor for Judah whom God will soon restore. In contrast to Judah's hopeful future, God will soon destroy the "tyrant" and "scoffer" in 29:20.

In verse 19, God is again given the title "the Holy One of Israel," an expression used throughout the book to refer both to God's utter distinction from humanity as well as God's choice to dwell with a specific nation (1:4 and so on). Notice that several verses later in this chapter God will be called "the Holy One of Jacob" in parallel with the title "the God of Israel" (29:23).

Isaiah 29:21. In the legal system of ancient Israel and Judah, law cases were conducted "in the gate," that is, in the public square just inside the main entrance to the town. Here the parties would meet to settle their disputes publicly (see Ruth 4:1-12 and Amos 5:12).

Isaiah 29:22-24. Touchingly, Jacob's "children" are claimed by God as "the work of my hands" (29:23). In the context of the chapter, one can't help thinking back on the image of the potter who shapes each object by hand only to be rejected by the assertion, "He did not make me!" (29:16). Perhaps the new "understanding" and "instruction" that is reached in 29:24 includes the basic realization that Judah depends on God for its very life. As in Proverbs 1:7, true knowledge and wisdom begins with the "fear of the LORD."

INTERPRETING THE SCRIPTURE

God's Strange Work: Worship and Politics

Throughout the Book of Isaiah, God does shocking deeds. In chapter 10, God speaks of using the military might of Assyria to God's own purposes: "Ah Assyria, the rod of my anger—the club in their hands is my fury!" (10:5). While it is surprising enough to hear that God will send Assyria to destroy and plunder enemy nations, Isaiah adds an additional surprise by declaring that God will bring Assyria in an attack on Jerusalem itself (10:6-11).

Now in Isaiah 29, the prophet declares that, in addition to military danger, God will also bring a spiritual insensitivity upon the people that will have sharp political consequences. The people will go about in a type of fog, stupefied and blinded by the hand of God: "the LORD has poured out upon you a spirit of deep sleep" (29:10). Although such a "deep sleep" was sent by God upon Adam in order to work a new work in the creation of Eve (Genesis 2:21), the consequences of this sleep in Isaiah are not nearly as welcome. This sleep involves a profound dislocation from God. The prophet also declares that God has impaired the work of the very people whose job it is to communicate regularly with the divine. The eyes of the prophets, the people whom the whole community relied upon to tell out the word of God, will be shut. In addition, the heads of the seers (people who likewise communicated with the divine) will be covered. This is a way of saying that they will be unable to receive direction from God. Isaiah emphasizes that these acts have not come through chance or bad luck. The dominant phrase in the grammar of 29:9-11 is the simple assertion, "For the LORD" (29:10). No matter what may *seem* to be true, the strange stupefaction has a divine source. All of the spiritual dullness of the people is attributable solely to God.

This spiritual insensitivity should be viewed in the political context. It is possible to relate this text to Judah's intrigue with Egypt in the nation's attempt to oppose Assyrian rule. (Later in chapters 30 and 31 the prophet sharply criticizes the idea of sending emissaries to Egypt without inquiring of the Lord.) In such a context the prophet declares that whatever might make the best "sense" on the political level might actually be senseless, conjured up by ineffectual advisors who are unable even to read.

In such ways Isaiah effectively links the religious world to the political one. Although contemporary Americans usually prefer to assume a division between "church and state," this concept is unimaginable within the polity of ancient Judah. But in chapter 29, the prophet declares that those in charge of seeking God's counsel will be unable to receive it.

This is strange work indeed. But perhaps, in the context of the entire book, even stranger is the fact that God's punishment has been withheld from the people for so long. Serving a holy God has serious consequences, as Isaiah emphasizes again and again. And when God holds back the divine hand of punishment, surely the proper response of humanity is thanksgiving and spiritual renewal. Yet when the delay brings about rather a multiplication of sin and the opportunity to become habituated to lives of unrighteousness, the prophet declares that God must act.

Our Strange Work: Worshiping Without the Heart

Part of this unrighteousness involves the people's worship. Although we may think of the Hebrew Bible as thick with strict commands about even the smallest details of worship, the text also expresses an overriding concern that the people also simply "draw near" to God and "honor" the deity (29:13). In some ways, these two verbs ("draw near" and "honor") are at the heart of the full and proper worship of God in the Bible.

In Isaiah 29, there is absolutely no critique of the outward expression of the people's worship. Externally, the congregation is in full conformity with the proper religious protocols, described here as drawing near with their mouths and honoring God

with their lips (29:13). Yet the prophet emphasizes that all outward acts of worship must always involve the correct attitude of the inner spirit. The most beautiful words that are repeated simply by rote, without any affirmation by the spirit or delight and wonder in one's deepest being are worth nothing at all in worship.

This theme of "empty worship" occurs regularly throughout the Prophets. In Hosea 7:14 God laments the people "do not cry to me from the heart." In Micah, God insists that proper worship must involve the moral life: "to do justice, to love kindness, and to walk humbly with your God" (Micah 6:8). And later in Isaiah, God laments that the people "delight" in worship and yet "oppress" their workers (58:2-3). There is a sense in which those who most fully experience the presence of God (that is, the prophets) are constrained to remind us again and again that there is no part of life that we can hide from God. God can see through our actions and discern our inner spirit, and God can remember what we affirmed in worship when we later make economic decisions that hurt the poor. As ones who are fully "captured" by God, the Prophets remind us that the fullest human admits of no divine estrangement in any aspect of life.

True worshipers find themselves in a world where tradition and ritual coexist alongside spontaneity and personal response. Although these elements may seem to contradict each other, in practice they are mutually supportive: Tradition gives us time-honored practices that generations have found fruitful, and spontaneity gives us the opportunity to respond fully from our own particular context. In some ways, an analogy to true worship is a dance in which specific moves are assigned to each partner that have been designed to elicit the most joy from the music and the human body. To truly enjoy the dance, the moves must be practiced and performed with skill. But these moves are not themselves the point of the dance. They are simply a structured framework that must be learned for true enjoyment. Once they have been learned, they are in some way "forgotten." The goal is to move beyond a focus on the correct movements (robotically repeating "step left, forward right") and become caught up in an enjoyment of one's partner. As with a dance, the true goal of worship is to learn the "rules" in order that we can be truly caught up in the profoundest enjoyment of God.

God's Amazing Response

God's response to the people who worship without the heart is described as something "shocking and amazing" (29:14). Just as in the political world, God can also surprise in the religious world as well. The surprise consists of turning over all that is credited by the established "knowers": "The wisdom of their wise shall perish, and the discernment of the discerning shall be hidden" (29:14). In the Psalms, "amazing" is often the adjective to describe God's original act of creation and in the Exodus (Psalms 77:12 and 78:11, for example, use the same Hebrew root word as "amazing" in 29:14). In Isaiah, the creator is the potter who truly knows us and is still capable of performing acts of amazement.

The reader is left to hope that, as the English translation of the Jewish Scriptures known as *Tanakh* reads, the "bafflement upon bafflement" that the prophet prophesies in 29:14 will be a sudden act of forgiveness. The chapter ends with a wonderful prophecy that Jacob's children will "stand in awe of the God of Israel," and even the ones who "err in spirit will come to understanding" (29:23-24).

SHARING THE SCRIPTURE

Preparing Our Hearts

Explore this week's devotional reading, found in Luke 8:9-14. Here Jesus discusses the purpose of parables and explains the one he has just told—the parable of the sower. From this parable we can learn that the one who truly hears is also the one who is fruitful. Think about this parable as you study today's reading from Isaiah, and draw a connection between what you hear and how you respond. Do you just parrot back what you have heard and then forget it, or do you truly take to heart what has been said and act on it?

Pray that you and the adult students will not only hear God's word but act appropriately on what you have heard.

Preparing Our Minds

Study the background Scripture from Isaiah 29 and the lesson Scripture from Isaiah 29:9-16a.

Consider this question as you prepare the lesson: *What is the danger involved in insincere speaking?*

Write on newsprint:
❑ information for next week's lesson, found under "Continue the Journey."
❑ activities for further spiritual growth in "Continue the Journey."

Review the "Introduction," "The Big Picture," "Close-up," and "Faith in Action." Consider how you will use this additional information, which immediately precedes the first lesson, for this session.

LEADING THE CLASS

(1) Gather to Learn

❖ Greet the class members. Introduce any guests and help them feel at home.

❖ Pray that those who have come today will be open to the presence of God in their lives.

❖ Read Howard Brinton's comment on worship: **Whatever is outward in worship must come as a direct result of what is inward—otherwise, it will be form without power.**

❖ Ask: **What kinds of problems may arise when people are not inwardly motivated to worship but appear to be worshiping anyway?**

❖ Read aloud today's focus statement: **People sometimes ritualistically repeat words or phrases that have little or no meaning for them. What is the danger involved in insincere speaking? Isaiah announces that those who honor God with their lips but not their hearts will face divine judgment.**

(2) Goal 1: Discover What Isaiah Says About Meaningless, Insincere Worship

❖ Use information from Understanding the Scripture from "Isaiah 29:1-2" through "29:6-8" to set today's lesson in context.

❖ Choose someone to read Isaiah 29:9-16a (ending with "regarded as the clay?")

❖ Discuss these questions:
  (1) What is God's purpose in pouring out "a spirit of deep sleep" (29:10)? (Add information from "God's Strange Work: Worship and Politics" in Interpreting the Scripture.)
  (2) What are God's concerns about the way people worship? (Add information from "Our Strange Work: Worshiping Without the Heart" in Interpreting the Scripture.)
  (3) What kind of response will God

make to this insincere worship? (Add information from "God's Amazing Response" in Interpreting the Scripture.)

(3) Goal 2: Examine the Meanings and Emotions Associated With the Words the Learners Use in Worship

❖ Distribute paper and pencils. Tell the students that you will read a list of phrases typically used in a service of worship. (Include on the list other phrases that may regularly be used in your own congregation.) The listeners are to respond by writing several words to describe how the phrase affects their worship experience. Would they describe each phrase as having a positive impact, having a negative impact, or being so trite that it has no impact?
  ■ **The Lord be with you. And also with you.** (The Great Thanksgiving of Holy Communion)
  ■ **Take, eat; this is my body which is broken for you.** (Word and Table Service 1)
  ■ **This is the Word of the Lord. Thanks be to God.** (words following the reading of Scripture)
  ■ **I believe in God the Father Almighty, creator of heaven and earth.** (Apostles' Creed)
  ■ **We renew our covenant faithfully to participate in the ministries of the church by our prayers, our presence, our gifts, and our service.** (United Methodist Baptismal Covenant)
  ■ **The peace of the Lord be with you. And also with you.** (passing of the peace)

❖ Invite the learners to talk about their responses to these words commonly used in worship. Encourage them to spotlight any of these (or others) that are especially meaningful to them. Also see if there are some phrases that have become meaningless to them. List their ideas on newsprint.

(4) Goal 3: "Freshen" a Common Component of Worship That Has Come to Be "Mere Words"

❖ Encourage the adults to review the list they just created. Ask:

(1) **What aspects of the service, if any, would we appreciate being changed?**

(2) **Why do these portions of the service need to be changed?** (Try to be specific. Are the words being used so outdated that people no longer understand them? Has a ritual, such as the passing of the peace, become so routine that no one really seems to speak sincerely? Do we "rattle off" certain words, possibly including the Lord's Prayer, to the point where they have become meaningless?)

(3) **Recognizing that there are historic traditions that guide our worship, what suggestions could we make about each portion of the service identified as needing a change? Are there contemporary words or images that could be used to convey the same ideas?**

❖ Enlist several volunteers to put the ideas in a logical, legible form and then approach the pastor or worship committee chair to discuss your ideas. Agree on a time when you would expect to hear back from the committee or pastor about how your suggestions are being addressed.

(5) Continue the Journey

❖ Pray that those who have come today will experience true worship of God.

❖ Read aloud this preparation for next week's lesson. You may also want to post it on newsprint for the students to copy.

    ■ **Title: The Glorious New Creation**

    ■ **Background Scripture: Isaiah 65**

■ **Lesson Scripture: Isaiah 65:17-21, 23-25**

■ **Focus of the Lesson: People desperately long for a time when there will be no more weeping and crying and the earth will be a place of happiness and peace. Will that time ever come? The God of truth and Creator of the earth promised through Isaiah that someday God's children would be so blessed.**

❖ Post these three activities related to this week's session on newsprint for the students to copy. Challenge the adults to grow spiritually by completing one or more of them.

(1) **Listen carefully to your own words this week. Do you express what is in your heart, or say something because you think that is what is expected of you? How does what you say reflect your beliefs and actions?**

(2) **Recall that today's passage from Isaiah concerns insincere, hypocritical worship. Would you rate your worship as sincere and focused on God? If not, what needs to change either in the service, in you, or in both?**

(3) **Talk with a friend who attends a church of another denomination. How does this person experience worship? Is there anything that he or she finds meaningless? What words or rituals particularly draw this person close to God? Be prepared to share your own worship experiences.**

❖ Sing or read aloud "O Worship the King."

❖ Conclude today's session by leading the class in this benediction, adapted from the key verse for June 9 from Isaiah 12:4: **Let us go forth continually giving thanks, proclaiming God's mighty deeds, and exalting God's holy name.**

UNIT 1: THE PROPHET AND PRAISE
THE GLORIOUS NEW CREATION

PREVIEWING THE LESSON

Lesson Scripture: Isaiah 65:17-21, 23-25
Background Scripture: Isaiah 65
Key Verses: Isaiah 65:17-18

Focus of the Lesson:
People desperately long for a time when there will be no more weeping and crying and the earth will be a place of happiness and peace. Will that time ever come? The God of truth and Creator of the earth promised through Isaiah that someday God's children would be so blessed.

Goals for the Learners:
(1) to identify the changes Isaiah claims God will make in the new creation.
(2) to describe their personal visions of the "new creation" God has promised.
(3) to discover worship experiences as rehearsals for what lies ahead in eternity.

Pronunciation Guide:
Achor (ay' kohr)　　　　　　　　Gibeon (gib ee' uhn)
Enosh (ee' nosh)　　　　　　　　Kenan (kee' nuhn)

Supplies:
Bibles, newsprint and marker, paper and pencils, hymnals

READING THE SCRIPTURE

NRSV
Lesson Scripture: Isaiah 65:17-21, 23-25

17　For I am about to create new heavens
　　　and a new earth;
　　the former things shall not be
　　　remembered
　　　or come to mind.

CEB
Lesson Scripture: Isaiah 65:17-21, 23-25

17Look! I'm creating
　　a new heaven and a new earth:
　　past events won't be remembered;
　　they won't come to mind.
18Be glad and rejoice forever

¹⁸ **But be glad and rejoice forever**
   in what I am creating;

for I am about to create Jerusalem as a joy,
   and its people as a delight.
¹⁹ I will rejoice in Jerusalem,
   and delight in my people;
no more shall the sound of weeping
   be heard in it,
   or the cry of distress.
²⁰ No more shall there be in it
   an infant that lives but a few days,
   or an old person who does not live
   out a lifetime;
for one who dies at a hundred years
   will be considered a youth,
   and one who falls short of a hundred
   will be considered accursed.
²¹ They shall build houses and
   inhabit them;
   they shall plant vineyards and
   eat their fruit.
²³ They shall not labor in vain,
   or bear children for calamity;
for they shall be offspring blessed
   by the LORD—
   and their descendants as well.
²⁴ Before they call I will answer,
   while they are yet speaking I will hear.
²⁵ The wolf and the lamb shall
   feed together,
   the lion shall eat straw like the ox;
   but the serpent—its food shall be dust!
They shall not hurt or destroy
   on all my holy mountain,
            says the LORD.

in what I'm creating,
   because I'm creating Jerusalem as a joy
   and her people as a source of gladness.
¹⁹I will rejoice in Jerusalem
   and be glad about my people.
No one will ever hear the sound
   of weeping or crying in it again.
²⁰No more will babies live only a few days,
   or the old fail to live out their days.
The one who dies at a hundred
   will be like a young person,
   and the one falling short of a hundred
   will seem cursed.
²¹They will build houses and live in them;
   they will plant vineyards
   and eat their fruit.
²³They won't labor in vain,
   nor bear children to a world of horrors,
   because they will be people
   blessed by the LORD,
   they along with their descendants.
²⁴Before they call, I will answer;
   while they are still speaking, I will hear.
²⁵Wolf and lamb will graze together,
   and the lion will eat straw like the ox,
   but the snake—its food will be dust.
They won't hurt or destroy
   at any place on my holy mountain,
   says the LORD.

UNDERSTANDING THE SCRIPTURE

Introduction. Chapter 65 consists of a long speech by God that responds to the prayer in the previous chapter. The prayer asked God to be revealed in power against the nation's enemies: "O that you would tear open the heavens and come down . . . to make your name known to your adversaries, so that the nations might tremble at your presence!" (64:1-2). In addition, the prophet confesses the sin of the people ("We have all become like one who is unclean" 64:6), and asks God to act with compassion toward the people ("Will you keep silent, and punish us so severely?" 64:12).

Isaiah 65:1-2. From the very first, God makes it clear that there was never any intention to hide from the people. In these verses, God speaks of a deep desire to be "found" by the people. The problem lay in the people's recalcitrance in seeking God. In a striking reversal of roles, God takes up the very words that Isaiah used when he heard his call: "Here am I!" (6:11). In God's repetition ("Here I am! Here I am!"), we see a vulnerable openness to the people who, again and again, "did not call on my name" (65:1).

Isaiah 65:3-4. Here God lists a number of religious practices, the first in a series throughout the chapter (see also 65:7, 11). Since sacrificing and offering incense were both central features of Israelite worship, the problem here seems to concern geography rather than practice. Sacrificing "in gardens" means that the worshipers have chosen to take their devotional acts outside the Temple, and the implication is that they have also chosen to worship gods other than the LORD.

"Sitting" and sleeping in "tombs" and "secret places" probably refers to practices of divination—that is, consulting the spirits for guidance. In the Hebrew Bible there are no sanctioned religious rituals that occur in tombs, but we do hear of sleeping by God's altar in order to see a vision or to communicate with the divine in a dream (an "incubation" rite). Solomon himself slept by the altar at Gibeon, and in his dream God appeared and promised to give him what he requested (1 Kings 3:4-14). It may be that, again, the problem is one of geography. By enacting such practices outside of the Temple area, the people are signaling their allegiance to other gods.

No matter where it is eaten, however, consuming pork was always forbidden in Israelite tradition (Deuteronomy 14:8).

Isaiah 65:5-7. By claiming "I am too holy for you" (65:5), the people assert that these illegitimate religious practices have somehow "worked," that the practitioners have received a blessing from their practices and become sanctified. God's anger at this ("These are a smoke in my nostrils," 65:5) reflects the divine displeasure that the nation has abandoned the commands concerning proper worship and is also blind to the consequences. The "Holy One of Israel" now promises judgment for the people ("I will indeed repay into their laps their iniquities," 65:6).

Isaiah 65:8-10. Within the anger, however, the Lord also promises to preserve a remnant, saving the "chosen" from Judah and God's "servants." Employing an agricultural saying, God turns away from the utter destruction of the people as a way to preserve the "blessing" in a cluster of grapes.

Just as even unlikely grapes can be separated and transformed into wine, God now promises more changes in the agricultural sphere. "Sharon" refers to a valley on the northern coastal plain of Israel, and "the Valley of Achor" is in the area west of the Dead Sea. The prophecy here envisions the land of Judah enveloped by productive, flock-supporting valleys.

Isaiah 65:11-12. Again we see the theme of maintaining proper geography within religious practice. "Forsaking" the Lord is equivalent to "forgetting" God's "holy mountain," that is, Jerusalem and the Temple. In Hebrew, the terms "Fortune" and "Destiny" are "Gad" and "Meni," and may refer to the Syrian gods of fate. With a play on words, God proclaims divine punishment upon their followers: Those who worship "Destiny" are "destined" to the sword.

Isaiah 65:13-14. Just as "my servants" were singled out as worth saving in the cluster of grapes in 65:8, now "my servants" will receive God's blessing and the others will be punished.

Isaiah 65:15. Having the name of the people now function as a "curse" effectively inverts God's promise to Abraham ("I will bless you, and make your name great, so that you will be a blessing," Genesis 12:2; see also Genesis 18:18 and 22:18).

Isaiah 65:16. Literally, "the God of faithfulness" mentioned here twice can also be read as "the God of Amen." (The Aramaic word on which we base the English "amen" is derived from the Hebrew word for "faithful.")

Isaiah 65:17. God's new creation is so astonishing that even the memory of the old world is shattered in its wake.

Isaiah 65:18. Although this is not reflected clearly in either the NRSV or the NIV, it is possible to read in this verse a divine "renaming" of the city and the people: "I am about to create Jerusalem 'Joy' and its people 'Delight.'"

Isaiah 65:19-23. Just as the new names of the city and its people suggest, life will no longer be marked by difficulty, and this is signaled by a prediction of human longevity. In the ancient world, a pregnancy often resulted in the early death of the child, and sometimes the mother as well. Stillborn or early infant deaths were a very common feature of life. Due to the poor diet and the hard physical labor demanded of people in agricultural societies, life spans over a hundred years were almost impossible in this period. The image of living past one hundred years points back to the biblical characters who lived before the flood, such as Adam, Seth, Enosh, Kenan, and Methuselah (see Genesis 5:3-32).

Isaiah 65:24. "Calling" upon God is a synonym for prayer throughout the Bible.

Isaiah 65:25. As in 11:6-9, the coming age is pictured as a time when enemies reconcile. The phrase "my holy mountain" refers to Jerusalem and signals God's special concern for the city.

INTERPRETING THE SCRIPTURE

Transformation

A central theme throughout this chapter is radical reformation. In Isaiah 65 we see God peering beyond present reality and giving us a picture of a future in which everything will be changed. For the original audience in the early postexilic period, this transformation entails nothing less than a total reconfiguration of a people who always stood in danger of losing life, land, and identity. Like the later author of the Book of Revelation, Isaiah points to a glorious future in which God will bring about a new heaven and a new earth (Revelation 21).

Given our own context, in which "transformation" may simply be a code word for something new that will quickly be replaced by the next "latest and greatest" enterprise, it may be helpful to notice at the very beginning that this work is expected to last for all future time. God is clear that the new creation will be sustained in the divine plan and worth an eternity of praise: "be glad and rejoice *forever* in what I am creating" (65:18, emphasis added).

The Transformation of Identity

The first feature of the divinely brought transformation is a renaming of the two entities most precious to God. In verse 18, Jerusalem becomes "Joy," and the people become "Delight." This is a surprising reversal for the city that just a chapter before was mourned by the prophet as a place of destruction: "Zion has become a wilderness, Jerusalem a desolation" (64:10). But in the new age, God declares that "his servants" will be given "a different name" (65:15). At this time the city and its people will be marked by a happy and full relationship with God: "I will rejoice in Jerusalem, and delight in my people" (65:19).

Identity changes, sometimes marked by a change in name, occur throughout the Book of Isaiah. In addition to the new names for Jerusalem and the people, Egypt and Assyria also receive new and surprising designations: "Blessed be Egypt *my people*, and Assyria *the work of my hands*" (19:25, emphasis added). Even God takes on a different title—in the new age, people shall swear and bless not by "the God of Israel" or "the God of the fathers" or any other such previously known epithet. In the future, people will bless and swear by "the God of faithfulness," or, in a different translation of the same Hebrew words, "the God of Amen" (65:16).

In some ways, these changes of names in the divine and human spheres are reflected in the animal world by a radical alteration in behavior and even eating habits. Instead of preying upon the lamb, the wolf will now eat alongside the young sheep. And instead of hunting for similar prey, the lion will now eat straw (65:25).

These new departures signal a far-reaching change in God's kingdom: "They shall not hurt or destroy on all my holy mountain" (65:25). But what has not changed is the ancient punishment on the very thing that helped to bring sorrow into the world at the very first: "but the serpent—its food shall be dust!" (65:25). According to the Book of Isaiah, the curse in Genesis 3:14 shall remain—the serpent will remain subjugated and never become strong enough to threaten humanity (65:25). God's holy mountain shall stand secure against all future hurt and destruction.

In the postexilic context, such radical changes of identity (and affirmations of ancient curses) must have been welcome indeed. Isaiah's audience had undergone major catastrophe, and they were still weak and despondent. They had experienced great destruction, terrible violence, and tragic loss at the hand of other powerful nations. They were always on the brink of extinction. Yet here God proclaims that a great change is coming. Predators would eat peaceably with their former prey, the desolate city would be named "Joy," and the people themselves would be known as God's delight. Such radical changes point to a much-welcomed future, brought by their God whose own new name reminds the people that God will remain "faithful" to the divine promises.

The Transformation of Life's Incompleteness

Verses 20 and 21 also give us a clear sense of what God understands to be the very opposite of the distress that can haunt one's life. Instead of the broken cries of weeping (65:19), the new Jerusalem will be filled with images that evoke a sense of satisfying completion. Human life will not now commence only to end too quickly: "No more shall there be in it an infant that lives but a few days, or an old person who does not live out a lifetime" (65:20). The verse goes on to assert that even one hundred years is too short to count as a lifetime: "for one who dies at a hundred years will be considered a youth" (65:20).

Long and satisfying life spans are also envisioned via architectural and agricultural images: "They shall build houses and inhabit them; they shall plant vineyards and eat their fruit" (65:21). The special preparation of the ground for vineyards and the eventual fruition of the slow-growing vines can take decades to accomplish. Thus, a lengthy period of time is envisioned so that the farmers can live to taste the fruit they planted.

The several images of a life begun and ended only after a century has passed, a house begun and lived in by the builder, and a vineyard enjoyed by its original planter are united by the theme of longevity. But this longevity is not simply the piling on of years for their own sake. The years are marked by an arc of wholeness, a context where each person can experience a full and fitting completion of what he or she has begun. No one will labor in vain, or fail to reap the rewards of his or her endeavors. For a people whose lives were marked by the violent disruptions of war and conquest, such a vision of the future must have seemed sweet indeed. And, given that political context, the chapter speaks to a true transformation that can only come from the hand of God.

The Transformation of Worship

Finally, God's vision in Isaiah 65 also involves a transformation of one of the core acts of worship: prayer. According to 65:24, in the new creation there will be no need even for the formal practice of calling on God because God will now hear even before such requests are uttered, and answer before the petitioners can finish their sentences.

In the context of the chapter, it is clear that this transformation does not involve any diminishment of the relationship that true prayer assumes and rests upon. God's "answering" and "hearing" still entails a human attempt to communicate with the divine. And the God who will take "delight" in the people (65:19) looks to a future of joyful intimacy. In the new world that God envisions, divine-human communication is not disregarded but rather becomes lost to time. Prayer will now no longer be tethered to a strict chronology of petitions that are later followed by answers. The boundaries between God and the people will now move so closely together that request and response will tumble over each other in glad abandonment.

SHARING THE SCRIPTURE

Preparing Our Hearts

Explore this week's devotional reading, found in Isaiah 42:1-9. Verses 1-4 of this passage are known as the first of the "Servant Songs." Verses 5-9 continue the themes of the song by describing the servant's mission and praising God the Creator and Sustainer. This familiar passage ties to today's Scripture lesson in verse 9, where we hear God saying, "The former things have come to pass, and new things I now declare." What new things is God doing in your personal life and in the life of your congregation? Thank God for marvelous opportunities that are coming your way.

Pray that you and the adult students will be alert to the new things that God is doing all around you and give thanks.

Preparing Our Minds

Study the background Scripture from Isaiah 65 and the lesson Scripture from Isaiah 65:17-21, 23-25.

Consider this question as you prepare the lesson: *Will a time ever come when there will be no more weeping and crying and the earth will be a place of happiness and peace?*

Write on newsprint:
- ❑ questions for "Discover Worship Experiences as Rehearsals for What Lies Ahead in Eternity."
- ❑ information for next week's lesson, found under "Continue the Journey."
- ❑ activities for further spiritual growth in "Continue the Journey."

Review the "Introduction," "The Big Picture," "Close-up," and "Faith in Action." Consider how you will use this additional information, which immediately precedes the first lesson, for this session.

LEADING THE CLASS

(1) Gather to Learn

❖ Greet the class members. Introduce any guests and help them feel at home.

❖ Pray that those who have come today will consider the possibility of a new and better world coming.

❖ Encourage the adults to give voice to their longings and hopes for a brighter future in a better world. Go around the room and ask each student to complete this sentence in a way that expresses his or her hopes: **If I could change the world I would . . .**

❖ Summarize, if possible, the kind of world that the group is seeking.❖

❖ Read aloud today's focus statement: **People desperately long for a time when there will be no more weeping and crying and the earth will be a place of happiness and peace. Will that time ever come? The God of truth and Creator of the earth promised through Isaiah that someday God's children would be so blessed.**

(2) Goal 1: Identify the Changes Isaiah Claims God Will Make in the New Creation

❖ Choose two volunteers, one to read Isaiah 65:17-21 and another, verses 23-25.

❖ Invite the learners to list on newsprint the changes that God will make in this new creation. Here are possibilities.

- 65:17—a future when former things will not be remembered.
- 65:18—a future characterized by joy and delight.
- 65:19—the elimination of weeping and distress.
- 65:20—an end to premature death.
- 65:21—homes to inhabit and food to eat.
- 65:22—long life.
- 65:23—blessings for the people and generations to come.
- 65:24—close communion with God.
- 65:25—peace even among former enemies in the natural world.

❖ Compare the hopes that the class members have to the list of changes that Isaiah claims God will make. Talk about any similarities and differences. Use information from Understanding the Scripture to clarify any of these changes.

❖ Conclude by discussing Isaiah's claims in light of life in the garden of Eden. Ask: **How might this new creation be like Eden?**

(3) Goal 2: Describe the Learners' Personal Visions of the "New Creation" God Has Promised

❖ Distribute paper and pencils. Write these words on newsprint:

Relationship to God
Social Structure
Economics
Behaviors
Attitudes
Politics
Generations/life span
Food supply
Housing

❖ Suggest that each person select one or two categories from the list and write about how he or she perceives God's new earth will operate in terms of that category.

❖ Call on volunteers to present their visions.

❖ Recognize that Isaiah's prophecy concerns a future time and is not available to us in the present. But, having said that, are there actions that we can take to move the earth and its people in the direction of God's promised future? For example, can we provide better prenatal care so that infants do not die at or shortly after birth? Can we help people around the globe obtain nourishing food at affordable prices? Can we make sure that everyone has a safe, decent place in which to live? Invite the class to identify any steps they could take now to move the world toward the kind of place that God intends.

(4) Goal 3: Discover Worship Experiences as Rehearsals for What Lies Ahead in Eternity

❖ Read "The Transformation of Worship" in Interpreting the Scripture.

❖ Distribute hymnals and turn to "Arise, Shine Out, Your Light Has Come" and "O Day of Peace That Dimly Shines." If your hymnal does not include these songs, select two substitutes that refer to the new heavens and earth of which Isaiah writes.

❖ Form two groups and assign each group one hymn. The groups are to discuss these questions, which you will post on newsprint, and then compare the hymnist's vision with that of Isaiah or with the students' own visions of what will come.

(1) What behaviors and attitudes will be characteristic of this future?

(2) According to the hymn writer, what can we expect to find in this new creation?

(3) Based on the words of the hymn, how will the new world be different from the one we know?

❖ Call the groups together to report their findings.

❖ **Option:** Sing one or both of the hymns the groups have studied.

❖ Conclude by asking: **How do our hymns, litanies, prayers, sacraments, and other facets of worship help you rehearse and be prepared for the transformed future that God promises us?**

(5) Continue the Journey

❖ Pray that today's participants will go forth with renewed hope for the future that God promises.

❖ Read aloud this preparation for next week's lesson. You may also want to post it on newsprint for the students to copy.

■ **Title: Joyful Worship Restored**
■ **Background Scripture: Ezra 1:1–3:7**
■ **Lesson Scripture: Ezra 3:1-7**
■ **Focus of the Lesson: People gratefully celebrate the happy turns of events in their lives. What are the marks of celebration for joyous** change of circumstances? **The writer of Ezra tells of the time when God's scattered and exiled people celebrated their return with sacred festivals and worship.**

❖ Post these three activities related to this week's session on newsprint for the students to copy. Challenge the adults to grow spiritually by completing one or more of them.

(1) **Investigate some utopias of the United States that gathered people into communities where all aspects of their lives were touched by their religious beliefs. The Shakers (formally known as United Society of Believers in Christ's Second Appearing and located in several states), Ephrata Cloister (Pennsylvania), Oneida (New York), and Amana (Iowa) are among the best known and most successful of these groups.**

(2) **Recognize that Isaiah's description of the "new heavens and a new earth" (65:17) peers into the future. Although God will bring about this ultimate transformation, what can you do now to help others have a better life?**

(3) **Speak to someone who seems depressed, perhaps feeling that there is no hope for a better future. Encourage this person to consider God's promises and focus on the possibility of new beginnings.**

❖ Sing or read aloud "Love Divine, All Loves Excelling."

❖ Conclude today's session by leading the class in this benediction, adapted from the key verse for June 9 from Isaiah 12:4: **Let us go forth continually giving thanks, proclaiming God's mighty deeds, and exalting God's holy name.**

UNIT 2: WORSHIPING IN JERUSALEM AGAIN (EZRA)
JOYFUL WORSHIP RESTORED

PREVIEWING THE LESSON

Lesson Scripture: Ezra 3:1-7
Background Scripture: Ezra 1:1–3:7
Key Verse: Ezra 3:4

Focus of the Lesson:

People gratefully celebrate the happy turns of events in their lives. What are the marks of celebration for joyous change of circumstances? The writer of Ezra tells of the time when God's scattered and exiled people celebrated their return with sacred festivals and worship.

Goals for the Learners:

(1) to identify the worship components described in the text and the reasons for the various actions.
(2) to describe a meaningful worship experience or celebration.
(3) to plan a worship festival for the class or congregation.

Pronunciation Guide:

Ammon (am' uhn)
Bigvai (big' vi)
Edom (ee' duhm)
Jeshua (jesh' yoo uh)
Jozadak (joh' zuh dak)
Shealtiel (shee al' tee uhl)
Sheshbazzar (shessbaz' uhr)

Sidon (si' duhn)
Sidonian (si doh' nee uhn)
Succoth (suhk' uhth)
Tishri (tish' ree)
Tyre (tire)
Tyrian (tihr' ee uhn)
Zerubbabel (zuh ruhb' uh buhl)

Supplies:

Bibles, newsprint and marker, paper and pencils, hymnals

READING THE SCRIPTURE

NRSV
Lesson Scripture: Ezra 3:1-7
   ¹When the seventh month came, and the Israelites were in the towns, the people gath-

CEB
Lesson Scripture: Ezra 3:1-7
   ¹When the seventh month came and the Israelites were in their towns, the people

ered together in Jerusalem. [2]Then Jeshua son of Jozadak, with his fellow priests, and Zerubbabel son of Shealtiel with his kin set out to build the altar of the God of Israel, to offer burnt offerings on it, as prescribed in the law of Moses the man of God. [3]They set up the altar on its foundation, because they were in dread of the neighboring peoples, and they offered burnt offerings upon it to the LORD, morning and evening. [4]And **they kept the festival of booths, as prescribed, and offered the daily burnt offerings** by number according to the ordinance, as required for each day, [5]and after that the regular burnt offerings, the offerings at the new moon and at all the sacred festivals of the LORD, and the offerings of everyone who made a freewill offering to the LORD. [6]From the first day of the seventh month they began to offer burnt offerings to the LORD. But the foundation of the temple of the LORD was not yet laid. [7]So they gave money to the masons and the carpenters, and food, drink, and oil to the Sidonians and the Tyrians to bring cedar trees from Lebanon to the sea, to Joppa, according to the grant that they had from King Cyrus of Persia.

gathered together as one in Jerusalem. [2]Then Jeshua, Jozadak's son along with his fellow priests, and Zerubbabel, Shealtiel's son along with his kin, started to rebuild the altar of Israel's God so that they might offer entirely burned offerings upon it as prescribed in the Instruction from Moses the man of God. [3]They set up the altar on its foundations, because they were afraid of the neighboring peoples, and they offered entirely burned offerings upon it to the LORD, both the morning and the evening offerings.

[4]**They celebrated the Festival of Booths, as prescribed. Every day they presented the number of entirely burned offerings required by ordinance for that day.** [5]After this, they presented the continual burned offerings, the offerings at the new moons, and at all the sacred feasts of the LORD, and the offerings of everyone who brought a spontaneous gift to the LORD. [6]From the first day of the seventh month, they began to present entirely burned offerings to the LORD.

However, the foundation of the LORD's temple had not yet been laid. [7]So they gave money to the masons and carpenters; and food, drink, and oil to the Sidonians and the Tyrians to bring cedarwood by sea from Lebanon to Joppa, according to the authorization given them by Persia's King Cyrus.

UNDERSTANDING THE SCRIPTURE

Introduction. The Book of Ezra begins with a royal proclamation that the newly victorious King Cyrus of Persia will allow the exiles to return to the land and rebuild God's Temple, which had been destroyed by the Babylonians in 587/586 B.C. Along with reconstructing the altar and Temple, the people also set about redefining their community as one that places the worship of God in Jerusalem at the center.

Before we get to the central passage of our lesson (Ezra 3:1-7), the book tells of the first return of the people from Babylon about 538 B.C. at the beginning of Cyrus's rule. The first group was led by a man named Sheshbazzar. This group was later followed by several more waves of immigration led by people such as Jeshua, Zerubbabel, and then Ezra himself. At points, these several returning groups are portrayed as if they are part of a second exodus, with the nation leaving their bondage in Babylon and traveling to the Promised Land. In other ways, the book describes these groups as making something closer to a pilgrimage, with different groups traveling with priests and cultic vessels to Jerusalem in order to worship. But no matter the imagery that lies behind the description of the travel, the text is emphatic that God has brought about their newfound freedom, and that they are to respond with the reinstitution of faithful worship in Jerusalem.

Ezra 1:1-4. With Cyrus's capture of Babylon in 539 B.C., a new empire was in power. With this political change came a new attitude toward those who had been exiled from the land by the Babylonians. The author of our text is clear that the return of the people is not to be understood solely in political terms, however; theology is also in play. The opportunity for the exiles to return and rebuild the Temple is due to God "stirring up" the spirit of Cyrus, foretold long ago by God's prophet Jeremiah (Ezra 1:1; see also Jeremiah 29:10). In addition, in his edict Cyrus declares that his very rise to power was to be attributed to "the LORD, the God of heaven" (1:2).

Ezra 1:5-11. "Return" in the Book of Ezra does not only entail a new residential address for the people; the text is clear that the people are able to return so that they can rebuild the Temple in Jerusalem. This was already signaled in Cyrus's edict ("permitted to go up to Jerusalem . . . *and rebuild* the house of the LORD," 1:3, emphasis added) and continues in this section: The people "got ready to go up *and rebuild* the house of the LORD" (1:5, emphasis added). The theme continues with notable attention given to the precious vessels that would furnish the Temple. In ancient warfare, the victor marked his conquest by removing the various statues and vessels from his enemy's temple and placing them into the temple of his own god as a sign of divine conquest and domination. When Cyrus returns the vessels that Nebuchadnezzar removed in 586 B.C., the Persian emperor makes a symbolic indication of what his edict already declared ("the LORD . . . has given me all the kingdoms of the earth," 1:2). The liberated vessels announce that, with the victory of Cyrus, God again reigns supreme over the empires of the day.

Ezra 2:1-67. Read quickly, this list appears to comprise a census of those who were part of the initial return to the land under Sheshbazzar's leadership in the first years of Cyrus. Yet several details indicate that it is more properly understood as a register of people who returned to the land in several waves over many years. Most notably, the list of leaders in 2:2 does not name Sheshbazzar, a surprising omission since he was the leader of the first group of returnees (1:8). Verse 2 also mentions a man named "Bigvai," and his Persian name likely indicates that he was born *after* the Persians came to power in 538 B.C. Regardless of the particular circumstances behind this list (and a very similar one found in Nehemiah 7), its details and length indicate that the author wanted to record the names of those who returned to the land.

Ezra 2:68-70. Before the people return to their hometowns, they present various offerings in Jerusalem in order that the Temple can be rebuilt. Calculated together, the returnees presented more than one thousand pounds of gold and six thousand pounds of silver along with one hundred robes for the priests.

The text notes that only some of the returnees lived in Jerusalem (2:70). Other biblical texts and archaeological excavation indicates that the population of the city was rather meager throughout the Persian period.

Ezra 3:1-7. The restoration of the altar occurs in the seventh month (named Tishri, corresponding to our September/October). This month contains several important holy days including the festival of booths/ Tabernacles (see Numbers 28–29 for the description of various offerings and festivals, and Leviticus 23:33-43 for the festival of booths/Tabernacles). The list of offerings in Ezra 3:3-5 is quite lengthy, and includes sacrifices that were offered every day (the morning and evening offerings), every month (the new moon offerings), and every year (the offerings for the festival of booths/Tabernacles). In addition, there were also "freewill" offerings (3:7). Such details clearly mark the emphasis of the text: The people of God worship regularly and with great frequency.

The "neighboring peoples" (3:3) mentioned here probably refer to the neighboring tribes of Edom and Ammon.

The material preparations for the rebuilding project in 3:7 echoes the description of David and Solomon's work in 1 Chronicles 22:2-4 and 2 Chronicles 2:1-10. Cedar beams from Lebanon were used in other public buildings and sanctuaries throughout the ancient world, including Solomon's Temple. In contrast to Solomon, however, who had to pay for the beams from his own treasury, here they are provided by King Cyrus (3:7).

INTERPRETING THE SCRIPTURE

Worshiping in Jerusalem Again

The proclamation of Cyrus in the first verses of the Book of Ezra prominently sets out some of the major themes of the entire book, including the restoration of the people of God. According to the edict, Cyrus's main concern (as directed by God's spirit) is to build God's house in Jerusalem: "the LORD . . . has charged me to build him a house" (1:2). Thus, the return of the people to the land is not an end in itself, but simply the way for Cyrus to accomplish this important task. In addition, the financial assistance given to those returning is not intended for their physical well-being during the journey but rather for the building project itself. Even before returning to their homesteads, they first present their gifts in Jerusalem (1:4; 2:68-69).

Our passage in Ezra 3 begins after this initial presentation in Jerusalem and after the people have begun to settle in their own towns. Their return to the city in "the seventh month" (3:1) marks the initiation of sacrificial worship in Jerusalem after the return. The detailed description of the worship and the preparation for the larger building project makes it clear that the author considered worship in Jerusalem of prime importance.

New Worship in Continuity With the Past

This emphasis on worship in Jerusalem is closely tied to another theme that is emphasized throughout the entire Book of Ezra: Worship in this city is in clear continuity with what was practiced in the past. Worshiping in the same geography is tightly linked with other parallels that connect the postexilic community to their forebears in worship.

Continuity with the worship traditions of an earlier time is initially indicated with the simple phrase "seventh month" (3:1). As mentioned in the Understanding the Scripture portion, there are several significant holy days in the month of Tishri, including the festival of booths (also known as the festival of Tabernacles or Succoth). By choosing to worship at this time in the year, the community indicates its desire to reenact the ancient calendar of worship "as prescribed"

(3:4) in books such as Numbers and Leviticus. The emphasis on following the directives of an earlier written text is also seen in 3:2 in the context of sacrificial worship on the altar: "as prescribed in the law of Moses the man of God." Thus, the timing and practice of the people's worship is not dictated simply by convenience but rather by tradition. In the midst of the work of resettlement, they leave their various tasks and gather in Jerusalem, in the presence of other returnees, and in continuity with the generations before who also worshiped at the same time and in the same place.

Continuity of worship is also marked with geography, personnel, and building materials. Although all of the people are gathered in Jerusalem, the restoration of the altar is led by "Jeshua son of Jozadak, with his fellow priests, and Zerubbabel son of Shealtiel with his kin" (3:2). Jeshua was the grandson of the last high priest who served before the exile (1 Chronicles 6:15), and Zerubbabel was a descendant of David (1 Chronicles 3:10-19). Ezra 3:3 also specifies that the altar was set up on its ancient foundations, indicating a geographical return to preexilic worship even before the Temple is completely rebuilt. Finally, the mention of stonecutters and cedar trees in 3:7 puts the readers in mind of the preparations for the first Temple, undertaken by David and Solomon as recounted in 1 Chronicles 22:2-4 and 2 Chronicles 2:1-10.

The Community of God

In terms of the formation of the community, Ezra 3 begins on a very hopeful note. The people have returned to the land, offered gifts in Jerusalem, and resettled in their various towns. And now, having returned to the holy city in the seventh month, the people are all together (3:1). The text is emphatic that the community of returnees joined collectively in Jerusalem: In a more literal translation, the people gathered "as one man."

It is in this context of solidarity that the returnees begin to restore the altar in order to reinstate the various sacrifices and festivals. But soon the text interjects an ominous note: Their work on the altar occurs while they are "in dread of the neighboring peoples" (3:3). The exact identity of these "neighboring peoples" cannot be established, but it may refer to the nearby tribes of Edom and Ammon. The reference to outside opposition here in Ezra 3:3 is the first mention of a theme that will be repeated in the next chapter: The community's work of rebuilding is threatened by other opposing groups. At times the opposition is referred to as "the adversaries of Judah and Benjamin" (4:1) or "the people of the land" (4:4), and the presence of such groups signals the sense of danger and peril felt by the returned community.

In our contemporary context of material wealth and comfort, it might be difficult to comprehend such a sense of threat. But for the ancient community, everything was at stake. Having just returned from an exile that they attributed to their sin and faithlessness, they must have been anxious to enact the precepts of God properly. And having preserved a remnant of the people of God through the geographic dislocation of exile, they must have been very concerned with maintaining strong communal boundaries. In addition, the returnees were also trying to re-form their community in a context that they have never before experienced. That is, before the exile, the people were united in one geographical area. Now some live again in the land, but others are still living in Babylon and other places such as Egypt as well. The worshipers of the Lord not only are in geographically diverse areas but also now live in the midst of other peoples who worship other gods. They must begin to think about how to maintain their distinct religious identity in a diverse context and (at times) at some distance from one another. Occasionally, this will prove to be a very taxing enterprise indeed.

During their first celebration of sacrifice in Jerusalem, the returned community must have been overjoyed that they could worship God together back in God's chosen city. And by enacting the worship practices from the First Temple, there is a sense in which the present community was also worshiping God together with their forebears as well. How moving it must have been to participate in these first acts of worship that reinstituted the worship of God in Jerusalem, and how fearful the community must have been that outside opponents would bring everything to naught. As hard as their experience might have been even up to this point, the task of rebuilding the Temple would continue to demand even more from them. Clearly, they would have to work together to accomplish their goal. How fitting that, in their first act of devotion after their initial resettlement, they join indivisibly together in the worship of God.

SHARING THE SCRIPTURE

Preparing Our Hearts

Explore this week's devotional reading, found in Matthew 23:29-39. In this denouncement of the scribes and Pharisees, which begins in verses 1-3, Jesus pronounces a series of woes. Verse 29 begins the seventh woe. The leaders about whom Jesus speaks descend from a long line of religious leaders who have rejected and killed God's messengers. Since these leaders are plotting Jesus' death, he too will experience their wrath. Jesus laments over Jerusalem as "the city that kills the prophets" (23:37) but in verse 39 quotes Psalm 118:26 to indicate that Israel will finally be saved. Do you see any evidence that the church today is trying to silence God's messengers? If so, what is happening—and where?

Pray that you and the adult students will care for those whom God has sent to lead, teach, and minister to you.

Preparing Our Minds

Study the background Scripture from Ezra 1:1–3:7 and the lesson Scripture from Ezra 3:1-7.

Consider this question as you prepare the lesson: *What are the marks of celebration for joyous change of circumstances?*

Write on newsprint:
❑ information for next week's lesson, found under "Continue the Journey."
❑ activities for further spiritual growth in "Continue the Journey."

Review the "Introduction," "The Big Picture," "Close-up," and "Faith in Action." Consider how you will use this additional information, which immediately precedes the first lesson, for this session.

Use the information from "Introduction" through "Ezra 2:68-70" in Understanding the Scripture to prepare a brief lecture for "Identify the Worship Components Described in the Text and the Reasons for the Various Actions."

LEADING THE CLASS

(1) Gather to Learn

❖ Greet the class members. Introduce any guests and help them feel at home.

❖ Pray that the adults who have come together today will experience God in their midst.

❖ Form small groups and give each group a sheet of newsprint and a marker. Challenge each group to choose one of the following events and quickly develop a supply list of items needed for the celebration: (1) birthday party, (2) Fourth of July party, (3) wedding shower, (4) baby shower.

❖ Provide time for the groups to present their lists.

❖ Ask: **How do these items add to the festivities?** (Point out that some items may be used because they are traditions for such an event.)

❖ Read aloud today's focus statement: **People gratefully celebrate the happy turns of events in their lives. What are the marks of celebration for joyous change of circumstances? The writer of Ezra tells of the time when God's scattered and exiled people celebrated their return with sacred festivals and worship.**

(2) Goal 1: Identify the Worship Components Described in the Text and the Reasons for the Various Actions

❖ Present the lecture you have prepared to provide background for the setting and context of today's lesson.

❖ Select a volunteer to read Ezra 3:1-7.

❖ Suggest that the students imagine themselves as eyewitnesses to this event. Ask the following questions:
  (1) **Who was present?**
  (2) **How would you describe their moods and actions?**
  (3) **When and where did this event take place?**
  (4) **What happened?**
  (5) **Why did this event occur?**
  (6) **Was there anything that particularly surprised you? If so, what?**

❖ Choose at least one person to act as a roving reporter. This person is to ask class members at random to tell about something they heard, saw, or did at this event that had great meaning for them.

❖ **Option:** Read "Worshiping in Jerusalem Again" from Interpreting the Scripture.

❖ Conclude this portion of the lesson by asking: **What facets of the worship experience seemed to be most important to these Israelites, who had been held captive in Babylon but at the time of this service had returned to their homeland?**

(3) Goal 2: Describe a Meaningful Worship Experience or Celebration

❖ Build a bridge between the Israelites restoring worship in Jerusalem and the students' current experience by asking: **What makes worship meaningful for you?** List their ideas on newsprint. These ideas may include any aspect of worship: *setting (such as the way the altar is arranged, banners, incense), type of music, musical instruments, use and frequency of sacraments, level of formality, use (or not) of clerical vestments and choir robes, type of sermon, use of traditional prayers and creeds, use (or not) of liturgical dance, participation of laypersons in leading worship, and so on.*

❖ Review the list. Students may have a wide variety of ideas, and some of those ideas may be in conflict. For example, one may appreciate quiet time for prayer whereas another thinks that there is too much silence at some points in the service.

❖ Look especially at those categories where some adults prefer one thing and some have very different preferences. Invite representatives from both groups to explain why whatever they have suggested is so meaningful to them. Encourage the students to get at the root of their preferences. In many cases, their preferences stem back to childhood memories, perhaps of worshiping in a certain way with a parent or grandparent. You may find it appropriate to add ideas from "New Worship in Continuity with the Past" from Interpreting the Scripture.

❖ Wrap up by asking: **How can we honor one another's preferences while still having an opportunity to experience those worship styles that nourish our own souls?**

*(4) Goal 3: Plan a Worship Festival for the
Class or Congregation*

❖ Post a sheet of newsprint on which you will write a Scripture that will be the basis for a sermon. Choose something very well known, such as the parable of the prodigal son from Luke 15, or the Beatitudes, or Psalm 23, or 1 Corinthians 13.

❖ Form small groups, distribute hymnals, and challenge each group to design a worship service around this Scripture. Time likely will be limited, so encourage the groups to choose two hymns, possibly a creed (found in the back of many hymnals), a psalm to use as a call to worship, and a sermon title.

❖ Call on each group to name its selections.

❖ **Option:** If time is available, choose ideas from each group and put together a very brief service to close this session.

(5) Continue the Journey

❖ Pray that today's participants will experience joy as they worship God.

❖ Read aloud this preparation for next week's lesson. You may also want to post it on newsprint for the students to copy.
- ■ **Title: Temple Restored**
- ■ **Background Scripture: Ezra 3:8-13**
- ■ **Lesson Scripture: Ezra 3:8-13**
- ■ **Focus of the Lesson: When people are separated from something they hold dear, restoration is usually a greatly anticipated goal. How do people respond to an accomplished goal? When the returned Israelite exiles laid the foundation stones to restore the Temple, they**

rejoiced and gave thanks to God with weeping, shouting, and playing of trumpets and cymbals.

❖ Post these three activities related to this week's session on newsprint for the students to copy. Challenge the adults to grow spiritually by completing one or more of them.

(1) Compare religious celebrations with national ones (such as the Fourth of July). What similarities do you see in terms of people's attitudes and modes of celebration? What meanings do these celebrations hold for those who participate? What role do traditions play in these celebrations?

(2) Check to see if there are any building projects slated for your church or a community facility. Why are people rallying to support this project? If this is a project that you can support with your time, talent, or treasure, what steps will you take to do so? How will you encourage others to become involved?

(3) Research the Festival of Booths, a festival also known as the Feast of Tabernacles or Sukkoth. How might this time be comparable to celebrations of Thanksgiving?

❖ Sing or read aloud "Praise to the Lord, the Almighty."

❖ Conclude today's session by leading the class in this benediction, adapted from the key verse for June 9 from Isaiah 12:4: **Let us go forth continually giving thanks, proclaiming God's mighty deeds, and exalting God's holy name.**

UNIT 2: WORSHIPING IN JERUSALEM AGAIN (EZRA)
TEMPLE RESTORED

PREVIEWING THE LESSON

Lesson Scripture: Ezra 3:8-13
Background Scripture: Ezra 3:8-13
Key Verse: Ezra 3:11

Focus of the Lesson:
When people are separated from something they hold dear, restoration is usually a greatly anticipated goal. How do people respond to an accomplished goal? When the returned Israelite exiles laid the foundation stones to restore the Temple, they rejoiced and gave thanks to God with weeping, shouting, and playing of trumpets and cymbals.

Goals for the Learners:
(1) to review the Israelites' story of obeying God's instructions for restoring the Temple.
(2) to identify their common responses when they reach long-anticipated goals.
(3) to retell acts of restoration in the life of their church.

Pronunciation Guide:
Asaph (ay' saf)   Jozadak (joh' zuh dak)
Binnui (bin' yoo ie)   Kadmiel (kad' mee uhl)
Darius (duh ri' uhs)   Levite (lee' vite)
Henadad (hen' uh dad)   Shealtiel (shee al' tee uhl)
Hodaviah (hod u vi' ah)   Zerubbabel (zuh ruhb' uh buhl)
Jeshua (jesh' yoo uh)

Supplies:
Bibles, newsprint and marker, paper and pencils, hymnals

READING THE SCRIPTURE

NRSV
Lesson Scripture: Ezra 3:8-13

⁸In the second year after their arrival at the house of God at Jerusalem, in the second

CEB
Lesson Scripture: Ezra 3:8-13

⁸In the second month of the second year after their arrival at God's house in

month, Zerubbabel son of Shealtiel and Jeshua son of Jozadak made a beginning, together with the rest of their people, the priests and the Levites and all who had come to Jerusalem from the captivity. They appointed the Levites, from twenty years old and upward, to have the oversight of the work on the house of the LORD. ⁹And Jeshua with his sons and his kin, and Kadmiel and his sons, Binnui and Hodaviah along with the sons of Henadad, the Levites, their sons and kin, together took charge of the workers in the house of God.

¹⁰When the builders laid the foundation of the temple of the LORD, the priests in their vestments were stationed to praise the LORD with trumpets, and the Levites, the sons of Asaph, with cymbals, according to the directions of King David of Israel; ¹¹and they sang responsively, praising and giving thanks to the LORD,

"For he is good,
for his steadfast love endures
forever toward Israel."

And **all the people responded with a great shout when they praised the LORD, because the foundation of the house of the LORD was laid.** ¹²But many of the priests and Levites and heads of families, old people who had seen the first house on its foundations, wept with a loud voice when they saw this house, though many shouted aloud for joy, ¹³so that the people could not distinguish the sound of the joyful shout from the sound of the people's weeping, for the people shouted so loudly that the sound was heard far away.

Jerusalem, Zerubbabel son of Shealtiel and Jeshua son of Jozadak and the rest of their kin—the priests and the Levites and all who had come from the captivity to Jerusalem—made a beginning. They appointed Levites 20 years old and more to oversee the work on the LORD's house. ⁹Then Jeshua with his sons and his kin, Kadmiel and his sons, Binnui and his sons, the sons of Judah, along with the sons of Henadad, the Levites, and their sons and kin, collaborated to supervise the workers in God's house.

¹⁰When the builders laid the foundation of the LORD's temple, the priests clothed in their vests and carrying their trumpets, and the Levites the sons of Asaph with cymbals, arose to praise the LORD according to the directions of Israel's King David. ¹¹They praised and gave thanks to the LORD, singing responsively, "He is good, his graciousness for Israel endures forever."

All of the people shouted with praise to the LORD because the foundation of the LORD's house had been laid. ¹²But many of the older priests and Levites and heads of families, who had seen the first house, wept aloud when they saw the foundation of this house, although many others shouted loudly with joy. ¹³No one could distinguish the sound of the joyful shout from the sound of the people's weeping, because the people rejoiced very loudly. The sound was heard at a great distance.

UNDERSTANDING THE SCRIPTURE

Introduction. After the dedication of the altar and recommencement of the sacrifices and annual festivals (3:1-7), the community now begins to work on the Temple building itself. They take as their first job the refurbishment of the Temple's foundations and celebrate the completion of their work with songs of praise and thanksgiving.

Because the official letter in Ezra 5 recounts an initial attempt at Temple building under the leadership of Sheshbazzar during the reign of Cyrus (5:13-16; see also 1:8), some commentators argue that the events retold in Ezra 3 happened during the later time of Darius (about 520 B.C.). In this reconstruction, a group returning with Sheshbazzar initiated the Temple building during the reign of Cyrus before they were thwarted by opposing forces (1:8; 5:13-16). Later, during the time of Darius, Jeshua and Zerubbabel reinitiated the project when the community was encouraged in their task by the prophets Haggai and Zechariah. If one would prefer to relate Ezra 3 to the reign of Cyrus (and date the events in 3:8-13 somewhere around 538 B.C.), one would have to explain Sheshbazzar's early work on the foundations (5:16). One would also have to assume that the Temple's construction languished sufficiently enough for Haggai to claim that the Temple lay in "ruins" about 520 B.C. (Haggai 1:4, 9).

Ezra 3:8-9. The text's designation that construction began "in the second month" refers to the month of Ziv (later named Iyyar). Agriculturally, this is a good time of the year to begin a building project because the winter rains had ended and the crops were sown. Beginning in the second month is also a way to link the Second Temple with the First Temple since this is the same month that Solomon began to build according to 1 Kings 6:1, 37; and 2 Chronicles 3:2.

The emphasis that the Book of Ezra places on Jerusalem as the center of the community is seen again twice here: The people don't simply return to the land, but rather to "the house of God at Jerusalem." In addition, the returnees are not those who come back to Yehud and settle in their former residences, they are those "who had come to Jerusalem from the captivity" (3:8). Even though many will resettle in their own towns and villages (2:70), the text gives special stress to their initial return to the holy city.

Such phrases not only highlight the significance of Jerusalem, they also serve to define the community. Under the leadership of Zerubbabel and Jeshua, those who build in Ezra 3 are defined here as "the rest of their people, the priests and the Levites and all who had come to Jerusalem from the captivity" (3:8). Significantly, this phrase includes only those members who had gone to Babylon in exile and then returned to the land. Those who stayed in the land throughout the exile are excluded from the building project, and rarely referred to throughout the Book of Ezra.

In other biblical texts, the Levites take on their duties at the age of twenty, twenty-five, or thirty (Numbers 4:3, 23, 30; 8:24; 1 Chronicles 23:3, 24, 27; 2 Chronicles 31:17). Perhaps, in choosing the relatively early age of twenty here in Ezra 3, the community is indicating that they need more Levites than they have in the older ranks.

Ezra 3:10-13. The verb used in "laid the foundations" can also mean "to establish" or "to found." Given the historical context, such an activity does not presume all new construction: The work would have also included the repair and the clearing out of the lower parts of the Temple that survived the Babylonian destruction (for an account of this destruction, see texts such as 2 Kings 25:9). The description of the work in Ezra 3 is similar to the widespread ancient practice of building "new" temples on the sites of older worship sites; communities in need of a worship area would usually just "reuse" the place where earlier communities had gathered for worship. Combining the term "laid the foundations" with a description of joyful shouts (3:11-12) is also found in poetic texts that speak of the earth's creation. For example, in Job 38:4-7 the sons of God "shouted for joy" when God laid the foundations of the earth. Perhaps the author poetically is relating the reestablishment of the Temple to the re-creation of the world.

"The sons of Asaph" were a subset of the Levites and functioned as the musicians for the community. Several of the psalms are ascribed to this group, including Psalms 50 and 73–83, where the superscription reads, "A Psalm of Asaph" or "A Maskil of Asaph." In 1 Chronicles 16 this group is also associated with singing and playing cymbals in public Temple worship. For David's organization of the priests and Levites (including the sons of Asaph), see 1 Chronicles 23–25.

Several psalms include a similar refrain to the one quoted in Ezra 3:11 ("For he is good"), including Psalms 100:5; 106:1; 107:1; 118:1; and 136:1 ("O give thanks to the LORD, for he is good, for his steadfast love endures forever"). Given the content of these psalms and the context of Ezra 3, it is likely that the worship described in this chapter included a lengthy recitation of God's past saving deeds regularly interspersed with responses repeated by the gathered congregation.

The combination of joyous shouts with loud weeping is an evocative feature of this text, and open to a variety of interpretations (some of which will be explored in the next section). Also striking is the fact that the combined shouts were "heard far away" (3:13), because the next chapter opens with the adversaries attempting to oppose the work once they "heard" that the Temple was being rebuilt.

INTERPRETING THE SCRIPTURE

Worship in Continuity With the Past

Considering the significance of the building program, it is interesting that the text gives very little detail about either the construction process or even the most basic feature of the architectural design. All we really know are the names of some of the leaders, including Jeshua, Kadmiel, Binnui, and others leading the work along with the Levites who were over the age of twenty. Such lack of specificity of anything other than personnel makes the emphasis of the passage even more apparent: the renewal of worship in Jerusalem. Instead of describing the process of rebuilding the foundations, the author prefers to tell about the worship that celebrated the completion of the work. It is here that the author spends a great deal of time, and describes for the readers the particulars of the instrumentation (trumpets and cymbals, 3:10), musicians (sons of Asaph, 3:10), lyrics ("For he is good," 3:11), and style of singing (responsively).

As with the information about the month in which the rebuilding began (3:8), and as well the information given in Ezra 3:1-7, these details also link the Second Temple to the protocols of earlier worship. This is made explicit in the phrase "according to the directions of King David of Israel" (3:10), but the careful reader can also point to specific texts that link the worship in Ezra 3 with liturgical precedents. The sons of Asaph played cymbals and were given responsibility for leading praise in worship by David according to 1 Chronicles 15:16; 16:7. In addition, the lyrics quoted in Ezra 3:11 ("For he is good, and his steadfast love endures forever toward Israel") are very similar to several psalms, including the first verses of Psalms 106 and 136 ("O give thanks to the LORD, for he is good, for his steadfast love endures forever"). It is probable that these psalms, like the refrain in 3:11, were sung responsively. Together these details emphasize that, for the author of Ezra, the Second Temple stands fully in the liturgical tradition of its predecessor.

This emphasis on the past throughout the chapter concludes with an announcement that some of the people at the dedication service "had seen the first house on its foundations" (3:12). These include "the priests and Levites and heads of families." Like the lyrics and instrumentation, these eyewitnesses are a link to the First Temple and their presence validates the renewed worship as faithful and authentic.

Highlighting this restoration of worship by the postexilic community might strike some as nothing more than hidebound liturgical conservatism, a drive to continue with the same leadership and the same hymns, in the same building with the same furnishings. For the people in Ezra 3, however, such continuity was not a means of liturgical repression but a heartfelt statement of faith. At the very beginning of the rebuilding project, with adversaries always close at hand, it must have taken a great deal of confidence to link the newly refurbished foundation stones with the glories of Solomon's Temple. Surely they realized that only God could bring this project to completion, so as they give praise for God's faithfulness, they also pray for God's enduring fidelity to the covenant community that worships together in Jerusalem.

Joyful Worship

With the Temple rebuilding project well on its way, the mood in the text is confident and hopeful, and during the worship that marked the completion of the Temple foundation, the people were "praising and giving thanks to the LORD" (3:11). Although we sometimes understand the terms "praise" and "thanksgiving" to be synonyms, they mark two distinct types of speech to and about God. Technically, "praise" is descriptive and speaks of God's attributes (that is, "God is good," "God is worthy to be praised," and so on). "Thanksgiving," however, is declarative and recounts specific acts of God in the past ("God has done marvelous things," "God saved me from the pit," and so on). Obviously, both are related, and together express a joyful eruption that comes from knowing who God is. But given the historical context portrayed in Ezra 3,

singing of God's nature *and* God's past activity is especially poignant. With exile such a recent memory, the community has every reason to praise God's very recent acts of deliverance. And it is such memories that the people need to hold on to as they press on to the work ahead: It is only in the remembrance of God's past faithfulness that they have confidence for the future and the ability to sing that God's steadfast love "endures forever toward Israel" (3:11).

Joy Mixed With Sadness

In the text, this confidence expressed in praise and thanksgiving is soon mixed with the tears of some of those who had seen Solomon's Temple: The "old people who had seen the first house . . . wept with a loud voice when they saw this house" (3:12). Curiously, the text does not give any explicit reason for the weeping, and this lack opens up a space in which the interpreter can meditate and imagine. Perhaps the tears emerged from a sense of disappointment in the construction itself: The newly refurbished foundations before their eyes seemed disappointingly measly when compared to the complete Temple that they remembered. Haggai 2:3 describes those who saw the First Temple thinking that the Second Temple looks "as nothing." In Zechariah 4:10, even God describes the time of Zerubbabel as a "day of small things." Or perhaps the tears were the result of a wave of nostalgia: Being in the Temple area together with those who returned may have reminded some of prior worship with those no longer present. Or, since building a Temple is a lengthy process (Solomon's Temple took seven years to complete according to 1 Kings 6:38), maybe the oldest members of the community were sad when they realized that they would probably not see the finished product.

Ezra 3:12 assigns the weeping only to those who had seen the First Temple, but perhaps they were joined in their grief with those who were making an inaugural visit to the sacred space. According to Psalm 137, the exiles in Babylon "remembered Zion," and these memories of an older generation surely informed those born after the deportation from the land. With expectations generated by stories and songs in exile, maybe the members of the younger generation were disappointed when they finally saw the rebuilt foundation. Their tears expressed their expectation that the new construction would be more impressive.

These shed tears clearly indicate that the community in Jerusalem were not entirely of the same mind: Many wept while "many shouted aloud for joy" (Ezra 3:12). Yet their disagreements could both be expressed together in worship, and one side could not drown out or fully extinguish the voice of the other: "The people could not distinguish the sound of the joyful shout from the sound of the people's weeping" (3:13). This description highlights the true diversity of perspective that worship is able to encompass.

Although this diversity is represented by different people in Ezra 3, it may be that we can recognize a similar diversity within our own selves: Sometimes when we achieve something that we have longed for, our joy is mixed. Maybe the acquisition makes us realize that the true goal lies elsewhere, or maybe the acquisition effectively reorders our values so that we now desire something else. Whatever the case, reaching long-anticipated goals may be combined with unanticipated emotions.

SHARING THE SCRIPTURE

Preparing Our Hearts

Explore this week's devotional reading, found in Psalm 66:1-12. In this psalm people are called to praise (66:1-4) and give thanks (66:5-7) to the God who has delivered them. Notice that "all the earth" (66:1) is called to worship God through song and praise. Write your own psalm or prayer or words of praise and thanksgiving for who God is and what God has done in your own life. Seek opportunities to share your praise and thanksgiving with others.

Pray that you and the adult students will focus your worship on the praise and thanks you give to God, rather than what you hope to get from God or from the service.

Preparing Our Minds

Study the background Scripture and the lesson Scripture, both of which are from Ezra 3:8-13.

Consider this question as you prepare the lesson: *How do people respond to an accomplished goal?*

Write on newsprint:
❑ information for next week's lesson, found under "Continue the Journey."
❑ activities for further spiritual growth in "Continue the Journey."

Review the "Introduction," "The Big Picture," "Close-up," and "Faith in Action." Consider how you will use this additional information, which immediately precedes the first lesson, for this session.

LEADING THE CLASS

(1) Gather to Learn

❖ Greet the class members. Introduce any guests and help them feel at home.

❖ Pray that the participants will respond with joy to the opportunity to study and worship together this day.

❖ Read the following information: **A sixty-year-old Baptist congregation in the Fukushima region of Japan was devastated by the March 2011 earthquake and tsunami that caused a nuclear plant meltdown. One of the church's four chapels, located just three miles from the plant, could not be rebuilt due to radiation. Despite losing loved ones, their church, their homes, and their jobs, this congregation stuck together and planned to rebuild. Their first priority was housing. Discriminated against due to concerns about their radiation exposure, and being in an area where rental housing was scarce, members of this congregation purchased a small apartment building where members could live. They began fund-raising efforts, sponsored in part by sales of their pastor's book,** *Exodus Church,* **which depicts the horrible events and a vision for recovery. Rev. Akira Sato said, "I was surprised the church never died because of this. . . . We became an every-day church, not a once-a-week church." He added, "We lost everything and we receive many things. We are very happy people."**

❖ Read aloud today's focus statement: **When people are separated from something they hold dear, restoration is usually a greatly anticipated goal. How do people respond to an accomplished goal? When the returned Israelite exiles laid the foundation stones to restore the Temple, they rejoiced and gave thanks to God with weeping, shouting, and playing of trumpets and cymbals.**

(2) Goal 1: Review the Israelites' Story of Obeying God's Instructions for Restoring the Temple

❖ Read aloud Ezra 3:8-13.
❖ Discuss these questions:
  (1) Why is it important to know that the foundations were laid during the "second month"? (See "Ezra 3:8-9" in Understanding the Scripture.)

  (2) What relationship will this Temple and its worship have with Solomon's Temple? (See "Worship in Continuity with the Past" in Interpreting the Scripture.)
  (3) How did people respond to the ceremony we see enacted in Ezra 3? (See "Joyful Worship" in Interpreting the Scripture.)
  (4) Why might some of the older people have wept? (See "Joy Mixed with Sadness" in Interpreting the Scripture.)
  (5) Had you been an outsider who witnessed this event, what conclusions might you have drawn about the roles of worship and the Temple in the lives of these returned exiles?

(3) Goal 2: Identify the Learners' Common Responses When They Reach Long-anticipated Goals

❖ Read aloud these scenarios and invite the adults to comment on responses they might make (or possibly did make at one time) to each situation:
  Scenario 1: A new driver has been dreaming of owning a car since he was fourteen years old. He's been doing odd jobs and saving any money he receives as a gift. He finally has enough money to purchase a used vehicle that he knows he will enjoy.
  Scenario 2: A struggling student has studied, done extra homework, and worked with a tutor to pass a required course. The final exam is now over and the anxious teen opens the report card to find a B for this subject.
  Scenario 3: A couple has scrimped while living in a small apartment to save enough money to buy a home of their own. With prices and interest

rates low, they realize that they can finally buy their own place.

Scenario 4: A college graduate decided that she wanted to hold a particular position by her thirty-fifth birthday. She would not compromise her ethics or ideals to reach this goal, but she would work hard and go the extra mile to show her employer that she was capable of assuming this responsibility. Her dream was fulfilled.

❖ Ask: **What are some of the common responses that many people make when a long-anticipated goal is finally reached?**

(4) Goal 3: Retell Acts of Restoration in the Life of the Learners' Church

❖ Note that unless a congregation is very new, most churches have had experiences with major changes: One building is torn down to make way for a newer one; a sanctuary is completely refurbished; an educational wing or family life center is added to the building; a church outgrows one location and must move to another; a church is damaged and must be rebuilt.

❖ Invite class members to recall such events in the life of this congregation. Include those who have not been members here long to recall such events in churches where they previously attended.

❖ Conclude by discussing how the memory of these renewals makes the adults feel about their congregation, and about God.

(5) Continue the Journey

❖ Pray that those who have come today will recall the joy of the Israelites and experience joy when they complete an important task.

❖ Read aloud this preparation for next week's lesson. You may also want to post it on newsprint for the students to copy.

■ **Title: Dedication of the Temple**

■ **Background Scripture: Ezra 6**
■ **Lesson Scripture: Ezra 6:13-22**
■ **Focus of the Lesson: People often assign great importance to specific locations. What makes a particular place so special? The Temple was special to the Israelites because God commanded them to rebuild it and because it gave them a place to commemorate with worship their original freedom from Egyptian bondage and more recently their Babylonian exile.**

❖ Post these three activities related to this week's session on newsprint for the students to copy. Challenge the adults to grow spiritually by completing one or more of them.

(1) **Spend time looking at photographs of places that have been important in your life: former homes, schools, neighborhoods, workplaces, or vacation sites. What makes these places so special for you? Why might some have a greater emotional attachment than others?**

(2) **Celebrate, preferably with a group, the completion of a task. Give credit to all who have worked together to make a vision become a reality.**

(3) **Work with the class to create something that can be used during worship, such as a banner, cushions for kneeling at the altar, paraments for the altar, a stole for the pastor, or Chrismons or Jesse symbols for a Christmas tree. Celebrate when your task has been completed.**

❖ Sing or read aloud "Christ Is Made the Sure Foundation."

❖ Conclude today's session by leading the class in this benediction, adapted from the key verse for June 9 from Isaiah 12:4: **Let us go forth continually giving thanks, proclaiming God's mighty deeds, and exalting God's holy name.**

UNIT 2: WORSHIPING IN JERUSALEM AGAIN (EZRA)
DEDICATION OF THE TEMPLE

PREVIEWING THE LESSON

Lesson Scripture: Ezra 6:13-22
Background Scripture: Ezra 6
Key Verse: Ezra 6:16

Focus of the Lesson:
People often assign great importance to specific locations. What makes a particular place so special? The Temple was special to the Israelites because God commanded them to rebuild it and because it gave them a place to commemorate with worship their original freedom from Egyptian bondage and more recently their Babylonian exile.

Goals for the Learners:
(1) to explore the story of the completion and dedication of the Temple and the observance of Passover.
(2) to identify what makes specific places of worship significant to them.
(3) to tell others the story of the dedication of their place of worship.

Pronunciation Guide:
Adar (ay' dahr)   Jeshua (jesh' yoo uh)
Artaxerxes (ahr tuh zuhrk' seez)   Shethar-bozenai (shee thar boz' uh nie)
Darius (duh ri' uhs)   Tattenai (tat' uh ni)
Ecbatana (ek bat' uh nuh)   Yehud (yeh hood')
Haggai (hag' i)   Zechariah (zek uh ri' uh)
Iddo (id' oh)

Supplies:
Bibles, newsprint and marker, paper and pencils, hymnals

READING THE SCRIPTURE

NRSV
Lesson Scripture: Ezra 6:13-22
    [13]Then, according to the word sent by King Darius, Tattenai, the governor of the province

CEB
Lesson Scripture: Ezra 6:13-22
    [13]Then Tattenai the governor of the province Beyond the River, Shethar-bozenai,

Beyond the River, Shethar-bozenai, and their associates did with all diligence what King Darius had ordered. ¹⁴So the elders of the Jews built and prospered, through the prophesying of the prophet Haggai and Zechariah son of Iddo. They finished their building by command of the God of Israel and by decree of Cyrus, Darius, and King Artaxerxes of Persia; ¹⁵and this house was finished on the third day of the month of Adar, in the sixth year of the reign of King Darius.

¹⁶**The people of Israel, the priests and the Levites, and the rest of the returned exiles, celebrated the dedication of this house of God with joy.** ¹⁷They offered at the dedication of this house of God one hundred bulls, two hundred rams, four hundred lambs, and as a sin offering for all Israel, twelve male goats, according to the number of the tribes of Israel. ¹⁸Then they set the priests in their divisions and the Levites in their courses for the service of God at Jerusalem, as it is written in the book of Moses.

¹⁹On the fourteenth day of the first month the returned exiles kept the passover. ²⁰For both the priests and the Levites had purified themselves; all of them were clean. So they killed the passover lamb for all the returned exiles, for their fellow priests, and for themselves. ²¹It was eaten by the people of Israel who had returned from exile, and also by all who had joined them and separated themselves from the pollutions of the nations of the land to worship the LORD, the God of Israel. ²²With joy they celebrated the festival of unleavened bread seven days; for the LORD had made them joyful, and had turned the heart of the king of Assyria to them, so that he aided them in the work on the house of God, the God of Israel.

and their colleagues carried out the order of King Darius with all diligence. ¹⁴So the elders of the Jews built and prospered because of the prophesying of the prophet Haggai and Zechariah, Iddo's son. They finished building by the command of Israel's God and of Cyrus, Darius, and King Artaxerxes of Persia. ¹⁵This house was completed on the third day of the month of Adar, in the sixth year of the rule of King Darius.

¹⁶**Then the Israelites, the priests and the Levites, and the rest of the returned exiles, joyfully celebrated the dedication of this house of God.** ¹⁷At the dedication of this house of God, they offered one hundred bulls, two hundred rams, four hundred lambs, and as a purification offering for all Israel, twelve male goats, according to the number of the tribes of Israel. ¹⁸They set the priests in their divisions and the Levites in their sections for the service of God in Jerusalem, as it is written in the scroll from Moses.

¹⁹On the fourteenth day of the first month, the returned exiles celebrated the Passover. ²⁰All of the priests and the Levites had purified themselves; all of them were clean. They slaughtered the Passover animals for all the returned exiles, their fellow priests, and themselves. ²¹The Israelites who had returned from exile, together with all those who had joined them by separating themselves from the pollutions of the nations of the land to worship the LORD, the God of Israel, ate the Passover meal.

²²They also joyfully celebrated the Festival of Unleavened Bread for seven days, because the LORD had made them joyful by changing the attitude of the king of Assyria toward them so that he assisted them in the work on the house of God, the God of Israel.

UNDERSTANDING THE SCRIPTURE

Introduction. The Book of Ezra includes regular notice of external opposition to the project of rebuilding the Temple, starting at the very beginning during the reign of Cyrus (4:5). By the first years of Darius (who reigned from 521–485 B.C.), the book records that the work had stopped completely (4:24). When the prophets Haggai and Zechariah encouraged the community to start again to rebuild (5:1-2, probably around 520 B.C.), we hear that the opposition also reactivated their campaign (see also Haggai 1:1-4; 2:1-3; Zechariah 4:9; 6:15). This time, the opposition is identified as the Persian governor of the province Beyond the River, the larger political territory in which Jerusalem and Yehud was a small entity. The governor, named Tattenai, was supported by Shethar-bozenai along with people simply named "their associates" (6:6). Perhaps in a bid to gain the support of Darius, Tattenai and his fellows wrote to the Persian emperor to tell him of the rebuilding (5:6-17). So Ezra 6 begins with a certain tension: Will Darius support governor Tattenai and stop the rebuilding or not? Within this tension, though, the community remains undaunted and continues to work on the Temple (5:5). Perhaps one should read the letter from Darius imagining the loud noise of building construction in the background.

Ezra 6:1-2a. Responding to the letter from the governor Tattenai and his associates, King Darius attempts to unearth Cyrus's original decree. Babylon was the city that Cyrus adopted as the new capital for the Persian Empire in 539 B.C., while Ecbatana was the former capital of Media and used as a summer residence for the Persian kings because the heat was less oppressive.

Ezra 6:2b-5. These verses contain the record of Cyrus's decree to rebuild and restore the Temple in Jerusalem. There are some additional details not included in Cyrus's declaration found in Ezra 1:2-4 that pertain to the Temple's dimensions and manner of construction (6:3-4). Significantly, the decree also specifies that the rebuilding is to be funded by the Persian treasury (6:4).

Ezra 6:6-12. After quoting Cyrus's original decree, King Darius added his own instructions to governor Tattenai and the people trying to stop the rebuilding. These instructions have two parts: The first is to cease any opposition ("Keep away!" 6:6), and the second is to fund all of the operations of the Temple with the tax revenue of the province (6:8). The significance of obeying the instructions is highlighted with threats (6:11-12).

Ezra 6:13-15. The governor and his associates, duly instructed by King Darius's letter, enact the decree "with all diligence" (6:13), and the Temple is finished in the sixth year of Darius's reign in the month of Adar, that is, March 12, 515 B.C. Credit for this completion is given to the prophesying of Haggai and Zechariah (6:14; see also 5:1), as well as the command of God and the decrees of the Persian emperors (6:14). According to the Book of Haggai, the prophet began his prophecy to encourage rebuilding on August 29, 520 B.C., and construction recommenced by September 21 (Haggai 1:1, 15). The mention of the emperor Artaxerxes here in Ezra 6 is somewhat confusing since he reigned later in this period (464–423 B.C.). Perhaps he is mentioned on the basis of what seems to be a later dispute recorded in Ezra 4:10-23, or in anticipation of his support for the Temple later in Ezra 7:15-17.

Ezra 6:16-18. The dedication is celebrated by the returnees with burnt offerings. Although some of the community still lived in exile (including Ezra and Nehemiah), all of the twelve tribes are represented by the twelve goats of the sin offering. In addition to celebrating the completion of the Temple building, part of the festival also included organizing the priests and the Levites so that the regular services could be performed. With the mention of Moses, we see the chronological reach envisioned by this service: The ongoing worship in the future will take as its precedent the protocols from the past. This ties together with the emphasis on "all Israel" at this service so that the rebuilt Temple links the entire community to its past and future.

Ezra 6:19-22. This portion resumes the Hebrew account in the text (Ezra 4:8–6:18 is written in Aramaic, the *lingua franca* [working language] of the Persian Empire). The festivals of Passover and Unleavened Bread are related to the Israelites' deliverance from Egypt when God "passed over the houses of the Israelites in Egypt" and struck the firstborn sons of the Egyptians (Exodus 12:26-27). In their rush to leave Egypt when Pharaoh finally gave them permission, the people brought only unleavened dough (Exodus 12:34, 39). Because of this association, unleavened bread is referred to as "the bread of affliction" in Deuteronomy 16:3. Although Exodus 12 envisions that the festivals of Passover and Unleavened Bread are to be celebrated in the home, Deuteronomy 16 commands that they be kept at the central sanctuary ("at the place that the LORD your God will choose as a dwelling for his name," Deuteronomy 16:6). It is this Temple-based worship that is enacted in Ezra 6. Of great significance in Ezra is the description of those who are included in the celebration: "the people of Israel who had returned from exile, and also by all who had joined them and separated themselves from the pollutions of the nations of the land to worship the LORD, the God of Israel" (Ezra 6:21). Throughout the Book of Ezra the community of returnees maintained firm boundaries for membership—here we see that these boundaries could, under strict circumstances, include converts as well.

The "King of Assyria" mentioned in 6:22 seems to be a reference to the Persian emperor who now ruled over the conquered territory of Assyria.

INTERPRETING THE SCRIPTURE

Persian Permission and Support

In this chapter and throughout the Book of Ezra, the whole of the Temple building project hinges on the support of the Persian authority. Although the people continued to build while official records were checked (5:5), there is no doubt that a negative word from the emperor would have stopped all construction.

As it is, Darius gives much more than just official permission. He also ensures that funding for the Temple comes out of the official Persian coffers. In addition to tersely instructing Tattenai, Shethar-bozenai, and their associates to "let the work on this house of God alone" (6:7), and threatening anyone who does anything to destroy "this house of God in Jerusalem" (6:12), he clarifies that the cost of the project is to be paid by provincial taxes (6:8). Effectively, Darius is taking from the royal coffers in order to provide for the worship of God in Jerusalem. By not taking any action before researching the prior mandates of King Cyrus, and by relating his own edicts to those of Cyrus, Darius emphasizes that his generosity is in line with generations of Persian rule.

Given this context of official support, it is small wonder that the emperors are attributed with the success of the building program alongside the word of God: "They finished their building by command of the God of Israel and by decree of Cyrus, Darius, and King Artaxerxes of Persia" (6:14). Linking the holy commands of Israel's God together with the decrees of secular emperors is not altogether common in the Hebrew Bible, but here the author of Ezra is very clear that the Temple rebuilding project is especially indebted to the support of the Persian kings. As a measure of thanks, Darius asks that, along with their sacrifices to God in the new Temple, the community also "pray for the life of the king and his children" (6:10).

Worship in God's House

According to 5:12, Jerusalem and its Temple were destroyed (587/586 B.C.) by Nebuchadnezzar, the king of Babylon, when God finally responded to the people's disobedience. Restoring the city and the Temple, and reviving worship again, was a task that called forth great faith and labor. Both the difficulties as well as the steadfast perseverance are in evidence throughout the Book of Ezra.

The Temple is often described through the Book of Ezra as God's "house." If a reader quickly reads through the book from the beginning, she or he will notice this term "house" used repeatedly, and I cite only some of the instances here: 1:2, 3, 4, 5; 3:8, 9; 4:24; 5:2, 3, 8; 6:3, 8, 13, 15, 16, 17; and so on. Obviously, the emphasis on worship in Jerusalem makes sense because within this city is the Temple, God's own "house."

But there is also a sense in the Book of Ezra that "God's house" designates the entire city of Jerusalem, rather than just the area enclosed by the Temple. There is reference to "the house of the LORD in Jerusalem" even *before* the Temple is built. In 2:68, people come to the "house of the LORD in Jerusalem," and *then* present offerings in order to begin the rebuilding process. Likewise, 3:8 begins the story of how Zerubbabel and Jeshua and the people began to rebuild the Temple's foundation "in the second year *after* their arrival at the house of God at Jerusalem" (emphasis added). So although the people celebrate the completion of God's Temple in 6:16-17, there is a sense in which God's dwelling place on earth is geographically larger than the Temple area.

There are strict limits on this geographical expansion, however, and we see this partially in the community's celebration of Passover and Unleavened Bread. As previously mentioned, the Bible maintains two traditions for where these festivals are to be kept. In Exodus 12, the festivals are based at the family home, but in Deuteronomy 16 they are to be cele-brated at the central worship area. By taking these festivals out of the home and celebrating them in Jerusalem, Ezra 6 highlights the central role of the city. God's "house" expands past the walls of the Temple, and the city of Jerusalem has a special role to play as the context for the people's worship.

Worshiping in this house of God in Jerusalem entails a certain amount of professional support and conformity with the tradition. Divine "ownership" of the Temple and its city demands careful and thoughtful worship. In Ezra 6:18 we hear that on the day of dedication the priests were set "in their divisions and the Levites in their courses" in order to serve God in Jerusalem. In a way, it's as if this verse insists on not making the celebration of the Temple a static moment fixed in time. Instead, dedicating the Temple involves setting up the structure of personnel that will ensure the proper workings of worship in the time ahead. Such "proper workings" in the present and future also involve a look to the past. By following the directives "written in the book of Moses" (6:18), the entire community will be able to participate in a religious life that they can trace back to earlier times. The worship in the Temple in Ezra 6 is a record of what happened on the specific day of dedication, to be sure, but it is also a gesture toward all future worshipers who will return to "God's house" to give thanks and praise.

Worship That Is Joyful

Both the celebration for the Temple's dedication and the festival of Unleavened Bread are described as "joyful" (6:16, 22). Although we also saw reference to joyful worship at the dedication of the foundation (3:11-13), there is not in Ezra 6 any mention of the weeping that was mixed with the joy in Ezra 3:13.

Joyfulness is usually thought of as something spontaneous and most people assume that it was largely absent in ancient worship. Readers familiar with other parts of the Bible will know that "joy" is an instituted feature of several Israelite festivals. Included in the instructions for the correct keeping of Passover and other festivals in Deuteronomy 16 is the repeated command that the entire community "rejoice" (Deuteronomy 16:11, 14). Although the biblical text does not give any reason for this rejoicing, one can provide several possible motivations. The elation could be related to the conscious reenactment of dangerous and threatening circumstances in a context of security. Remembering slavery in Egypt after the community has been liberated by God elicits a joyful thankfulness that bubbles over during the festival. In addition, the connection of these celebrations with the completion of the spring and autumn harvests surely would also have elicited a sense of pleasure.

In Ezra 6, the community once again reenacts the dangers of the flight from Egypt, and so the remembered threat and present bounty may have given rise to joy. In this chapter, of course, the people are also celebrating the festivals for the first time after the completion of the rebuilt Temple. The joy that they experience includes the liberation from Pharaoh's power *and* the procurement of Persian favor that has now allowed them to rebuild the Temple in Jerusalem.

SHARING THE SCRIPTURE

Preparing Our Hearts

Explore this week's devotional reading, found in Ezra 5:1-5. Here we see Tattenai, a government official in the area Beyond the River, that is, the Euphrates, trying to derail the rebuilding of the Temple. The Jews working on the Temple were not deterred, even though Tattenai sent word to King Darius to find out what should be done. How often have you had direction from God only to find that someone else had other ideas? How has your church responded when it felt led to reach out to the community only to find that someone there—perhaps even a government official—disapproved of your plans?

Pray that you and the adult students will be sensitive to God's leading and willing to move forward even when someone tries to throw up roadblocks.

Preparing Our Minds

Study the background Scripture from Ezra 6 and the lesson Scripture from Ezra 6:13-22.

Consider this question as you prepare the lesson: *What makes a particular place so special that people often assign great importance to it?*

Write on newsprint:
- ❑ information for next week's lesson, found under "Continue the Journey."
- ❑ activities for further spiritual growth in "Continue the Journey."

Review the "Introduction," "The Big Picture," "Close-up," and "Faith in Action." Consider how you will use this additional information, which immediately precedes the first lesson, for this session.

Choose an option for "Tell Others the Story of the Dedication of the Learners' Place of Worship." Make arrangements with any speakers you wish to invite.

LEADING THE CLASS

(1) Gather to Learn

❖ Greet the class members. Introduce any guests and help them feel at home.

❖ Pray that those who have come today will experience joy as you study and fellowship together.

❖ Read this list of familiar places and invite the students to comment on any meaning that these special places may have for them. Notice that some places will have strong personal connections, whereas others may have national or historic significance.

> **Home**
> **School or college they attended**
> **Church**
> **Jerusalem**
> **Washington, D.C.**
> **Times Square, New York City**
> **Ellis Island**
> **Mississippi River**
> **Disney World**
> **Golden Gate Bridge**

❖ Read aloud today's focus statement: **People often assign great importance to specific locations. What makes a particular place so special? The Temple was special to the Israelites because God commanded them to rebuild it and because it gave them a place to commemorate with worship their original freedom from Egyptian bondage and more recently their Babylonian exile.**

(2) Goal 1: Explore the Story of the Completion and Dedication of the Temple and the Observance of Passover

❖ Introduce today's lesson by reading or retelling "Introduction" through "Ezra 6:6-12" in Understanding the Scripture.

❖ Choose two volunteers, one to read Ezra 6:13-18 and a second to read verses 19-22.

❖ Note that behind the hard work of the people stood two prophets, Haggai and Zechariah, urging them on, according to Ezra 5:1; 6:14. In his book, written between August 29, 520 B.C. and December 7, 518 B.C., Haggai calls and encourages the people to rebuild the Temple. Form two groups and assign one to Haggai 1:1-15 and a second to Haggai 2:1-9. The groups are to skim their assigned verses and report to the class the main message of their passage.

❖ Discuss these questions. Use information from Understanding the Scripture and other suggested sources to fill in the discussion.

(1) **What role did the Persian government play in the rebuilding of the Temple?** (Use "Persian Permission and Support" from Interpreting the Scripture to add information.)

(2) **How did the people celebrate the dedication of the Temple?** (See "Ezra 6:16-18" in Understanding the Scripture.)

(3) **Who participated in the Passover celebration in the newly rebuilt Temple?** (See "Ezra 6:19-22" in Understanding the Scripture.)

(4) **What was the mood of this Passover observance?** (See "Worship That Is Joyful" in Interpreting the Scripture.)

(3) Goal 2: Identify What Makes Specific Places of Worship Significant to the Learners

❖ Note that different people are moved by different types of sacred space. Some prefer the grandeur of a European cathedral, whereas others feel closest to God in a country clapboard church. Some delight in spaces that call upon their senses—the feel of carved wood, the smell of incense, the shimmering light of stained glass, the echo of marble floors as a huge organ resounds—whereas others prefer whitewashed walls and pegged wooden floors. There is no one "right" or "wrong" kind of worship space. Where one feels at home with God is the "right" space for that believer.

❖ Brainstorm answers to this question, and record ideas on newsprint: **What makes a worship space special for you?**

❖ Form several small groups and encourage participants to talk about the kinds of worship space they prefer and how the church where they worship does (or does not) meet their needs. They may also talk about worship spaces that may make them feel uncomfortable—and why. Remind them again that there are no "correct" answers.

❖ **Option:** Distribute unlined paper and pencils. Invite the learners to sketch a worship space that they would prefer. Or they may want to sketch some of the items they would like to find in that space, such as a stained glass window, an organ, candles, and so on. Provide time for the learners to share with a partner what they have drawn.

(4) Goal 3: Tell Others the Story of the Dedication of the Learners' Place of Worship

❖ **Option 1:** Make arrangements with the church historian or one or more long-standing members of the congregation to speak with the class about the construction and dedication of your church building(s). Set a time limit for this presentation, and allow time for questions from the group. Encourage the speaker(s) to bring any pictures they have of this event. Suggest that the speaker(s) not only give "the facts" but also try to recount the mood of the congregation as they anticipated and then dedicated their new structure.

❖ **Option 2:** Use "Faith in Action: Building Our Church" to learn more about the history of your congregation and the dedication of its building(s). If you choose this option, be sure to do some research prior to class and have documents available for the students to use as they begin to research and discuss the information. Additional time will need to be scheduled to complete the suggested projects.

(5) Continue the Journey

❖ Pray that today's participants will joyfully celebrate opportunities to worship God.

❖ Read aloud this preparation for next week's lesson. You may also want to post it on newsprint for the students to copy.
- ■ **Title: Fasting and Praying**
- ■ **Background Scripture: Ezra 8:21-23**
- ■ **Lesson Scripture: Ezra 8:21-23**

■ **Focus of the Lesson: As people journey through life, they pause to assess their strengths and weaknesses for reaching their destination. How can people prepare themselves to make this assessment? Ezra and his entourage stopped on their way to Jerusalem to prepare themselves by fasting and praying for God's protection on their journey.**

❖ Post these three activities related to this week's session on newsprint for the students to copy. Challenge the adults to grow spiritually by completing one or more of them.

(1) **Envision a special place from your childhood. What warm memories do you recall? Why was this place so important to you?**

(2) **Learn whatever you can about the history of your church building's dedication by reading or talking with those who attended, if that is possible. Perhaps you were present and can recall this vividly. If you were, share with newcomers what happened during this event. Try to convey the mood of the congregation.**

(3) **Remember an important event in your country's history. Perhaps you recall the assassination of John F. Kennedy or Dr. Martin Luther King Jr., or the events of September 11, 2001. Maybe you were present when a major hurricane devastated your area. What emotional connection did you feel with others who experienced this event with you? How did this event somehow shape the witnesses into a community?**

❖ Sing or read aloud "God Is Here."

❖ Conclude today's session by leading the class in this benediction, adapted from the key verse for June 9 from Isaiah 12:4: **Let us go forth continually giving thanks, proclaiming God's mighty deeds, and exalting God's holy name.**

UNIT 2: WORSHIPING IN JERUSALEM AGAIN (EZRA)
FASTING AND PRAYING

PREVIEWING THE LESSON

Lesson Scripture: Ezra 8:21-23
Background Scripture: Ezra 8:21-23
Key Verse: Ezra 8:23

Focus of the Lesson:
As people journey through life, they pause to assess their strengths and weaknesses for reaching their destination. How can people prepare themselves to make this assessment? Ezra and his entourage stopped on their way to Jerusalem to prepare themselves by fasting and praying for God's protection on their journey.

Goals for the Learners:
(1) to research Ezra's experience with prayer and fasting.
(2) to reflect on times when prayer made their journey easier.
(3) to design a discipline of prayer and fasting each learner may use.

Pronunciation Guide:
Ahava (uh hay' vuh)
Artaxerxes (ahr tuh zuhrk' seez)
Casiphia (kuh sif' ee uh)
Jabash-gilead (jay bish gil' ee uhd)
Jehoshaphat (ji hosh' uh fat)

Supplies:
Bibles, newsprint and marker, paper and pencils, hymnals

JULY 21

READING THE SCRIPTURE

NRSV

Lesson Scripture: Ezra 8:21-23

21Then I proclaimed a fast there, at the river Ahava, that we might deny ourselves before our God, to seek from him a safe journey for ourselves, our children, and all our

CEB

Lesson Scripture: Ezra 8:21-23

21Then I called for a fast there at the Ahava River so that we might submit before our God and ask of him a safe journey for ourselves, our children, and all our possessions.

possessions. ²²For I was ashamed to ask the king for a band of soldiers and cavalry to protect us against the enemy on our way, since we had told the king that the hand of our God is gracious to all who seek him, but his power and his wrath are against all who forsake him. **²³So we fasted and petitioned our God for this, and he listened to our entreaty.**

²²I had been ashamed to ask the king for a group of soldiers and cavalry to help us in facing enemies on the way, because we had told the king, "The power of God favors all who seek him, but his fierce wrath is against all who abandon him." **²³So we fasted and prayed to our God for this, and he responded to us.**

UNDERSTANDING THE SCRIPTURE

Introduction. Between the text that we dealt with in the last lesson (ending with Ezra 6:22) and our current text (8:21-23), there has been a significant development: Ezra has been sent by the Persian emperor to Jerusalem. Since Ezra is a major character in the text for this lesson and in succeeding ones, it is worth spending a bit of time examining the way that the text presents him.

First of all, Ezra is called a priest, and, although he is not designated as the community's high priest, the text lays out his genealogical relation to the high priest Aaron (7:1-5). The text also calls him "a scribe skilled in the law of Moses that the LORD the God of Israel had given" (7:6), and one who "had set his heart to study the law of the LORD, and to do it, and to teach the statutes and ordinances in Israel" (7:10).

The emphasis on Ezra's relationship to the law helps make sense of the reason that the text gives for King Artaxerxes to send him to Jerusalem. In the letter of Artaxerxes to Ezra that is recorded in 7:11-26, the king instructs Ezra to "make inquiries about Judah and Jerusalem according to the law of your God" (7:14). In addition, Ezra is to set up a legal system in the land, appointing judges and teaching the precepts, and strictly punish those who run afoul of "the law of your God and the law of the king" (7:25-26). Along with legal reform, Ezra is to

also ensure that the functioning of the Temple is supported: He is to transport the offering from the king and the people and buy offerings to be offered in the Temple (7:15-17), transport various Temple vessels from Babylon to Jerusalem (7:19), and provide anything else needed by the Temple with funds from the king's treasury (7:20).

Ezra was not alone in his journey to Jerusalem. According to the summary of the trip recorded in 7:7-10, Ezra was accompanied by other members of his community ("some of the people of Israel" is how verse 7 puts it) as well as Temple personnel such as priests, singers, gatekeepers, and the Temple servants (7:7). Although Levites are also mentioned in this list, they seem to have joined the group after they initially set out; the text in 8:15-20 recounts the story about what happened when Ezra "reviewed the people and the priests" at the beginning of the journey. Realizing that they had no Levites among them, he sent several leaders along with two men designated as "wise" to Casiphia to gather from there Levites who could go with them to Jerusalem.

Ezra 8:21. The first verse of our narrative continues in the voice of Ezra. Although the entire book is named after him, his first-person account only begins at the end of chapter 7 and continues through chapter 9.

The precise location of the river Ahava remains unknown, but it is clear that Ezra's group reaches it close to the beginning of their journey and stays there as they prepare for their trip (ensuring that they have the proper number of Levites with them, devoting themselves to prayer and fasting, and assigning various priests and Levites to carry the precious offerings; see Ezra 8:15, 21, 24-25). Thus it is most likely that the river is a tributary of the Euphrates. The city of Babylon itself was built on the Euphrates, and a variety of canals were built to defend and provide for the city. It is on such a waterway that the community had earlier hung their harps on the willow trees when they were asked to sing a song of Zion (Psalm 137). Now in a similar place where before they could not sing of the holy city, they are making final preparations for their return journey to Jerusalem.

The literal meaning of "safe journey" is a "straight or level way." This is exactly what Isaiah prophecies will signal the beginning of the postexilic period, the time when the people can return to the land and when God's glory will once again be manifested to the whole world:

A voice cries out:
"In the wilderness prepare the way
 of the LORD,
  make straight in the desert a
   highway for our God.
Every valley shall be lifted up,
 and every mountain and hill be
  made low;
the uneven ground shall become level,
 and the rough places a plain.
Then the glory of the LORD shall
 be revealed,
  and all people shall see it together,
   for the mouth of the LORD has
    spoken." (Isaiah 40:3-5)

Ezra 8:22. With the phrase "the enemy on our way," the text telegraphs that Ezra's concern was not simply physical ease related to level roads with few or no hills. Rather, Ezra's prayer for a "straight or level way" also relates to the real and always present danger involved in travel in the ancient world. Numerous accounts tell of the threat of robbers and other dangers. Surely his worry about potential attacks was also heightened by the presence of children among their retinue, as well as the large amount of silver, gold, and Temple vessels that they carried (8:21, 26-27).

In the second part of the verse, Ezra recounts his prior statement to the king, a more literal rendering of which is "the hand of our God is on/over all who entreat him, for (their) good."

Ezra 8:23. We are not given any real details about the fasting and petitioning in which the group engaged. We do not know how long the fast lasted, and no prayer is quoted in the text. Matthew 6:16-18 gives us some hint about what may have been involved in a fast (besides, of course, the voluntary denial of food), namely the denial of any ritual associated with personal appearance such as putting oil on one's head and washing one's face.

Although details concerning the *how* of fasting are absent in Ezra 8, the text is clear that the fast accomplished its purpose: God, we are told, "listened to our entreaty" (8:23). The reader is not told how the people know that this is so, and we are struck by their faithful confidence. And then, in the strength of such knowledge of divine heed, the group confidently makes its final preparations and sets out for Jerusalem.

INTERPRETING THE SCRIPTURE

Prayer and Fasting

As Ezra, the priests and Levites, and the people prepare for their journey, they take time to pray and to fast. The practice of fasting is mentioned throughout the Old Testament in a variety of contexts. At some points it is associated with the ritual mourning of the dead: The people of Jabash-gilead fast when they mourn Saul and his sons after they were slain in battle (1 Samuel 31:13). David and his people also fast when they mourn these same deaths (2 Samuel 1:12).

In a related way, the mourning of the destruction of Jerusalem is also marked by fasting. After the city was destroyed by the Babylonians, a tradition developed in which the people fasted and prayed in the fifth month throughout the many years of exile until the Temple was rebuilt (see Zechariah 7:2-7).

In addition to mourning, a story from the life of David points toward another related purpose of prayer and fasting. When his son lay dying, David fasted and pleaded with God (2 Samuel 12:16). Following in the tradition discussed above, David's servants thought that his behavior was more appropriate during the mourning period itself. Yet David clearly fasts for a different reason: "While the child was still alive," he says to the servants, "I fasted and wept, for I said, 'Who knows? The LORD may be gracious to me, and the child may live.' But now he is dead; why should I fast? Can I bring him back again? I shall go to him, but he will not return to me" (2 Samuel 12:22-23). David clearly links fasting with intercessory prayer, and hopes that the practice will be met with a gracious response from God.

Mourning and intercession are surely in view again when we hear of yet another related reason for fasting that was present in the postexilic community: contrition for wrongdoing. When, under Ezra's leadership, the community came to realize that they had committed sin, they begin to fast (Ezra 10:6; Nehemiah 9:1). They also engaged in other practices associated with mourning such as dressing in sackcloth and putting dirt on their heads. Clearly they are mourning their sin and at the same time praying for divine mercy.

Outside of the context of mourning and contrition, the community also fasted and prayed when it was in great distress and especially needed God's guidance and protection. Usually this was done in the context of a national emergency. This is the case in Judges 20:26-28, when, after its defeat at the hands of the Benjaminites, Israel mourned its loss and sought to discern whether it would stand to fight the same army for a second time (Judges 20:26-28). Fasting is also associated with great military peril in 2 Chronicles 20 in a story that tells of the time of King Jehoshaphat of Judah. With several armies set to invade and in a time of great fear, the king "set himself to seek the LORD, and proclaimed a fast throughout all Judah" (2 Chronicles 20:3). A few verses later we read of his prayer to God: "We do not know what to do, but our eyes are on you" (2 Chronicles 20:12). In response to their prayers and pleas for help, God has the invading armies fight each other to the death and Judah is victorious without needing a single weapon.

The Book of Esther also tells of fasting during a time of national threat. When the queen realizes that her whole community is in mortal danger, she asks the people to fast together with her before she presents the request to the king that will ultimately save their lives (Esther 4:16).

Finally, after King Solomon dedicated the Temple, God appeared to him and promised to respond favorably to the people's prayers and acts of humility during times of famine:

"If my people who are called by my name humble themselves, pray, seek my face, and turn from their wicked ways, then I will hear from heaven, and will forgive their sin and heal their land" (2 Chronicles 7:14).

It is particularly these practices associated with King Jehoshaphat, Queen Esther, and King Solomon that seem most akin to that called for by Ezra in our passage. The people are not in mourning, but they clearly are in danger: They are about to set out on a difficult journey, while carrying a great deal of precious treasure. We learn later in the chapter that this group carried an astonishing amount of gold, silver, and bronze (8:26-27). The danger that Ezra's caravan faced stemmed not only from the predictable bandits that threatened all travelers but also the political unrest that would spring up in the Persian Empire on occasion.

Ezra's Vow and the People's Support

Given the danger, some have suggested that Ezra's vow to the king was rash: "We had told the king that the hand of our God is gracious to all who seek him, but his power and his wrath are against all who forsake him" (8:22). Surely the king would understand that the proof of God's character does not hinge on the number of guards protecting a small band of worshipers on their way to Jerusalem. Other biblical texts from this period speak of military escorts for such journeys as a matter of course. For example, Nehemiah was accompanied by armed guards when he traveled from Susa to Jerusalem, and this fact never puts his piety in doubt (Nehemiah 2:9). Whether or not Ezra's vow betrays an overabundance of earnestness (earnestness that even he

may have regretted!), it is significant to note that the text records no grumbling on the part of his fellow travelers. Together they all fast and pray, and together they make the journey without a hint of complaint.

Preparing for What Lies Ahead

Thinking about the fasting and prayer that preceded the journey in Ezra 8 (as well as in the stories of Jehoshaphat, Esther, and Solomon) may put us in mind of the ways that we go about preparing for journeys or significant decisions in our own lives. At times, perhaps the anticipated danger of a significant journey leads us into practices that we hope will draw us nearer to God. Alone, or in the context of our faith community, we set out only when we have properly prepared ourselves by engaging in the spiritual disciplines that strengthen our souls and draw us closer to the heart of God. Ironically, we may find ultimate strength by engaging in acts that render us temporarily weak (Psalm 109:24). Fortified together by such practices, the community can embark on momentous and even perilous journeys knowing that they will not be undone by rancor and infighting. At other times, of course, we may embark upon journeys or make decisions while never giving the accompanying dangers a second thought. But the dangers are no less real simply because we are oblivious to them in advance. Perhaps Ezra 8 is a good reminder that we should get into the habit of the types of practices that will sustain us and our community in our relationship with God even when the pilgrimage journey takes unexpected and even dangerous turns.

SHARING THE SCRIPTURE

Preparing Our Hearts

Explore this week's devotional reading, from 2 Chronicles 7:12-18. In 2 Chronicles 1:7-12 God appeared to Solomon in a vision and asked the king what he would like. Solomon's reply—wisdom to rule God's people—greatly pleased God. In chapter 7, God again appears to Solomon in the night and says that his prayers have been heard. Notice that God promises to heal the Israelites' land if they turn from their evil ways and repent (7:14). Humble yourself and offer your own prayer of repentance. Be assured that God will hear and grant you forgiveness.

Pray that you and the adult students will humbly come before God's throne of grace to make your prayers known.

Preparing Our Minds

Study the background Scripture and the lesson Scripture, both of which are from Ezra 8:21-23.

Consider this question as you prepare the lesson: *How can people prepare themselves to assess their strengths and weaknesses?*

Write on newsprint:

❑ Scripture passages for "Design a Discipline of Prayer and Fasting Each Learner May Use."

❑ information for next week's lesson, found under "Continue the Journey."

❑ activities for further spiritual growth in "Continue the Journey."

Review the "Introduction," "The Big Picture," "Close-up," and "Faith in Action." Consider how you will use this additional information, which immediately precedes the first lesson, for this session.

LEADING THE CLASS

(1) Gather to Learn

❖ Greet the class members. Introduce any guests and help them feel at home.

❖ Pray that today's participants will find new and deeper meaning in prayer.

❖ Read the following: **In an April 2011 Web post, Ashley wrote about her concerns related to December 2012 when the world will end as we know it—at least according to her understanding of the Mayan calendar. This mother is trying hard to be prepared and has written to see if others are making preparations too. She mentions the supplies she has been gathering and comments: "There seems to be a lot involved in planning for something this serious, preparing mentally has been quite strenuous on my mind and emotions as well. Learning to balance my emotions about the possibilities that we face is quite scary. I often find myself feeling very anxious, overwhelmed, and very much alone."**

❖ Ask: **As you peer into the future, what steps are you taking to prepare yourself?** (You may wish to add information from "Preparing for What Lies Ahead" in Interpreting the Scripture.)

❖ Read aloud today's focus statement: **As people journey through life, they pause to assess their strengths and weaknesses for reaching their destination. How can people prepare themselves to make this assessment? Ezra and his entourage stopped on their way to Jerusalem to prepare themselves by fasting and praying for God's protection on their journey.**

(2) Goal 1: Research Ezra's Experience With Prayer and Fasting

❖ Use "Introduction" in Understanding the Scripture to help the class get to know Ezra and what he is called to do.

❖ Choose a volunteer to read Ezra 8:21-23.

❖ Discuss these questions. Add information from "Ezra 8:21," "Ezra 8:22," and "Ezra 8:23" in Understanding the Scripture to the discussion.

(1) **For what reason does Ezra proclaim a fast?**

(2) **Why did Ezra refuse to ask the king for a military escort?**

(3) **Compare the preparations that Ezra calls the Israelites to make with those that Ashley (in "Gather to Learn") was concerned about and calling others to make. Which type of preparations are you most likely to make?** (Note that Ezra's preparations were spiritual, whereas Ashley's were focused on stockpiling material goods and having enough "stuff" to survive.)

(4) **What do these brief verses teach you about the power of prayer and fasting?**

(3) Goal 2: Reflect on Times When Prayer Made the Learners' Journey Easier

❖ Distribute paper and pencils. Invite the adults to recall a challenging time in their lives when prayer really kept them afloat. Suggest that they each write a letter to God expressing what the opportunity to pray and know that they were heard meant to them.

❖ Encourage several volunteers to either read their letters or briefly state an important point about the power of prayer that they learned from their experience.

(4) Goal 3: Design a Discipline of Prayer and Fasting Each Learner May Use

❖ Read "Prayer and Fasting" from Interpreting the Scripture to help the students see examples of how these spiritual practices were used in ancient Israel.

❖ Post these Old Testament Bible passages on newsprint. Assign ten individuals, partners, or groups to each look up one of these passages to learn the purpose and meaning of fasting in each case:

    2 Samuel 12:15-23
    1 Kings 21:1-29
    2 Chronicles 20:1-4
    Esther 4:12-17
    Isaiah 58:3-6
    Jeremiah 14:11-12
    Jeremiah 36:4-10
    Joel 1:13-16
    Jonah 3:1-5
    Zechariah 8:18-19

❖ Call on the students to recount briefly what they have learned from these passages. Point out that although we did not survey the New Testament, examples of fasting are found there as well. Jesus himself speaks of fasting.

❖ Encourage the students to identify a church event, community issue, or national concern that needs to be undergirded with prayer and fasting. Work together to plan a way that the students could engage in a period of prayer and fasting. Perhaps they will spearhead a congregational event, such as a twenty-four-hour prayer vigil. Maybe they will agree to pray at a specified time or for a certain length of time each day. Possibly those who are physically able will agree to fast from food for one or more meals on a particular day of the week. Challenge the students to implement their plan and report within two weeks as to how the plan is working.

(5) Continue the Journey

❖ Pray that those who have come today will recognize the value of prayer, fasting, and other spiritual disciplines as they walk daily with God.

❖ Read aloud this preparation for next week's lesson. You may also want to post it on newsprint for the students to copy.

- Title: Gifts for the Temple
- Background Scripture: Ezra 8:24-30
- Lesson Scripture: Ezra 8:24-30
- Focus of the Lesson: People often make gifts to others whom they revere. What inspires one to give in this manner? As an act of worship, Ezra prepared gifts of precious metals to be carried by the priests and Levites to the house of God in Jerusalem.

❖ Post these three activities related to this week's session on newsprint for the students to copy. Challenge the adults to grow spiritually by completing one or more of them.

(1) Spend time in prayer each day for a specific issue or person. If you are physically able, consider fasting, even one meal per day, as part of your spiritual discipline.

(2) Check out types of fasts. Although biblical fasts involved abstaining from food, some modern writers, such as Marjorie Thompson (*Soul Feast*), suggest other things we can give up to spend more quality time with God. See if any of these ideas will work for you.

(3) Keep a prayer journal. Write a brief note or name along with the date of your prayer. When this prayer appears to be answered, add another note and a date. Give thanks to God for answered prayer, and continue praying for those concerns and persons for whom your prayers do not yet seem to be answered.

❖ Sing or read aloud "Not So in Haste, My Heart."

❖ Conclude today's session by leading the class in this benediction, adapted from the key verse for June 9 from Isaiah 12:4: **Let us go forth continually giving thanks, proclaiming God's mighty deeds, and exalting God's holy name.**

UNIT 2: WORSHIPING IN JERUSALEM AGAIN (EZRA)
GIFTS FOR THE TEMPLE

PREVIEWING THE LESSON

Lesson Scripture: Ezra 8:24-30
Background Scripture: Ezra 8:24-30
Key Verse: Ezra 8:28

Focus of the Lesson:
People often make gifts to others whom they revere. What inspires one to give in this manner? As an act of worship, Ezra prepared gifts of precious metals to be carried by the priests and Levites to the house of God in Jerusalem.

Goals for the Learners:
(1) to review the principles of financial accountability Ezra put in place.
(2) to reflect on being generous givers to the church as an act of worship to God.
(3) to present their offering as an act of worship to God.

Pronunciation Guide:
daric (dair' ik)
Hashabiah (hash uh bi' uh)
Sherebiah (sher uh bi' uh)

Supplies:
Bibles, newsprint and marker, paper and pencils, hymnals

READING THE SCRIPTURE

NRSV
Lesson Scripture: Ezra 8:24-30

²⁴Then I set apart twelve of the leading priests: Sherebiah, Hashabiah, and ten of their kin with them. ²⁵And I weighed out to them the silver and the gold and the vessels, the offering for the house of our God that the king, his counselors, his lords, and all Israel there present had offered; ²⁶I weighed out

CEB
Lesson Scripture: Ezra 8:24-30

²⁴Then I selected twelve of the leading priests, Sherebiah and Hashabiah and ten of their relatives with them. ²⁵I weighed out to them the silver and the gold and the equipment, the offering for the house of our God that the king, his counselors, his officials, and all Israel present there had offered. ²⁶I

into their hand six hundred fifty talents of silver, and one hundred silver vessels worth . . . talents, and one hundred talents of gold, ²⁷twenty gold bowls worth a thousand darics, and two vessels of fine polished bronze as precious as gold. ²⁸And I said to them, **"You are holy to the LORD, and the vessels are holy; and the silver and the gold are a freewill offering to the LORD, the God of your ancestors.** ²⁹Guard them and keep them until you weigh them before the chief priests and the Levites and the heads of families in Israel at Jerusalem, within the chambers of the house of the LORD." ³⁰So the priests and the Levites took over the silver, the gold, and the vessels as they were weighed out, to bring them to Jerusalem, to the house of our God.

weighed out into their keeping six hundred fifty kikkars of silver, one hundred silver containers weighing a certain number of kikkars, one hundred kikkars of gold, ²⁷twenty gold bowls worth one thousand darics, and two containers of highly polished copper, which were as precious as gold. ²⁸**I said to them, "You are holy to the LORD, and the equipment is holy; the silver and the gold are a spontaneous gift to the LORD, the God of your ancestors.** ²⁹Guard them carefully until you weigh them out in Jerusalem before the officials of the priests, the Levites, and the heads of the families of Israel, within the rooms of the LORD's house." ³⁰So the priests and the Levites received the silver and the gold and the utensils as they were weighed out, in order to bring them to Jerusalem, to our God's house.

UNDERSTANDING THE SCRIPTURE

Ezra 8:24. There are two possibilities for translating this verse, and these are both represented in the NIV and the NRSV translations. Literally, the text reads "Then I set apart from the leaders of the priests twelve, to Sherebiah and Hashabiah and ten of their relatives." Because Sherebiah and Hashabiah were identified as Levites in the previous section (Ezra 8:18-19), and because the caretakers of the treasure include both priests and Levites in Ezra 8:30, the NIV chooses to render the text as if it describes a twenty-four-member group made up of twelve priests and twelve Levites. By using a colon, the NRSV implies that there are only twelve members in the group, and it consists of an undisclosed mix of priests and Levites along with Sherebiah and Hashabiah. Regardless of the different options that the two translations take, both retain the original emphasis that the ancient text puts upon the presence of both priests

and Levites among the group and on the number twelve.

Ezra 8:25. Similar to the presentation throughout the Book of Ezra, this verse explicitly names the Persian royal court as active financial supporters of the Jerusalem Temple. In this verse, the king, the royal counselors, and the lords of Persia make contributions to God's house in Jerusalem. The rest of the community in Persia ("all Israel there present") also added its contribution to the royal donation.

Ezra 8:26. Again the NRSV and the NIV make different decisions regarding how to interpret the number of talents that the one hundred silver vessels named here weigh. Literally, the text reads "one hundred silver vessels weighing talents." The NRSV prefers to indicate that there seems to be something missing in the text, and shows this by using ". . ." (that is, "one hundred silver vessels worth . . . talents").

The NIV, on the other hand, takes the number "one hundred" to indicate the number of talents rather than the number of vessels (that is, "silver articles weighing 100 talents"). In either case, the amount of silver is very large. In addition to the silver vessels, the text also records an additional 650 talents of silver. If a talent weighs about 75 pounds, then these 650 talents amount to an astronomical 24.3 tons of silver.

Although Ezra leads the group, he decides that the treasure should be guarded by a group of people that does not include him. By weighing out the offering into the "keeping" of the priests and Levites, he is enlarging the circle of those who are responsible for the valuable treasure. Given the potential for danger involved in ancient travel, this is a wise decision. It allows for the division of the treasure, so that if one of those who carries it is robbed, the entire consignment is not at risk. It also releases Ezra from sole blame in the case of theft.

Ezra 8:27. This verse completes the list of the great amount of treasure that the group conveyed to Jerusalem. Added to the one hundred vessels or talents of silver vessels and the additional 24.3 tons of silver listed in 8:26 is one hundred talents of gold calculated to weigh just under four tons. In addition, some estimate that the twenty gold bowls would add an additional twenty pounds to the total of gold. To this is added two more vessels made of "polished bronze as precious as gold." Although the text clearly indicates that this metal was valuable, its exact identity is not entirely clear. Some have suggested orichale, which was a metal made of a copper alloy highly valued in the ancient Near East.

Altogether, the silver, gold, and polished bronze make for a grand offering indeed! Some have suggested that the great amount of treasure indicates that the list is pure fabrication. However, two facts point against such a conclusion. The first is that only portions of the list are incredible: The 24.3 tons of silver is admittedly a very large amount, but the total of twenty gold vessels and two copper ones hardly seems unreasonable. The second fact is that the list proceeds in an orderly and logical manner: The amount of silver is followed by the amount of silver vessels, then the amount of gold is followed by the amount of the gold vessels, and the amount of special items concludes the list. Perhaps it is best to assume that only parts of the original list have been confused in the text's transmission.

By measuring and listing the exact contents of the treasure before the journey begins, Ezra helps ensure that nothing will go missing before the group reaches Jerusalem.

Ezra 8:28. Before they leave on their journey, Ezra reminds everyone that both the precious vessels and their guards are "holy," and that the silver and the gold are a votive/freewill offering to God. The designation "holy" is an explicit indication that the treasure and its custodians were set apart for service to God. On a literal level, holiness in the Old Testament has a geographical aspect to it: People or items that were removed from profane spaces and spent time in the worship area where God dwelled were uniquely consecrated to God. By designating the treasure and its guards "holy," the text implies that God would take some responsibility for protecting these holy people and objects. In addition, some have suggested that this "reminder" about the holiness of the guards and their treasure is a canny way for Ezra to discourage any potential theft.

Ezra 8:29-30. The "chambers of the house of the LORD" were rooms along the outside perimeter of the Temple building. These are described in connection with the First Temple in 1 Kings 6:5-10, and it is likely that something similar is meant here. In the other texts describing these rooms in the Second Temple (that is, Ezra 10:6 and

Nehemiah 10:38-39; 13:5, 8), such rooms are used for the storage of offerings, tithes, and Temple vessels, as well as housing for the priests. With the treasure safely in tow, the priests and Levites were ready to journey to God's house in Jerusalem.

INTERPRETING THE SCRIPTURE

Generous Gifts for the Temple

As noted in the Understanding the Scripture comments, the treasure that the people are carrying makes for a very large sum. When it is all added together, it comprises about 24.3 tons of silver (plus an additional one hundred silver vessels), just under four tons of gold (plus an additional twenty gold bowls), and two bowls of polished bronze.

This amount is surprising not just because of its enormity but also because of its source. According to the narrative, it was the gift of the Persian emperor and his counselors and his lords, supplemented by the people of Israel who were still in Babylon (8:25; and see also 7:14). Certainly the text means to emphasize that the Jerusalem Temple had official support by the highest authorities. In the face of extreme antagonism from opposing forces, such support must have meant a great deal.

The text briefly mentions that the gifts also came from the community in exile, and such generosity might also seem surprising. Setting aside specific gifts for the use of the Temple in Jerusalem points to a set of priorities that might seem strange in the contemporary world. Supporting the rebuilding of a temple so far away (that the givers might not even see!) can only be called a statement of faith.

Those who carried this gift and added to it their own contributions also surprise us with their generosity. At the very moment when they were attempting to rebuild their own settlements, and in a time when they must have felt the most financially vulnerable on a personal level, they give generously to God's service in the Temple. Clearly this community understood that its own flourishing would not be possible unless it first reestablished the Temple and its work.

A similar theme is sounded in the Book of Haggai, in a text that tells the story of the time before the Second Temple was rebuilt. Again and again the prophet tells the people that they would not succeed until they set the rebuilding of the Temple as their first concern. Rhetorically, God has the prophet ask the people, "Is it a time for you yourselves to live in your paneled houses, while this house lies in ruins?" (Haggai 1:4). Only once the returnees build the house in which God will delight and be honored will the community thrive (Haggai 1:7-11). In Ezra's account, it seems as if he and the people have understood this message.

Returning the Temple Vessels

One aspect of some of these generous gifts that might not be immediately obvious is their theological and political import. Some of these gifts consist of Temple vessels, and it is likely that these are meant to parallel those that the returnees take with them in Ezra 1, namely the sacred objects taken from Jerusalem by the conquering forces at the beginning of the exilic period (1:7).

Throughout the ancient world, removing sacred items from conquered temples was a way that empires signaled their dominance in the political as well as the religious spheres. Back in the days of the prophet Samuel, when the Philistines gained the upper hand over Israel, they captured the ark of God and placed it in their temple beside their chief god Dagon (1 Samuel 5:1-2). The Philistines, like the Babylonians after them, were demonstrating the belief that a nation that could capture notable religious objects showed forth its ascendant power over the god or gods to whom these objects were related. (For the very interesting story of how God convinced the Philistines to return the ark, see 1 Samuel 5:1–7:2.)

With the return of the Temple's vessels to Jerusalem during the time of Ezra, the text emphasizes that, even though the Persians are in current political control, it is Israel's LORD who reigns supreme. The return also indicates that the Jerusalem Temple is considered to be the proper and legitimate place to worship this powerful and matchless God.

Ezra's Leadership

As we noted in last week's reading, Ezra made something of a rash comment. He had previously told the king that "the hand of our God is gracious to all who seek him, but his power and his wrath are against all who forsake him" (8:22). Later, as he and his company set out for Jerusalem, he realized that it would now be difficult to ask for armed protection from royal reserves. Given the vulnerability of the people and their large treasure on their journey, making theological claims that would then necessitate foregoing prudent security seems ill-considered and impetuous.

Now, in 8:24-30 we see Ezra acting with thoughtfulness and consideration. In the very next set of verses he carefully selects a number of "leading priests" and Levites, divides up the treasure, and weighs it out to each man in turn. He then pronounces the men and their treasure as consecrated to God: "You are holy to the LORD, and the vessels are holy" (8:28). Finally, he charges them with their responsibility: "Guard [the vessels] and keep them until you weigh them before the chief priests and the Levites and the heads of families in Israel at Jerusalem, within the chambers of the house of the LORD" (8:29). Later in the passage, when we are told that the company arrived in Jerusalem, we also read that those who carried the treasure handed it over to the appropriate authorities. The text retains the notice that "the total was counted and weighed, and the weight of everything was recorded" (8:34).

Such deliberation can make for slow reading, but in this very slowness we see Ezra's careful leadership. Although he had forgone extra security forces, he is at pains to show that he is not careless in keeping the travelers and their treasure accounted for. He apportions a clerical guard from two different groups (priests as well as Levites), carefully records what each man received, and notes that everything was offered to the proper Temple authorities at the end of the journey. He also announces that both the men and their treasure are holy, that is, consecrated to God, and thus specially considered by God. At the very least, such a public announcement would discourage theft! In all of these acts, Ezra appears to be the very paragon of responsibility.

Considering these two stories of Ezra in rapid succession makes for interesting reading indeed. Those who think that Ezra had been rash in 8:21-23 can see in 8:24-30 that he had quickly learned from his mistakes. Or, at the very least, every reader can see that biblical actors can be flexible and adapt their decision-making to the specific task at hand. Since there is no notice of any dissent on the journey, the text implies that his co-travelers trusted their leader and their God even in the context of challenging and changing circumstances.

SHARING THE SCRIPTURE

Preparing Our Hearts

Explore this week's devotional reading, found in Mark 12:38-44. After denouncing the religious leaders for taking money from vulnerable widows, Jesus points to a widow who had given "all she had to live on" (12:44). Her generosity far outshone that of those with far greater resources. Her contribution contrasted greatly with the leaders who managed the financial affairs of widows, supposedly to protect them, but who in the process were lining their own pockets. How do you determine the amount of your gifts to God? Are you freely returning to God a portion of what has been entrusted to you?

Pray that you and the adult students will think seriously about why and how much you give to God.

Preparing Our Minds

Study the background Scripture and the lesson Scripture, both of which are from Ezra 8:24-30.

Consider this question as you prepare the lesson: *What inspires people to give gifts to others whom they revere?*

Write on newsprint:

❑ information for next week's lesson, found under "Continue the Journey."

❑ activities for further spiritual growth in "Continue the Journey."

Review the "Introduction," "The Big Picture," "Close-up," and "Faith in Action." Consider how you will use this additional information, which immediately precedes the first lesson, for this session.

Prepare the suggested lecture for "Review the Principles of Financial Accountability Ezra Put in Place."

LEADING THE CLASS

(1) Gather to Learn

❖ Greet the class members. Introduce any guests and help them feel at home.

❖ Pray that today's participants will think carefully about how, why, and to whom they give gifts.

❖ Briefly retell O. Henry's familiar short story of 1906, "The Gift of the Magi": **Della and Jim Dillingham Young were a young couple who lived quite modestly in a furnished flat that cost $8 per week. When Jim was forced to take a pay cut, their finances were stretched to the limit. Despite her best efforts to save, Della had just $1.87 on Christmas Eve to buy Jim a present. To raise money to buy a fob for his prized watch, Della had her long hair cut. Meanwhile, Jim had sold his watch to get money to buy the tortoiseshell combs that Della had admired. Each had sacrificed his or her most treasured possession to give a gift to the other.**

❖ Read aloud today's focus statement: **People often make gifts to others whom they revere. What inspires one to give in this manner? As an act of worship, Ezra prepared gifts of precious metals to be carried by the priests and Levites to the house of God in Jerusalem.**

(2) Goal 1: Review the Principles of Financial Accountability Ezra Put in Place

❖ Choose a volunteer to read Ezra 8:24-30.

❖ Present a brief lecture based on information in Understanding the Scripture to help the adults recognize the great value of the treasure for which the priests were responsible.

❖ List on newsprint the steps that Ezra took to ensure that treasures belonging to God were kept safe and the people in charge of them were held accountable. (Add information from "Ezra's Leadership" in Interpreting the Scripture as appropriate.)

❖ Ask: **How would you rate Ezra's plan in terms of its potential to keep people accountable?**

(3) Goal 2: Reflect on Being Generous Givers to the Church as an Act of Worship to God

❖ Read these quotations about generosity and invite the learners to respond as to how each quotation does—or does not—reflect their own beliefs about giving.

(1) **Giving is a joy if we do it in the right spirit. It all depends on whether we think of it as "What can I spare?" or as "What can I share?"** (Esther York Burkholder)

(2) **Giving is the thermometer of love.** (anonymous)

(3) **God does not need our money. But you and I need the experience of giving it.** (James C. Dobson, 1936–)

(4) **Let us give according to our incomes, lest God make our incomes match our gifts.** (Peter Marshall, 1902–49)

(5) **Not how much we give, but what we do not give, is the test of our Christianity.** (Oswald Chambers, 1874–1917)

(6) **You do not have to be rich to be generous. If he has the spirit of true generosity, a pauper can give like a prince.** (Corinne U. Wells)

❖ Distribute paper and pencils. Invite the learners to complete this sentence: **When I think about being a generous giver to the church** . . . Tell the students that they will not be asked to share their responses.

(4) Goal 3: Present the Learners' Offering as an Act of Worship to God

❖ Form several small groups and ask them to discuss this question: **What does the motivation with which we give money to the church say about our relationship with God?** Caution the groups to be careful not to equate a large gift with greater spirituality; some people give with the idea that they are taking out an insurance policy: *If I give to God, God will take good care of me,* they reason. A small gift, such as the widow's tiny coin, given freely and with love is far more valuable to God than a major gift given for the wrong reasons.

❖ Call the groups together and ask: **How does the way that we receive offerings in our congregation help or hinder the notion that offering is an act of worship?** (Help the students see that money freely given out of love for God within the context of worship can be a valuable worship experience because it brings glory to God and prompts the givers to reflect on God's love and gracious gifts given to them. Problems may arise when the offering is an afterthought, such as when a plate is left at the back of the worship space where people may just throw in envelopes without any meditative time or prayer.)

(5) Continue the Journey

❖ Pray that as the students go forth they will give serious consideration as to what God may be calling them to do in terms of gift giving.

❖ Read aloud this preparation for next week's lesson. You may also want to post it on newsprint for the students to copy.

◼ **Title: Festival of Booths**
◼ **Background Scripture: Nehemiah 7:73b–8:18**
◼ **Lesson Scripture: Nehemiah 8:13-18**
◼ **Focus of the Lesson: People use festivals and celebrations as observances of things most important to them in life. What are some times or events we celebrate? The festival of booths and Ezra's reading were observations of the**

Israelites' wilderness exile and the giving of the law, which the people celebrated joyously, followed by solemn contemplation.

❖ Post these three activities related to this week's session on newsprint for the students to copy. Challenge the adults to grow spiritually by completing one or more of them.

(1) Research the biblical concept of tithing, or the giving of 10 percent. Some congregations insist that all members tithe. Others encourage tithing, while still others see it as a minimum level of giving. Where do you stand on tithing? What do you do with whatever percentage of money that you do not return to God?

(2) Explore your motives for giving to God. Do you give with the hope that God will reward you? Do you want to do your "fair share" in supporting your congregation's expenses? Do you give out of habit? Do you give as a sign of gratitude for all that God has given you, especially the gift of Jesus? Prayerfully consider your motives. Write your thoughts about giving in your spiritual journal.

(3) Review a copy of your church's budget. Is the congregation being good stewards of the money that it receives? What percentage of the money goes to internal affairs? What percentage goes to outreach and missions projects? How is the church accountable for the way it spends the money entrusted to it? If you have questions or concerns, talk with your treasurer or finance chairperson to clarify any issues.

❖ Sing or read aloud "What Gift Can We Bring."

❖ Conclude today's session by leading the class in this benediction, adapted from the key verse for June 9 from Isaiah 12:4: **Let us go forth continually giving thanks, proclaiming God's mighty deeds, and exalting God's holy name.**

UNIT 3: WORSHIPING IN JERUSALEM AGAIN (NEHEMIAH)
FESTIVAL OF BOOTHS

PREVIEWING THE LESSON

Lesson Scripture: Nehemiah 8:13-18
Background Scripture: Nehemiah 7:73b–8:18
Key Verse: Nehemiah 8:17

Focus of the Lesson:
People use festivals and celebrations as observances of things most important to them in life. What are some times or events we celebrate? The festival of booths and Ezra's reading were observations of the Israelites' wilderness exile and the giving of the law, which the people celebrated joyously, followed by solemn contemplation.

Goals for the Learners:
(1) to compare the Nehemiah text with the decree in Leviticus 23:33-43 that established the festival of booths.
(2) to explore human emotions associated with being given rules for life.
(3) to encourage all the faith community to study God's Word as Ezra modeled.

Pronunciation Guide:
Artaxerxes (ahr tuh zuhrk' seez)   Susa (soo' suh)
Ephraim (ee' fray im)   Tishri (tish' ree)
Gihon (gi' hon)   Yehud (yeh hood')
Jeshua (jesh' yoo uh)   Zerubbabel (zuh ruhb' uh buhl)
Succoth (suhk' uhth)

Supplies:
Bibles, newsprint and marker, paper and pencils, hymnals

READING THE SCRIPTURE

NRSV
Lesson Scripture: Nehemiah 8:13-18
   [13]On the second day the heads of ancestral houses of all the people, with the priests and the Levites, came together to the scribe Ezra

CEB
Lesson Scripture: Nehemiah 8:13-18
   [13]On the second day, the heads of the families of all the people, along with the priests and the Levites, gathered together around

in order to study the words of the law. [14]And they found it written in the law, which the LORD had commanded by Moses, that the people of Israel should live in booths during the festival of the seventh month, [15]and that they should publish and proclaim in all their towns and in Jerusalem as follows, "Go out to the hills and bring branches of olive, wild olive, myrtle, palm, and other leafy trees to make booths, as it is written." [16]So the people went out and brought them, and made booths for themselves, each on the roofs of their houses, and in their courts and in the courts of the house of God, and in the square at the Water Gate and in the square at the Gate of Ephraim. [17]And **all the assembly of those who had returned from the captivity made booths and lived in them;** for from the days of Jeshua son of Nun to that day the people of Israel had not done so. **And there was very great rejoicing.** [18]And day by day, from the first day to the last day, he read from the book of the law of God. They kept the festival seven days; and on the eighth day there was a solemn assembly, according to the ordinance.

Ezra the scribe in order to study the words of the Instruction. [14]And they found written in the Instruction that the LORD had commanded through Moses that the Israelites should live in booths during the festival of the seventh month.

[15]They also found that they should make the following proclamation and announce it throughout their towns and in Jerusalem: "Go out to the hills and bring branches of olive, wild olive, myrtle, palm, and other leafy trees to make booths, as it is written."

[16]So the people went out and brought them, and made booths for themselves, each on the roofs of their houses or their courtyards, in the courtyards of God's house, in the area by the Water Gate, or in the area by the Gate of Ephraim.

[17]**The whole assembly of those who had returned from captivity made booths and lived in them.** This was something that the people of Israel hadn't done since the days of Joshua, Nun's son, and there was very great rejoicing.

[18]He read from God's Instruction scroll every day, from the first until the last day of the festival. They kept the festival for seven days and held a solemn assembly on the eighth day, just as the Instruction required.

UNDERSTANDING THE SCRIPTURE

Introduction. The first several chapters of this book begin with the story of Nehemiah, and relate how he left the capital city of Susa in order to repair the exterior wall of Jerusalem. In chapter 8, we pick up again with the story of Ezra.

Nehemiah 7:73b–8:2. The "seventh month" is Tishri, that is, September/October, a month marked by the harvest as well as many significant religious festivals. On the first day of this month was what became known as the New Year festival, celebrated by the people resting from their labor, gathering together, hearing loud trumpet blasts, and offering sacrifices to the Lord (Leviticus 23:33-43; Numbers 29:1). This feast was followed by the Day of Atonement on the tenth day, and the week-long festival of booths beginning on the fifteenth day. According to Deuteronomy 31:10-13, Moses commanded that every seventh year the law be read to the people gathered together for the festival of booths. It is probably this association that gave rise to the people's request that Ezra read them the law.

The "Water Gate" was probably associated with the major water source of the city of Jerusalem, the Gihon Spring.

Nehemiah 8:3-8. These verses contain a long and detailed description of Ezra's proclamation, and the reader is able to easily visualize the event. The details include a description of Ezra as he reads: He stands above the people on a wooden platform (literally, a "tower") with the scroll opened in front of him along with several men whose names are specified (8:4). The text also describes the people: The men and women and "those who could understand" listened attentively (8:3; literally, "the ears of all the people [were] toward the book of the law"). They stand when the Book of the Law is opened as a sign of respect (see also Judges 3:20; Ezekiel 2:1). Then they lift their hands to indicate their total dependence (Nehemiah 8:6; Psalm 28:2) and say "Amen, Amen" when Ezra blesses them to mark their agreement (Nehemiah 8:6). Finally they bow their heads with their faces toward the ground in order to worship the Lord (8:6). The description also includes the names of those who stood with Ezra (8:4), and those who "helped the people to understand the law" (8:7). The latter were probably translating the Hebrew text into the Aramaic language with which the people were more familiar and also explaining the sense.

Nehemiah 8:9-12. The immediate reaction of the people to this reading and interpretation of the law is grief. The reader gets the sense that this grief stems from realizing the immensity of their failure. And their sense of personal failure may have been deepened in the context of imperial threat: King Artaxerxes' directive to Ezra included the stipulation that "all who will not obey the law of your God and the law of the king, let judgment be strictly executed on them, whether for death or for banishment or for confiscation of their goods or for imprisonment" (Ezra 7:26). The leadership is quick to try to quell the remorse of the people by

reminding them that this day is "holy to our LORD," and that "the joy of the LORD is your strength" (Nehemiah 8:10). Religious festivals are often associated with joy in the Hebrew Bible (Deuteronomy 12:12; 16:11), so the advice of Ezra, Nehemiah, and the Levites ("do not be grieved," Nehemiah 8:10, 11) is entirely appropriate in this context. The people respond by eating and drinking (and sending "portions" to their neighbors) and making a "great rejoicing" (8:12).

Nehemiah 8:13-15. The designation "the second day" (8:13) is set in context by 7:73b and 8:2, when the people gathered in Jerusalem on the first day of the seventh month to celebrate the new year. After the community-wide feast that marked the end of the first day (8:12), the heads of the houses, priests, and Levites gathered to Ezra to hear more from the law. The "law, which the LORD had commanded by Moses" (8:14) refers to Mosaic regulations. Something similar to Ezra 8:14-15 is found in Leviticus 23:33-43 (see also Numbers 29:12-38; Deuteronomy 16:13-15). During the festival of the seventh month, the people were to make booths or tabernacles for themselves and their families out of branches and live in them for seven days. The alternative designation for this festival is "Succoth," which is the English translation of the Hebrew word for "booths." This festival probably derived from a celebration of the harvest, indicated by the time of year as well as the production of temporary dwellings that mimic those used by those who work in the fields to gather the crops.

Nehemiah 8:16-18. The celebration of the festival of tabernacles is marked by a joyful week living in booths made out of branches. The assertion in verse 17—"from the days of Jeshua [or Joshua] son of Nun to that day the people of Israel had not done so"—is confusing for a number of reasons. Other biblical texts describe the community celebrating this festival between the time of the settlement and the events in Nehemiah 8. It was in the context of this festival that Solomon dedicated the Temple (1 Kings 8:2). Even more striking is the fact that Ezra 3:4 tells of the group who returned from Babylon with Jeshua and Zerubbabel "keeping the festival of booths" when they reached Jerusalem. (See also references to annual festivals in Judges 21:19 and 1 Samuel 1:3.) Perhaps the text in Nehemiah 8 uses hyperbole in order to emphasize this particular celebration. Or it may be a way to make an explicit link between the two groups who "had returned from captivity" (8:17), both the captivity in Egypt and in Babylon.

INTERPRETING THE SCRIPTURE

The Study of God's Word

In Ezra 7, Ezra was designated "scribe of the law of the God of heaven" by the Persian emperor Artaxerxes and instructed to teach this law in Yehud (Ezra 7:21, 25). This imperial command parallels what we are told about his own inner motivation: "Ezra had set his heart to study the law of the LORD, and to do it, and to teach the statutes and ordinances in Israel" (Ezra 7:10). Given these two factors, it is not surprising that we now find him reading the law at a communal gathering for five to six hours ("from early morning until midday" according to Nehemiah 8:3). Choosing the "seventh month" for such an event was probably influenced by the tradition now found in Deuteronomy 31:10-13, where the law is to be read to the people every seventh year in the seventh month.

But the emphasis on *Ezra's* connection to the law does not at all preclude the active role of the *people* in learning God's word. The text in Nehemiah 8 is very clear that the whole community was involved in Ezra's reading, and this is emphasized in several ways. A small detail at the very beginning sets the tone in that it is not Ezra himself who chooses to begin reading the law but rather part of the community who takes the lead: "They told the scribe Ezra to bring the book of the law of Moses, which the LORD had given to Israel" (8:1).

The text is also very clear that Ezra's reading is not simply for the enrichment of a chosen few, but has an inclusive reach: Twice the text states "both men and women and all who could hear with understanding" were present (8:2; also 8:3), and he stands on a specially constructed platform (literally, a "tower") so that he could read "in the sight of all the people" (8:5). In addition to this all-encompassing *presentation* of the law, the community is also very involved in the law's *interpretation*: Levites engage in their traditional role of teachers to help the people comprehend the reading (8:7-8, notice that the people's "understanding" is mentioned twice). Finally, just as the study of the law occurs in the context of the community, the description of the following celebration also has an encompassing reach: "All the people" (8:12) ate and drank the special food, and they sent "portions" to their neighbors as well to ensure that everyone could participate in the celebration.

Celebrating the Festival of Booths Together

Noticing the emphasis on the work of both Ezra *and* the community in the beginning of chapter 8 is significant for the proper understanding of verses 13-18. Here the law that Ezra brought with him from Babylon is enacted in the celebration of the festival of booths, and the depiction of this celebration clearly emphasizes the central role of the community.

In 8:13-18, Ezra is again explicitly related to the law just as he was previously, and once again it is the people who take a very active role in learning and enacting its precepts. The morning after the great public-law reading and celebration, a smaller group of leaders seek out Ezra "in order to study the words of the law" (8:13). The very first item that they find in this law is a regulation for another community-wide festival, the festival of booths. The Bible contains several passages that describe how this festival is to be kept, including Leviticus 23:33-36, 39-43; Numbers 29:12-38; and Deuteronomy 16:13-15. Careful readers will notice that Leviticus 23 contains the most details that are subsequently enacted in Nehemiah 8, including the date (seven days during the seventh month), the undertaking (collecting tree branches and living in booths for seven days), and the conclusion of the festival (a "solemn assembly" on the eighth day).

By enacting the festival legislation now found in Leviticus 23 by setting up their booths, the community signals that it is actively taking its place alongside its ancient forebears. The people living in the Persian Empire reanimate the law of Moses by reading it again and doing what it commands. They join themselves with the crowd of witnesses who annually mark the holy week with prescribed rituals, and actively keep the celebration "as a statute forever throughout your generations" (Leviticus 23:21).

The connection that the community draws from prior generations consists of more than ritual repetition: The community is also marking its connection with those who escaped from Egypt long before. According to the law in Leviticus, the festival of booths was a reenactment of the events surrounding the Exodus. Adopting the voice of God, the Mosaic code clearly specifies that the people are to build temporary dwellings from branches in order to "re-remember" the Exodus: "so that your generations may know that I made the people of Israel live in booths when I brought them out of the land of Egypt: I am the LORD your God" (Leviticus 23:43). Now in Nehemiah, those who have returned from out of the land of Babylon can take strength from the story and experience of those who escaped from Egypt and set up their new dwellings in the land that God had chosen.

Alongside this connection with the community and the ritual in Leviticus 23, the festival celebration in Nehemiah has several unique elements not found in the Mosaic law. One of the main differences is the mention of a country-wide notification. According to Nehemiah 8:15, the community was to "publish and proclaim" the festival protocols "in all their towns and in Jerusalem." By means of such proclamation, the entire community was able to hear about the festival, and thus participate in it all together.

The other difference between the festivals in Leviticus 23 and Nehemiah 8 is the emphasis put on the reading of the law. For the people in the time of Nehemiah, their initial acquaintance with the festival seems to have come while the leaders were gathered together with Ezra "to study the words of the law" (8:13). And these words continued to be read during the festival itself: "from the first day to the last day, he read from the book of the law of God" (8:18). The festival regulations in Leviticus 23 do not prescribe such a reading. But perhaps this group, recently returned from Babylon, wanted and needed to hear again the great story of its God and its people. It knew that its true identity was located in its ancient story, and it was thirsty to hear more and more.

Joyful Reading, Joyful Worship

It may come as a bit of a surprise for a contemporary reader to read of the easy combination in this story of law and ritual along with communal enjoyment. The text is clear that, in the middle of the festival of booths "there was very great rejoicing" (8:17). Lengthy readings from the Mosaic legal code and precise enactments of ancient religious festival regulations are not always considered natural prerequisites for days of delight. Yet such delight is exactly the experience of those in Nehemiah 8. Perhaps this text is exactly what contemporary communities need to read to see how to make the true connection between a holi-day and a holy-day.

SHARING THE SCRIPTURE

Preparing Our Hearts

Explore this week's devotional reading, found in Exodus 23:12-17. Here the importance of the sabbath is lifted up: The people may work six days but on the seventh day they are to rest. And this command applies not only to the Israelites themselves but also to their "homeborn slave" and "resident alien" and the animals who work as beasts of burden. The people are again reminded that God and God alone is to be worshiped. How do you take a sabbath rest as God commanded? How do you observe other important holidays on the Christian calendar?

Pray that you and the adult students will recognize that the commandment to honor the sabbath and participate in festivals is actually a gift of God.

Preparing Our Minds

Study the background Scripture from Nehemiah 7:73b–8:18 and the lesson Scripture from Nehemiah 8:13-18.

Consider this question as you prepare the lesson: *What are some times or events that we celebrate?*

Write on newsprint:
❑ information for next week's lesson, found under "Continue the Journey."
❑ activities for further spiritual growth in "Continue the Journey."

Review the "Introduction," "The Big Picture," "Close-up," and "Faith in Action." Consider how you will use this additional information, which immediately precedes the first lesson, for this session.

Prepare the suggested lecture for "Encourage All the Faith Community to Study God's Word as Ezra Modeled."

LEADING THE CLASS

(1) Gather to Learn

❖ Greet the class members. Introduce any guests and help them feel at home.

❖ Pray that all who have come today will experience the joy of worshiping God.

❖ Distribute paper and pencils. Then read these partial sentences aloud so that the adults may complete them.

(1) When I was a child, my favorite holiday was _____ because _____.

(2) As a child, my least favorite holiday was _____ because _____.

(3) Now that I am an adult, my favorite holiday is _____ because _____.

(4) As an adult, my least favorite holiday is _____ because _____.

❖ Call the learners back together and ask:

(1) Were you surprised by any of your responses?

(2) Why do you think most people, young and old alike, are so eager to join in holiday celebrations?

❖ Read aloud today's focus statement: **People use festivals and celebrations as observances of things most important to them in life. What are some times or events we celebrate? The festival of booths and Ezra's reading were observations of the Israelites' wilderness exile and the giving of the law, which the people celebrated joyously, followed by solemn contemplation.**

(2) Goal 1: Compare the Nehemiah Text With the Decree in Leviticus 23:33-43 That Established the Festival of Booths

❖ Choose someone to read Leviticus 23:33-43 to explain how the festival of booths was established. Invite another volunteer to read Nehemiah 8:13-18, which describes how this festival was celebrated in Nehemiah's day. Suggest that the audience listen closely in order to compare the two descriptions.

❖ Encourage the adults to call out how, according to Leviticus, the festival is to be celebrated, and list these ideas on newsprint. Prompt the students to look at the Nehemiah passage in their Bibles and point out any similarities and differences between that passage and Leviticus. (See the second paragraph of "Celebrating the Festival of Booths Together" in Interpreting the Scripture.)

❖ Discuss these questions:
    (1) Given the fact that the instructions in Leviticus seem clear, why do you think the people had not celebrated this festival for some time?
    (2) What took place at Nehemiah's festival that had not been commanded in Leviticus? (Note that reading from God's Word was not prescribed, but the people clamored to hear it read and explained.)

(3) Goal 2: Explore Human Emotions Associated With Being Given Rules for Life

❖ Look again together at Nehemiah 8:13-18 and ask:
    (1) What does this passage tell you about how the people felt as they worshiped? (You may wish to follow up with "Joyful Reading, Joyful Worship" in Interpreting the Scripture.)
    (2) Are these the kinds of emotions that you would associate with the reading of God's rules for life as found in the law? If not, what did you expect and why is the people's joyful response so surprising to you?

(4) Goal 3: Encourage All the Faith Community to Study God's Word as Ezra Modeled

❖ Point out that Nehemiah 8:18 reports that the law of God was read to the people.

❖ Present a brief lecture based on "The Study of God's Word" in Interpreting the Scripture and Nehemiah 8:3-8 in Understanding the Scripture to help the class members figure out how the people studied the Word together and why it made such an impact on them.

❖ Select several volunteers to participate in an informal debate on this topic: **Ezra's model for studying God's Word is similar to the one used by many contemporary Christians.** To have a lively debate, be sure you have selected students who will support this idea and those who will debunk it.

❖ Ask:
    (1) What differences might we see in our churches and homes if more people studied God's Word using methods that Ezra led his people in doing?
    (2) How would this model empower the students so they are able to get something relevant from Scripture study?

(5) Continue the Journey

❖ Pray that the learners will go forth rejoicing because they have had an opportunity to study and worship together this morning.

❖ Read aloud this preparation for next week's lesson. You may also want to post it on newsprint for the students to copy.

■ **Title: Community of Confession**
■ **Background Scripture: Nehemiah 9:1-37**
■ **Lesson Scripture: Nehemiah 9:2, 6-7, 9-10, 30-36**
■ **Focus of the Lesson: It is often hard to tell the truth about ourselves, especially our misdoings. What brings us to be honest about our shortcomings? The writer shows us that confession and repentance are necessary acts of worship, because God is merciful in every generation and gives people another chance.**

❖ Post these three activities related to this week's session on newsprint for the students to copy. Challenge the adults to grow spiritually by completing one or more of them.

(1) **Identify those practices that may be as helpful to you in practicing your Christian faith as the festi-** val of booths was for the Israelites in the days of Ezra and Nehemiah. What special activities do you undertake? How does the reading of Scripture enter into your celebration?

(2) **Recall that there was great rejoicing among the people as they celebrated this festival (Nehemiah 8:17). Choose several holy days that you observe and remember the emotions you experience. Would you say that, on the whole, worship is a joyous experience for you? Why or why not?**

(3) **The Israelites sent portions (8:12) to those who could not attend the festival in person. What tangible action can you take this week to let someone who cannot regularly attend church know that the congregation cares for him or her?**

❖ Sing or read aloud "Glorious Things of Thee Are Spoken."

❖ Conclude today's session by leading the class in this benediction, adapted from the key verse for June 9 from Isaiah 12:4: **Let us go forth continually giving thanks, proclaiming God's mighty deeds, and exalting God's holy name.**

UNIT 3: WORSHIPING IN JERUSALEM AGAIN (NEHEMIAH)
COMMUNITY OF CONFESSION

PREVIEWING THE LESSON

Lesson Scripture: Nehemiah 9:2, 6-7, 9-10, 30-36
Background Scripture: Nehemiah 9:1-37
Key Verse: Nehemiah 9:2

Focus of the Lesson:
It is often hard to tell the truth about ourselves, especially our misdoings. What brings us to be honest about our shortcomings? The writer shows us that confession and repentance are necessary acts of worship, because God is merciful in every generation and gives people another chance.

Goals for the Learners:
(1) to link the public reading of God's Word to personal acts of confession and repentance.
(2) to hear God's Word confess shortcomings.
(3) to write personal covenants with God as a result of hearing God's Word and confessing shortcomings.

Pronunciation Guide:
Artaxerxes (ahr tuh zuhrk' seez)   Heshbon (hesh' bon)
Bashan (bay' shuhn)   Ur (oor)
Chaldean (kal dee' uhn)

Supplies:
Bibles, newsprint and marker, paper and pencils, hymnals

READING THE SCRIPTURE

NRSV
Lesson Scripture: Nehemiah 9:2, 6-7, 9-10, 30-36

²Then those of Israelite descent separated themselves from all foreigners, and stood and confessed their sins and the iniquities of their ancestors.

CEB
Lesson Scripture: Nehemiah 9:2, 6-7, 9-10, 30-36

²After the Israelites separated themselves from all of the foreigners, they stood to confess their sins and the terrible behavior of their ancestors.

[6]And Ezra said: "You are the LORD, you alone; you have made heaven, the heaven of heavens, with all their host, the earth and all that is on it, the seas and all that is in them. To all of them you give life, and the host of heaven worships you. [7]You are the LORD, the God who chose Abram and brought him out of Ur of the Chaldeans and gave him the name Abraham.

[9]"And you saw the distress of our ancestors in Egypt and heard their cry at the Red Sea. [10]You performed signs and wonders against Pharaoh and all his servants and all the people of his land, for you knew that they acted insolently against our ancestors. You made a name for yourself, which remains to this day.

[30]"Many years you were patient with them, and warned them by your spirit through your prophets; yet they would not listen. Therefore you handed them over to the peoples of the lands. [31]Nevertheless, in your great mercies you did not make an end of them or forsake them, for you are a gracious and merciful God.

[32]"Now therefore, our God—the great and mighty and awesome God, keeping covenant and steadfast love—do not treat lightly all the hardship that has come upon us, upon our kings, our officials, our priests, our prophets, our ancestors, and all your people, since the time of the kings of Assyria until today. [33]You have been just in all that has come upon us, for you have dealt faithfully and we have acted wickedly; [34]our kings, our officials, our priests, and our ancestors have not kept your law or heeded the commandments and the warnings that you gave them. [35]Even in their own kingdom, and in the great goodness you bestowed on them, and in the large and rich land that you set before them, they did not serve you and did not turn from their wicked works. [36]Here we are, slaves to this day—slaves in the land that you gave to our ancestors to enjoy its fruit and its good gifts."

[6]You alone are the LORD. You alone made heaven, even the heaven of heavens, with all their forces. You made the earth and all that is on it, and the seas and all that is in them. You preserve them all, and the heavenly forces worship you.

[7]LORD God, you are the one who chose Abram. You brought him out of Ur of the Chaldeans and gave him the name Abraham.

[9]You saw the affliction of our ancestors in Egypt and heard their cry at the Reed Sea.

[10]You performed signs and wonders against Pharaoh, all his servants, and the people of his land. You knew that they had acted arrogantly against our ancestors. You made a name for yourself, a name that is famous even today.

[30]You were patient with them for many years and warned them by your spirit through the prophets. But they wouldn't listen, so you handed them over to the neighboring peoples.

[31]In your great mercy, however, you didn't make an end of them. Neither did you forsake them, for you are a merciful and compassionate God.

[32]Now, our God, great and mighty and awesome God, you are the one who faithfully keeps the covenant. Don't treat lightly all of the hardship that has come upon us, upon our kings, our officials, our priests, our prophets, our ancestors, and all your people, from the time of the kings of Assyria until today.

[33]You have been just in all that has happened to us; you have acted faithfully, and we have done wrong.

[34]Our kings, our officials, our priests, and our ancestors haven't kept your Instruction. They haven't heeded your commandments and the warnings that you gave them.

[35]Even in their own kingdom, surrounded by the great goodness that you gave to them, even in the wide and rich land that you gave them, they didn't serve you or turn from their wicked works.

[36]So now today we are slaves, slaves in the land that you gave to our ancestors to enjoy its fruit and its good gifts.

UNDERSTANDING THE SCRIPTURE

Nehemiah 9:1-3. The twentieth-fourth day of "this" month seems to indicate the month of Tishri (September–October) and follows the weeklong festival of booths that was described in the preceding chapter. Fasting, wearing sackcloth, putting earth on one's head, and confessing sins are acts associated with mourning and repentance (see 1 Chronicles 21:16; Job 1:20; 2:12; Joshua 7:6; Daniel 9:3-4; Jonah 3:5, 8). The "separation" from foreigners may relate to the dissolution of mixed marriages referred to in Ezra 9–10, although the following confession does not specifically refer to this. Perhaps the people simply intended to separate themselves for the duration of the confession of their sins and those of their ancestors. Literally, "those of Israelite descent" is "the seed of Israel." "A fourth part of the day" signifies three hours (9:3).

Nehemiah 9:4-5. It is difficult to say exactly what (or where) the "stairs of the Levites" (9:4) are since they are not mentioned elsewhere in the Bible. Perhaps they are similar to the wooden platform (or "tower") mentioned in Nehemiah 8:4, although here they are reserved for the Levites alone. The term for "crying out" has the sense of pleading for deliverance in a time of distress.

Nehemiah 9:6. Many translations follow the ancient Greek version and put the following speech into the mouth of Ezra, although his name is missing in the Hebrew. Heavenly "hosts" refers to heavenly bodies such as the stars, sun, and moon (Genesis 2:1). Although sometimes such "hosts" were objects of worship in the ancient world (see Deuteronomy 4:19), this prayer emphasizes that they actually worship the Lord.

Nehemiah 9:7-8. Following creation, the prayer turns to the story of Abraham. By recalling the divine name change from "Abram" to "Abraham," the prayer emphasizes God's miraculous gift of fertility, such that Sarai and Abram had a child in their old age (see Genesis 17:5-8). The more literal translation of "you have fulfilled your promise" is "you established your words."

Nehemiah 9:9-11. For the story of slavery in Egypt, the plagues, and God's deliverance at the Red Sea, see the Book of Exodus, chapters 1–15. The "Red Sea" is also known as the "Sea of Reeds." "Making a name" for oneself is an expression signaling the completion of a deed that brings renown.

Nehemiah 9:12-15. For the events of the wilderness wanderings (including the giving of manna and water and the law), see Exodus 16–40; and Numbers 11:7-9; 20:7-11. Verse 15 describes the ancient gesture of oath making: A more literal translation of "land that you swore to give them" (9:15) is "the land which you lifted up the hand to give them."

Nehemiah 9:16-21. The verb for "acting presumptuously" in verse 16 is fairly rare in the Old Testament, but used twice in this chapter. By using this term for both the Egyptians in verse 10 and the ancestors in verse 16, the author makes a striking and unflattering parallel. There is another remarkable assertion in verse 17 when the prayers tell that the people were "determined to return to their slavery in Egypt." For the story of the golden calf, see Exodus 32.

Nehemiah 9:22-31. Entering into and living in the land is yet another occasion when God's goodness is met with the people's rebellion. Both Heshbon and Bashan are on the east side of the Jordan River, thus these victories occurred before the people entered into the Promised Land on the west side of the river. For more details about these battles, see Numbers 21:21-35 and Deuteronomy 2:24–3:11. "You [God] handed them over to the people of the lands" in 9:30 describes the capture of Jerusalem and the Babylonian exile.

Nehemiah 9:32-37. With the phrase "Now therefore," the long historical recital ends and a single petition is made: "Do not treat lightly all the hardship that has come upon us . . . since the time of the kings of Assyria until today" (9:32). This simple petition is followed by more description of God and the human community both in the past and in the present. Pointedly, the prayer recalls that the people who "did not serve" God in the past (8:35) have now become "slaves" even in the land of promise (8:36). Also, by using the Hebrew term for "given" to describe the process by which the people came to be ruled by foreign rulers (literally, "the kings you have given over us because of our sins," 9:37), the author is able to contrast God's earlier gift of the land (9:22). The Persian Empire demanded a fair amount of financial resources from its colonies to support its military campaigns, administration, and building programs. Verse 37 mentions military conscription and forced labor as well as the requisitioning of livestock; other biblical texts also speak of taxes in this period (including Ezra 4:13; 7:24 and see the high rates spoken of in Nehemiah 5:4). It is striking to note that although the Persians allowed the people to return to the land, and Nehemiah is additionally grateful that Artaxerxes allowed him to leave his duties and rebuild the wall of Jerusalem in a time of distress (Nehemiah 2), criticisms against the empire occasionally emerge in the biblical texts.

The prayer does not conclude at the end of chapter 9 but rather continues with a signed pledge in the next chapter. In the pledge, the people agree that they will not intermarry with the "peoples of the land," they will not buy grain on the sabbath day or any holy day, and every seven years they will forgive debts and let the land lie fallow (10:30-31). They also agree to support the Temple with agricultural gifts and a one-third shekel annual tax (10:32-39).

INTERPRETING THE SCRIPTURE

Prayer and Confession

Although the Bible has many prayers that praise God and give thanks for all of God's gracious acts, we also see some prayers that are confessional. Many times these are meant simply for an individual to say as a way to confess one's sins and beg for mercy. Nehemiah 9, though, is a confessional prayer that rehearses the sinfulness of present and past generations of God's people, and it has the entire community in mind.

The inclusion of a long historical narrative is also a feature of this kind of confessional prayer that can be found in other biblical texts. Psalms such as 105, 135, and 136 all contain long historical recitals that are meant to be prayed. Prayers that contain long historical recitals were also found in the Dead Sea Scrolls. In terms of the actual stories that are retold, Psalm 106 is probably the closest parallel that we have to Nehemiah 9. Both texts retell the story of the Exodus and settlement, and contain a similar pattern of rehearsing several cycles of people's rebellion and God's forgiveness. And although Psalm 106 starts out with praise in verses 1-2, after the historical recital the text ends like Nehemiah 9 with a prayer that God deliver the people from their distress (Psalm 106:47).

In the contemporary world, we might find it strange to include in our confession not only our own sins but those of our ancestors (9:2). However, as we shall see, the acts of previous generations and the mercies of God were central to the correct understanding of the current situation.

God's Acts and God's Mercies

Strikingly, the central feature of this communal confession is not really the community at all, but rather the deeds and nature of God. The first statement of the prayer is the short but significant line "You are the LORD, you alone" (9:6). The following verses begin with God's deeds in creation and then continue to tell of God's acts in history. Notice the simple repetition of the divine "You" throughout these verses: "You made heaven" (9:6), "You chose Abram" (9:7), "You performed signs and wonders against Pharaoh" (9:10), "You made a name for yourself" (9:10), "You divided the sea" (9:11), "You led them by day with a pillar of cloud" (9:12), "You came down also upon Mount Sinai" (9:13), "you made known your holy Sabbath to them" (9:14), and "For their hunger you gave them bread from heaven . . . you brought water for them . . . you told them to go in to possess the land that you swore to give them" (9:15).

By retelling history as the deeds of God, the prayer highlights the intense involvement of the divine actor. God has been active and part of human history from the very inception of the world. Implicitly, the prayer also says something about the chosen people even before they are mentioned, namely, that every moment of their lives has been dependent upon God. God has been their source of liberation from Egypt, their guide and guardian in the desert, and the One who promised them the land.

When the text finally mentions the people responding to this recitation in verse 16, it comes as a shock, and begins with the strategic word "but." Verse 16, of course, goes on to fill out the content of that strategic word, but the reader already knows from the very beginning that things will not go well: "But they and our ancestors acted presumptuously and stiffened their necks and did not obey your commandments" (9:16). The description of the ancestor's response could hardly be more condemnatory: By using the Hebrew term translated "presumptuously," the author is linking this verse to 9:10 (where the NRSV translation is "insolently"), and making a dramatic parallel between the ancestors and Egyptians. Just as Pharaoh and

his people acted "presumptuously" against the ancestors, so now the ancestors themselves act "presumptuously" against the very God who liberated them from Egypt.

Maybe even more surprising than the "but" that begins the account of Israel's response is the story of God's next act: "But you are a God ready to forgive, gracious and merciful . . . you did not forsake them" (9:17). God's gracious acts are responded to with impunity, and yet God acts with grace again. And in the verses that follow, we hear of several more cycles in which God acted with mercy only to have the people respond with disobedience followed by prayers for deliverance.

The cycles end with the verses that our lesson focuses on, namely verses 30-36. After God continued to respond to the people's sin with graciousness, things take a different turn in 9:30: "You handed them over to the peoples of the lands." Finally, God acts in a more reciprocal manner. Yet this divine destruction was still not the final word. It's as if God's habitual acts of grace were too ingrained in the divine character to be completely obliterated. In the very next words we hear again of God's mercy: "Nevertheless, in your great mercies you did not make an end of them or forsake them" (9:31). In the end, it seems, God's acts and God's mercies are one and the same.

History as Prayer

Students of biblical history will no doubt notice that the account in Nehemiah 9 looks different from other accounts of Israel's history in both what it includes and what it leaves out. For example, the list of the nations whose land was given to Abraham is different in Nehemiah 9:8 than it is in Genesis 15:19-21. The Abrahamic covenant is the only covenant mentioned in Nehemiah 9; there is no explicit mention of the covenant with either Noah or David. Neither is there any mention made of Joshua in its version of the conquest.

But of course, the point of *this* retelling of

God's acts is not historical reflection for its own sake. Although the text certainly rehearses some of the major points of Israel's history, the retelling is a prayer. Like the psalms that also retell Israel's history mentioned above (namely Psalms 105, 106, 135, and 136), Nehemiah 9 recounts the past with a clear focus on the present.

But what, exactly, is being asked for in this prayer? And how does the retelling of the past function in this prayer? Surprisingly, the actual petition does not occur until very late in the passage, with verse 32 to be exact: "Do not treat lightly all the hardship that has come upon us."

At first glance, this seems such a simple request. God is not even asked to take these "hardships" away but simply to take due consideration of them ("do not treat lightly"). One might even wonder if such a limited request is worth the long historical prelude. But perhaps praying the nation's history is the only way to make *any* request of God. For just as such a history reminds the people of their faithlessness and short-comings, it also reminds God of God's sur-prising (and unearned) acts of mercy. The history of this mercy may, in the end, be the only proper content of prayer.

SHARING THE SCRIPTURE

Preparing Our Hearts

Explore this week's devotional reading, found in Luke 15:1-10. Here we have the first two parables—the parable of the lost sheep and the parable of the lost coin—that Jesus tells in response to the religious leaders who are upset about the people with whom Jesus associates. The third parable in this group is the parable of the prodigal and his brother. The point of the first two parables, as seen in verses 7 and 10, respectively, is the joy experienced in heaven when one sinner repents. Search your heart. Are there sins of omission or sins of commission that you need to repent of right now?

Pray that you and the adult students will identify and confess your sins so that you may be forgiven and reconciled to God.

Preparing Our Minds

Study the background Scripture from Nehemiah 9:1-37 and the lesson Scripture from Nehemiah 9:2, 6-7, 9-10, 30-36.

Consider this question as you prepare the lesson: *What brings us to be honest about our shortcomings?*

Write on newsprint:
❑ information for next week's lesson, found under "Continue the Journey."
❑ activities for further spiritual growth in "Continue the Journey."

Review the "Introduction," "The Big Picture," "Close-up," and "Faith in Action." Consider how you will use this additional information, which immediately precedes the first lesson, for this session.

LEADING THE CLASS

(1) Gather to Learn

❖ Greet the class members. Introduce any guests and help them feel at home.

❖ Pray that those who have come to class today will recognize and confess their shortcomings.

❖ Read this very brief information about Reverend Arthur Dimmesdale, a main char-acter in Nathaniel Hawthorne's 1850 classic, *The Scarlet Letter*. Since this book is often read in high school and college literature courses, many students may be very familiar with it and able to add other details. **Thought to be a pious Puritan, Reverend Arthur Dimmesdale was revered as a holy man by his congregation. Yet lurking behind his apparently humble facade and self-effacing references to himself as a worthless creature was a troubled man. He had had an affair with Hester Prynne and had fathered her child, Pearl. Although Hester was forced to wear a scarlet "A" to denote her shameful status as an adulteress, Dimmesdale struggled internally with the idea of publicly acknowledging his daughter and his relationship with Hester. He was keenly aware of and tormented by his sin, yet could not bring himself to tell the truth about his illicit behavior. When he did finally confess to the townspeople, he fell down dead.**

❖ Ask: **Why are we so reluctant to tell the truth about ourselves?**

❖ Read aloud today's focus statement: **It is often hard to tell the truth about ourselves, especially our misdoings. What brings us to be honest about our shortcomings? The writer shows us that confession and repentance are necessary acts of worship, because God is merciful in every generation and gives people another chance.**

(2) Goal 1: Link the Public Reading of God's Word to Personal Acts of Confession and Repentance

❖ Select four volunteers to read Nehemiah 9:2-3, 6-7, 9-10, and 30-36.

❖ Note that the people heard God's Word read and then offered their confession as a nation. Ezra begins this prayer in verse 6, a description of who God is and what God does. Form two groups, distribute newsprint and markers, and ask both groups to look at verses 6-7, 9-10, and 30-36. (If time permits, invite them to look at verses 6-37, which include all of today's background Scripture.) One group is to list

words and phrases that describe God. The other group is to list God's actions.

❖ Call time and bring the groups together to report their findings. Then ask: **What do these verses teach us about God, particularly in relationship to sinful people?**

❖ Summarize this segment of the session by reading "God's Acts and God's Mercies" from Interpreting the Scripture.

(3) Goal 2: Hear God's Word and Confess Shortcomings

❖ Invite the class to be in a meditative mood as three volunteers read a communal prayer of confession from Psalm 106. Ask one volunteer to read verses 1-12, another to read verses 13-31, and a third to read verses 32-48.

❖ Read "Prayer and Confession" from Interpreting the Scripture to help the class draw parallels between Psalm 106 and Nehemiah 9.

❖ Challenge the adults to confess their shortcomings as a church and as a community. List their ideas on newsprint.

❖ Compare the confessions mentioned in Nehemiah 9 and Psalm 106 with those that the class has made. Try to identify similarities and differences.

❖ Ask these questions:
  (1) What do you think causes the people of our church and community to sin as a body? (Notice that the emphasis is on communal sin, not the sin of an individual.)
  (2) What might be the consequences of our corporate sin?
  (3) How might we work together to study God's Word, become aware of our sins, and regularly confess them?
  (4) If we are able to identify sins, what steps might we take to ask forgiveness from anyone we have harmed?

*(4) Goal 3: Write Personal Covenants With
God as a Result of Hearing God's Word
and Confessing Shortcomings*

❖ Distribute hymnals and invite the students to turn to the section where they will find confessions of sins. (If you have access to *The United Methodist Hymnal*, see pages 890–93.) Notice that confessions may be followed by words of assurance and pardon. Lead the group in reading at least one of these confessions aloud.

❖ Distribute paper and pencils. Encourage the adults to respond to their confession by writing a personal covenant. This need not be a formal document, but the learners need to pledge to take action. They may use the words of confession they just read, or one of the biblical passages we have considered, to prompt their thinking. For example, if we have confessed that we are not the loving people that God calls us to be, what can we do to become more loving? Or if we confess that we have strayed from God, what steps will we take to return home? What help or guidance will we need?

❖ Recognize that these covenants are private documents, but call on anyone who volunteers to share all or part of what he or she has written.

❖ Affirm the relationship between hearing the Word of God and confessing one's sins.

(5) Continue the Journey

❖ Pray that today's participants will recognize and confess their sins.

❖ Read aloud this preparation for next week's lesson. You may also want to post it on newsprint for the students to copy.
  ■ **Title: Dedication of the Wall**
  ■ **Background Scripture: Nehemiah 12:27-43**
  ■ **Lesson Scripture: Nehemiah 12:27-36, 38, 43**
  ■ **Focus of the Lesson: A sense of**

pride, joy, and thankfulness goes with the accomplishment of tasks. What triggers people to desire to celebrate specific accomplishments? Nehemiah's portrayal of the dedication of the wall is an act of worship thanking God and celebrating a community being restored.

❖ Post these three activities related to this week's session on newsprint for the students to copy. Challenge the adults to grow spiritually by completing one or more of them.

(1) **Read Psalm 51, which is attributed to David and occurs after he hears from the prophet Nathan concerning his adulterous relationship with Bathsheba. This psalm in which David confesses his sin and seeks God's forgiveness prompts readers to think about the nature of sin and guilt. How does this psalm compare with the confession in Nehemiah 9?**

(2) **Read Augustine's *Confessions*, a preeminent book of personal confession written by one of the most important shapers of the Christian church. Consider ways in which your life is similar to that of Augustine.**

(3) **Identify communal sins of your nation. Are there people who have been harmed by your nation's policies? If so, are there ways to make restitution to them? Have national practices harmed God's good earth? If so, what might be done to help the earth recover?**

❖ Sing or read aloud "When the Church of Jesus."

❖ Conclude today's session by leading the class in this benediction, adapted from the key verse for June 9 from Isaiah 12:4: **Let us go forth continually giving thanks, proclaiming God's mighty deeds, and exalting God's holy name.**

UNIT 3: WORSHIPING IN JERUSALEM AGAIN (NEHEMIAH)

DEDICATION OF THE WALL

PREVIEWING THE LESSON

Lesson Scripture: Nehemiah 12:27-36, 38, 43
Background Scripture: Nehemiah 12:27-43
Key Verse: Nehemiah 12:43

Focus of the Lesson:

A sense of pride, joy, and thankfulness goes with the accomplishment of tasks. What triggers people to desire to celebrate specific accomplishments? Nehemiah's portrayal of the dedication of the wall is an act of worship thanking God and celebrating a community being restored.

Goals for the Learners:

(1) to unpack the narrative of the dedication of the wall as a joyous but formal praise service.
(2) to identify their feelings upon completing a significant task.
(3) to develop worship that celebrates specific accomplishments of the community.

Pronunciation Guide:

Ammonite (am' uh nite)	Jezrahiah (jez ri hi' uh)
Artaxerxes (ahr tuh zuhrk' seez)	Maai (may' i)
Asaph (ay' saf)	Mattaniah (mat' uh ni' uh)
Azarel (az' uh rel)	Meshullam (mi shool' uhm)
Azariah (az uh ri' uh)	Micaiah (mi kay' yuh)
Azmaveth (az' muh veth)	Milalai (mil' uh li)
Beth-gilgal (beth gil' gal)	Nethanel (ni than' uhl)
Geba (gee' buh)	Netophathite (ni tof' uh thite)
Gilalai (gil' uh li)	Sanballet (san bal' at)
Hanani (huh nay' ni)	Shemaiah (shi may' yuh)
Horonite (hor' uh nite)	Tobiah (toh bi' uh)
Hoshaiah (hoh shay' yuh)	Zaccur (zak' uhr)

Supplies:

Bibles, newsprint and marker, paper and pencils, hymnals

READING THE SCRIPTURE

NRSV

Lesson Scripture: Nehemiah 12:27-36, 38, 43

27Now at the dedication of the wall of Jerusalem they sought out the Levites in all their places, to bring them to Jerusalem to celebrate the dedication with rejoicing, with thanksgivings and with singing, with cymbals, harps, and lyres. 28The companies of the singers gathered together from the circuit around Jerusalem and from the villages of the Netophathites; 29also from Beth-gilgal and from the region of Geba and Azmaveth; for the singers had built for themselves villages around Jerusalem. 30And the priests and the Levites purified themselves; and they purified the people and the gates and the wall.

31Then I brought the leaders of Judah up onto the wall, and appointed two great companies that gave thanks and went in procession. One went to the right on the wall to the Dung Gate; 32and after them went Hoshaiah and half the officials of Judah, 33and Azariah, Ezra, Meshullam, 34Judah, Benjamin, Shemaiah, and Jeremiah, 35and some of the young priests with trumpets: Zechariah son of Jonathan son of Shemaiah son of Mattaniah son of Micaiah son of Zaccur son of Asaph; 36and his kindred, Shemaiah, Azarel, Milalai, Gilalai, Maai, Nethanel, Judah, and Hanani, with the musical instruments of David the man of God; and the scribe Ezra went in front of them.

38The other company of those who gave thanks went to the left, and I followed them with half of the people on the wall, above the Tower of the Ovens, to the Broad Wall.

43They offered great sacrifices that day and rejoiced, for God had made them rejoice with great joy; the women and children also rejoiced. The joy of Jerusalem was heard far away.

CEB

Lesson Scripture: Nehemiah 12:27-36, 38, 43

27When it was time for the dedication of Jerusalem's wall, they sought out the Levites in all the places where they lived in order to bring them to Jerusalem to celebrate the dedication with joy, with thanks and singing, and with cymbals, harps, and lyres.

28The singers also gathered together both from the region around Jerusalem and from the villages of the Netophathites, 29also from Beth-hagilgal and from the region of Geba and Azmaveth, because the singers had built themselves villages around Jerusalem. 30After the priests and the Levites purified themselves, they purified the people, the gates, and the wall.

31Then I brought the leaders of Judah up onto the wall and organized two large groups to give thanks. The first group went in procession on the wall toward the right, in the direction of the Dung Gate. 32Following them went Hoshaiah and half the officials of Judah, 33along with Azariah, Ezra, Meshullam, 34Judah, Benjamin, Shemaiah, and Jeremiah. 35There were also some young priests with trumpets—Zechariah son of Jonathan son of Shemaiah son of Mattaniah son of Micaiah son of Zaccur son of Asaph— 36along with his associates Shemaiah, Azarel, Milalai, Gilalai, Maai, Nethanel, Judah, and Hanani. They brought the musical instruments of David the man of God. Ezra the scribe went in front of them.

38The second group went in procession to the left. I followed them with half of the people along the wall past the Tower of the Ovens to the Broad Wall.

43They offered great sacrifices on that day and rejoiced, for God had made them rejoice with great joy. The women and children also rejoiced, and the sound of the joy in Jerusalem could be heard from far away.

UNDERSTANDING THE SCRIPTURE

Introduction. After the great prayer in Nehemiah 9, the people rededicate themselves to following God's commandments and supporting the Temple, and they mark their dedication with a signed pledge (Nehemiah 10). Chapter 11 then lists the tribal leaders who went to live in Jerusalem, and chapter 12 continues with additional census lists. The story of the dedication of Jerusalem's walls begins in Nehemiah 12:27.

Nehemiah 12:27-30. The account of the dedication starts with the assembling of the three main groups of religious and liturgical leaders: the Levites, the priests, and the companies of singers (literally, "the sons of the singers"). Some members of these groups seem to have lived permanently in Jerusalem, while others apparently lived in villages close by and stayed in the city for the duration of their time of service. The settlements mentioned are fairly close to Jerusalem; most are less than six miles away.

The purification ritual that precedes the dedication service here is not described, but other biblical passages may give us some clues. The purification of *people* can involve fasting, sexual abstinence, washing one's clothes, making sacrifices, and being sprinkled with water or blood (for abstaining from sex and washing clothes in preparation to meet God, see Exodus 19:11-15; for purification involving shaving, washing clothes, and the sprinkling of water, see Numbers 8:7-8; for bathing, shaving, washing one's clothes, and being sprinkled with blood to be purified after a skin disease, see Leviticus 14:4-7). The purification of specific *structures* such as gates and a city wall reflects a ritual about which we read very little in the Bible. It may have involved the sprinkling of water, similar perhaps to what we read of in Numbers 19:18 when the tent of someone who had recently died is purified by sprinkled water.

Nehemiah 12:31-37. Verse 31 returns the narrative to the voice of Nehemiah himself, picking up from 7:5 and continuing through the end of the book. Commentaries often refer to this section as part of a "Nehemiah Memoir," that is, a biography written by Nehemiah himself. In the section of this "memoir" that begins in 12:31, Nehemiah describes the great procession around the city walls by two separate but similar groups, walking past various gates and landmarks. The first group heads southward on the walls, walking counterclockwise. Careful readers will notice that the two groups are numerically and functionally parallel: following a thanksgiving choir (12:31, 38) comes one half of the lay leadership (led by Hoshaiah in 12:32 and Nehemiah in 12:38), followed by groups of musicians including seven priests with trumpets (12:33-35, 41), a music director (Zechariah in 12:35 and Jezrahiah in 12:42), and finally eight musicians from the Levites (12:36, 42). The scribe Ezra is said to lead the first group in 12:36, but curiously, his name is mentioned at the end of the list.

It is difficult to reconstruct precisely the procession and the walls of Jerusalem at this time. Some of the textual details are obscure, and the archaeological remains admit of several possibilities for interpretation. However, although the exact details of the various gates and towers may be lost to us now, the existence of a secure wall around Jerusalem was clearly a much-treasured ambition of this period.

The mention of the "house of David" in 12:37 may refer to the original palace of the Davidic kings, presumably in ruins after the Babylonian destruction. It is also possible that it refers, rather, to the tomb of David and his household, mentioned in Nehemiah 3:16 in the description of the people building the wall.

Nehemiah 12:38-42. The second procession heads northward on the walls (the

Hebrew in 12:38 reads, literally, "opposite").

Nehemiah 12:43. At the end of the procession, the two groups come to the Temple, where they reassemble and enter into the holy area. The "great" (that is, "many") sacrifices offered that day certainly included thank offerings or offerings of well-being. According to Leviticus 3, for such offerings the layperson would present to the priests an unblemished animal at the entrance to the worship space. Then the priests would offer the kidneys and fat (sometimes called "suet") to the Lord by burning them on the altar ("an offering by fire of pleasing odor to the LORD," according to Leviticus 3:5). Then the rest of the animal would be eaten by the priests and the family who offered it. In this way, God, the priests, and the people all joined together in a kind of communion meal, and this seems the kind of celebration that is in view in Nehemiah 12.

The careful reader will note the repetition of the verb "rejoice," followed by mention of the "joy of Jerusalem"—as a verb or a noun the term is used five times within this single verse. Clearly the author wanted to emphasize the celebratory aspect of the dedication service. This emphasis on joy, along with the mention of the presence of women and children, puts one in mind of prior celebrations of the postexilic community in Jerusalem. The description of the noise in 12:43 ("The joy of Jerusalem was heard far away") also forms a link to earlier festivities. When the people celebrated the dedication of the altar in Ezra 3, "the people shouted so loudly that the sound was heard far away" (Ezra 3:13). On that occasion, however, the joy was mixed with the weeping of "many of the priests and Levites and heads of families, old people who had seen the first house on its foundations" (Ezra 3:12). The noisy celebration in Nehemiah 12 is an example of unalloyed joy, more similar to that of the community celebrating the dedication of the Temple in Ezra 6:16-17 with a multitude of sacrifices and burnt offerings.

INTERPRETING THE SCRIPTURE

The Importance of the Walls of Jerusalem

The Book of Nehemiah begins with the dramatic announcement in Babylon that the residents of Jerusalem are in great distress: "The wall of Jerusalem is broken down, and its gates have been destroyed by fire!" (1:3). Nehemiah responds in great shock, and acts as if one of his closest relatives had just died: "When I heard these words I sat down and wept, and mourned for days, fasting and praying before the God of heaven" (1:4). With the permission of the Persian emperor Artaxerxes, Nehemiah journeys to Jerusalem on a mission to rebuild the walls (2:7-11).

As is clear from his initial reaction to the news of their destruction, Nehemiah regards the state of the city's walls as much more than simply a public-works project. For him and his contemporaries, the city walls are inextricably linked with the very well-being of the entire nation. This is partially seen in the various reactions to the news of the rebuilding project. When Nehemiah's enemies Sanballet the Horonite and Tobiah the Ammonite hear that the building materials for the walls have been secured, they become angry that "someone had come to seek the welfare of the people of Israel" (2:10). The deeper significance of the walls is also seen in the speech that Nehemiah gives to the city leaders in order to motivate them in the task of rebuilding: "Come, let us rebuild the wall of Jerusalem, so that we may no longer suffer disgrace" (2:17).

Completing the Walls of Jerusalem

It is this connection of the walls with national well-being that explains the long list of names in Nehemiah 12 of those who took part in the dedicatory procession. Such lists may seem dull and overly long to contemporary readers, and sound a clashing note in the context of a joyous celebration. Yet they point to the significance that the entire community placed upon these walls, and their pride in being part of the building project. In some ways, this list provides a satisfying balance to the list in Nehemiah 3 that names the individuals and groups who repaired the walls, as well as the specific sections for which they were responsible. The task of rebuilding was arduous as well as dangerous. At one point the text tells us that Nehemiah received intimidating letters and death threats (6:10, 19), and the builders worked with weapons ready at their sides (4:15-18). Jerusalem's walls (and the national well-being that they represent) were built and celebrated by particular individuals, and their dedication is marked in such lists for future generations to read. There were surely others who worked on these walls whose names are not recorded in any list in Nehemiah or anywhere else for that matter—and just as surely all of the builders, named and unnamed, who joined together in the work also joined together in celebrating the completion of their task.

Dedicating the Walls of Jerusalem

Fittingly, those who dedicated themselves to the building of the walls and their gates now themselves dedicate these same walls and gates. In addition, they also give thanks to the God whose hand was very much in evidence throughout the building process. In Nehemiah 12 we see the community responding to God with joyous gratitude upon the wall's completion. They celebrate the fulfillment of their difficult task as a way of acknowledging God's deci-

sive role in the endeavor. In Nehemiah's account, this role was evident to the people who built, as well as even to the adversaries who tried to thwart the project. When news that the wall was completed spread abroad, their enemies were "afraid . . . for they perceived that this work had been accomplished with the help of our God" (6:16).

It might seem that such explicitly religious celebrations would be more in keeping with the dedication of a religious space such as a temple rather than the more "secular" arena of the city walls and gates. Including priests and Levites with the laity in the procession, purifying the walls and gates and marking the occasion with sacrifices seems to be a clear violation of the contemporary notion of the separation between church and state. Yet such separation was clearly of little import to the postexilic community. In fact, the author of Nehemiah 12 makes a clear parallel between the city walls and the central religious symbol, namely the Temple.

This parallel is made, primarily, by the repetition of key features in the description of the dedication of the altar in Ezra 3, the dedication of the rebuilt Temple in Ezra 6, and the dedication of the walls here in Nehemiah 12. Central to the act of "dedicating" is giving something over to God's protection and use. Although we may think of God's relationship with Jerusalem's Temple as quite distinct from God's relationship to its walls, the "dedication" in chapter 12 belies such an assumption. In addition to the very use of the term "dedication" for the walls, we see other similar features in the dedication services of the Temple and walls.

The first is the participation of the laity along with the ordained ranks. At the Temple's dedication "the people of Israel, the priests and the Levites, and the rest of the returned exiles" joined together to celebrate (Ezra 6:16). The procession around the walls included two groups of lay leaders, followed by priests and Levites (Nehemiah 12:31-36, 40-42).

In a related way, the choice to include *seven* trumpet-bearing priests in the procession around the walls may be an explicit link with another religious procession, namely when David brought the ark to Jerusalem as retold in 1 Chronicles 15:24. By making a parallel in personnel, the author of Nehemiah is highlighting the parallels between the city walls and the Temple's furnishings.

An additional parallel is the offering of many sacrifices to mark the occasion of dedication. In Nehemiah 12, the community offers "great sacrifices" (12:43). The sacrifices in Ezra 6 are also numerous, namely one hundred bulls, two hundred rams, four hundred lambs, and twelve goats (Ezra 6:17).

The most dramatic parallel between these dedication accounts is the incorporation of loud and joyful music, and the emphasis on joy. According to Ezra 6:16, the community marked the Temple's dedication "with joy." The dedication of the altar was also marked with joyous shouts and praise sung by responsive choirs, although there were also those present who wept (Ezra 3:11-13). The dedication in Nehemiah 12 is pure joy, however. After the thanksgiving choirs and the trumpets processed around the walls, the community gathered at the Temple and "rejoiced" so greatly that "the joy of Jerusalem was heard far away" (12:43).

Seeing these parallels between the dedication services of the Temple and the walls makes clear a central tenet of the postexilic community: The religious and the secular are one. This is a people for whom the urban space of Jerusalem is first and foremost a religious space. In ways similar to the Temple, the walls of Jerusalem are a symbol of the community itself, and God's presence with that community. The Temple and the walls both are central features of the "holy city" (11:1).

SHARING THE SCRIPTURE

Preparing Our Hearts

Explore this week's devotional reading, found in Psalm 96. The psalmist celebrates the enthronement of the Lord as king. In the three stanzas of this song God is praised as the creator and ruler of the universe. God is also portrayed as a savior and deliverer who is the righteous judge of all. Because this psalm's text can be traced to other psalms and to Isaiah 40–55, some commentators view this song as the parent of hymnody. Try reading this psalm aloud, preferably from several translations. Which one really "sings" for you? Make this psalm your hymn of praise for the week.

Pray that you and the adult students will worship God joyfully.

Preparing Our Minds

Study the background Scripture from Nehemiah 12:27-43 and the lesson Scripture from Nehemiah 12:27-36, 38, 43.

Consider this question as you prepare the lesson: *What triggers people to desire to celebrate specific accomplishments?*

Write on newsprint:

❑ information for next week's lesson, found under "Continue the Journey."

❑ activities for further spiritual growth in "Continue the Journey."

Review the "Introduction," "The Big Picture," "Close-up," and "Faith in Action." Consider how you will use this additional information, which immediately precedes the first lesson, for this session.

Contact two class members early in the week who will be prepared to play the roles of Ezra and Nehemiah for "Unpack the Narrative of the Dedication of the Wall as a Joyous but Formal Praise Service."

Be prepared to read the Scripture. The "Pronunciation Guide" will be of help to you.

Use information from all of Interpreting the Scripture to summarize the importance of the walls and their dedication in the "Unpack the Narrative of the Dedication of the Wall as a Joyous but Formal Praise Service" segment.

LEADING THE CLASS

(1) Gather to Learn

❖ Greet the class members. Introduce any guests and help them feel at home.

❖ Pray that those who have gathered for class today will experience joy in the Lord and a sense of accomplishment in whatever they are able to do.

❖ Invite the adults to think back to a time when their church building was consecrated or rededicated after a major renovation. As you read the following excerpt of a prayer from *The United Methodist Book of Worship*, encourage the learners to recall how they felt at the dedication, or might have felt had they been present at such a dedication.

O eternal God, mighty in power and of incomprehensible majesty, whom the heavens cannot contain, much less the walls of temples made with hands, you have promised your special presence whenever two or three are assembled in your name to offer praise and prayer.

By the power of your Holy Spirit *consecrate* this house of your worship. Bless us and sanctify what we do here, that this place may be holy for us and a house of prayer for all people.

Guide and empower in this place by the same Spirit the proclamation of your Word and the celebration of your Sacraments, the pouring out of prayer, and the singing of your praise, professions of faith and testimonies to your grace, the joining of men and women in marriage, and the celebration of death and resurrection.

❖ Ask: **What would be your response to the completion of such a major task as you participated in the dedication of a building to the service of God?**

❖ Read aloud today's focus statement: **A sense of pride, joy, and thankfulness goes with the accomplishment of tasks. What triggers people to desire to celebrate specific accomplishments? Nehemiah's portrayal of the dedication of the wall is an act of worship thanking God and celebrating a community being restored.**

(2) Goal 1: Unpack the Narrative of the Dedication of the Wall as a Joyous but Formal Praise Service

❖ Read "Introduction" in Understanding the Scripture to bridge the gap between last week's lesson and this one.

❖ Present the summary you have developed of the entire Interpreting the Scripture portion to help the students understand why the walls themselves were so important and, in turn, why their dedication prompted such a major celebration.

❖ Prepare to read Nehemiah 12:27-36, 38, 43 yourself, since it includes many names that are found in the "Pronunciation Guide."

❖ Invite two volunteers with whom you spoke early in the week to give a firsthand report of the events related to the dedication of the city wall. One may play the role of Ezra; the other, Nehemiah. They are to talk about how the celebration, music, procession, and so on, as recorded in Nehemiah 12:27-43, affected them.

❖ **Option:** If you did not arrange for these firsthand accounts based on Scripture, invite volunteers from the audience to discuss this praise service from their perspective.

(3) Goal 2: Identify the Learners' Feelings Upon Completing a Significant Task

❖ Prompt the learners to recall their feelings as they considered the dedication of a church building in the "Gather to Learn" portion.

❖ Invite the participants to think of other significant tasks and the feelings associated with completing them. Go around the room and give each person an opportunity to state in two or three sentences what the task was and the emotions its completion evoked.

❖ Ask: **Why do we feel so gratified— and perhaps relieved—when a major task is completed?**

(4) Goal 3: Develop Worship That Celebrates Specific Accomplishments of the Community

❖ Distribute hymnals, paper, and pencils. Write this list on newsprint:

Hymn(s)   Sermon Title
Prayer   Scriptures

❖ Form several small groups. Challenge each one to think of the completion of some task that your congregation could celebrate. Then they are to choose hymns, Scriptures, and a sermon title for this occasion, and write a prayer of praise and thanksgiving to God for enabling them to complete the task.

❖ Call the groups together and let each one share the worship elements they have selected.

❖ **Option:** Instead of asking the groups to name their selected elements, if time permits encourage them to present a portion of the worship they envision. The class should be able to discern the tone of the service.

(5) Continue the Journey

❖ Pray that those who have attended today will celebrate the accomplishments of their own congregation.

❖ Read aloud this preparation for next week's lesson. You may also want to post it on newsprint for the students to copy.

■ Title: Sabbath Reforms

■ **Background Scripture: Nehemiah 13:4-31**

■ **Lesson Scripture: Nehemiah 13:15-22**

■ **Focus of the Lesson: People sometimes make demands of those who are breaking community rules. Which community rules are important enough for everyone to follow consistently? Keeping the sabbath was so important to the welfare of God's community that Nehemiah ordered the gates shut to prevent the Israelites from breaking this law.**

❖ Post these three activities related to this week's session on newsprint for the students to copy. Challenge the adults to grow spiritually by completing one or more of them.

(1) Recall significant tasks that your congregation has undertaken in the past several years. As each task was finished, how did the members celebrate? If you have not celebrated, consider finding ways to celebrate now. You may focus on a "bricks-and-mortar" type task, or a program of ministry or outreach that helped others.

(2) Thank someone in the congregation or community who was instrumental in completing a major task.

(3) Research the role of the Levites, who figure prominently in this week's Scripture lesson. Use concordances, Bible dictionaries, study Bibles, or online resources. Compare what you find in your research with the role that the Levites played in the dedication of the walls of Jerusalem.

❖ Sing or read aloud "When in Our Music God Is Glorified."

❖ Conclude today's session by leading the class in this benediction, adapted from the key verse for June 9 from Isaiah 12:4: **Let us go forth continually giving thanks, proclaiming God's mighty deeds, and exalting God's holy name.**

UNIT 3: WORSHIPING IN JERUSALEM AGAIN (NEHEMIAH)
SABBATH REFORMS

PREVIEWING THE LESSON

Lesson Scripture: Nehemiah 13:15-22
Background Scripture: Nehemiah 13:4-31
Key Verse: Nehemiah 13:22

Focus of the Lesson:
People sometimes make demands of those who are breaking community rules. Which community rules are important enough for everyone to follow consistently? Keeping the sabbath was so important to the welfare of God's community that Nehemiah ordered the gates shut to prevent the Israelites from breaking this law.

Goals for the Learners:
(1) to explore what Nehemiah said and did about the inviolability of the sabbath.
(2) to examine their feelings about the importance of sabbath and the ways they may violate it.
(3) to compare and contrast the sabbath practices in Nehemiah's day with ours today.

Pronunciation Guide:
Ammon (am' uhn)
Artaxerxes (ahr tuh zuhrk' seez)
Ashdod (ash' dod)
Eliashib (i li uh shib)
Jehoiada (ji hoi' uh dih)
Levite (lee' vite)

Moab (moh' ab)
Sanballet (san bal' at)
Tobiah (to bi' uh)
Tyre (tire)
Tyrian (tihr' ee uhn)

Supplies:
Bibles, newsprint and marker, paper and pencils, hymnals

READING THE SCRIPTURE

NRSV
Lesson Scripture: Nehemiah 13:15-22
   ¹⁵In those days I saw in Judah people treading wine presses on the sabbath, and

CEB
Lesson Scripture: Nehemiah 13:15-22
   ¹⁵In those days I saw people in Judah using the winepresses on the Sabbath. They

bringing in heaps of grain and loading them on donkeys; and also wine, grapes, figs, and all kinds of burdens, which they brought into Jerusalem on the sabbath day; and I warned them at that time against selling food. [16]Tyrians also, who lived in the city, brought in fish and all kinds of merchandise and sold them on the sabbath to the people of Judah, and in Jerusalem. [17]Then I remonstrated with the nobles of Judah and said to them, "What is this evil thing that you are doing, profaning the sabbath day? [18]Did not your ancestors act in this way, and did not our God bring all this disaster on us and on this city? Yet you bring more wrath on Israel by profaning the sabbath."

[19]When it began to be dark at the gates of Jerusalem before the sabbath, I commanded that the doors should be shut and gave orders that they should not be opened until after the sabbath. And I set some of my servants over the gates, to prevent any burden from being brought in on the sabbath day. [20]Then the merchants and sellers of all kinds of merchandise spent the night outside Jerusalem once or twice. [21]But I warned them and said to them, "Why do you spend the night in front of the wall? If you do so again, I will lay hands on you." From that time on they did not come on the sabbath. [22]And **I commanded the Levites that they should purify themselves and come and guard the gates, to keep the sabbath day holy.** Remember this also in my favor, O my God, and spare me according to the greatness of your steadfast love.

were also collecting piles of grain and loading them on donkeys, as well as wine, grapes, figs, and every kind of load, and then bringing them to Jerusalem on the Sabbath. I warned them at that time against selling food.

[16]In addition, people from Tyre who lived in the city were bringing in fish and all kinds of merchandise and selling them to the people of Judah on the Sabbath. This happened in Jerusalem itself!

[17]So I scolded the officials of Judah: "What is this evil thing that you are doing?" I asked. "You are making the Sabbath impure! [18]This is just what your ancestors did, and God brought all this evil upon us and upon this city. And now you are bringing more wrath upon Israel by making the Sabbath impure!"

[19]So when it began to grow dark at the gates of Jerusalem before the Sabbath, I gave orders that the doors should be shut. I also ordered that they shouldn't be re-opened until after the Sabbath. To make sure that no load would come into the city on the Sabbath, I stationed some of my own men at the gates. [20]Once or twice the traders and sellers of all kinds of merchandise spent the night outside Jerusalem. [21]But I warned them: "Why are you spending the night by the wall? If you do that again, I will lay hands on you!" At that point, they stopped coming on the Sabbath. [22]**I also commanded the Levites to purify themselves and to come and guard the gates in order to keep the Sabbath day holy.**

Remember this also in my favor, my God, and spare me according to the greatness of your mercy.

UNDERSTANDING THE SCRIPTURE

Introduction. The last chapter of Nehemiah tells of his "second" term as governor, or leader, in Jerusalem. In 13:6, Nehemiah mentions that he left Jerusalem in Artaxerxes' thirty-second year (about 432 B.C.) and returned to Babylon. Although the text does not give the length of his absence from Jerusalem, he returns to the city with a great deal of authority over the Temple buildings, the Temple's funding, and the city gates. It is interesting to note that in this second period, Nehemiah's leadership has a different profile than his first: In chapters 1–12 he is concerned primarily with building the wall, but in the final chapter he turns his attention to matters more explicitly religious.

Nehemiah 13:4-9. The Book of Nehemiah mentions Tobiah the Ammonite, who tries to thwart the plans of Nehemiah. In 2:10, Tobiah and Sanballat the Horonite are greatly displeased that Nehemiah has come to Jerusalem to rebuild the city's walls. And in 6:17-19 we hear that Tobiah was kept informed of Nehemiah's plans by letters sent to him by the leaders in Judah, and that Tobiah also sent out his own letters in an effort to "intimidate" Nehemiah. Although Nehemiah was able to complete the walls, Tobiah clearly maintained some power and, according to verse 5, was able to convince Eliashib to install him in a Temple apartment (previously occupied by vessels and offerings)—quite a remarkable place for a layperson and a foreigner to occupy.

When Nehemiah learns of this news, the text relates his anger at the defilement of holy space. Notice that, in this account, the word "temple" is never used; the sacred precinct is called "the house of God" or "the house of our God" three times (13:4, 7, 9), emphasizing the divine association. And after he throws out Tobiah's furniture, Nehemiah realizes that it is not enough to clean and then ritually "cleanse" the room.

All of the areas in the surrounding "chambers" must also be purified (13:9). It is only after this that the room is ready for its proper use: the storage of ritual vessels, as well as the frankincense and the grain offering.

Nehemiah 13:10-14. Nehemiah's attention to the Temple rooms now expands to the welfare of the Temple's worship leaders. Realizing that lack of financial support for some of the Levites and the Temple singers has forced them to leave Jerusalem and return to "their fields" (13:10), Nehemiah takes several steps to alleviate the situation. First of all, he scolds the officials, asking them, "Why is the house of God forsaken?" (13:11). Then he brings the worship leaders back to Jerusalem. Finally, once Judah brings in their various offerings, Nehemiah then sets up trustworthy leaders to distribute the goods (13:12-13). Nehemiah closes this story with a prayer to God, asking that his "good deeds" (literally, works motivated by covenant loyalty) not be "wiped out" by God.

Nehemiah 13:15-18. Having dealt with sacred space (namely, the chambers of the Temple) and sacred people (namely, the Levites and singers who lead the Temple's worship), Nehemiah now turns his attention to sacred time, namely, the sabbath.

As he did when he realized that the worship leaders were not supported, Nehemiah takes his complaint to the leaders of Judah (13:17, see also 13:11). His words are harsh, and reach their sharpest pitch when he contrasts "your ancestors" with "our God," thus disassociating himself from the sinful nation (13:18).

Nehemiah 13:19-22. Ancient city walls were protected by large wooden gates into which were set smaller doors that could be closed with greater ease. The area in front of the gates was a place to congregate, where legal cases could be heard (as in the story of

Ruth 4:1-2), and merchandise could be sold. When Nehemiah realizes that barring the gates on the sabbath did not completely solve his problem (the merchants could simply bed down by the walls), he resorts to threats: "If you [sleep by the wall] again, I will lay hands on you!" (13:21). As after the story of cleansing the Temple from Tobiah's residence, Nehemiah concludes this story with a prayer that God "remember" him and spare his life based on God's covenant loyalty (13:22).

Nehemiah 13:23-29. In the last account of his work in Jerusalem, Nehemiah tells how he had the community take an oath promising that they would not intermarry with the neighboring tribes of Ashdod, Ammon, and Moab. Of particular concern for him is the issue that the children of such unions "could not speak the language of Judah" (13:24), meaning that they would not be able to engage the history and the law except in translation. For Nehemiah, mixed marriages would lead to "sin," and he cites the example of King Solomon's wives (1 Kings 11:1-8). Although the text is not explicit, the implication is that marriage with a foreigner leads to a division in loyalty with regard to religious worship. Or, as Nehemiah himself puts it, doing "all this great evil and act[ing] treacherously against our God" (13:27). Given the consequences of such marriages, Nehemiah takes extreme actions, including reproaching and cursing the guilty parties, beating them, pulling out their hair, and making them take an oath against such marriages (13:25). Pulling out the hair is an expression both of grief (Ezra 9:3) and an example of degrading punishment (Isaiah 50:6).

The son of Jehoiada, son of the high priest Eliashib, comes under particular censure from Nehemiah in verse 28 since priests were mandated to "marry a virgin of his own kin" (Leviticus 21:14). This story of the oath against intermarriage ends with an interesting twist: Instead of Nehemiah praying that God "remember" him for his good deeds as he did in 13:14, he prays that God "remember" priests such as Jehoiada's son "because they have defiled the priesthood, the covenant of the priests and the Levites" (13:29).

Nehemiah 13:30-31. Nehemiah closes his account with a final notice of additional accomplishments, and a final prayer that God "remember" him, "for good" (13:31).

INTERPRETING THE SCRIPTURE

Sacred Time

Central to this passage is a concern with the proper keeping of the sabbath day. Twice within two verses Nehemiah accuses the "nobles of Judah" of "profaning the sabbath," and thus threatening the entire community with God's wrath (13:17-18).

The offense that Nehemiah is dealing with is stated clearly in verses 15 and 16: People in Judah were treading winepresses, loading foodstuffs onto donkeys, and bringing this merchandise into Jerusalem on the sabbath. In addition, Tyrians were bringing fish and other products and selling them in Jerusalem on the sabbath.

Nehemiah is clearly engaging with the rules and traditions about the sabbath day that we now find recorded throughout parts of the Bible. In the version of the Ten Commandments found in Exodus 20, the fourth command states that on the seventh day, the people and all in their community were not to work: neither "you, your son or your daughter, your male or female slave, your livestock, or the alien resident in your towns" (Exodus 20:10).

Similar sabbath rulings appear in different texts, and they are interesting to compare because they often convey slightly different emphases—emphases that Nehemiah himself may have been trying to enact. Unique within the Ten Commandments given in Exodus 20, the sabbath rule includes a kind of justification based on divine precedent: "For in six days the LORD made heaven and earth, the sea, and all that is in them, but rested the seventh day" (Exodus 20:11). Also unique to this command is a statement about God's blessing: "The LORD blessed the sabbath day and consecrated it" (Exodus 20:11).

In other texts we see different variations on the justification. In Exodus 23:12 the text mentions the need for rest: "On the seventh day you shall rest, so that your ox and your donkey may have relief, and your homeborn slave and the resident alien may be refreshed." For anyone who may be tempted to read this justification as a savvy business strategy (promising a "carrot" at the end of a workweek as a way to boost productivity), the expansion in Deuteronomy 5:12-15 explicitly links this rest with the plight of the worker: "Remember that you were a slave in the land of Egypt, and the LORD your God brought you out from there with a mighty hand and an outstretched arm; therefore the LORD your God commanded you to keep the sabbath day" (Deuteronomy 5:15).

Still other versions contain other differences. After the people break the covenant during the incident of the golden calf (Exodus 32), the text records another set of commandments in Exodus 34 that includes the sabbath ruling. Here, however, there is no justification given but rather a clarification stipulating that at no times during the year can the sabbath be disregarded: "Six days you shall work, but on the seventh day you shall rest; even in plowing time and in harvest time you shall rest" (Exodus 34:21).

Clearly Nehemiah considered that workers treading winepresses and loading merchandise, animals forced to carry burdens, and anyone involved in commercial transactions were violating the sabbath command. Although he does not name any one of the particular justifications for the ruling (*divine precedent, need for rest, or identification with the plight of the worker*), he clearly understands the stakes. When the ancestors acted similarly, God brought "disaster" upon them. Now the people are themselves bringing "more wrath on Israel by profaning the sabbath" (13:18).

Sacred Spaces

Although the passage in this lesson has a clear emphasis on the sabbath, attention to this sacred time should not totally obliterate the text's concern with sacred space. Properly understanding the issue of the sabbath in Nehemiah 13 demands that we also look at the way the text presents various geographies.

When Nehemiah returns to Jerusalem from Babylon for the second time, he finds that his work on the wall now must be supported by work on other aspects of communal life in Jerusalem. As important as it was to build and repair the walls, Nehemiah finds that he must also tend to the areas now enclosed by these walls. He begins with the Temple. First he cleans the rooms previously occupied by Tobiah and then returns them to their proper use as storerooms for Temple vessels, the grain offerings, and the frankincense (13:4-9). Second, in the course of these tasks, he realizes that the Temple is not being properly staffed. So he reactivates the tithing program that will allow the Levites and the Temple singers to tend to their proper duties (13:10-13). After completing both of these measures designed to support the Temple, he links them together in his prayer to God: "Do not wipe out my good deeds that I have done for the house of my God and for his service" (13:14).

When he next turns his attention to the sabbath, his concern is linked to geography, this time not of the Temple but rather of the city. Notice the frequency of the phrase "in Jerusalem" throughout this passage. It is not simply *the work* on the sabbath that is the problem; it is also the fact that this work is done *within the city*. Nehemiah does not threaten the merchants for their various sabbath dealings unless they sell inside Jerusalem or camp so close as to tempt the inhabitants of Jerusalem (13:20-21). Fittingly, those same walls that took so much effort to complete now function not simply as a military defense of the city's space, they also protect the ways that the city has defined and sanctified its time.

Sin and Consequences

To the contemporary reader, Nehemiah's concerns with sacred spaces and sacred times may appear overly zealous. For those of us who don't hesitate to stop by the supermarket on our way home from church, reading chapter 13 may seem strange indeed. But regardless of the sizable "gap" between our contemporary worldview and that of Nehemiah, this story still may have much to teach us.

First and foremost is the seriousness with which Nehemiah takes sin. For him, profaning sacred spaces and sacred times is, quite simply, "evil" (13:17). The strength of his reaction is found in the enormity of the possible consequences. By consecrating the sabbath (Exodus 20:11), God says something about the significance of keeping it holy. And when the human community consistently flaunts this consecration, we may be doing ourselves irreparable harm. This is the very harm that Jeremiah saw, and he prophesied before the exile that fire would be kindled in the gates of Jerusalem if the people continued to shun the sabbath in Jerusalem (Jeremiah 17:19-27).

Nehemiah knew that his community was already extremely vulnerable: It had just been allowed to return to Jerusalem from exile and miraculously rebuilt the wall. The threat of a new exile or even just a temporary political setback must have seemed very real. His clear goal was to organize his community in such a way that it continued to flourish in God's "steadfast love" (13:22).

SHARING THE SCRIPTURE

Preparing Our Hearts

Explore this week's devotional reading, found in Mark 2:23-27. Here Jesus is involved in a controversy with some Pharisees who accuse his disciples of acting unlawfully on the sabbath because they were plucking grain from the fields. Jesus uses this confrontation as a teaching moment to explain that the sabbath was made for humanity, not the other way around. Jesus defends his disciples by citing a story concerning David, who was on the run from Saul. Read 1 Samuel 21:1-6 to find out what had happened. How do you view the sabbath? How do your actions reflect your beliefs?

Pray that you and the adult students will honor the sabbath and keep it holy.

Preparing Our Minds

Study the background Scripture from Nehemiah 13:4-31 and the lesson Scripture from Nehemiah 13:15-22.

Consider this question as you prepare the lesson: *Which community rules are important enough for everyone to follow consistently?*

Write on newsprint:
- ❑ information for next week's lesson, found under "Continue the Journey."
- ❑ activities for further spiritual growth in "Continue the Journey."

Review the "Introduction," "The Big Picture," "Close-up," and "Faith in Action." Consider how you will use this additional information, which immediately precedes the first lesson, for this session.

Be prepared to read or retell the segments from Understanding the Scripture noted in "Explore What Nehemiah Said and Did About the Inviolability of the Sabbath."

LEADING THE CLASS

(1) Gather to Learn

❖ Greet the class members. Introduce any guests and help them feel at home.

❖ Pray that the adults who have come will be open to hearing what God has to say to them through today's lesson.

❖ Brainstorm answers to this question, which you will write on newsprint: **What rules or laws seem to be important to our community?** Encourage the students to think of all kinds of rules, such as those pertaining to traffic, dogs, skateboard use, teens (perhaps special driving or curfew laws apply), or housing covenants.

❖ Discuss these questions:
  (1) **Which of these rules or laws seems to be most stringently enforced? Why?**
  (2) **How is the community harmed when one of these laws is broken?**

❖ Read aloud today's focus statement: **People sometimes make demands of those who are breaking community rules. Which community rules are important enough for everyone to follow consistently? Keeping the sabbath was so important to the welfare of God's community that Nehemiah ordered the gates shut to prevent the Israelites from breaking this law.**

(2) Goal 1: Explore What Nehemiah Said and Did About the Inviolability of the Sabbath

❖ Set the stage for today's lesson by reading or retelling "Introduction," "Nehemiah 13:4-9," and "Nehemiah 10-14" in Understanding the Scripture. Focus on the reforms that Nehemiah tried to make in terms of the Temple and worship.

❖ Select a volunteer to read Nehemiah 13:15-22, which focuses on sabbath reforms.

❖ Read "Sacred Time" in Interpreting the Scripture and ask these questions:
  (1) **What are three justifications, according to Scripture, for keeping the sabbath?** (Divine precedent, a need for rest, and identification with the plight of workers are mentioned.)
  (2) **How were people profaning the sabbath?**
  (3) **Who were these people?**
  (4) **What reforms did Nehemiah institute to keep the sabbath holy?**
  (5) **How did the merchants respond to Nehemiah's order that the gates must be shut and remain so until the sabbath had ended?**
  (6) **Do you find Nehemiah to be too authoritarian? Why or why not?**

(3) Goal 2: Examine the Learners' Feelings About the Importance of Sabbath and the Ways They May Violate It

❖ Read these anonymous words: **You see, God, it's like this: We could attend church more faithfully if your day came at some other time. You have chosen a day that comes at the end of a hard week, and we're all tired out. Not only that, but it's the day following Saturday night, and Saturday night is one time when we feel we should go out and enjoy ourselves. Often it is after midnight when we reach home, and it is impossible to get up on Sunday morning. We'd like to go to church** and know we should; but you have just chosen the wrong day.

❖ Choose two volunteers for a role-play. One person is to agree with the words about sabbath that have just been read and try to defend his or her apparently regular violation of the sabbath. The other is to express his or her feelings about what sabbath is and how he or she tries to observe it faithfully.

❖ Invite other students to express their feelings about sabbath and the way they observe it.

(4) Goal 3: Compare and Contrast the Sabbath Practices in Nehemiah's Day With Ours Today

❖ Read "Sin and Consequences" from Interpreting the Scripture to help the learners better understand why the sabbath observance and the sacred space in which these observances took place were so important to Nehemiah.

❖ Choose volunteers to read these passages concerning the sabbath:

Exodus 20:8-11   Exodus 23:12
Exodus 34:21   Deuteronomy 5:12-15

❖ Read these anonymous words concerning the way many in our society view the sabbath: **Our great-grandfathers called it the holy Sabbath; our grandfathers, the Sabbath; our fathers, Sunday; but today we call it the weekend.**

❖ Distribute paper and pencils. Form two groups, or multiples of two if the class is large. Set up an informal debate wherein one group is to argue that the biblical practices of sabbath are to be observed regardless of what the rest of society is doing. The other group is to argue that in a modern society with people adhering to multiple religious beliefs—and some to no beliefs—it is impossible to impose a biblical standard on everyone. Even Christians who would like to observe the sabbath may have no choice but to work at a paying job on Sunday. Allow time for group members to jot down their ideas before the debate begins.

❖ Conclude this time, which has likely focused on the differences between sabbath practices in Nehemiah's day and ours, with a discussion on how our practices may be similar.

(5) Continue the Journey

❖ Pray that as the students go forth on this sabbath they will recall and act on ways to keep this day holy.

❖ Read aloud this preparation for next week's lesson. You may also want to post it on newsprint for the students to copy.

■ **Title: God Creates**
■ **Background Scripture: Psalm 104**
■ **Lesson Scripture: Psalm 104:5-9, 24-30**
■ **Focus of the Lesson: All humans have some basic needs that must be supplied in order to sustain their daily lives. Where can Christians find a reliable source to assist them in acquiring what is needed? The psalmist tells the reader that God's hands are full to overflowing with the resources needed by everything that God created.**

❖ Post these three activities related to this week's session on newsprint for the students to copy. Challenge the adults to grow spiritually by completing one or more of them.

(1) **Research blue laws in your state. These laws that were designed to enforce sabbath rest by prohibiting commerce have either been repealed or are unenforced. Talk with someone about how these laws may have helped the community—or overregulated it.**

(2) **Think about how and when you observe the sabbath. The sabbath for Jews is from Friday sundown until Saturday sundown. Most Christians consider Sunday, the**

day of Jesus' resurrection, to be their sabbath.

(3) Talk with older people about how the sabbath was celebrated years ago. If you are a senior adult, compare what happens on the sabbath now with what was allowed when you were growing up—or stories you heard from parents and grandparents about what was allowable when they were younger. Do you think community life is better or worse because of the way the sabbath is now observed?

❖ Sing or read aloud "Sent Forth by God's Blessings."

❖ Conclude today's session by leading the class in this benediction, adapted from the key verse for June 9 from Isaiah 12:4: **Let us go forth continually giving thanks, proclaiming God's mighty deeds, and exalting God's holy name.**